Lecture Notes in Computer Science 4564

Commenced Publication in 1973
Founding and Former Series Editors:
Gerhard Goos, Juris Hartmanis, and Jan van Leeuwen

Douglas Schuler (Ed.)

Online Communities and Social Computing

Second International Conference, OCSC 2007
Held as Part of HCI International 2007
Beijing, China, July 22-27, 2007
Proceedings

 Springer

Volume Editor

Douglas Schuler
The Evergreen State College and The Public Sphere Project
(Computer Professionals for Social Responsibility)
2700 Evergreen Parkway NW, Olympia, WA 98505-0002, USA
E-mail: dschuler@evergreen.edu

Library of Congress Control Number: 2007929549

CR Subject Classification (1998): K.4-6, K.8, C.2, H.5, H.4, H.3, J.1, J.3

LNCS Sublibrary: SL 3 – Information Systems and Application, incl. Internet/Web
and HCI

ISSN   0302-9743
ISBN-10   3-540-73256-X Springer Berlin Heidelberg New York
ISBN-13   978-3-540-73256-3 Springer Berlin Heidelberg New York

Springer is a part of Springer Science+Business Media

springer.com

© Springer-Verlag Berlin Heidelberg 2007
Printed in Germany

Typesetting: Camera-ready by author, data conversion by Scientific Publishing Services, Chennai, India
Printed on acid-free paper   SPIN: 12081837   06/3180   5 4 3 2 1 0

Foreword

The 12th International Conference on Human-Computer Interaction, HCI International 2007, was held in Beijing, P.R. China, 22-27 July 2007, jointly with the Symposium on Human Interface (Japan) 2007, the 7th International Conference on Engineering Psychology and Cognitive Ergonomics, the 4th International Conference on Universal Access in Human-Computer Interaction, the 2nd International Conference on Virtual Reality, the 2nd International Conference on Usability and Internationalization, the 2nd International Conference on Online Communities and Social Computing, the 3rd International Conference on Augmented Cognition, and the 1st International Conference on Digital Human Modeling.

A total of 3403 individuals from academia, research institutes, industry and governmental agencies from 76 countries submitted contributions, and 1681 papers, judged to be of high scientific quality, were included in the program. These papers address the latest research and development efforts and highlight the human aspects of design and use of computing systems. The papers accepted for presentation thoroughly cover the entire field of Human-Computer Interaction, addressing major advances in knowledge and effective use of computers in a variety of application areas.

This volume, edited by Douglas Schuler, contains papers in the thematic area of Online Communities and Social Computing, addressing the following major topics:

- Designing and Developing On-line Communities
- Knowledge, Collaboration, Learning and Local On-line Communities

The remaining volumes of the HCI International 2007 proceedings are:

- Volume 1, LNCS 4550, Interaction Design and Usability, edited by Julie A. Jacko
- Volume 2, LNCS 4551, Interaction Platforms and Techniques, edited by Julie A. Jacko
- Volume 3, LNCS 4552, HCI Intelligent Multimodal Interaction Environments, edited by Julie A. Jacko
- Volume 4, LNCS 4553, HCI Applications and Services, edited by Julie A. Jacko
- Volume 5, LNCS 4554, Coping with Diversity in Universal Access, edited by Constantine Stephanidis
- Volume 6, LNCS 4555, Universal Access to Ambient Interaction, edited by Constantine Stephanidis
- Volume 7, LNCS 4556, Universal Access to Applications and Services, edited by Constantine Stephanidis
- Volume 8, LNCS 4557, Methods, Techniques and Tools in Information Design, edited by Michael J. Smith and Gavriel Salvendy
- Volume 9, LNCS 4558, Interacting in Information Environments, edited by Michael J. Smith and Gavriel Salvendy
- Volume 10, LNCS 4559, HCI and Culture, edited by Nuray Aykin
- Volume 11, LNCS 4560, Global and Local User Interfaces, edited by Nuray Aykin
- Volume 12, LNCS 4561, Digital Human Modeling, edited by Vincent G. Duffy

- Volume 13, LNAI 4562, Engineering Psychology and Cognitive Ergonomics, edited by Don Harris
- Volume 14, LNCS 4563, Virtual Reality, edited by Randall Shumaker
- Volume 16, LNAI 4565, Foundations of Augmented Cognition 3rd Edition, edited by Dylan D. Schmorrow and Leah M. Reeves
- Volume 17, LNCS 4566, Ergonomics and Health Aspects of Work with Computers, edited by Marvin J. Dainoff

I would like to thank the Program Chairs and the members of the Program Boards of all Thematic Areas, listed below, for their contribution to the highest scientific quality and the overall success of the HCI International 2007 Conference.

Ergonomics and Health Aspects of Work with Computers

Program Chair: Marvin J. Dainoff

Arne Aaras, Norway
Pascale Carayon, USA
Barbara G.F. Cohen, USA
Wolfgang Friesdorf, Germany
Martin Helander, Singapore
Ben-Tzion Karsh, USA
Waldemar Karwowski, USA
Peter Kern, Germany
Danuta Koradecka, Poland
Kari Lindstrom, Finland

Holger Luczak, Germany
Aura C. Matias, Philippines
Kyung (Ken) Park, Korea
Michelle Robertson, USA
Steven L. Sauter, USA
Dominique L. Scapin, France
Michael J. Smith, USA
Naomi Swanson, USA
Peter Vink, The Netherlands
John Wilson, UK

Human Interface and the Management of Information

Program Chair: Michael J. Smith

Lajos Balint, Hungary
Gunilla Bradley, Sweden
Hans-Jörg Bullinger, Germany
Alan H.S. Chan, Hong Kong
Klaus-Peter Fähnrich, Germany
Michitaka Hirose, Japan
Yoshinori Horie, Japan
Richard Koubek, USA
Yasufumi Kume, Japan
Mark Lehto, USA
Jiye Mao, P.R. China
Fiona Nah, USA
Shogo Nishida, Japan
Leszek Pacholski, Poland

Robert Proctor, USA
Youngho Rhee, Korea
Anxo Cereijo Roibás, UK
Francois Sainfort, USA
Katsunori Shimohara, Japan
Tsutomu Tabe, Japan
Alvaro Taveira, USA
Kim-Phuong L. Vu, USA
Tomio Watanabe, Japan
Sakae Yamamoto, Japan
Hidekazu Yoshikawa, Japan
Li Zheng, P.R. China
Bernhard Zimolong, Germany

Human-Computer Interaction

Program Chair: Julie A. Jacko

Sebastiano Bagnara, Italy
Jianming Dong, USA
John Eklund, Australia
Xiaowen Fang, USA
Sheue-Ling Hwang, Taiwan
Yong Gu Ji, Korea
Steven J. Landry, USA
Jonathan Lazar, USA

V. Kathlene Leonard, USA
Chang S. Nam, USA
Anthony F. Norcio, USA
Celestine A. Ntuen, USA
P.L. Patrick Rau, P.R. China
Andrew Sears, USA
Holly Vitense, USA
Wenli Zhu, P.R. China

Engineering Psychology and Cognitive Ergonomics

Program Chair: Don Harris

Kenneth R. Boff, USA
Guy Boy, France
Pietro Carlo Cacciabue, Italy
Judy Edworthy, UK
Erik Hollnagel, Sweden
Kenji Itoh, Japan
Peter G.A.M. Jorna, The Netherlands
Kenneth R. Laughery, USA

Nicolas Marmaras, Greece
David Morrison, Australia
Sundaram Narayanan, USA
Eduardo Salas, USA
Dirk Schaefer, France
Axel Schulte, Germany
Neville A. Stanton, UK
Andrew Thatcher, South Africa

Universal Access in Human-Computer Interaction

Program Chair: Constantine Stephanidis

Julio Abascal, Spain
Ray Adams, UK
Elizabeth Andre, Germany
Margherita Antona, Greece
Chieko Asakawa, Japan
Christian Bühler, Germany
Noelle Carbonell, France
Jerzy Charytonowicz, Poland
Pier Luigi Emiliani, Italy
Michael Fairhurst, UK
Gerhard Fischer, USA
Jon Gunderson, USA
Andreas Holzinger, Austria
Arthur Karshmer, USA
Simeon Keates, USA

Zhengjie Liu, P.R. China
Klaus Miesenberger, Austria
John Mylopoulos, Canada
Michael Pieper, Germany
Angel Puerta, USA
Anthony Savidis, Greece
Andrew Sears, USA
Ben Shneiderman, USA
Christian Stary, Austria
Hirotada Ueda, Japan
Jean Vanderdonckt, Belgium
Gregg Vanderheiden, USA
Gerhard Weber, Germany
Harald Weber, Germany
Toshiki Yamaoka, Japan

George Kouroupetroglou, Greece
Jonathan Lazar, USA
Seongil Lee, Korea

Mary Zajicek, UK
Panayiotis Zaphiris, UK

Virtual Reality

Program Chair: Randall Shumaker

Terry Allard, USA
Pat Banerjee, USA
Robert S. Kennedy, USA
Heidi Kroemker, Germany
Ben Lawson, USA
Ming Lin, USA
Bowen Loftin, USA
Holger Luczak, Germany
Annie Luciani, France
Gordon Mair, UK

Ulrich Neumann, USA
Albert "Skip" Rizzo, USA
Lawrence Rosenblum, USA
Dylan Schmorrow, USA
Kay Stanney, USA
Susumu Tachi, Japan
John Wilson, UK
Wei Zhang, P.R. China
Michael Zyda, USA

Usability and Internationalization

Program Chair: Nuray Aykin

Genevieve Bell, USA
Alan Chan, Hong Kong
Apala Lahiri Chavan, India
Jori Clarke, USA
Pierre-Henri Dejean, France
Susan Dray, USA
Paul Fu, USA
Emilie Gould, Canada
Sung H. Han, South Korea
Veikko Ikonen, Finland
Richard Ishida, UK
Esin Kiris, USA
Tobias Komischke, Germany
Masaaki Kurosu, Japan
James R. Lewis, USA

Rungtai Lin, Taiwan
Aaron Marcus, USA
Allen E. Milewski, USA
Patrick O'Sullivan, Ireland
Girish V. Prabhu, India
Kerstin Röse, Germany
Eunice Ratna Sari, Indonesia
Supriya Singh, Australia
Serengul Smith, UK
Denise Spacinsky, USA
Christian Sturm, Mexico
Adi B. Tedjasaputra, Singapore
Myung Hwan Yun, South Korea
Chen Zhao, P.R. China

Online Communities and Social Computing

Program Chair: Douglas Schuler

Chadia Abras, USA
Lecia Barker, USA

Stefanie Lindstaedt, Austria
Diane Maloney-Krichmar, USA

Amy Bruckman, USA
Peter van den Besselaar,
  The Netherlands
Peter Day, UK
Fiorella De Cindio, Italy
John Fung, P.R. China
Michael Gurstein, USA
Tom Horan, USA
Piet Kommers, The Netherlands
Jonathan Lazar, USA

Isaac Mao, P.R. China
Hideyuki Nakanishi, Japan
A. Ant Ozok, USA
Jennifer Preece, USA
Partha Pratim Sarker, Bangladesh
Gilson Schwartz, Brazil
Sergei Stafeev, Russia
F.F. Tusubira, Uganda
Cheng-Yen Wang, Taiwan

Augmented Cognition

Program Chair: Dylan D. Schmorrow

Kenneth Boff, USA
Joseph Cohn, USA
Blair Dickson, UK
Henry Girolamo, USA
Gerald Edelman, USA
Eric Horvitz, USA
Wilhelm Kincses, Germany
Amy Kruse, USA
Lee Kollmorgen, USA
Dennis McBride, USA

Jeffrey Morrison, USA
Denise Nicholson, USA
Dennis Proffitt, USA
Harry Shum, P.R. China
Kay Stanney, USA
Roy Stripling, USA
Michael Swetnam, USA
Robert Taylor, UK
John Wagner, USA

Digital Human Modeling

Program Chair: Vincent G. Duffy

Norm Badler, USA
Heiner Bubb, Germany
Don Chaffin, USA
Kathryn Cormican, Ireland
Andris Freivalds, USA
Ravindra Goonetilleke, Hong Kong
Anand Gramopadhye, USA
Sung H. Han, South Korea
Pheng Ann Heng, Hong Kong
Dewen Jin, P.R. China
Kang Li, USA

Zhizhong Li, P.R. China
Lizhuang Ma, P.R. China
Timo Maatta, Finland
J. Mark Porter, UK
Jim Potvin, Canada
Jean-Pierre Verriest, France
Zhaoqi Wang, P.R. China
Xiugan Yuan, P.R. China
Shao-Xiang Zhang, P.R. China
Xudong Zhang, USA

In addition to the members of the Program Boards above, I also wish to thank the following volunteer external reviewers: Kelly Hale, David Kobus, Amy Kruse, Cali Fidopiastis and Karl Van Orden from the USA, Mark Neerincx and Marc Grootjen from the Netherlands, Wilhelm Kincses from Germany, Ganesh Bhutkar and Mathura

Prasad from India, Frederick Li from the UK, and Dimitris Grammenos, Angeliki Kastrinaki, Iosif Klironomos, Alexandros Mourouzis, and Stavroula Ntoa from Greece.

This conference could not have been possible without the continuous support and advise of the Conference Scientific Advisor, Gavriel Salvendy, as well as the dedicated work and outstanding efforts of the Communications Chair and Editor of HCI International News, Abbas Moallem, and of the members of the Organizational Board from P.R. China, Patrick Rau (Chair), Bo Chen, Xiaolan Fu, Zhibin Jiang, Congdong Li, Zhenjie Liu, Mowei Shen, Yuanchun Shi, Hui Su, Linyang Sun, Ming Po Tham, Ben Tsiang, Jian Wang, Guangyou Xu, Winnie Wanli Yang, Shuping Yi, Kan Zhang, and Wei Zho.

I would also like to thank for their contribution towards the organization of the HCI International 2007 Conference the members of the Human Computer Interaction Laboratory of ICS-FORTH, and in particular Margherita Antona, Maria Pitsoulaki, George Paparoulis, Maria Bouhli, Stavroula Ntoa and George Margetis.

Constantine Stephanidis
General Chair, HCI International 2007

HCI International 2009

The 13th International Conference on Human-Computer Interaction, HCI International 2009, will be held jointly with the affiliated Conferences in San Diego, California, USA, in the Town and Country Resort & Convention Center, 19-24 July 2009. It will cover a broad spectrum of themes related to Human Computer Interaction, including theoretical issues, methods, tools, processes and case studies in HCI design, as well as novel interaction techniques, interfaces and applications. The proceedings will be published by Springer. For more information, please visit the Conference website: http://www.hcii2009.org/

General Chair
Professor Constantine Stephanidis
ICS-FORTH and University of Crete
Heraklion, Crete, Greece
Email: program@hcii2009.org

Table of Contents

Part I: Designing and Developing On-Line Communities

Part II: Knowledge, Collaboration, Learning and Local On-Line Communities

Part I

Designing and Developing On-Line Communities

User-Centred Design Approach for a Community Website with Social Software

Ilse Bakx

Centre for Usability Research (CUO)
Katholieke Universiteit Leuven
Parkstraat 45 Bus 3605 - 3000 Leuven, Belgium
Ilse.Bakx@soc.kuleuven.be

Abstract. Social software and web 2.0 live on the fact that people want to share and collaborate. This feeling of connecting with each other as well as helping and sharing information can be used in different domains. We think social software can be used to build dynamic online communities and subsequently can be used to improve the relationships between community members and stimulate them to be more active community members. To make sure the website is usable by all people and to make it approachable for all people to be active on a community website, we involved the users in an early stage of the design process. With the results of the user studies we designed the website, after which iterative usability tests took place. In this paper, we discuss a case study of the design of a community website around an interactive page in a local newspaper, using social software and their interaction with the real life community.

Keywords: Social software, online community, user-centred design, usability.

1 Introduction

In this paper, we discuss the possibilities of using social software in a community website developed with a user-centred design approach. The community website is built around an interactive page in a newspaper; called WegWijs. WegWijs is a two weekly page in two regional newspapers of Media Groep Limburg (MGL) "Het Limburgs Dagblad" and "Dagblad de Limburger" in the southern province of The Netherlands "Limburg". Limburg is a province with a very strong feel of identity and has its own dialect. These newspapers have a very large reach in this province, 64,6% of the civilians of the province of Limburg who are 13 year and older read one of the two newspapers, although the largest group of readers are 50+ [9].

The WegWijs page is a page where people can send in original questions which will be answered by editors with the help of experts. Examples of questions are. "How exists a family coat of arms?", "Why is a toilet roll divided in separate sheets?" "How long takes a dream?" (see figure 1 for an example of a question). Moreover they can place personal ads and contribute with limericks and personal thoughts. It is a highly successful page, with a long queue of questions and submissions, it takes about half a year before a submission appears in the newspaper. The main target

D. Schuler (Ed.): Online Communities and Social Comput., HCII 2007, LNCS 4564, pp. 3–11, 2007.
© Springer-Verlag Berlin Heidelberg 2007

group, making use of this page, consists of people over 55. The newspaper decided to translate this concept to the Internet, but stressed that the same target group should be able to interact with it, and the high commitment should be retained. This project is done as part of a bigger project VIP-lab ("Virtual Lab for ICT Experience prototyping"), with the aim of making small and medium-sized businesses in the region aware of the advantages of ICT Experience Prototyping and user-centred design [3].

To make sure the website will fit the expectations of the readers of the newspaper, and will be usable for all people, also the people with very few Internet experience, we developed the website in a user-centred design approach. There is an international standard (ISO 13407: human-centred design process) that is the basis for many user-centred design methodologies. This standard defines a general process for including human-centred activities throughout a development life-cycle [6]. This means the readers and the editors of the WegWijs page in the newspaper were involved in all stages of development. In the following paragraphs we will describe the different phases of the user-centred design process, starting with a contextual inquiry and Internet survey, followed by an iterative phase of design and several usability tests, concluding with a field test.

2   Enhancing the WegWijs Experience

In order to gain insight into the way the WegWijs page is being used now, we performed a contextual inquiry and an Internet survey. Contextual inquiry is a field data-gathering technique to arrive at a full understanding of the work practice across all users [1]. An important benefit of contextual inquiry is that the interviewees are observed in their context, therefore is it not only possible to discover the user's opinion and experiences, but also understanding the user's motivations and context. Besides that, this technique makes unarticulated knowledge explicit [1,5]. The contextual inquiry took place at people's homes, observing how they read this particular page and interviewing them about the interaction they have with WegWijs (see figure 2 for an example). The Internet survey was a questionnaire which could be filled in on the Internet.

We interviewed and observed 7 readers of this page, mean age 56 (between 41 and 75 years of age) spread over the province of Limburg. They all had some computer and Internet experience. During the observations the subjects were reading the page in the newspaper for the first time that day. We asked questions about the reading sequence of the different sections, their favourite sections, etc. These readers were recruited by sending an email to all the readers of the WegWijs page who ever had contacted the WegWijs editors by email. This means these people were already active by reacting on WegWijs items in the newspaper. We received a lot of enthusiastic reactions on our request, for that reason we decided to conduct an Internet survey as well.

During the Internet survey with 50 readers of the WegWijs page, just as during the observation and interviews, we asked their opinion about the WegWijs page published in the newspaper and what their expectations were for an interactive version of this page on the Internet. The average age of readers who filled in the survey was 55 (between 13 and 86 years of age). They used the Internet at least once a week, especially for emailing or surfing the web.

This contextual inquiry and Internet survey showed us that most of the readers were willing to visit the future WegWijs website and participate in the interaction, although some people asked themselves why everything should be digitized. Most of them were afraid that they did not have enough technological knowledge to really interact with the website. They were for example saying: "I don't have much experience with computers" or "I will interact if I know how to do this". The readers did not really had a fixed reading sequence on the WegWijs page, although most of them said the WegWijs page was the first page they read of the whole newspaper. The majority of the time, they first read their favourite section or the section which stands out the most by colour or subject. Overall they did not want the online version to be an exact copy of the paper version of WegWijs, and they preferred to keep it small and local.

When we asked them why they contribute to the WegWijs page, they gave several reasons for this. A frequently given answer was that they wanted to help other people: "just to be helpful", "to pass knowledge", "I like to help other people this way". Some of them were wondering about a question and did not know how to find the answer, and they saw WegWijs as their solution: "I would like to know the answer and I think others want too". Other people were just curious, wanted to learn ("you are never too old to learn"), wanted to know the opinion of other people, liked it to come in contact with other people, or did it just for fun. Another frequently seen explanation was that they like to see things they contributed, their own names or their home town in the newspaper ("to make sure my town is not underrepresented").

Overall, the reactions on the WegWijs page in the newspaper were very enthusiastic. Also the amount of reactions we got on our requests for participation in the research confirmed the strong bonding with the page in the newspaper.

Fig. 1. Example of question and answer on WegWijs page in the newspaper

Fig. 2. Observation WegWijs reader

3 Prototyping the Wegwijs Website with Social Software

Based on the contextual inquiry and the Internet survey we wrote two scenarios of the current situation with the WegWijs page in the newspaper and two future scenarios describing how the interaction with an interactive version of the WegWijs page on the web could be. Scenarios are made up stories of people who want to reach their goals with a product. The stories are detailed and also design suggestions can be discussed [15]. These scenarios and the results of the contextual inquiry and the Internet survey were used as input for the design decisions on how the interface should function and what it should look like. We will explain some different aspects of the community website by clarifying why we made these design implications.

The readers already had a strong tie with the WegWijs page in the newspaper and they indicated they really liked the looks of the page. Therefore we wanted the website to be recognizable for the WegWijs readers. We used the same graphical elements and colours like the newspaper so the users will have a feeling of trust and comfort. The decision of which sections would be translated to the Internet was based on the most favourite sections of the readers.

The WegWijs page in the newspaper has already a strong bond with their readers. The readers indicated they talk about the page with their friends, family and colleagues regularly. To support this feeling of connecting with each other and wanting them to share information and opinions with each other, we decided to implement social software concepts in the WegWijs website to make it a community website. Different definitions of social software can be found [11,16], often in combination with some other buzz words in the same domain, like Web 2.0 and Rich Internet Applications. All these terms express the feeling that the web is where we live. New sites like MySpace, Last.fm, del.icio.us and Flickr are not just places to go, but contain things to do, ways to express yourself, means to connect with others and they extend your own horizons [7]. They live on the fact that people want to share and collaborate, which makes it easier to build a community in a natural way. Using social software can even increase the involvement of the WegWijs readers in the community. Despite the vibrancy of online communities, large numbers of them fail. Often, designers do not have a solid understanding of why [8]. On Web 2.0 websites, users are not only trying to interact with the technology or information, they are also trying to interact with others. This makes the user interface a social interface. Because social interactions are complex and unpredictable, we certainly have to focus on usability problems concerning social software. Social interface issues can be far more difficult to deal with than conventional user interfaces because the interaction of technology, users or communities involves interdependencies that exceed the reach of conventional design techniques [2].

Users have to create a personal profile, if they want to contribute to the website. They can fill in their interests, where they live, upload their own photo, etc. People who have registered can see the profile pages from all the registered users, including a list of all the contributions to the website someone has made. The homepage gives an indication of the number of registered users, and the number of online users. This makes the website more personal and enables communication between users with similar interests in the future.

We changed the way questions were answered compared to the original WegWijs page, partly to spare the editors, but more important to support the community. Users can still ask questions, but the answers will not be given by the editors but by other users. To approach the reliability of the newspaper, other users can indicate if they agree or disagree with the answers. They can also just react on the answer by writing down their own opinion. Another indication of reliability can be the interests of the writer. For example if you see the writer was a former mine worker, you can presume that the answer he gave about the question about the mines is correct. Further, the readers indicated that they thought it was a shame that after a question was answered, the subject was closed. On the website they can still ask substantial questions or react on the answers. Another benefit is that the long queue of questions can be solved because the activity of the editors will be reduced.

Users can also put their own rhymes and aphorisms online. In the paper version the editors choose the best submissions and publish them in the newspaper. Readers indicated they felt proud to see their own name and contribution in the newspaper. To simulate this feeling in the web version of WegWijs, users can give positive votes on these writings if they like them, like giving a complement, similar to Digg, a news website with a user-based ranking system. At the end of every week, the rhyme and aphorisms with the most votes will appear on the homepage. This way the writers can still feel proud, just like in the newspaper.

Fig. 3. Screenshot of Visio WegWijs prototype   **Fig. 4.** Screenshot question page

4 Usability Tests with the WegWijs Website

To involve the users in the next stages of the design process, we conducted several usability tests and a field test in an iterative process. First we made a prototype with Microsoft Visio, to get first reactions of users on the idea. We tested the website with 5 people. Not the whole website was worked out but only a few pages, see figure 3 for a screenshot of the Visio prototype. With this prototype there was interaction possible, with working links and buttons, but input fields were inactive. Because it was still a prototype and not all parts were functional, the usability test was accomplished in an informal way. As a result we received a lot of feedback of the users on the design. Taking into account the results of this first usability test, the website was built and a second and third usability test was carried out with this beta version of the website.

During the usability tests the users had to accomplish several tasks with the WegWijs website while thinking aloud. Thinking aloud means they say out loud everything that they are thinking and trying to do, so their thought processes are externalized [14]. Examples of tasks are creating a personal profile and voting on a limerick. After the test they had to fill in a questionnaire about their opinion of the prototype and about specific interaction techniques. The usability tests were carried out with a portable usability lab at the editorial office at MGL in Sittard.

The second usability test was carried out with 9 WegWijs readers. The older adults are our primary target group, therefore we tested with 6 users aged between 60 and 75. Because the WegWijs page is also read by younger people, for example school classes send in questions regularly, we also selected 2 users about 45 and 1 user aged 17. Half of the subjects had very few computer and Internet experience. Another usability test was carried out with the 3 editors of the WegWijs page. Because the editors had very few experience with community websites and the website contained some extra features for them, we wanted to know if the website was also user friendly for them.

During the tests we saw some usability problems, especially with the users with less computer experience. The overall impression of the website was good. The users really liked the identification with the page in the newspaper. They said it was clear, familiar, and it was "peaceful for the eyes". Most people were very pleased with the possibility of voting on other people's submissions, like rhymes and aphorisms ("Nice to see if you have the same taste as other people" and "It is a stimulation to submit more"). They did not mind if other people were voting on their input, most of them even really appreciated it ("Nice to see what others think of it"). They also liked the opportunity to indicate if they agree or disagree with answers on questions ("You get a better idea of degree of truthfulness"). Most of them had enough faith the correct answer to their questions will eventually appear ("There are always people who know the answer") (see figure 4 for an example of a question and answers). They also liked the idea they could take a look at other people's interests and their submissions, although some people indicated they feel no need for it. They especially wanted to know more about people with the same interests, even more than was possible now. Most of the subjects had the feeling they could get in contact with other people who are registered through this website, and they liked this, especially with people with the same interests. The majority of the subjects indicated they even wanted to contact other people directly. They did not mind that other people could see their personal information, like hometown or their personal interests, although one person thought the photo was overdone. The younger people even wanted to go one step further, they would like to send messages to other users and wanted to know why people vote on rhymes. They also indicated that they would more easily publish something on the website then send it to the newspaper.

5 Field Test with the WegWijs Website

With the results of the usability tests, the website was improved and a field test was carried out. Thirty-one WegWijs readers were asked to use the WegWijs community website intensively and were asked to participate during a period of 3 weeks. To make sure we had a balanced variation in the group, we made a selection out of 150 readers who already had contact with the editors of WegWijs page and wanted to participate. The selection criteria were based on age, computer and Internet experience and profession. The participants were aged between 11 and 87 (mean 50). They were asked to fill in a diary every time they visited the WegWijs website. They had to answer questions about their experience with different parts of the website. The amount of time they spend on the website and what they were doing on the website was automatically logged. We also visited 7 of these testers at their homes, observing and interviewing them while they were visiting the WegWijs website.

Before the 31 testers visited the WegWijs website, they had to fill in a questionnaire with some general question about their experience with computer, Internet and the WegWijs page in the newspaper. The results of this questionnaire indicated that all testers had experience with computers and Internet, but on different levels. Half of them visited the Internet every day and only half of them had experience with forums or newsgroups. Most of them (25) had reacted already on an item on the WegWijs page in the newspaper. Most of them (25) indicated they talk about the content of the WegWijs page in the newspaper with family, colleagues or friends regular.

All the testers visited the website during the test period. On average the website was visited about 22 times per person during the 3 weeks, with a mean time of 16 minutes and about 42 pages per visit. During the first week we saw a peak in the amount of votes compared with the other weeks as well as compared with other actions, properly because this was an easy first step to participate on the website. One person was very active and took care of 15% of all actions during the 3 testweeks on the website. Thirteen testers took care of 62% of all actions, 2 people only visited the website without being active, this means the remaining 23% of actions was done by the rest of the testers, 15 testers. This means we had much more active people on the website than normally is the case mentioned by Preece et al. [12] and Nielsen [10].

During the home visits people reacted very enthusiastic about the website. Some people indicated the website was good for their general knowledge. They also used their own reference books much more because they wanted to answer questions from other users.

The diaries showed that there were still some minor usability problems, although most testers really appreciated the website and thought it was a cosy and lively environment. After the first week, we saw that the testers became friendlier to each other, they thanked for example each other for answers on questions. The page with all the registered users was visited often. Some people wrote that the first thing they did when visiting the website was checking if there were new registered people and checking their profile to see if it would match their own profile. If someone's question was answered, they received automatically an email with a link to the answer on the WegWijs website. The testers really appreciated this, actually it felt for them like an invitation to contribute more. The testers also told us that they often checked their own submissions to see if they got compliments or answers to their questions. This means the implemented features encourage people to participate, were working.

The testers would appreciate it if there would be more interaction between the website and the paper version of WegWijs. This will be a point of attention in the future, because it was not realisable during the test period. They want to place some items from the website in the newspaper and the other way around. Some people also indicated they want the editors to contribute more, especially after a lively discussion about a question. So, they still miss the reliability of the newspaper.

6 Discussion and Conclusion

During this user-centred design process we saw that during the early design stages some WegWijs readers were a bit sceptical about the WegWijs website on the Internet and their ability to use it. By involving the users during the whole design cycle and through analyzing the users' needs and expectations we could design a community website adapted to their needs and skills. As a result we saw during the usability tests that most users could easily use the website and had an enjoyable experience when discovering those new social software components. This resulted in a contribution of almost every user on the WegWijs website during the field test. Half of the testers were above average active and took care of the majority of all the activities on the website. As already mentioned before, this is much more than normally is the case with community websites, probably partly caused by the fact that it was a test case of 3 weeks and people were encouraged to participate. But the results of the field tests showed confidence for the community website, that the people were encouraged by the features build in. During the field test we also saw that a lot of the features we had build in were working well, like the mission statement, rewarding contributions, the personal information in the website. This confirmed that the strategies to encourage people to become an active community member mentioned by Preece et al. [13] were working. Furthermore, there was not only a strong bond between the readers and the newspaper, but during the field test we saw that the users felt more connected with each other. This can be of major advantage for the newspaper to strengthen and secure their bond with their readers.

Acknowledgements. VIP-lab is financed by the "Interreg Benelux-Middengebied" authorities and is co-financed by Province of Limburg (B), Province of Limburg (NL), Ministry of Economic Affairs (NL) and Ministry of Flemish Government/Economic Affairs (B). We acknowledge the contribution of our consortium partners: EDM (B), EC/DC (B), De Vlijt (B) and TU/e (NL). Our thanks go to the editors of WegWijs from MGL for their co-operation and to Mieke Haesen, Tom Kooy, Codruta Ancuti and Els Maes for their contribution and hard work.

References

1. Beyer, H., Holtzblatt, K.: Contextual Design: Defining Customer-Centered Systems. Morgan Kaufmann Publishers, San Francisco, CA (1997)
2. Chan, A.: Social Interaction Design. Examples of social navigation (2006) Gravity 7 (http://www.gravity7.com/G7_Soc_Int_Design _3-27.pdf)
3. Coninx, K., Haesen, M., Bierhoff, J.: VIP-lab: A virtual lab for ICT experience prototyping. In: Proc. Measuring Behavior 2005, Wageningen, The Netherlands (2005)
4. Cooper, A., Reinman, R.: About Face 2.0, The Essentials of Interaction Design. Wiley Publishing, Inc., Indiapolis, USA (2003)
5. Hackos, J.T., Redish, J.C.: User and Task Analysis for Interface Design. Wiley & Sons Inc, New York (1998)
6. ISO 13407:1999 Human-centred design processes for interactive systems (April 2004)
7. Levy, S., Stone, B.: The new wisdom of the Web. Newsweek (2006) April 3, 2006 issue (http://www.msnbc.msn.com/id/12015774 /site/newsweek)

8. Ludford, P., Cosley, D., Frankowski, D., Terveen, L.: Think Different: Increasing Online Group Community Participation Using Uniqueness and Group Dissimilarity. In: Proceedings of CHI 2004, Vienna, Austria (2004)
9. Media Groep Limburg (2006) Bereikcijfers (http://www.mgl.nl)
10. Nielsen, J.: Participation Inequality: Encouraging more users to contribute (2006) (http://www.useit.com/alertbox/participation_inequality.html)
11. O'Reilly, T.: What is Web 2.0: Design patterns and business models for the next generation of software (September 30, 2005)
12. Preece, J.: Online communities: Designing Usability, Supporting Sociability. John Wiley & Sons, Chichester, England (2000)
13. Preece, J., Nonneke, B., Andrews, D.: The top 5 reasons for lurking: Improving community experiences for everyone. Computers in Human Behavior 2, 1 (2004)
14. Preece, J., Rogers, Y., Sharp, H.: Interaction Design: beyond human-computer interaction. Wiley & Sons Inc, USA (2002)
15. Rosson, M.B., Carrol, J.M.: Usability engineering: scenario-based development of human-computer interaction. Morgan Kaufmann Publishers, San Francisco, CA (2001)
16. Shirkey, C.: A Group Is Its Own Worst Enemy. A speech at ETech (2003) April, 2003 and published July 1, 2003 on the "Networks, Economics, and Culture" mailing list http://www.shirky.com/writings/group_enemy.html

What Would Jiminy Cricket Do? Lessons from the First Social Wearable

Timothy W. Bickmore

Northeastern University College of Computer and Information Science
360 Huntington Ave WVH202, Boston, MA 02115
bickmore@ccs.neu.edu
http://www.ccs.neu.edu/home/bickmore/

Abstract. Work towards the development of a "wearable conscience" that helps individuals make healthy decisions in their everyday lives is described. To be effective, such a system must be portable, sense key elements of the user's environment, have knowledge of counseling and health behavior change techniques, be able to effectively communicate with the user, and have social competencies for maintaining an ongoing working relationship. The design of a prototype system is presented, along with results from a series of design and usability studies. Current and future directions for the research are also discussed.

Keywords: social agent, relational agent, embodied conversational agent, health behavior change, wearable computer.

1 Introduction

Imagine an external conscience that goes everywhere with you, experiences everything that you do, and whispers suggestions about the "right" thing to do in your ear. Such a system could help you make healthy lifestyle decisions, such as choosing healthy over unhealthy foods, taking the stairs rather the elevator, or avoiding situations in which significant social pressure would exist to engage in unhealthy behavior such as smoking or eating or drinking too much.

Such a system could have a significant impact on society. Poor lifestyle health behaviors, such as lack of physical activity and unhealthy dietary habits, are among the leading causes of death and chronic disease in the United States [22]. In addition, adherence to prescribed medical treatments — such as medication regimens — is estimated to average only 50%, and represents another significant source of morbidity, mortality and healthcare cost to the nation [13]. Each of these large classes of health behavior problems could be more effectively addressed if the right information and counseling could be delivered to someone at the moment they are trying to decide whether to engage in a healthy behavior or not. Importantly, however, this positive impact will only be realized if such a conscience is carefully designed so that it is not perceived to be annoying or intrusive.

1.1 Lessons from a Cricket

Perhaps the earliest conceptualization of such a "wearable conscience" was Jiminy Cricket, who accompanied Pinnochio on many of his escapades, offering advice on

D. Schuler (Ed.): Online Communities and Social Comput., HCII 2007, LNCS 4564, pp. 12–21, 2007.

the long-term consequences of Pinnochio's actions. In the original story, Jiminy's advice was not readily accepted; in fact Pinnochio strikes and kills the cricket with a hammer in their first meeting after he provides unwanted counsel [8]. There are important lessons to learn from this, and Jiminy can be used as a case study to understand the requirements for a digital version of the wearable conscience:

- **Social and Relational Competency.** Given the lesson above, one of the most important abilities for such a system to have is the same range of social competencies any good human coach, counselor or friend has, including the ability to establish and maintain a good working relationship with the person being helped, and the knowledge of when and how to offer suggestions in order to maximize long-term benefit. Such a conscience must interrupt and speak persuasively to have any effect at all, yet long-term effectiveness is curtailed if the user simply smashes it with a hammer after the first few pieces of advice are delivered. Beyond simply providing reminders (e.g., in the form of audio alerts), such systems must be able to counsel and persuade users in non-trivial ways, thus requiring the use of natural language. It is also important that these systems be able to use the same range of verbal and nonverbal relational behaviors that people use to build and maintain good working relationships in face-to-face interaction. These behaviors include such things as facial displays of emotion to convey empathy and the use of social dialogue for building trust. Relational agents are systems that employ such competencies to establish long-term social-emotional relationships with users [5].

- **Adeptness at Interruption.** The system must be adept at knowing not only how, but when to interrupt a user in order to maximize long-term compliance with a health regimen. Knowledge of a user's schedule and current task context would enable the system to know the precise moment when, for example, the user should be interrupted and reminded to take a morning dose of medication or given the suggestion to take a break from work and go for a walk.

- **Portability.** Obviously, the conscience should be portable so that it can accompany users wherever they go. This is important so that: (1) it can intervene at the moment the user is making a relevant decision, wherever and whenever that occurs; (2) it is available whenever the user actively seeks counsel on a relevant topic; and (3) it can give the user the perception that it shares in a significant portion of their life, important for the establishment of credibility and a good working relationship.

- **Sensing Ability.** In order for the system to actively intervene, it must be able to detect when the user is at a point of decision making, or perhaps has just started to engage in an unhealthy behavior. Different health behaviors require different sensors, but some examples that have been developed include: accelerometers for detecting physical activity [15]; microphones for detecting chewing [1]; smoke detectors for identifying cigarette lighting; and GPS for detecting proximity to locations known to present the user with difficult health choices (e.g., stairs vs. elevator, fast food restaurant, grocery store, etc.).

- **Persistence.** In order to establish long-term working relationships with users, and to effectively change behavior over time, a wearable conscience must retain memory of past interactions with users. Persistent memory should ultimately be represented as an episodic store recording details of all (or key) past interactions with users. At a minimum, however, it can be designed to record specific facts that can be referenced in future conversations. Examples in the physical activity coaching domain include remembering the name of a user's walking buddy or favorite walking location, as well as purely social (off-task) facts, such as the user's favorite television program and whether they had any big plans for the upcoming weekend .

- **Health Behavior Change Counseling Competency.** Finally, it is not enough that the system recognize when a user is about to do something unhealthy and tell them not to. Over the last few decades the field of behavioral medicine has produced a range of theories and counseling techniques for achieving effective health behavior change over time [11], and at least some of this knowledge must be codified into the system.

2 Related Work

Although there is a significant and growing literature on technologies to promote health behavior change, very few of these technologies involve real-time or wearable interventions. One notable exception is a body of research on reminder systems for individuals with cognitive impairment using pagers [14] and PDAs [18].

Several systems have also been developed to provide older adults with real-time reminders to perform various activities of daily living (including medication taking). The ILSA system used automated phone to calls to provide real-time reminders to older adults living alone, but the calls were not always effective and users did not like them [12]. Pollack *et al.* developed the AutoMinder system, which could reason about whether, when and how to give a reminder based on a deep understanding of the tasks involved and the user's schedule (e.g., "If you take your medicine now, I won't have to interrupt you during your favorite TV show later") [23]. Preliminary evaluation indicated that acceptance among older adult users was high, although efficacy results have not been reported.

2.1 Handheld Conversational Agent-Based Health Interventions

Johnson, *et al*, developed DESIA, a psychosocial intervention on a handheld computer that features an animated conversational agent who uses balloon text and optional recorded speech output for the agent utterances [17]. Outcome evaluations have yet to be reported.

2.2 Task Interruption Studies

There has been considerable research done in the area of task interruption of computer users in recent years. Much of this work is primarily concerned with the impact of interruptions on task performance, while the concern here is primarily on user responsiveness to the interruption.

A number of studies have shown that, in terms of supporting human performance of all kinds, negotiation-based methods in which users are alerted that there is a notification, but are able to control whether or when the full content of the notification is displayed, are preferable to simpler models in which the full notification is delivered immediately [20,21,24]. Czerwinski *et al.* also found that delivering a pre-interruption warning prior to the delivery of the content of the interruption can also have a significant positive effect on performance [9].

Arroyo, *et al.* found that different interface modalities (e.g. heat, light, sound, odor) carry varying degrees of "disruptiveness" [2]. However, they did not investigate different stimuli within a modality (e.g., multiple sounds), nor did they measure short or long-term compliance to an interruption-based request.

There is also evidence that the use of empathy in interruptions can create a more positive user experience. Liu and Picard developed a wearable system that periodically interrupted users and asked them (via text-based prompts) to annotate whether or not it was a good time to interrupt, and to specify their current stress level and activity [19]. The use of empathic language in the system prompt was varied within subjects, who showed (via self-report) significantly higher desire to continue using the empathic version of the system. Additionally, subjects perceived a lower frequency of interruptions when using the empathic system. However, they also did not investigate the impact of empathic interruption on compliance, or compare their approach to other interruption coordination strategies (users were required to either acknowledge an interruption or cancel it immediately).

3 Prototype System

My research group at Northeastern University has been working to develop a general purpose relational agent interface for use on handheld computers that can meet the requirements set forth in Section 1.1 (see Fig. 1). The animated agent appears in a fixed close-up shot, and is capable of a range of nonverbal conversational behavior, including facial displays of emotion; head nods; eye gaze movement; eyebrow raises; posture shifts and "visemes" (mouth shapes corresponding to phonemes). These behaviors are synchronized in real time with agent output utterances, which are displayed in a text balloon rather than using speech, for privacy reasons. The words in the agent utterance are individually highlighted at normal speaking speed and the nonverbal behavior is displayed in synchrony. User inputs are constrained to multiple choice selections and time-of-day specifications at the bottom of the display.

Interaction dialogues are scripted in an XML-based hierarchical state-transition network, which allows for rapid development and modification of system behavior. Scripts consist primarily of agent utterances (written in plain text), the allowed user responses to each agent utterance, and instructions for state transitions based on these responses and other system events (timers, sensor input, etc.). Once a script is written, it is preprocessed using the BEAT text-to-embodied-speech engine [7], which automatically adds specifications for agent nonverbal behavior.

Interruption behavior can be very flexibly defined using a variety of wait states and state transitions conditioned on events. During specified wait states, the PDA's display shuts off, and the interface remains dormant until some condition is met. Example conditions include specific times of day, changes in user behavior as measured by sensor input, or other factors. The particular modality of an interruption can consist of various combinations of audio tones and/or visual cues presented on an arbitrarily complex schedule.

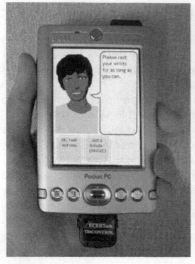 

Fig.1. PDA and Relational Agent Interface

Fig. 2. Experimental Setup for Interruption Studies

The run-time software was developed entirely in Macromedia Flash, and we are using Dell Axim X30 Pocket PC computers for development and experimentation. We have also developed a custom case for the PDA, which can be worn either on the waist like a large pedometer or pager, or in a shoulder harness. The initial application domain for the handheld agent is exercise promotion using an integrated accelerometer so the agent can tell whether a user is currently exercising or not.

4 Preliminary Evaluation Studies

Preliminary design and usability studies of the PDA-based system have been conducted and are described in this section. A longitudinal field study is also underway, and is described in more detail in Section 5.1.

4.1 Modality Study

In the first study, the impact of four different agent display modalities on the ability of a PDA-based agent to establish a social bond with the user was evaluated [4]. The four versions evaluated were: (FULL) the full version of the animated interface (animation, text and recorded speech consisting of backchannels and discourse markers only); (ANIM) the animated interface without the speech; (IMAGE) the interface showing only a static image of the character; and (TEXT) the interface without any character. These modalities were evaluated in a counterbalanced within-subjects experiment in which a subject conducted a brief social dialogue with each agent then filled out a self-report questionnaire evaluating the agent.

Results from the 12 subjects indicated that social bonding and perceived caring were significantly greater in the two animated conditions (FULL and ANIM) compared to the other two conditions (see Fig 2). Credibility of the information delivered by the agent was also rated higher in the FULL and ANIM conditions, but not significantly.

4.2 Task Interruption Studies

For users who happen to be sitting idly when a reminder to perform a healthy behavior is triggered, the interruption may result in a relatively high compliance rate. However, as many recent studies in task interruption have shown, responsiveness to an interruption (in this case, compliance with a recommended health behavior) depends crucially on what the user is doing at the time the interruption presents itself [15], in addition to many other factors such as the emotional state of the user [16] and the modality of the interruption [2].

To explore the range of possible interruption strategies that a PDA-based relational agent could use to maximize long-term health regimen compliance, a series of studies were conducted in the laboratory with the prototype system. For this purpose "wrist rests" were used as the health behavior to be promoted, and web searching and typing answers to questions on a desktop computer was used as the representative office task that a user may be engaged in when a health-related interruption occurs (Fig 2 shows the experimental setup). The PDA-based agent was programmed to discuss the importance of taking frequent breaks from typing in order to avoid repetitive stress injury and other upper body musculoskeletal disorders, and to interrupt users periodically with a request to rest their wrists. Prevention of such disorders is an important problem in its own right: in 2002 they accounted for two thirds of all reported occupational illness in the US, and intervention studies that promote wrist rests for computer workers have demonstrated significant reductions in self-reported symptoms [10].

A dilemma was presented to subjects, in which the research assistant running the study periodically reminded them to complete their work on the desktop computer as quickly as possible, while the PDA-based agent explained the importance of taking wrist rests and periodically (twice per session) asked them to take breaks from typing for as long as possible. The dilemma could often be visibly observed in subjects' behavior following each interruption (e.g., false starts at task resumption).

Primary measures used in the interruption studies included the duration of wrist rests taken by subjects, as a measure of short-term compliance (REST1 and REST2, dual-coded from video, with inter-rater reliability of 0.99), self-reported "desire to continue use" as a proxy for long-term adherence (CONTINUE), and other self-report assessments of the agent including: politeness of the agent (POLITE), satisfaction with the agent (SATISFIED), relationship with the agent (RELATION), and how much they liked the agent (LIKE).

4.2.1 Politeness and Compliance
A very insistent or annoying interruption may be effective at gaining compliance in the short term, but individuals may be likely to use the agent less frequently in the long run (or discontinue use altogether, as Jiminy Cricket discovered), resulting in an overall loss of compliance. On the other hand, an extremely polite interruption may have the inverse effect: it may not be very effective at gaining compliance at any particular moment (e.g., if the user is engrossed in a task), though individuals may be

more likely to continue use of the agent over time. Thus, a curvilinear relationship between the perceived "politeness" of interruption strategies and long-term health regimen adherence was hypothesized, holding all other factors constant.

To test this hypothesis, a range of interruption techniques were compared that were designed to vary only in their perceived politeness by just varying the audio alarm used to signal the start of each PDA interruption. Four alert sounds were selected which varied from very polite (AUDIO1, a subtle "ping") to very impolite (AUDIO4, a loud klaxon).

The study had a counterbalanced within-subjects design, and 29 subjects completed the protocol. Participants did perceive a difference in politeness across conditions (manipulation check), which varied directly with their ratings of how much they liked the advisor, how satisfied they were with the advisor, and their relationship with the advisor (greater politeness leading to closer relationships, Fig. 3). Desire to continue using the advisor varied directly with politeness ratings, confirming part of our hypothesis.

Fig. 4 shows short-term compliance behavior (rest time) for the two interruptions in each evaluation session. Rest time following initial exposure to each stimulus sound (REST1) did appear to vary according to our hypothesis (subjects rested longer for less polite sounds), but this variation was not significant. By the second exposure to each stimulus sound (REST2), the hypothesized longitudinal effects were already visible, with a curvilinear relationship between politeness and compliance, and the most annoying sound resulting in the shortest rest time.

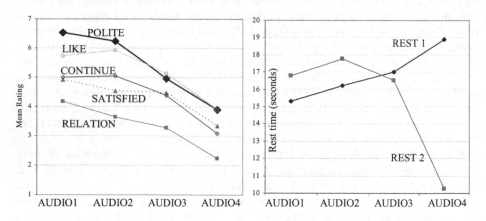

Fig. 3. Self-Report Ratings   **Fig. 4.** Compliance(Rest Times)

4.2.2 Interruption Negotiation Strategies

In the second interruption study, the effect of several interruption coordination strategies on long-term health behavior adherence was compared. According to McFarlane, negotiation-based methods, which give subjects more control over the interruption process, should provide the greatest overall performance [20]. Accordingly, two negotiation methods were evaluated, one which gave users control over the start of the interruption (NEGOTIATED, via a "snooze" button) and one which gave subjects a warning that an interruption was about to occur (FOREWARN). Given that a wearable health counselor also requires social competencies, the efficacy of empathic interruptions on long-term adherence was also evaluated, following the results of Liu and Picard [19]. In this condition (SOCIAL), the agent apologizes for interrupting the subject, assesses their emotional state at the time of the interruption and, if warranted, provides empathic feedback. The final condition compared these three against a simple audio alarm from the previous study (BASELINE, identical to AUDIO3 above).

The study had a counterbalanced within-subjects design, and 16 subjects completed the protocol. Results indicated that subjects actually rested the longest in the SOCIAL condition, but the difference among conditions was not statistically significant. When asked which method they thought was most effective at getting them to rest, subjects also rated the SOCIAL condition the highest, and this difference in ratings was significant. Long-term compliance, as measured by subjects' reported desire to CONTINUE use, was also highest for SOCIAL, and the pair-wise difference between BASELINE (lowest rating) and SOCIAL was significant, although the overall ANOVA was not. Interestingly, the NEGOTIATED condition was rated as the least effective, although actual rest times were second only to SOCIAL. Subjects did perceive a significant difference in politeness across conditions, with SOCIAL rated as significantly more polite than the other three conditions, and FOREWARN rated as the least polite.

Thus, overall, the SOCIAL condition was both the most preferred and the most effective at gaining health behavior compliance.

5 Conclusion

The design studies completed to date indicate the importance of social and relational competencies in wearable systems that work with users to motivate health regimen adherence. Users demonstrated a preference for personified, animated counselors to less social media. Our hypothesis about the relationship between politeness and compliance in interruptions recommending a health behavior was supported, and the use of social behaviors such as empathy outperformed other interruption negotiation strategies from the recent literature on task interruption.

5.1 Future Work

There are many interesting directions of future research in this area. The next study planned involves manipulation of the perceived social distance between the user and advisor. Following Brown & Levinson's theory of politeness [6], we expect this to moderate the relationship between politeness and compliance, such that as familiarity grows, users actually expect and prefer less polite forms of interruption. Techniques from studies such as this on the *best way* to interrupt someone should be combined with techniques for determining the *best time* to interrupt someone (e.g., [15]) to design systems that have the overall best chance of promoting long-term health behavior regimen adherence.

The initial "wearable conscience" under development using the prototype system described in Section 3 is an exercise coach that is able to sense a user's walking behavior and intervene in real time in order to promote physical activity among sedentary adults [3]. Users are prompted daily to schedule times at which they commit to go for brisk walks, and if the system senses that they are not walking when they should be, it interrupts and engages them in a "problem solving" motivational dialogue. The longitudinal field study will compare this "just in time" intervention to one in which the same motivational dialogue is delivered during an end of day session. The study is intended to demonstrate the importance of the "just in time" concept, together with the importance of social and relational competencies, for health regimen adherence.

Acknowledgements. Thanks to Daniel Mauer for his work on the design and implementation of the experimental platform, and to Francisco Crespo and Thomas Brown for their help in running the evaluation studies. Jennifer Smith provided many helpful comments on the paper. This work was supported by NIH National Library of Medicine grant R21LM008553.

References

1. Amft, O., Stäger, M., Lukowicz, P., Tröster, G.: Analysis of Chewing Sounds for Dietary Monitoring. In: Beigl, M., Intille, S.S., Rekimoto, J., Tokuda, H. (eds.) UbiComp 2005. LNCS, vol. 3660, pp. 56–72. Springer, Heidelberg (2005)
2. Arroyo, E., Selker, T., Stouffs, A.: Interruptions as multimodal outputs: which are the less disruptive? 4th IEEE International Conference on Multimodal Interfaces, pp. 479–482 (2002)
3. Bickmore, T., Gruber, A., Intille, S., Mauer, D.: A Handheld Animated Advisor for Physical Activity Promotion. American Medical Informatics Association Annual Symposium (2006)
4. Bickmore, T., Mauer, D.: Modalities for Building Relationships with Handheld Computer Agents. ACM SIGCHI Conference on Human Factors in Computing Systems (CHI) (2006)
5. Bickmore, T., Picard, R.: Establishing and Maintaining Long-Term Human-Computer Relationships. ACM Transactions on Computer Human Interaction 12(2), 293–327 (2005)
6. Brown, P., Levinson, S.C.: Politeness: Some universals in language usage. Cambridge University Press, Cambridge (1987)
7. Cassell, J., Vilhjálmsson, H., Bickmore, T.: BEAT: The Behavior Expression Animation Toolkit. SIGGRAPH '01, pp. 477–486 (2001)
8. Collodi, C.: Adventures of Pinnochio (1881) (checked 2/12/07) English translation available at http://www.gutenberg.org/etext/500
9. Czerwinski, M., S., C., Schumacher, B.: The effects of warnings and display similarities on interruption in multitasking environments. SIGCHI Bulletin 23(4), 38–39 (1991)
10. Galinsky, T., Swanson, N., Sauter, S., Hurrell, J., Schleifer, L.: A field study of supplementary rest breaks for data-entry operators. Ergonomics 43(5), 622–638 (2000)
11. Glanz, K., Lewis, F., Rimer, B.: Health Behavior and Health Education: Theory, Research, and Practice. Jossey-Bass, San Francisco, CA (1997)
12. Haigh, K., Kiff, L., Ho, G.: The Independent LifeStyle AssistantTM (I.L.S.A.): Lessons Learned. Assistive Technology 18, 87–106 (2006)
13. Haynes, R., McDonald, H., and Garg, A.: Helping Patients Follow Prescribed Treatment. JAMA 288, 22, pp. 2880-2883 (2006)

14. Hersh, N., Treadgold, L.: Neuropage: The rehabilitation of memory dysfunction by prosthetic memory and cueing. NeuroRehabilitation 4, 187–197 (1994)
15. Ho, J., Intille, S.S.: Using Context-Aware Computing to Reduce the Perceived Burden of Interruptions from Mobile Devices. CHI (2005)
16. Hudson, J.M., Christensen, J., Kellogg, W.A., Erickson, T.: I'd Be Overwhelmed, but It's Just One More Thing to Do: Availability and Interruption in Research Management, pp. 97–104 (2002)
17. Johnson, W., LaBore, C., Chiu, Y.: A Pedagogical Agent for Pyschosocial Intervention on a Handheld Computer. AAAI Fall Symposium on Dialogue Systems for Health Communication (2004)
18. Kim, H., Burke, D., Dowds, M., Robinson Boone, K., Park, G.: Electronic Memory Aids for Outpatient Brain Injury: Follow-up Findings. Brain Injury 14(2), 187–196 (2000)
19. Liu, K., Picard, R.: Embedded Empathy in Continuous, Interactive Health Assessment. CHI Workshop on HCI Challenges in Health Assessment (2005)
20. McFarlane, D.C.: Comparison of Four Primary Methods for Coordinating the Interruption of People in Human-Computer Interaction. Human-Computer Interaction 17(1), 63–139 (2002)
21. McFarlane, D.C., Latorella, K.A.: Coordinating the Interruption of People in Human-Computer Interaction. IFIP TC.13 International Conference on Human-Computer Interaction, pp. 295–303 (1999)
22. Mokdad, A.H., Marks, J.S., Stroup, D., Gerberding, J.: Actual causes of death in the United States, 2000. JAMA 291, pp. 1238–1245 (2004)
23. Pollack, M.E., Brown, L., Colbry, D., McCarthy, C.E., Orosz, C., Peintner, B., Ramakrishnan, S., Tsamardinos, I.: Autominder: An Intelligent Cognitive Orthotic System for People with Memory Impairment. Robotics and Autonomous Systems 44, 273–282 (2003)
24. Robertson, T.J., Prabhakararao, S., Burnett, M., Cook, C., Ruthruff, J.R., Beckwith, L., Phalgune, A.: Impact of interruption style on end-user debugging CHI, pp. 287–294 (2004)

Using Design Critique as Research to Link Sustainability and Interactive Technologies

Eli Blevis, Youn-kyung Lim, David Roedl, and Erik Stolterman

Sustainable Interaction Design Research Group,
School of Informatics, Indiana University at Bloomington,
901 East 10th Street, Bloomington IN USA 47408
{eblevis,younlim,droedl,estolter}@indiana.edu

Abstract. This paper echoes and points to work we have presented elsewhere on establishing the links between issues of sustainability and interaction design. The significant contribution of this paper is a description of the use of design critique as a research method and an argument for its importance to HCI researchers, especially with respect to very complex design contexts—the link between sustainability issues and interaction design research and practice, in particular.

Keywords: Design critique, design research, sustainable interaction design, research methods, design ethics and values, value sensitive design, social context of interaction design.

1 Introduction

In other work, we have argued that sustainability can and should be a central focus of the research and practice of design with the materials of interactive technologies [2,3], a perspective that has been echoed and articulated in several other sources we enumerate below. In this paper we first explain what we mean by sustainability and re-iterate a rubric and a framework we have developed for understanding how sustainability can be considered as a factor in design with the materials of interactive technologies. As a unique contribution of this particular paper and presentation, we argue that an important way of understanding the relationship between sustainability and interactive technologies is the method of *design critique*. It has been argued by some in the HCI literature and frequently in the design literature that design critique has not been generally understood as a method for research within HCI [37]. As a complement to other methods familiar in HCI—such as methods borrowed from ethnography, prototyping methods, field work and observations, case studies, surveys, interviews, and so forth—design critique is an important addition that allows interaction designers to achieve a nuance in their design research that can only be achieved by understanding *particular* designs and environments in very specific terms as opposed to *general* ones. This approach is common in design disciplines, and has been characterized by Nelson and Stolterman as the *designerly* notion that design understanding concerns the "ultimate particular" [23].

D. Schuler (Ed.): Online Communities and Social Comput., HCII 2007, LNCS 4564, pp. 22–31, 2007.

When it comes to issues of sustainability, the design issues under consideration are particularly complex and demand a nuanced approach. For example, the inter-relationships between such issues as software, hardware, fashion, form, content, marketing, and copyright that affect our understanding of the Apple iPod as an example of a particular interactive device create a complex morass of effects, many of which have implications for sustainable and unsustainable behaviors. Before such issues can be understood in precise, measurable ways, we must first enumerate all of the factors and environmental contexts that play a role and doing so demands informal, phenomenological techniques like design critique to begin such a discourse.

Significance: The links between sustainability and interactive technologies are not often cited and yet, the consumption of computing technologies driven by the cycle of mutual obsolescence in which hardware and software are the key actors has great importance for the future of our collective human environments and conditions. There have been hundreds of millions of computers purchased new in the world in the last 5 years—with nearly a third purchased in the United States [2]. If advancing economies like China and India adopt western habits of consumption, the electronic trash generated by such practices predict potentially disastrous effects on the global environment.

Relevance: From the perspective of sustainability and interaction technologies, we repeat a rubric and framework for assessing the sustainable and unsustainable factors of particular interactive devices. The rubric relates to possible material effects that may result from the use and marketing of interactive devices, such as disposal, reuse, remanufacturing, sharing for maximal use, and other possibilities. The framework relates to design principles for promoting sustainable interactive design such as linking invention to disposal, or promoting renewal and reuse. In this paper and in referenced sources, we hope that this rubric and framework are sufficiently articulated that others in HCI will be able to apply them and understand them as a theoretical model and structure for evaluation. The notion of design critique is also situated within more familiar theoretical frameworks in HCI. The notion of design critique as research has been argued in the general literature, and this literature is referenced and situated in relation to the theoretical literature in HCI.

2 Design Critique

In a well-known article, Daniel Fallman [8] distinguishes between *design-oriented research*—research targeted at building design knowledge, and *research-oriented design*—design as an activity which makes use of tools of research. Our notion of design critique applies to both cases—that is, design critique is a way of creating design knowledge and design critique is also a tool in the practice of design. Without question, design critique is at least tacitly within the repertoire of tools used within the practice of interaction design. Understanding design critique as a foundational tool for developing design knowledge is much less well accepted within the scholarly literature on HCI. We argue that design critique deserves recognition within the HCI community and moreover, that it is oftentimes at least as appropriate as empirical methods in many and certain interaction design contexts where the complexity of effects is larger than what can be isolated as variables for experimental methods.

Definition. We define *design critique* as *a process of discourse on many levels of the nature and effects of an ultimate particular design.* Design critique may be regarded to be a research method and the act of design criticism can make use of intellectual and conceptual frameworks as a supporting mechanism of structure. Nonetheless, it is possibly an act without controversy to claim that design critique is better understood as part of a reflective practice of design than as science [6,23,30].

Design critique involves looking at an ultimate particular example in a non-reductive immediate way. The focus of a design critique in the context of interactivity can range from a particular model of cell-phone to a particular system of services that scaffold an interactive device to an understanding of the cultural and environmental effects that accrue from a particular co-mingling of hardware and software. The role of the design critic is to comment on the qualities of an ultimate particular from an holistic perspective, including reason, ethics, and aesthetics as well as minute details of form and external effects on culture.

The emphasis in the definition above on the notion of ultimate particular designs as being a designerly way of understanding owes to [23] and the notion of designerly ways of knowing is characterized more generally in [6], as well as Fallman [8]. The notion of the value of design critique as a method in-and-of its own right will have been introduced by Zimmerman, Forlizzi, & Evenson [37] with some anticipated controversy at this year's ACM CHI conference by the time this present paper appears. There are a number of attributes of design critique that make it important for consideration as a distinguished technique within the HCI community that is concerned with design, specifically

(i)   design critique accommodates the need to understand the effects and context of any particular interaction design on a number of different levels denoting a number of different contexts—for example, the level and context of individual use, the level and context of how interaction design mediates between individuals, the level and context of how some interaction design may creates advantages for some groups while preserving or adding to the disadvantages of others, and so forth,

(ii)   design critique provides a mechanism for nuanced discourse and understanding of particular interaction designs, especially when to do otherwise would lead to overly reductive discourse and understandings,

(iii)   design critique can be fast compared to empirical studies; moreover, design critique can make use of secondary sources, especially compiling the insights that emerge from secondary readings of empirical studies into complex and nuanced wholes,

(iv)   further to point (i) above, design critique accommodates and fosters discourse at individual, communal, and societal levels about the nature and effects of particular interaction designs,

(v)   design critique accommodates and invites contrast and comparison between particular interaction designs and historically significant examplars— contrasts and comparisons which yield an historically informed and predictive view not easily managed by empirical studies alone,

(vi)   design critique accommodates and provides a mechanism for comparisons that are massively multi-dimensional and cross-contextual, including contexts of interaction design that are formed from characterizations of fashion, form, color, appearance, operation semantics, function, and other dimensions,

(vii)   design critique accommodates and provides a mechanism for the consideration of ethics, aesthetics, and reasoning with respect to understanding interaction design

(viii)   the integration of design critique as part of a designerly reflective practice—the term reflective practice owes to [30] and is echoed throughout the design and education literatures—is key to providing the designerly experience and judgment that can allow interaction designers to more effectively create meaningful and ethically-sensitive designs.

Comparison to other methods: There are of course many ways to inform interaction design in the context of complex conditions and levels of concern. Our claims above concern the reasons why design critique should be counted among such means, and specifically not that design critique is the only method that interaction designers should employ. An inventory of general design methods from the critical view of design in the context of information technologies is presented in [16]. A related discussion of the role of ethnography as a means of building knowledge in-and-of itself and achieving nuanced discourse is presented in [7].

3 Sustainable Interaction Design

One of the central notions of Sustainable Interaction Design (SID) is that the durability of interactive devices and the ability to reconstitute interactive devices with minimal or no waste in the presence of changing needs and requirements and in the presence of technological advances is part of the design of an interactive device. In other words, SID prescribes an ethical imperative to create things that last, that can be maintained, and that can be adapted as an aesthetic preference to things that are easily obsoleted and frequently disposed. As an ethical design principle within SID, we could say:

> Make nothing that is disposable and make everything of such high quality that each thing endures and continues to delight and invites maintenance and renewal even as it passes from one person or context of use to another.

Reflections on an aesthetic of high quality durable things: First, this notion of an aesthetic of high quality durable things is not the only constituent notion of the idea of SID. Sustainability can be broadly construed to apply to the ongoing conservation and preservation of resources and well-being in terms of the environment, public health, global economic conditions, and many other aspects of the human condition and the condition of the earth.

Second, this notion of an aesthetic of high quality durable things stands in direct opposition to some enterprise models which require a constant cycle of obsolescence and acquisition for their own survival, irrespective of the survivability of those who may be effected including those who are the apparent primary beneficiaries of the profit motives which such enterprises serve. There are enterprises which create high quality enduring and renewable products. There are businesses that do both well and good [32]. Sadly, few if any such enterprises within the marketplace for interaction design seem to be actively looking for opportunities to escape the enterprise model of what we have elsewhere termed "invention and disposal" [2,3].

Third, conservation and preservation of things is not always the best thing to do from the perspective of sustainability—at least theoretically. Sometimes new things are more resource efficient than old things to the point where it makes more sense from a conservation point of view to retire the old and use the new. This circumstance is almost never entirely clearly the case. The most obvious example is automobile technology, where one can reasonably consider if the environmental cost of manufacturing and using a new hybrid electric vehicle over its potential lifespan is less than the cost of adapting an older vehicle to new, cleaner or otherwise alternative fuel technologies such as propane, hydrogen, or bio-fuels. The answer to this question is not at all clear one way or the other. In the case of interactive devices design with the materials of information technologies, the question is also difficult to answer in any particular case. The US Environmental Protection Agency (EPA) offers a program to certify certain computer hardware as "Energy Star" compliant. According to the EPA site (www.energystar.gov), the criteria for this certification include: *"If left inactive, ENERGY STAR qualified computers enter a low-power mode and use 15 watts or less. New chip technologies make power management features more reliable, dependable, and user-friendly than even just a few years ago. Spending a large portion of time in low-power mode not only saves energy, but helps equipment run cooler and last longer. Businesses that use ENERGY STAR enabled office equipment may realize additional savings on air conditioning and maintenance. Over its lifetime, ENERGY STAR qualified equipment in a single home office (e.g., computer, monitor, printer, and fax) can save enough electricity to light an entire home for more than 4 years."*

Especially with respect to the forth statement above, the question of if it is better from an environmental sustainability point of view to replace a computer which is not Energy Star compliant with one that is depends on if the energy savings more than offset the environmental cost of manufacture of the new device and disposal of the old one. This question is still not easy to answer and only underscores the complexity of understanding the environmental impacts of interactive design decisions. Moreover, if new chip technologies and software with better power management features are available for new computers, such technologies and software could cause enormous good if they become popular as consumer-installed upgrades that enable the preservation of old ones. Such good can only come from alternative models of enterprise to the present ones adopted by computer manufacturers.

This notion of an aesthetic of high quality things turns out to be a complex design context, as one begins to think about it deeply from a design point of view, especially from the point of view of design with the materials of information technologies.

A rubric and some principles: In [2], we give a rubric of material effects that can be used to understand by interaction designers as a kind of checklist to analyze and predict the environmental effects of particular interaction designs as a means of sorting through such complexities. The items of the rubric are: *disposal, salvage, recycling, remanufacturing for reuse, reuse as is, achieving longevity of use, sharing for maximal use, achieving heirloom status, finding wholesome alternatives to use,* and *active repair of misuse.* This rubric of material effects is further refined and developed in [3]. Also in [2], we give five principles that are intended as hypotheses about how interaction designers can consider promoting less harmful material effects over more harmful ones. In [3], these principles are elaborated to include meanings of *critical design*—essential acts of design and *design criticism*—the analysis of design. The principles are *linking invention & disposal, promoting renewal & reuse, promoting quality & equality,* and *de-coupling ownership & identity.*

Additional sources: There are many other sources which relate to the notion of SID. The rubric and principles above are inspired by notions of sustainability and design described in [13,34,35]. A Special Interest Group meeting on the subject will have occurred at the 2007 ACM CHI conference [17]. In what follows, we discuss the case of cell phones, a case which has been investigated from the perspective of sustainability in [4,22]. The issue of sustainability in connection with ubiquitous computing has been articulated in [5,14,19,36]. The connection of sustainability to value sensitive design has been noted in [9] and value sensitive design in general is described in [9-12]. Designing interactivity to promote sustainable behaviors is described specifically in [18,33]. The use of design critique within HCI is in some sense pioneered by Norman in [24-27]. Sustainability and design are connected in [21,28,29,31,32].

4 Linking Sustainability and Interaction Design by Means of Design Critique

In [3], we give many examples of design criticism applications of the rubric described in section 3. We conclude this essay by sketching how the rubric and principles can be used in a critical design sense to generate considerations and concepts for how cell phones as an example may be designed as interactive devices in accordance with notions of SID.

Some background: In [22], the social implications of cell phone use and disposal are considered from the point of view of environmental sustainability. The authors point out the duality of utility and harm that arise from the design conceptualization of cell phones as disposable objects:*"Disposable cell phones combine utility and toxicity in one indivisible package. It is likely that the environmental hazard from these phones will be significant because they have a large potential market, promising immense usefulness and usability to currently underserved customers. "*

In a survey we ourselves conducted of 435 undergraduates students (IUB IRB #06-11332) in October 2006, we asked about the number of cell phones owned by the participants in their lifetime. Most of the participants were in their late teens or early twenties. The responses were extraordinary: "morc than 15"=0.9% N=4; "9-15"=3.9% N=17; **"4-8"=32.8% N=142;** "3"=30.5% N=132; "2"=23.6% N=102; "1"=7.9% N=34; "0"=0.5% N=2; "No response" N=2. The survey responses suggest that cell phones, disposable by design or not, are effectively disposable in practice. Other survey results showed that the participants for the most part expressed a preference to change cell phones once a year or more (66%, N=428) if money were not an object. As a conjecture, the desire to stay fashionable is possibly the motivation for such rapid replacement, rather than technical utility.

Linking invention & disposal: Cell phones are interactive devices that form part of systems of communications which can vary widely from one context to another. In some markets, such as China, cell phones are not commonly provided by the service carriers, but purchased from independent vendors. In the US market, cell phones are provided by service carriers with the effect that switching carriers requires switching cell phones. The differences in features of one service provider's plans over another's in the US enterprise model co-mingle with the features of the actual hardware itself. Clearly, the Chinese model may promote less premature disposal of cell phones. The invention of new cell phones which integrate wireless internet and other features not yet common is a more troubling predictor of the early demise and disposal of many existing cell phones.

Promoting renewal & reuse: The separation of service providers from hardware vendors is just one way to promote less disposal. Separating aspects of a system promotes the kind of modularity that allows for renewal and reuse as an alternative to invention and disposal. Products like smart phones do exactly the opposite— integrating functions of various products into a single product predicts the early demise of that product as soon as any one of the integrated elements becomes obsolete. Smart phones that embed user-upgradeable operating systems and software in a manner that is backwards-compatible with the hardware remain an elusive promise. A better design for cell phones from the perspective of SID might involve separating at least the case, display, keypad, software, and internal electronic components into modules which may be replaced independently.

Promoting quality & equality: The separation of a cell phone into independently renewable components would allow for some of the high-touch components to made of enduring materials that create the sense of quality for owners and the desire to maintain and renew rather than dispose and acquire. The cases on such a cell phone may be made of metals or other high quality materials rather than inexpensive plastics, since that portion of the product may be expected to endure. People who have invested in a cell phone case with the quality of an object of high fashion such as many kinds of watches or items of jewellery may be more inclined to update the internal components rather than discard the whole appliance. Furthermore, the value of the cell phone in promoting equality of experience may be better preserved by such design as ownership transfers. Similarly the internal components may be built to higher standards with more resistance to shock or moisture in order to promote longevity of use.

De-coupling ownership & identity: With things that have high fashion, the uniqueness and exclusivity and enduring qualities of an object matters. Items of apparel and jewellery in all manner of global cultural contexts can convey much about personal identity. See [20] for a wonderful photographic treatment of this phenomenon. With the things that emphasize only high status, having the latest invention or style may matter more than enduring qualities. Again, the separation of a cell phone into independently renewable components may allow for the endurance and uniqueness of the visible components themselves to convey sense of identity, rather than the need to convey sense of status that accrues from having the very latest thing. The uniqueness and exclusivity that creates cell phone fashion may primarily be about high status— the newest design is sold at a premium price that only the rich can afford and the rest covet until the price drops when a still newer design arrives. In other contexts (clothing, music) fashion is driven by personal style, participation in subculture, and so forth. In addition to high quality enduring materials, perhaps the fashion of new technology can be replaced by the fashion of new original *digital content*. One example where this already occurs is ring-tones, where personal identity is expressed by having the latest most original ring-tone. See [15] for example.

Using natural models & reflection: In [1], the notion of *structure-preserving transformations* as a design principle is defined as the goal to make the built environment operate more like nature in which things evolve over time and the materials of old structures are preserved as part of the birth and growth of new ones. It is hard to imagine a cell phone achieving heirloom status, but perhaps some of its visible components can—especially the ones with which people interact directly.

Summary: An interactive device like a cell phone underscores the need for interaction designers to think beyond the scope of mere human-computer interaction. Cell phones incorporate interactive software, hardware, and services. Cell phones vary widely by context of use from one country to another, from one demographic group to another. Cell phones can be fashion and status statements. Cell phones can be made to be modular and selectively upgradeable if the enterprise models and will are present to do so. Interaction designers need to take all of these and other factors into account in the design of such devices. Such complexity demands that interaction designers engage in design critique of what is at present in order to inform the critical design of what is possible.

5 Conclusions

In this paper we have presented the fundamental idea that sustainability is an increasingly important concern with respect to the design of interactive products. We have argued that he complexity of this concern demands the use of design critique and that design critique needs at its foundation to (i) emphasize the ultimate particular, and (ii) be centered in a well developed intellectual and conceptual framework.

Our belief in design critique stems from an understanding that design is always about the ultimate particular. In designed products, all design considerations at all levels must be explained together as a single whole account. We also believe that such a whole account cannot be understood by an approach that is based only on reductive analytical thinking. Issues concerning sustainability cannot be reduced to individual measurable properties of a design. Instead, sustainability is always about the whole, and about how all possible aspects are composed into one. Design critique, as we have defined it here, has the potential to address the question of the whole. It is a process that is massively parallel through the appreciation of all qualities as a whole. Such an approach requires a developed sense of quality, as well as a sensibility of the particular. Experience and insights based on an abstract conceptual understanding must be coupled to a pragmatic and intimate relation to actual real designs.

Design critique is a way to foster such a sensibility of the particular over time within the mind of a designer. It requires an ongoing exposition of ultimate particular designs, and a constant struggle with trying to critique each particular design, not as an example but as a real design, as a whole. The reflection between an intellectual abstraction—here the rubric and the framework presented—and the particular designs fosters an understanding both of the particular designs but also of the intellectual abstraction.

In order to link the design of interactive technologies with a sustainability issues, we propose that the field of interaction design has to develop both intellectual abstractions (such as the rubric and principles) that are not only theoretical constructs but are suitable as supporting frameworks for pragmatic design critique. In this paper we have described such a supporting framework that we believe would be suitable in relation to sustainability. We also propose that there is a need to develop the notion and understanding of design critique, not only as a process to gain insight of a particular design, but also as a way to develop insights that can further push intellectual foundations. In this paper we have presented a first characterization of the design critique process, as a necessary step in linking sustainability and interaction design.

References

1. Alexander, C.: The Nature of Order. vol. II. The Center for Environmental Structure. Berkeley, CA (2002)
2. Blevis, E.: Sustainable Interaction Design: Invention & Disposal, Renewal & Reuse. In: Proc.of CHI '07, ACM Press, New York, NY (2007)
3. Blevis, E.: Advancing sustainable interaction design: two perspectives on material effects. Design Philosophy Papers #04/2006 (2006)
4. Bhuie, A., Ogunseitan, O., Saphores, J., Shapiro, A.: Environmental and economic trade-offs in consumer electronic products recycling: a case study of cell phones and computers. IEEE International Symposium on Electronics and the Environment, pp. 74–79 (2004)
5. Coroama, V., Kostakos, V., Magerkurth, C., de Vallejo, I.: UbiSoc 2005: first international workshop on social implications of ubiquitous computing. In: Ext. Abs. of CHI '05, pp. 2111–2112. ACM Press, New York, NY (2005)
6. Cross, N.: Designerly ways of knowing: design discipline versus design science. Design Issues (MIT Press) 17(3), 49–55 (2004)
7. Dourish, P.: Implications for design. In: Proc. of CHI '06, pp. 541–550. ACM Press, New York, NY (2006)
8. Fallman, D.: Designing design: design-oriented human-computer interaction. In: Proc. of CHI '03, pp. 225–232. ACM Press, New York (2003)
9. Friedman, B., Kahn, P., Borning, A.: Value sensitive design and information systems. In: Zhang, P., Galletta, D. (eds.) Human-Computer Interaction and Management Information Systems: Foundations. M.E. Sharpe, New York, pp. 348–372 (2006)
10. Friedman, B.: Value sensitive design, pp. 76–774. Berkshire Publishing, Great Barrington, MA (2004)
11. Friedman, B., Kahn Jr., P.: Human values, ethics, and design. In: Jacko, J., Sears, A. (eds.) The human-computer interaction handbook, pp. 1177–1201. Lawrence Erlbaum Associates, Mahwah, NJ (2003)
12. Friedman, B.: Human Values and the Design of Computer Technology. CSLI Press, Stanford, CA (1997)
13. Fry, T.: A New Design Philosophy: An Introduction to Defuturing. NSWU Press, New South Wales, Australia (1999)

14. Jain, R., Wullert, J.: Challenges: environmental design for pervasive computing systems. In: Proc. of the 8th Annual international Conference on Mobile Computing and Networking, pp. 263–270. ACM Press, New York, NY (2002)
15. Liu, C.M., Donath, J.S.: Urbanhermes: social signaling with electronic fashion. In: Proc. of CHI'06, ACM Press, New York, NY (2006)
16. Löwgren, J., Stolterman, E.: Thoughtful Interaction Design. MIT Press, Cambridge (2004)
17. Mankoff, J., Blevis, E., Borning, A., Friedman, B., Fussell, S., Hasbrouk, J., Sengers, P., Woodruf, A.: Sustainability and interaction (SIG). In: Ext. Abs. of CHI'07, ACM Press, New York, NY (2007)
18. Mankoff, J., Matthews, D., Fussell, S.R., Johnson, M.: Leveraging social networks to motivate individuals to reduce their ecological footprints. In: Proc. of HICSS (2007)
19. Makelberge, N.: Computing against the grain. Design Philosophy Papers. #04/2003 (2003)
20. Menzel, P.: Material World: A Global Family Portrait. Sierra Club Books. San Franciso, CA (1994)
21. Nardi, B.A., O'Day, V.L.: Information Ecologies: Using Technology with Heart. MIT Press, Cambridge (1999)
22. Nardi, B.A., & Others.: (2003) A social ecology of wireless technology by Critical Friends of Technology. First Monday, vol. 8(8) (August 2003)
23. Nelson, H., Stolterman, E.: The Design Way—Intentional Change in an Unpredictable World. Educational Technology Publications, New Jersey (2003)
24. Norman, D.: Emotion and design: attractive things work better. Interactions Magazine ix(4), 36–42 (2002)
25. Norman, D.: Affordances, conventions, and design. Interactions, 38–43 (May 1999)
26. Norman, D.: The Invisible Computer: Why Good Products Can Fail, the Personal Computer Is So Complex, and Information Appliances Are the Solution. MIT Press, Cambridge (1998)
27. Norman, D.: The Design of Everyday Things, 2nd edn. Doubleday, New York (1990)
28. Papanek, V.: Design for the Real World: Human Ecology and Social Change, 2nd edn. Academy Chicago, Chicago (1985)
29. Reed, C., Wang, H., Blevis, E.: Recognizing individual needs and desires in the case of designing an inventory of humanity-centered, sustainability-directed concepts for time and travel. In: Proc. of DPPI '05 Designing Pleasurable Product Interfaces. Eindhoven, NL, pp. 181–212 (2005)
30. Schön, D.: The Reflective Practitioner. Temple Smith, London (1983)
31. Stegall, N.: Designing sustainability: a philosophy for ecologically intentional design. Design Issues 22(2), 56–63 (2006)
32. Thackara, J.: In the Bubble: Designing for a Complex World. MIT Press, Cambridge, MA (2005)
33. Wash, R., Hemphill, L., Resnick, P.: Design decisions in the RideNow Project. In: Proc. SIGGROUP, pp. 132–135 (2005)
34. Willis, A.M.: Ontological designing. Design Philosophy Papers. #02/2006 (2006)
35. Winograd, T., Flores, F.: Understanding Computers and Cognition: A New Foundation for Design. Addison-Wesley, Inc., New York (1986)
36. Woolley, M.: Choreographing obsolescence - ecodesign: the pleasure/dissatisfaction cycle. In: Proc. of DPPI '03 Designing Pleasurable Products and Interfaces, pp. 77–81. ACM Press, New York, NY (2003)
37. Zimmerman, J., Forlizzi, J., Evenson, S.: Research through design as a method for interaction design research in HCI. In: Proc.of CHI '07, ACM Press, New York, NY (2007)

An Analysis of Involvement of HCI Experts in Distributed Software Development: Practical Issues

Görkem Çetin[1], Damiano Verzulli[2], and Sandra Frings[3]

[1] Gebze Institute of Technology
gcetin@gyte.edu.tr
[2] CINECA
damiano@verzulli.it
[3] University of Stuttgart
sandra.frings@iao.fraunhofer.de

Abstract. Traditionally, free and open source software (F/OSS) developers have focused more on the features of a specific application, most of the time ignoring the necessity of user-centric design. This has mainly stemmed from the fact that developers have little interaction with HCI studies, knowledge bases and reports. Moreover, the lack of user interface designers has resulted in a lack of awareness of this area. As a consequence, the user centric design phenomenon within F/OSS applications has been neglected. In this paper, we have mentioned various problems that would slow down a F/OSS project development towards a user-engineered software, and investigated the ways that HCI experts and developers interact with each other and researched bug reporting systems by means of eligibility to issue usability bugs. For the conclusion part, we have explored possible ways to achieve a user-centric design in a project with asynchronous interaction among geographically distributed developers.

Keywords: F/OSS, HCI, usability, open source, distributed usability, user centric design.

1 Introduction

Ignoring the necessity of user centric design [2] by the developers of the same project has been a global problem of project managers since the very beginning of software development paradigm. There has been a notorious conflict between the developer seeking for an extended ability bundled with paranormal features of the software and the project manager trying to convince the developer to build a framework exploiting user centric development methodologies. For a long time, the project managers and the developers of many open source projects have been pointing to the same person, so this problem has been solved in a manner that it has never existing. As a result, user centric design phenomenon within F/OSS applications has been neglected [3]. Starting from the beginning of 2000, commercialization of open source software has opened the possibility for the masses to realize the effects of "an open project does not mean it should suffer from usability" paradigm. End users, developers and

D. Schuler (Ed.): Online Communities and Social Comput., HCII 2007, LNCS 4564, pp. 32–40, 2007.
© Springer-Verlag Berlin Heidelberg 2007

customers have become the main sources of reporting usability bugs. However, there's still room for HCI experts to take part in this table as the fourth player.

Problems above can be seen as a conseguence of the particular history of the F/OSS community. Right after the birth of the F/OSS community, in 1983[1], all the developer efforts were spent for the development of technical applications targeting computer scientists. At that time there was no previous F/OSS applications and the development of the building-blocks (editor, compiler, linker, debugger, etc.) was necessary as the first step. Once becoming production-ready, these building-blocks could have acted as enablers for a much wider community of programmers that, with such tools, would have been able to develop many other kinds of applications.

Although there have been some attempts to simplify the usage of several F/OSS applications, nothing serious happened until 1996. At that time end-user personal computers were running a proprietary operating system together with a certain number of proprietary applications. Being driven by marketing needs, software corporations developed such applications focusing of several factors, including usability: "...the effectiveness, efficiency and satisfaction with which users can achieve tasks..." by the way of such operating system and applications [4].

It was in this timeframe and context that something new happened within the F/OSS community. Following the announcement of the KDE project (1996) and the GNOME project (1997), F/OSS community started taking care of end-users needs and, as such, building two completely new desktop environments. Both KDE and GNOME had the end-users needs within their mission remit, recognising usability as a critical factor from the beginning of both projects.

Comparing the way usability norm was approached by proprietary vendors and by the F/OSS community, it is worth nothing that, due to the commercial nature of proprietary software vendors, usability was (and still is) seen as a revenue generator: the more usable the software, the more licenses sold, the more revenues generated. This issue can heavily impact the development process as companies, being driven by the business needs, will force the adoption of usability requirements even if they are often underestimated by many programmers due to their technical mindset. Within the F/OSS community things are much different [5] as the main driver for the developing activities is the "freedom" of the movement itself. A freedom that, as such, does not imply and/or enforce nothing in terms of usability compliance.

Several other factors have had a critical role in taking the F/OSS community to completely ignore, or to heavily limit, the necessity of a User Centric Design (UCD). With the launch of the KDE project, for the first time, the F/OSS community focused on end-users. Communications with such users, the understanding of their needs, their approach to computer usage and lots of other issues were completely new problems that the F/OSS community needed to face. Moreover, while since the early days the F/OSS community succeeded relying only on its internal competences, with the advent of F/OSS desktop computing the situation quickly changed and a completely new set of skills was needed. Interface design, visual communication and information

---

[1] Here we identify the F/OSS community with the GNU project, as this was the first attempt to formally develope a "free" operating environment. The GNU project have been officially started by Richard Stallman on Sep 27th 1983, with the announcement stated on http://www.gnu.org/gnu/initial-announcement.html

architecture became mandatory concepts for a winning desktop environment. Those concepts were mostly unknown and unavailable within the F/OSS community member [6].

Furthermore, if it were easy to put F/OSS programmer around the same table discussing about applications technical details, the rising of desktop F/OSS required the establishment of new links between F/OSS community and HCI community. Actually, it was (and still is) hard to establish such new links as both communities grow among different roots.

Based on what have been written above, we think that to improve the usability level of F/OSS applications, and specifically, to increase the current involvement of HCI experts in whole development process, several actions need to be jointly adopted. We refer to the need, for the F/OSS community and HCI experts' community, to create a distributed development, involvement, evaluation and reporting methodology for every F/OSS usability issues. It's also fundamental that usability requirements needs to be taken in proper account since the very beginning of every F/OSS projects: all programmers know that application requirements need to be formally defined before the start of the developing activity; in the same way usability requirements need to be specified and defined well before the development activity. Finally, the need to maintain or even increase the current trend in desktop F/OSS development will surely impact the usability of future F/OSS applications: the development trend of projects like KDE and GNOME follows a very tight time-frame, with improvements, also in usability area, that are much visible in respect to proprietary counterparts. Should such progress continue for the future releases, it is easy to expect a very comfortable and usable future F/OSS desktops.

2 Interaction Issues

In a distributed environment, limited and asynchronous information flow leads to a problem of low performance among developers, compared to collocated teams. In such a team, most of the communication is ideally conducted electronically (e-mails, phone, teleconferencing, emails, etc) – sometimes all team members meet in a predefined location with changing periods. For example, most KDE developers meet at least twice in a year, but some less technical and low-profile projects' developers may find it unnecessary and expensive even to meet annually. The Internet can both be a viable and a problematic way of collaboration, since it has a dull side which limits vocal peer conversation. However F/OSS developers can benefit from distributed intelligence where there is always room for usability experts. Low-budget projects can also have an opportunity to find usability people, and merge them into their projects to increase the usability profile of the resulting product [7].

Reitmayr and Mühling [8] define three basic problems that would slow down the development towards a user-engineered software:

1. The basis of usability work, a clear definition of the target users, their tasks and their requirements are often missing.
2. Missing hierarchical decision paths may pose a problem in larger projects where a usability expert needs to convince each relevant developer instead of the head of department.

3. A traditional focus on technical rather than GUI-related issues may require a major redesign of the information architecture and interaction design of software.

It's convenient to add the following items about why usability experts face problems while taking an active part in F/OSS development.

1. With usability experts taking an active part in the project, the time-to-market is slowed down.
2. A developer should cope with other roles – now he is not the only decision maker.
3. The developer without knowing its user base assumes that the requirements for the new application are the same as the requirements in all other applications.
4. The necessity of a user interface developer is questioned after introduction, adoption and exploitation of interface design software by non-designers.

As we have stated before, the fact of problematic way of having collaboration leads to a low profile of interaction modalities. Bug reports may be well hidden from the project volunteers, the documentation subsystem may not benefit from the modern application development interfaces, or the lack of consistent and coherent software including a scheduling tool, task list or a trouble ticket system may yield to a frustration of the HCI expert. Vast variety of tools geared towards high tech developers, always questioned efficiency of high volume mailing list traffic, and a lack of initiative to amend the requests of the usability expert pose a diverse working environment than a model where the usability expert joins a project from the very beginning, sets the requirements, initiates a user centric design under project manager's acknowledgement, conducts necessary usability tests with predefined tasks matching the focus user group.

3 Focusing on Usability Reporting Tools

Bug reporting tools vary with the way they work. While some utilities (i.e. crash reporting tools) involve little end user activity by only sending proper crash debugging information, others can request a plea of subjective and objective input from the end user. A few applications, when clicked on a specific menu item, forward the user to the application development web page and requests to answer the qualitative and quantitative questions asking the degree of users' satisfaction [9].

There are some prototypes [10] to report usability bugs, having a major redesign of a generic user reporting tools and real world examples which has a working backend to support interested developers [11]. Communication channels between the end user and developer is limited, so application-bundled can be an effective solution. However, in free software world, application developers tend to rely on web based bug reporting tools like Bugzilla and Mantis, ignoring the necessity to bundle their application with a consistent feedback tool. While this approach is changing over the recent years with more applications return feedback from users, we believe that the ignorance of developing a bug reporting interface which collects not only textual data but hypermedia from users seldomly makes it complicated to exchange proper information among developer and the reporter.

Current tools are not convenient for reporting usability issues with the following reasons:

- They don't have a mechanism to interactively record, upload, show, maintain and comment on user submitted videos, images and voice.
- There's no way to merge a note to an attachment to show the submitters' and developers' opinion, annoyance and feedback. Trying to spot a minor usability issue may not be explained verbally, and hence needs a graphical representation. Unfortunately, not all computers are bundled with a painting and drawing application.
- Current bug reporting tools have an increased complexity which is trying to spot all kinds of problems on the direction of the developer, ignoring the mental model of the user.
- An average bug reporting tool requires to fill a considerable amount of information, some of which are not immediately pertinent to the end user or HCI expert, making it sometimes impossible to submit a bug thus leave the HCI expert out of the scope of the project.

Under the light of the facts above, the lack of a suitable usability reporting interface results in some issues. First, number of reporters and reports thereof decreases. Most of the critical bugs never go into the bug database, rendering it unusual to increase the quality of the code. Second, usability reports are handled by the mailing lists and forums instead of a database, which is hard to follow, fix and give proper feedback to the reporter. And finally, since the aim of the bug reporting tool is often misunderstood, the end user (sometimes the usability expert) starts to discuss about an issue and/or report a problem he cannot solve, mostly ending up with closing the bug because of misusing the bug reporting tool.

4 Analyzing Bug Reports

There has been related empirical researches showing findings in F/OSS development community [12], however there's a lack of researching how developers really exploit the presence of HCI experts and usability bugs. In this study, KDE (K Desktop Environment) project has been identified as core materials to be investigated. 100 random samples have been taken from KDE, and usability and non-usability bugs have been identified and classified according to their severity. For a side by side study, a cross-comparison can be practiced with the bug database of a Linux distribution to see the differences in usability bugs with respect to maturity of the project, development phase, number of developers, number of active HCI experts, and awareness of the project. This comparison will also identify the main deviations of bug results of a desktop OS vs. desktop applications.

The following considerations and assumptions are taken during the analysis of bug database.

1. File attachments are not counted as another thread item
2. Application crashes are not counted as usability bugs
3. Number of threads also includes the first post
4. Duplicate information in the thread is not counted as another thread item

Table 1. KDE bugs analysis. The bug numbers are randomly taken from bugs.kde.org between years 2001-2005.

Heading level	Total number	Average number of threads	Number of closed bugs (rate)
All bugs	100	2,75	80 (80%)
Usability bugs	27	2,78	27 (100%)
Non-usability bugs	73	2,74	53 (73%)

From this table, we can immediately see that roughly a quarter of all bugs are usability related. While the detailed investigation of the bug reports haven't been carried, it sill remans a question whethera bug reporting tool with usability extensions mentioned in chapter 3 would:

- Increase the rate of usability bugs compared to non-usability bugs
- Increase the average number of threads because more people can be involved in the discussion since the report is more comprehensive and hypertext-based.
- Decrease the average number of the threads since the reports are more meaningful, thus eliminating the repetitive questions from developers asking for clarification of the issue.

5 Behaviour Patterns

Lack of HCI experts have always been a delaying and erosing factor of usability paradigm in F/OSS projects. The basic rule of thumb of "far away syndrome" where the developers cooperate with an asynchronous collaboration framework also hits the usually non-technical HCI experts, resulting in an alienation to the project. Up to now, many papers have investigated the hybrid form of developing and implementing F/OSS software, and also identified several key factors shaping the collaboration between the developers in a community [13] or defined success measures of F/OSS projects [14], however none of them had considered the usability experts' involvement and behaviour patterns in F/OSS projects and the relationship between the project success and the degree of user centric design in the project.

The time at which a usability expert becomes involved in a F/OSS project is critical. Early involvement offers a better chance of a strong influence on the product user interface, since the acceptability of the interface designer will likely be higher within the project. In this way, a paper prototyping is possible, allowing continuous amendment cycles during the product design stage. Moreover, the usability expert will not only develop user requirements and develop user profiles, but he will also be able to consistently fix and/or offer usability bugs found within the product at an early stage. The table below shows different involvement stages of an usability expert in a F/OSS project and their outcomes [15].

This analysis shows that if the HCI involvement is high, then influence on the product interface, acceptance of the expert in the community, and applicability of the paper prototyping is also high. For the late involvement scenario, the focus point of

Table 2. A table showing the degree of sustainability and progress and degree of mutual interaction. Communication hub refers to various collaborative media (i.e forums, mailing lists, bugzilla interface) project stakeholders are involved in.

Discussion model	Characteristic of usability discussions	Possible results
Between-developer	• Subject to lose focus in time • Limited to mutual understanding of a concept with limited knowledge about HCI • Usually via mailing lists or instant messaging environments • Short living discussion • No potential mechanism to maintain and sustain the discussion • Subjective	Likely yields to a successful feedbacking of other project developers if the mutual mailings are carried on at mailing lists
Between HCI expert and developer	• Usually initiated and directed by the expert • Progression is directly related to expert's behaviour as well as the complexity of request • Seldomly yields to an initiative to start a UI refactoring • Perceived usability is generally a dominant feedback context	The expert should convince the developer
Between HCI expert and communication hub	• Qualitative as well as quantitative discussions • Well maintained, generally long lasting • Yields to providing reports • Objective and methodological rather than depending on personal ideas	Generally yielding a far more better result, however this model is not much widely exploited

Table 3. Different involvement stages and their outcomes

Discussion model	Early involvement	Involvement on halfway	Late involvement
Influence on the product user interface (UI)	High	Moderate	Less likely
Acceptance of the expert	High	Moderate	Moderate
Applicability of paper prototyping	For all UI elements	For the upcoming UI elements	Almost none
Focus point of usability expert	Developing user requirements	Amendment of UI	Crucial usability bug fixing

the usability expert narrows to crucial usability bug fixing. Unfortunately, we have found evidences that the acceptance of the HCI expert in the community considerably lowers in the case of late involvement.

6   Results and Discussion

In this paper, we focused on the involvement and the adoption of usability experts into F/OSS projects. We analysed the problems and how to overcome them in a straightforward manner. One way to get usability experts into F/OSS projects is to make developers more aware of basic usability principles. The outcome of this action can be stated as follows:

1. Developers will be able to evaluate their own projects, which in turn yields better quality and usable software.
2. There will be a mutual understanding of two groups (i.e. developers and interaction designers).
3. A usability expert will show the user's perspectives and focus on user profiles, finely defining the target groups.

We see the absence of key components like usability reports, usability laboratories, usability experts and companies specialising in usability for F/OSS, to be taken in appropriate consideration during all of the development process. Moreover, there's a lack of usability bug reporting tool which can be used to submit, store, modify and maintain user submitted videos, audio files and pictures showing the usability issues on a particular software UI.

For a radical change of the current status, not only it is necessary to take into account usability standards requirements, but it is critical to adopt them as early as possible in the development process. Such an approach, in effect, can be seen like an adaptation and/or a simplification of the directives specified by current proprietary standards provided by external organizations [16].

Acknowledgments. We would like to thank the KDE developers for providing their Bugzilla data for this study to analyze their bug database

References

1. Nichols, D.M., Twidale, M.B: The usability of Open Source, First Monday issue 8.1 (2003)
2. Frans E.: Open source usability is a technical problem we can solve our own, reached at http://www.newsforge.com/article.pl?sid=04/07/07/1640244
3. Muehling, J., Reitmayr, E.: Integrating Usability with Open Source Software Development: Case Studies from the Initiative OpenUsability: tOSSad OSS 2006 Workshop proceedings, pp. 65 (2006)
4. ISO 9241-11:1998 Ergonomic requirements for office work with visual display terminals (VDTs) – Part 11: Guidance on usability

5. Meeting the challenge of open source software usability, by Benson, C.: British HCI Group – (Autumn 2004) (Interfaces 60) – http://www.bcs-hci.org.uk/interfaces/interfaces60.pdf
6. OpenUsability.org: Usability and Open Source Software, by Muehlig, J., Paul, C.L.: British HCI Group – (Spring 2006) (Interfaces 66) http://www.bcs-hci.org.uk/interfaces/interfaces66.pdf
7. Çetin, G., Frings, S., Verzulli, D., Jovanovic, U.: Usability involvement in F/OSS projects, a usability guideline. tOSSad project report, funded by EU FP6-IST3 contract no 015981.
8. Muehling, J., Reitmayr, E.: Integrating Usability with Open Source Software Development: Case Studies from the Initiative OpenUsability: tOSSad OSS 2006 Workshop proceedings, pp. 65 (2006)
9. OpenOffice.org office software web page, reached at http://www.openoffice.org
10. Nichols, D.M., McKay, D., Twidale, M.B: Participatory Usability: supporting proactive users, pp. 4
11. Likeback feedback software, reached at http://basket.kde.org/likeback.php
12. Sandusky, R.J., Gasser, L., Ripoche, G.: Bug Report Networks: Varieties, Strategies, and Impacts in a F/OSS Development Community
13. Lin, Y.: Hybrid innovation: The dynamics of collaboration between the FLOSS community and corporations: Journal of Knowledge, Technology and Policy, 18(4) (Winter 2006)
14. Crowston, K., Annabi, H., Howison, J., Masango, C.: Towards A Portfolio of FLOSS Project Success Measures. In: Collaboration, Conflict and Control: The 4th Workshop on Open Source Software Engineering, International Conference on Software Engineering (ICSE 2004), Edinburgh, Scotland (May 25, 2004)
15. Çetin, G., Frings, S., Verzulli, D., Jovanovic, U: Usability involvement in F/OSS projects, a usability guideline. tOSSad project report, funded by EU FP6-IST3 contract no 015981
16. Jokela, T., Iivari, N., Matero, J., Karukka, M: The Standard of User-Centred Design and the Standard Definition of Usability: Analyzing ISO 13407 against ISO 9241-11.

Modelling and Matching: A Methodology for ePlanning System Development to Address the Requirements of Multiple User Groups

Yun Chen[1], Maria Kutar[2], and Andy Hamilton[1]

[1] Rearch Institute for the Built and Human Environment, University of Salford. Room 10, Technology House, Lissadel Street, Manchester, M6 6AP, U.K
[2] Salford Business School, University of Salford. Room 505c, Maxwell Building, 43 The Cresent, Manchetser, M5 4WT, U.K
Y.Chen1@pgr.salford.ac.uk , A.Hamilton@salford.ac.uk,
M.Kutar@salford.ac.uk

Abstract. In this paper the authors present the Modelling and Matching methodology (M&M), developed to ensure that ePlanning systems meet the needs of their users. Designed to address the requirements of multiple and diverse user groups, the methodology intends to offer an operational guidance to ePlanning system developers. M&M combines elements of UML, Soft Systems Methodology, Object-Oriented Methodology and Rapid Development Methodology, and embeds them into a five-step process to reflect a human-centred approach. The methodology will be elucidated further in the paper together with its application and evaluation in a multi-partner, geographically distributed ePlanning system development project, called Virtual Environment Planning System (VEPs) project. The reflection of this application will be discussed at last, in terms of the learning recorded with respect to the methodology (i.e. M&M) itself and the effects it caused.

Keywords: ePlanning Systems, Information System Development Methodologies (ISDMs), Multiple User Groups, Modelling and Matching (M&M).

1 Introduction

The strategic goal for 2010 set for Europe is 'to become the most competitive and dynamic knowledge-based economy in the world, capable of sustainable economic growth with more and better jobs and greater social cohesion. [1] ' This new style of society is defined as the 'Information Society', in which low-cost information and Information Communication Technologies (ICTs) are in general use. eGovernment has been defined as one of the most important goals in achieving the Information Society, which intends to provide the public with the services of government [2]. As one of the most important services to be provided by the eGovernment, ePlanning is about using ICTs to facilitate the urban planning process [3]. With varying levels of knowledge, experience and computer literacy, different stakeholders may use the ePlanning system in a large number of application areas. For instance, a local authority could use the

D. Schuler (Ed.): Online Communities and Social Comput., HCII 2007, LNCS 4564, pp. 41–49, 2007.

ePlanning system to disseminate planning information and thus promote transparency of activities and public awareness of planning and sustainability issues [4]; citizens could comment on local and strategic urban planning to participate in the process via the ePlanning system [5]; the ePlanning system could also facilitate professionals to create different planning alternatives and to forecast their outcomes [6]. Accommodating such a wide spectrum of needs and the effective use of technologies to facilitate the interaction of various stakeholders is a challenge. As a result, a well-understood and feasible development methodology is needed to bridge this gap.

The work of this research is focused on the design of a methodology to facilitate the development of complex ePlanning systems so that they can be fitted to the expectation of users, whilst still being suitable to facilitate the urban planning process. This paper firstly focuses on the preliminary investigation of ePlanning systems and Information System Development Methodologies (ISDMs). Based on the findings of the preliminary investigation, the core work of this research is implemented during the development and evaluation of a proposed methodology for ePlanning system development in a project called Virtual Environmental Planning Systems (VEPs) [7]. This development methodology is called 'Modelling and Matching' (M&M). The M&M development methodology offers a roadmap for ePlanning system developers to transform the initial planning scenario to the final system solution. This methodology together with its application and reflection are discussed in the subsequent sections of this paper.

2   Background

2.1   ePlanning Systems

In Europe, many local governments have employed new ICTs to provide eGovernment services. ICTs offer many opportunities to improve the quality of the built environment through new forms of better planning, urban and building design tools as well as through improved planning processes [8]. ePlanning, as an important part of eGovernment, can enable easy access to high quality information, guidance and services that support and assist planning applicants and streamlined means of sharing and exchanging information amongst key players. With the emergence of the ePlanning concept, the information system is used to realise the concept, namely the ePlanning system. The ePlanning system is a new product of the information age to facilitate the urban planning process, based on a range of ideas and technologies. The point of an ePlanning system is to make the urban planning process more effective and efficient with appropriate ICTs. It intends to offer considerable opportunity for enhancing public participation, with an emphasis on electronic delivery [9]. In addition, the ePlanning system has specific positive effects on social inclusion, allowing people to become more effectively involved in the planning process. It consists of the data of electronic information and is hosted on the Internet. The main body of an ePlanning system includes one base and two centres – infrastructure and spatial data as base; government information centre and public information centre.

Implementing ePlanning systems requires high-level vision supported by 'What' and 'How' strategies to ensure continuous sustainable improvements in service delivery [3]. In order to get a clear picture of ePlanning systems, *'characteristics of ePlanning system'* and *'criteria for an effective ePlanning system'* are summarised as below:

Characteristics of ePlanning Systems. As a special product emerged during last few years, evidence indicates that the ePlanning system has its own characteristics distinguishing itself from other information system, summarised as below:

- From the process perspective, ePlanning system development is a complex and iterative process, which has a gap between initial development stage and final system specification.
- From the social perspective, ePlanning systems have a wide range of stakeholders involving complicated interaction. Its target users tend to have a diverse range of computer literacy, worldviews, cultural backgrounds, knowledge and preferences. In addition, their interests and benefits may be in conflict.
- From the technical perspective, producing an ePlanning system is normally based on a historical 'technique heritage', especially including geo-spatial technologies In addition, the development of ePlanning system is restricted to certain physical development standards.

Criteria for an Effective ePlanning System. An effective ePlanning system should facilitate the urban planning process to enhance public participation and social inclusion via proper technologies. In Figure 1 below the assertions (A) to (D) concern the basic technical development of ePlanning systems, which can be assessed in the short term. The realisation of these assertions can support higher levels in the 'assertion pyramid'. The assertions (E) to (G) describe more concrete criteria related to an effective ePlanning system. The assertions (H) and (I) illustrate the positive social influences an effective ePlanning system should make.

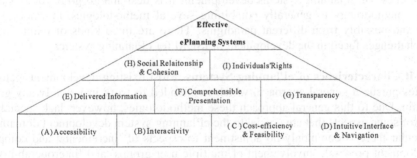

Fig. 1. Effective ePlanning systems assertions

2.2 ISDMs

ISDM is a rapidly developing area of research. In the 1960s, IS were largely developed depending on individual programmers' experience and expertise, without explicit or formalized development methodologies [10]. But many different ISDMs can now be found in the literature. Avison and Fitzgerald (2006) [11] refer to it as "the methodology jungle."

There is no widely accepted framework for studying ISDMs. They can be categorised by their underpinning paradigms and approaches, ranging from the 'hard' rationalistic ones that have a technical development focus to 'soft' hermeneutic ones with a social and human focus. However, as developers face increasing uncertainty and complexity in IS development situations and diverse problem situations, they found that they could not be served by an either single 'soft' or 'hard' methodology (e.g. [12]; [13]). Hence, researchers started to think about combining both 'hard' and 'soft' methodologies into a multi-methodology, which is a new product in post-methodology era [13] [14]. Mingers (1997) [15] argues that 'Multi-methodology' is not the name of a single methodology, or of a specific way of combining methodologies. Rather, it refers in general to utilizing a plurality of methodologies or techniques, both qualitative and quantitative, within a real-world intervention. The purpose is to generate a richer and more effective way of handling the problem situation.

We argue that to develop complex systems like ePlanning systems, the multi-methodology is the most appropriate approach. There are two arguments to support this statement: First, all real-world problems existing in the complex urban planning process have personal, social and technical dimensions. Combining methodologies to deal with all these characteristics should therefore be more effective. Second, a typical IS development passes through several stages, from an initial exploration and appreciation of the situation, through analysis and assessment, to implementation and action. Individual methodologies and techniques have their strengths and weakness with regard to these various stages.

3   The M&M Framework and Methodology

3.1   Requirements and Challenges of ePlanning System Development

As discussed above, in order to make the most effective contribution in dealing with the richness of ePlanning systems development, it is desirable to go beyond using a single methodology to generally combining several methodologies, in whole or in part, and possibly from different paradigms. There are three kinds of requirements and challenges faced in the development of ISDM for ePlanning systems.

To Fit Characteristics of ePlanning Systems. Most existing development methodologies pursue a general approach, which is intended to work in virtually any given domain. Due to this general approach these methodologies, however, lack specialisation for some aspects that are crucial to the ePlanning system development domain. In particular there is commonly no adjustment to aspects of 'incremental and complex development process', 'involvement of multiple user groups' and 'interoperability of applications'.

To Ensure Assertions of Effective ePlanning Systems. A set of nine assertions for effective ePlanning systems are identified in Figure 1. The desired development methodology should facilitate produced ePlanning systems to meet these criteria, so that the quality of 'methodology delivery' can be ensures.

To Address Multi-Methodology Combination Issues. It is undoubted that the multi-methodology involving both 'soft' paradigm and 'hard' paradigm is desirable and feasible for ePlanning systems. However, mixing methodologies, particularly from different paradigms, does present some problems need to be addressed, such as philosophically in terms of paradigm incommensurability, theoretically in terms of effectively fitting methodologies together, and practically in terms of the wide range of knowledge, skills and flexibility required of practitioners [15].

3.2 The Theoretical Framework of M&M

Based on the peculiarities of ePlanning system development, the authors consider that the possible approaches to ePlanning systems development can be conducted through four processes: *Modelling Process, Matching Process, Iterative Process* and *Evaluation Process*. In theory these processes are proposed in terms of specific characteristics of ePlanning systems, and thus have significant implications for the effective ePlanning system development. The four-process framework is underpinned by both objectivist ('hard') viewpoints and interpretivism ('soft') viewpoints to ensure that social context, stakeholders, activities and technologies are all covered during the whole development process. The following figure illustrates the general layout of the framework:

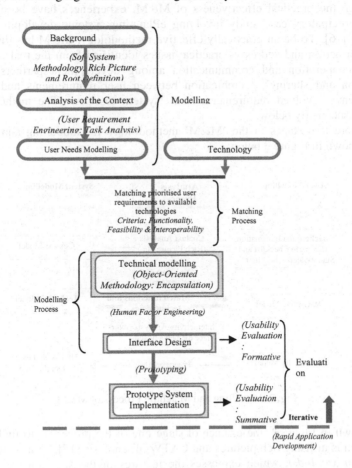

Fig. 2. The Theoretical Framework of M&M

As illustrated in Figure 2, the first modelling process is to model its context and user needs. Second way of using models in the framework is to model technologies for reuse, which happens after the matching between available technologies and user models in terms of *functionality, feasibility* and *interoperability*. The modelling and matching processes take place in the iterative cycle together with evaluation. In summary, the main concept of this framework is the separation of requirement elicitation and system modelling into views reflecting the peculiarities of the ePlanning system. This results in models of sub-problems, which are then matched and combined to an overall model of the system. As a result, modelling and matching processes are two main processes in the proposed framework, complemented by iterative and evaluation processes.

3.3 The Practical Methodology of M&M

To enhance the practical effectiveness of M&M, experiences have been extracted from a participatory case study involving ePlanning systems development named IntelCities [16]. To be an practically effective methodology, M&M has distinct procedures for action and addresses practical issues identified from the real case study, such as 'cooperation and communication among development partners', 'results presentation and sharing', 'combination between user requirements and technical development', 'evolved requirements 'and 'system test' etc. The methodology is elucidated succinctly below.

There are five stages in the 'M&M' methodology for modelling and matching process, shown in Figure 3 below.

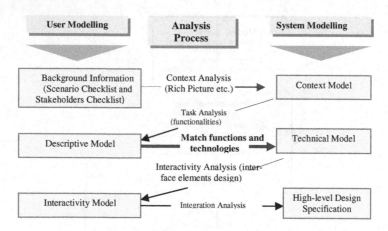

Fig. 3. Modelling and Matching Process of M&M

As shown in Figure 3, the essence of stage one of the process is to find out what the problem is utilising rich pictures and CATWOE analysis [17]. That is summarised in the *Context Model*, which expresses the features of the situation and its stakeholders. Stage two undertakes task analysis. Although it similarly concerned with system definition as stage one, it is driven by the needs of external stakeholders rather than any inherent purpose of the ePlanning system development project. The outcomes from stage two are presented in the *Descriptive Model*, which tends to focus inwardly on use cases and stakeholders interacting with the system. It is hoped that the combination of *Context Model* and *Descriptive Model* can yield a more balanced view of system definition and provide a systematic development path from high-level context analysis down into an object-oriented implementation. In stage three, the matching process occurs which facilitates the establishment of a feasible and interoperable development solution against the system functionality identified in previous stages. The solution is 'elucidated' by the object-oriented language (i.e. Unified Modelling Language) in the *Technical Model*, which needs to be handed over to technical developers for realisation. Stage four concerns the interface design issues based on proposed technologies. The interface elements and their arrangement are presented in the *Interactivity Model* by storyboards. The final stage of M&M (i.e. Stage five) is an integration process to construe the high-level design specification based on outcomes produced from above four stages, as another 'methodology delivery' besides established ePlanning system. Although the stages described above show the similarity with ones in Multiview model [13], they are distinguishing with regards to several points. Basically speaking, Multiview is an organization-oriented ISDM, which attempts to address business-related questions such as' what do we hope to achieve for the company as a result of installing a computer?'. While M&M is a public-sector-oriented ISDM, which has different concerns such as accessibility and interoperability. In addition, M&M is intended to offer a more operational methodology, rather than a general 'framework' like Multiview which 'gives insufficient guidance in certain situations' [18].

Besides the process, evaluation is another integral part of the M&M methodology. There are two evaluation activities occurring during M&M. One is call 'design evaluation' when the interactive model is produced. Cognitive walk-through [19] is applied in this evaluation step for usability assessment. The second evaluation activity is 'prototype evaluation' which will use questionnaires and empirical evaluation to check whether functional and non-functional requirements grasped in the early stage are met in the final prototype system. The context and descriptive model serve as the criteria for system functionality evaluation.

4 Application of M&M

M&M has been applied in an EU-funded project, called Virtual Environmental Planning Systems (VEPs), a collaborative project which has eight academic and industry partners located across Europe alongside associated planning authorities [7]. It aims to improve the knowledge base on the potential of ICTs for territorial development in the North West European (NWE) region specifically on the use of ICT for ePlanning, consultation and communication of citizens' views on planning issues. Under the guidance of M&M, two prototypes were developed for interactive participation concerning urban regeneration in Rosensteinviertel (Germany), the location of one of the demonstration projets in VEPs. These are the *Commenting System* and the *Discussion Forum*. Two techniques were adopted to evaluate the 'methodology use' and 'methodology delivery' after the development of these prototypes, namely questionnaires to end users and interviews with project partners.

In the evaluation using the questionnaire, the test website (i.e. www.vp.salford.ac.uk/testpage) was distributed to twenty citizens in UK. In addition, ten pairs of questionnaires (for Commenting System and Discussion Forum separately) were brought to attendees in the workshop at Urban Data Management System International Conference 2006 (UDMS2006) held in Aalborg. 21 were returned out of 30 (70 % response rate). The results of questionnaires illustrate the positive argument that first rapid prototype for Rosensteinviertel demonstration project is effective as an ePlanning system. Simultaneously, the evaluation indicates two weaknesses of the development. The first is the geo-spatial interface design and the second is the long-term effective evaluation regarding the social inclusion and selflessness issues. Further empirical fieldwork and evaluation needs to be carried out to assess how satisfactory the geo-spatial interface is for novices and how useful the system is in enabling the social inclusion and selflessness.

In the evaluation using the interview technique, two interviews were conducted with team members in the Rosensteinviertel project. The highlights in using the methodology observed in the interview include:

- The methodology presents a very precise ideas and development plans for project cooperation
- The methodology provides profound structure and control for development process.
- The methodology documents back-up cognitions of stakeholders' profiles, stakeholder requests and technical must-bes.
- The methodology encourages the good communication among partners.
- The methodology is effective in combining 'hard' issues with 'soft' issues during development process to avoid technique bias.
- The methodology integrates the evaluation plan into the process to facilitate the rapid prototyping, which does help for iterative development process.

The lowlights in using the methodology reported in the interview include:

- Letting all project partners follow an agreed methodology is a challenge because every methodology needs some time to be learned, M&M is the same.
- It is difficult to involve target users into the interface design. This methodology did not show the concrete idea about how to achieve this aim.
- Integrating with existing prototypes which was developed by other partners is not easy. A common system interface needs to be developed to realize the integration.

5 Conclusion

In this paper, we have illustrated that ePlanning systems present a number of challenges for IS development and have proposed a methodology (i.e. M&M) to enable effective ePlanning system development. The design of the M&M methodology focuses on multiple user groups, the wide variety of user needs and the complexity in urban planning process. Initial evaluation of the methodology following its application in the VEPs indicates that it facilitates the documentation and analysis of user profiles and request together with technical must-bes, and encourages the good communication among partners in the real development project. The evaluation also suggests that some areas of work remain, such as the involvement of users into the interface design and the integration with existing prototypes. Future work will focus on more extensive application and evaluation of the methodology following adjustments to address the issues raised in the initial evaluation.

References

1. European Commission, i2010: A comprehensive strategy for the information society 2005 –2010 (2005a) available at: http://europa.eu.int/information_society/eeurope/i2010/ introduction/index_en.htm
2. European Commission, eGovernment Research & Development (2005b) available at: http://ec.europa.eu/information_society/activities/egovernment_research/index_en.htm
3. I-documentsystems, Implementing E-Planning in England and Wales (2002) available at http://www.i-documentsystems.com/idox/downloads/whitepapers/Implementing%20E-Planning%20in%20England%20and%20Wales.pdf
4. Haklay, M.E.: Public access to environmental information: past, present and future. Computers, Environment and Urban Systems 27, 163–180 (2003)
5. Song, Y., Hamilton, A., Trodd, N., Zhang, X.: Public participation in urban planning facilitated by an Internet based Geographic Visual Information System. In: The Proceedings of the 3rd International Postgraduate Research Conference in the Built and Human Environment. 3rd – 4th Apr 2003, ESAI, Lisbon, pp. 797–805 (2003)
6. Laurini, R.: Information Systems for Urban Planning: A hypermedia co-operative approach. Taylor & Francis, New York (2001)
7. VEPs (2006) VEPs Project Home Page, available at: http://www.veps3d.org
8. IntelCity (2003) IntelCity Project Home Page, available at: http:// ndmodelling.scpm.salford.ac.uk/intelcity/
9. The Planning Service (2004) Electronic Planning (ePlanning), available at: http:// www.planningni.gov.uk/Corporate_Services/PlanningToDeliver/eplanning/eplanning.htm
10. Avison, D., Fitzgerald, G.: Where Now for Development Methodologies? Communications of the ACM 46(1), 79–82 (2003)
11. Avison, D., Fitzgerald, G.: Information System Development: Methodologies, Techniques and Tools, 4th edn. The McGraw-Hill Companies, Inc., New York (2006)
12. Miles, R.: Combining 'Soft' and 'Hard' Systems Practice: Grafting or Embedding? Journal of Applied System Analysis 15, 55–66 (1988)
13. Avison, D., Wood-Harper, T.: Multiview methodology. Blackwell Scientific Publishers, Oxford (1990)
14. Bell, S., Wood-Harper, T.: How to Set Up Information Systems: a non-specialist's guide to the Multiview approach, Earthscan Publications Ltd (2003)
15. Mingers, J., Brocklesby, J.: Multimethodology: for Mixing Towards a Framework Methodologies. Omega (Elsevier Science Ltd.) 25(5), 489–509 (1997)
16. IntelCities (2004) IntelCities Project Home Page, available at: ttp://www.Intelcitiesproject.com
17. Checkland, P.: Soft Systems Methodology In Action – includes a 30-year retrospective. John Wiley & Sons, Ltd, UK (1999)
18. Stowell, F.: Information Systems Provision: The Contribution of Soft Systems Methodology. McGraw-Hill International Ltd., UK (1995)
19. Nielsen, J.: Usability Engineering. Morgan Kaufmann, San Diego, CA (1993)

The Need for Technology to Support Creative Information Sharing Whilst Mobile: Identified Activities and Relationship Groups

Yan Chen, Tracy Ross, and Val Mitchell

Ergonomics and Safety Research Institute (ESRI), Loughborough University,
Holywell Building, Holywell Way, Loughborough, LE11 3UZ, UK
{Y.Chen3,T.Ross,V.Mitchell}@lboro.ac.uk

Abstract. Social computing technologies are becoming increasingly popular as it allows people to create and share their own content. Given that most social computing technologies are limited to fixed environments, this paper outlines an exploratory study which investigates the characteristics of people's creative information sharing process; identifying user needs and difficult scenarios during the process, focusing particularly on mobile scenarios. The results give an indication about people's potential needs to create and share whilst mobile. It describes the characteristics of creative information sharing process and suggests that supporting the process of information sharing by harnessing context-aware elements could be a potential solution.

Keywords: social computing, mobile environment, context-awareness.

1 Introduction

Social computing, as one of the growing fields of HCI, aims to support people's social interaction, knowledge sharing, and collaboration in multi-user environments ranging from working in small groups to participating in virtual communities and forums. Social computing technologies (e.g. Blogs, Wikis) are moving from niche to mass market and becoming increasingly important in people's lives by enabling individuals to increasingly take cues from one another rather than from institutional sources such as corporations, and media outlets [3].

Mobile devices have traditionally been used for communicating, and more recently, accessing information. The recent wave of innovations including increased connectivity (e.g. Bluetooth, WIFI, etc), processing power, storage space and enhanced multimedia capabilities, is supporting an increased social interaction (e.g. create and share) based on mobile computing. One trend, discussed by both the academic and popular press, is that people are starting to create and share their own content using mobile facilities although at the moment this is limited to basic content, such as photos [4], [5], [6]. A recent press article [12] on the dismal uptake of 3G multimedia revealed that the network companies have failed to persuade the consumer to buy premium content so far. Consumers' genuine demands were strongly stated in the

D. Schuler (Ed.): Online Communities and Social Comput., HCII 2007, LNCS 4564, pp. 50–59, 2007.
© Springer-Verlag Berlin Heidelberg 2007

report as easily creating and sharing their own content, which reflects the basic human need for self-actualization [11]. This trend is also compatible with Shneiderman's view that "following *information* technology and *communications* technology, is *innovative* technology" that supports creativity and dissemination within the community [14]. To assist in the development of technology innovation, he separates creative information sharing process into four stages: *collect* (e.g. read), *relate* (e.g. ask questions), *create* (e.g. write), *donate* (e.g. advise).

However, further research is needed to determine how technologies can help improve user experience of social interaction, knowledge sharing and collaboration whilst mobile as well as in a fixed environment.

The aim of the research in this paper is to capture and analyse the characteristics of the creative information sharing process, and also to identify user needs and difficulty scenarios during the process, focusing particularly on real life mobile scenarios. The objectives of the research were:

- to understand the characteristics of people's current creative information sharing processes when mobile, and with whom they need to share;
- to identify requirements/difficulties in the creative process;
- to identify the contexts in which the needs arose.

2 Method

A field study approach is the most appropriate for identifying needs whilst mobile because it enables the research to be carried out in 'the real world', rather than a laboratory setting, to match the target environment of mobile use. Moreover, it enables a better understanding of 'context' which is critical to mobile applications [7]. Therefore, an exploratory field study approach was adopted to identify requirements of creative information sharing process whilst in a mobile environment (two terms used to describe people's environment are 'fixed' and 'mobile'. 'Fixed' is defined as people working on a fixed PC with a relatively stable context, whereas 'Mobile' is defined as all other scenarios).

The study adopted a three phase approach incorporating the following techniques:

1. Shadowing;
2. Diary Studies;
3. Semi-interview.

Shadowing enabled rich context data to be gathered and was not reliant on participant recall. However, one potential limitation of shadowing is that the amount of time spent shadowing only represents a small proportion of participants' time. Another potential problem is that participants may mask their normal behavior. These limitations were overcome by extending the period using other two techniques and by there being no pressure placed on the participant to produce a certain amount of 'data'. *Diary Studies* were used to cover a longer period of time to capture a wider range of needs. *Semi-interviews* were used to validate the experiments interpretation of the collected data and to further explore problems and solutions.

2.1 Participants

The sample chosen was based on a high need to create and share content and potential for use of mobile devices. Young adults have been identified as the primary mobile user group with a focus on maintaining their social group by Nokia's business to consumer market summary [8]. Married, professional parents with lack of time were identified as having a very tight schedule and strong information needs. They are also proved to be heavy mobile users [2], [10].

Due to the exploratory nature and resource-heavy methods, a small group of 10 participants (two groups) were involved. They were: 'Young adults', aged 18-30, unmarried, with no dependants, working or studying full-time; 'Working parents', aged 31-45, married and with dependants, working part-time.

2.2 Procedure

All the studies were carried out within a town in Central England (population 60,000) between July and August, 2006. To gather rich data and avoid the limitations of each method if used singly, for every participant a three phase approach was applied. Before the trial, a participant information sheet was given out which explained the process of the study and stated that the information required in this study was details about obtaining information from people and sharing information with people. Moreover, each participant was asked to draw a social communication map [1] to show all the people with whom that person had regular social contact and described the related information, e.g. how the group interacts what image & role the participant has in the group, issues of privacy& trust,. The preparation before the trial was mainly to help the participant understand the trial and to help the experimenter to plan the following steps (e.g. choosing the time period for shadowing).

Shadowing. Each participant was asked to choose a period of 2-3 hours which would represent a typical time period when performing several tasks and being very mobile. For the working parents group, this tended to be a period focused around school drop-off and pick-up time, with the latter often involving follow-on activities (e.g. swimming lessons). For the young adults, this tended to be leisure/hobby periods (e.g. shopping trip, meeting friends).

Diary Study. Following the shadowing period, each participant was asked to record the activities for the rest of a 24 hour period in a diary book. S/he was asked to record the content and context data (see Table 1) each time s/he has an impulse to search and/or share information.

Semi-structured Interview. Each participant was asked to validate the shadowing data and diary data interpreted by the experimenter and also to provide extra information about difficulties with the creative information process and potential solutions.

3 Results

The data collected from both groups on the shadowing, diary studies, and the semi-structured interviews were combined in a database. All data where participants were actively using a fixed device with information and communication capabilities (e.g. working at a PC) were eliminated from the analysis. As a result, there were 165 qualified instances of creative information sharing needs (e.g. a pedestrian whilst using a dangerous crossing will have the need to report the crossing to the local authority as well as warn other road users) gathered in the study and each of them was described according to 4 main sections of attributes listed in Table 1.

Shneiderman's framework on creative information sharing process was used to help analyse the data [14]. According to the framework, each activity was classified into four stages. For example, in the purchase of a car, the first stage is to *collect* information (e.g. read brochures); the second is to *relate* communication (e.g. ask questions from trusted parties); the third is to *create* an idea (e.g. a decision about which car to purchase) and, finally, to *donate* or disseminate (e.g. share feedback with the community). Apart from the activity classification, the framework also classifies human relationships into four growing circles: *self* (e.g. person him/herself), *intimate* (family & friend), *regular encounters* (e.g. neighbors) and *citizen & market* (e.g. ebay participants) according to size difference and the degree of interdependence, shared knowledge, and trust.

Table 1. Description of Recorded Data

Sections	Attributes
Activity-Relationship (section 3.1)	Activity description; Activity classification Relationship classification
Current ability to achieve Needs (section 3.2)	Level of difficulty (e.g. easy, hard, or impossible); Reason for difficulty; Consequence (e.g. damage, frustration, annoying, or no consequence)
Content (section 3.3)	What type of information do people share?
Context data (section 3.4)	Data collection phase; Date; Time; Location; Current task; Triggers (what caused the need to occur)

3.1 Activity-Relationship Data

This data was collected to capture the details of activity & relationships-- who does what, with whom. Two properties (i.e. activities and relationships) were combined to build an Activity-Relationship Table (see Table 2). Also, for each creative information sharing need, participants were asked to rate how hard it was to accomplish the activity. A three point difficulty scale was used: *impossible*, *hard*, and *easy*. To avoid bias, the framework (i.e. classification of activities and relationship) was validated by three other experienced human factor researchers and a consensus was reached.

The total number of creative information sharing needs which were identified in the study is listed in each cell. For example, the first cell shows there are 9 needs gathered in the study. It is a result of the human relationship category = 'Self' e.g. himself/herself and the activity stage = 'Collect' e.g. internet searching, in sum, 9 instances of someone collecting information him/herself (e.g. search information online).

Table 2. Combined Activity- Relationship Table

	Collect	Relate	Create	Donate	Total
Self	9	0	**29** [1]	0	38
Close Intimates	10	**31**	6	6 [2]	53
Regular Encounter	10	**25**	13	13	61
Citizen & Market	13	3	18	18	52
Total [3]	42	59	66	37	

1 Bold represents a figure which is greater than 20 (which is double the value of the average participant);
2 A shaded cell represents where more than three quarters of participants expressed difficulty;
3 These figures may add up to more than 165 because some of the data could be classified into more than one category.

The most frequently stated needs were:

- Relate-Close intimate (31 instances), e.g. "I need to call my sister to ask my nephew's top size. Tomorrow is his birthday. I still haven't got anything for him yet". (Female, 25)
- Relate-Regular encounters (25 instances), e.g. "I cannot believe I forgot it again! I need to ask Jane (neighbor) if she can take care of the cat when I am on holiday next week". (Female, 43)
- Create-Self (29 instances), e.g. "I have to remember to buy envelope on my way home". (Male, 37)
- The difficult scenarios were mainly with create and donate information:
- Donate-Close intimates, e.g. "I would like to tell all my friends who love exercises, especially Tom, the gym on campus is absolutely great .The program I got worked really well on me! Look…but I always forget when I meet him". (Male, 25)
- Create&Donate-Regular encounters, e.g. "Sharing the idea- really I wanted to share my thoughts with all other parents in school about the new coming school events. It would be very nice to know other parents' opinion. Maybe we can even make some constructive suggestions together. But our communication relies on random chatting…" (Female, 42)
- Create&Donate-Citizen&market, e.g. "The health & safety problem around this area is getting worse. People who go past should really pay more attention. How to let them know? Maybe put a big sign here…" (Female, 43)
- Collect-Citizen&market, e.g. "What do I need to know about road regulations in France? I really have no time to read the whole document". (Female, 43)

In this study, as rated by participants, *create* and *donate* information are identified to be a lot more difficult than the first two stages of activities. It suggests that the first two types of needs are supported well by current information technology (e.g. Internet, phone communication). The next section describes in more detail the difficult scenarios as identified by the shaded areas in Table 2 as the participants rated these information sharing needs to be more difficult to achieve.

3.2 Current Ability to Achieve Needs

In order to analyse the qualitative data obtained from the descriptions given by the participants in the level of difficulty it takes to accomplish an individual information sharing need the 2x2 Thinking approach was adopted. Lowy *et al.* defines this as 'a thoughtful analysis of the nature of the conflict between the X and Y axes in a 2x2 matrix, as well an explanation of how changing the context of the problem space helps to iterate the issues to the point where new and more powerful solutions emerge [9].' This approach was used to analyse the difficult scenarios related to the shaded areas in Table 2 above.

Table 3 adopts this approach. The 'X' axis refers to the 'difficulty level' (impossible, hard, easy). For this axis the rating anchors 'impossible' and 'hard' were redefined as 'High Difficulty' and 'easy' as 'Low Difficulty'. The 'Y' axis refers to the 'consequence descriptors' (damage, frustration, annoyance, no consequence). Here 'damage' and 'frustration' were grouped into 'Major consequence and 'annoyance' and 'no consequence' were grouped into 'Minor consequence'. This group of data was very informative and plays an important role in identifying the difficult scenarios together with the Activity-Relationship data. More details are displayed in the table below:

Table 3. Difficulty vs. Consequence

	Low Difficulty	**High Difficulty**
Minor consequence	- Self-reminder; - Relate to Intimates;	- Self-reminder; - Create(organize event) for Regular; - Share recommendations to Citizen;
Major consequence	- Relate with Regular; - Relate with Intimates;	- Share experience with Citizen; - Relate with Intimate; - Self reminder.

3.3 Content

Overall, the *Content* that people share mainly included plans (e.g. event plans), experiences (e.g. holiday experience), and recommendations. More details are shown in Fig. 1.

3.4 Context Data

In this section, context data is made up of 3 subsections – location, task and trigger.

By analysing the *Location* data (see Fig 2), 'Home' and 'Car' were two locations where the activities occurred most frequently.

For the *Current Task* (see Fig 3), 'Moving around' and 'relaxing' were identified as being the most commonly performed task by both groups. 'Moving around' includes driving and walking; 'relaxing' includes shopping, having a shower, watching TV, eating, doing exercises, etc.

Trigger (see Fig 4), which is important to describe the situation, has 9 different options that represent different influencing contexts. The most common were 'current task', 'what does the participant see/hear', 'relevant history'.

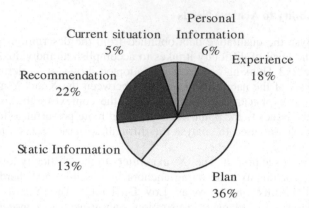

Fig. 1. The type of content shared

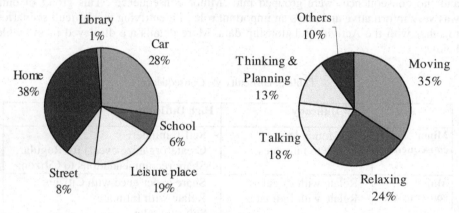

Fig. 2. The location where the need occurred   **Fig. 3.** The current task when the need occurred

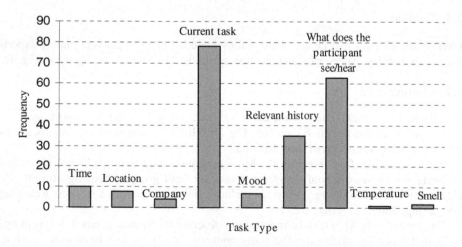

Fig. 4. The 'trigger' for the need

4 Discussion

The research findings are discussed in relation to the four circles of relationship to help clarify the problems and difficulties. Each section also describes the findings in relation to the four stages of activity defined by Schneiderman [14].

Self. Within this relationship level, people's creation mainly concerns self-reminders. The problem with forgetting things was highlighted as high difficulty with possible major consequence for people who have a heavy work load. The study showed that the time when participants think about the potential tasks wasn't the time when they actually were able to do them. Trying to remember and be triggered to perform the task caused heavy memory load and stress for people. The study suggests that reminders could be harnessed by context-based triggers.

Trigger, as the important factor for reminder, has proved to be slightly different from previous research. Rather than identifying location as the common trigger [13], 'task', 'history', and 'What they see at that moment' proved to be the most regularly identified triggers.

The Close Intimates. Within this level, people have been identified as having needs to relate communication with family and friends. However, lacking the knowledge of their availability is still an unsolved problem that has been identified in the study. Also, the need to create and share within this group is very common. The main information shared is experiences and knowledge which is characteristically context-triggered (e.g. current task) and generally succinct. It is probably because this group has much shared knowledge and a high level of trust. Also, more details could be further shared through other approaches, such as, face-to-face or phone communication. Within this level, a common problem is sharing rather than creating: the content is succinct and creation could be achieved using current multimedia capture abilities of the mobile facilities. The main problem in the creative information sharing process is that the person receiving the information does not currently have this information 'filtered' for them on the basis of context.

The Regular Encounters. This group is the group that remains in most frequent contact. Compared to the intimate group, the communication is generally a daily connection, and therefore was called 'the basic connection that needs to be maintained' by the participants. The current communication mainly relies on random face-to-face moments (e-mail & phone calls were also an option available to some groups, such as among colleagues), which creates inefficient contact within the certain types of group.

Problematic scenarios within these groups were identified mainly as creating, i.e. planning an event or organising a social event (e.g. resident meeting planning, school events arrangement, children's activity planning). More specifically, group-awareness (e.g. be aware of members' backgrounds) and trust building (e.g. personal information exchanging, such as calendar between group members who are involved with certain event) are two potential barriers to information sharing.

Sharing is also problematic as people within this group tend to only have a basic connection because of the low level of interdependence and trust, i.e.: they tend not to exchange email addresses and contact numbers within the group. Also, this group contains larger numbers of people (i.e. 50-5000 people) than the Intimates group, which makes the logistics of communication even harder.

The Citizen & Market. The results show a high level of demand but potential problems for collection, creation and donation within this group.

The main content sharing within this group is experience and reviews (e.g. about services, products, holiday). For collecting, the main problems they met were 'too much unrelated information' and getting information that 'fits into my situation/background'. For creating, the problems focused on a lack of ways to create more detailed information when on the move. For sharing, rather than sharing reviews with anybody, people usually have a specific condition regarding who s/he wants to share with. It includes: 1) People who need the information to make corresponding changes (e.g. city council, complaint manager of leisure centre); 2) People who share a similar background (e.g. share the review about one type of skincare product with others who have the similar type of skin). Also, for an individual, these groups are likely to be fluid and change over time.

Therefore, an extra relationship layer, *Potential Community*, was separated from the Citizen and Market circle. It could be used in future studies to point towards groups of people who share some links but don't currently know each other, e.g. have the similar skin texture, park in the same car park, share the same interests or reviews about the certain product / service.

5 Conclusions

This exploratory study gives an indication that people do have needs to create and share a range of content whilst mobile and supports Shneiderman's prediction that future technologies should be used to support people's desire to create and share information with others. Moreover, it describes the scenarios in which these activities may occur and the current difficulties in the creative information sharing process. It describes the content of shared inforamtion when people are mobile as mainly plan/experience/recommendations. Creative information sharing needs are usually context-triggered (e.g. current task, what does the participant see, relevant history), instant and succinct. For longer, more detailed sharing, a fixed environment is required.

The study indicates that creating (i.e. capturing) experiences is now a lot easier with the development of mobile technologies, but the process of sharing is still problematic. It suggests that supporting the process of information sharing by harnessing context elements could be a potential solution. Further research will be conducted to fully understand this scenario for a larger sample and propose mobile HCI solutions to support these aspects of the creative information sharing process and to find out how to harness the possibilities of the mobile context together with the fixed environment to support people's creative information sharing process.

References

1. Anderson, B., Gale, C., Gower, A.P., France, E.F., Joes, M.L.R., Lacohee, H., Mcwilliam, A., Tracey, K., Trimly, M.: Digital Living-People Centered Innovation and Strategy. BT Technology Journal 20(2), 11–29 (2002)
2. Beech, S., Geelhoed, E., Murphy, R., Parker, J., Sellen, A., Shaw, K.: The Lifestyle of Working Parents: Implication and Opportunities for New Technology. HPL-2003-88 (R.1). HP Laboratories Bristol (2004)
3. Charron, C., Favier, J., Li, C.: Social Computing: How Networks Erode Institutional Power, And What to Do About It. Forrester Research (February 13, 2006)
4. Counts, S., Fellheimer, E.: Supporting Social Presence Through Lightweight Photo Sharing On and Off the Desktop. In: Proc. CHI, pp. 599–606 (2004)
5. Elliott, S.: The Media Business: Advertising; Round-the-Clock News, With a British Accen, Business/Financial Desk. Late Edition - Final, Section C, Page 3, Column 1, (2006)
6. Espinoza, F., Person, P., Sandin, A., Nyström, H., Cacciatore, E., Bylund, M.: GeoNotes: Social and Navigational Aspects of Location-Based Information Systems. In: Abowd, G.D., Brumitt, B., Shafer, S. (eds.) Ubicomp 2001: Ubiquitous Computing. LNCS, vol. 2201, pp. 2–17. Springer, Heidelberg (2001)
7. Kjeldskov, J., Graham, C.: A Review of Mobile HCI Research Methods. LNCS, pp. 317–335. Springer, Heidelberg (2003)
8. Lindgren, M., Jedbratt, J., Svensson, E.: Beyond Mobile: People, Communications and Marketing in a Mobilized World. Palgrave. Chapter 8 (2002)
9. Lowy, A., Hood, P.: The Power of the 2x2 Matrix: Using 2x2 Thinking to Solve Business Problems and Make Better Decisions. Jossey-Bass (2004)
10. Hoefnagels, S.: Designing for a Frictionless Mobile Lifestyle. HPL-2003-143. Mobile & Media Systems laboratory, HP Laboratories Bristol (2003)
11. Maslow, A.: Toward a Psychology of Being, 2nd edn. Van Nostrand Reinhold, New York (1968)
12. Pritchard, S.: It Cost £22.5bn to Deliver, and All We Want is a Crazy Frog, the Independent on Sunday (April 30, 2006)
13. Schmidt, A., Beigl, M., et al.: There is More to Context than Location. Computers & Graphics-UK 23(6), 893–901 (1999)
14. Shneiderman, B.: (1947) Leonardo's Laptop: Human Needs and the New Computing Technologies. MIT, Cambridge, MA, London (2002)

Aspects of Augmented Social Cognition: Social Information Foraging and Social Search

Ed H. Chi, Peter Pirolli, and Shyong K. Lam

Palo Alto Research Center
3333 Coyote Hill Road, Palo Alto, CA 94304 USA
echi@parc.com, pirolli@parc.com

Abstract. In this paper, we summarized recent work in modeling how users socially forage and search for information. One way to bridge between different communities of users is to diversify their information sources. This can be done using not only old mechanisms such as email, instant messages, newsgroups and bulletin boards, but also new ones such as wikis, blogs, social tags, etc. How do users work with diverse hints from other foragers? How do interference effects change their strategies? How can we build tools that help users cooperatively search? We seek theories that might help us answer these questions, or at least point us toward the right directions.

Keywords: social processes, information search, information foraging.

1 Introduction

"There is a growing mountain of research. But there is increased evidence that we are being bogged down today as specialization extends. The investigator is staggered by the findings and conclusions of thousands of other workers - conclusions which he cannot find time to grasp, much less to remember, as they appear. Yet specialization becomes increasingly necessary for progress, and the effort to bridge between disciplines is correspondingly superficial." -- V. Bush [6]

V. Bush envisioned a device he called the Memex that would allow scholars to forage through personal stores of multimedia documents, and to save traces of paths through content that could then be shared with other scholars as a way of communicating new findings [6]. The Memex was envisioned as a tool that would increase the capacity of individuals to attend to greater spans of emerging knowledge, and would increase the cooperative information sharing that Bush viewed as necessary to improvements in scientific discovery, which he expected to result in increased benefits to society. Bush's vision was not only to improve the foraging ability of the individual user, but to also improve communication and collaboration. There appears to be a number of intuitions about why collaboration might improve productive work.

(1) Like over-the-horizon radar, an individual analyst may receive information otherwise unseen because of the information flowing to him or her from a social network of collaborators.

D. Schuler (Ed.): Online Communities and Social Comput., HCII 2007, LNCS 4564, pp. 60–69, 2007.

(2) Collectively, by arranging the spotlights of attention of individual users to insure maximum, exhaustive coverage of the available information, one can diminish the chances of failing to bring to light some crucial data that might otherwise be missed.

(3) Coordinated teams of experts may be assembled in order to exploit years of specialized skill and relevant knowledge about background and precedents, in order to better recognize and interpret data and information.

(4) Diversity of viewpoints can be brought to bear to provide mutually corrective forces to overcome the cognitive heuristics and biases that often create blindness to impending threats.

Each of these beneficial effects is crucial to overcoming the most frequent impediments to situation awareness and knowledge sharing [9]. Each of these effects has been the focus of some fields of research that we draw upon for theoretical guidance.

Despite a large amount of Computer Supported Cooperative Work research and literature in this area, significant progress still can be made. For example, what has been amazing is the amount of new social mechanisms invented on the Internet for social foraging. To some extent, the Web, blogs, email, internet groups, wikis, and other mundane technologies are all aimed at supporting cooperative information sharing and their success implies their effectiveness.

However, there is also a considerable body of evidence from social psychology and decision support systems that indicates that collaborative work often results in worse outcomes than working alone. Further, it is common knowledge that collaboration involves overhead costs that, for the individual, act as disincentives for collaborative activities. Despite the potentially negative features of collaboration, many new tools for social information foraging have emerged as disrupting technologies on the Internet including peer-to-peer information sharing, social search, and blogs. The aim of this paper is to develop theory, evaluation techniques, and disruptive technology to increase the benefits and reduce the costs of augmented social information foraging.

The major question confronting the field, therefore, is to not only understand how these mechanisms are different or the same as previous generation of tools, but also build models of how social foraging appears to be benefiting individuals, and how these models might in turn tell us how to build new collaboration tools.

In this article, we outline several explorations on models of social information foraging, and how some of these ideas might impact social search engines. We will touch upon general results concerning the costs and benefits of cooperative foraging, the effects of group diversity, and patterns of social structuring that are correlated with innovative discovery.

2 Costs and Benefits of Cooperative Foraging

2.1 Problems of Specialization, Bias Barriers, and Tools

Specialization is a natural consequence of too much public knowledge for the individual mind to comprehend. The worry is that knowledge specialization leads to situations in which all the information required to make an important discovery is in the available record somewhere, but it is distributed across specialization boundaries with no single set of eyes in a position to see it all and make sense of it. In the information retrieval and library sciences, this is known as the *undiscovered public knowledge problem*. These problems may include hidden refutations, hidden cumulative strength of individually weak studies, or other hidden links in the logic of discovery.

Indeed, in the intelligence analysis community, since 9/11, there has been increasing focus on the need to reduce individual bias in analysis. Some barriers to information sharing has been systematically studied and publicly debated, including computer security issues, political turf concerns, and multiple intelligence agencies with differing sources of information.

While much of the problem remain organizational, analysts also lack the most basic tools for information sharing, such as the ability to identify the experts in a particular domain, search in a database that has been tagged with the most promising leads, or automatically download and attend to the most promising information sources. The tools are truly quite impoverished.

2.2 Studies of Existing Solutions

Existing research showed that the benefits of social information foraging can be systematically studied and understood. Cooperation may yield more benefits than simply making search more parallel and making it less prone to failure. Membership in a group provides actual or potential resources that can be utilized or mobilized to achieve individual goals. This is known as *social capital* [4,17].

Pirolli and Card [16] describe a business intelligence agency whose analysts were tasked to write monthly newsletters about core areas such as computer science or materials science. In addition to culling material for their own newsletters, analysts would also notice articles pertinent to the specialties of other analysts, and would have such articles copied and routed to the appropriate specialist. An analyst would typically receive about 6–12 relevant articles per month from other analysts, at very little cost. The general belief of the analysts was that such cooperation enhanced the individuals' search capabilities, and reduced the risk of missing something relevant to a specialty area that had emerged in a non-specialty publication. The social network amongst the analysts is precisely their social capital for solving complex problems of their own.

Interestingly, recent recommender systems use an implicit form of these social networks to provide social capital to their users. Recommender systems exploit social information to make recommendations (documents, movies, music) to individuals. These include collaborative filtering systems [10] in which people typically indicate their preference for items in some way (e.g., by rating things such as books), and they receive recommendations based on the preferences of others with similar tastes.

2.3 Effects of Group Diversity

Existing research studied the effects of group diversity on cooperative information foraging, as well as the theory that people who provide brokerage of ideas across social clusters are often in position to make valuable novel discoveries.

Organization and management studies [8] suggest that effective work groups are ones that share information and know-how with external members, and that effectiveness is improved by *structural diversity* of the group. *Structural diversity* is variability in features of the group that expose members to different sources of task information, know-how, and feedback. Such features include geographic locations, functional assignments, number of mangers to whom members report, and number of business units associated with the group.

The findings of Cummings [8] are consistent with the theory of social structural holes (*structural holes theory*) proposed by Burt [5]. Typically, such social networks of information flow will contain densely connected clusters. The sparse linkages between such clusters constitute *structural holes*. People who bridge such structural holes have an advantage of exposure to greater diversity of information and know-how, and *brokerage* across structural holes becomes a form of *social capital* that translates into the discovery of greater amounts of useful, productive knowledge.

2.4 Epidemiological Model

One of the exciting prospects for the study of social information foraging is improved ability to find and measure social networks using on-line resources. For instance, it appears that e-mail flow and Web links among personal home pages provide data that can be used to accurately construct social networks [12] and to study information flow.

Recent researchers have tried to model the information flow in a social network of information foragers. One set of models for such flow is based on epidemiological models [12,21]. The model of Wu et al. [21] is based on the application of random graph theory [3,14] to the epidemiological models of the spread of diseases. The key idea is that information spreads from person to person in ways analogous to the spread of an infection from person to person. Wu et al. [21] assume a social network whose nodes have an outdegree distribution that follows a scale-free power law. This means that there are a few members of the social network who have a very large number of social connections, but the typical number of connections is small (and less than the arithmetic mean).

Information tends to be selectively passed on to people that the host believes will find the information useful. Individuals tend to form social associations based on the similarity of their characteristics (known as *homophily*), and Wu et al. assume that the similarity of two people diminishes as a function of their distance in a social network (a common observation in sociometrics). One is lead to infer that transmission probabilities for information should decay as a function of network distance from the host source.

The sum of all the predicted infected individuals across all distances from the host provides a measure of the average total size of an "outbreak" (the number of individuals "infected" by the information). Interestingly, Wu et al. showed that the assumption of decay in transmissibility with network distance typically leads to outbreaks of finite size. Empirical studies of samples of email, and numerical simulations using parameters based on observation and a social network graph based on email patterns suggest that outbreaks in an organization of about 7000 people is typically limited to under 50 people.

2.5 Social Information Foraging Model

Pirolli [15] derived a basic model of social information foraging based on the Information Foraging Theory. The basic model derivation is too complex to present in detail here. Instead, we will provide a brief summary here. A key insight of the theory is that there is an intricate relationship between the interference costs of collaboration and the benefits of the diversity of view of point.

The model seeks to understand the effect of the diversity of information foragers and their hints to each other, and how this diversity directly affects the size of cooperating groups.

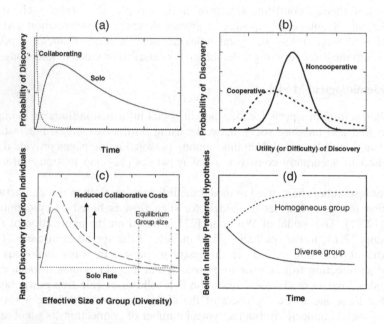

Fig. 1. Key predictions of an Augmented Social Cognition theory. (a, top left): collaboration in a diverse group improves chances of discovery; (b, top right): cooperation improve chances of discovering the more important facts; (c, lower left): cost and benefit of collaboration determine effective group size; (d, lower right): diversity decreases confirmation bias.

Figure 1 summarizes key predictions of the theory. This model assumes that there are some processing steps that are required to find useful patches of information and this can be modeled as a Poisson process. Cooperating information hints from other foragers can be modeled as the number of search steps that are eliminated due to a distinct hint.

The model suggests that so long as the diversity of agents increases with group size, then the size of a group increases the overall power of cooperative discovery. As individual foragers increase the diversity of their cooperating contacts they will improve in performance.

Figure 1a shows how collaboration with a diverse group improves the rate of return to the individual analyst. Being embedded in a cooperative social network of analysts provides the individual analysts with the ability to explore more of the space of information more rapidly than could be done alone -like an over-the-horizon radar [5].

Figure 1b shows how the theory predicts how cooperation among a set of analysts improves the probability of making important (or difficult) discoveries. This means that unseen patterns, connections, inferences that are latent in the raw data may come to light as the number of diverse but cooperative analysts increases [19].

The model also showed that, assuming there are interference costs that grow with the number of members in a group, these interference costs may reduce the social capital of group foraging down to the level of individual foraging, at which point one expects an equilibrium group size.

Figure 1c illustrates that a combination of expected benefits and interference costs to an individual determines the effective size of a group. People typically join a group only if the benefits (to the individual) outweigh the costs of cooperation [7].

Figure 1c also illustrates how a reduction in the costs of collaboration is predicted to increase the effective size of the collaborating group. Lowering the costs of collaboration leads naturally to larger groups of collaborating analysts.

Figure 1d illustrates the effects of diverse heuristics and biases in a cooperative group on the mitigation of confirmation bias [11,20]. Diversified groups show greater mitigation of confirmation biases than homogenous groups [2].

3 Implications from the Models

The effects of group diversity and the social foraging models tell us that the structure, composition, and the size of the social network are extremely important.

In terms of **composition**, Cummings research show that the diversity of hints is important in bringing fresh information into a group.

In terms of **structure**, the findings from Burt suggest that if we can locate structural holes in the social network, we will be able to bridge across these holes by enabling information to directly flow across more efficiently. One way this can be operationalized is by identifying two workgroups that has tight information sharing, and finding the highest connected members from each group to inform each other.

In terms of **size**, the results from Pirolli and Wu et al. [21] suggest that there is an optimal size of the information outbreak for a given situation. Too large of an outbreak will generate interference, while too small of an outbreak causes information to be disseminated too inefficiently.

The crushing pressure of information overload leads to specialization by people in fields of knowledge discovery. Overspecialization may lead to increases in undiscovered public knowledge [19]—a failure for any one mind to grasp and connect all the dots. Information sharing is usually recognized as a strategy for extending the grasp of the solitary mind across specializations, to reduce the risk of failing to make discoveries implicit in the existing collections of data. To the extent that individual members of a core specialty can devote some effort to exploring related peripheral specialties, and sharing possible leads with others, then one might expect the group to perform more effectively.

There are still other open questions, such as issues surrounding trust and privacy. An information sharing tool should enable further enhancement of trust between users or at least not diminish it. Much more difficult to design for, the privacy of the user must be protected. These are open future research issues.

4 Social Search

We have been interested in applying these findings and implications to the design of a social search engine. In considering the implications of composition and structure, we first wanted to understand the variety of information that different people look at and if there is enough structure and composition in these groups to cover many topics but with enough commonalities to infer possible structural holes to bridge.

We wanted to do this analysis to understand how well people can collaborate in their search process.We do this by first comparing the history and bookmarks of some real users. We performed some analysis of user browsing histories and their bookmarks, trying to understand to what extent their information sources are diverse but yet overlap. Given the vastness of the web, it turns out that there is a lot more overlap than we might otherwise have expected.

USERS	3x3eyes	biotech	creap	dinopixel	ed	elindbloom	fabio	ffg	gbuser6	guruzilla	jilim	jugglebird	lowellk	rainer	terrorism
3x3eyes	-	0.00%	2.13%	6.80%	0.02%	2.02%	0.06%	0.46%	0.01%	0.52%	1.07%	1.77%	1.71%	0.61%	0.00%
biotech	0.00%	-	0.00%	0.00%	0.00%	0.00%	0.00%	0.00%	0.00%	0.00%	0.00%	0.00%	0.00%	0.00%	0.00%
creap	2.13%	0.00%	-	4.66%	0.01%	2.10%	0.00%	0.08%	0.00%	0.04%	0.54%	1.60%	0.93%	0.40%	0.00%
dinopixel	6.80%	0.00%	4.66%	-	0.01%	6.13%	0.02%	0.59%	0.00%	0.13%	1.18%	2.41%	2.63%	0.34%	0.00%
ed	0.02%	0.00%	0.01%	0.01%	-	0.01%	0.72%	0.04%	0.03%	0.00%	0.03%	0.03%	0.01%	0.00%	0.00%
elindbloom	2.02%	0.00%	2.10%	6.13%	0.01%	-	0.00%	0.20%	0.00%	0.00%	0.60%	1.90%	0.78%	0.16%	0.00%
fabio	0.06%	0.00%	0.00%	0.02%	0.72%	0.00%	-	0.00%	0.08%	0.02%	0.02%	0.00%	0.02%	0.00%	0.00%
ffg	0.46%	0.00%	0.08%	0.59%	0.04%	0.20%	0.00%	-	0.00%	0.28%	0.35%	0.55%	0.18%	0.27%	0.00%
gbuser6	0.01%	0.00%	0.00%	0.00%	0.03%	0.00%	0.08%	0.00%	-	0.00%	0.03%	0.00%	0.06%	0.00%	0.00%
guruzilla	0.52%	0.00%	0.04%	0.13%	0.00%	0.00%	0.02%	0.28%	0.00%	-	0.14%	0.19%	0.03%	0.09%	0.00%
jilim	1.07%	0.00%	0.54%	1.18%	0.03%	0.60%	0.02%	0.35%	0.03%	0.14%	-	0.60%	0.45%	0.21%	0.00%
jugglebird	1.77%	0.00%	1.60%	2.41%	0.03%	1.90%	0.00%	0.55%	0.00%	0.19%	0.60%	-	0.41%	0.37%	0.00%
lowellk	1.71%	0.00%	0.93%	2.63%	0.01%	0.78%	0.02%	0.18%	0.06%	0.03%	0.45%	0.41%	-	0.23%	0.00%
rainer	0.61%	0.00%	0.40%	0.34%	0.00%	0.16%	0.00%	0.27%	0.00%	0.09%	0.21%	0.37%	0.23%	-	0.00%
terrorism	0.00%	0.00%	0.00%	0.00%	0.00%	0.00%	0.00%	0.00%	0.00%	0.00%	0.00%	0.00%	0.00%	0.00%	-

Fig. 2. Browsing history overlap study show (1) overlap between random del.icio.us users is surprisingly high; (2) Experts (such as gbuser6) may be foraging in entirely different areas of the Web than curated collections (terrorism and biotech)

The figure above depicts our analysis results. The user profiles "ed", "fabio", and "gbuser6" (highlighted in yellow and orange) are history traces we obtained by directly examining the browser histories. They all contain 3-6+ months of data. "Biotech" and "terrorism" (highlighted in green) are bookmarks from the Open Directory Project curated listings. Finally, we also examined ten bookmark histories from a social bookmarking site called del.icio.us (users with no highlights). The profiles ranged from 831 URLs to over 9211 (Mean=2243). There are some striking results:

- Ed and Fabio's profiles only overlapped with each other strongly, but not with other profiles. This is interesting, especially since they were co-workers.
- Gbuser6's profile is a real intelligence analyst profile that mainly consists of terrorism and biological weapon URLs. This profile did not overlap with the curated Biotech and Terrorism profiles, and in fact showed very little overlap with any other profiles, despite having 9211 in his profile. This indicates that he used very different information sources. Biotech and Terrorism also had no overlap with other profiles.
- The del.icio.us users overlap strongly with each other, forming their own little community. This is true despite the fact that we have no evidence that these users know each other at all. In particular, dinopixel overlapped with 3x3eyes by 6.8%, which means roughly every 1 in 15 URLs were viewed by both of them! One possible explanation is that they are all uber-geek technologists who tend to use similar information sources on the net such as Slashdot.

What these results seem to suggest are:

- Users with similar interests tend to skim the same surfaces on the web, if they might be using similar news sources in their everyday browsing activities. Co-workers and communities are most likely to skim the same surfaces, but they are not always getting to the same pages. Given the vastness and diversity of the web, people actually get pretty close to each other, and could easily inform each other of sources that they should not have missed.
- People in related fields but not in the same community do not skim the same surfaces on the web, and are prime candidates for more information sharing. These results seem to confirm that structural holes do exist. Gbuser6 is well poised to benefit from both biotech and terrorism profiles, and serve as a bridge between the two communities.
- The similarity between profiles could be used as input to a social search engine. It could be used to find experts in particular areas, share new information sources, and bridge across structural holes. We could use the overlap between users to help find related users, related queries, and result pages.

We are currently constructing foraging agents that build upon personalized search technology developed at PARC. A preliminary version of this system called Proximal Search. Foraging agents can be seeded with starting points and search/browsing histories extracted from the individual users and their knowledge resources. Using social network search one may gain access to the results produced by foraging agents working on behalf of experts, or users with different sensemaking viewpoints.

In this system, context focused foraging is achieved by a focused crawler that has the goal of seeking out and indexing parts of the Web that are highly relevant to a particular user, based on the search history, tags, and other knowledge resources. Such search agents can find deep parts of the Web that are unindexed by common search engines, and provide search results that have higher precision and recall for the specific interests of the user.

One aspect is the ability to exploit social connections to gain access to expertise outside of one's own. Membership in a group provides actual or potential resources that can be utilized or mobilized to achieve individual goals. Cooperation, such as collaborative tagging, may yield more benefits than simply making search more parallel and making it less prone to failure. Systems such as Dogear can be combined with social search [13].

Expert location using social network search can be used to guide peer-to-peer meta search to retrieve from expert search indexes produced by those expert's agents. Professional knowledge workers, such as scientists, who are engaged in making sense of information and making discoveries, typically search through their networks of social relations in order to find experts on matters on which they themselves are unfamiliar. Searching for expertise in a social network in the electronic world is known as the *expert location problem* [1,22]. A variety of search algorithms have been explored in simulation studies [22], but remain to be implemented.

5 Concluding Remarks

In this short paper, we summarized recent work in the understanding of social information foraging, and models of how users socially foraging with diverse hints.

Information overload results in knowledge specialization, which increases the need to communicate between analysts with diverse viewpoints. Communications lead to interference costs, which can be mitigated by technology. Less interference costs will enable more effective collaboration and cooperation amongst analysts.

In communities of practice that depend on foraging in overly rich information environments, there appears to be pressure to self-organize into a balance of some division of labor, plus some degree of cooperation. It appears that the division of labor is necessary because of the limits of human attention, but some investment in cooperation can lead to increased returns and less risk of missing something important. The power of cooperation is related to the amount of diversity of the information foragers. Greater diversity leads to greater returns for the group and the individual. This is related to the notion that brokerage (diverse social contacts) provides social capital, and there is evidence that brokers in the flow of information are more likely to be sources of innovative discoveries. Although there are benefits to cooperation, those benefits trade against interference effects.

Recent emerging tools such as blogs, podcasts, and other internet groups serve to bridge across structural holes, but they must at the same time eliminate their potential for interference effects and overwhelm the users.

One way to bridge between different communities of users is to diversify their information sources. We have been examining the possibility of using a collaborative search engine to achieve this effect. Initial studies suggest that a social search engine build with the understanding of the implications of composition, structure, and size of communities should be able to inform users of new potential information sources without creating much additional interference overhead for the users.

References

1. Adamic, L.A., Adar, E.: How to search a social network. Social Networks 27(3), 187–203 (2005)
2. Billman, D., Convertino, G., Shrager, J., Massar, J.P., Pirolli, P.: Collaborative intelligence analysis with cache and its effects on information gathering and cognitive bias, Human Computer Interaction Consortium Workshop. Boulder, CO (2006)

3. Bollobas, B.: Random graphs. Academic Press, London (1985)
4. Bourdieu, P.: The forms of capital. In: Richardson, J.G. (ed.) Handbook of theory and research in the sociology of education, Greenwald Press, New York (1986)
5. Burt, R.S.: Structural holes and good ideas. American Journal of Sociology 110(2), 349–399 (2004)
6. Bush, V.: As we may think. Atlantic Monthly, 176, 101–108 (1945)
7. Clark, C.W., Mangel, M.: The evolutionary advantages of group foraging. Theoretical Population Biology 30(1), 45–75 (1986)
8. Cummings, J.N.: Work groups, structural diversity, and knowledge sharing in a global organization. Management Science 50(3), 352–364 (2004)
9. Grabo, C.M.: Anticipating surprise: Analysis for strategic warning. Joint Military Intelligence College, Washington, DC (2002)
10. Herlocker, J.L., Konstan, J.A., Terveen, L.G., Riedl, J.: Evaluating collaborative filtering recommender systems. ACM Transactions on Information Systems 22(1), 5–53 (2004)
11. Heuer, R.J.: Psychology of intelligence analysis. Center for the Study of Intelligence, Washington, DC (1999)
12. Huberman, B.A., Adamic, L.A.: Information dynamics in a networked world. In: Ben-Naim, E., Frauenfelder, H., Toroczkai, Z. (eds.) Complex networks, Springer, Heidelberg (2004)
13. Millen, D.R., Feinberg, J., Kerr, B.: Dogear: Social bookmarking in the enterprise. In: Proceedings of the SIGCHI Conference on Human Factors in Computing Systems. CHI '06, Montréal, Québec, Canada, April 22 - 27, 2006, pp. 111–120. ACM Press, New York, NY (2006)
14. Newman, M.E.J.: Spread of epidemic disease on networks. Physical Review E (Statistical, Nonlinear, and Soft. Matter Physics) 66(1), 16128 (2002)
15. Pirolli, P.: Chapter 8: Social Information Foraging. Information Foraging (2007)
16. Pirolli, P., Card, S.K.: Information foraging. Psychological Review 106, 643–675 (1999)
17. Putnam, R.: Bowling alone: The collapse and revival of american community. Simon and Schuster, New York (2000)
18. Sandstrom, P.E.: Scholarly communication as a socioecological systems. Scientometrics 51(3), 573–605 (2001)
19. Swanson, D.R.: Undiscovered public knowledge. The. Library Quarterly 56(2), 103–118 (1986)
20. Tversky, A., Kahneman, D.: Judgment under uncertainty: Heuristics and biases. Science 185, 1124–1131 (1974)
21. Wu, F., Huberman, B.A., Adamic, L.A., Tyler, J.R: Information flow in social groups. Physica A: Statistical and Theoretical Physics 337(1-2), 327 (2004)
22. Zhang, J., Ackerman, M.S.: Searching for expertise in social networks: A simulation of potential strategies. In: Proceedings of the 2005 international ACM SIGGROUP conference on Supporting group work, ACM Press, Sanibel Island, Florida, USA (2005)

First Design of a Ubiquitous System for Affective Bonding and Support with Family and Friends

Sébastien Duval and Hiromichi Hashizume

National Institute of Informatics
Hitotsubashi 2-1-2, Chiyoda-ku, Tokyo 101-8430, Japan
{duval,has}@nii.ac.jp

Abstract. We consider the design of a ubiquitous system whose objective is to strengthen affective bonding and allow affective support, especially for distant relationships with the family and friends. It is based on wearable computers that evaluate emotions, transmit information to authorized persons, and enable interactions. Our most significant contribution is the provision of the design for a complete system usable in everyday life, based on emotional design and on multi-cultural feedback.

Keywords: Cultures, Emotional design, Emotions, Family, Friends, HCI, Ubiquity, Wearable.

1 Introduction

Ubiquitous systems can improve our quality of life by satisfying fundamental needs [1] and gratifying wishes. Here we consider relationships, and more particularly with the family and friends. The aim is to complement existing technologies and services, which are mainly based on voluntary linguistic input: e-mails, chat, voice over IP, etc. For this we propose, like others before us [2], to share information about emotions. Combining language and physiology in real-time is a promising strategy that allies continuous to occasional, conscious to unconscious, and explicit to implicit input. Leaving aside technological and algorithmic obstacles for a moment, we have to acknowledge the criticality of human needs for the proper design of everyday things:

> "[…] the emotional side of design may be more critical to a product's success than its practical elements", Norman [3, p5].

Our prior investigations confirmed the priority of psychological expectations over potential gains from emotional displays [4]. Social distance appeared decisive, with services dedicated to families and friends emerging as most propitious, leading to the current project. Our strategy is based on these results, on emotional design [3] to create desirable systems, and on feedback of potential users from multiple cultures to allow smart variations.

We first describe the system as a whole, then detail the user interfaces, and finally discuss emotional design with feedback from potential users.

D. Schuler (Ed.): Online Communities and Social Comput., HCII 2007, LNCS 4564, pp. 70–79, 2007.
© Springer-Verlag Berlin Heidelberg 2007

2 Overview of the System

We first present scenarios to identify significant features then provide a global view of the system, and finally describe its components.

2.1 Scenarios and Critical Features

To clarify functional requirements and illustrate useful applications, we propose three scenarios: (1) *Hospitalized child*, (2) *Friends' holidays*, and (3) *Lonely grand-parents*. We then extract from them critical features.

Scenario 1. A 10-year old French boy is hospitalized for several months. His parents have difficulties visiting him regularly because of their work and of the distance. The boy continuously wears a bracelet that monitors his heartbeats and skin conductivity. A server processes the information to evaluate his emotional state. When high arousal is detected, the server sends an e-mail to his parents' cell-phone.

Scenario 2. A group of Korean students visits various countries during the summer. Each of them wears a networked watch that monitors physiological states and displays graphics. When they send e-mails from Internet cafés, a server extracts smileys and keywords. Combining physiological and textual information, it tracks the evolution of users' emotional state. This information is regularly sent to registered friends' watches and displayed using a customized visual metaphor. When one appears joyful, the others send simple messages using the watch interface to e.g. ask what happens.

Scenario 3. Two old Japanese live far from their family. They dislike wearables and refuse *monitoring watches* for both medical and affective purposes. However they enjoy e-mails to organize their activities and keep in touch with friends. When they send e-mails, a server processes the text to evaluate their state. Every Friday, their son logs on a secured web site that displays a summary of their emotions. When it highlights sadness, he visits his parents during the week-end.

According to the scenarios the system should evaluate emotions from physiological signals and/or content of outgoing e-mails. The analysis of e-mails implicitly requires algorithms adapted to different languages (sets of characters, grammar) and cultures.

For practical uses, visualization and interaction should be possible with standard *and* dedicated technologies; for instance the Web, cellular phones and wearable computers. A proper visual metaphor is required to check in a glance the state of family members and friends. Interactions should at least include the transmission of predefined messages.

Finally, when dedicated equipment is provided, it should be accessible to children, adults, and seniors. The location of sensors needs to be determined; the wrist may not be the most reliable place to monitor heartbeats and skin conductivity in an everyday setting.

2.2 Global View

To support affective communication with family members and friends, we propose to acquire emotion-related data from each user, process it on a server, and transmit personalized information to acquaintances (figure 1). Emotion-related data is acquired from physiological sensors embedded in a personal wearable, and from copies of e-mails received by the server from registered e-mail addresses. After processing the data, the server checks which users should get updates and accordingly creates updates based on the originator's and recipients' preferences.

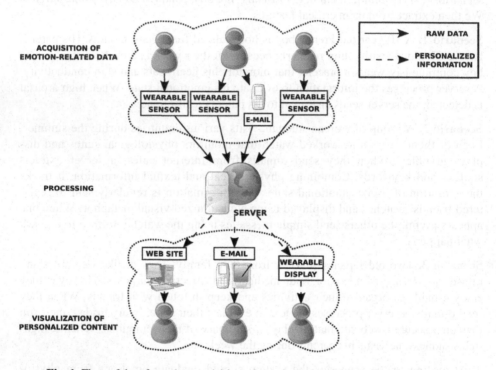

Fig. 1. Flow of data from the acquisition of emotion-related data to the visualization

The core of the system runs on a server, which stores the personalization and privacy information. Because of its sensitivity, the data should be protected; we suggest applying encryption and a storage retention policy. We currently evaluate benefits and drawbacks of pushing the raw data into versus pulling it from the server. Processing and networking should be limited due to the limitations in energy of wearables.

2.3 Description of Components

The main components deal with the management of personal information, processing of emotion-related information, encryption/decryption, management of messages, and visualization. Figure 2 details elements of the three first components.

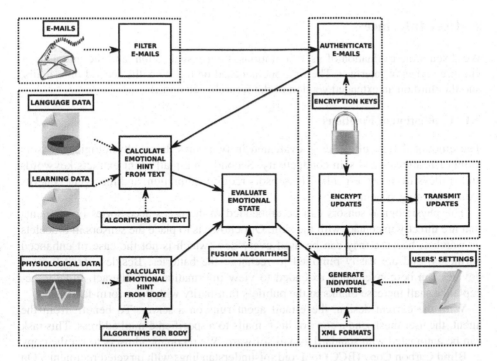

Fig. 2. Components involved in the evaluation of emotions on the server, and transmission

Emotional Information Management. This component evaluates emotions from data provided by physiological sensors embedded in the wearable computer, and text from outgoing e-mails. Because focus is on global design rather than precise evaluation, we can use simple algorithms. The intensity of emotions can be inferred from the speed of heartbeats or increases in skin conductivity, and the type (e.g. joy, anger [5]) from words compared to language-specific databases. Results are then fused.

Personal Information Management. This component lists information to provide to acquaintances. It checks the originator's preferences, identifies recipients, and the accuracy/frequency authorized by the originator and requested by each recipient. It then generates updates in appropriate formats from XML descriptions.

Encryption/Decryption. We propose to use GPG to authentify the origin of e-mails received by the server, and to encrypt updates sent by the server. We still have to find a satisfactory method to protect the transmission of physiological data.

Message Management. The manager possesses a list of predefined messages that can be sent and received through the interface. It deals with eventual translations.

Visualization. This component displays the state of family members, and eventual messages, on the screen. The default style, *bubbles*, is presented hereafter.

3   User Interfaces

We discuss the evaluation of users' emotions, their visualization, and the interactions via three types of interface. The first one is based on the Web, the second on e-mails, and the third on an extended version of the wearable computer.

3.1   Evaluation of Emotions

The emotional state of a user is evaluated in two ways. First, physiological sensors monitor heartbeats and skin conductivity. Second, an e-mail agent extracts keywords and smileys from sent e-mails. The sensors require calibration, and the agent benefits from a learning system.

The physiological sensors can be embedded in the user's accessories or garments that are directly in contact with the skin. Our choice is to place the sensors in bracelets or watches, because they can be used every day (which is not the case of enhanced garments) and are easily removed to recharge the batteries. Besides, wrist-located devices can be conveniently extended to view information and interact. Finally, acceptance shall increase thanks to the public's familiarity with these form-factors.

With the current design, the e-mail agent runs on a server. To benefit from the agent, the user must send a copy of his e-mails to a specified e-mail address. This task can be automated with standard e-mail software. We recommend users to set the copy as Blind Carbon Copy (BCC) to avoid misunderstandings with targeted recipients. On reception, the agent processes the e-mail to acquire hints about the user's emotional state. A summary is conserved for a week, and the user can access it with the web interface to provide feedback for the learning process.

Discussions with potential users, based on sketches, suggest that a simple interface could satisfy English speakers. This interface would show e-mails one by one, the aspect of words varying to reflect emotions. Using colors for kinds (happy, angry) and font sizes for intensities appears natural. It is unclear whether this method could be successfully employed with languages based on ideograms, such as Japanese.

3.2   Display of Emotions

After evaluating the emotional state, the server relays the information to authorized family members and friends. The information is then either pulled or pushed. First, users can access a graphical representation on a web site (pull), after identification. Second, they can receive e-mail alerts (push). Third, the information can be continuously updated on a wearable display (push). These methods provide flexibility for various life-styles, contexts, wishes, and needs.

The web interface lets users visualize in detail the state of acquaintances and check their own evaluated status. The state of family members and friends is displayed using a *soap bubble* metaphor (figure 3) in which the background color represents the state of the group, and colored bubbles the state of individuals. The speed of the upward flow reflects the speed of variations. Three views are possible: "current", "day" and "week".

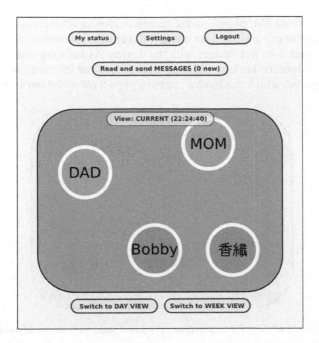

Fig. 3. Example of view for acquaintances' current state with the Web interface

With the e-mail interface, users receive e-mail alerts that summarize the states of acquaintances at specific moments, or indicate important changes (figure 4).

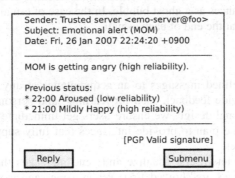

Fig. 4. Example of e-mail alert about a family member

The wearable interface (figure 5) is similar to the web interface. Acquaintances' state is displayed using the *soap bubble* metaphor but the options (e.g. switching from the "day" to "week" view) are not visible. A frame indicates the current view, and a click allows users to change it. This GUI works with a touch-sensitive display embedded in a watch, or with semi-transparent glasses combined to mobile input devices.

Visualization with wrist-located wearables poses several problems; notably that bystanders can see the display. The color scheme provides a first way to hide meaning. A polarized film placed on the screen is also an efficient low-tech solution. Besides, to preserve privacy and save energy, information is only displayed for a short time when the user does not interact with the device. As for semi-transparent glasses, privacy is not a concern because only the wearer sees the information. However eye contact is hampered, which can have a negative impact on social interactions.

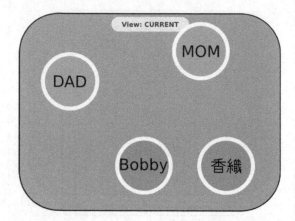

Fig. 5. Example of view for acquaintances' current state with the wearable interface

Several potential users requested the addition of a function to visualize their own evaluated status. They felt it is important in order to feel comfortable with the system, to monitor correctness, and to disable the system if it sends incorrect or embarrassing information. We consider several implementations such as letting users view their state among acquaintances as a ghost bubble. In the case of e-mail alerts, a descriptive line can be appended at the end of each e-mail.

3.3 Interactions

Users can send predefined messages to an acquaintance at any moment, get details about their state, provide feedback used for learning, and personalize their interface. To favor good emotional design, we ensure users get immediate and useful feedback about their actions. We plan to provide interfaces that fully support French, English and Japanese languages.

The web interface lets users visualize and send messages through a "Messages" screen. Recent messages are showed first. When a message is received through the system, the user can comment it and save it, reply to it, or delete it. Users can also check their status with the "My status" screen. It provides the current evaluated state, as well as a description of its evolution over the day and week. Feedback exploited by the learning component is provided here. The "Settings" screen is used to register new acquaintances and set the accuracy/frequency of information to transmit, on an individual basis. It is also used to register personal e-mail addresses and to set the e-mail address on which alerts are sent.

When receiving an e-mail alert, the user can send a message to the person concerned. The message goes through the server, where it is processed. If specific keywords are found at the top, predefined messages take their place. For example a simple message "help?" would be replaced by "Do you need any help?". In the absence of keywords, the message is transmitted without modification to the recipient. The message is sent with an indication about the context such as the sender's evaluated state.

The wearable interface lets users visualize and send messages through a "Messages" screen. This interface does not currently allow text input so, when a message is received through the system, the user can just save it, reply to it with predefined messages through icons, or delete it. To send a message, the user clicks on the bubble corresponding to the receiver.

To support privacy, we also propose personalization functions. These include the selection of the type of information gathered and transmitted; for example, restrict the system to indicate only three states: "positive", "neutral" and "negative" rather than detailed emotional states such as "happy" or "angry". A second element of personalization is rendering: colors can be chosen by users. Color theory should guide the default settings. Changes in colors can increase comfort and prevent bystanders from understanding displayed information. Finally, one can request automatic notifications about states at regular intervals.

4 Emotional Design with Feedback from Potential Users

Emotional design is based on visceral, behavioral, and reflective dimensions, which influence any design [3]. We discuss them in the frame of our current design and of comments from six potential users (25-37 year old): two Japanese mothers, a French couple, a German male, and a Japanese male.

4.1 Visceral Dimension

Visceral design deals with shapes, physical feel, textures of materials, and weight. Its bases are valid for everybody:

> "The principles underlying visceral design are wired in, consistent across people and cultures. If you design according to these rules, your design will always be attractive, even if somewhat simple", Norman [3, p67].

Although this paper mainly describes the system and graphical elements, the aspect of the device itself should not be neglected. Wearables containing sensors can be created with various materials, shapes and colors, notably influenced by fashion. We recommend starting with bright colors, warm and soft materials.

To induce a positive affect, we use a bright/warm (yellow) background for the graphical user interface, round shapes, and the *soap bubbles* metaphor. Round shapes are applied to buttons, frames, and to the screen itself. We also suggest the display of sans serif fonts. The bubble representation can induce positive reactions because of slow motions, round and symmetric shapes with a bright (white) contour, and because soap bubbles tend to evoke fond memories of childhood.

Other senses could have a similar influence, such as simple soothing sounds played as feedback about actions. The French male suggested sending supportive messages by caressing a part of the device, with tactile stimulation on reception. One of the two Japanese mothers similarly suggested cold/heat stimulations under the bracelet.

4.2 Behavioral Dimension

Behavioral design deals with performance. This includes the provision of appropriate functions as well as understandable and usable implementations.

Because we propose an innovative system, it is difficult to know how people will use it and what functions are required; tests in real environments and revisions will be necessary. In this paper, we focus on a minimal set of functions and on clear feedback. The design respects the activities of users, avoiding interruptions (no beeps, no vibrations), except in the case of e-mail alerts, which depends on equipment used: cellular phone, laptop, etc. In the successive implementations and improvements of the design, we will consider how to notify users while preserving this important feature:

> "We need technologies that provide the rich power of [human] interaction without the disruption: we need to regain control over our lives.", Norman [3, p159].

The *bubble* metaphor was selected for its visceral, behavioral and reflective characteristics. It provides a good understanding of the data because it shows data as volatile (bubbles burst and vanish, data is retained for short periods only), because it reflects the passing of time with an upward flow, and because each bubble is independent but from the same source (individuals are from the same family or group of friends). Finally, this metaphor is appropriate to convey feelings related to the *family*, because soap bubbles are usually made with one's parents, siblings, or children.

4.3 Reflective Dimension

Reflective design deals with self-image, personal satisfaction, and memories. The quality of the experience cannot be assessed without tests in real world environments. However, we considered the heightening of the quality of the experience, and added the possibility to save and comment messages to *create memories*.

4.4 General Comments

Some of the comments gathered from the potential users concerned the acceptance and usability of the system.

The Japanese mothers looked most interested in the system, especially to know what happens during babysitting. The three Europeans objected to having their typed thoughts (e-mails) being monitored, and similarly rejected the idea of acquire and process voice with the wearable or cellular phones. Local processing, with the e-mail agent serving as proxy before transmitting e-mails, appears more acceptable to them. The presence of a function switching transmissions on and off was much appreciated, as well as the attention paid to security and privacy issues.

The proposed form-factors may be inappropriate for children and seniors. In the case of children, weight and screen size can pose problems. In the case of seniors, reading watch-size screens may be difficult due to reduced sight. Also, Parkinson's disease may prevent the fine manipulations required to interact with touch screens. Finally, equipment placed at the tip of sleeves or in bracelets can be inconvenient–or at risk–for wearers doing house tasks or taking care of babies.

The *soap bubble* representation is considered easy to understand however it raises predictable problems for large groups of friends, and for people that keep contact with their extended family. Similarly e-mail alerts can become unwieldy when used with large groups and very sensitive persons.

5 Future Works

Our future works are to improve the design of the system, evaluate its usability, and study its psychological and social impact.

First, we need to improve our equipment. The cheap sensors provided with the game *Wild Divine* and *Shimadzu*'s semi-transparent glasses *Data Glass 2* are inappropriate for everyday uses by laymen. To favor long-term use, we will consider ways to make the system more fun while carrying out tests and implementing improvements.

Usability will be evaluated in a mobile environment, including visual performance and comfort while walking on a treadmill and in the street, while sitting in a car, train, or coffee shop. We will consider movements, noise, light, and weather.

The psycho-social impact will be studied with French and Japanese families. We expect them to reveal cultural variations in reactions to the service, leading to a better understanding of the creation of ubiquitous systems. We also expect the system to act as a social facilitator and to increase social presence.

Acknowledgments

Thanks to Nadine Richard (NII, Japan) for comments on earlier versions of this publication.

References

1. Maslow, A.: Motivation and personality (1987)
2. Picard, R.: Affective Computing (1997)
3. Norman, D.: Emotional Design – Why we love (or hate) everyday things (2004)
4. Duval, S., Hashizume, H., Andrès, F.: First evaluation of Enhanced Jackets' Potential to Support First Encounters with Photo Slideshows and Emotional Displays. 8th Virtual Reality International Conference, pp. 75–84 (2006)
5. Ekman, P., Davidson, R.: The nature of emotions – Fundamental questions (1994)

PixelWish: Collective Wish-Making and Social Cohesion

Catherine Hu[1] and Simon M.S. Law[2]

[1] Interaction Design Lab
School of Design
The Hong Kong Polytechnic University
Hung Hom, Kowloon,
Hong Kong, China
sdcathhu@polyu.edu.hk
[2] Philips Design
3/F, Philips Electronics Building
5 Science Park Avenue
Hong Kong Science Park, Shatin, NT
Hong Kong, China
Simon.law@philips.com

Abstract. This paper discusses the concept of a network-mediated system for making wishes and sending them remotely to people whom we care about. Particularly at occurrences of critical events, i.e. crises, when shared emotional connection [1] and group bond is most likely to develop, we believe this system will have positive emotion effects on both the wish-senders and the wish-receivers. We propose this to be a novelty design of community-ware, and believe it has strong potentials in utilizing information technologies to turn 'digital divide' into 'digital cohesion'. [2]

Keywords: Online communities, community-ware, wish-making, social cohesion, emotional connection, Graphical User Interface (GUI).

1 Introduction

Wish-making is a common human behavior. Ancient Greeks threw coins into wells, hoping to keep the wells from drying up. Today, people throw coins in fountains to make their wishes come true. Fetishism aside, making wishes is as natural as breathing for many of us. When a wish is made, there is always the desire that it might be granted. Wishing is hence closely linked to *hope*, one of the identified character strengths in the study of *Positive Psychology* that contributes to the mental wellness of mankind. [3]

Generally speaking, people make two types of wishes: the "me-oriented" wishes that aim to bestow oneself with good fortune, and the "them-oriented" wishes that ask for well-being for others whom we care about. While the former is usually concealing in nature, the wisher for the latter is usually glad to communicate the wish to its

D. Schuler (Ed.): Online Communities and Social Comput., HCII 2007, LNCS 4564, pp. 80–85, 2007.

intended receiver. Sending well wishes to someone is synonymous with sending your blessings, and the positive emotions involved are essential in cultivating understandings and mutual bond. This project explores network-supported exchanges of well wishes as a cohesive force in promoting healthy communities and cross-cultural understandings.

1.1 Collective Wish-Making

In addition to sending well wishes to friends and families, as citizens of societies and the world at large, we also collectively send wishes to show concern for our fellow men. This was evident during the SARS outbreak in 2003 in Hong Kong, and the Tsunami incident that scourged SE Asia in 2005. In the former, throughout the months of dark period when the only news on television was about locations of outbreak and the day's death-roll, people in Hong Kong were touched by the professsionalism and courage of frontline medical personnel who risked their lives in treating patients who contracted SARS. In order to show their gratitude and moral support, people voluntarily posted little heart-shaped memos with written wishes and thank you notes onto notice boards at hospitals. Doctors and nurses responded to these wishes with even greater commitment to their duties of saving lives, and it was this constant exchange of blessings that had helped people in Hong Kong through the difficult times of SARS.

The Tsunami attack witnessed a slightly different form of emotional exchange and collective wish-making. Touched by stories of the disaster, communities all over the world felt the need to express their concern for the less fortunate people in Indonesia, and so candle nights were organized and Mass was particularly dedicated to remotely pray and wish for the victims.

1.2 Supporting Shared Emotional Need

These two incidents show that empathy is very likely to develop during crisis situations, resulting in positive social actions of collective wish-making. When this happens, it is in fact the most favorable opportunity to build human bonds. Unfortunately, as was evident in both cases, this shared emotional need of sending others well wishes is not currently supported by effective methods, thus impeding its great potentials: pinning up of paper wishes was confined geographically with limited participation only by residents in the neighborhood of hospitals, and Tsunami victims and their families remained ignorant to the invisible blessings from afar, which might well have brought much needed comfort and strength to face their miseries.

We thus argue that if this strong emotional need of collective wish-making is properly channeled and effectively supported, it will promise to generate positive forces in promoting social cohesion, and might well result in resolving conflicts and overcoming other negative emotions amongst individuals and communities. While most information and communication technologies (ICTs) systems are for supporting general purpose communication, we identify the exchange of well wishes as a niche communication area to support, offering new design opportunities.

2 Design Concept

Our motivation for this project is threefold: to provide a common platform for collective wish-making to meet the psychological need of bestowing others with our blessings, to facilitate greater participation from local communities, and to promote global, cross-cultural understandings. The proposed PixelWish system combines collective wish-making with basic concepts of an online message board, except that visuals replace text as the main mode of communication.

2.1 System Overview

The basic configuration of the proposed PixelWish system comprises dedicated terminals for sending and retrieving wishes, and a large screen display to show a cumulative view of sent wishes. The system is proposed to be installed in the heart of the city in public spaces like shopping malls or subway stations, providing easy access to the community. People access PixelWish terminals to interact with the system. Pixel Wishes could be sent to cell phone numbers as well as to the virtual entity of the 'PixelWish Tree'. All sent wishes will be shown on the large screen display. When a Pixel Wish is sent to a mobile phone number, a QR Code representing the wish will be sent instead. The wish receiver will then need to physically access the PixelWish terminals to have the QR code scanned in order to retrieve the respective Pixel Wish.

Fig. 1. The PixelWish system is proposed to comprise of dedicated terminals for sending and viewing wishes, and a large, projected or LCD screen to display uploaded Pixel Wishes

2.2 Pixel Wishes as Pictograms

Each Pixel Wish is comprised of a pictogram coupled with a simple text message. Since initial user surveys confirmed the interests in a visual rather than a textual interface, the pictogram is proposed as a mandatory representation of a Pixel Wish while the text message is optional. Unless restricted by the wish sender, all Pixel Wishes sent through the system could be freely viewed by others. People click onto each Pixel Wish pictogram to view its attached text message.

To create a Pixel Wish, a user clicks on a 7x7 dot matrix graphic in the 'Make-a-Wish' interface. The use of low resolution dot matrix pictogram is intended to ease people's fear of drawing while providing a reasonable degree of creative freedom at the same time. Our goal is to design a system that provokes self-expression and stimulates new form of communication, as well as one that is less restricted by language barriers.

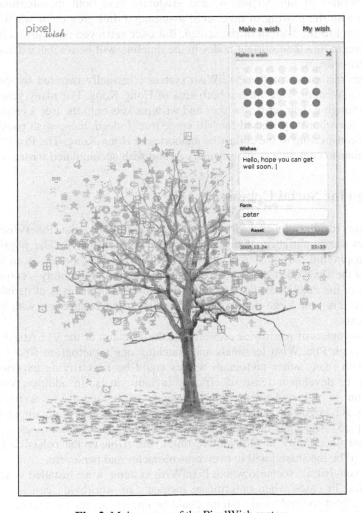

Fig. 2. Main screen of the PixelWish system

To test whether a 7x7 dot matrix is capable of producing recognizable shapes and decent pictograms, paper prototypes were made with perforated holes in the same configuration. To make a pictogram, people selectively punched through these perforations with a sharp instrument like using the tip of a pencil. About a hundred of these paper cards were distributed for testing, resulting in a good variety of pictogram designs that confirmed the viability of the 7x7 matrix. The test also received favorable feedback on the personalization and playfulness of creating one's unique pictogram design.

2.3 Hierarchy of Pixel Wish Messages

Each Pixel Wish appears as its representational pictogram hanging on the digital image of a tree. The display of Pixel Wishes follow a generic timeline, with the latest uploaded wishes in full brightness, and gradually fade both in saturation and in luminance with the passing of time, until assuming a dull grey color when they will eventually fall to the bottom of the screen. But once retrieved and viewed by a user, wishes disregarding their current nodes in the timeline will be revitalized and assume full brightness again.

The tree metaphor for the PixelWish system is actually inspired by the famous 'Lam Tsuen Wishing Tree' in a suburb area of Hong Kong. For many years, people have been hanging their written wishes and wish packets onto the tree's branches with the belief that what they wished for will come true. Indeed, these wish packets could be seen as constituting to the collective memories of Hong Kong. The PixelWish Tree interface aims to capture a similar memory notion with accumulated wish exchanges.

3 Design for Social Cohesion

Rather than residing in the virtual world as a website, the PixelWish system emphasizes the importance of a physical presence in the city. The physicality of publicly displaying current and accumulative Pixel Wishes is seen as an important attribute of the PixelWish system. The goal is to reveal a community's current issues of concern or the emotional states of a city right in front of the eyes of its inhabitants. We believe this will forge people's understandings and connection with their own local contexts.

For catastrophes of worldwide concern like the Tsunami or the 911 Attack, sending wishes through PixelWish terminals and watching one's pictogram wish lighted up together with many other pictogram wishes could be a gratifying experience, and could help to develop a sense of efficacy in individuals. In addition, one's civic participation is acknowledged, and the sense of belonging to a much larger community is recognized, both of which being essential features in maintaining social cohesion. [4, 5] And since the social cohesiveness of a society determines its response to fears and uncertainty in unfavorable times, the stronger the cohesive force, the mightier will be the shared will to overcome obstacles and persevere.

We also envision a scenario where PixelWish systems were installed worldwide in global cities. In cases when unfortunate incidents of worldwide concern occurred, geographically dispersed local systems could be opened up for international linkages and be networked together to form a united communication platform. For instance, at different time slots, the system could be broadcasting PixelWish Trees from different overseas cities. In this manner, Pixel Wishes from all over the world could genuinely reach the local community that was experiencing the crisis. We believe this will have positive effect in cultivating understandings and bonds across nations.

4   Conclusion

In this paper, we described a networked system that aims to support collective wish-making to express our concern for our fellow men. We have pointed out a real emotional need and a virtuous behavior that has great potentials in alleviating differences and in promoting fellowship. The proposed PixelWish system is a novelty design concept that aims to sensitively support this need in order to cultivate social cohesion. Although interactions amongst users of the PixelWish system are comparatively limited compared to other online communities, we nonetheless argue that users of the PixelWish system constitute a valid community as they commonly share the significance and value of bestowing their fellow men with blessings. This common motivation to participate actually transcends personal needs or professional interests – the common ties for most other online communities. We believe the PixelWish system offers a positive contribution in building the strengths and virtues that enable communities to thrive.

Acknowledgments. Pixelwish was developed by Simon Law as an undergraduate final year project, supervised by Catherine Hu at School of Design, the Hong Kong Polytechnic University. We thank Doris Cheung, Jim Tse and Kenneth Sin for their contributions to the project.

References

1. McMillan, D.W., Chavis, D.M.: Sense of Community: A Definition and Theory. American Journal of Community Psychology 14(1), 6–23 (1986)
2. Culture & Society: eInclusion. Europa – Information Society http://ec.europa.eu/information_society/soccul/eincl/index_en.htm
3. Seligman, M.: Authentic Happiness: Using the New Positive Psychology to Realize Your Potential for Lasting Fulfillment. Free Press, New York (2002)
4. Putnam, R.D.: The Prosperous Community: Social Capital and Public Life. The American Prospect, vol. 4(13) (1993)
5. Blanchard, A., Horan, T.: Social Capital and Virtual Communities. Social Science Computer Review 16, 293–307 (1998)

Computing Social Networks for Information Sharing: A Case-Based Approach

Rushed Kanawati[1] and Maria Malek[2]

[1] LIPN – CNRS UMR 7030, 99 Av. J.B. Batiste F-93430 Villetaneuse
rushed.kanawati@lipn.univ-paris13.fr
[2] LAPI – EISTI, 11 Av. du Parc F-95011 Cergy
maria.malek@eisti

Abstract. In this paper we describe a peer-to-peer approach that ails at allowing a group of like-minded people to share relevant documents in an implicit way. We suppose that user save their documents in a local user-defined hierarchy. the association between documents and hierarchy nodes (or folders) is used by a supervised hybrid neural-CBR classifier in order to learn the user classification strategy. This strategy is then used to compute correlations between local folders and remote ones allowing to recommend documents without having a shared hierarchy. Another CBR system is used to memorize how good queries are answered by peer agents allowing to learn a dynamic community of peer agents to be associated with each local folder.

Keywords: Collaborative Document Sharing. Peer To Peer, Case-based reasoning; Community identification.

1 Introduction

Social networks based information searching and dissemination approaches have gained recently an increasing attention as a promising approach to handle the problem of information searching on the Internet. The idea is to provide a computer-mediated support that allow organized group of like-minded people to share their experiences in information searching. Actually, it is reasonable to expect enhancing the outcome of a personal information searching process by providing the user with some access to searching experiences of other like-minded users [4, 7]. Useful experiences include: a) relevant founded documents, b) interesting information sources as well as c) usage information indicating how to better use existing searching tools. In this work we focus on the problem of documents sharing among an organized group of like-minded people. Examples are shared bookmark systems [10, 11, 12, 13], and collaborative bibliographical data management systems [2, 6, 9]. The problem here is to recommend users that are interested in some topic T with documents that are effectively relevant to T by exploring the set of judgments made by the group's members about the relevancy of documents to interest topics. Relevancy judgment can be made explicitly by users or inferred, in an implicit way, by observing user's actions.

D. Schuler (Ed.): Online Communities and Social Comput., HCII 2007, LNCS 4564, pp. 86–95, 2007.

Interests topics are usually organized in a hierarchy. The goal is to ease document indexing and recall processes. Hierarchies can either be user-defined as it is the case of individual web bookmarking tools, or system-defined such as the case of using some domain ontology to index the documents. According to the sharing degree of the interests topic' hierarchy among the users we classify document sharing approaches into three classes:

1. *Class 1*: Systems where users share the same topic hierarchy with the same interpretation of each topic. Most existing systems fall into this class. Such systems have often a centralized architecture [1, 3]. Users register, in an implicit or in an explicit way, relevancy judgment into a central repository. The problem here is to compute (or to predict) how relevant would be a document d for a user u knowing the relevancy of this document to other users [3].
2. *Class 2*: Systems where users share the same hierarchy of interest' topics but each has her/his own interpretation of topics. A document is judged relevant to a topic T by one user may be judged relevant to other topics (related to T) by others. In addition to the problem of predicting document relevancy for each user, systems belonging to this class should also handle the problem of heterogeneity of topics interpretation [9]
3. *Class 3:* Systems where each user manages her/his own topic' hierarchy. This class can be seen as a generalization of the previous one. In addition to the above mentioned problems, systems from this class should find a mapping between the different topics hierarchies used by different users.

In this paper we describe a collaborative case-based reasoning (CBR) approach for implementing systems from the third class. The basic idea of the proposed approach is to associate with each user a CBR classifier that learns how the user classifies documents relevant to her/his own hierarchy of interest topics. The use of a CBR classifier is motivated by the incremental learning capacities that can handle dynamic changing in user's classification strategies. Mapping topics defined by user $U1$ to those defined by another user $U2$ is computed by classifying documents provided by $U1$ using the classification knowledge (i.e. cases) related to $U2$. In other words the similarity measure between two topics (defined by two different users) is itself computed by a CBR system. This mapping function is used to infer, for each user and for each topic, the most appropriate social network to fed the local topic with relevant documents. The reminder of this paper is organized as follows: The document recommendation approach is described in section 2. Subsection 2.1 gives a general overview of the approach. Then the three main components of the approach : Learning to classify, learning to recommend and community learning are describes inn subsequent subsections. Ann example of applying the recommendation approach tor implementing a bookmark recommendation approach is given with first experimental results are given in section 2.5. Related work are reported in section 3 and a conclusion is given in section 4.

2 Our Approach

2.1 General Description

The goal of the proposed document sharing approach is to allow a group of like-minded people to share their documents in an implicit way [7]. Let U be the group of users. $U = \{u_1, u_2,..., u_n\}$ where n is the number the group members. The sharing system functions as follows: each user u_i manages her/his own document collection. We assume that each user u_i organizes his/her documents in a collection of folders $F_{ui} = \{f_{ui}^j\}$. The same document d can be saved to more than one local folder. Each user u_i is associated with a personal software assistant agent A_{ui}. The role of this agent is to learn to map, if possible, each local folder f_{ui}^j with folders managed by other users. In other words the task of agent A_{ui} is to learn a mapping function $M_{ui} : F_{ui} \rightarrow \prod_j F_{uj} \, j \neq i$. Computing this mapping function requires computing a correlation measure between local and remote folders. A local folder f_{ui}^j will be mapped to highly correlated remote folders. The huge number of available documents does not allow to use simple folder correlation measure such as $correlation(f_1, f_2) = /f_1 \cap f_2 // /f_1 \cup f_2|$ since two effectively highly correlated folders may have a low correlation degree computed by such a function. A document similarity function could be used to cope with this problem. Correlation between two folders could be expressed by how much documents in f_1 are similar to those in f_2. Another problem to cope with is that folders do not necessarily express a class of documents. Folders are basically defined by users as a document organization entity. Different users apply different document classification criteria. Therefore using a mere document similarity function ay lead to poor folder correlation detection. In our approach we propose to compute folder correlation as a function of their usage similarity. More precisely, a correlation degree between folder f_{ui} (created by user u_i) and folder f_{uj} (created by another user u_j) is given by the ratio of documents in folder f_{uj} that would be classified in folder f_{ui} according to user u_i classification scheme. Hence in order to compute the mapping function we first need to model each user classification scheme. This is performed by using a incremental supervised classifier. Classes to be recognized are defined by the set of folders created by the user. The proposed classifier is described in next section. A collaboration protocol is described in section IV that allow each agent to compute correlation between its local folders and remote ones. Documents added to remote folders that are highly correlated to a local folder f will be recommended to be added to f. From the classification learning point of view, each document recommendation will constitute either as a positive example (if the recommendation is accepted by the user), or either as a negative example (if the recommendation is rejected by the user). The classification learning and the older correlation computation are described in the next two following sections.

2.2 Learning to Classify

In order to learn the user document classification scheme, each personal agent implements an incremental hybrid neural/case-base reasoning classifier. This classifier called PROBIS and initially proposed in [14] is based on the integration of a prototype-based neural network and a flat memory devised into many groups, each of them is represented by a prototype. PROBIS contains two memory levels, the first level contains prototypes and the second one contains examples. The first memory level is composed of the hidden layer of the prototype-based neural network. A prototype is characterized by:

1. *The prototype's center.* This is given by the co-ordinates in the m-dimensional space (each dimension corresponding to one parameter), these co-ordinates are the center of the prototype.
2. *The prototype's influence region.* This is determined, by the region of the space containing all the examples represented by this prototype.
3. *The class* to which belongs the prototype. In our application the class is the folder identifier in which the document is saved.

The second memory level is a simple flat memory in which examples are organised into different zones of similar examples. These two levels are linked together, so that a memory zone is associated with each prototype. The memory zone contains all examples belonging to this prototype. A special memory zone is reserved for *atypical examples*. These are examples that do not belong to any prototype. Documents that belongs to more than one folder will be typically saved in this memory zone. The classifier system operates either in learning mode or in classification mode. The system can switch from one mode to another at any moment. Before the first learning phase, the system contains neither prototypes nor zones of examples. Examples for training are placed initially in the atypical zone. Prototypes and associated zones are then automatically constructed. An incremental prototype-based neural network is used to construct the upper memory level. Particular and isolated examples are kept in the atypical zone whereas typical examples are transferred to the relevant typical zones. This memory organization helps to accelerate the classification task as well as to increase the system's generalization capabilities. In addition adding a new example is a simple task, the example is added in the appropriate memory zone and the associated prototype is modified. The learning procedure is the following:

1) If the new example does not belong to any of the existing prototypes, a new prototype is created (this operation is called assimilation). This operation is accomplished by adding a new hidden unit to the neural network. The co-ordinates of this prototype and the radius of the influence region is initialized to a maximal value (this is a system parameter). A new memory zone is also created and linked to the prototype. The new example is added to the new memory zone.

2) If the new example belongs to a prototype whose class value is the same as the example, the example is added to the associated zone of the second level memory. The prototype co-ordinates are modified according to the *Grossberg* learning law [5] to fit better the new example (this operation is called accommodation). The vector representing the prototype co-ordinates and memorized in the weights of the links going from the input layer to this prototype is modified as follows:

$$W_{pro}(t+1) = W_{pro}(t) + g(t)*Sim\,(b_i - W_{pro}(t))$$

where b_i is the vector representing the document to classify, $g(t)$ is a decreasing series which tends to 0, and *Sim* is the document similarity function.

3) If the new example belongs to a prototype whose class value is not the same as the example, the radius of this prototypes is decreased in order to exclude the new example of this prototype (this operation is called differentiation). The new example is introduced again to the neural network and the most similar prototype (if any) is activated again and one of the three previous conditions is right.

2.3 Learning to Recommend

The goal of an assistant agent is to gather form peer agents documents that can be relevant to be added to a local folder. Given a target local folder f, an agent applies the following steps for computing documents relevant to f : First, the agent computes summery of f. Actually, the summery is a keyword list containing the k-most frequent keywords that are listed in descriptions of documents stored in f. Then the agent applies the community formation algorithm, described in section 2.4, in order to get the list of peer agents that are likely to provide most relevant documents. A recommendation request is sent to each member of the computed community. A recommendation request contains the following informations: the sender agent identifier, the target folder identifier, the folder summery and the list of document descriptions of documents in f. Selected peer agents respond to a recommendation request by sending back : a list of relevant folder's identifiers and a list of recommended agents. Local folders whose correlation degree with the received folder is above a given threshold t are said to relevant to the recommendation request. The correlation between folder f and a local folder g is given by:

$$correlation(f,g) = |d_i \text{ in } f : Class(d_i) = g| / |f|$$

Where Class(x) is a function giving the predicted class, according to the local classifier, of document d_i. With each sent folder, the agent associate the computed correlation degree.

The list of recommended agents is computed by applying the local community formation algorithm (see section 2.4) using the received folder summery. This facility allow to propagate among agents of the system the *expertise* of the different agents. Notice that either of the both answer lists (recommended folders end agents) can be empty. Upon receiving answers for the selected peer agents, the initiator agent used the lists of relevant folders with their correlation degrees for updating a local folder correlation matrix (FCM). The FCM is a $m \times n$ matrix where m is the number of folders in the local repository and n the number of peer agents known to the agent. An entry $FCM[i, j]$ is a set of couples $<f_{jk}, cor_{ij}>$ where f_{jk} is a folder identifier maintained by user u_j and cor_{ij} is the correlation degree between the folder f_{jk} and the folder f_{ik} maintained by local agent.

The *FCM* matrix is used by an assistant agent in order to determine which remote folders are highly correlated to a given local folder f. A *folder request message* is then sent for agents that have the selected remote folders. Upon receiving a folder request message, an agent send back all documents contained in the requested folders. The initiator agent merges the list of received documents (in case it requests downloading more than one remote folder) and the top K-documents will be presented to the associated user when accessing the local folder f. K is a user defined parameter that allow the user to limit the number of new documents to be recommended at once when accessing a local folder. This two step document recommendation computation process aims at reducing the network traffic by transmitting over the networks only documents to be effectively recommended to the user.

Received lists of recommended agents are used by the community formation module, described in the next section, in order to complete its information about the peer community associated to a given local folder. The user evaluates the recommended documents by simply accepting or refusing each of these documents. Recommendations provided by a given agent are evaluated using the classical precision and recall criteria defined as follows:

$$\text{Precision (summery, } a_i) = |\text{ accepted recommendations provided by } a_i | / |\text{ recommended documents }|$$

$$\text{Recall (summery, } a_i) = |\text{ accepted recommendations provided by } a_i | |\text{ accepted recommended documents }|$$

The user feed back is used, on one hand, to update the the local agent classification knowledge as described in section 2.2. On another hand, it is used to evaluate the recommendations provided by peer agents. This evaluation is used by the community computation module, as described in the next section.

2.4 Community Computation

In order to avoid sending recommendation requests to all known peer agents, we provide each assistant agent with learning capability that allow to compute for each local folder a set of peer agents that are most likely to provide relevant documents. We call these agents, the *folder community*.

We use a second CBR reasoner in order to compute folder's communities. A source case is classically composed of a problem part and a solution part []. In this subsystem, the problem part is given by a keyword list that summarize a folder content while the solution part is composed of the list of peer agents identifiers. With each agent identifier is associated a the highest correlation degree obtained from this agent and, if it exists, the user evaluation of the recommendations provided by this remote agent answering a recommendation request using the folder summery provided in the problem part.

Initially, the case base is empty. As a consequence, the local agent will send the recommendation request to all known agents. Upon receiving recommendations and a the user feedback, a new source case can be added to the case base. The recommendation evaluation criteria are used to compute a *trust degree* in the concerned remote agent. The trust degree is defined as the product of the computed precision and recall. Notice that only agents that have answered a folder request message (see previous section) can be evaluated. All other agents that have answered a recommendation request message will be assigned a neutral trust degree (i.e. 0.25 on a scale from 0 to 1, that to say that both precision and recall are equal to 0.5).

Before sending a new recommendation request with a target folder f, the agent computes the new summery of f. The summery of a folder changes in function of the actual set of documents that are stored in f but also in function of the summery of other local folders. the case retrieval phase computes the similarity between the new folder summery and the problem part of each stored case. Cases with similarity measure above a given threshold t_r will be retrieved. Each retrieved case provides a set of agents to contact. The obtained lists of agents are then merged and the result list is sorted in function of the trust degree. The top K-agent (where K is another system parameter) will form the folder community.

2.5 Application: Collaborative Bookmarking

In oder to illustrate our document recommendation approach, we have applied the proposed approach in the context a collaborative bookmark management system. In this application a document is represented by a bookmark. A bookmark is described by a couple : 1) the address of the indexed web site (i.e. the site URL) and 2) by a set of keywords that summarize the content of the indexed page. Hence the similarity between two bookmarks is defined as a weighted sum of two basic similarities defined overs URL and keyword lists.

$$sim(b1, b2) = \alpha\, URLSim(b1.url, b2.url) + (1-\alpha)\, ContSim(b1.Cont, b2.cont)$$

Where $0<\alpha<1$ is weight of the address similarity. The address similarity *URLSim* function is defined as follows:

$$URLsim(a,b) = 0 \text{ if a and b have different web servers.}$$
$$URLSim(a,b) = 1- h(a.FP, MSCA(a.FP,b.FP) \quad +$$
$$h(b.FP,MSCA(a.FP,b.FP) /h(a.FP,root) +h(b.FP,root)$$

Where the function $h()$ returns the number of links between two nodes in the documents tree and $MSCA()$ returns the most specific common ancestor of two nodes in a tree. This similarity measure is based on the hypothesis that two documents that are placed in the same directory on the same server are similar to each other. More the directory is deep in the server hierarchy more the documents are related to each other.

The content similarity function is defined by : $ContSim(u,v) = | u \cap v | / | u \cup v |$.

In order to validate our approach we have applied the following experimentation protocol. We start by forming a synthetic collection of bookmarks. The total number of bookmarks is 300. These bookmarks are grouped in 30 folders. The mean number of bookmarks per folder is 10. Starting from this bookmark collection we randomly generated ten other collections by modifying each by up to 35%. Two types of operations are possible in order to modify a folder: 1) delete a bookmark from the entire collection ,2) move a bookmark to another folder. Notice that we assume that a bookmark may not belongs to two different folders at the same time. The generated bookmark collections verify, by construction, this property. The modification percentage (i.e. 35%) ensures a suitable overlapping between the different collections of bookmarks. The system performances are evaluated by two criteria:

- The learning ratio that measures for each classifier the precision of good classifications of examples belonging to the learning set (i.e. local bookmarks used to build the classifier)

- The generalization ratio that measures the precision of recommending a bookmark of the right folder. The right folder of a bookmark is the original folder where the bookmark was in the initial collection.

A set of ten different experiences has been conducted. The average obtained learning ratio is 93,3% and the average generalization ratio 86,2%. While these figures are encouraging, we should admit that these will not be the same is real world settings where overlapping ration among bookmark folders is far below the artificial overlapping threshold we have imposed in our experimental work.

3 Related Work

A number of document sharing and recommendation systems are proposed in the scientific literature. Most of existing systems fall in the first two classes defined in section 1.

Pharos [1] and *KnoweldgePump* [3] provide users with the possibility to share a centralized document repository. The repository hierarchy is defined by a system administrator. Both systems provide also customization service in order to recommend users with documents that are more interesting for them in given folder. Recommendation computation is made by applying a collaborative filtering mechanism that is base on matching the characteristics of bookmarks added and accessed by each user.

GAB is a shared bookmark system that allows merging different user bookmark repository in a virtual centralized bookmark [16]. No recommendation mechanism is provided. It is up to the users to navigate in the merged repository to find bookmarks they are interested in. A comparable approach is also implemented in the *Power-Bookmarks* systems [11]. *CoWing* in a peer-to-peer (P2P) multi-agent collaborative bookmarking system [7, 8]. *CoWing* is the our first prototype of document sharing system. In this early prototype agents send recommendation request to all known agents and all agents respond directly with the set of documents to recommend. No Community formation function is provided. *Bibster* [2, 6] is a P2P bibliographical data sharing system. In this system, each agent publishes its own expertise for all agents. The published expertise is used to match agents to actual need of recommendation expressed by an agent.

Most related to our approach are the *COBRAS* system [9] and the *REMINDIN* approach [15]. Both systems provide a query routing in a P2P network based on observing queries that are successfully answered by peer agents, these queries are memorized locally. Subsequently, a peer uses this information in order to select others peers to forward request to.

4 Conclusion

In this paper we've proposed a new approach for allowing a a group of like-minded people to share documents in an implicit and intelligent way. Users are not required to do extr effort to get document recommendations from others. They are only required o maintain their personal documents in a hierarchy of folders (as most do). Personal software agents observes users in order to learn document classification rules. This knowledge is used to compute a correlation degree between local folders and remote ones. In addition, agents uses feed-back provided by the user when accepting or rejecting recommendations in order to learn to associate a community of peer agents for each local folder. Recommendation request concerning a local folder is only sent to the community avoiding broadcasting the request to all known peers.

References

1. Bouthors, V., Dedieu, O.: Pharos, a Collaborative Infrastructure for Web Knowledge Sharing. In: Abiteboul, S., Vercoustre, A.-M. (eds.) ECDL 1999. LNCS, vol. 1696, pp. 215–233. Springer, Heidelberg (1999)
2. Brockstra, J., et al.: Bibster: A semantic-based bibliographic P2P syste. In: Proceedings of the second workshop on semantics in P2P & grid computing, New York, pp. 3–22 (May 2004)
3. Glance, N., et al.: Making recommender systems work for organization. In: proceedings of PAAM'99, London (April 1999)
4. Delgado, J., Ishii, N., Ura, T.: Intelligent Collaborative Information Retrieval. In: Coelho, H. (ed.) IBERAMIA 1998. LNCS (LNAI), vol. 1484, pp. 170–182. Springer, Heidelberg (1998)
5. Grossberg, S.: Competitive learning: From interaction activation to adaptive resonance. Cognitive Science 1, 23–63 (1987)
6. Hasse, P., Ehrig, M., Hotho, A., Scnizler, B.: Personnalized Information Access in a bibliographic Peer-to-Peer System. In: Staab, S., Stuckenschmidt, H. (eds.) Semantic web and Peer-to-Peer, Decentralized management and exchange of knowledge and information, pp. 144–157. Springer, Heidelberg (2006)
7. Kanawati, R., Malek, M.: Informing the design of shared bookmark systems. In: proceedings of RIAO'2000: Content-based Multimedia information access, Paris (2000)
8. Kanawati, R., Malek, M.A.: multi-agent system for Collaborative Bookmarking. In: proceedings of fourth international Workshop on Agent-oriented Information System (AOIS'02), CEUR , vol. 59, Bologna, pp. 84–97 (July, 2002)
9. Karoui, H., Kanawati, R., Petrucci, L.: COBRAS: Cooperative CBR System for Bibliographical Reference Recommendation. In: Roth-Berghofer, T.R., Göker, M.H., Güvenir, H.A. (eds.) ECCBR 2006. LNCS (LNAI), vol. 4106, pp. 76–90. Springer, Heidelberg (2006)
10. Keller, R.M., Wolf, S.R., Chen, J.R., RabinowitzJ., L., Mathe, N.A: Bookmaking Service for Organizing and Sharing URLs. In: Proceedings of the 6th International Conference on the World Wide Web, Santa Clara, CA (April 1997)
11. Li, W., Vu, Q., Agrawal, D., Hara, Y., Takano, H.: PowerBookmarks: A system for Personnalizable Web Information Organization, Sharing and Management. In: proceedings of the 8th International World Wide Web Conference (WWW'8), Toronto, Canada (May 1999)
12. Lim, J-G.: Using Cool-lists to Index HTML Documents in the Web. In: Proceedings of the 2nd International Conference on the World Wide Web (WWW'2) Chicago, IL, 1994 pp. 831–938 (1994)
13. Maarek, Y.S., Ben Shaul, I.Z.: Automatically Organizing Bookmarks per Contents. In: Proceedings of the 5th International World Wide Web Conference, Paris (May 6-8, 1996)

14. Malek, M.: Hybrid approaches Integrating Neural Networks and case based reasoning: from Loosely Coupled to Tightly Coupled Models. In: Sankar, K.P., Tharam, S.D., Daniel, S.Y. (eds.) Soft Computing in Case-based Reasoning, pp. 73–94. Springer, Heidelberg (2000)
15. Tempich, C., Staab, S.: Semantic Query Routing in Unstructured Networks Using Social Metaphors. In: Staab, S., Stuckenschmidt, H. (eds.) Semantic web and Peer-to-Peer, Decentralized management and exchange of knowledge and information, pp. 107–123. Springer, Heidelberg (2006)
16. Wittenburg, K., Das, D., Hill W., Stead, L.: Group Asynchronous browsing on the World Wide Web. In: Proceedings of the 6th International Conference on the World Wide Web (WWW'6) (1997)

Presentation Desire of Digital Identity in Virtual Community

Hee-Woong Kim and Eunice Que

National University of Singapore
{kimhw,EuniceQue}@comp.nus.edu.sg

Abstract. Recently digital items have been widely used by people in the online space including virtual communities and online games. Some Internet companies even in the context of virtual community (VC) generate revenue from the sales of digital items to their online members. The sales of digital items provide insights for Internet companies and virtual community providers who are suffering from the lack of a profitable business model. This study examines why people pay for digital items from the self-presentation perspective in the context of VC by introducing a new construct, digital identity, and developing a conceptual framework of presentation of digital identity. The findings of this study show that the presentation desire of digital identity leads to the intention of purchasing digital items. This study identifies the significance of online group norm and online group involvement on the presentation desire from the social digital identity perspective and the significance of personal innovativeness from the personal digital identity perspective. These findings help to advance theory and offer practical insights in the context of Internet business and VC.

1 Introduction

Recently, virtual communities (VCs) like MySpace (www.myspace.com) and Friend-ster (www.friendster.com) as well as online game providers have developed a virtual icon called Avatar— a graphical representation and articulation of a user in the virtual environment. In addition to Avatar, online game providers like WorldWarCraft (www.worldofwarcraft.com) and NeoPets (www.neopets.com) have started developing digital items (e.g., game character) and selling them for generating revenue. VCs have also started developing and selling digital items to their users. Digital items (e.g., avatar, clothes and hats for the avatar, digital wallpapers, background music, and weapons used in online games) are online products which can be employed by users for representation and articulation and as a multipurpose platform in the online space. Cyworld (us.cyworld.com) is a representative success case with its unique and profitable business model based on the sales of digital items in the context of VC.

Cyworld is a VC where members build relationships with other members and share their interests and information. Cyworld enables its members to form online clubs of similar interests (e.g., online recipe club, stock investment club, travel information club). Compared to other VCs, Cyworld has a unique feature called a mini-hompy, which is similar to a weblog. Upon registration in Cyworld, each member gets an

D. Schuler (Ed.): Online Communities and Social Comput., HCII 2007, LNCS 4564, pp. 96–105, 2007.
© Springer-Verlag Berlin Heidelberg 2007

empty mini-hompy. Mini-hompy consists of each member's profile, journal, mini-room, photo album, and guestbook. Members communicate through the mini-hompies. Popular pastimes involve the user clicking through his circle of friends or his friend's circle of friends, reading their profiles, looking at their photo albums, listening to music from their jukebox, and leaving them messages. Members are under no obligation to decorate their mini-hompies but that would be similar to entertaining visitors in an empty living room.

Cyworld has developed several digital items (e.g., avatar, clothes, hats, shoes, furniture, pets, wallpapers, music, and works of art) which can be purchased by members with prices varying from US$0.2 to US$0.5 for each digital item. Members can buy these digital items and use them to decorate their mini-hompies. Most of the digital items have a certain life span varying from one week to one year. After expiry of the digital items, members need to purchase them again. According to company information, Cyworld had around 13 million members (8% of them are in 10s, 79% of them are in 20s, 8% in 30s, 5% in 40s and above; 60% of them are female) in 2004 and made an average of US$200,000 in sales each day by selling digital items. Cyworld has further expanded its business from Korea (www.cyworld.com) to US (us.cyworld.com), Japan (jp.cyworld.com), China (www.cyworld.com.cn), Taiwan (tw.cyworld.com) and Europe in the near future.

While Cyworld clearly illustrates a new and profitable business model in the context of VC, the members' purchase behavior has not been explained. This study aims to examine the purchase behavior of people in VCs like Cyworld. Specifically, this paper seeks answers to two research questions: (1) what factors motivate the intention of purchasing digital items in the online space? and (2) how do the factors affect the purchase intention? The rest of the paper is organized as follows. The next section presents the conceptual background of this research. The research model and hypotheses follow. We then describe the research methodology applied. After interpreting the empirical results, we discuss the implications and conclude with a summary of this study.

2 Digital Identity and the Presentation

Identity is often characterized by one's personality traits, interpersonal characteristics such as the roles and relationships one takes on in various interactions, the skills one possesses, and one's personal values or moral beliefs (Calvert 2002). It would be difficult to explain how one person is different from others without using identity. There is an inherent unity to the self as one body corresponding to one particular identity in offline context (Donath 1998). Self-presentation of identity in the offline context is also affected by many factors beyond our control such as age, race, and gender.

However, the Internet has provided a new context for identity exploration because of its anonymity and flexibility. An identity established online is not necessarily tied to the identity of same person established offline. For example, one person can establish very active and cheerful identity in the online context while (s)he has a different identity characterized by shyness in the offline context. One person can also join a special online club and actively participate in that club's activities while (s)he does not want to or can not join such a club in the offline context. It would also be easy to establish and change one's identity in the online context while it would be very difficult to establish and change one's identity in the offline context. In addition, it takes less time and effort for the self-presentation of identity in the online context while it takes a lot of time and effort for the self-presentation of identity in the offline context. This study proposes a new construct, digital identity, to represent any identity established online. Same as the self-concept consisting of personal identity and social identity in the offline context (Ashforth and Mael 1989), digital identity may consist of a personal digital identity and a social digital identity.

Digital identity then leads to the online presentation. Establishing digital identity, people want to make a desired impression to others online and project a wanted online image. Online image is the opinion or concept of the identity that is held by the public in the online space. There could be two main approaches in expressing one's digital identity in the online space: textual communication and symbolic communication. In textual communication, linguistic cues (e.g., language intensity and lexical diversity) and paralinguistic cues (e.g., typographical marks and emoticons) could be used to form the online image in cyberspace (Jacobson 1999). As a type of textual communication, there is also synchronous communication like chatting to reflect spontaneity and the more thoughtful style of asynchronous communication as in message boards (Suler 2002). In symbolic communication, presentation of digital identity is mediated by digital items (e.g., avatar). Digital items are like physical possessions and functions as tangible symbols of identity. Thus, by studying an individual's digital items portfolios, others gain access to the possessor's intangible image (Schau and Gilly 2003).

However, presentation of digital identity is constrained by the digital representations constructed by interactive systems. For example, people can use different features such as homepage, avatar, music, photo, message board for representing digital self only if the interactive system provides them. Especially, for the presentation of personal digital identity, an individual may need to use any of the mediums (e.g., blog and message board) which can show his or her accomplishments, characteristics, and unique things. Regarding the presentation of social digital identity, social digital identity can be exemplified by the online groups one belongs to as well as the digital signs and digital symbols that point to an affiliated identity like logos or a sports team color. People thus use digital items for presenting digital identity only if the interactive system provides.

3 Research Model and Hypotheses

Based on the conceptual background discussed above, we develop a research model (see Figure 1). From the personal perspective of self-concept, an individual's personality traits affect the establishment of identity (Baumeister 1998). This study selects personal innovativeness as a personality trait because it is a good indicator of how likely an individual is to try out new ideas and new things and all individuals possess it in varying intensities (Hirschman 1980). As a key personality trait helping to establish one's personal identity, personal innovativeness is defined as *the degree to which an individual is receptive to new ideas and makes innovative decisions independently of the communicated experience of others* (Midgely and Dowling

1978). Personal innovativeness thus boosts confidence to perform new and unknown tasks and seek out new and stimulating experiences (Venkatraman 1991), which leads an individual to desire to present his or her digital identity in an attempt to mirror personal innovativeness in the online space, especially in online groups like VCs. Hence, we hypothesize:

H1: Personal innovativeness has a positive effect on the presentation desire of digital identity in the context of online group.

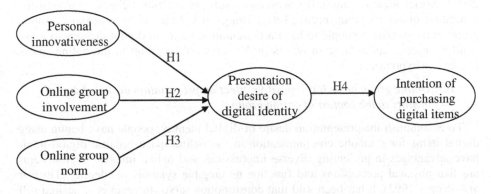

Fig. 1. Research Model

Regarding the social perspective of self-concept, self-categorization is the process of taking the self as an object and categorizing, classifying and naming itself in particular ways in relation to social categories and classifications (Turner, Hogg, Oakes, Reicher, and Wetherell 1987). Social categorization then leads to the formation of one's social identity. Categorizing oneself as a group member shifts the self-concept to bring it in line with the characteristics of the focal group. It is a cognitive assimilation of the self to the group prototype which describes and prescribes perceptions, attitudes, feelings, and behaviors of the group members (Hogg and Terry 2000). With respect to self-categorization, this study identifies online group involvement as one factor responsible for initiating and managing self-categorization process and helping to establish one's social identity in the online space. Following the concept of group involvement (Havitz and Dimanche 1997), this study defines online group involvement as *a state of motivation, arousal or interest toward a focal online group.* The more attached an individual is to a group, the more he or she will value social interactions directed at the group audience, which increases the person's inclination to project a desired self-image and consistently perform coherent and complementary behaviors to maintain the desired impression (Rice, Grant, Schmidt, and Torobin 1990; Schlenker 1980). Online group involvement thus leads people to desire to self-present in accordance with the same online group members through social-categorization in the online space. Hence, we hypothesize:

H2: Online group involvement has a positive effect on presentation desire of digital identity in the context of online group.

Another assertion from the social perspective of self-concept says that people as group members tend to adhere to group norms (Barreto et al. 2000). Group norms specify what group members are expected to do when faced with a given situation (Turner 1985). Group members then perform the actions that exemplify and reinforce group norms (Terry and Hogg 1996). As an individual categorizes himself or herself into an online group, the person will be more likely to behave (e.g., projecting online image) in accordance with the online group norm in the online space (Madrigal 2000). Online group norm means social influence on the group members (Venkatesh et al. 2003). Social identity thus influences one's self-presentation behavior through the mediation of online group norm (Terry, Hogg, and White 1999). Likewise, online group norm motivates people to have a presentation desire of digital identity to make similar impressions to those of others in the same online group in the online space. Hence, we hypothesize:

H3: Online group norm has a positive effect on presentation desire of digital identity in the context of online group.

To accomplish the presentation desire of digital identity, people have begun using digital items for symbolic communication in the online space because digital items have advantages in presenting diverse impressions and online images. Digital items are like physical possessions and function as tangible symbols of identity (Dittmar and Pepper 1992). It has been said that consumption serves to produce a desired self through the images and styles conveyed through one's possessions (Thompson and Hirschman 1995). The consumption of digital items thus enables users to associate themselves with objects that make their selves more tangible and visitors who land on their online sites perceive as surrogates for the individual who produced them (Schau and Gilly 2003). By examining an individual's digital item portfolios, others gain access to the possessor's intangible image (Schau and Gilly 2003). In contrast, textual communication is severely limited when it comes to self-presentation online. People can get digital items from their online group providers. For example, if a VC provider provides digital items for free then people can use them without purchase for the actual presentation of their digital identities. However, if the VC provider sells digital items then people should buy them for the self-presentation. Presentation desire also affects consumer behavior because it is associated with the degree of interest in maintaining a front through products that are used as props to convey an image of the self to other people (Cass 2001). Hence, we hypothesize:

H4: Presentation desire of digital identity has a positive effect on the intention of purchasing digital items in the context of online group.

4 Research Methodology

This study employed the survey research methodology because it enhances generalizability of results. We chose Cyworld (www.cyworld.com) as the context of our study. After logging into Cyworld, people can visit other members' mini-hompies. We randomly selected 500 mini-hompies (some of them are very well decorated and others are barely decorated) and left a survey invitation message with the URL of the online survey web site in the guestbook of each mini-hompy. The owners of the 500 mini-hompies and visitors to the mini-hompies could read the invitation message and participate in the survey. As incentive, we paid each participant US$5 worth of Cyworld currency. A total of 217 complete and valid responses were collected over one week: age (mean = 24.6 years, s.d. = 6.7) and gender (male = 43.8%, female = 56.2%). More than 80% of respondents were in 20s and 30s.

For the development of the measurement instrument, we adopted existing validated scales and empirical procedures wherever possible. To measure purchase intention, we adapted scales from Dodds et al. (1991) by indicating target (digital items) and time (within the next six months). As for presentation desire of digital identity, we self-developed the scales because the construct is unique to our study. We adapted the personal innovativeness scales from Joseph and Vyas (1984) and Oliver and Bearden (1985) by considering innovativeness as personality traits. Scales for online group involvement were taken from Kyle et al. (2004). As for online group norm, we adapted scales from Taylor and Todd (1995) by considering the study context. We modified the self-efficacy scales from Taylor and Tod (1995) by considering the object of behavior and behavior context. The questionnaire employed the seven-point Likert scale (1 = strongly disagree, 7 = strongly agree).

5 Data Analysis and Results

We assessed the constructs for convergent validity and discriminant validity via confirmatory factor analysis (CFA) using LISREL. After establishing the convergent validity and discriminant validity, we examined the structural model based on the measurement model.

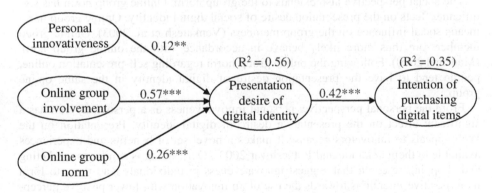

Fig. 2. Standard LISREL Solution normed χ^2 = 2.01, RMSEA = 0.061, GFI = 0.86, AGFI= 0.83, CFI = 0.98, NFI = 0.96 (**: p < 0.01, ***: p < 0.001, ns: insignificant at the .05 level)

The structural model had good fit indices except goodness-of-fit index (GFI) (see Figure 2). GFI (0.87) was below the recommended threshold, but adjusted goodness-of-fit index (AGFI) was 0.83, which is above the cut-off value of 0.8. These results suggest that the structural model adequately fits the data. The standardized path coefficients could then be used for testing the hypotheses relevant to the main effects.

Personal innovativeness (H1), online group involvement (H2), and online group norm (H3) had significant effects on the presentation desire of digital identity, explaining 56 percent of the variance. Presentation desire of digital identity (H4) had significant effect on the intention of purchasing digital items, explaining 35 percent of the variance.

6 Discussion of Findings

There are several interesting findings in this study. This study first found that presentation desire of digital identity has a significant effect on the intention of purchasing digital items in the context of online group. Presentation desire of digital identity takes the role of key motivator of actual self-presentation online (Maslow 1943). People are more likely to use digital items for the presentation of digital identity in the online space because digital items have advantages in presenting diverse impressions and online images from the symbolic communication perspective. Thus, people should purchase digital items for the presentation of their digital identity.

This study also found that presentation desire of digital identity is influenced by self-concept from its personal perspective and social perspective. From the social perspective, an individual's involvement in a focal online group has significant effects on the presentation desire of his or her social digital identity in the online group. Group involvement influences pro-social behavior of the members towards the group (Ellemers, Spears, and Doosje 2002). A good case would be in the realm of sports, where high levels of team involvement lead to group behaviors such as wearing a team uniform.

The social perspective also extends to the group norm. Online group norm has significant effects on the presentation desire of social digital identity. Online group norm means social influence on the group members (Venkatesh et al. 2003). Online group members are thus more likely behave in accordance with the online group norm (Madrigal 2000). Following the online group norm regarding self-presentation online, people tend to have the presentation desire of digital identity in the same online group.

From the personal perspective, personal innovativeness as a personality trait has a significant effect on the presentation desire of digital identity. Presentation on the Web appeals to innovators because it makes a novel set of benefits and experiences available to them (Ziamou and Ratneshwar 2003). Our finding is similar to marketing and shopping research that suggest innovativeness in individuals lead them to form more positive intentions towards the use of an innovation with fewer positive perceptions to support them. It explains that people with higher level of innovativeness have higher presentation desire of their digital identities.

7 Conclusion and Implications

This study has examined why people pay for digital items in the context of VC by proposing a new construct, digital identity. This study highlights the significance of presentation desire of digital identity as a factor leading to the intention of purchasing digital items. This study also identifies the significance of online group norm and online group involvement in enhancing the presentation desire from the social digital identity perspective and the significance of personal innovativeness from the personal digital identity perspective. These findings help to advance theory and offer practical insights in the context of Internet business and VC.

This research offers several implications for theory and practice. From the theoretical perspective, this study introduces a new construct, digital identity, and its corresponding presentation desire in the online space. Self-concept reflects the characteristics of the person and determines his or her behavior (Stets and Burke 2000; Verkuyten and Hagendoorn 1998). However, the Internet has provided a new context for identity exploration. It has been posited that one can have as many electronic personas as one has time and energy to create in the online space (Donath 1998). An identity established online is not necessarily tied to the identity of same person established offline. This study thus proposes a new construct, digital identity, to represent the identity established online.

This study explains how digital identity as a self-concept leads to the presentation of digital identity as self-presentation. While the concept of self-presentation had been studied in other fields (Ashforth and Mael 1989; Baumeister 1998; Turner et al. 1987; Verkuyten and Hagendoorn 1998), this is one of the first studies which examined it in the context of electronic commerce and virtual community. Especially, this study has explained the role and usage of digital items in the presentation of digital identity. Compared to the self-presentation in the offline space, presentation of digital identity in the online space is constrained by the digital representations constructed by interactive systems. This study has thus examined how the presentation desire of digital identity leads to the intention of purchasing and using digital items which are the digital representations constructed by interactive systems in the context of online group, VC.

From the practice perspective, this study shows how Internet companies can generate revenue from selling digital items especially in the context of VCs. While previous VCs had limitations in generating income, this study shows a new way of generating revenue from the sale of digital items which can be used for presenting digital identities in the online space. It highlights people's underlying desire to self-present online and their intent to purchase digital items for presentation in the VC context. Hence, it is definitely worthwhile for an Internet company as a provider of online group or VC to invest in efforts that can enhance the presentation desire of digital identity of its members.

References

1. Ashforth, B.E., Mael, F.: Social Identity Theory and the Organization. Academy of Management Review 14(1), 20–39 (1989)
2. Barreto, M., Ellemers, N.: You can't always do what you want: Social identity and self-presentational determinants of the choice to work for a low-status group. Personality and Social Psychology Bulletin, (26), pp. 891–306 (2000)
3. Baumeister, R.F.: The self. In: Gilbert, D.T., Fiske, S.T., Lindzey, G. (eds.) Handbook of social psychology, pp. 680–740. McGraw-Hill, New York (1998)

4. Calvert, S.L.: Identity construction on the Internet. In: Calvert, S.L., Jordan, A.B., Cocking, R.R. (eds.) Children in the digital age: Influences of electronic media on development, Praeger, Westport, CT, pp. 57–70 (2002)
5. Cass, A.O.: Consumer Self-Monitoring, Materialism, and Involvement in Fashion Clothing. Australasian Marketing Journal 9(1), 46–60 (2001)
6. Dittmar, H., Pepper, L.: Materialistic Values, Relative Wealth, and Person Perception: Social Psychological Belief Systems of Adolescents from Different Socio-Economic Backgrounds. In: Rudmin, F., Richins, M. (eds.) Meaning, Measure, and Morality of Materialism, Association for Consumer Research and School of Business, Provo, UT, pp. 40–45 (1992)
7. Donath, J.S.: Identity and Deception in the Virtual Community. In: Kollock, P., Smith, M. (eds.) Communities in Cyberspace, University of California Press, LA (1998)
8. Dodds, W.B., Monroe, K.B., Grewal, D.: Effects of Price, Brand and Store Information on Buyers' Product Evaluations. Journal of Marketing Research XXVIII, 307–319 (1991)
9. Ellemers, N., Spears, R., Doosje, B.: Sticking together or falling apart: ingroup identification as a psychological determinant of group commitment versus individual mobility. Journal of Personal Social Psychology (72), 617–626 (1997)
10. Havitz, M.E., Dimanche, F.: Leisure involvement revisited: Conceptual conundrums and measurement advances. Journal of Leisure Research (29), 245–278 (1997)
11. Hirschman, E.C.: Innovativeness, novelty seeking and consumer creativity. Journal of Consumer Research (7), 283–295 (1980)
12. Hogg, M.A., Terry, D.J.: Social identity and self-categorization processes in organizational contexts. Academy of Management Review (25), 121–140 (2000)
13. Jacobson, D.: Impression formation in cyberspace: Online expectations and offline experiences in text-based virtual communities. Journal of Computer-Mediated Communication, vol. 5(1) (1999)
14. Joseph, B., Vyas, S.J.: Concurrent validity of a measure of innovative cognitive style. Journal of the Academy of Marketing Sciences 12(2), 159–175 (1984)
15. Kyle, G., Graefe, A., Manning, R., Bacon, J.: Predictors of Behavioral Loyalty Among Hikers Along the Appalachian Trail. Leisure Sciences, vol. 26(1), pp. 99–118 (2004)Madrigal, R.: The influence of social alliances with sports teams on intentions to purchase corporate sponsors' products. Journal of Advertising, vol. 29(4), pp. 13–24 (2000)
16. Maslow, A.H.: A theory of human motivation. Psychological Review (50), 370–396 (1943)
17. Midgely, D.F., Dowling, G.R.: Innovativeness: The Concept and Measurement. Journal of Consumer Research 4, 229–242 (1978)
18. Oliver, R.L., Bearden, W.O.: Crossover effects in the theory of reasoned action: A moderating influence attempt. Journal of Consumer Research (12), 324–340 (1985)
19. Rice, R., Grant, A., Schmitz, J., Torobin, J.: Individual and network influences on the adoption and perceived outcomes of electronic messaging. Social Networks 12(1), 27–55 (1990)
20. Schau, H.J., Gilly, M.C.: We Are What We Post? Self-Presentation in Personal Web Space. Journal of Consumer Research 30(3), 385–404 (2003)
21. Schlenker, B.R.: Impression management: The self-concept, social identity, and interpersonal relations Brooks/Cole, Monterey, CA (1980)
22. Stets, J.E., Burke, P.J.: Identity Theory and Social Identity Theory. Social Psychology Quarterly 63(3), 224–237 (2000)

23. Suler, J.R.: Identity Management in Cyberspace. Journal of Applied Psychoanalytic Studies (4), 455–460 (2002)
24. Taylor, S., Todd, P.A.: Understanding information technology use: A test of competing models. Information Systems Research 6(2), 144–173 (1995)
25. Terry, D.J., Hogg, M.A.: Group norms and the attitude-behavior relationship. A role for group identification. Personality and Social Psychology Bulletin 22, 776–793 (1996)
26. Terry, D.J., Hogg, M.A., White, K.M.: The theory of planned behavior: Self-identity, social identity, and group norms. British Journal of Social (38), 225–244 (1999)
27. Thompson, C.J., Hirschman, E.C.: Understanding the socialized body: a poststructuralist analysis of consumers' self-conceptions, body images, and self-care practices. Journal of Consumer Research 22(2), 139–154 (1995)
28. Turner, J.C., Hogg, M.A., Oakes, P.J., Reicher, S.D., Wetherell, M.S.: Rediscovering the social group: A self-categorization theory. Basil Blackwell, Oxford, England (1987)
29. Turner, J.C.: Social categorization and the self-concept: A social cognitive theory of group behavior. In: Lawler, E.J. (ed.) Advances in group processes: Theory and research, pp. 77–122. JAI Press, Greenwich, CT (1985)
30. Venkatesh, V., Morris, M., Davis, G.B., Davis, F.D.: User acceptance of information technology: Towards a unified view. MIS Quarterly 27(3), 425–478 (2003)
31. Venkatraman, M.P.: 'The impact of innovativeness and innovation type on adoption. Journal of Retailing 67(1), 51–67 (1991)
32. Verkuyten, M., Hagendoorn, L.: Prejudice and self-categorization: The variable role of authoritarianism and in-group stereotypes. Personality and Social Psychology Bulletin (24), 99–110 (1998)
33. Ziamou, P., Ratneshwar, S.: Innovations in Product Functionality: When and Why Are Explicit Comparisons Effective? Journal of Marketing 67, 49–61 (2003)

Grand Challenges in Design Research for Human-Centered Design Informatics

Youn-Kyung Lim, Eli Blevis, and Erik Stolterman

School of Informatics, Indiana University, Bloomington, USA
{younlim,eblevis,estolter}@indiana.edu

Abstract. The idea of *design informatics* as a distinguished discipline is a new one, with little precedence. This paper argues for the importance of a human-centered perspective with respect to the emergence of this newly nascent field of design informatics—a perspective which may be termed *Human-Centered Design Informatics* (HCDI). The paper proposes four grand challenges that are essential to the foundations of HCDI, specifically (i) understanding the *living nature* of information, (ii) understanding the relationships between interaction design and information, (iii) understanding how to design for sustainable and engaging social interactions mediated by information technologies, and (iv) understanding the multi-cultural and globalization issues implied by the use of the materials of information technologies in design.

Keywords: design informatics, information and communications technology (ICT), human-centered design, design education, design research, human-computer interaction (HCI).

1 Introduction

It can be said without controversy that we face grand challenges in every aspect of design research and practice in HCI as new information and communication technologies emerge. The explosion of information and communications technologies (ICTs) that are now available to people everywhere has implications for changing the way we think about design. The more that information becomes intrinsic to our daily lives, the more important it is to establish the field of *design informatics*. In this paper, we propose four grand challenges that can be the initial attempt to be addressed as design research agenda in order to achieve the foundation for *human-centered design informatics*. We promote the term, *design informatics*, in this paper, instead of human-computer interaction, in order to encompass larger perspectives of the relationships between design and the materials of information technologies in all contexts and not just the interactive ones.

The term, *design informatics*, has lately started to gain some attention from both design disciplines and information science disciplines. Some examples include the approach by Harvard Design School, the Center for Design Informatics (CDI) [18] where *design informatics* was defined as "research on the impact of information technology and the Internet on the real estate, design and construction industry, on

D. Schuler (Ed.): Online Communities and Social Comput., HCII 2007, LNCS 4564, pp. 106–115, 2007.

multi-media and visualization, and on Internet-based learning," which is from a design discipline perspective, and the approach by David Hendry in University of Washington, Information School, who views *design informatics* as a study area that enables "a deeper understanding for design that can be obtained by taking an information perspective on design activities," [9] which is more from an information science perspective.

We appreciate both directions on defining *design informatics*, but in this paper, we like to define it in a way that may cover both perspectives. We define *design informatics* as having two important dimensions, namely (i) the application of information technologies to design as an agency in the world, and (ii) design using the materials of information technologies, through the emphases on design values, design actions, and design reasoning. We view it as a field of study of what the digital information age enabled people to do, behave, and live with new information technologies, and how various insights induced by such research can inform the design of new ICTs. This perspective resonates with various researcher perspectives including "Information Ecologies" by Nardi and O'Day [15], "Smart Mobs" by Rheingold [19], and "Infotopia" by Sunstein [23].

In this proposal of a definition of *design informatics*, we are particularly interested in establishing a human-centered perspective of design informatics. Many ICT examples, which are not anymore only about the interactions between a person and a computer, have led us to focus on *people-to-people interactions* mediated by computing-enabled tools and *experiences* emerging from interactions with such tools. Starting from human activities and their experiences becomes inevitable. In this regard, we like to propose that *design informatics* itself should imply the importance of the human-centered perspective.

Examining what emerges from the relationships between people and technologies and how technologies take place in our daily activities made us realize that supporting the design of the emerging forms of technologies to address those two foci becomes even more difficult than ever. In earlier days, there was an obvious setup of the interactions between human and computer when the forms of computers were rather homogeneous. In those days, computers were also more for "non-discretionary" use rather than activities people can choose for what to do with computers [8]. It was far easier to predict what people would do to interact with computers back then. It was far easier to formalize design processes and to measure the effects of design outcomes. However, with these two emerging foci now, it is impossible to think about design in such ways. In this regard, these two foci motivated us to deeply think about what the significant challenges we face in establishing human-centered design informatics which will be able to address those two foci.

In this paper, we particularly propose the challenges which we face especially when we think about the *design research perspective* when developing new ICTs rather than computer science and engineering or information science oriented research perspectives. By design research perspective, we mean the study to improve design knowledge and activities for designing systems. What needs to be addressed is how to advance design knowledge to create better systems which will benefit to human well-being and society welfare.

We propose four grand challenges as an initial proposal when we target to establish the field of *human-centered design informatics*. They include 1) understanding the living nature of information behaviors that emerge from its abundance and pervasive-ness—e.g. "ambient findability" [14] and "everyware" [7]—through the understand-ing of the nature of digital materials which are what enable the abundance and pervasiveness of information, 2) understanding the relationships between interaction design and the living nature of information, 3) understanding how to design for more sustainable and more engaging social interactions, and 4) understanding multi-cultural and global issues.

In what follows, we will discuss in detail why each challenge is important, as well as its definition, examples that show the importance of the challenge for human-centered design informatics, and keys to be considered in design research to address the challenge.

2   The First Challenge: Understanding the Living Nature of Information

We believe that the first challenge is to understand *the living nature of information that emerge from its abundance and pervasiveness* caused by the advent of new tech-nologies—this nature may be construed as a complex system of *living* information. Nardi and O'Day introduced the term, "information ecology", to describe and empha-size the nature of the system that involves "people, practices, values, and technolo-gies" as a coevolving collection [15]. They viewed that the system of this collection behaves like a biological ecology system. Every part of the information ecology adapts to its own ecology to be able to survive and optimize itself to dynamically changing conditions. The ecology is evolving, has its own history, has interconnec-tions among the components within it, and is never static [15].

The most interesting here for us to think about is why in this system the technolo-gies which connect people with information and with other people become also an active part of the ecology rather than fixed tools that can be fully controlled by people and their practices. We believe that this is possible due to the power of digital tech-nologies which created the *living nature of information*. Instant creation and publish-ing of information, unbounded and unconfined sharing of information, and access to information without physical bounds are what become possible due to the digital technologies and what made information behave like living creatures which actively take a part in an *ecology*.

We have observed this nature of information from various existing examples. Some examples of big successes to be self-sustainable and pervasively used web applications especially in US include youtube.com [27] and wikipedia.org [26]. Ano-nymity, instant responses, ratings, and tags are all important features that enabled such success. With information technologies, people smartly utilize and exploit what is available to them to be able to achieve their needs and desires. It is not anymore for people to use them only to achieve certain predefined tasks. What we now face is the uncontrollable expansion and use of information available to almost everyone. The Time Magazine assigned the Person of the Year for 2006 as "You" [22]. The Manag-ing Editor of the Time Magazine, Richard Stengel says, "you, not we, are transform-ing the information age" (p.8) [22].

We believe that this nature of information must be carefully understood for better design of ICTs. And it is a grand challenge because it is impossible to see the whole *ecology* in a clear picture, and impossible to predict what will happen in the whole system.

When we face this challenge, we must make sure that design should not try to figure out a fixed structure of information to visualize or to provide interface to access to the information without accommodating the *living nature of information*. The design case of iPod, shows a good evidence of the tight relationship between the properties of the data and the ways to interact with them. The reason for coming up with the wheel interface was to manipulate more than 200 or 300 songs far more smoothly than pushing a plus button "a thousand times" which was popularly used in regular mp3 players at that time [12].

We must also understand the nature of *digital material* which is the cause of the living nature of information. The term, *digital material*, is carefully examined in this sense by Löwgren and Stolterman [13]. In the process of digitizing information we are creating vast amounts of digital material. Digital material has unusual properties that are the reason for the success of modern information technology. Digital material makes common material properties like reproducibility, storage, and transportation mean new things. At the same time, common economic principles such as the relation between abundance/scarceness and prize are radically challenged. Designers are traditionally professionals who deeply understand and manipulate the natures of materials they need to deal with for ultimate designs. When designers create information technology applications, it is critical to understand what digital technologies—basically *digital material*—have enabled in this current world as well as what will be enabled in future. Understanding digital material is not about studying engineering or science of digital material, but more about studying the consequences that may influence user experiences and society due to their nature.

This definitely has implications for the methods designers use when designing ICT products, the discourse that defines design philosophy, and the notion of design research and education.

3 The Second Challenge: Understanding the Relationships Between Interaction Design and Information

We believe that the second challenge is to understand *the close relationships between interaction design and the living nature of information*. No one has specifically emphasized or identified that the living nature of information is what matters for how we design interactions of ICT products. This is a challenge since, first, without understanding the living nature of information, which is the first challenge we identified in the previous section, it is impossible to identify the relationships between the two, and second, it is a space people have not much explored as a design consideration yet although people have been unconsciously addressing it. The example of iPod's wheel interface design described in [12] clearly shows us the importance of this issue as we mentioned in the previous section. The nature of information and data, which the device provides the access to, was what drove the design of its interface and interaction technique. And various innovative ways of visualizing and manipulating information have been created, and there is also a blog, namely, "Information Aesthetics" [5] where the collection of such new approaches has shared. The core idea here is the living nature of information created new ways of visualizing and interacting with information, and it is not anymore confined to few ways of controlling or interacting with it. What becomes important here is the quality of experiencing the information.

We propose that it is important to clearly conceptualize this space as an important design consideration within which we can closely identify how interaction techniques should be designed to support the access, sharing, and manipulation of different types of information used for different purposes. People have much more focused on new features, new interaction techniques, and new forms of devices without a close examination of how the types of information, the amount of data, and the purpose of the use of information, and the nature of the content in relation to the context of its use and manipulation are related to the design and creation of such new interaction techniques. Although the information visualization area has been thriving, people in this area have not closely examined in relation to the interaction techniques to manipulate such information, or vice versa. Those two areas were rather separately researched rather than seeing the relationships. We here claim that understanding the relationships between these two areas is what we need for better and successful design of ICT products.

One way to address the issue of understanding these relationships is to consider the differences and similarities between *digital* and *analog* qualities of experiences. When we look at these relationships, it is not just about the creation of new forms of devices or about real (physical) and virtual representations. It becomes more about how people perceive and experience the information through the mediated interaction techniques to manipulate various types of information, which can be categorized as *digital experiences* and *analog experiences* although all the technologies are digital.

Digital experiences are commonly described by such terms as *replicable, precise, artificial, discrete, scientific, objective, clean, modern, cold,* and *hard.* **Analog** experiences are commonly described by such terms as *imprecise, continuous, proximate, warm, emotional, sensual, natural, soft, rough, retro,* and *humane.* Ironically, the abundance and collaborative creation of information through digital technologies justifies a metaphor of *living information* to denote the dynamic, organic behavior of information in the modern milieu—which means that digital information itself behaves like *analog* information. As a consequence, the manipulation of digital information becomes more of an analog experience as well. For example, browsing huge amounts of information is no longer an issue of precision. It is an issue of discovery, proximity, and exploration. New ways of visualizing information also mirror the analog aspects of human experiences as well. Since humans live in an analog world, it is natural for them to interpret digital information in terms of the qualities of analog experience. Thus, designers need to account for how digital material will be interpreted in terms of analog experiences.

Many examples in "ambient intelligence" [24] show how the analog quality of experience of perceiving information can be designed through digital technologies. For example, Ambient Orb [2] can visualize various types of information such as weather, stock market, and horoscopes with a glowing color light spectrum (Figure 1(a)). The Orb does not tell you precisely any textual information, but it proximately describes the level of information so that people can quickly capture the information they need.

This is a very analog quality since it is continuous, proximate, and imprecise. Due to these qualities, the way people experience this information is very different from the way people experience when they directly log into websites which precisely show such types of information with rich texts that is more of a digital quality of experience.

Another example includes Attenex Patterns [3] which is a product for information discovery and search. Attenex Patterns (Figure 1(b)) is a tool that discovers useful patterns and facts from information-rich documents "to rapidly identify relevant content for litigation, investigations and regulatory response projects" [3]. In order to enable this, it provides unique ways of exploring information with analog-like interfaces. The query interface allows a user to put a chunk of texts in a search box, which are related to or precisely same with what they like to find among a ton of documents in their database. Then a slide-bar in the query interface that is analogous to an analog quality enables the user to adjust different thresholds for defining the level of relatedness to the queried texts among different documents in the database.

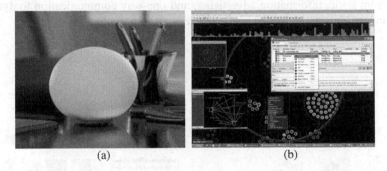

(a)   (b)

Fig. 1. (a) Ambient Orb (the source of picture: http://www.ambientdevices.com); (b) Attenex Patterns (the source of picture: http://www.attenex.com/products/documentMapper/visual/)

Earlier fears about information overload proved to be unfounded and people turn out to be comfortable with this abundance of information. Information was always a part of the human environment, even before the digital age. And now with digital technology, it supports new ways of creating, sharing, and using information that contrast old ways. These new ways have changed our interactions with information and our understanding of the very nature of information. Our interactions with information have become abundant, pervasive, and ubiquitous. With the advent of mobile devices, especially those that are internet connected, we have pervasive access to information that augments our natural memory. Such extensions of ourselves imply the need for new ways of thinking about the design of products which embed the materials of information and communications technologies.

With these technologies, we now not only have a pervasive access to information but also an ability to create new information anytime anywhere by anyone. In this regard, we not only think about how the *access* to different information types drives the ways of thinking about interaction design, which was the primary discussion above, but also we must think about how the interaction design to support the *creation* of information affects the ways of information behaviors and its *ecology*. An example for this would be the case of the success of SecondLife.com where attracted almost

3.5 million people [20]. The fact that it allows people to be able to create their own spaces and objects in their virtual world is what makes it different from other virtual online social spaces which may be less popular than Second Life, due to the fact that people are confined by what is given, and do not have much freedom to expose their creativity in such spaces unlike Second Life.

4   The Third Challenge: Understanding How to Design for Social Interactions

We believe that the third challenge is to understand *how to design for social interactions* mediated by ICTs that support the social nature of human activities. The form of interactions with information on the web has significantly changed over time. A new term denoting the new trend in web culture—Web 2.0 [16]—has transformed web culture from static, information advertising, and one-way communication to dynamic, social-centered business models, and multiple-way communications.

(a)   (b)

Fig. 2. (a) Kodak EasyShare Gallery (www.kodakgallery.com); (b) Flickr (www.flickr.com)

In order to explore how the design of digital information media influences the social nature of people, we compared two websites, one representing the characteristics of the first generation of web sites, Kodak EasyShare Gallery [11], and the other one representing the characteristics of the new generation of web sites, Flickr [25] (Figure 2 (a) & (b)). Kodak EasyShare Gallery which originally called Ofoto was launched in 1999, and Flickr was launched in 2004. Although Flickr started far later than Kodak EasyShare Gallery, Flickr was ranked as the 41st place of the most popular websites in Alexa.com on February 11, 2007 [1], and Kodak EasyShare Gallery was not even in the list for the top 500 sites. Although it may still be arguable if the number of page-viewers and the number of visits, which are the major units to determine the most popular websites by Alexa.com, are more important measurements to evaluate the level of support for the social activities than the market share of visits— according to [17], Kodak EasyShare Gallery had a slightly higher market share of visits than Flickr on June 21, 2006—we think that the number of page-views and visits to the site are better measurements to understand how actively the site users are involved in the community for the sharing of photos. Our comparison of the designs of these two sites is described in Table 1.

Table 1. Comparing the designs between Kodak EasyShare Gallery and Flickr

Compared Aspects of Design	Kodak EasyShare Gallery	Flickr
Used terms	• Album-oriented—individual photos are hidden under albums (e.g. my new album, sample album) • Relationship-oriented (e.g. friends)	• Photo-oriented—individual photos are visible at the first place (e.g. your photos, photos from your contacts, everyone's photos) • Undefined relationships (e.g. contacts, groups)
Link organization	• Sharing photos is 5 steps deep • Commenting on photos is 5 steps deep • Viewing the comments is 3 steps deep	• Sharing photos is 2 steps deep • Commenting on photos is 2 steps deep • Viewing the comments is 1 step deep
Photo browsing and organization	• Album oriented • Comments are hidden • Updates in friends' albums are not visible	• Individual photo oriented • Comments are visible • Updates in contacts' photos are visible

Through this analysis, we realized that what need to be considered for the design of social interactions are as follows:

• how it will allow sharing information,
• what terminology it will use for links and interface elements,
• how it will create a sense of community, and;
• how the focal point of the application and its interface design will be oriented to social features.

These four considerations above are not the ones which can easily be addressed in design without any additional social research support. To be able to accommodate these considerations successfully, we must understand the nature of social context, social desires, and the nature of bonding experiences. This will require even more active research collaborations between social sciences, social informatics, and design informatics.

5 The Fourth Challenge: Multi-cultural and Global Issues

We believe that the fourth challenge is to understand *multi-cultural and global issues* even with the introduction of identical technologies in the different parts of the world, such as information sharing issues caused by language differences or cultural characteristics. In addition, an even more important thing is to understand the fact that not every country or culture has same ways to interact with information. For example, wikipedia.org [26] is not much popular in South Korea comparing to US or other countries which have highly populated Internet users, although South Korea is one of the top countries with the highest internet penetrations [10]. The interesting thing is that the countries like Portugal and Netherlands are shown as places where the number of articles in the Wikipedia is very high [26] and they are not even listed as the top 20 countries of internet users in [10]. Such data imply that the ways people use and create information through digital technologies are different according to cultures, lifestyles, values, and countries.

To be able to understand what causes such patterns, it is important to be able to elicit tacit cultural assumptions and patterns. There are several established methods for this such as ethnomethodology-based methods with which researchers can reveal implicit patterns through defamiliarization [4], using technologies as probes to understand "how people perceive and work with technology" [21], and the cultural probes technique with which we use commonly known artifacts as probes to trigger "inspirational" and tacit responses from the targeted participants whose culture is unknown to designers [6].

We need more of research and development for such methods and techniques, and the research on cultural characteristics in relation to the use of information technologies should be much more published and shared within the HCI and design informatics field.

6 Conclusion

In order to address these four challenges in the design education and the design field, we should develop systematic education and research programs that help designers establish *interdisciplinary, culturally and socially sensitive, and integrated mindsets*. Educating designers who can communicate and work with people in other fields is one essential part of the equation that needs to be established for human-centered design informatics. The issue of creating a culturally and socially sensitive mindset is particularly important when we think about the third and the fourth challenges, although the first two challenges are indirectly related as well. All these discussions lead to the discussion of establishing the new direction of design research—*human-centered design informatics*. We will further discuss what design research activities need to be addressed and implemented in our field as future agenda in the full paper.

Acknowledgments. We like to thank Marty Siegel, Jeffrey Bardzell, Skip Walter and Yvonne Rogers for their insightful comments on our ideas.

References

1. Alexa Web Search – Top 500, Alexa Internet, Inc. (February 11, 2007) http://www.alexa.com/ site/ds/top_sites ?ts_mode=global&lang=none
2. Orb, A.: The Ambient Information Network, Inc. (June 27, 2006) http://www.ambientdevices.com/
3. Attenex Patterns, Attenex, Inc. (June 27, 2006) http://www.attenex.com/products/eDiscovery/

4. Bell, G., Blythe, M., Sengers, P.: Making by making strange: Defamiliarization and the design of domestic technologies. ACM Trans. Comput.-Hum. Interact. 12(2), 149–173 (2005)
5. Data Visualization and Visual Design – Information Aesthetics (11 February, 2007) http://www.infosthetics. com/
6. Gaver, B., Dunne, T., Pacenti, E.: Design: Cultural probes. Interactions 6(1), 21–29 (1999)
7. Greenfield, A.: Everyware: The Dawning Age of Ubiquitous Computing. New Riders Press, Berkeley, CA (2006)
8. Grudin, J.: Is HCI homeless?: in search of inter-disciplinary status. Interactions 13(1), 54–59 (2006)
9. Hendry, D.G.: Design Informatics: Information Needs in Design. Converging on a Science of Design through the Synthesis of Design Methodologies, CHI 2007 Workshop (2007)
10. Internet Users – Top 20 Countries – Internet Usage, Miniwatts Marketing Group (January 11, 2007) http://www.internetworldstats.com/top20.htm
11. Kodakgallery.com: Print, Store & Share Digital Photos, Kodak Imaging Network, Inc. (February 11, 2007) http://www.kodakgallery.com/
12. Levy, S.: The Perfect Thing, Wired 14. 11(November 2006) http://www.wired.com/wired/archive/14.11/ ipod.html
13. Löwgren, J., Stolterman, E.: Thoughtful Interaction Design: A Design Perspective on Information Technology. MIT Press, Cambridge, MA (2004)
14. Morville, P.: Ambient Findability. O'Reilly Media Inc., Sebstopol, CA (2005)
15. Nardi, B., O'Day, V.: Information Ecologies: Using Technology with Heart. MIT Press, Cambridge, MA (1999)
16. O'Reilly, T.: What Is Web 2.0: Design Patterns and Business Models for the Next Generation of Software, O'Reilly Media, Inc. (September 30, 2005) http://www.oreillynet.com/pub/a/oreilly/tim/news/2005/ 09/30/what-is-web-20.html
17. Prescott, L.: PhotoBucket Leads Photo Sharing Sites (June 21, 2006) Flickr at #6 http://weblogs.hitwise.com/leeann-prescott/2006/06/photobucket_leads_photo_sharin.html
18. Research matters: Center for Design Informatics, Research Matters at Harvard University (February 5, 2007) http://www.researchmatters.harvard.edu/program.php?program_id=349
19. Rheingold, H.: Smart Mobs: The Next Social Revolution. Perseus Books Group, Cambridge, MA (2002)
20. Second Life: Your World. Your Imagination. Linden Research, Inc (February 11, 2007) http://secondlife. com/
21. Sengers, P., Kaye, J., Boehner, K., Fairbant, J., Gay, G., Medynskiy, Y., Wyche, S.: Culturally Embedded Computing. IEEE Pervasive Computing 3(1), 14–21 (2004)
22. Stengel, R.: Now It's Your Turn. Time Magazine (Saturday, December 16, 2006)
23. Sunstein, C.R.: Infotopia: How Many Minds Produce Knowledge. The MIT Press, Cambridge, MA (2006)
24. Tscheligi, M.: Introduction. Interactions, vol. 12(4) (July 2005)
25. Welcome to Flickr – Photo Sharing, Yahoo! Inc. (February 11, 2007) http://flickr.com/
26. Wikipedia, Wikipedia.org (February 11, 2007) http://www.wikipedia.org/
27. YouTube – Broadcast Yourself, YouTube, Inc (February 11, 2007) http://www.youtube.com/

A Study on Content and Management Style of Corporate Blogs

Shanshan Ma and Qiping Zhang

Drexel University 3141 Chestnut Street, Philadelphia, PA 19104
Long Island University 720 Northern Blvd, Brookville, NY 11548
shanshan.ma@drexel.edu, qiping.zhang@liu.edu

Abstract. Corporate blogs are used by companies to talk with customers. We did a study into 262 blog entries in 9 corporate blogs. The study revealed three corporate blog content types; three corporate blog management styles, and relatively shorter blog length and lower update frequency.

Keywords: Blog, Corporate blog, blog content, blog management, update frequency.

1 Introduction

Blog was used for publishing online journal when it was first introduced. Personal bloggers use blog for personal expression and communication. Nardi et al. [14] discovered five major motivations for blogging: documenting one's life; providing commentary and opinions; expressing deeply felt emotions; articulating ideas through writing; and forming and maintaining community forums. Blogging has also been used a lot as a knowledge management tool. Experts in a particular field can use their blogs to publish and distribute their acquired knowledge about the subject area [4]. People who read such blogs can interact with the experts and make their own voice heard by leaving comments as reviewers.

Other than personal use, blogs can be created and maintained by multiple authors within a workplace, a team, a family as a computer mediated communication tool. Corporate blog is an example in this category. Fredrik [8] defined corporate blog as *"a blog published by or with the support of an organization to reach that organization's goals. In external communications the potential benefits include strengthened relationships with important target groups and the positioning of the publishing organization (or individuals within it) as industry experts. Internally blogs are generally referred to as tools for collaboration and knowledge management."* Early practitioners in corporate blog include Microsoft, Sun Microsystems, SAP developers, Oracle, Macromedia and etc. Although people predicted that blog will be commonplace for most marketers in the future, it seems that currently most marketers are still taking the wait-and-see approach [16]. Statistics from Socialtext show that currently only 5.8 percent of the top Fortune 500 corporate blogs.

It seems a trend to start a corporate blog for companies, but it is not so clear what people are doing with them. What kind of content should be posted on a corporate

D. Schuler (Ed.): Online Communities and Social Comput., HCII 2007, LNCS 4564, pp. 116–123, 2007.

blog? How should a corporate blog be managed? The purpose of the research is to study on the popular corporate blogs at present and provide insight in corporate blog content, management styles, and posting volume.

2 Corporate Blogs

Blog has "coincided with and helped to impel an irreversible surge in faster, easier, more ubiquitous publishing to a web of increasingly indexable, searchable, findable and collaborative information" [7]. Blog has great potential to influence our daily life, although it was claimed that blog is neither a new nor a unique genre in the ecology of interactive web technology, but rather a bridge between multimedia HTML documents and text-based computer-mediated communication [10]. Blog could also be a promising tool for knowledge management.

There are many tools developed to serve the function of knowledge management across organizations. Tools like bulletin boards, discussion forum, chat rooms have been employed by companies to build up community and communicating with customers. Different tools have different functions, and work most efficiently in the most suitable environment. Corporate blogs enable people to accumulate knowledge as well as sharing and managing it. Knowledge is synthesized by communication between people who come to this community formed around corporate blogs. Blogs facilitate this by making people easier to find, and providing immediate and direct communication channels once contacts have been established. Bloggers do not merely publish information, but also use the blogosphere as a source for increasing their own knowledge and supporting or disproving their claims.

The launch and maintenance of corporate blogs is mainly driven by business reasons. Cohen [5] identified four business reasons for blogs: establish expertise, create alternative media, extend corporate communications, and build community. First, leading companies in certain fileds use corporate blog as a tool to provide professional opinion. A company can establish itself as industry expert by offering domain knowledge. Second, corporate blogs can serve as an extra media for advertisement purpose. New product and new features can be announced through blog posts. Third, corporate blog can serve as a direct communication channel to customers. It can act really quickly when unpredictable event happens. What's more important, it is a two-way communication channel in that customers can speak up by leaving comments. The employees are blog authors and the customers are commentators. Fourth, a community composed of enthusiastic customers would be built up as corporate blog develops. In general, for most companies that launch corporate blogs, blog provides a way to enable corporation to talk directly with their customers with a human face and voice, rather than "hollow, flat, literally inhuman" to online audiences [12]. Customers are then connected with the company in a personalized, immediate way.

Other than the four business reasons above, corporate blogs are used for more practical purposes such as optimizing search engine ranking. Because the current popular search engines like google and yahoo usually give high credits to constantly-updated and link-rich web pages like blog posts. Small business can use blog as a tool to make itself visible among numerous search results.

2.1 Content Types of Corporate Blogs

Based on the overall purpose of blogs, Blood [3] identified three basic types of blogs: filters, personal journals, and notebooks. The content of filters is external to the blogger (world events, online happenings, etc). The content of personal journals is internal (the blogger's thoughts and internal working). Notebooks are usually long focused essays. Herring et al. [10] replaced the category of notebook with k-log, which "functionally resemble hand-written project journals in which a researcher or project group makes observations, records relevant references, and so forth about a particular knowledge domain". Bar-Ilan [2] listed three categorizations of blogs based on content: associative, personal and self-expressive, and topic oriented. In his categorization, topic blogs refer to blogs which aims at talking about topics relating to a hobby or to the author's profession or business.

It seems that different researchers have very different opinions regarding blog types. In the case of corporate blog, Dugan [6] identified three big corporate blog models: intranet blogs, event blogs, and product blogs. Intranet blogs, blogs maintained inside a company, are not applicable to corporate blogs that are open to public. Thus only event blogs and product blogs should be included in our case. Borrowed from previous study in personal blogs, we believe that there should be one more kind of blog type in corporate setting: knowledge blog. Therefore, we suspect that there are three types of corporate blogs: event blog, product blog, and knowledge blog.

2.2 Corporate Blog Management Style

Management is less a problem for personal blogs than for corporate blogs. Personal blogs are maintained by individuals who can only reach a certain amount of audience. The effect of personal blogs is much less than corporate blogs. Open corporate blogs empower employees to talk freely with their colleagues, customers, partners in an open environment. It is considered another official channel that people get company information from. Certain topics like financial information can be very sensitive under such circumstances. There usually are statements on web pages or corporate blogs specifying what kinds of blogs are appropriate and not appropriate in corporate blogs.

The ability to monitor and control what is being published is a big concern for companies. The problem gets more complicated if the company has a large number of employees. Some companies set their corporate blogs as only open to employees. For them, corporate blogs are served as a group communication tool which helps employees to communicate with each other without any outsiders' peeking. Some other companies control the content on corporate blogs by only giving a few people the power to publish blogs. Different companies have different strategy, which varies with the company culture, size of the company, industry, and etc.

2.3 Posting Volume and Update Frequency

Bloggers have to update their blogs on a certain level to keep their blogs alive. But how often is often enough and how long each post should be are not clear for bloggers. Louis [13] did a length analysis into blog entries on five A-list blogs. He found out that the top five bloggers created an average of 30 entries in one day, with each entry being under 150 words. Liao [11] suggested that blog posts should be human sized pieces in that people won't be able to read long articles. Although it sounds reasonable that shorter posts makes more frequent updating possible and more posts are better for generating readership with RSS and in search engines, other issues, like topic, comprehensive coverage, quality of post, reader attention span [15], are deserve considering when bloggers decide the proper posting volume and update frequency.

Corporate blogs aim at building up long term relationship with customers. Posting volume and update frequency of corporate blogs can affect company image on a certain level. We are interested in looking into the overall patterns in posting volume and update frequency among corporate blogs.

3 Method

9 corporate blog sites were monitored for one month, from June 1st to June 31st 2006. Sundar [19] reported a list of top 10 corporate blogs based on the number of inbound links provided by technorati [20]. 9 out of the top 10 corporate blogs were chosen in our study (The one we don't include in this study is an aggregation of personal employee blogs). Among these 9 companies, there are 3 search engines (Google, Yahoo! Search, and Ask.com), 1 software manufactures (Sunbelt software), 2 online media learning companies (The otter group and O'Reilly Rader), 1 automaker (GM fast lane), and 1 online management consultancy (Tom Peters), 1 small business company (English cut). A total number of 262 blog entries from the 9 corporate blog sites were analyzed. For each blog entry, information about author, topic, posting length is recorded. Content analysis was conducted to decide the content category of the blog entry.

For each corporate blog, basic information about every blog post during the whole month was recorded. Basic information includes posting date, authorship, number of internal links, number of comments, number of trackback (if applicable), number of pictures, number of audio and video, and posting length, etc. Each post was read by the author to decide which type it belongs to.

Table 1. Company and corporate blogs

Company	URL of Blog Site	Industry
Google	http://googleblog.blogspot.com/	Search engine company
O'Reilly Radar	http://radar.oreilly.com/	Online media learning company
Yahoo! Search	http://www.ysearchblog.com/	Search engine
Tom Peters	http://www.tompeters.com/	Online management consultancy
Ask.com	http://blog.ask.com/	Search engine
GM Fast Lane	http://fastlane.gmblogs.com/	Automaker
SunBelt Software	http://sunbeltblog.blogspot.com/	Software manufacture
English Cut	http://www.englishcut.com/	Small business
The Otter Group	http://www.ottergroup.com/	Online media learning company

4 Findings

4.1 Content Types of Corporate Blogs

As we suspected, three types of corporate blogs were identified in our study based on their contents: event blog, product blog and knowledge blog. Event blogs are announcements or the broadcast of current events of the company. Product blogs refer to the entries that introduce the company's new product or describe the new features of the product. Knowledge blogs refer to the entries that discuss the general topic in the field without a direct relationship with the company's products or services, such as industry information, relevant literature [1]. Overall, among the 262 blog posts, there were 23% event blogs, 21% product blogs, and 56% knowledge blogs.

There are different patterns in the distribution of three types of blogs among different companies. For search engine companies, 40-60% of their blog entries fall into product blogs.

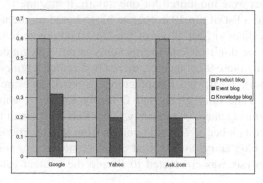

Fig. 1. Percentage of three types of blogs among three search engine companies

Three online companies are all short on product blogs and event blogs. Most of their blogs are knowledge blogs, which talking about general topics in the filed and discussion on current trends, etc.

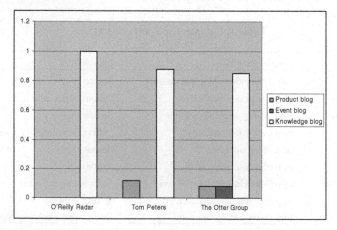

Fig. 2. Percentage of three types of blogs among three online companies

4.2 Management Style

Centralized Style. Centralized corporation blog is managed by one moderator and written by multiple authors. The moderator acts like an editor. Company employees send the moderator entries that he/she wants to post. The moderator would then decide whether to post it or not. When a blog entry is posted, usually the author's name and the position are displayed.

Companies with large number of employees and multiple departments would like to adopt this style. For instance, Google's official blog (http://googleblog.blogspot.com/) is managed in centralized style. Individual employees send their articles to the moderator and the moderator publishes their articles as blog entries. In the 9 cases we studied, 4 of them are managed this way. They are Google, Yahoo, Ask.com, and GM fast lane blog.

There are some advantages of this style. First, it's easy to control what content is published. The moderator's role guarantees that the content published is in line with company's policy. Second, blogs can be published with a more consistent tone, so that they don't only represent the single authors, but also the company as a whole.

Distributed Style. Distributed corporate blog is managed by a small number of contributors. They blog as a team and they post their own entries based on their own preference. We found that corporate blogs managed by group bloggers have the highest update frequency. Because more than one blogger can contribute to the blog and they can update the corporate blog whenever they feel that they have something new to say.

Usually, companies in this category are the one which don't have a large number of employees. Mostly they are online small companies. In the 9 companies we studied, 2 are managed by distributed style. For example, O'reilly Radar's blog (http://radar.oreilly.com/) is managed by five writers, who basically constitute the whole company. The other one is The Otter Group. For these companies, the blog team and the company team are the same group of people. They blog independently from each other yet represent the company as a whole.

Mono Style. Mono style corporate blogs are written and managed by one single person. The single person writes blogs and publishs it under the name of the company. Usually it applies to small business companies. For example, English Cut (http://www.englishcut.com/), an English tailor company's corporate blog, is managed by the tailor himself. In the 9 cases we studied, 3 of them are managed by mono style, which are Tom Peters, Sunbelt software, and English Cut.

4.3 Posting Volume and Update Frequency

All corporate blogs showed short blog length. The overall average length of blog entries is 300 words with a minimum of 114 words and a maximum of 570 words. The observation is in accordance with our assumption based on previous study. Corporate blogs want to catch reader's attention by not providing so much at one time.

As for update frequency, corporate blogs in our study showed varied patterns. The most frequently updated blog posted 2.83 entries a day (Sunbelt software), while the least frequently updated blog only posted 2 blog entries during the whole month we studied (English cut). Overall the average updating frequency is 1 blog post per day.

5 Conclusion

Corporate blog could be used by companies to communicate with customers more directly. We did a study into 9 corporate blogs. The study revealed three types of blog content: product blog, event blog and knowledge blog. Three management styles are identified: centralized style, distributed style and mono style. We also found that corporate blogs have relatively shorter blog entry and lower updating frequency. In addition, our study established a framework for analyzing corporate blog usage and contents. It helps practitioners to understand how other corporations manage their blogs.

References

1. Angeles, M.: K-Logging: Supporting KM with Web Logs. Library Journal (April 15, 2002)
2. Bar-Ilan, J.: An Outsider's View on "Topic-oriented" Blogging. WWW2004, New York, New York, USA (2004)
3. Blood, R.: The Weblog Handbook: Practical Advice on Creating and Maintaining Your Blog. Perseus Publishing, Cambridge, MA (2002)
4. Brady, M.: Blogging, personal participation in public knowledge-building on the web. Chimera Working Paper, 2 (2005)
5. Cohen, H.: Corporate Blogs, Measure Their Value http://www.clickz.com/ showPage.html?page=3517546 (2005)
6. Dugan, K.: Emerging Corporate Blog Models (2004) http://prblog.typepad.com/ strategic_public_relation/2004/11/emerging_corpor.html
7. Ellsworth, E.: CIO Michael Fitzgerald Exemplifies Open Corporate Blogging Style (2006) http://www.businessblogwire.com/2006/07/cio_michael_fitzgerald_exempli.html
8. Fredrik, W.: Your Guide to Corporate Blogging http://www.corporateblogging.info/ 2004/06/corporate-blog-short-definition.asp
9. Herring, S.C., Scheidt, L.A., Kouper, I., Wright, E.: A longitudinal content analysis of weblogs: 2003-2004. In: Tremayne, M. (ed.) Blogging, Citizenship, and the Future of Media (2006)
10. Herring, S.C., Scheidt, L.A., Bonus, S., Wright, E.: Bridging the gap: A genre analysis of weblogs. In: Proceedings of the 37th Hawai'i International Conference on System Sciences (HICSS-37) (2004)
11. Liao, B.: Scoble on Tips for joining the A-list http://www.stoweboyd.com/ message/2006/02/scoble_on_tips_.html (2006)
12. Levine, R., Locke, C., Searls, D., Weinberger, D.: The Cluetrain manifesto. Perseus Publishing, Cambridge, MA (2000)
13. Louis, T.: Secrets of the A-list bloggers: lots of short entries (2005) http://tnl.net/blog/2005/05/24/secrets-of-the-a-list-bloggers-lots-of-short-entries/

14. Nardi, B.A., Schiano, D.J., Gumbrecht, M., Swartz, L.: Why We Blog. Communications of the ACM 47(12), 41–46 (2004)
15. Rowse, D.: Post length- how long should a blog post be? (2006) http://www.problogger.net/archives/2006/02/18/post-length-how-long-should-a-blog-post-be/
16. Rendon, P.: Blog Talk (2004) http://www.masterfile.com/info/products/open/037.html?eid=open037
17. Socialtext http://www.socialtext.com/
18. Stocker, C.: Measuring Blog Popularity (2005) http://blog.bitflux.ch/archive/2005/10/10/measuring-blog-popularity.html
19. Sundar, M.: Top 10 Corporate Blogs (technorati ranked) (2006) http://mari-osundar.wordpress.com/2006/07/16/top-10-corporate-blogs-technorati-powered/
20. Technorati www.technorati.com

Chameleon-Based Deniable Authenticated Key Agreement Protocol Secure Against Forgery

Chunbo Ma[1,3], Jun Ao[2], and Jianhua Li[1]

[1] School of Information Security Engineering
Shanghai Jiao Tong University, Shanghai, 200030, P.R. China
{machunbo,lijh888}@sjtu.edu.cn
[2] State Key Laboratory for Radar Signal Processing,
Xidian University, Xi'an, Shanxi, 710071, P.R. China
Junjunao1@263.net
[3] The State Key Laboratory of Information Security,
Institute of Software of Chinese Academy of Sciences
Beijing, 100049, P.R. China

Abstract. As a useful means of safeguarding privacy of communications, deniable authentication has received much attention. A Chameleon-based deniable authenticated key agreement protocol is presented in this paper. The protocol has following properties. Any one of the two participants can't present a digital proof to convince a third party that a claimed agreement has really taken place. Once a forgery occurs, the original entity can present a digital proof to disclose the forgery.

Keywords: Chameleon, Deniability, Authentication, Key Agreement.

1 Introduction

Key agreement is one of most important security mechanisms in the area of secure communications. Such protocols allow two entities to exchange information between them and establish a shared secret over an insecure open channel. Later, they can encrypt actual data using a fast symmetric cipher keyed by the shared secret. The first two-party key agreement is the Diffie-Hellman protocol given in their seminal paper [1]. Currently, how to design an efficient and secure key agreement protocol have received much attention.

Due to lack of authentication, the original Diffie-Hellman protocol is vulnerable to "man-in-the-middle" and some other attacks. In order to solve this issue, many two-party authenticated key agreement protocols have been proposed [2][3][4][5]. Authenticated two-party key agreement allows two users to establish a common secret key and ensures nobody besides them can possibly learn the secret key.

However, in some applications [6], deniability is needed to prevent an authorized user from disclosing information it receives legitimately. For example, Alice and Bob have complemented an authenticated key agreement protocol and established a session key (shared secret). Later, Bob presents a digital proof to convince Carol that Alice

D. Schuler (Ed.): Online Communities and Social Comput., HCII 2007, LNCS 4564, pp. 124–133, 2007.
© Springer-Verlag Berlin Heidelberg 2007

once sent some message to him. In this process, Bob discloses Alice's some information without Alice's authorization and impinges upon Alice's privacy.

To solve above issue, Alice and Bob can use deniable authenticated key agreement protocol. Under such circumstances, Bob can't present proof to convince the third party Carol that there is a certain key agreement protocol occurred between Alice and him. The deniable authenticated key agreement protocol is seldom investigated, though there is a lot of research on deniable authentication technology, such as [7] and followed by a series of papers including [8][9]. Raimondo et al. [10] recently extended the work of Dwork from deniable authentication to deniable agreement protocol, and proved the deniability features of SKEME [11] and SIGMA [12].

We can't prevent a deniable key agreement protocol from being forged even though we design it with some secure technologies. One of the reasons is that we don't have a method to prove the protocol secure against any attacks including know and unknown. In other words, after completing the a deniable key agreement protocol, Bob can produce a forged protocol using the message once transmitted and announces that the protocol has executed between him and Alice. And then, Bob submits corresponding information to convince the third party Carol that the forged protocol is true. Alice's privacy may be impinged while Carol can't judge the protocol's reality. Hence, we need a mechanism to disclose a forgery in case of occurrence.

Chameleon Hash has some special properties, and can be used to design signature and some other cryptography mechanism. To the Chameleon-based signature, the recipient can't convince the third party of the identity of the signer, as the recipient has the ability to forge the signature. In the case of forgery occurrence, the original signer can disclose the forgery in non-interactive manner. The first to present the Chaemelon Hash were Krawczyk [13] in 2000, followed by papers [14][15]. The properties of Chameleon Hash are very useful to our designing two-party deniable authenticated key agreement protocol.

Motivated by above statement, we design a two-party key agreement protocol with Chameleon Hash and signature. In our mechanism, either sender or recipient has ability to deny his communication. Furthermore, any one of them can disclose a forgery. For example, if Bob forges a protocol between Alice and him, Alice can get Bob's private key with the forged message, and consequently presents a digital proof to disclose the forgery.

2 Related Works

At present, recipient in many crypto schemes is designated, i.e. only the designated recipient can validly execute the schemes. Some signature schemes with designated recipient are proposed in [20] [21]. In these schemes, only the designated recipient can verify the signature. Another important property about these schemes is that the recipient can't convince the third party of the identity of the signer as well as the content that signed by the signer. Hence, this kind of signature has the property of deniability. An interesting signature, ring signature, is proposed in [18]. It can hide the identity of signer and achieve the goal of deniability.

Deniable key agreement protocol is studied in [16] and also can be found in [17] [11]. Dwork et al. [7] first formally treat the deniable authentication problem, followed by paper [16] [19]. Raimondon et al. [10] extend the work of Dwork and carry on thorough analysis to the deniable authenticated key agreement protocol. Krawczyk first presented the Chameleon function in 2000. Due to the interesting properties of Chameleon function, it is used to design some crypto schemes [14] [15].

3 Background

3.1 Preliminaries

Let G_1 be a cyclic multiplicative group generated by g, whose order is a prime q and G_2 be a cyclic multiplicative group of the same order q. Assume that the discrete logarithm in both G_1 and G_2 is intractable. A bilinear pairing is a map $e: G_1 \times G_1 \rightarrow G_2$ and satisfies the following properties:

1. *Bilinear:* $e(g^a, p^b) = e(g, p)^{ab}$. For all g, $p \in G_1$ and $a, b \in Z_q$, the equation holds.
2. *Non-degenerate:* There exists $p \in G_1$, if $e(g, p) = 1$, then $g = O$.
3. *Computable:* For g, $p \in G_1$, there exists an efficient algorithm to compute $e(g, p)$.

Typically, the map e will be derived from either the Weil or Tate pairing on an elliptic curve over a finite field. Pairings and other parameters should be selected in proactive for efficiency and security.

3.2 Chameleon Hash

Let G_1 and G_2 be two groups that support a bilinear map as defined in section 2.1. PKG random chooses $v \in Z_q^*$ as the private key of the system, and computes the matching public key $PK_{pub} = g^v$, and then random chooses $a \in Z_q^*$ and generates Alice's key pair ($SK_A = g^{v \cdot a}, PK_A = g^a$). Similarly, PKG generates Bob's key pair $(SK_B, PK_B) = (g^{v \cdot b}, g^b)$. Alice chooses $x_A \in Z_q^*$ and $R_A \in G_1$ uniformly at random, and generates Chameleon Hash.

$$T_A(PK_A, x_A, R_A) = e(R_A, g)e((PK_A)^{x_A}, P_{pub}).$$

The Chameleon Hash function has following properties.

- Alice who has known (T_A, x_A, R_A) random chooses $x_A' \in Z_q^*$ and computes $R_A' = g^{a \cdot v \cdot (x_A - x_A')} \cdot R_A$, which satisfies $T_A(PK_A, x_A, R_A) = T_A(PK_A, x_A', R_A')$. We have

$$T_A(PK_A, x_A', R_A')$$

$$= e(g^{a \cdot v \cdot (x_A - x_A')} \cdot R_A, g) e(g^{a \cdot x_A'}, PK_{pub})$$

$$= e(g^{a \cdot (x_A - x_A')}, PK_{pub}) e(R_A, g) e(g^{a \cdot x_A'}, PK_{pub})$$

$$= e(g^{a \cdot x_A}, PK_{pub}) e(R_A, g)$$

$$= T_A(PK_A, x_A, R_A).$$

In the circumstances of having known (x_A, R_A), if Alice can compute another (x_A', R_A') that satisfies above relationship, we say that Alice can successfully forge (T_A, x_A, R_A).

- To the given $T_A(PK_A, x_A, R_A) = T_A(PK_A, x_A', R_A')$, anyone can compute and get Alice's private key as follows.

$$T_A(PK_A, x_A, R_A) = T_A(PK_A, x_A', R_A')$$

$$e(R_A, g) e(g^{a \cdot x_A}, g^v) = e(R_A', g) e(g^{a \cdot x_A'}, g^v)$$

$$R_A \cdot g^{a \cdot v \cdot x_A} = R_A' \cdot g^{a \cdot v \cdot x_A'}$$

$$g^{a \cdot v} = (R_A \cdot (R_A')^{-1})^{(x_A' - x_A)^{-1}}$$

3.3 Deniable Key Agreement Protocol

Our definition of the notions of deniability follows essentially the definition from Dwork et al. [7] and Raimondon et al. [10].

A protocol is deniable if a recipient Bob can't convince a third party Carol that a given sender Alice once executed a claimed key agreement protocol with him. In other words, a key agreement protocol is deniable if the recipient's view of the protocol can be perfectly simulated by a simulator SIM that doesn't know the secret key of the sender Alice. When Bob tries to convince Carol that he has executed a protocol with Alice, he will be failed since Carol knows he can simulate the view by manipulating the simulator SIM.

Assume that there exists an adversary $\mathbf{A}$ in the protocol, acting as the recipient on input any auxiliary input $aux \in AUX$, where AUX is a set that comprises some extra information that $\mathbf{A}$ might have gathered in some other form, such as eavesdropping. We denote the interaction between **A** and sender as $View_A^S(PK, aux)$, where PK is the public key of sender.

Definition 1 [7]. We say that (KG, S, R) is a deniable key agreement protocol if for any adversary **A**, acting as the recipient on input PK and any auxiliary input $aux \in AUX$, there exists a simulator SIM_A^S running on the same inputs, produces a simulated view which is indistinguishable from the real one. In other words, we have the following two probability distributions.

$$\mathrm{Re}\,al(aux) = [(SK, PK) \leftarrow KG(1^n); (aux, PK, View_A(PK, aux))]$$

$$Sim(aux) = [(SK, PK) \leftarrow KG(1^n); (aux, PK, SIM_A(PK, aux))].$$

For all probabilistic polynomial time machine **P** and all $aux \in AUX$, we have

$$\left| \mathrm{Pr}_{x \in \mathrm{Re}\,al(aux)}[\mathbf{P}(x) = 1] - \mathrm{Pr}_{x \in Sim(aux)}[\mathbf{P}(x) = 1] \right| \le \varepsilon.$$

Then we say that the key agreement protocol is deniable.

Definition 2 [10]. We say an encryption scheme is PA-1 plaintext-aware if for any adversary **A** that on input PK can produce a valid ciphertext c, there exists a "companion" machine $\mathbf{A}^*$ that, running on the same inputs, outputs the matching plaintext.

Definition 3 [22]. We say an encryption scheme is PA-2 plaintext-aware if for any adversary **A** on input $c \notin AUX$, the "companion" machine $\mathbf{A}^*$ is defined to yield matching plaintext. Otherwise the machine $\mathbf{A}^*$ outputs $\bot$.

4   Key Agreement Protocol

When Alice and Bob want to establish a session key, they can execute the following protocol as shown in Figure 1.

Let G_1 and G_2 be two groups that support a bilinear map as defined in section 2.1. The keys distribution is as defined in section 2.2. Assume that there exists a secure signature $Sign$ and IND-CCA2 encryption algorithm (Enc, Dec). The two entities Alice and Bob will execute the protocol as following steps.

1.   Alice chooses $x_A, y_A \in Z_q^*$ uniformly at random, and computes $T_B = e(g^{y_A}, g)e(g^{b \cdot x_A}, g^v)$, and then signs T_B using secure signature algorithm $Sign$. Alice sends $\sigma_A = Sign_{SK_A}(T_B)$ and T_B to Bob. Similarly, Bob produces $\sigma_B = Sign_{sk_B}(T_A)$ and sends it and T_A to Alice.

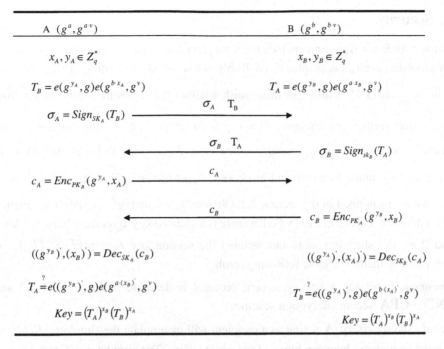

Fig. 1. Proposed two-party deniable authenticated key agreement protocol

2. Alice encrypts x_A and g^{y_A} using Bob's public key, and sends $c_A = Enc_{PK_B}(g^{y_A}, x_A)$ to Bob. Bob does the same things as Alice, and sends $c_B = Enc_{PK_A}(g^{y_B}, x_B)$ to Alice.

3. Alice gets $(x_B)'$ and $(g^{y_B})'$ by decrypting c_B, and then verifies the values as follows.

$$T_A \overset{?}{=} e((g^{y_B})', g)e(g^{a \cdot (x_B)'}, g^v) \tag{1}$$

If above equation holds, Alice produces the session key $Key = (T_A)^{x_B}(T_B)^{x_A}$. Bob does the same things as Alice, and verifies $(x_A)'$ and $(g^{y_A})'$ by the following equation.

$$T_B \overset{?}{=} e((g^{y_A})', g)e(g^{b \cdot (x_A)'}, g^v) \tag{2}$$

If above equation holds, Bob produces the session key $Key = (T_A)^{x_B}(T_B)^{x_A}$.

5 Security

Neither Alice nor Bob can convince the third party Carol that a claimed key agreement protocol has really taken place. To Bob's signature $\sigma_A = Sign_{SK_A}(T_B)$, and the values x_A and g^{y_A}, Carol can distinguish whether the signature really comes from Alice, and verifies the equation $T_B \overset{?}{=} e(g^{y_A}, g)e(g^{b \cdot x_A}, g^v)$, but she can't judge whether the two values x_A and g^{y_A} come from Alice since Bob has the ability to forge the two values. Bob can random choose x'_A and forge $g^{y'_A} = g^{a \cdot v \cdot (x_A - x'_A)} \cdot g^{y_A}$ as we have mentioned in the section 2.2. Obviously, x'_A and $g^{y'_A}$ satisfy the equation (2). Therefore, Carol can't tell whether there is a claimed key agreement between Alice and Bob, also she can't work out whether the session key $Key = (T_A)^{x_B} (T_B)^{x_A}$ is generated by them. We have following result.

Theorem 1. we say a key agreement protocol is deniable if Enc is a PA-2 and $IND - CPA$ secure encryption scheme.

Proof. The adversary **A** acting as a recipient will manipulate the simulator SIM_A^S to simulate a protocol between him and the sender Alice. The simulator will use Alice as an oracle to yield the signature.

The simulator SIM_A^S chooses $r_A, z_A, x_A, y_A \in Z_q^*$ uniformly at random and computes T_B, then uses Alice as an oracle to generate matching signature $\sigma_A = Sign_{SK_A}(T_B)$. The simulator SIM_A^S sends (T_B, σ_A) to the adversary **A**. Upon receiving the signature, **A** sends the signature (T_A, σ_B) to the simulator SIM_A^S. Due to the publicly verifiability, the signatures can be verified by adversary **A** and SIM_A^S. Since the signature from SIM_A^S is indistinguishable from that of Alice, the protocol executed between simulator and adversary is indistinguishable from that of a real protocol executed between adversary **A** and sender Alice.

The adversary **A** sends c_B to the simulator SIM_A^S. The simulator recalls machine $\mathbf{A}^*$ to yield matching plaintext. If $c_B \in AUX$, the machine $\mathbf{A}^*$ outputs $\perp$. In this situation, the adversary doesn't know the plaintext of c_B since c_B may be gathered in some other form as defined in section 3.3 rather than generated by himself. If $c_B \notin AUX$, i.e. c_B is generated by the adversary himself, the simulator recalls $\mathbf{A}^*$ and outputs the matching plaintext (g^{y_B}, x_B). Since the response from $\mathbf{A}^*$ is indistinguishable from those of real decryption oracle then the simulation between adversary **A** and simulator SIM_A^S is indistinguishable from the simulation between adversary **A** and the real sender Alice. The simulator SIM_A^S can verify the plaintext gotten from $\mathbf{A}^*$ by the equation $T_A \overset{?}{=} e(g^{y_B}, g)e(g^{a \cdot x_B}, g^v)$ and generate the session key $Key = (T_A)^{x_B}(T_B)^{x_A}$.

It is easy to see that the above simulation is perfect, so the key agreement protocol is deniable.

Theorem 2. We say that either sender or recipient can disclose a protocol forgery directed at him, if the signature Sign is unforgeable, the encryption is IND-CCA2 and the CDH assumption holds.

Proof. Assume that if Bob can forge a key agreement protocol and get the message $(T_B, x_A', g^{y_A''})$ after his agreement with Alice, we can say that Alice can compute Bob's private key in the case of having known $(T_B, x_A', g^{y_A''})$. Considering the assumptions, T_B must be a value that Alice has signed and sent to Bob, so Alice can find corresponding (T_B, x_A, g^{y_A}) in her recorder. Then we have

$$e(g^{y_A}, g)e(g^{b \cdot x_A}, g^v) = e(g^{y_A''}, g)e(g^{b \cdot x_A'}, g^v)$$

$$g^{y_A} \cdot g^{b \cdot v \cdot x_A} = g^{y_A''} g^{b \cdot v \cdot x_A'}$$

$$g^{b \cdot v} = (g^{y_A''} / g^{y_A})^{(x_A' - x_A)^{-1}}$$

Therefore, Alice has the ability to get Bob's private key $g^{b \cdot v}$, and work out other two values $g^{y_A''}$ and x_A'' that make $(T_B, x_A'', g^{y_A''})$ satisfies the equation (2). Alice can find the values in this way. First she chooses $x_A'' \in Z_q^*$ uniformly at random and then computes $g^{y_A''} = g^{b \cdot v \cdot (x_A - x_A'')} \cdot g^{y_A}$. We have

$$T_B = e(g^{y_A''}, g)e(g^{b \cdot v \cdot x_A''}, g^v)$$

If Alice presents $(T_B, x_A'', g^{y_A''})$ that satisfies above equation, then we can say that Bob forges a protocol with $(T_B, x_A', g^{y_A''})$.

6 Conclusion

In some communication scenarios, deniability is playing an important role in protecting privacy. A Chameleon-based deniable authenticated key agreement protocol is presented in this paper. In our mechanism, the two-party who participant the communication can't present digital proof to convince the third party that a claimed key agreement protocol is executed between them. If any participant forges a key agreement protocol and produces a session key, the original entity can work out the forger's private key and then discloses the forgery by giving other two values that satisfy the requirement. The key agreement protocol has such properties due to Chameleon hash function.

References

1. Fiffie, W., Hellman, M.: New directions in cryptography. IEEE Transactions on Information Theory 6, C644–654 (1976)
2. Smart, N.P.: An Identity-based Authenticated Key Agreement Protocol based on the Weil Pairing. Electronic Letters 38, 630–632 (2002)
3. Scott, M.: Authenticated ID-based Key Exchange and Remote Log-in with Insecure Token and PIN Number
4. Chen, L., Kudla, C.: Identity Based Authenticated Key Agreement Protocols from Pairings. Available at Http://Eprint.iacr.org/2002/184
5. McCullagh, N., Barreto, P.S.L.M.: A New Two-Party Identity-Based Authenticated Key Agreement. In: Menezes, A.J. (ed.) CT-RSA 2005. LNCS, vol. 3376, pp. 262–274. Springer, Heidelberg (2005)
6. Katz, J.: Efficient and Non-Malleable Proofs of Plaintext Knowledge and Applications. In: Biham, E. (ed.) EUROCRPYT 2003. LNCS, vol. 2656, pp. 211–228. Springer, Heidelberg (2003)
7. Dwork, C., Naor, M., Sahai, A.: Concurrent Zero-Knowledge. In: Proc. of 30th Symposium on Theory of Computing (STOC), pp. 409–418. ACM Press, New York (1998)
8. Di Raimondo, M., Gennaro, R.: New Approaches for Deniable Authentication. In: Proc. of 12nd ACM Conference on Computer and Communications Security (CCS'05), pp. 112–121. ACM Press, New York (2005)
9. Pass, R.: On Deniability in the Common Reference String and Random Oracle Model. In: Boneh, D. (ed.) CRYPTO 2003. LNCS, vol. 2729, pp. 316–337. Springer, Heidelberg (2003)
10. Di Raimondo, M., Gennaro, R., Krawczyk, H.: Deniable Authentication and Key Exchange. Available at http://eprint.iacr.org/2006/280
11. Krawczyk, H.: SKEME: a versatile secure key exchange mechanism for Internet. In: Proc. of 1996 IEEE Symposium on Network and Distributed System Security (SNDSS'96), pp. 114–127
12. Krawczyk, H.: SIGMA: The 'SiGn-and-Mac' Approach to Authenticated Diffie-Hellman and Its Use in the IKE Protocols. In: Boneh, D. (ed.) CRYPTO 2003. LNCS, vol. 2729, pp. 400–425. Springer, Heidelberg (2003)
13. Krawczyk, H., Rabin, T.: Chameleon signatures. In: Proc. of NDSS, 2000, pp. 132–154 (2000)
14. Ateniese, G., de Medeiros, B.: Identity-based chameleon hash and applications. http://eprint.iacr.org/2003/167
15. Zhang, F., Safavi-Naini, R., Susilo, W.: ID-based Chameleon hashes from bilinear pairings http://eprint.iacr.org/2003/208
16. Di Raimondo, M., Gennaro, R.: New approaches for deniable authentication. In: Proc. of 12nd ACM Conference on Computer and Communications Security (CCS'05), pp. 112–121. ACM Press, New York (2005)

17. Di Raimondo, M., Gennaro, R., Krawczyk, H.: Secure Off-the-Record Messaging. In: Proc. of 2nd ACM Workshop of Privacy in the Electronic Society, pp. 81–89. ACM Press, New York (2005)
18. Rivest, R., Shamir, A., Tauman, Y.: How to Leak a Secret. In: Boyd, C. (ed.) ASIACRYPT 2001. LNCS, vol. 2248, pp. 552–565. Springer, Heidelberg (2001)
19. Katz, J., Sako, K., Impagliazzo, R.: Designated Verifier Proofs and Their Applications. In: Maurer, U.M. (ed.) EUROCRYPT 1996. LNCS, vol. 1070, pp. 143–154. Springer, Heidelberg (1996)
20. Laguillaumie, F., Vergnaud, D.: Designated Verifiers Signature: Anonymity and Efficient Construction from any Bilinear Map. In: Blundo, C., Cimato, S. (eds.) SCN 2004. LNCS, vol. 3352, pp. 107–121. Springer, Heidelberg (2005)
21. Steinfeld, R., Bull, L., Wang, H., Pieprzyk, J.: Universal Designated Verifier Signatures. In: Laih, C.-S. (ed.) ASIACRYPT 2003. LNCS, vol. 2894, pp. 523–543. Springer, Heidelberg (2003)
22. Bellare, M., Palacio, A.: Towards plaintext-aware public-key encryption without random oracles. In: Franklin, M. (ed.) CRYPTO 2004. LNCS, vol. 3152, pp. 273–289. Springer, Heidelberg (2004)

ConnectDots: Visualizing Social Network Interaction for Improved Social Decision Making

Deidra Morrison and Bruce Gooch

Northwestern University
2133 N. Sheridan Rd. Suite 3-209
Evanston, IL 60208 USA
d-morrison2@northwestern.edu
University of Victoria
EECS Bldg. Rm 504
P.O. Box 3055 STNCSC
Victoria, B.C Canada V8W3P6
bgooch@cs.northwestern.edu

Abstract. There has been a fairly large body of research surrounding decision making theory and ways in which choice framing and judgment are major contributing factors to decision outcome and future practice. The purpose of this study is to use abstract visual stimulus as an application for information organization and display, in order to aid in decision making practices. In this paper, we will introduce ConnectDots, a visualization tool that will allow users to be able to view this large data set of interaction information and more easily perceive the patterns of interaction therein. With this information, a person can also become more aware of their current decision making practices for their social network, and observe how their relationships are affected.

1 Introduction

Decision making involves evaluating information related to choices and finding a selection that will satisfy the purposes of the decision task. As people in today's society, there is so much to decide on that we hardly realize that we go through our day making decisions about what we wear in the morning or which restaurant to go to for lunch. Inherent in all of these decisions is a notion of "goal-importance" [5] – understanding how much of a life impact that this decision will have for an individual – and the potential risk associated with choosing between different options in a decision task. There has been a history of investigation of decision making theory of individuals [1][9] This research has been done extensively with choice problems involving probability and statistical average as presentations in the domains of marketing, finance, politics, economics and other fields. When investigated in social contexts, the everyday choices revolving around social interactions for an individual are made based on the exorbitant amount of information that is available through the many media sources used for communication and their pre-existing sociality models [4]. When evaluating the outcomes of interaction choice in social situations, the social

D. Schuler (Ed.): Online Communities and Social Comput., HCII 2007, LNCS 4564, pp. 134–140, 2007.
© Springer-Verlag Berlin Heidelberg 2007

model in which an individual views their relationship with another plays a large role in the perception of satisfaction or success of the social decisions.

The increasing use of technology for information collection and organization has made the amount of information that we can apply to our decision process seem unmanageable. In addition, the advent of new communication technologies such as email, instant messaging, handheld computers, and cell phones which also provide text messaging opportunities, give those who previously would have only communicated face to face or through written correspondence an abundance of options for interaction with their social and business circles. We seek to find a correlation between the quantitative information surrounding personal social interaction through email and instant messaging and the sociality models in which a person attributes to those within their social network.

This paper will continue on to discuss related work in the domain of information visualization for social spaces. There will then be an introduction to sociality theory and its importance in understanding relationship interactions. It will then continue into an explanation of the ConnectDots architecture, and the visual metaphor implemented. There will then be a discussion of planned long term user study and evaluation, and finally the conclusion and future work.

2 Related Works

The use of information visualization techniques to help in the understanding of complex and diverse types of large information collections has been done for many different disciplines. Information analysts that work for government agencies have deployed visualization tools that enable 3D visualization of query results of related intelligence information. Climatologists use visualizations as predictive tools for natural weather phenomena and understanding regional and global climate trends and how different events relate and affect others. Even in the social information domain, there have been graph theory, node network, and abstract representational visualization techniques used to show social networks, online group activity history, and user-centric data portraits. These visual displays allow for the layering of information using symbol and textual mapping to help a person better view the different dimensions in which data can be viewed [7].

2.1 Social Visualization Tools

When creating tools for visualization of social information, there has been a large body of work focused on understanding group interactions and social spaces. Prominent work with network applications such as newsgroups, web logs, and online communities, focused on visualizing group dynamics. The interest in understanding the patterns of communication and interaction practices between the many members of a community were motivated by the desire to understand the "personality" or "identity" of the community, so that newcomers would be able to better establish a place there. Additional motivation came from the desire to understand the online identity of potential new contacts.

One of the most studied and well established online community used as a foundation for these visualizations, is Usenet. Visualization projects such as Treemaps [6], Loom [3], and PeopleGarden [10] take different approaches to the visualization of newsgroup posting and commenting activities within Usenet. These different visualization techniques seek to create a "data portrait" of the individuals and other group members based on interaction data. Treemaps applies a nested box based layout of groups and subgroups to the individual groups and child groups. The size and color and location of the box represent number of posts, age and popularity of particular groups. This visualization has been tailored to many other data problems that have a specific hierarchy that can be applied to them as well as chronological sequencing. Loom, is a networked display that shows connections between individual messages, and there are color codes to indicate subject and suffix differences in message postings. There is also a way to track message thread progression over time. PeopleGarden uses an intuitive nature based visual metaphor of petals, flowers, and gardens to show the posting and commenting history of users within groups in Usenet. Color, size, grouping, and height represent parts of the data such as age, popularity, response amount, and time spent in group.

We draw from previous social visualization techniques in ConnectDots, by incorporating visual metaphors to create a data portrait that is specific to an individual's social personality based not only on the data retrieved from their interactions. What is different about our approach, however, is that we also apply information and data gained through surveying users on their perceptions of relationship status and health with the individuals whom we've collected interaction data about. ConnectDots correlates social information gained from survey with the frequency of interaction and modes of media used, to give users a more detailed and individual visual representation of the communication practices that they use.

3 Relationships and Sociality Models

Social decision making is tied to the sociality models that individuals associate with others in their social circles. A.P. Fisk created a paradigm of human social life that argues that people construct their social environments based on relationships with others, and that four models of relationships are applied to all social interactions with people. These four models are *communal sharing, authority ranking, equality matching,* and *market pricing*. These models are used to interpret behaviors of interaction partners and make decisions about appropriate ways in which to interact with others.

The *communal sharing* relationships are denoted by a concept of affiliation with a group where the status of all members is equivalent. Persons who fit within this model would be those an individual felt a close bond with and expected equality in treatment and social initiations. In *authority ranking* relationships there is a distinct understanding of hierarchy and the social responsibilities assigned to each level at which a person is considered. There are clear ideas about whether an individual is higher or lower in standing than the individual and interactions and behaviors are expected to be deferential with those of higher rank, and preferential behavior is expected of those of lower rank. The *equality matching* relationship is one where egalitarian, even balanced interaction is expected. The order or frequency, of interactions, is not as important as the need to keep all interactions equal and fair. A person who an individual shares an equality matching relationship with would expect the same amount of action or attention as has been given to them. Finally, the *market pricing* relationship is based on cost-benefit and monetary or value-relevant features of the interactions in the relationship. There is an expectation of personal value being calculated and compared to the person with whom the relationship has been formed, and typically there is a desire to increase individual value relative to the value of the other member of the relationship.

Although these models are not typically applied alone to relationships, there is generally one model that can describe the overall structure of interactions.

4   ConnectDots Visualization Tool

4.1   Architecture

The ConnectDots visualization tool collects information on the frequency of interaction with members of one's social network and the frequency of use of different media types. The visualization tool was created in Macromedia Flash MX and information is gathered from the user with forms that pass the user information and email and instant messenger logs to web based scripts written in Perl and PHP. These scripts dissect the interaction data and store this and the user information in the database (Figure 1).

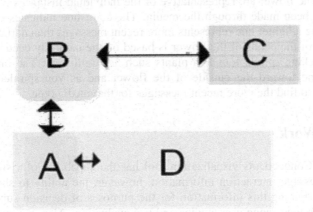

Fig. 1. The architecture of the ConnectDots system. (A) Flash ActionScript that passes information between scripts that interface with database and generates visualization of information. (B) Perl and PHP scripts that take in information from the user and store and retrieve data from database for visualization in flash. (C) MySQL database system that stores user information and network data. (D) Visualization pane where visualization is viewed and explored.

Once this information is collected the user is queried with surveys to acquire their perceived relationship with all of the individuals within their network. Using questions drawn from scales used to measure affiliation and dominance rating within social relationships, along with expected interaction patterns of relationships of different sociality models this information is correlated with the quantitative information and stored in the database as well. Once the organization and storage of data is completed, a user can immediately return to the visualization and explore the patterns of interaction throughout their social network.

4.2 Organic Visual Metaphor

The visual metaphor that is used is a tree based metaphor, with indicators of relationship status, health, and age indicated by naturally occurring visual cues. The visualization is a user-centric view of their social network, with branches representing the connections that the user has with those within their network.

Each branch of the tree represents one individual with the user's social network. The frequency of interaction that the user has with this person is represented by the length of the branch. The type of sociality model that is widely representative of the type of relationship that the user has with this person is represented by the height at which you would find the branch positioned in the tree. Also the health of the relationship would be represented by width of the branch. Branches that are thinner, would be representative of fragile relationships and less healthy, where as thicker branches would indicate stronger healthier relationships.

For each branch there is a flower that represents the interaction history that the user has with the person represented over the different media types (i.e. email, IM, etc.). There is a color distinction for the flowers based on the type of media it represents. The petals of the flower are representative of the individual instances of communication that have been made through the media. The color hue indicates the age of the message, where a lighter hue represents more recent messages than darker hues.

The layout of the petals of the flower is based on the naturally occurring phenomena of interlocking spirals found in plants such as sunflowers. The older messages would be found toward the outside of the flower and as you spiraled inward you would be able to find the more recent messages for that media type.

5 Future Work

Currently the ConnectDots visualization tool has the capability of visualizing email and instant message interaction information, however, the ability to show the effectiveness of navigating this information for the purposes of decision support needs to be studied with long range user studies and use evaluation. Also, being able to incorporate more communication media types into the visualization is a priority.

Although the current visualization is useful in gaining an insight into social decision habits, a more complete view would be gained by incorporating interaction information relative to cellular phone interactions and text messaging behavior. The ability to access and download logs of this type of information requires development of information extraction and sharing for mobile devices. A proposed plan is to work on implementations of possible web-based logging and transfer software for mobile device communication records.

Another relevant issue is the inability for ConnectDots to currently do automatic updates of data to the system. The proposed use of the system would be administrative and used to keep a person updated on the status of their social decision making behaviors. With the ability for the system to automatically upload information from communication media, would allow for a more regular use of the tool and a less time intensive operation of the visualization.

Measuring the effectiveness of this tool for decision support for social interaction practices will require a study of not only usability factors and issues with the interface, but an extended study of the task of social decision making and the tools currently used to perform these tasks. We propose conducting user studies that observe the affects of the decision tasks with the aid of visual stimulation and of those without to see differences in the resulting impacts that these decisions have made.

To conduct this test, a study of the current decision task performance methods will be evaluated by methods of observation and interviews or surveys. The study participants will then be asked to complete decision tasks using their current methods. Quantitative information about the time it takes to complete decision tasks and the quantity and frequency that information sources are access will be recorded and a survey about attitudes toward the process will be given to the participants. The participants will then be given the visual tools to use in the same type of decision task and the process of data recordings and survey collection will be repeated.

6 Conclusion

Through the presentation of this information, users will be able to view this large data set of interaction information and more easily perceive the patterns of interaction therein. With this information, a person can also become more aware of their current decision making practices for their social network, and observe how their relationships are affected. This will allow for the opportunity to engage in interventions to prevent relationship dissolution, as well as give better indicators to users of their methods for establishing and maintaining what they perceive as successful relationships. Through the use of tools that will allow for faster exploration of information and quicker development of choice options a decision maker would make more satisfying and well rounded decisions. This work will also contribute to current efforts to find means of evaluating information visualization systems for their effectiveness in comparison to currently used tools or decision making processes.

References

1. Abelson, R.P., Levi, A.: Decision making and decision theory. In: The Handbook of Social Psychology, 3rd edn., pp. 231–309. Random House, New York (1995)
2. Beisswanger, A,.: Risk Taking in Relationships: Differences in Deciding for Oneself versus for a Friend. Basic & Applied Social Psychology 25(2), 121 (2003)
3. Boyd, D., Lee, H.-Y., Ramage, D., Donath, J.: Developing legible visualizations for online social spaces. In: Proceedings of the Hawaii International Conference on System Sciences. (Janaury 7–10, 2002, Big Island, Hawaii) (2002)

4. Fiske, A.P.: The four elementary forms of sociality: Framework for a unified theory of social relations. Psychology Review 99, 689–723 (1992)
5. Schwartz, B. (ed.): The Paradox of Choice: Why More is Less. HarperCollins Publisher, New York, NY (2004)
6. Shneiderman, B.: Tree visualization with treemaps: a 2-d space-filling approach. ACM Transactions on Graphics 11(1), 92–99 (1992)
7. Sutton, S.A.: The role of attorney mental models of law in case relevance determinations: An exploratory analysis. Journal of the American Society for Information Science 45(3), 186–200 (1994)
8. Tufte, E.: Envisioning Information. Graphics Press, Cheshire, CT (1990)
9. Tversky, A., Kahneman, D.: Rational Choice and the Framing of Decisions. The Journal of Business, vol. 59 (1986)
10. Xiong, R., Donath, J.: PeopleGarden: Creating Data Portraits for Users. UIST 1999, Asheville, NC. CHI Letters, vol. 1(1) (1999)

Recognition of Affect Conveyed by Text Messaging in Online Communication

Alena Neviarouskaya[1], Helmut Prendinger[2], and Mitsuru Ishizuka[1]

[1] University of Tokyo, Department of Information and Communication Engineering, Japan
lena@mi.ci.i.u-tokyo.ac.jp, ishizuka@i.u-tokyo.ac.jp
[2] National Institute of Informatics, Japan
helmut@nii.ac.jp

Abstract. In this paper, we address the task of affect recognition from text messaging. In order to sense and interpret emotional information expressed through written language, rule-based affect analysis system employing natural language processing techniques was created. Since the purpose of our work is to improve social interactivity and affective expressiveness of computer-mediated communication, we decided to tailor the system to handle style and specifics of online conversations. Proposed algorithm for affect analysis covers symbolic cue processing, detection and transformation of abbreviations, sentence parsing, and word/phrase/sentence-level analyses. To realize visual reflection of textual affective information, we have designed an avatar displaying emotions, social behaviour, and natural idle movements.

Keywords: Affective computing, affective user interface, avatar, emotions, online communication, language parsing and understanding, text analysis.

1 Introduction and Motivation

There is a wide perception that the future of human-computer interaction is related to affective computing. The necessity to design intelligent user interfaces and to create rich mediating environments for social interactions is a strong incentive for many researchers to analyze natural language with regard to affective information. Recognition, classification and understanding of opinionated or emotional text are challenging tasks for natural language researchers.

In order to support applications based on language recognition and language production, the linguistic resource for a lexical representation of affective knowledge, WordNet-Affect, was introduced by Strapparava and Valitutti [17]. In [7], authors describe how the structure of the WordNet database might be used to assess affective or emotive meaning. Kim and Hovy [8] developed an automatic algorithm for obtaining opinion-bearing and non-opinion-bearing words, and described a method for detection of sentence-level opinion. An approach to analyzing affect content in free text using fuzzy logic techniques was proposed by Subasic and Huettner [18].

Statistical language modelling techniques have been applied by researchers to learn the characteristics of 'happy' and 'sad' moods indicated in the blog entries [11], and

D. Schuler (Ed.): Online Communities and Social Comput., HCII 2007, LNCS 4564, pp. 141–150, 2007.

to classify online diary posts by mood [9], [12]. However, the main limitations of the "bag-of-words" approach to textual affect classification are neglect of negation constructions and syntactical relations in sentences.

Keyword spotting technique was employed by the emotion recognition system proposed by Olveres et al. [15], and it was used as a method in an approach to multimodal emotion recognition from speech signals and textual content described in [19]. However, a simple word-level analysis model cannot output an appropriate emotional state in cases where affect is expressed by phrases requiring complex phrase/sentence-level analysis or when a sentence carries affect through underlying meaning. A pure affective keyword spotting technique will fail even with simple sentences like "*I saw this movie without interest*".

More advanced systems for textual affect recognition, such as the Text-to-Emotion Engine [2] or Empathy Buddy [10], perform sentence-level analysis. Both systems use a small set of emotions, the six "basic" types as defined by Ekman [5]. The parser described in [2] generates emotional output only if an emotional word refers to the person himself/herself and the sentence is in present continuous or present perfect continuous tense. We think that such limitations greatly narrow the potential of textual emotion recognition. As the result, sentences like "*Onion pie is disgusting*" and "*It was the most joyous feeling!*" are disregarded by the parser despite the fact that they evidently carry affect. An approach aimed at understanding the underlying semantics of language using large-scale real-world commonsense knowledge is proposed by Liu et al. [10].

Style and level of formalism of written natural language differ greatly depending on situation. In news, reports, scientific papers etc., text is syntactically correct and written in a formal style, while in private correspondence, online messaging, and blogs, text is informal and may include special symbols, emoticons, abbreviations and acronyms.

The weakness of most affect recognition systems integrated with a chat or e-mail browser is that they do not take into account crucial aspects of informal online conversation such as its specific style and evolving language. In order to account for the peculiarity of this medium, and to ensure satisfactory results on real examples, we investigated style, linguistic and interactional features of online conversations (details are given in [14]), and considered them while constructing our Affect Analysis Model.

Social interactions among people play an important role in the establishment of genuine interpersonal relationships and communities. However, computer-mediated communication lacks such signals of face-to-face communication as spoken language, intonation, gaze, facial expressions, gestures, and body language. The main goal of our research is thus to enrich social interactivity and affective expressiveness of online Instant Messaging (IM) communication. Here, a key issue is to support the automation of multiple expressive channels so that the user does not have to worry about visual self-presentation as in standard IM systems, but can focus on the textual content of the conversation. Our approach is based on deep word/ phrase/sentence-level analyses of affect in text, and the visual reflection of affective states and communicative behaviour through use of a 2D cartoon-like avatar.

2   Basis for Text Categorization

A fundamental task for any automatic emotion detection system is to first choose the basis for text categorization.

2.1   Emotion and Communicative Function Categories

In a face-to-face communication, people prefer to interact with a person who is expressive, because displayed emotion gives the impression that the speaker is significantly more sociable, open and humorous. Interaction in online conversations might be supported by the expressiveness too.

Facial expressions, gestures, body postures and movements have great communicative power [1], [3], [16]. All types of expressive means are dependent on context.

As the purpose of affect recognition in an IM system is to relate text to avatar emotional expressions, emotional categories were confined to those that can be visually expressed. For text categorization, we have decided to use (the relevant) nine emotional states taken from a set of ten emotions defined by Izard [6]: 'anger', 'disgust', 'fear', 'guilt', 'interest', 'joy', 'sadness' ('distress'), 'shame', and 'surprise'.

In our work, we aim at recognition of not only affective information conveyed by textual messages but also communicative functions that can be performed by avatar communicative behaviour ('greeting', 'thanks', 'posing a question', 'congratulation', and 'farewell').

2.2   Affect Database

In order to handle abbreviated language and to interpret affective features of emoticons, abbreviations, and words, we created the database using MySQL 5.0 [13].

While accumulating affect database entries, we collected 364 emoticons, both of American and Japanese style (for example, ":">" and "=^_^=" for 'blushing'), and the 337 most popular acronyms and abbreviations, both emotional and non-emotional (for example, "LOL" for 'laughing out loud', and "4U" – 'for you'). From the source of affective lexicon, WordNet-Affect [17], we have taken 1620 words: adjectives, nouns, verbs, and adverbs. We added not only words that refer directly to emotions, mood, traits, cognitive states, behaviour, attitude, sensations, but also words (especially, verbs) that carry the potential to provoke affective states in humans to our database. Since interjections, such as "alas", "wow", "yay", "ouch", etc. are specific indicators of communicated emotion caused by unexpectedness, a long-awaited joyful event, or pain, they were collected as well. Moreover, we included modifiers (e.g. "very", "extremely", "less", "not", etc.) into our database because they influence the strength of related words and phrases in a sentence.

Emotion categories and intensities were manually assigned to affect-related entries of database by three independent annotators. Intensity values range from 0.0 to 1.0, and describe the intensity degree of affective states from 'very weak' to 'very strong'. Annotators conformed to our guideline with the description of emotional state gradation within intensity levels. For example, 'cheerful', 'glad', 'happy', 'joyful' and 'elated' all correspond to the 'joy' emotional state, but to a different degree of intensity. Emoticons and emotional abbreviations were transcribed and related to named affective states, whereby each entry was assigned to only one category (examples are listed in Table 1). The inter-rater agreement was calculated using Fleiss' Kappa statistics. The Kappa coefficients for emoticons and abbreviations are 0.94 and 0.93, respectively, showing good annotation reliability.

Table 1. Examples of emoticons and abbreviations taken from affect database

Symbolic representation	Meaning	Category	Intensity
:-)	happy	Joy	0.6
:-o	surprise	Surprise	0.8
:-S	worried	Fear	0.4
/(^O^)/	very excited	Joy	1.0
(~_~)	grumpy	Anger	0.3
m(._.)m	bowing, thanks	Thanks	-
JK	just kidding	Joy	0.3
4gv	forgive	Guilt	0.6
PPL	people	-	-

Considering the fact that some affective words may express more than one emotional state, annotators related those words to more than one category. For instance, 'anger' and 'sadness' emotions are involved in the annotation of word "frustrated" with intensities 0.2 and 0.7, respectively (Table 2).

Table 2. Examples of words taken from affect database

Affective word	Part of speech	Category	Intensity
cheerfulness	noun	Joy	0.3
amazing	adjective	Surprise	1.0
frustrated	adjective	Anger	0.2
		Sadness	0.7
dislike	verb	Disgust	0.4
hopefully	adverb	Interest	0.2
		Joy	0.3

Variance of data from the mean was taken into consideration in order to eliminate errors in resulting intensity estimation due to subjective judgements. If the variance was not exceeding the threshold in 0.027, the resulting intensity was measured as the average of intensities given by three annotators. Otherwise, the intensity value responsible for exceeding the threshold was removed, and only the remaining values were taken into account.

As for the modifiers, coefficients for intensity degree strengthening or weakening were given (e.g. 1.4 for "very").

3 Affect Analysis Model

The algorithm for analysis of affect in text consists of five stages:

1. symbolic cue analysis;
2. syntactical structure analysis;
3. word-level analysis;
4. phrase-level analysis;
5. sentence-level analysis.

The working flow of the Affect Analysis Model is presented in Fig. 1.

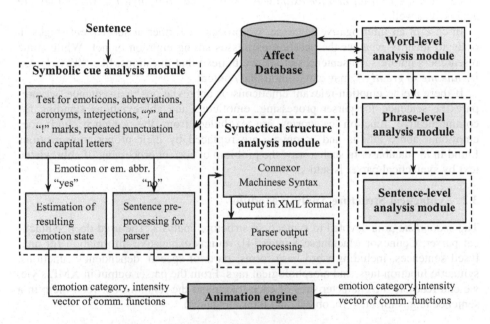

Fig. 1. Working flow of the Affect Analysis Model

3.1 Symbolic Cue Analysis Module

In the *first stage*, the sentence is tested for occurrences of emoticons, abbreviations, acronyms, interjections, "?" and "!" marks, repeated punctuation and capital letters.

First of all, punctuation marks of a sentence are delimited from words in order to disambiguate sentence punctuation marks from those belonging to emoticons. The "!" mark, repeated punctuation and capital letters are considered as an emphasis of the communicated emotion.

If there is an emoticon or abbreviation related to an emotional state, no further analysis of affect in text is performed based on the assumption that the emoticon (or abbreviation) dominates the affective meaning of the entire (simple or compound) sentence. It is known that people type emoticons and emotional abbreviations to show actual feeling, or to avoid misleading the other participants, for instance, after irony or joke. On the other hand, if there are multiple emoticons or emotion-relevant abbreviations in the sentence, we determine the prevailing (or dominant) emotion based on the following two rules: (1) when emotion categories of the detected emoticons (or abbreviations) are the same, the higher intensity value is taken for this emotion; (2) when they are different (e.g. 'sad': 0.5 and 'joy': 0.2), the category (and intensity) of the emoticon occurring last is dominant.

Regarding the visualisation by the avatar, when both emotional state and communicative function category appear in a sentence (for example, 'joy' and 'thanks'), two animations are sequentially displayed.

As interjections are added to text to reflect an author's feelings, like in the sentences *"Oh no, I forgot that the exam was today!"* and *"But anyways, yay!"*, they are analysed as well.

In case of an interrogative sentence, we process it further at subsequent stages in order to identify whether the question expresses strong emotion or not. While some researchers ignore such sentences at all, we believe that questions, like *"Why do you irritate me so greatly?"* may carry emotional content.

If there are no emotion-relevant emoticons or abbreviations in a sentence, we prepare the sentence for parser processing: emoticons and abbreviations standing for communicative function categories are excluded from the sentence, and non-emotional abbreviations and acronyms are replaced by their proper transcriptions found in the database. In such a way, the problem of correct processing of abbreviated text by syntactical parser is settled.

3.2 Syntactical Structure Analysis Module

The *second stage* is devoted to syntactical structure analysis. The used deep syntactical parser, Connexor Machinese Syntax [4], returns exhaustive information for analysed sentences, including word base forms, parts of speech, dependency functions, syntactic function tags, and morphological tags. From the parser output in XML style, we can read off the characteristics of each token and the relations between them in a sentence (e.g. subject, verb, object, and their attributes).

3.3 Word-Level Analysis Module

After handling the result from the previous analysis stage, the system transfers the data to the *third stage*, word-level analysis.

For each word found in the database, either the communicative function category is taken as a feature or the affective features of a word are represented as a vector of emotional state intensities e = [anger, disgust, sadness, fear, guilt, interest, joy, shame, surprise] (e.g. e = [0.2, 0, 0.7, 0, 0, 0, 0, 0, 0] for word "frustrated").

In the case of a modifier, the system identifies its coefficient.

Since the database contains words only in their dictionary form, one important system function on this stage is to increase the intensity of the emotional vector of an adjective if it is in comparative or superlative form. Currently, the intensity of an adjective is multiplied by the values 1.2 or 1.4, depending on its form.

3.4 Phrase-Level Analysis Module

In the *fourth stage*, phrase-level analysis is performed. The purpose of this stage is to detect emotions involved in phrases. Words in a sentence are interrelated and, hence, each of them can influence the overall meaning and sentiment of a statement.

We have defined general types of phrases, and rules for processing them with regard to affective content:

- adjectival phrase ("extremely sad"): modify the vector of adjective;
- noun phrase ("wonderful peace"): output vector with the maximum intensity within each corresponding emotional state in analysing vectors (for instance, e1=[0..0.7..] and e2=[0.3..0.5..] yield e3=[0.3..0.7..]);
- verb plus noun phrase: if verb and noun phrase have opposite valences ("break favourite vase", "enjoy bad weather"), consider vector of verb as dominant; if valences are the same, output vector with maximum intensities in corresponding emotional states for positive ("like honey"), and output null vector for negative;
- verb plus adjective phrase ("is very kind", "feel bad"): output vector of adjective phrase.

The rules for modifiers that influence the emotional vectors of related words are as follows:

- intensifiers multiply or decrease emotional intensity values;
- negation modifiers such as "no" or "not", and connector "neither...nor" cancel (set to zero) vectors of the related words, i.e. "neutralize the emotional content";
- prepositions such as "without", "except", "against", "despite" cancel vectors of related words.

We think that negation constructions do not reverse emotional meaning of words from positive to negative or vice versa. For example, "not splendid" is not necessarily reverse of "splendid".

Statements with words like "think", "believe", "sure", "know" and with modal operators such as "can", "may", "need" etc. are not considered by our system because they express a modal attitude towards the proposition. Conditional clause phrases beginning with "if", "when", "whenever", "after", "before" are disregarded as well.

3.5 Sentence-Level Analysis Module

In the *fifth and final stage*, the overall affect of a sentence and its resulting intensity degree are estimated. The emotional vector of a simple sentence (or of a clause) is generated from emotional categories and their intensities resulting from phrase-level analysis.

It is important to note that the developed system enables the differentiation of the strength of the resulting emotion depending on the tense of a sentence and availability of first person pronouns. We introduce this idea based on psychological literature.

As Paul Ekman states, "sometimes when people give an account of an emotional experience they unexpectedly begin to re-experience the emotion" [5]. "Genuine" emotion expressions display that emotion is now felt, whereas so-called "referential" expressions occur most often when people talk about past or future emotional experiences. Therefore, we assume that the strength of emotions conveyed by text depends on tense.

As to first person pronouns, people tend to use them to underline the strength of an emotion. For example, emotion conveyed through sentence like "*I am charmed by cherry flowers of Japan*" is stronger than in case of "*Cherry flowers of Japan are charming*".

According to our proposal, the emotional vector of a simple sentence (or of a clause) is multiplied by the corresponding empirically determined coefficient of intensity correction (Table 3).

Table 3. Coefficients of intensity correction

Tense	First person pronouns	
	yes	no
present	1	0.8
past	0.8	0.4
future	0.4	0

For compound sentences, we defined two rules:

- with coordinate connectors "and" and "so" (e.g. "*Exotic birds in the park were amazing, so we took nice pictures.*"): output the vector with the maximum intensity within each corresponding emotional state in the resulting vectors of both clauses;
- with coordinate connector "but" (e.g. "*Canada is a rich country, but still it has many poor people.*"): the resulting vector of a clause following after the connector is dominant.

After the dominant emotion of the sentence is determined, the relevant parameters are sent to the animation engine.

4 Visualization of Affect

We created an emotively expressive avatar for visual reflection of textual affective information. Animation engine of the developed system is responsible for the display of animations in an appropriate sequence, and for the decision on their duration (depending on sentence length). The strength of the displayed emotion is directly related to the intensity of the emotion derived from the text message.

To achieve believable emotion visualization, the avatar can display various emotions, behaviour associated with communicative functions, and idle states giving a sense of "liveliness".

Examples of 'greeting' and 'surprise' expressions are shown in Fig. 2.

Fig. 2. 'Greeting' and 'surprise' expressions

5 Conclusion

This paper has introduced a rule-based syntactical approach to affect recognition from text messaging. Typically, researchers in this field deal with grammatically and syntactically correct textual input. By contrast, our analysis of affect is inspired by the evolving language as seen in online conversation. The purpose of our work is to improve expressiveness and interactivity of computer-mediated communication. For textual input processing, the proposed analysis model takes into consideration features of IM conversation. Affect in text is classified into nine emotion categories, and information that can be displayed by avatar gestures as communicative behaviour is identified. The strength of a displayed emotional state depends on emotional vectors of words, relations among them, tense of sentence and availability of first person pronouns. A designed graphical representation of a user, avatar, performs various expressive patterns, contributing thus to rich interactivity.

Acknowledgments. We would like to express our gratitude to Dzmitry Tsetserukou and Shaikh Mostafa Al Masum who have contributed to annotations of affect database entries for their efforts and time.

References

1. Allwood, J.: Bodily Communication Dimensions of Expression and Content. In: Multimodality in Language and Speech Systems, pp. 7–26. Kluwer Academic Publishers, Netherlands (2002)
2. Boucouvalas, A.C.: Real Time Text-to-Emotion Engine for Expressive Internet Communications. In: Being There: Concepts, effects and measurement of user presence in synthetic environments, pp. 306–318. IOS Press, Amsterdam (2003)
3. Cassell, J.: More than Just Another Pretty Face: Embodied Conversational Interface Agents. Communications of the ACM 43(4), 70–78 (2000)
4. Connexor Oy. http://www.connexor.com/
5. Ekman, P.: Facial Expression and Emotion. American Psychologist 48(4), 384–392 (1993)
6. Izard, C.E.: Human emotions. Plenum Press, New York, NY (1977)
7. Kamps, J., Marx, M.: Words with attitude. In: Proceedings of the 14th Belgian-Netherlands Conference on Artificial Intelligence, BNAIC'02, pp. 449–450 (2002)
8. Kim, S.-M., Hovy, E.: Automatic Detection of Opinion Bearing Words and Sentences. In: Dale, R., Wong, K.-F., Su, J., Kwong, O.Y. (eds.) IJCNLP 2005. LNCS (LNAI), vol. 3651, Springer, Heidelberg (2005)
9. Leshed, G., Kaye, J.: Understanding How Bloggers Feel: Recognizing Affect in Blog Posts. In: Extended Abstracts of CHI'06, pp. 1019–1024 (2006)
10. Liu, H., Lieberman, H., Selker, T.: A Model of Textual Affect Sensing using Real-World Knowledge. In: Proceedings of IUI'03, pp. 125–132 (2003)
11. Mihalcea, R., Liu, H.: A Corpus-based Approach to Finding Happiness. In: Proceedings of the AAAI Spring Symposium on Computational Approaches to Weblogs (2006)
12. Mishne, G.: Experiments with Mood Classification in Blog Posts. In: Proceedings of the First Workshop on Stylistic Analysis of Text for Information Access (2005)
13. MySQL 5.0. http://www.mysql.com/
14. Neviarouskaya, A., Prendinger, H., Ishizuka, M.: Analysis of Affect Expressed through the Evolving Language of Online Communication. In: Proceedings of IUI'07, pp. 278–281. ACM Press, New York (2007)
15. Olveres, J., Billinghurst, M., Savage, J., Holden, A.: Intelligent, Expressive Avatars. In: Proceedings of WECC'98, pp. 47–55 (1998)
16. Poggi, I., Pelachaud, C.: Performative Faces. Speech Communication 26, 5–21 (1998)
17. Strapparava, C., Valitutti, A.: WordNet-Affect: an Affective Extension of WordNet. In: Proceedings of LREC'04, pp. 1083–1086 (2004)
18. Subasic, P., Huettner, A.: Affect Analysis of Text Using Fuzzy Semantic Typing. In: IEEE Transactions on Fuzzy Systems, vol. 9(4) (2001)
19. Chuang, Z.-J., Wu, C.-H.: Multi-Modal Emotion Recognition from Speech and Text. Computational Linguistic and Chinese Language Processing 9(2), 45–62 (2004)

Ranking Method for Mediators in Social Network

Ryosuke Saga and Hiroshi Tsuji

Graduate School of Engineering
Osaka Prefecture University
1-1 Gakuen-Cho, Naka-ku, Sakai, Japan 5998531
saga@mis.cs.osakafu-u.ac.jp, tsuji@cs.osakafu-u.ac.jp

Abstract. This paper proposes a method for ranking mediators where a mediator is defined as node having an important role in a social network. To precisely rank the mediators in order of their importance, a method is used based on changes in the average shortest path length. However, the computational complexity for this method is $O(N^5)$, so an unreasonable amount of time it is required to determine complexity for a massive network. Our ranking method, whose complexity is no more than $O(N^2)$, is based on the relationships among adjacency nodes. Although the method does not provide a precise but an approximate rank, we found that there is a strong correlation between the ranks generated using the strict and the developed methods. Results on a variety of generated networks confirmed the feasibility of our method for a massive network.

Keywords: Social Network, Mediator, Rank Mining, Community Computing, Graph Theory.

1 Introduction

Let us imagine the following organization: members openly share their knowledge and exchange ideas not only within groups but also with groups outside the organization. Additionally, members within the organization work cooperatively with external experts and other skilled persons to assist and support each other. This type of organization is called an *open innovation* organization [1]. Intel, IBM, etc. have succeeded in actively making open innovation organizations.

Within an organization, a social network can exist and consists of nodes and links in which each node indicates a person and each link shows the relationship of the dyad. If an organization is expressed as a social network, the central people in the network are called *leaders*, and many people work around the leaders. However, to express plural organizations which work collaboratively in open innovation, each company is required to have mediators who communicate outside the borders of organizations. Such people are not always leaders but are sometimes considered just as important as leaders. In order to manage and drive such mediators, it is necessary to find and rank them, and the method to rank mediators uses changes in the average shortest path length. However, the method has a problem that it takes a lot of time to compute the method because of large complexity.

D. Schuler (Ed.): Online Communities and Social Comput., HCII 2007, LNCS 4564, pp. 151–159, 2007.
© Springer-Verlag Berlin Heidelberg 2007

In this paper, we evaluated a new method for ranking a mediator's importance. Our fast approximation method is based on the relationship among adjacency nodes of potential mediators. The approximation method focuses on local nodes, even though a strict method is required to handle all the nodes within a network.

The reminder of this paper is structured as follows: Section 2 is a literature review of the importance of mediators and their influence to a network. Section 3 outlines two ranking methods: a strict method, which uses the average shortest path, and our approximation method. We compared the strict method with our method. Section 4 checks feasibility of our method. Section 5 discusses related and future works. Finally, we conclude this paper in Section 6.

2 Role of Mediator

If a mediator leaves an enterprise described as open innovation organization, the enterprise will lose some critical communication paths and some nodes will fail to collaborate. Moreover, the associated enterprise connected by the mediator will also not be able to work effectively either and will need to invest additional costs to compensate their weak points. The cost may be wasted, and the related enterprises may incur additional costs when working out the costs. Therefore, mediators can be thought as influencing an entire network.

According to research about patents and inventors Fleming et al. [2], reported that some inventors play a role of gatekeeper and make innovation more progressive in a network. Such inventors can be regarded as a mediator in a network. In the management science area, Malone et al. [3] proposed a team form called the X-team. Mediators have the same importance as key decisions makers in the X-team who cooperate with other related projects. Leydesdorff [4] indicated that new developments may occur at the borders of disciplines, that is, interdisciplinary relationships are formed. Girvan et al.[5] shows that any group connected to each other through a small number of mediators in a collaborative network Research has shown that large internet service providers seldom connect directly each other [6], which highlights the importance of mediators.

Any mediator plays an important role in their organization, and therefore, it is important to develop a method to manage and drive mediators. Ranking mediators based on their existence value for management is an effective method for manage. Consequently, we evaluated, as described in the following section two ranking methods: strict method based on the average shortest path length and our approximation method based on the links created by adjacency nodes.

3 Ranking Methods

In the following sections, we assumed that a link has neither direction nor weight.

3.1 Strict Solution

Mediators affect not only adjacency nodes but also the entire network. The degree of influence is high when a node is removed from a network and affects the network path length. This is because mediators exist in the shortest path between specific nodes.

Accordingly, we focused on the change in the average shortest path length. Note that the average shortest path length is the average of the distance, d_{ij}, between two arbitrary nodes called node i and node j in a network where N nodes exist. Distance d_{ij} is the number of the required links to connect node i and node j. We can get the average length, L_i, of node i by using formula (1):

$$L_i = \frac{1}{N-1}\sum_i d_{ij} \ . \tag{1}$$

Calculating L_i for all nodes, we can calculate the average shortest path length in the network by using formula (2):

$$L = \frac{1}{N}\sum_i L_i \ . \tag{2}$$

By using the average shortest path length in a network, we can assign mediators' ranks as follows:

1. Remove a node individually,
2. Calculate the average shortest path for each, and
3. Measure the change in length and rank them.

However, there is a problem about computational complexity. Under the premise that Dijkstra's algorithm [7] is used to compute the distance between nodes. Assuming that Dijkstra's algorithm, which is a representative method, is used to compute the distance, formula (1) needs $O(N^3)$ because the complexity of Dijkstra's algorithm is $O(N^2)$. For computing formula (2), the computational complexity becomes $O(N^4)$. Additionally, this process should be repeated for all nodes. As a result, the final complexity is $O(N^5)$ in practice. Therefore, this method is impractical for a massive network.

3.2 Proposed Method: Approximation Method

To highlight the difference between the methods, we will describe a local structure and the relationships formed. Fig. 1(a) and Fig. 1(b) indicate the importance of the node. These figures represent situations when node v has the same number of adjacency nodes in a dense network with a focus on node v and another less dense network. Even if node v is removed from the network, the effect on adjacency nodes is small because there are many alternative links. Therefore, node v can be regarded as an unimportant mediator. Contrary to this, assuming that the relationship among adjacency nodes is weak, as shown in Fig. 1(b), several adjacency nodes would not able to communicate when node v is removed from the network. In this case, the role of node v as a mediator is considered more important than in the preceding case.

From the above features, we hypothesize the following:

Hypothesis 1. Nodes whose adjacency node has a small number of direct links to others have higher importance than mediators than other nodes.

Hypothesis 2. The importance of a mediator is indicated by the importance of its adjacency nodes.

For the first hypothesis, let us consider Fig. 1(a). We can regard node v as an unimportant mediator because the numbers of links from adjacency nodes to other nodes do not change even when node v is removed. On the other hand, the numbers of links from adjacency nodes to other nodes shown in Fig. 1(b) are less than those shown in Fig.1 (a). This means that node v shown in Fig. 1.(b) can be regarded as a more important mediator than node v shown in Fig.1.(a).

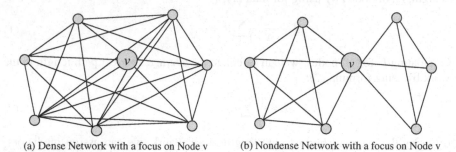

(a) Dense Network with a focus on Node v   (b) Nondense Network with a focus on Node v

Fig. 1. Relation among node v and its adjacency nodes

For the second hypothesis, the effect of the neighbors' influence is made high-lighted by several methods. For example, the concept of PageRank assumes that a web page linked by important pages is also important [7]. Thus, we consider that the degree of importance a mediator has reflects the influence of adjacency nodes.

Consequently, we can compute a node's rank for a mediator based on the two hypotheses. We assume that node v has adjacency nodes v_i (where i = 1, ..., n) in which the number of its links is E_i and define r_i as the short number of links for node v as compared to a complete graph. When node v is removed from the network, b_i, which links the decline rate of node v_i, is given as follows:

$$b_i = \frac{r_i}{n-1} = \frac{n-1-E_i}{n-1}.$$ (3)

As a result, B_v which is a mediator score of node v, is shown as follows:

$$B_v = \sum_{i=1}^{n} b_i = n - \sum_{i}^{n} \frac{E_i}{n-1}$$ (4)

Arranging the values shown in formula (4) in descending order, we can obtain the node rank for each mediator.

Next, we will consider the computational complexity of our method. Our algorithm needs the most computational complexity when a network creates a complete graph because formula (4) needs O(N) per each node. Therefore, the total complexity is $O(N^2)$, which is by far smaller than previous strict methods $O(N^5)$.

3.3 Simple Example

The difference between the two methods can be shown using a simple example, like that network shown in Fig. 2 We will initially show the example using the strict method. Table 1 lists the distances necessary to create the average shortest path length about Node0. Note that when the distance is 10, a node cannot reach another node.

The average shortest path of Node0 is 5.41, as listed in Table 1. Finally, the computed values and ranks are listed in Table 2.

When our method is used, the value of Node0 is computed as follows:

$$6 - \frac{0+0+0+2+2+2}{6-1} = 4.8 \ . \tag{5}$$

For iteration of our method in the same way as the strict method, the values of the nodes are listed in Table 3. Thus, our method indicates that a node is zero if adjacency nodes of the node under review form a complete graph within themselves.

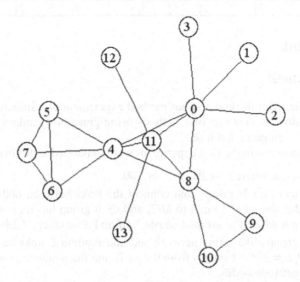

Fig. 2. Example of simple network having 14 nodes

Table 1. The number of hops when node0 is removed. (When a node is not reachable to another, the value is 10.).

Node (From\To)	1	2	3	4	5	6	7	8	9	10	11	12	13
1		10	10	10	10	10	10	10	10	10	10	10	10
2	10		10	10	10	10	10	10	10	10	10	10	10
3	10	10		10	10	10	10	10	10	10	10	10	10
4	10	10	10		1	1	1	1	2	2	1	2	2
5	10	10	10	1		1	1	2	3	3	2	3	3
6	10	10	10	1	1		1	2	3	3	2	3	3
7	10	10	10	1	1	1		2	3	3	2	3	3
8	10	10	10	1	2	2	2		1	1	1	2	2
9	10	10	10	2	3	3	3	1		1	2	3	3
10	10	10	10	2	3	3	3	1	1		2	3	3
11	10	10	10	1	2	2	2	1	2	2		1	1
12	10	10	10	2	3	3	3	2	3	3	1		2
13	10	10	10	2	3	3	3	2	3	3	1	2	

Table 2. Values and ranks of strict method

Node	0	1	2	3	4	5	6	7	8	9	10	11	12	13
Value	5.41	2.14	2.14	2.14	5.1	2.17	2.17	2.17	4.33	2.14	2.14	4.44	2.13	2.13
Rank	1	8	8	8	2	5	5	5	4	8	8	3	13	13

Table 3. Values and ranks of proposed method

Node	0	1	2	3	4	5	6	7	8	9	10	11	12	13
Value	4.8	0	0	0	3.6	0	0	0	3	0	0	3.5	0	0
Rank	1	5	5	5	2	5	5	5	4	5	5	3	5	5

4 Experiment

4.1 Network Model

We compared the strict method and our method experimentally. Initially, we checked the rank correlation between the two methods using generated random networks, and then measured the computation time.

In Random networks in the first experiment were generated as follows:

Step1. Make N nodes where N is 20,30, ... or 100.

Step2. Divide them into M groups and connect the links between nodes in the same group. Reduce the size of M from 5 to $M/7$, and each group has mi nodes based on a normal distribution where the average equals N/M and a variance of 2 is used.

Step3. Connect groups like a ring network and add random L links between selected nodes. Note that $L = N * t$, t ranges from 0.1 to 1, and the distance is set to infinity if there is no path between nodes.

The sample network is shown in Fig. 3.

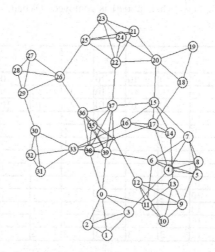

Fig. 3. Generated sample network having 40 nodes

The second experiment involving computation time was when we produced networks consisting of nodes (*N*) and density (*D*) (that is, the networks have links of $D*N*(N-1)/2$). The number of nodes ranged from 20 to 300, and the density ranged from 0.1 to 1(that is, a complete graph).

4.2 Result

Table 4 lists and Fig. 4 shows the correlation of rank between the strict method and our approximation method. We found a strong correlation that was greater than 0.8 for most cases. We also found that the correlation does not depend on the t value.

Table 4. Correlation between node and rate of random link

t\Node	20	30	40	50	60	70	80	90	100	Average
0	0.87	0.86	0.85	0.84	0.86	0.88	0.82	0.85	0.87	0.86
0.1	0.83	0.86	0.84	0.85	0.83	0.80	0.83	0.81	0.85	0.83
0.2	0.18	0.83	0.79	0.70	0.81	0.78	0.84	0.77	0.81	0.75
0.3	0.81	0.75	0.84	0.81	0.88	0.81	0.85	0.89	0.73	0.82
0.4	0.87	0.81	0.83	0.77	0.90	0.72	0.91	0.90	0.79	0.84
0.5	0.84	0.85	0.74	0.81	0.68	0.81	0.90	0.81	0.82	0.81
0.6	0.76	0.79	0.84	0.92	0.90	0.84	0.77	0.93	0.78	0.84
0.7	0.87	0.81	0.88	0.76	0.76	0.88	0.81	0.78	0.81	0.82
0.8	0.73	0.77	0.90	0.83	0.78	0.96	0.83	0.90	0.73	0.82
0.9	0.66	0.71	0.86	0.82	0.95	0.92	0.94	0.93	0.93	0.86
1	0.57	0.82	0.96	0.76	0.82	0.70	0.87	0.77	0.75	0.78
Average	0.73	0.81	0.84	0.80	0.83	0.82	0.85	0.84	0.82	0.82

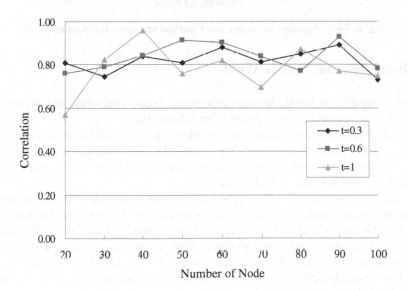

Fig. 4. Correlation when the rate of additional link *t* is 0.3, 0.6 and 1

The results of the computational time are shown in Fig. 5. Note that only one case is shown for the strict method because the results are similar for each other. The results in this figure show that our method reduced the computation time when compared to the strict method. We understand that our method depends on density. For example, the computation time in networks of density 1 is more than 10 times of that in the networks of density 0.1.

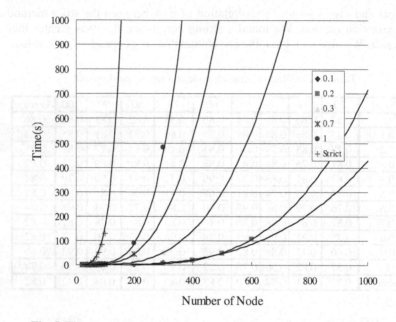

Fig. 5. Time consumption among strict method and approximation methods

5   Discussion and Future Work

Various centrality methods: *closeness centrality, degree centrality,* and *betweenness centrality,* have already been proposed to rank nodes [9].

Closeness centrality is an index that considers a node important when the distances among nodes is short. Degree centrality is an index that considers a node important when the nodes have many adjacency nodes. However, these indices measure centrality and do not measure the rank of the mediator.

On the other handWhereas, betweenness centrality is an index that determines the importance of each node based on the actual number of shortest paths between vertices it has. This index is also useful when ranking mediators. However, all the network data need when measuring them globally. Thus, computational complexity used to measure betweenness centrality is well-known as $O(N^3)$. Therefore, the betweenness centrality is not appropriate measure for massive networks in terms of time complexity. Additionally, one can argue that processing is possible when there are many short paths in a network, even though the concept of betweenness centrality is relatively easy to understand.

Our method ranks nodes based on the local relationship among adjacency nodes. Thus, the method is able to compute a node's ranks even when not all network information is known and is also able to minimize complexity $O(N^2)$. However, we consider that arguments about precision and correlation and betweenness centrality have not been discussed in the current research. This is a future work in our research.

6 Conclusion

We developed an approximation method to rank mediators. Initially, we introduced a strict method and highlighted the problem of computational complexity. To solve this complexity, we developed a method based on the relationships among adjacency nodes. By comparing our method and the strict method, we found that a strong correlation exists between the results produced by each test and that our method can reduce computation time drastically.

References

1. Chesbrough, H.W.: Open Innovation, Harvard Business School Press (2003)
2. Fleming, L., Adam, J.: A Network of Invention, Harvard Business Review, vol. 82(4) (2004)
3. Malone, T.W.: The Future of Work: How the New Order of Business Will Shape Your Organization, Your Management Style, and Your Life. Harvard Business School Press, Boston, MA (2004)
4. Loydesdorff, L.: "Betweenness Centrality" as an Indictor of the "Interdisciplinarity" of Scientific Journals, Journal of the American Society for Information Science and Technology (forthcoming) (2007)
5. Girvan, M., Newman, M.E.J.: Community structure in social and biological networks, Proc. Natl. Proc. Natl. Acad. Sci. USA 99, 8271–8276 (2002)
6. Pastor-Satorras, R., Vazquez, A., Vespignani, A.: Dynamical and correlation properties of the internet, Phys. Rev. Lett. vol. 87(25) (2001)
7. Dijkstra, E.W.: A note on two problems in connection with graphs. Numerische Mathematik 1, 269–271 (1959)
8. Google: http://www.google.com
9. Freeman, L.C.: Centrality in social networks: Conceptual clarification. Social Networks 1, 215–239 (1979)

The Relationship Between Social Presence and Group Identification Within Online Communities and Its Impact on the Success of Online Communities

Diana Schimke, Heidrun Stoeger, and Albert Ziegler

University of Ulm, Faculty of Computer Science, Department Educational Psychology,
Albert-Einstein-Allee 47, 89069 Ulm, Germany
{Diana.Schimke,Heidrun.Stoeger,Albert.Ziegler}@uni-ulm.de

Abstract. In order to encourage more girls to choose STEM-study courses (Science, Technology, Engineering, and Mathematics) we created an online community and e-mentoring program for German high school girls and women engaged in STEM vocational fields. Within the online community, we brought together girls and female role models. A community platform was offered for getting to know and exchange with other community members. Within this community, we used quantitative methods to measure the students' levels of social presence and group identity, and tested to see if a correlation between those two factors exists. We further evaluated if the group identity has an impact on the girls interest and willingness to participate in STEM.

Keywords: Online communities, e-mentoring, social presence, group identity, STEM, gender.

1 Introduction

Girls and women are underrepresented in the areas of mathematics as well as the hard sciences chemistry and physics in comparison to boys and men [12, 17]. This is true from both a professional aspect [29] – and in particular with respect to academic careers and leadership positions – as well as the scholastic area [4, 6]. Interesting here is that these gender specific disparities grow with increasing ability levels [29]. The low levels of participation among girls in the international Olympics, which serve to identify and promote young talents in these areas, demonstrate this for the subjects of biology, chemistry, mathematics, physics and computer science [13].

Although massive gender differences were recorded in studies during the 1970's and 80's for performance in the areas of mathematics and the natural sciences [4, 15], performance levels seem to be evening out in these subjects for the time being [1, 8]. However, by the time they reach adolescence, girls in many countries demonstrate poorer achievement levels than boys [3].

Regardless of the degree of difference, or of the presence of achievement differences in the area of science, technology, engineering and mathematics (STEM), it

D. Schuler (Ed.): Online Communities and Social Comput., HCII 2007, LNCS 4564, pp. 160–168, 2007.

must be stressed that the slight discrepancy in performance cannot explain the phenomenon that women and girls almost completely avoid subjects in the areas of mathematics and the natural sciences. Consequently, the psychological approaches used to explain the poor levels of participation of women and girls in the areas of STEM have focused increasingly in the last decade on a lack of female role models in these talent domains [11].

1.1 CyberMentor-Community

Due to the lack of female role models in STEM and the low participation rates of women and girls in STEM in Germany, we created an online community to bring together women engaged in STEM vocational fields and German high school girls.

CyberMentor is an e- mentoring program that aims to foster interest and participation of high school girls in STEM through a web-based approach [19]. It provides suitable role models via mentoring, which involves a one-to-one relationship between women who work in the field of STEM (researchers, professors, engineers) and female high school students. The girls communicate with their mentors via e-mail. In addition to the e-mail communication between mentors and mentees, the members have access to a community platform with feasibilities to communicate synchronous and asynchronous with other girls and mentors. For asynchronous communication there is a discussion forum and an internal messaging system. The discussion forum is used for questions concerning STEM but also for personal exchange. The posts in the forum are visible to all the other members. If wanting to communicate privately with only one other person, the participants can use the community-intern messaging system called CyberMail. For both, the forum and the internal messaging, users can subscribe e-mail notification which informs them about new messages getting in. The platform also offers the feasibility for synchronous communication. Participants find a chat room where they can have spontaneous meetings with other mentees and mentors as well as arranged chats with their mentors or other girls. On a regular term, chat meetings are being held and STEM-topics are being discussed. Mentors can act as experts and invite interested girls to their expert chats.

Furthermore, CyberMentor offers personal pages with pictures for each member to introduce herself and get to know other online community members. Each personal page includes a guestbook and the users can post on each other's pages. A web journal, called CyberNews, appears once a month and offers interesting articles about STEM, quizzes and interviews with female students talking about their study courses in the domain of STEM. Mentees and mentors can also write their own articles and upload them via an online submission form.

2 Background

"Social Presence is the degree of person-to-person awareness, which occurs in the computer environment." [24, p.34] Short, Williams, and Christie define Social

Presence as the *"degree of salience of the other person in the interaction and the consequent salience of the interpersonal relationships"* [21, p.65]. Gunawardena sees social presence as *"the degree to which a person is perceived as a 'real person' in mediated communication"* [9, p.151]. Biocca further explains *"the minimum level of social presence occurs when users feel that a form, behavior, or sensory experience indicates the presence of another intelligence."* [5, sect. 7.2]

Social presence has been recognized as an important factor in the context of computer-mediated communication, online learning or virtual communities. Gunawardena and Zittle report findings that in a computer-mediated communication system, social presence is a strong predictor of satisfaction [10]. Different researchers report that social presence affects the degree of social interaction taking place in computer-supported collaborative learning environments [9, 22, 23, 25, and 26]. Venkatesh and Johnson found positive effects of social richness, which is an important indicator of presence, on motivation, subsequently leading to a higher system usage [27]. Furthermore Perse, Burton, Kovner, Lears and Sen recognized a positive relationship between social presence and a student's perception of his/her own computer expertise [18]. Concerning the participation rate within online environments, social presence is also an important indicator. Leh found that when social presence within an environment is lacking, the participants see it as impersonal and the amount of information shared with others decreases [16].

Asch found with his conformity study that people generally want to fit in groups [2]. At a collective level fitting behavior happens, when one sees trends in the behaviors of others, e.g. clothing, and changes his/her own style in dressing to fit in. Whiteman states *"People feel more comfortable around us when they believe we share a kinship or common values"* [28, p.8]. Further do Shaffer and Anundsen believe that communities are built on a person's sense of belonging and yearning to belong; when people share identities and values, communities are constructed [20]. An experiment by Cosley, Lam, Albert, Konstan, and Riedl showed that people generally want to fit in their group [7]. In their experiment within an online movie rating system, they divided all subjects into four groups. The groups were seated in separate rooms and told to rate movies they had seen before. Groups A, B, and C saw system-predicted ratings for the films they were rating. Group D did not get this information. The result of this experiment show that a significant proportion of the rating given by groups A, B, and C correlated with the system-predicted values those groups had been seen before rating. This shows that users tried to conform to the predictions [7].

The statements and studies mentioned above show that social presence and belonging to a group (group identity) both are important factors in online environments. In our study we want to find out if there is a relationship between social presence and group identity in online communities, and if a higher level of group identity affects the interest level of girls in STEM and their willingness to get involved with STEM.

3 Empirical Study

In our empirical study we wanted to test the hypotheses that (H1) the level of Social Presence has an impact on the level of Group Identification, (H2) the level of Group Identification influences the interest-level in STEM, and that (H3) the level of Group Identification furthermore has a positive impact on the involvement with STEM.

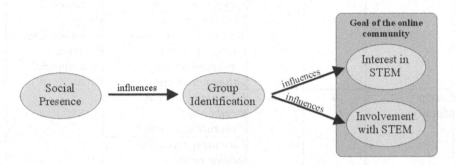

Fig. 1. Hypotheses we want to test with our empirical study

3.1 Online Community and Its Members

The Online Community we are referring to in our research was created in October 2005. 107 volunteering mentors engaged in STEM-vocational fields and 107 girls visiting grades six to thirteen (M = 9.35, SD = 2.12) were members of the Online Community. Each high school girl was matched with one mentor. Besides exchanging with their mentoring partners via e-mail, the online community members had access to an interactive community platform described above.

After being a member of the online community for nine months, the girls were asked to participate in a voluntary web based survey which included the question-naires mentioned in the following paragraph. 51 online community members took part in the survey and answered the questions.

3.2 Measurement Tools

To test our hypotheses we used quantitative methods. The Group Identification was measured with an adapted and translated version of Henry, Arrow and Carini's group identification scale [14]. We adapted the questionnaire and used six items instead of nine. The 6-item questionnaire was highly reliable with α = .90. For measuring the level of social presence, we translated and adapted Gunawardena and Zittles' Social Presence Scale [10]. In our version we used 12 items instead of 14. The α-value of our Social Presence scale was .90. Interest in STEM was measured with a 6-item questionnaire (α = .89), Involvement with STEM with a 5-item questionnaire   (α = .90). Table 1 shows the measuring tools we used and lists two example items of each scale. The answer options reached from *"1-completely disagree"* to *"6- completely agree"*.

Table 1. Information about the measuring tools we used

Scale for measuring...	Number of Items	Alpha	Example Questions	Answer Options
Social Presence	12	.90	*The CyberMentor-Community is an excellent medium for social interaction.*	1 - completely disagree
			I felt comfortable conversing via e-mail, forum, chat and cybermail within the online community.	2 - disagree 3 - rather disagree 4 - rather agree 5 - agree 6 - completely agree
Group Identity	9	.90	*I am happy to be a member of the CyberMentor group.*	
			I see myself as quite similar to other members of the group.	
Interest in STEM	6	.89	*I like STEM classes at school.*	
			Getting good grades in STEM-classes is important to me.	
Involvement with STEM	5	.90	*I can imagine choosing a STEM class as a major in High School.*	
			I can imagine studying a STEM course when going to college.	

3.3 Results

51 users filled out our questionnaire about social presence. We grouped those users according to their level of social presence by the help of a median split. Those users with a value above 4.4 on a 6-point likert scale were grouped to "High SP", users with a value of 4.4 and lower were grouped to "Low SP" (see table 2).

Table 2. Group statistics: social presence

Group	SP value	N	Mean	S.D.
High SP	> 4.4	25	4.91	.43
Low SP	<= 4.4	26	3.66	.54

To test hypothesis **H1**: "*The level of Social Presence has an impact on the level of Group Identification.*" a t-test was computed for the grouping variable "Social Presence group" and the test variable "Group Identity". The responses were measured on a 6-point likert scale (from 'strongly disagree' (1) to 'strongly agree' (6)). A significant difference between the two groups 'High SP' and 'Low SP' could be found using a t-test ($p<.01$; $t=6.97$; $df=47$). Table 3 presents the mean values and standard deviations for the groups 'High SP' and 'Low SP'.

Table 3. Mean values of 'Group Identity' for the groups 'High SP' and 'Low SP'

Group	N	Mean value group identity	S.D.
High SP	25	5.06	.53
Low SP	24	3.73	.79

The users who filled out our questionnaire about group identity were again grouped into two groups according to their level of group identity by the help of a median split. Users with a group identity value greater than 4.5 were grouped to "High GI", while users with the value 4.5 and lower were assigned to "Low GI" (see table 4).

Table 4. Group statistics: group identity

Group	SP value	N	Mean	S.D.
High GI	> 4.5	25	5.17	.40
Low GI	<= 4.5	24	3.67	.65

Another t-test was computed to test **H2**: *"The level of Group Identification influences the interest-level in STEM"*. Grouping variable was the "Group Identity group" (see table 4) and the test variable was "Interest in STEM". The same was done for **H3**: *"The level of Group Identification has a positive impact on the involvement with STEM"* with the test variable "Involvement with STEM". Figure 2 shows the mean values of the two groups 'High GI' and 'Low GI' for both test variables. The t-test results proved significant differences between both groups concerning 'Interest in STEM' ($p<.01$; $t= 3.28$; $df=40$) and 'Involvement with STEM' ($p<.01$; $t=3.39$; $df=40$).

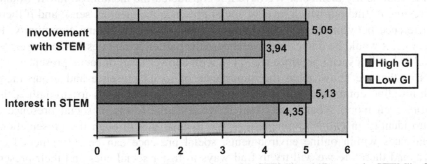

Fig. 2. Mean values of the variables "Involvement with STEM" and "Interest in STEM" of the two groups (High GI and Low GI)

Table 5 summarizes our results. With our study we found that the level of social presence does have an impact on the identification with the online group. If the users' levels of social presence are higher, their identification with the online group is also higher. Further, the group identity does positively influence the members' interests in STEM and also the involvement or willingness to get involved with STEM.

Table 5. Summary results for our hypotheses

Hypothesis	Confirmed
H1: *The level of Social Presence has an impact on the level of Group Identification.*	Yes
H2: *The level of Group Identification influences the interest-level in STEM.*	Yes
H3: *The level of Group Identification has a positive impact on the involvement with STEM.*	Yes

4 Discussion and Future Prospects

The results we gained through our empirical study showed that social presence is a crucial factor within online communities. Other studies mentioned above proved for example, that social presence is an important factor concerning the participation rate [9, 16, 22, 23, 25, 26, and 27] within online communities or satisfaction within an online environment [10]. With our study we could expand the list of positive impacts social presence has within online environments. We showed that social presence influences the users' identification with the group, which in turn is an important factor within online communities as well. In the case of our online community, the factors *Interest in STEM* and *Involvement with STEM* were important. We showed that higher group identification strengthens those factors. A higher identification with the group leads to greater interest in and more involvement with STEM. This demonstrates that group identity is a factor which positively influences the groups' goals.

In this study we only measured the level of social presence among the student online community members. We have not considered the mentors so far. It would be interesting to find out which level of social presence the mentors sense and if there is a difference between the student and adult members of the online community. Furthermore, it would be interesting to compare the participation rates of those users with a higher level of social presence and those with a lower level of social presence.

Now that we know about the importance of social presence and group identity within online communities, our next goal will be to find ways to strengthen those factors even more. What leads to an increase in the levels of social presence and group identity in online communities? We assume that through the presentation of social cues within online environments, social presence can be strengthened even more, and therefore we will try to find ways to foster social cues and their presentation within online communities.

Acknowledgments. We gratefully acknowledge Carolina Cozacu for her efforts in helping implement the online community and working for the CyberMentor project. Thanks also go to Iris Woersdoerfer who is presently a member of the CyberMentor team. The CyberMentor-project was supported by a state ministry (Ministerium für Ernährung und ländlichen Raum) of Baden-Württemberg, Germany.

References

1. Arnot, M., Gray, J., Rudduck, J.: Recent research on gender and educational performance. The Stationery Office/Office for Standards in Education, London (1998)
2. Asch, S.E.: Effects of Group Pressure upon the Modification and Distortion of Judgments. In: Guetzkow, H. (ed.) Groups, Leadership, and Men, pp. 177–190. Carnegie Press, Pittsburgh (1951)
3. Beller, M., Gafni, N.: International Assessment of Educational Progress in Mathematics and Sciences: The gender differences perspective. Journal of Educational Psychology (Washington) 88, 365–377 (1996)
4. Beerman, L., Heller, K.A., Menacher, P.: Mathe: nichts für Mädchen? Begabung und Geschlecht am Beispiel von Mathematik, Naturwissenschaft und Technik (Math: Nothing for girls? Talent and gender in the subjects of Mathematics, Natural Sciences and Technology). Huber, Bern (1992)
5. Biocca, F.: The Cyborg's dilemna: Progressive embodiment in virtual environments. Journal of Computer Mediated Communication, vol. 3(2) (1997)
6. Colley, A., Comber, C., Hargreaves, D.J.: Gender effects in school subject preferences: A research note. Educational Studies 20, 13–18 (1994)
7. Cosley, D., Lam, S.K., Albert, I., Konstan, J., Riedl, J.: Is Seeing Believing? How Recommender System Interfaces Affect Users' Opinions. CHI Letters, ACM Conference on Human Factors in Computing Systems 5(1), 585–592 (2003)
8. Freeman, J.: Cultural influences on gifted gender achievement. High Ability Studies 15, 7–23 (2004)
9. Gunawardena, C.N.: Social presence theory and implications for interaction and collaborative learning in computer conferences. International Journal of Educational Telecommunications 1, 147–166 (1995)
10. Gunawardena, C.N., Zittle, F.: Social presence as a predictor of satisfaction within a computer mediated conferencing environment. American Journal of Distance Education 11(3), 8–25 (1997)
11. Hackett, G., Esposito, D., O'Halloran, M.S.: The relationship of role model influences to the career salience and educational and career plans of college women. Journal of Vocational Behavior 35, 164–180 (1989)
12. Heller, K.A., Ziegler, A.: Gender differences in mathematics and the natural sciences: Can attributional retraining improve the performance of gifted females? Gifted Child Quarterly 40, 200–210 (1996)
13. Heller, K.A., Lengfelder, A.: Wissenschaftliche Evaluation der Internationalen Schülerolympiaden in Mathematik, Physik und Chemie (1977-1997): Abschlussbericht zur deutschen Olympiastudie mit kulturvergleichenden Analysebefunden [Evaluation of the international student Olympics in mathematics, physics and chemistry instruction: final report]. Institut für Pädagogische Psychologie. München (1999)
14. Henry, K.B., Arrow, H., Carini, B.: A tripartite model of group identification: Theory and measurement. Small Group Research 30(5), 558–581 (1999)

15. Hyde, J.S., Fennema, E., Lamon, S.J.: Gender differences in mathematics performance: A meta-analysis. Psychological Bulletin 107, 139–155 (1990)
16. Leh, A.S.: Computer-Mediated Communication and Social Presence in a Distance Learning Environment. International Journal of Educational Telecommunications 7(2), 109–128 (2001)
17. Lupart, J.L., Cannon, E., Telfer, J.A.: Gender Differences in Adolescent Academic Achievement, Interests, Values and Life Role Expectations. High Ability Studies 15, 25–42 (2004)
18. Perse, E.M., Burton, P.I., Kovner, E.S., Lears, M.E., Sen, R.J.: Predicting computer-mediated communication in a college class. Communication Research Reports 9, 161–170 (1992)
19. Schimke, D., Cozacu, C., Stoeger, H., Ziegler, A.: Development of a community platform for girls interested in STEM. In: Auer, M.E. (ed.) Interactive Computer Aided Learning ICL, Lifelong and Blended Learning. University Press, Kassel [CD-ROM] (2006)
20. Shaffer, C., Anundsen, K.: Creating Community Anywhere. Perigee Books, New York (1993)
21. Short, J., Williams, E., Christie, B.: The social psychology of telecommunications. John Wiley, London (1976)
22. Tammelin, M.: From telepresence to social presence: the role of presence in a network-based learning environment. In: Tella, S. (ed.) Aspects of media education, pp. 219–231. Media Education Publications, Helsinki (1998)
23. Tu, C-H.: On-line learning migration: from social learning theory to social presence theory in a CMC environment. Journal of Network and Computer Applications 23, 27–37 (2000)
24. Tu, C-H.: The measurement of social presence in an online learning environment. International Journal on E-Learning 1(2), 34–45 (2002)
25. Tu, C-H.: The impacts of text-based CMC on online social presence. The. Journal of Interactive Online Learning 1, 1–24 (2002)
26. Tu, C-H., Isaacs, M.: An examination of social presence to increase interaction in online classes. American Journal of Distance Education 16, 131–150 (2002)
27. Venkatesh, V., Johnson, P.: Telecommuting Technology Implementations: A Within- and Between- Subjects Longitudinal Field Study. Personnel Psychology 55(3), 661–687 (2002)
28. Whiteman, J.A.M.: Interpersonal Communication in Computer Mediated Learning, White/opinion paper (2002)
29. Zorman, R., David, H.: Female achievement and challenges towards the third millenium. Henrietta Szold Institute Press, Jerusalem (2000)

From Clicks to Touches: Enabling Face-to-Face Shared Social Interface on Multi-touch Tabletops

Chia Shen

MERL - Mitsubishi Electric Research Laboratories
201 Broadway, Cambridge, MA, USA
shen@merl.com

Abstract. Making the interactions with a digital user interface disappears into and becomes a part of the human to human interaction and conversation is a challenge. Conventional metaphor and underlying interface infrastructure for single-user desktop systems have been traditionally geared towards single mouse and keyboard, click-and-type based, WIMP interface design. On the other hand, people usually meet in social context around a table, facing each other. A table setting provides a large interactive visual and tangible surface. It affords and encourages collaboration, coordination, serendipity, as well as simultaneous and parallel interaction among multiple people. In this paper, we examine and explore the opportunities, challenges, research issues, pitfalls, and plausible approaches for enabling direct touchable, shared social interactions on multi-touch multi-user tabletops.

1 Introduction

Multi-touch has been a buzz word of much media attention and technological discussion. One only needs to type in the keyword "multi-touch" in any search engine today to reveal the fervor. Bill Buxton's recent article [2] offers a historical account into how the form factor of this enabling technology has slowly evolved, in the past twenty five years, from universities and laboratories around the world.

Much of the research so far has mainly focused on innovation of multi-touch multi-user input and display devices including tabletops and walls [4] , and the demonstration of individual interaction techniques [1] [3] [5] [15] [21]. Very little is understood and has been studied with respect to full-blown user interfaces and shared interactions that can be deployed in actual applications and our day-to-day lives. What is largely missing is a holistic approach that examines the social, technological, as well as the cognitive potentials, and shortcomings, of this emerging form factor.

On the other hand, one can't help but notice that there are over a billion mice in use today as inputting devices to interact with computers [8]. This is not just a mere commercial success, it underscores the user acceptance and an entire user culture that have developed around this tiny device, after thirty years from the time when the mouse was invented by Engelbart and English in 1965. Inside the quiet offices and homes, in the midst of banking facilities and stock traders, upon the school classroom desks and lab benches, and amongst the hustle and bustle of airports, cafes and bus

D. Schuler (Ed.): Online Communities and Social Comput., HCII 2007, LNCS 4564, pp. 169–175, 2007.

terminals, we hear billions of clicks each day around the world. So it is almost a daunting task for anyone to think about researching another input modality, and to endeavor to develop a user culture around it. Nevertheless, this is the task some of us took on a few years ago.

There have been many earlier and recent attempts at human-computer interactions using touches, gestures, speech and tactile. 1980's Bolt's Put-That-There [3], and the more recent movie "the Minority Report" are two such examples. These projects/designs have provided inspirations, yet not systematic and scientific studies to offer a path and reason for user acceptance beyond the "*wow*" factor.

In the following sections, I will relate the challenges and research issues, and attempt to describe plausible approaches for enabling direct touchable, shared social interactive applications on tabletops.

2   Why Tables? a Paradigm Shift

In social settings, people often gather around a table, let it be a meeting room table, a coffee table, a dinner table or a game table. It is not hard to envision how computational augmentation on these tabletops can enrich and enhance the group experience. Figure 1 illustrates one of our early visions in this paradigm shift. Given the nature of social interaction where the fluidity and expressiveness of the input device, in supporting interactive casualness and serendipity, are inducible to mutual engagement, one would expect that multi-touch and multi-user affordances might be two of the key desirable capabilities for digital tabletops.

Fig. 1. A paradigm shift: Two images from *ACM CHI 2001*. (Left) PhotoFinder [11] demonstration. (Photo courtesy Bill Kules, University of Maryland). (Right) Design of a tabletop story-sharing system called Personal Digital Historian [16], presented at the Design Expo Session.

Since a direct touch interactive table serves both as a visual display and as the user's immediate direct input device, natural hand gestures and intuitive manipulations may be employed to improve the fluidity and reduce the cognitive load of interaction between the user and the digital content. By leveraging the tendency to gather around a table for face-to-face interaction, a horizontal tabletop surface offers affordances and opportunities for building and enhancing co-located collaborative social environments. Moreover, large surfaces such as tabletops offer a spacious work area that may influence meeting styles and group dynamics. The larger area also provides a larger visual field, which may be utilized as external physical memory in order to extend the working memory capacity of people, and as an external cognitive medium.

Although the cynical may see a digital tabletop as simply a vertical touch sensitive display laid down horizontally, this mere re-orientation of the display surface breaks down much of the usual usage patterns and conventions. People treat vertical desktop displays as personal information spaces. Tabletops bear no such connotation. Now, instead of a personal display, it leaps out at the users' visual field and invites them to touch and interact, *together*.

3   Tabletop Opportunities and Challenges for Social Interaction

Physical, non-computationally augmented, tables existed long before computers were invented. Yet, we do not have much experience in the design and implementation of digital tables that provide direct multi-touch affordances. Here we discuss experiences and challenges that tabletop designers may face. Digital tabletop is still in its infancy, design challenges fall into at least three categories: (1) social and psychological effects, (2) UI and interaction techniques, and (3) human tactile and perceptual implications. Some of these challenges stem from the aforementioned "click" centric human-computer interaction culture that has been ingrained for the past few decades. Given that much research has been focusing on the UI and interaction techniques in the recent years [1] [3] [4] [15] [21], the following sections will discuss the social and human tactile/perceptual aspects.

3.1   Social Challenges: Group Interaction, Walk-Up Usage and Shared Multi-device Ecology

When group activities are mediated by a digital tabletop, the group dynamics can be different from when the mediation is through other form factors, such as vertical displays. One set of our controlled studies has shown these effects [7]. In [7], we compared groups' working on either a single vertical display, an array of four vertical displays, or sitting around a horizontal display. An interesting outcome of the study indicated that groups sitting around a tabletop display may not work as fast as sitting in front of a row of multiple displays when given a specific visual search task, but the groups do carry out more inter-personal discussions and communicate more around the tabletop. The egalitarian seating arrangement around a tabletop seems to encourage comfortable interaction amongst participants.

In a broad sense, digital touch tabletops, differing desktop displays and electronic wall displays or whiteboards, have at least two unique personas – (a) offering equal access (almost), and (b) inviting social interaction.

Equal access can imply both shared usage and a lack of permanent ownership. Anyone and everyone can claim the temporary possession of a table for the intended usage session or meeting, then can also just as easily to walk away. Moreover, most of the people today carry one or more personal digital devices with contents that they might want to show and share during these social meetings and encounters. They can leverage the large display space of a digital table.

A multi-touch surface invites all participants to reach out and touch in an egalitarian manner. This entirely deviates from the conventional one-mouse, one-keyboard, single-control interaction, or the one-scribe, one-moderator meeting dynamics. With a non-computationally augmented tabletop, everyone around the table has a socially well-understood personal space [12] [19], and physical documents and objects have a well-defined protocol for handling and sharing. With a multi-touch digital table, there are no established protocols and conventions yet.

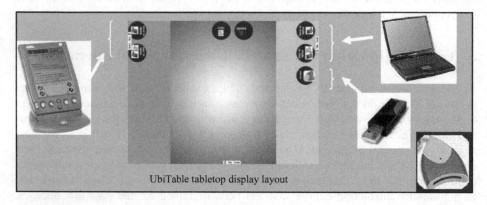

UbiTable tabletop display layout

Fig. 2. UbiTable: Tabletop view and the devices that can share data with the tabletop

One of the social interactive tabletop environment that we have developed is called UbiTable [18]. The UbiTable was intended to provide "walk-up" usage for people to fluidly share the viewing and manipulation of contents from their personal devices, such as PDAs or laptops. In our observational study [5], some interesting user experience and problems arose from group interaction on document sharing.

Since UbiTable used DiamondTouch [cite Dietz] as the physical tabletop platform, we were able to provide two special computational support to the users. First, since the DiamondTouch can tell which seated user is touching which location of the table, this capability was used to designate ownership of documents on the table. If a document is put on the table from a particular user's laptop, that user has full control of the sharing semantics of that document. During our user studies, we used documents with similar contents from different users' laptops and used color borders around the digital display of the documents to indicate the ownership when they are placed on the tabletop. This mechanism seemed to work fine until the users needed to bring (copy) the documents from the tabletop back to their respective laptop. Since the user task required them to take copies of documents that were originated from both each of their own laptop and their meeting partner's laptop, the ownership of documents become blurred.

Second, DiamondTouch allows users to simultaneously touch any location on the tabletop. Therefore, using the UbiTable, the users are able to write and annotate on the exactly the same document at exactly the same time. This brought out unexpected "conflict" resolution issues. Some people took turns to modify a document by verbally negotiating whose turn it is, while others had near-physical 'collisions' (i.e., hands collided inside the same document).

Many opportunities and challenges still remain to be investigated with respect to the value of digital tabletops for social interaction.

3.2 Human Perception and Tactile Input

When people interact over a direct touch surface, some of the problems that one may incur include imprecision with fingers as input devices, occlusion by the operating hand, meaningful usage of multi-hand gestures, multi-user widgets, multiple input tools and multi-modal input. Much of previously published research has addressed these issues and proposed technical solutions [15] [22]. On the other hand, there has not been a body of systematic examination on the effects of direct touch interaction compared with conventional mouse on a tabletop, and the visual effects of viewing information horizontally.

Visual distortion is a phenomenon that people encounter and are accustomed to daily. Given sufficient contextual information, people are good at correctly perceive what appear to be distorted. However, in social settings, the presentation of information to be perceived on a horizontal tabletop surface may need to be carefully thought out so that the orientation, rotation, and position of information to be shared can be most conducive for the collaboration and flow of conversation. Figure 3 illustrates this difference between information perceivable on a vertical display (right) and that on a tabletop (left). From our first set of user evaluations, our findings indicate that data values encoded in position (as in x, y axis on a tabletop) are less accurately perceived on a tabletop than those encoded in length (as in bar charts).

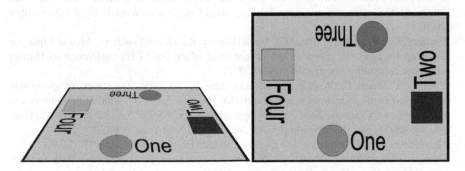

Fig. 3. Perceptual distortion due to planar rotational distortion [wigdor 07]

One of the compelling usage scenarios of a direct touch tabletop is when people can use bimanual (two-handed) interactive metaphors to manipulate digital objects, such as those described in [1] [22]. However, when it comes to performance in terms of speed, error and user preference, do bare hands outperform the well-accepted, well-understood mice? Our most recent study [6] suggests that people benefit from bimanual direct bare hand input techniques on a tabletop, while for single point inter-action, a mouse would be a better choice for performance.

4 Let There Be Touches

In this paper, we have offered a brief look at some of the challenges, opportunities and issues regarding the support for interactions around multi-touch digital tabletops. We focused on how simultaneous touches, horizontality, group interaction and visual information encoding can be challenging in the design of tabletop user interfaces and interaction techniques. We have only made initial strides in examining the effects of various aspects of multi-touch tabletop designs on human perception and tactile op-erations.   Much still remains to be studied in order to derive full benefits for social interaction using this exciting new form factor.

References

1. Benko, H., Wilson, A.D., Baudisch, P.: Precise Selection Techniques for Multi-Touch Screens. In: Proc. ACM CHI 2006 (CHI'06: Human Factors in Computing Systems), pp. 1263–1272 (2006)
2. Buxton, B.: (Retrieved on January 30 2007)
   http:// www.billbuxton.com/ multitouchOverview.html
3. Bolt, R.A.: Put-that-there: Voice and gesture at the graphics interface. In: Proc ACM Conf. Computer Graphics and Interactive Techniques Seattle, pp. 262–270 (1980)
4. Dietz, P., Leigh, D.: DiamondTouch: a multi-user touch technology. In: Proceedings of the 14th Annual ACM Symposium on User interface Software and Technology. UIST '01, Or-lando, Florida, November 11 - 14, 2001, pp. 219–226. ACM Press, New York, NY (2001)
5. Everitt, K., Forlines, C., Ryall, K., Shen, C.: Observations of a Shared Tabletop User Study, ACM Conference on Computer Supported Cooperative Work (CSCW) (November 2004)
6. Forlines, C., Wigdor, D., Shen, C., Balakrishnan, R.: Direct-Touch vs. Mouse Input for Tabletop Displays. To appear in the Proceedings of the 2007 CHI conference on Human factors in computing systems (In press) (2007)
7. Forlines, C., Shen, C., Wigdor, D., Balakrishnan, R.: Exploring the effects of group size and display configuration on visual search. In: Proceedings of the 2006 20th Anniversary Conference on Computer Supported Cooperative Work. CSCW '06, Banff, Alberta, Can-ada, November 04 - 08, 2006, pp. 11–20. ACM Press, New York, NY (2006)
8. Hutchinson, A.: CHI pioneers. The Ottawa Citizen (Thursday, September 07, 2006)
9. Ryall, K., Ringel Morris, M., Everitt, K., Forlines, C., Shen, C.: Experiences With and Ob-servations of Direct-Touch Tables, In: First IEEE International Workshop Proceedings of the Horizontal Interactive Human-Computer Systems, TableTop 2006 (Adelaide, South Australia, 2006), pp. 89–96 (2006)
10. Ryall, K., Forlines, C., Shen, C., Morris, M.R.: Exploring the effects of group size and ta-ble size on interactions with tabletop shared-display groupware. In: Proceedings of the 2004 ACM Conference on Computer Supported Cooperative Work. CSCW '04, Chicago, Illinois, USA, November 06 - 10, 2004, pp. 284–293. ACM Press, New York, NY (2004)
11. http://www.cs.umd.edu/hcil/photolib/

12. Scott, S.D.: Territoriality in Collaborative Tabletop Workspaces. Ph.D. thesis, Department of Computer Science, University of Calgary (2005)
13. Sears, A., Shneiderman, B.: High precision touchscreens: design strategies and comparisons with a mouse. International Journal of Man.-Machine Studies 34(4), 593–613 (1991)
14. Shneiderman, B., Kang, H., Kules, B., Plaisant, C., Rose, A., Rucheir, R.: A photo history of SIGCHI: evolution of design from personal to public. ACM Interactions 9(3), 17–23 (2002)
15. Shen, C., Vernier, F.D., Forlines, C., Ringel, M.: DiamondSpin: an extensible toolkit for around-the-table interaction. In: Proceedings of the SIGCHI Conference on Human Factors in Computing Systems. CHI '04, Vienna, Austria, April 24 - 29, 2004, pp. 167–174. ACM Press, New York, NY (2004)
16. Shen, C., Lesh, N., Moghaddam, B., Beardsley, P., Bardsley, R.S.: Personal digital historian: user interface design. In: CHI '01 Extended Abstracts on Human Factors in Computing Systems. CHI '01, Seattle, Washington, March 31 - April 05, 2001, pp. 29–30. ACM Press, New York, NY (2001)
17. Shen, C., Lesh, N.B., Vernier, F., Forlines, C., Frost, J.: Sharing and building digital group histories. In: Proceedings of the 2002 ACM Conference on Computer Supported Cooperative Work. CSCW '02, New Orleans, Louisiana, USA, November 16 - 20, 2002, pp. 324–333. ACM Press, New York, NY (2002)
18. Shen, C., Everitt, K., Ryall, K.: UbiTable: Impromptu Face-to-Face Collaboration on Horizontal Interactive Surfaces. In: Dey, A.K., Schmidt, A., McCarthy, J.F. (eds.) UbiComp 2003. LNCS, vol. 2864, pp. 281–288. Springer, Heidelberg (2003)
19. Sommer, R.: Personal Space: The Behaviour Basis of Design. Prentice-Hall, Englewood Cliffs, NJ (1969)
20. Tse, E., Shen, C., Greenberg, S., Forlines, C.: How Pairs Interact Over a Multimodal Digital Table. To appear in the Proceedings of the 2007 CHI conference on Human factors in computing systems (In press) (2007)
21. Wigdor, D., Shen, C., Forlines, C., Balakrishnan, R.: Perception of Elementary Graphical Elements in Tabletop and Multi-Surface Environments. To appear in the Proceedings of the 2007 CHI conference on Human factors in computing systems (In press) (2007)
22. Wu, M., Shen, C., Ryall, K., Forlines, C., Balakrishnan, R.: Gesture Registration, Relaxation, and Reuse for Multi-Point Direct-Touch Surfaces. In: First IEEE International Workshop Proceedings of the Horizontal Interactive Human-Computer Systems, TableTop 2006 (Adelaide, South Australia, 2006), pp. 183–190 (2006)

Physical Representation Social Presence with Interactive Grass

Jui Hang Shih, Teng-Wen Chang, Hui-Mei Hong, and Tian-Chiu Li

Graduate School of Computational Deisgn, National Yunlin University of
Science and Technology
{g9434707,tengwen,g9434713,g9434714}@yuntech.edu.tw

Abstract. The hypothesis that happy team members are more cooperative than sad team members has become a popular presumption in social and applied psychology. The member negatively may affect the emotion, mood or attitudes, and continually annoys the rest in the team, and positive either. Also, how do es team member learn more adaptive emotion strategies in complex relationship. This paper introduces a research program on social presence theory and practice of technology creation based on application of emotional physical device. The simple concept of our study is to create an interactive system of expression in the following areas: (1) Theoretical Research: research of social presence and the team members in adopted an emotion system; we will study social media concept in scientific fields, and then establish a program of slow theology. (2) The interactive table as human emotion.

Keywords: Emotion, Social media, Adaptive, Affective, Interactive Behavior, Corporation design.

1 Introduction

The interface problem within an office is not a fancy media or a high-tech innovated design, but a social surface between office workers and their cooperated members. Furthermore, emotional control is the most needed but very difficult to achieve requirement for an efficient working environment.

A typical office environment will have a higher productivity only if they have an efficient and sometime happiness atmosphere as a working environment. Plants, office furniture and the desktop software that lie on every desktop of people in the office are affecting everyday's working life.

In addition, with current state-of-the-art technology developed over the years such as calm technology [1], ubiquitous computing and ambient intelligence, computing has got a social status that has never been achieved before. Computing has become a social media and aiding social and collaboration further with more activities and social psychology studies.

2 The Problem

Experiences of positive emotions can transform us into more creative, resilient, socially integrated, and healthy individuals [2]. We found that group mood is typically

D. Schuler (Ed.): Online Communities and Social Comput., HCII 2007, LNCS 4564, pp. 176–181, 2007.

awareness at team. Most members have traditionally express on facial expression. As such, to learn what the best adaptive way is and let most team members learn to manage their emotions by observing others in the workplace.

Hide negative or positive emotions. Hidden emotional control and the visualization of such hidden emotion. Even a team member wants to achieve a better productive but still will be affected by the implicit emotional acts and turn this will not discuss about meaning emotional acts.[6] Emotional acts still affect the mood of cooperation and atmosphere of working environment.

Slow technology. With the technology described above, we propose a system to collect and represent a new communication process. With the timing process, the concept of slow technology has been used for the time/slowness of such interaction. Time is the cue.

2.1 Calm Technology

Calm technology is the very important design problem of the twenty-first century [1], we do not watch at it or near it to take advantage of its peripheral clues and it will communicate both light and network by integrating with human information processing. You do not need to take any space on your existing computer screen or contain a computer at all.

2.2 Silence/Ambient Media

Silence the simply defined is the absence of sound. There are two aspects to sound: Its generation and its perception. An ambient in which events and states in both physical and computational environment is reflected in the form of intrusive audio cues. [1]

2.3 Ambient Furniture

Ambient lighting or component system integrated with furniture can be changed by reversal of the yoke of one or more supporting fixture heads for mounting structures [3].

2.4 What Are the Domains We Are Aiming and Studying for This Problem?

How to use interactive interface to utilize emotional information for social objective have been noted, including: (1) individuals differ in workgroup how to harness their own emotion but represent in some other way; (2) What kind of emotions information and moods is used to motivate and assist in improved whole team performance; (3) Discover that moods may be able to facilitate more creative or affection responses and native doesn't. (4) Press blurred emotions and moods information can subtly and systematically influence certain strategies components and affecting workgroup relationship.

3 Related Works

With the technology described above, we propose a system to collect and represent a new communication process. With the timing process, the concept of slow technology has been used for the time/slowness of such interaction.

Collecting information: we cannot sense or collect implicit biological information such as emotion, intention, speaking tone and attitudes and eyes' sight. Even so, some technology like forum, such as blog, MSN title and anonymous email and bulletin board will somehow unleash the inner feeling of personal emotion.

We can not convey most things as accurately as usually required. But when talking about something such as emotions, feelings and sensations we can only relate to someone else's experience through reference to our own. What we see, hear and what we can diagrammatically think are close to what others seeing but when it comes down to feeling, emotion and other kinds of we can not sensation. But describing human emotion directly without the use of any other perceptions information, sensory or what the following feelings like is difficult. [4]

MSN Messenger offers consumers integrated and easy ways to communicate the way they want with the people they care about paging colorful and capabilities icons, like smiley faces, that let them express their emotions in IM conversations, all from the MSN Messenger user interface. It has experienced lets people successful personalize emotions such as happiness, sadness or love using the new face and heart icons.

4 How We Approach

With the technology described above, we propose a system to collect and represent a new communication process. With the timing process, the concept of slow technology has been used for the time/slowness of such interaction. [5]

Our own emotional state and our perception of that of others with which we collaborate influence the Outcome of cooperative work. The evolution of media has decreased the significance of physical device in the experience of people's emotion. One can understand how an audience to a social concept is with being physically present and one can communicate not directly with others without facing in the same place. With the growing grass and computational support for the recognition and representation of emotions, there is a clear interest in adding such facilities to social media and to evaluate the positive and negative effects of using this emotion icon from personal computers by internet. In this paper we discuss the social presence with involved in supporting a new type of collaborative awareness in Physical representation system.[6]

The emotional awareness also present more adventured and invaded, intruded emotion-based applications. [7] It means how if one privately affects other's grass. If you have more passive emotion you also make some way to push the weather comptroller and change the whole situation maybe someone be encouraged cause the "silent helping". Then we will provide new generation "*table lawn*" grass social presence system.

The new computational model of emotion-based applications in real time affective-cognitive of physical receive from nonverbal cues such as head and growing displays of grass, and communicates these inferences by the intruded wearer [8]. While the social media with computing is still relative new, further motivated and exciting work in this area within the social presence of collaborative community has started to motivate and inspire more researchers like us nowadays [9].

5 The Implementation

"Grass" is an affective and inactive people emotion representation system that explores ways to augment and enhance the physical emotional-social intelligence (shown in Fig. 1).

We make a working table with real grass and weather control system inside, the regimen right for "table lawn" care will vary, according to the group or team member emotion, if their expression changes to happy, the "planting cultural system" adapts so that the water and sun light are vibrant and more subtly applied (shown in Fig. 2).

There are numerous ways in which emotional awareness can be used in personal *Widget emotion online tool*. The user's privately "emotion icon" of widget emotion tool needs to identify the positive and negative implications of computer-mediated affective communications whether your lawn is composed of a warm season   turf grass or a cool season turf grass. Examples of each "emotion icon" are given. The planting cultural system likes the real weather central by each person. We think the emotion face's information just temporary, our digital device and online software can receive more referable information. In this project, not just switch the weather system, we have some analysis processing and methodology. We do not want to represent the each member's for a short time period. In addition, we want to see the affection in a gradual change of whole team and "grass".

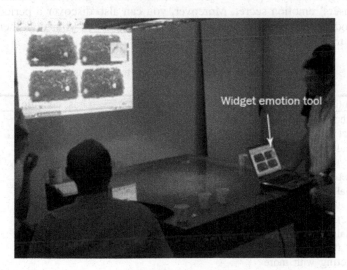

Fig. 1. Using Grass online with widget

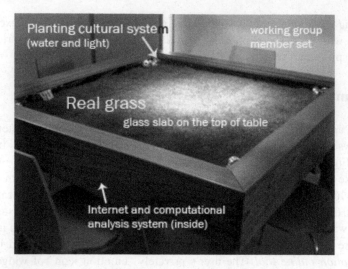

Fig. 2. Grass table's structure

5.1 Framework

The Grass was divided into three parts. One is the emotion information receive area, another one is ecological area and the last one is weathering area. The emotion information receive area will collect the emotion sight from each member then process and analysis to order weather system change the whether inside table. We have the real nature plants in table, the effect just do to living things. Members' emotion will express on the grass. If you pass the grass not only see the grass, but you can also see this table users' emotion secret. Moreover, you can also discover a period of somebody's mood silently privately and make you a metaphor of your own then the emotion begins to communicate with each other.

Table 1. Weather type related to emotions

Emotional style	The following weather	Grass condition
1st-the emotion is quiet with less social activities	**Light raining**	Growing slowly
2nd- the emotion is quiet with more social activities	**Heavy light**	Growing steady but die slowly
3rd- the emotion is exacting with less social activities	**Heavy light and steady rain**	Growing fast
4th- the emotion is exacting with more social activities	**Heavy light and rain**	destruction

5.2 The Weather Analysis

We collate the team member's emotion information and try to simulate the most approaching real mood. Further, we also compare the social activity information. It is the better way to analyze the member's mood, because the emotion is related to relationship of workgroup.

6 How We Learn from Grass

The relationship of team members have outcomes in hidden or blurry way and express the emotions on indirectly performance will grow some cues to let the stoical subtraction to adapt real emotions.

The value of the project is affording new interface for hidden emotion but can still commutate. In addition, the metaphor of emotion each discovered can develop new communication and new social media. Furthermore, we can conclusion in noted point: (1) if individuals differ in workgroup could express their own emotion; the group will have some well mood regulation. (2) Will any emotions information and moods is very easily used to discover and the whole team mood directly affects workgroup relationship.

References

1. Mark, W., John Seely, B.: Designing Calm Technology. Xerox PARC (1995)
2. Douglas, J.: Configurable furniture integrated ambient lighting system and method. NSI Enterprises, Inc (1999)
3. Fredrickson, B.L.: The role of positive emotions in positive psychology: The broaden-and-build theory of positive emotions. Psychologist American, 218–226 (2001)
4. Short, J.A., Williams, E., Christie, B.: The social psychology of telecommunications. John Wiley & Sons, New York (1976)
5. Dyer, M.G.: Emotions and their computations: Three computer model. Cognition & Emotion (1987)
6. McCauley, T.L., Franklin, S.: An Architecture for Emotion. AAAI Fall Symposium Emotional and intelligent (1998)
7. Ortony, A.: Is Guilt an Emotion? Cognition & Emotion I, pp. 283–298 (1987)
8. Pfeifer, R.: Artificial Intelligence Models of Emotion Congnitive Perspectives on Emotion and Motivation, pp. 287–320 (1988)
9. Picard, R.: Does HAL cry digital tears? Emotion and computers. 2001's Computer as Dream and Reality (1997)

Artistic Data Visualization:
Beyond Visual Analytics

Fernanda B. Viégas and Martin Wattenberg

Visual Communication Lab, IBM Research, 1 Rogers St,
Cambridge, MA 02142, USA
{viegasf,mwatten}@us.ibm.com

Abstract. Information visualization is traditionally viewed as a tool for data exploration and hypothesis formation. Because of its roots in scientific reasoning, visualization has traditionally been viewed as an analytical tool for sensemaking. In recent years, however, both the mainstreaming of computer graphics and the democratization of data sources on the Internet have had important repercussions in the field of information visualization. With the ability to create visual representations of data on home computers, artists and designers have taken matters into their own hands and expanded the conceptual horizon of infovis as artistic practice. This paper presents a brief survey of projects in the field of artistic information visualization and a preliminary examination of how artists appropriate and repurpose "scientific" techniques to create pieces that actively guide analytical reasoning and encourage a contextualized reading of their subject matter.

Keywords: Visualization, Art.

1 Introduction

Data visualization is usually viewed as a tool to support analytic reasoning. This reflects its roots in science—ranging the economic charts of William Playfair to Richard Feynman's diagrams for performing calculations in quantum field theory. Researchers in the scientific visualization community have naturally focused on supporting scientific analytic tasks.

In recent years there has been a renewed interest in infovis' role as an intelligence tool for military and national security applications. (This too has historical roots: several visualizations of war have become touchstones for information designers: e.g., the 1869 chart by Minard of Napoleon's march to Moscow and Florence Nightingale's diagram of patient mortality in military field hospitals.) Visual analytics, the combination of infovis and mathematical deduction to extract patterns in massive, dynamically changing information spaces has, of late, become one of the main themes of the visualization academic community. As with research that supports scientific visualization, the emphasis has been on visualization as a tool for dispassionate analysis.

This relentless focus on visualization as a neutral tool may appear to be a forced move. At first, bias in a visualization might seem like a technical problem, much like

D. Schuler (Ed.): Online Communities and Social Comput., HCII 2007, LNCS 4564, pp. 182–191, 2007.
© Springer-Verlag Berlin Heidelberg 2007

chromatic aberration in a telescope. Yet a recent, separate stream of thought in visualization calls this assumption into question.

109 Homes for Sale,
Seattle/Tacoma

117 Homes for Sale,
Chicagoland

124 Homes for Sale,
The 5 Boroughs

121 Homes for Sale,
LA/Orange County

114 Homes for Sale,
Dallas/Ft. Worth Metroplex

112 Homes for Sale,
Miami-Dade County

Fig. 1. Homes for Sale, Digital C-prints by Jason Salavon

In the past decade a second very different type of information visualization has flourished. Art based on data has been featured at institutions such as the Whitney Museum of American Art [4] and the San Francisco Museum of Modern Art. [1]. Often such artwork is directly based on techniques first explored by the academic community. At the Austrian Ars Electronica art festival in 2004, a visitor could see interactive treemaps in one exhibit [18], play with an installation by Brad Paley based on social network analysis [10], and hear Josh On talk about his use of graph drawing a discussion panel.

While the basic techniques used by these artists would be familiar to those in the scientific visualization community, their motivations and creations are new and different. In this paper we explore the implications of the surge of artistic interest in visualization. In section 2, we define our terms and describe some useful context. Section 3, the core of the paper, consists of a set of analyses of several prominent examples of artistic visualizations. Finally, in section 4 we make some suggestions about what the academic visualization community might learn from artists on visualization.

2 Definitions and Background

Defining what constitutes "artistic" visualization is hard, if only because defining art itself is hard. To sidestep that philosophical question, our working definition in this paper is that artistic visualizations are visualizations of data done by artists with the intent of making art. This definition may seem like a tautology, but in fact it specifies a coherent and interesting class of work.

First, the artworks must be based on actual data, rather than the metaphors or surface appearance of visualization. Many artists have used diagrammatic imagery as a base for their projects. One example is Simon Patterson, whose "Great Bear" relabels the famous map of the London Underground [10], and whose "J.P.233 in C.S.O. Blue" [12] appropriates imagery from a map of airline routes. While Patterson's work has many merits, it cannot be said to be data visualization since there is no underlying mapping between data and image.

A second point is that our definition avoids the issue of beauty: we do not contend that beautiful scientific visualizations are automatically artistic, or that visualization art must be pretty. Thus a microscope photograph taken as part of a scientific experiment would not qualify under our definition: no matter how beautiful the colors, the photograph would lack artistic intent. As the examples below show, focusing on intent rather than surface aesthetics provides a coherent category of work with important distinguishing characteristics from scientific visualizations.

A natural question is why this new type of visualization (or this new style of art) has emerged. Any answer to this question is speculative, but two particular factors are relevant. First is the emergence of software tools that are appropriate for artistic production of data visualizations. Today one does not require a supercomputer or fluency in C++ to create visualizations. Instead, it is possible to create sophisticated visualization software using cheap hardware and friendly development environments such as Flash (www.adobe.com/) or Processing (www.processing.org).

A second factor is that data has become part of the cultural discourse on several levels. Thanks to the internet, complex data sets such as SEC filings are available with a few clicks. Indeed, the internet itself can be viewed as a massive database. Moreover, government and corporate collections of data now play a critical role in the lives of citizens of many nations. As a result, it is natural that artists want to grapple with the issues raised by the controlling power of data.

3 Artistic Visualization Projects

To understand the issues raised by artistic visualization, it is helpful to have a set of concrete examples in mind. In this section we provide descriptions of projects that have been successful in the artistic community and that use sophisticated visualizations of data. This is, by no means, supposed to be an exhaustive survey of the area—such an undertaking is well beyond the scope of this paper. Instead, we have chosen to focus on a purposeful sample of projects that highlight some of the central qualities of artistic visualizations.

3.1 Jason Salavon and the Power of Colored Pixels

If information visualization enables the viewer to see unexpected patterns in a body of data, Jason Salavon's art pieces confront the viewer with inescapable, pervasive patterns in everyday life [13]. From innocuous mementos such as high-school year books (Fig. 2) to racy centerfolds of adult magazines (Fig. 3), Salavon blurs individual pieces to focus our attention on the collective aggregation of human experience.

Take, for instance, *Homes for Sale* (Fig. 1), which shows a series of realtor photos of single-family homes for sale in different cities around the U.S. Each piece encompasses a collection of homes on the market in a given metro region in the median price range for that area. The images are constructed by taking the mean averaging color of every photo, pixel by pixel. The result is a blurred view of an area's weather pattern and ghostly images of the houses for sale. Miami boasts the bluest sky whereas Dallas has the greenest grass. Seattle, on the other hand, seems awash in an assortment of gloomy grays.

Salavon utilizes the same averaging technique to explore a wide variety of themes that permeate visual culture. *The Class of 1988* and *The Class of 1967* (Fig. 2), for instance, are part of a series of pieces investigating rites of passage—in this case, high school graduation—and the conventional visual mementos that get produced to celebrate such events.

The Class of 1988

The Class of 1967

Fig. 2. Class of 1988 and The Class of 1967, by Jason Salavon

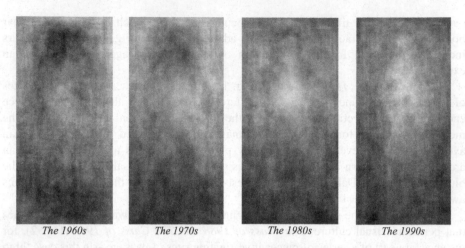

The 1960s   The 1970s   The 1980s   The 1990s

Fig. 3. Every Playboy Centerfold, The Decades (normalized), by Jason Salavon

In *Every Playboy Centerfold, The Decades* (Fig. 3), the colored images confirm the formulaic compositions of the adult industry and the change in taste over the years. Skin tones and hair color get lighter as time goes by.

To be certain, the technique of averaging the color of pixels in a collection of images is not new. In fact, computer scientists have utilized the same mechanism in a variety of applications in the field of image processing [16]. Whereas the intent in most of these applications is to use pixel manipulations as input to face recognition algorithms, Salavon's subverts this original goal. The artist exposes the technique as the output of his piece by letting the collection of individual images dissolve into a field of color that carries meaning in itself.

Expanding on the theme of pure color, Salavon has also explored the concept of narrative through the arrangement of colored pixels in an image. For *The Top Grossing Film of All Time, 1 x 1* (Fig. 4), the artist digitized the movie *Titanic* in its entirety and extracted individual frames. Each frame was averaged to a single color best representative of that image. Reading from left-to-right and top-to-bottom, the narrative is laid out in color. One can see the rich golden tones depicting the luxurious interior of the ship half-way through the movie. Towards the end, there is a highly "pixilated" band of color that reflects the climatic point in the story where the ship sinks and the camera moves frantically between scenes. Finally, almost at the bottom of the image, deep tones of blue dominate, reminding us of the chilling scenes where passengers float scattered in the ocean.

3.2 Golan Levin and the Power of Numbers

Is the number 7 trendier than the number 13? Why is 2323 more popular than 2354? *The Secret Lives of Numbers* [7] is an interactive system that invites the viewer to

Fig. 4. The Top Grossing Film of All Time, 1 x 1

explore how the usage patterns of numbers reflect culture, history, and biology. The data represents the "popularity" of every integer between 0 and 100000, collected between 1997 and 2002 from a popular web search engine. The results form an unexpected portrait of our cultural relationship to integers: we love certain numbers and disregard others.

In this piece, Golan Levin borrows heavily from the formal vocabulary of scientific visualization. By juxtaposing multiple, coordinated panels of information, the artist succeeds in building a dashboard-like display where the viewer can query a sizable amount of data. Whereas the middle panel displays a histogram-like representation of the popularity of numbers, the right pane contains a matrix of the same information. Numbers on the matrix run left-to-right, top-to-bottom, where each pixel represents an integer. The lighter a pixel is, the more popular that number is. The viewer can immediately see patterns such as the band of popular number at the top of the matrix (0 to 1,000) and the diagonal line of light pixels (numbers with repeated digits such as 1212 and 4545). Finally, a white band of numbers representing years reminds us of our fierce dependence on time.

The remarkable twist in this piece is its seemingly random data set: a collection of numbers with no strings attached. The fact that Levin places the data set in such a traditional infovis setting, with amazing interaction capabilities—smooth transitions, beautiful brushing and querying capabilities—increases the feeling of neutrality and scientific purpose. In fact, the artist reveals just how culturally meaningful even the most arbitrary data set might be.

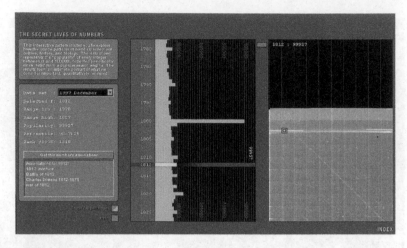

Fig. 5. The Secret Lives of Numbers, by Golan Levin and collaborators

3.3 Last Clock

Given the widespread presence of surveillance cameras in cities, video output has become one of the most pervasive kinds of data around. Artists have taken notice of this abundance and are experimenting with ways to capture some of the most evocative aspects of the medium.

South Kensington, London   *BBC 2, Golf*   *Big Brother, Channel 4*

Fig. 6. Last Clock, by Jussi Ängeslevä & Ross Cooper

Last Clock [2] uses video footage to record time. Like an analogue clock, it has a second hand, a minute hand and an hour hand. The hands are arranged in concentric circles, the outermost circle being seconds, the middle circle is minutes, and the innermost circle hours. Each of the hands of the Last Clock are made from a slice of live video feed. As the hands rotate around the face of the clock they leave a trace of what has been happening in front of the camera.

After a few hours running, the clock becomes a unique emblem of its surroundings. Not useful for either surveillance or video watching, the visualization succeeds in creating a powerful record of time and place.

3.4 They Rule

Social networks have become powerful tools of analysis and discourse over the past decade [17]. Visualizations of social networks followed along, becoming quite popular as well [6]. The scientific community is awash with node-and-link graphs showing clusters of connections in communities ranging from small villages to massive web sites for teenagers.

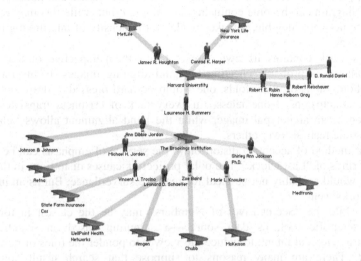

Fig. 7. "Why Harvard Doesn't Fund Alternative Health Care Research," created by Shojo on the They Rule web site

In *They Rule* [9], Josh On utilizes this scientific method to reveal power structures in American companies. The web site visualizes the members of directory boards of some of the most powerful U.S. companies, which share many of the same directors. The graphs reveal that some individuals sit on multiple companies, exposing webs of inbred influence that the viewer might not have been aware of (Fig. 7). The site allows users to browse through these interlocking directories and run searches on boards and companies. Users can also save maps of connections and email links of these maps to others.

Josh On follows in the steps of previous artists who appropriated the grammar of social network theory to create narratives of unsuspected influence in society. Mark Lombardi [8], for instance, was an abstract painter who created a series of hand-drawn node-and-link graphs to illustrate the way money flows in western countries; from banking institutions to the Catholic Church, from corporations to political organizations, and so forth. *They Rule* contributes to this tradition by adding the element of updateable data sets and interactive capabilities.

4 Discussion and Conclusion

All these projects share one characteristic that distinguishes them from traditional visualization tools: Each embodies a forceful point of view. In a sense, the artworks derive their power from the fact that the artists are committing various sins of visual analytics. It is worth reviewing the projects in this light.

"Theyrule" guides the viewer to a particular type of conclusion about capitalist power structure. (To use it for executive recruiting would miss the point.) It accomplishes this through a variety of mechanisms—the austere color scheme and the careful imagery used in its icons, for instance. More subtly, it deliberately exploits some of the pitfalls of network visualizations. If too many nodes and links are on the screen, the diagram can become confusing and tangled: but while this may make the details of the network illegible, it makes readable the density of interlinking between circles of power.

Salavon's work contains its own "sins." From the perspective of a computer scientist, Salavon is probably cheating by hand-aligning images. In his images of yearbook photographs or centerfolds, one would be hard pressed to draw any sort of quantitative conclusions. Nonetheless, this very lack of crispness translates into a poetic notion of an archetypal image, while the hand alignment allows Salavon to emphasize some features over others.

A similar method of accepting distortion in the service of emphasis can be seen in the circular rings of "Last Clock." The polar projection causes distortions in the video images and would probably not be ideal for real-life surveillance. But as an image of a clock it works well.

Finally, while the "Secret Lives of Numbers" may be the closest in form to a traditional scientific tool, its data source—a sampling based on search engine results—betrays its real intent: to induce the viewer to ponder the roles of numbers in our culture. There are many reasons to suppose that search result counts are inaccurate and biased, but this fact in no way detracts from the value of the piece.

These distortions are not mistakes on the part of the artists. The value of the artworks rests on the fact that their creators recognize the power of visualization to express a point of view. By contrast, traditional analytic visualization tools have sought to minimize distortions, since these may interfere with dispassionate analysis.

Is it possible that this focus on minimizing "point of view" is misguided? For one thing, it is generally impossible to create a visualization that is truly neutral, just as it is impossible to create a flat map of the Earth's surface without distorting distances. Indeed, cartographers have long recognized that these distortions cannot be ignored. Perhaps instead of seeking simply to minimize the intrusion of point-of-view, a more realistic attitude for a designer of a visualization should be, as with traditional maps, to choose which perspective is the right one for a given analytic task.

A more radical change in attitude would be to embrace the fact that visualizations can be used to persuade as well as analyze. Neutral analysis is not the only important task in life. It's easy to associate persuasion with the sales-oriented "pitch culture" decried by Edward Tufte [15], but there are often valid reasons to want to change the way people think and it may be that much of the value of visualization comes from its ability to change attitudes. A useful context for this line of thinking is the study of "captology" or technology used in the service of persuasion [5] as well as the classical study of rhetoric and oratory.

To summarize, we have seen a surge of interest in data visualization in the artistic community. Many data-oriented artworks use sophisticated visualization techniques that have been developed in academia, but at the same time the techniques are used in a very different style. The information visualization community has a long interdisciplinary tradition, and it is worth asking what might be learned from the current artistic explorations. We suggest that one answer to this question might lie in the artistic use of a particular point of view or persuasive goal. Should data visualization researchers investigate ways to support making a point, as well as disinterested analysis?

References

1. 010101, Exhibit at the San Francisco Museum of Modern Art (2001)
2. Ängeslevä, J., Cooper, R.: Last Clock http://www.lastclock.co.uk/
3. Chung, P., Thomas, J.: Visual Analytics. Retrieved on Feb 6 2007 from: http://infoviz.pnl.gov/pdf/visualAnalytics.pdf
4. Data Dynamics Exhibit, Whitney Museum of American Art (2001)
5. Fogg, B.J.: Persuasive Technology: Using Computers to Change What We Think and Do. Morgan Kaufman, San Francisco (2002)
6. Freeman, L.: Visualizing Social Networks. Journal of Social Structure, vol. 1 (2000)
7. Levin, G., Wattenberg, M., Feinberg, J., Becker, D., Elashoff, D., Wynecoop, S.: The Secret Lives of Numbers. http://www.turbulence.org/Works/nums/
8. Lombardi, M., Hobbs, R.C., Richards, J.: Mark Lombardi: Global Networks. Independent Curators (2003)
9. On, J.: They Rule (2001) http://www.theyrule.net/
10. Paley, W., Han, J.: Trace Encounters. Ars Electronica, Linz, Austria (2004)
11. Patterson, S.: The Great Bear. Tate Museum Collection, lithograph on paper (1992)
12. Patterson, S.: J.P.233 in C.S.O. Tate Musuem Collection, household emulsion paint installation (1992)
13. Salavon, J.: The Salavon Studio. http://salavon.com/
14. Thomas, J.J., Cook, K.A.: Illuminating the Path: The Research and Development Agenda for Visual Analytics. IEEE CS Press, Los Alamitos (2005)
15. Tufte, E.: Beautiful Evidence. Graphics Press, Cheshire (2006)
16. Turk, M., Pentland, A.: Face recognition using eigenfaces. In: Proc. IEEE Conference on Computer Vision and Pattern Recognition, pp. 586–591 (1991)
17. Wellman, B., Berkowitz, S.D. (eds.): Networks as Personal Communities. In: Social Structures: A Network Analysis, pp. 130–184, Cambridge University Press, Cambridge, UK (1988)
18. Weskamp, M.: Newsmap (2004) http://www.marumushi.com/apps/newsmap/

Social Puppets: Towards Modular Social Animation for Agents and Avatars

Hannes Vilhjalmsson[1], Chirag Merchant[2], and Prasan Samtani[3]

[1] CADIA, Reykjavík University
Kringlan 1, IS-103 Reykajvík, Iceland
hannes@ru.is
[2] USC Institute for Creative Technologies
13274 Fiji Way, Marina del Rey, CA 90292, USA
merchant@ict.usc.edu
[3] USC Information Sciences Institute
4676 Admiralty Way, Marina del Rey, CA 90292, USA
samtani@isi.edu

Abstract. State-of-the-art computer graphics can give autonomous agents a compelling appearance as animated virtual characters. Typically the agents are directly responsible for controlling their graphical representation, but this places too much burden on the agents that already deal with difficult high-level tasks such as dialog planning. This paper presents work, done in the context of an interactive language and culture training system, on a new kind of engine that fits between the high level cognitive agent models and the animated graphics that represent them. This is a social engine that generates socially appropriate nonverbal behavior based on rules reflecting social norms. Similar to modular physics engines, the social engine introduces a re-usable component that can heighten believability of animated agents in games and simulations with relatively little effort.

1   Introduction

Autonomous agents that interact with humans are found in applications ranging from health intervention to computer games. It is important for many of these applications to create a sense of face-to-face interaction with the agents and therefore they have benefited from modern graphics hardware that is capable of rendering a realistic physical appearance in real-time. After the agent software processes user input and generates agent responses, it typically calls a graphics engine to deliver speech and animation through an articulated face or body. This may suffice in a relatively constrained dialog environment, but take this into a dynamic 3D environment, such as the interactive world of games, and the physical delivery of spoken responses becomes more complex.

How does the animated body know that it is within hearing distance of its addressee before speaking? How does it visually indicate to those around it that it has something to say? How does it perform a specific co-verbal gesture when the spatial configuration of participants changes? How does it know it is not speaking out of turn? It is hard to avoid awkward social moments when the division between mind and body is absolute,

D. Schuler (Ed.): Online Communities and Social Comput., HCII 2007, LNCS 4564, pp. 192–201, 2007.
© Springer-Verlag Berlin Heidelberg 2007

such as is the case when agent software, oblivious to physical surroundings, hands responses off to a graphics engine that is oblivious to the social situation.

It is possible to extend the original autonomous agent model to deal with all of these physical factors, but that places a lot of burden on a process that already has its hands full with coming up with the next thing to say. Besides, we should be able to generalize and re-use a model that carries out nonverbal behavior according to social norms. They are called norms for a reason.

In fact, this is similar to the situation where we have an agent that we want to behave realistically inside a world governed by Newtonian physics while also pursuing its high level goals. It would make for poor portability if we needed to re-implement our laws of physics every time we changed our agent models. Similar to attaching skeletal geometry to a "rag-doll" object inside a specialized physics engine and giving the physical simulation full control over its joints when the laws of physics need to apply, one can imaging plugging an agent into a social structure that ensures that the rules of social nonverbal behavior are observed as the agent pursues its goals in the world.

This paper describes work that was done as part of developing a system for rapidly teaching new languages and culture through an engaging social game environment. This overall system will be described in section 3 after the following review of related work. The role and implementation of the novel Social Puppets module will be discussed in section 4, followed by future work and conclusions.

2 Related Work

Agents simulating groups of people interacting with each other with or without a human in the loop, typically appear more believable when they act according to coherent social or psychological models, inspired by scientific theory and empirical data, than when they act in ad-hoc or random ways, even if their visual appearance is photo realistic [1], [13], [23]. This has encouraged researchers to build computational models and incorporate them into their agents' decision process. Implemented models include group dynamics [13], social role awareness [14], social relationship [2], politeness [24], emotion [7], [12] and personality, which tends to factor into many of these other models.

While all of the models mentioned address believability, they focus on the computation of the abstract inner state of agents and then how that state reveals itself through a choice of verbal action or perhaps facial expression. The nonverbal coordination of the social situation is often a secondary concern, which can leave these rich minds stranded in an awkwardly stiff or uncoordinated body.

Embodied Conversational Agents (ECA) [3] specifically address the nonverbal aspect of social conduct. This research generally draws from the study of human face-to-face conversation and applies rules that relate abstract description of communicative intent to observable physical behavior, which is realized through real-time multi-modal behavior production. Early ECAs, such as Gandalf [20] and Rea [4], demonstrated the importance of separating content generation and interaction control. It was argued that how and what an agent chooses to say in a given situation is highly domain specific whereas the ability to deliver the chosen content through face-to-face interaction with others is a broad skill and re-usable across domains.

Another important idea that came out of early ECA research was to keep the planning of communicative intent and planning of its surface form as separate stages in the production process. Wide adoption of this view and interest in sharing system components has lead to the formalization of a multi-modal behavior generation framework called SAIBA [9]. This framework defines an interface at the level of communicative intent, called Function Markup Language (FML) and another interface at the level of form description, called Behavior Markup Language (BML).

Primarily used as interface agents, Embodied Conversational Agents have mostly been built for one-on-one conversations with users in a relatively fixed physical setting. When moving into a dynamic 3D game environment, more behaviors and more complex patterns of interaction need to be considered, for example to deal with a larger numbers of participants and longer locomotion distances. Research into the generation of believable communicative behavior in multi-party settings is growing, but has for the most part focused on one or two kinds of behavior at a time such as posture or gaze [6], [15].

Another kind of research into the generation of multi-party social behavior deals with crowds, which has for a long time been at a level of detail that is too low for close quarters environments. However, recent work on autonomous pedestrians suggests the implementation of a coupling between cognitive control and reactive behavior control at the individual level to attain a higher level of realism in social locomotion [17] and work has started on simulating believable smaller sized crowds with a collection of rules based on statistical data on observed behavior in human gatherings [11]. While the detail in this work is not high enough to support face-to-face interaction, the gap that has existed between the deep modeling of a single individual in a very limited environment and the broader modeling of a large number of individuals in a complex environment is getting smaller. This trend is perhaps driven by the requirements of densely populated but highly interactive game worlds that are now possible.

It is important to build tools and flexible system frameworks to bring models of behavior into real-world applications and to speed up the development of new models and environments for testing. Such tools both exist for the more abstract socio-psychological models [16], [18] and for the rule-based generation of nonverbal behavior [5], [10]. The work presented here on Social Puppets, a special tool for game environments, is very much influenced by the latter, with roots in the Spark framework for animating online avatars [22] and its core engine which itself was based on the BEAT nonverbal behavior toolkit [5]. The Social Puppets approach aims to accommodate any kind of higher level agent models and lower level animation systems by supplying a clear behavior interface. The approach extends previous work by starting to address both the depth of face-to-face conversation and the existence of an extended 3D social game environment. The Social Puppets have been realized in the context of a real-world application which will be discussed next.

3   The Language and Culture Training System

The work presented in this paper was done as an important component of the DARPA funded Tactical Language and Culture Training System (TLCTS) which teaches adults basic communication skills in a foreign language and culture [8]. The overall system combines several advanced technologies including speech recognition, dynamic learner modeling, adaptive feedback, interactive autonomous agents and a 3D game environment. Learners pick up new communication skills in a multimedia tutoring environment and get to practice them by switching to a game environment where they carry out related tasks within an interactive story. Advancing through the story relies on building trust with automated characters by speaking with them in their language and behaving in a culturally sensitive manner. Modules for Levantine Arabic, Iraqi Arabic and Pashto were developed at ISI and other languages and cultures are forthcoming from Alelo Inc., a spin-off that licensed the technology for commercialization.

The simulated social encounters in the game and the engaging story give learners a strong context for practicing the new language as well as learning about the culture. Nonverbal behaviors play an important role in any face-to-face interaction and are therefore a very important part of any language and culture training. From the inception of the project, it was clear that an accurate rendition of nonverbal behavior was essential.

A screenshot from the game in an early Pashto version of TLCTS is shown in Fig. 1. The learner, represented by an avatar (1), has just entered an Afghan village and is greeted by a group of children. Behind the learner stands a native guide who can assist if the learner stumbles (4). To interact with the children, the learner starts by crouching down, taking of his shades, to make eye-contact, and then greeting the children. The learner accomplishes the greeting by facing the children, selecting a hand-over-heart gesture with the mouse and speaking into a microphone (2). The way that the learner conducts himself affects the agents that control the characters of the children, possibly resulting in increased or decreased trust as indicated by an animated plus or a minus sign, and the movement of an accumulative trust bar underneath each character's portrait (3).

The TLCTS is a modular system with many well defined interfaces, several of which contribute to the game environment experience. For a description of all modules and the interaction between them, see [21]. The graphics are rendered in the Virtual Culture (VC) game engine from Alelo Inc., a modified version of the Unreal Engine from Epic Games. The VC engine has a character animation interface that supports procedural motor skills for communication, such as gaze control, facial expressions, pointing and detailed body locomotion and orientation.

Considerable work went into adding this repertoire of interpersonal behavior into the game engine because the original Unreal games were only concerned with combat related behavior. The game engine is also responsible for rendering and maintaining the graphical environment that serves as the stage for the interactive stories.

While the game engine carries out the final low level realization of character action, the decision about how a character responds to the learner's input, is taken at a much higher level in what is called the agent code. The agents, as well as the rest of the high-level processing in TLCTS, are written in Python and plug right into a flexible framework that supports message routing between components. In fact, two very different implementations of the agent code were built, and switching between them is quite trivial. The former implementation is a full-blown multi-agent system with deep social reasoning that includes theory of mind. Originally developed as a

Fig. 1. A scene from the Pashto version of TLCTS where the learner has encountered a group of children in an Afghan village

general social simulation tool called PsychSim, a special version called Thespian was created for TLCTS. Thespian addresses two important needs that arise in an interactive drama setting. The first being able to give the agents a pre-written story script as a guideline for their behavior through a process called fitting [19] and the second being able to enforce common social norms that govern conversation, including multi-party conversation [18]. The second agent implementation is based on finite state machines, and was created as a less computationally intensive alternative to the first one to improve agent response time at the cost of reduced reasoning power and dynamism. Both types of agent modules receive the learner input in the form of speech acts and return agent responses also in the form of speech acts.

The deliberation at the level of speech acts does not involve any detailed coordination of nonverbal behavior or in fact any interaction with the simulated physical environment. This is not necessarily a fundamental limitation of the underlying agent technologies, but has more to do with the fact that they were authored around mental models rather than physical ones. Not only does this leave a gap between the decisions that the agents make and their manifestation in the environment, but also begs the question what happens while the agents are not producing speech acts? This is where the Social Puppets come in. They ground the agents in their physical bodies within the environment as the next section will explain.

4 The Social Puppets

Instead of having the agent code interface directly with the game engine, each agent interfaces with a *Social Puppet* (see Fig. 2). While each puppet represents an individual, all the puppets belong to a single social environment overseen by a social engine or a manager that enforces social order. This social engine communicates with the game engine through an executive module that takes care of executing behavior scripts once they have been generated by the puppets.

To use Social Puppets, a system first needs to instantiate a Social Puppets Manager. Through the manager, individual Social Puppets are created and named, one for each agent and one for the human learner. The Manager keeps track of all the puppets, routes special communicative messages between them and dynamically organizes them into interaction groups. The manager needs to receive updates about learner input and a few perceptual updates from the game engine, but is otherwise self-contained with respect to generating appropriate reactive nonverbal behavior for all the puppets. The agent code can have as much control over its corresponding puppet as it wants, but generally it only interfaces with it when it wants to speak or when it wants to change a context parameter (see below).

While running, the manager turns learner input and character perceptual data, into meaningful communicative events described in an early version of the Function Markup Language (FML). These events are then routed to any puppets that are

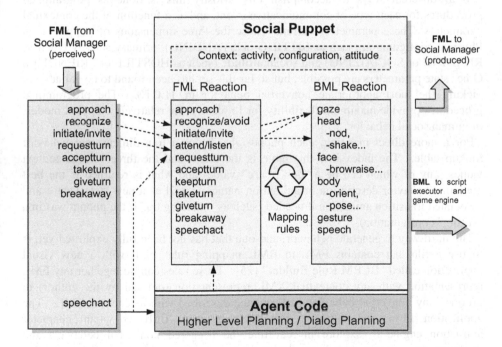

Fig. 2. The Social Puppet is coupled with an autonomous agent and takes care of adding non-verbal behavior, both in reaction to external communicative events and when the agent itself wishes to communicate (dashed arrows are example mappings)

possibly affected by the event, based mainly on how they are grouped. Everyone in a group gets to observe the same events, even if the event does not directly target them. For example, if the learner initiates contact with one member of a group, the other group members react.

When a puppet receives an FML event, it generates a communicative reaction, described at the same abstract FML level. The incoming event typically maps directly to a reaction such as accepting a conversation turn that has been given to the puppet. However, in some cases contextual parameters stored as a state vector in each puppet, have to be consulted. For example, a certain attitude can cause a puppet not to respond well to the approach of another puppet.

In the Pashto system, the learner might choose to approach an Afghan woman standing by herself near a well. As the learner approaches the woman, her puppet receives an approach message from the learner's puppet. The woman's puppet finds that its attitude parameter is negative and therefore selects avoidance as a reaction rather than recognition (see Fig. 3). The attitude value had been set as part of initializing the scene with proper cultural information. In this case it's part of Pashtun culture to condemn attempts from strangers, especially men, to interact with local women.

Once a puppet has chosen the appropriate reaction at the level of communicative intent, it now has to plan nonverbal behaviors that support this intent. There are several different ways to accomplish this. Mostly this is done as programmed procedures for each type of communicative event, and as a function of the contextual parameters. These parameters currently describe three dimensions of puppet state: Physical configuration (such as SITTING or STANDING), primary activity (such as READING or SOCIAIZING) and social attitude (such as HOSTILE or FRIENDLY). Other state parameters are possible, but so far this set has been found to be valuable in picking the most appropriate nonverbal behavior in TLCTS. The programmed procedures provide maximum flexibility for implementing relatively complex models of human social behavior.

For a more direct mapping, each puppet also keeps a four-dimensional behavior lookup table. The index into this table is the intent and the three current context values (any of which can be a "don't care" value) and what is returned is the best matching behavior description or animation name, as well as a new state vector and associated transition animation if needed (such as "standing up" if the puppet was in a "sitting" configuration).

The third way to generate behavior, and one that has not been fully exploited yet, is to use a file that contains FML to BML mapping rules built with a new visual application called "BCBM Rule Builder" [25]. These rules can tie together any FML representation with any contextual XML representation (defined by the author) to produce any nonverbal behavior performance described with a block of BML. The application allows the author to test the rules on a BML compliant character animation engine to explore in real-time the triggered nonverbal behavior, and therefore can greatly speed up the authoring process. A prototype with this functionality is already in Social Puppets.

Fig. 3. Examples of communicative intent turning into visible behavior in the Social Puppets. Avoidance (Left). Speaking and listening (Right).

After the puppet is done producing a behavior description in the form of a BML-level script, it is passed on to an execution module which in turn feeds the game engine with individual behavior commands that drive the character animation. The puppet's intent is also broadcast to any other relevant puppets through the manager to continue the sequence of events.

In some cases, the manager itself can choose to generate a sequence of events according to a particular behavior model. For example, the manager in Tactical Pashto implements the turn-taking model from [22] where it is assumed that the turn is returned to whomever spoke before the current speaker if no explicit turn action is taken. Because the manager keeps track of all puppets and their groups, it is a good place for implementing top-down behavior models for group behavior, whereas the puppets themselves are a better place for bottom-up rules that are meant to result in some emergent social order.

Speech acts are a special kind of communicative event in the social engine. These either come from the learner or the agent code as mentioned above. The pathway for these events is different from other communicative events. Speech acts from the learner trigger turn-taking events in the social puppets, including the puppet that represents the learner, but the acts are also routed to the agents so they can generate a response. The response from an agent is a speech act that gets passed through the agent's puppet, generating nonverbal behaviors, before finally coming out in the environment as a multi-modal performance.

5   Conclusions and Future Work

The Social Puppets have not been formally evaluated as a component by themselves, but the rigorous testing and subsequent release of the overall TLCTS to thousands of end users speaks well of the module's robustness, and the warm reception, of its quality of output. Furthermore, the module visibly improved development time, not least because it provided a new middle-level for scripting prototype characters that didn't require any agent code to be present. Currently, one of the biggest problems with the approach is that while channels for communicative events and behaviors are well defined, other required information, such as perceptual data and contextual parameters, hasn't lent itself to clear-cut modularization and therefore some ad-hoc connections still remain. Future work will involve cleaning this up, extending the range of communicative intent and behaviors, and including dynamic locomotion planning using social anchor points such as formations and environmental features.

Acknowledgements. This project was a part of the DARWARS Training Superiority Program of the Defense Advanced Research Projects Agency and was conducted while the first author was working at USC/ISI. The authors wish to acknowledge the contributions of the members of the Tactical Language team and the BCBM team at Micro Analysis and Design. Many thanks to W. Lewis Johnson, Andre Valente and Stacy Marsella for their leadership and support.

References

1. Bailenson, J., Blascovich, J.: Avatars. In: Bainbridge, W.S. (ed.) Encyclopedia of Human-Computer Interaction. Berkshire Publishing Group, pp. 64–68 (2004)
2. Cassell, J., Bickmore, T.: Negotiated Collusion: Modeling Social Language and its Relationship Effects in Intelligent Agents. In: User Modeling and User-Adapted Interaction, vol. 13, pp. 89–132. Kluwer Academic Publishers, Boston (2003)
3. Cassell, J., Sullivan, J., Prevost, S., et al. (eds.): Embodied conversational agents. MIT Press, Cambridge (2000)
4. Cassell, J., Bickmore, T., Billinghurst, M., et al.: Embodiment in Conversational Interfaces: Rea. CHI, pp. 520–527. ACM Press, New York (1999)
5. Cassell, J., Vilhjalmsson, H., Bickmore, T.: BEAT: The Behavior Expression Animation Toolkit. SIGGRAPH, pp. 477–486. ACM Press, New York (2001)
6. Gillies, M., Ballin, D.: A Model of Interpersonal Attitude and Posture Generation. In: Rist, T., Aylett, R., Ballin, D., Rickel, J. (eds.) IVA 2003. LNCS (LNAI), vol. 2792, pp. 88–92. Springer, Heidelberg (2003)
7. Gratch, J., Stacy, M.: Evaluating the Modeling and use of Emotion in Virtual Humans. In: Autonomous Agents and Multi-Agent Systems, ACM Press, New York (2004)
8. Johnson, W.L., Marsella, S., Vilhjalmsson, H.: The DARWARS Tactical Language Training System. The Interservice/Industry Training, Simulation and Education Conference, SSA (2004)
9. Kopp, S., Krenn, B., Marsella, S., et al.: Towards a Common Framework for Multimodal Generation in ECAs: The Behavior Markup Language. In: Gratch, J., Young, M., Aylett, R., Ballin, D., Olivier, P. (eds.) IVA 2006. LNCS (LNAI), vol. 4133, Springer, Heidelberg (2006)
10. Lee, J., Marsella, S.: Nonverbal Behavior Generator for Embodied Conversational Agents. In: Gratch, J., Young, M., Aylett, R., Ballin, D., Olivier, P. (eds.) IVA 2006. LNCS (LNAI), vol. 4133, pp. 243–255. Springer, Heidelberg (2006)
11. Patel, J., Parker, R., Traum, D.: Simulation of Small Group Discussions for Middle Level of Detail Crowds. Army Science Conference (2004)
12. Pelachaud, C., Bilvi, M.: Computational model of believable conversational agents. In: Huget, M. (ed.) Communication in MAS: Background, Current Trends and Future, Springer-Verlag, Heidelberg (2003)

13. Prada, R., Paiva, A.: Synthetic Group Dynamics in Entertainment Scenarios. In: International Conference on Advances in Computer Entertainment Technology, ACM Press, New York (2005)
14. Prendinger, H., Ishizuka, M.: Social Role Awareness in Animated Agents, AGENTS'01. ACM Press, New York (2001)
15. Rehm, M., Andre, E., Nisch, M.: Let's Come Together - Social Navigation Behaviors of Virtual and Real Humans. In: Maybury, M., Stock, O., Wahlster, W. (eds.) INTETAIN 2005. LNCS (LNAI), vol. 3814, pp. 124–133. Springer, Heidelberg (2005)
16. Rehm, M., Endrass, B., Andre, E.: A Plug-and-Play Framework for Theories of Social Group Dynamics. In: Gratch, J., Young, M., Aylett, R., Ballin, D., Olivier, P. (eds.) IVA 2006. LNCS (LNAI), vol. 4133, pp. 465–466. Springer, Heidelberg (2006)
17. Shao, W., Terzopoulos, D.: Autonomous Pedestrians. In: ACM SIGGRAPH Symposium on Computer Animation, ACM Publishing, New York (2005)
18. Si, M., Marsella, S., Pynadath, D.: Thespian: Modeling Socially Normative Behavior in a Decision-Theoretic Framework. In: Gratch, J., Young, M., Aylett, R., Ballin, D., Olivier, P. (eds.) IVA 2006. LNCS (LNAI), vol. 4133, pp. 369–382. Springer, Heidelberg (2006)
19. Si, M., Stacy, M., Pynadath, D.: Thespian: Using Multi-Agent Fitting to Craft Interactive Drama. In: International Conference on Autonomous Agents and Multi-Agent Systems, pp. 21–28. ACM Press, New York (2005)
20. Thorisson, K.R.: Real-Time Decision Making in Multimodal Face-to-Face Communication. In: Autonomous Agents, pp. 16–23. ACM Press, New York (1998)
21. Vilhjalmsson, H., Samtani, P.: MissionEngine: Multi-System Integration using Python in the Tactical Language Project. PyCon, Python Software Foundation (2005)
22. Vilhjalmsson, H.: Animating Conversation in Online Games. In: Rauterberg, M. (ed.) ICEC 2004. LNCS, vol. 3166, pp. 139–150. Springer, Heidelberg (2004)
23. Vinayagamoorthy, V., Gillies, M., Steed, A., et al.: Building Expression into Virtual Characters. EUROGRAPHICS State of The Art Report, vol. 2006. The Eurographics Association (2006)
24. Wang, N., Johnson, W.L., Mayer, R.E., et al.: The Politeness Effect: Pedagogical Agents and Learning Outcomes. In: International Journal of Human-Computer Interaction, vol. 22, Lawrence Erlbaum Associates, Mahwah (2007)
25. Warwick, W., Vilhjalmsson, H.: Engendering Believable Communicative Behaviors in Synthetic Entities for Tactical Language Training: An Interim Report. Behavior Representation in Modeling and Simulation, SISO (2005)

A Cross-Cultural Study of Flow Experience in the IT Environment: The Beginning

Alexander E. Voiskounsky

Psychology Department,
Moscow State University
Russia
vaemsu@gmail.com

Abstract. Flow (optimal) experience is being widely investigated in the IT environments: in human-computer interaction, computer-mediated communication and exploratory behaviour, consumer and marketing applications, educational practice, playing computer, video and online games, psychological rehabilitation of the disabled, web usability testing, etc. Though a universal experience, flow can be expected to be culture specific and culture dependent. Optimal experience has only rarely been studied from a cross-cultural perspective, mainly in the field of gaming activities. An overview of the earliest works in the field is presented, as well as empirical evidences of a study referring to the flow experience and interaction patterns inherent to the samples of Russian and French online players.

Keywords: Optimal Experience, Flow, Interaction, Information Technologies, Culture, Online Games, Multy-Player Games, MUD, Cross-Cultural Study.

1 Introduction

Flow, or optimal experience, has been introduced by Mihaly Csikszentmihalyi. While interviewing dancers, chess players, rock climbers, surgeons and many others, he has selected often reported characteristics of a feeling which is related to what they believe constitute an optimal level of their experience. They produced almost identical verbal descriptions regardless of the particular sort of the preferred activity: 'being in the midst of a flow', or "flowing from one moment to the next" [1]. The interviewed people reported that at these moments they had been performing to the utmost. This sort of holistic experience was called flow, or else optimal experience [1].

Flow experience takes place when people are engaged in the preferred activity, including work, homework or hobbies, and is not likely to occur when they relax. Flow cannot be qualified as a regular attribute of one's engagement and absorption with the preferred activity; instead, every time it is a sort of a happening. Prior to experiencing flow, a person has to acquire competence in the preferred activity. Flow happens or not irrespectively of the nature of the activity itself. Processes of pursuing a desired result are reported to be more pleasing and self-rewarding that the result itself [1], [2]. From the fact that enjoyment is associated with the process of goal achievement, it can be concluded that repetitions of these processes are expected and wanted.

D. Schuler (Ed.): Online Communities and Social Comput., HCII 2007, LNCS 4564, pp. 202–211, 2007.

Flow experience is presented manifold: as a high-level methodological construct applicable within/outside the field of psychology [2], [3], as a major factor of biocultural evolution and selection [3], [4], as a theory of creativity, good-work and development of talented adolescents [1], [5], as a developmental psychology theory [2], [6], as a cognitive artifact [1], [7], as a basis for psychological rehabilitation practice [4], [8], not to mention further. Also, the flow methodology has been successfully applied to diverse professions and occupations, including those that include the IT use.

2 Characteristics of Flow Used in Empirical Research Projects

The variety of flow related research in the IT environments includes learning to handle and adapt novel software and hardware pieces; online instruction and distant education; computer- and Internet-mediated communication; instant messaging and chatting; consuming web media sources and online entertainment; web marketing, e-shopping, business web applications; online gaming, video gaming and playing computer games; web navigation, exploratory online behavior, search of content items on the web; illegal penetrations in the cyberspace field, in particular hacking; psychological rehabilitation by means of immersive virtual reality equipment and software; measurement of web-site attraction and friendliness, usability testing and adaptation of web sources to target populations. The whole line of research begins in the early 1990s [9].

Theoretically and empirically, Csikszentmihalyi [1], [2] has selected the following major characteristics of flow: clear and distinct goals; loss of self-consciousness; distorted sense of time; actions and awareness merge; immediate feedback; concentration on the task; high level of control over it; balance (precise matching) between the available skills and the task challenges; activity seems worth doing for its own sake. A recent paper [10] says that "these factors may not be the only ones that contribute to flow, but Csikszentmihalyi identifies them as the most commonly exhibited ones (p. 83)". Other researchers have made efforts to use more characteristics and to validate them. For example, some authors [11-13] found additional characteristics to accompany the known ones: for example, interest, discovery and curiosity, excitement, positive affects, time urgency, quality of computer interfaces, etc.

In an influential study [14] the model of flow experience in the IT environments was introduced; it included such characteristics as vividness and interactivity which cumulatively induce the parameter of (tele)presence, or "mediated perception of an environment" [14]; later the inclusion of additional characteristics (for example, presence and interactivity) into the revised model was empirically validated [15]. The inclusion of media-specific characteristics referring to the mediated environments seems a reasonable thing to do; for example, 'presence' was not once named by respondents in interviews and/or surveys [12], [13], [16].

Often specialists share the view that the flow dimensions may be variable, dependent on the particular type of activity human beings are engaged in. Thus, in order to qualify flow experience it is important that some of the dimensions are marked, not necessarily all of them. Indeed, a sensation of flow experienced while online shopping might be described with a set of characteristics only partly matching the parameters describing flow experienced while online gaming, or navigating the web, etc. As Rettie [17] states, "while respondents recognized most of Csikszentmihalyi's dimensions, the merging of action and awareness and loss of self-consciousness were not really relevant (p. 111)".

The sets of characteristics differ, taken for example less vs. more competent (in the same types of activities) respondents; with the change of activities, the levels of competence may become the opposite, as it often happens. Possibly there are sets of flow dimensions (or characteristics), which can be informally called "flow dialects"; these 'dialects' strongly depend on task specificity, competence in this or that task, emotional state, quality of computer/web interfaces, software applications, type of prior instruction, and probably on other parameters which have not yet become obvious.

Flow may be expected when the available skills match task challenges one chooses, provided both are close to the person's utmost. Precise matching means a perspective for personal growth. Such a balance is often adopted as an antecedent of flow [14], [18]; sometimes, however, it is not discovered as a significant parameter [16].

3   Cross-Cultural Studies of Flow Experience in IT Environments

3.1   Culture Related Studies

Traditionally, research projects in the optimal experience field include cross-cultural comparisons. Not so in the IT environments: little can be said about non-English and non-Taiwanese IT users. Some studies have been carried out within German students [19-21], Russian gamers and hackers [22-24], Korean online gamers [25], and Scandinavians – speakers of Norway [26], Swedish [27], [28], and Finnish [29]. Pioneer studies have also been carried out in Israel within groups chatting in Hebrew [30] and within a population of Brazilian journalists, active in the IT use [31]. Neither of these works is, nevertheless, comparative and might be qualified a cross-cultural study, although IT environments are global and intercultural. For many other IT-related areas (for example, the digital divide, gender issues in e-shopping, attitudes towards IT, computer anxiety, etc.) the interest toward intercultural comparisons is significant.

Hopefully, the current lack of interest to cross-cultural specifics of flow experience in the IT environments will not last long. At the moment we are able to refer to a comparative investigation of flow patterns displayed while navigating through a marketing website; bilingual speakers of Spanish and English participated [32]. One of researchers' goals was to create a cross-cultural model of web related flow experience, and to trace the impact of several cultural factors (including for example within-site navigation using first or second language verbal skills) on attitudes toward the website and on participants' actual cognitive schemes; besides, marketing parameters were of interest: purchases from the e-shop and intentions to revisit it.

3.2 A Cross-Cultural Study of Optimal Experience While Playing MUDs

Another research project will be described in more details; it is targeted on culture specific aspects of flow experience in samples of Russian and French online gamers. It has been planned as a cross-cultural work and consists of two independent studies administered under the equal methodology and procedure. Full reports are published: the study carried out within the sample of gamers speaking Russian [22], [23] and within the sample of gamers speaking French [33]. The study was held in collaboration with Dr. Olga Mitina and Ph.D. student Anastasiya Avetisova.

The cross-cultural research was planned and held within communities of MUD gamers – MUDs represent the earliest text-only version of the MMORPG class of games. Playing MUDs is a typically global activity; non-native speakers of English were involved in MUDding when there were no options to use a language other than English, but with years passing, various national-language scripts of MUDs became acceptable. MUD is a class of online games being continuously played since 1978 [34].

The reasons to compare the two particular samples of gamers – the French and the Russian – are as follows [35]. First, there are MUD servers and MUD players in both the countries (Russia and France); the two cultures exhibit neither particular prejudices nor particular sympathies toward online gaming. No prior research of flow experienced while playing MUD is known in any of these two countries.

Second, online speakers of French as well as online speakers of Russian include citizens of countries other than the two metropolitan states. The speakers of French (francophones) are located, besides France, in Canadian Quebec, in European countries neighboring France, and in French-speaking African countries; speakers of Russian are located, besides Russia, in post-Soviet countries (including the Ukraine, the population of which is close to that of the France), as well as in the USA, Israel, Germany, Australia and other countries. Since the speakers of the two languages are distributed, it is reasonable to suppose that the respective online populations are also distributed.

Third, we find parallels in the ways the two metropolitan countries became late in acquiring global access to the Internet: the Russians due to the totalitarian nature of the Soviet state for which free exchange of views was alien; the French due to the pioneer development of the videotex system Minitel. With time passing, the Minitel penetration is a barrier [35] to the advance of the Internet: "France was the first to develop a public telematic system", but "the French telematic system now appears outmoded (p. 37)".

Fourth, the two online audiences seem to be comparable in their amounts. Since no reliable statistics of MUD players is known, we can at best suppose that the two supposedly comparable online audiences contain a supposedly comparable number of gamers in general and finally a supposedly comparable number of MUD players. Thus, we have to compare the audiences by the time when research was held, 2003-2004.

First we estimate the Russian online audience. The reliable sociological bureau, the Foundation for Public Opinion (www.fom.ru) informs that by the end of 2003 the audience was equal to 13.1 M citizens of Russia, aged 18+. Thus, Russian-speaking non-citizen and younger generations – the two categories of frequent and competent users – stay outside the sociological survey. It is usually stated (see arguments at [36]) that at the time research was held the citizens of Russia formed a little more than half and certainly less than two thirds of the total online audience of speakers of Russian; the amount of children and adolescents before 18 on the Web is estimated as about a half of the adult audience. Thus, a rough estimation says the Russian online audience which includes non-citizens and teenagers, active in 2003, may be approximated as close to 30 M (but not reaching this amount).

To estimate the online francophones audience, we take the data placed at the "Global Reach" (http://www.glreach.com/globstats/), classified by languages. Quoting the 2004 reference (http://global-reach.biz/globstats/refs.php3#6) we get the following estimation:

> There are 22.4 M people in France online (source: Nielsen/NetRatings, Feb., 2004). French-speaking Canada follows at 2.3 M people online (according to The Daily Statistics (Canada), March, 2001. One must add 1.0 M French-speakers in Switzerland (23% of the 4.3 M Swiss online, according to Nielsen NetRatings marketing research, Feb., 2004). Among the 3.4 M people online in Belgium (see latest survey from GfK and InSites), one-quarter of them, or 0.9 M, are from the French-speaking provinces. Next to Belgium, Luxembourg has 170 K people online (source: ITU, 2003). Another 95 K Americans who access the Internet in French (50% of the French-speaking American population). (We will not count the French-speaking users in Africa, although there are a good 7 to 10 M Africans who speak French there: Internet access is simply not readily available in most African countries.) This gives a total of 33.3 M French-speaking people online.

We conclude, by the time of cross-cultural study the francophone online audience outscored the Russian online audience by 10 per cent. Though this is a difference, we state that the two audiences are comparable and reasonably close. Supposedly, the populations of MUD players are comparable in approximately the same proportion as the online audiences. We compare the two populations of MUD players taken as a whole, i.e. irrespectively of the particular MUD-type games they use to play.

The cross-cultural methodology included the adaptation of the prior (Russian) questionnaire of 40 questions (including 8 questions on demography, on longevity and frequency of playing sessions) in order to get the French questionnaire culturally and linguistically equal. The procedure consisted of translating the Russian questionnaire into French; trial testing within a small sample of MUD gamers; putting questions to French speakers, not necessarily online gamers; inserting appropriate changes into the questionnaire to be adapted, and testing once more [33]. The data collecting procedure was that of an online survey, it was held in 2003 (Russian part) and 2004 (French part).

Analysis of research results includes [22], [23], [33] the analysis of respondents' demography and all the questionnaires' items, explorative and confirmatory factor analyses, comparative analysis of questionnaires' items, qualitative analysis of the factor models allocated to the Russian and the French samples. Since the current overview paper is not the full report of the comparative study, we do no more than describe the two factor models, referring to the Russian and the French samples, and correlations between the factors and the particular questionnaires' items.

The total number of participants is 347 speakers of Russian and 203 francophones. As anticipated, both samples included non-citizens of respectively Russia and France. Explorative factor analysis provided a six-factor model for the Russian sample [22], [23] and a three-factor model for the French sample [33]. The factors can be viewed at the Fig. 1, which provides correlations between factors and questionnaire items (non-demographic ones); the latter is loosely translated into English. Both factor models include the Flow factor; the models are significant, intercorrelations between the factors are reasonably high [22], [23], [33]. A brief discussion of the factor models follows.

The Russian factor model includes all the factors characterizing the French one: Flow, Achievement, Cognition and Interaction – the latter means social interaction, not between the user and the system [25]. Hence, factor models characterizing the Russian and the French samples are partly similar. Besides, in the factor model characterizing the Russian sample there are two more factors, namely Activity/ Passivity and Thoughtfulness/Spontaneity. In the French sample Interaction and Cognition merge, while for the Russians these represent independent factors. In a way, the Russian factor structure is more transparent: the four factors common for the two samples and characterizing prevalent gamestyles do not merge, unlike the factor structure of the French sample. On the other side, the French factor structure shows that in MUD games Cognition presupposes Interaction in the form of social perception, i.e. gaining knowledge about fellow players: thus, the merge of the two factors looks reasonable.

The analysis of the data at the Figure 1 presents a special perspective for discussion. One can easily notice that the French-sample major factor, i.e. Achievement, includes all the questionnaire items referring to the Russian-sample Achievement factor plus several additional parameters referring to Flow factor (mostly common to the Russian and the French samples). Thus, for the Frenchmen Achievement includes elements of Flow: 'focused attention', 'mobilization', and 'perception of reality' – the latter, we believe, may refer to 'presence'. In other words, the desire for Achievement, characteristic for the French sample, includes some standard characteristics of Flow. The Russian-sample desire for Achievement does not include characteristics alien to this desire. Also, for the Russians Achievement is not the first factor, unlike the French sample.

Thus, flow is a really significant component of online games, it turns out to be either the major factor (in the Russian sample) or included into the major factor as its important component (in the French sample). In the both samples flow is a significant factor. This outcome seems to be important both in the cross-cultural context, and in the context of the gamers' attitudes toward playing MUDs. That means, a probable reason for long-time devotion to MUDs (a sort of old-fashioned, i.e. text-only games without rich modern graphics) is that playing MUDs provokes flow experience, an expected feeling highly estimated by the players. This is shown to be true for at least two national samples of online gamers; the more reasons to investigate it in more samples and applied to a more diverse class of games, not necessarily MMORPG-like games.

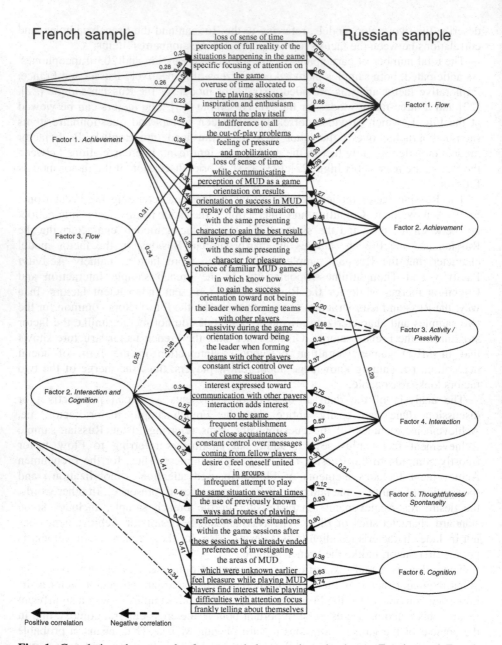

Fig. 1. Correlations between the factors and the questionnaire items (Russian and French samples)

Although thorough analysis of data gained in the two investigations (partly presented at the Figure 1) may provide more interesting findings, we will not go into further details of this cross-cultural study. We believe the importance of this type of investigation will be constantly increasing.

4 Conclusions

Optimal, or flow experience represents an important parameter inherent of various IT related behaviors. For example, a possible explanation of players' years-long, if not decades-long attachment to text-only group roleplays like MUD is that they experience flow and are fond of the feeling. Dependent on task specificity, personal competence, type of prior instruction, and probably on other parameters which have not yet become obvious, there are what may be called "flow dialects", i.e. partly different sets of flow-related dimensions characterizing optimal experience. Although people experiencing flow have been identified in all the investigated cultures, and thus flow is universal, at the same time the particular characteristics of optimal experience are expected to be culture sensitive. This is supposedly true, taken IT related activities which are about the most universal types of activity. Very few culture related studies have been done in the field up to now; the available results confirm the conclusion that cross-cultural analysis of flow experience in the IT environments provides good perspectives for gaining new knowledge. For example, flow is a significant factor and at the same time it is differently located in the factor models characterizing the two investigated samples of players in online role games like MUDs: the sample of speakers of Russian and the sample of francophones.

Acknowledgments. Research was supported by the Russian Foundations for Humanities, project # 06-06-00342a.

References

1. Csikszentmihalyi, M.: Beyond boredom and anxiety: Experiencing flow in work and play. Jossey-Bass, San-Francisco (first published in 1975) (2000)
2. Csikszentmihalyi, M.: Flow: The psychology of optimal experience. Harper and Row, New York, NY (1990)
3. Csikszentmihalyi, M.: The evolving self: A psychology for the third millennium. HarperCollins, New York, NY (1993)
4. Optimal experience: psychological studies of flow in consciousness. In: Csikszentmihalyi, M., Csikszentmihalyi, I.S. (eds.) Cambridge Univ. Press, New York, NY (1988)
5. Csikszentmihalyi, M.: Creativity. Flow and the psychology of discovery and invention. HarperPerennial, New York, NY (1996)
6. Csikszentmihalyi, M., Larson, R.: Being adolescent: Conflict and growth in the teenage years. Basic Books, New York, NY (1984)
7. Csikszentmihalyi, M.: Attention and the holistic approach to behavior. In: Pope, K.S., Singer, J.L. (eds.) The stream of consciousness, pp. 335–359. Plenum Press, New York, NY (1978)
8. Delle Fave, A., Massimini, F.: Bringing subjectivity into focus: Optimal experiences, life themes, and person-centered rehabilitation In: Linley, P.A., Joseph, S. (eds.) Positive psychology in practice, pp. 581–597. Wiley & Sons, Hoboken, NJ (2004)
9. Trevino, L.K., Webster, L.: Flow in computer-mediated communication. Communication research 19(5), 539–573 (1992)

10. Finneran, C.M., Zhang, P.: Flow in computer-mediated environments: Promises and challenges. Communications of the Association for information systems 15, 82–101 (2005)
11. Chen, H.: Flow on the net – detecting web users' positive affects and their flow states. Computers in human behavior 22, 221–233 (2006)
12. Chen, H., Wigand, R.T., Nilan, M.S.: Optimal experience of web activities. Computers in human behavior 15(5), 585–608 (1999)
13. Pace, S.: A grounded theory of the flow experiences of web users. International journal of human-computer studies 60(3), 327–363 (2004)
14. Hoffman, D.L., Novak, T.P.: Marketing in hypermedia computer-mediated environments: Conceptual foundations. Journal of marketing 60(3), 50–68 (1996)
15. Novak, T.P., Hoffman, D.L., Duhachek, A.: The influence of goal-directed and experiential activities on online flow experiences. Journal of consumer psychology 13(1-2), 3–16 (2003)
16. Skadberg, Y.X., Kimmel, R.: Visitors' flow experience while browsing a web site: Its measurement, contributing factors and consequences. Computers in human behavior 20(3), 403–422 (2004)
17. Rettie, R.: An exploration of flow during Internet use. Internet research: Electronic networking applications and policy 11(2), 103–113 (2001)
18. Pearce, J.M., Howard, S.: Designing for flow in a complex activity. In: Masoodian, M., Jones, S., Rogers, B. (eds.) APCHI 2004. LNCS, vol. 3101, pp. 349–358. Springer, Heidelberg (2004)
19. Konradt, U., Filip, R., Hoffmann, S.: Flow experience and positive affect during hypermedia learning. British journal of educational technology 34(3), 309–327 (2003)
20. Konradt, U., Sulz, K.: The experience of flow interacting with a hypermedia learning environment. Journal of educational multimedia and hypermedia 10(1), 69–84 (2001)
21. Tzanetakis, R., Vitouch, P.: Flow-experience, the Internet and its relationship to situation and personality. Abstract of a paper presented at the Internet Research 3.0: Net/Work/Theory (Maastricht, The Netherlands) (2002) available at: http://aoir.org/2002/program/tzanetakis.html
22. Voiskounsky, A.E., Mitina, O.V., Avetisova, A.A.: Playing online games: Flow experience. PsychNology journal 2(3), 259–281 (2004)
23. Voiskounsky, A.E., Mitina, O.V., Avetisova, A.A.: Communicative patterns and flow experience of MUD players. International journal of advanced media and communication 1(1), 5–25 (2005)
24. Voiskounsky, A.E., Smyslova, O.V.: Flow-based model of computer hackers' motivation. CyberPsychology & behavior 6(3), 171–180 (2003)
25. Choi, D., Kim, J.: Why people continue to play online games: In search of critical design factors to increase customer loyalty to online contents. CyberPsychology & behavior 7(1), 11–24 (2004)
26. Heidman, L., Sharafi, P.: Early use of Internet-based educational resources: Effects on students' engagement modes and flow experience. Behaviour & information technology 23(2), 137–146 (2004)
27. Montgomery, H., Sharafi, P., Heidman, L.R.: Engagement in activities involving information technology: Dimensions, modes, and flow. Human factors 46(2), 334–348 (2004)
28. Sharafi, P., Heidman, L., Montgomery, H.: Using information technology: Engagement modes, flow experience, and personality orientations. Computers in human behaviour 22(5), 899–916 (2006)

29. Pilke, E.M.: Flow experiences in information technology use. International journal of human-computer studies 61(3), 347–357 (2004)
30. Shoham, A.: Flow experiences and image making: An on-line chat rooms ethnography. Psychology and marketing 21(10), 855–882 (2004)
31. Manssour, A.B.B.: Flow in journalistic telework. CyberPsychology & behavior 6(1), 31–39 (2003)
32. Luna, D., Peracchio, L.A., de Juan, M.D.: Cross-cultural and cognitive aspects of web site navigation. Journal of the academy of marketing science 30(4), 397–410 (2002)
33. Voiskounsky, A.E., Mitina, O.V., Avetisova, A.A.: Flow experience and interaction: Investigation of francophone online gamers. In: Sudweeks, F., Hrachovec, H., Ess, C. (eds.) Cultural attitudes towards technology and communication. Proceedings, 5th international conference, Tartu, Estonia, 28 June – July, pp. 385–396. School of information technology, Murdoch University, Murdoch, Australia (2006)
34. Bartle, R.: Designing virtual worlds. New Riders Publishing, Indianapolis, IN (2003)
35. Lemos, A.: The labyrinth of Minitel. In: Shields, R. (ed.) Cultures of Internet: Virtual spaces, real histories, living bodies, pp. 33–48. Sage, New Delhi, Thousand Oaks, London (1996)
36. Voiskounsky, A.: Internet culture in Russia. Internet-based teaching and learning (IN-TELE) 99. In: Proceedings of IN-TELE 99 conference. Frankfurt a/M: Peter Lang, pp. 36–44 (2001)

Cultural Institutions, Co-creativity and Communities of Interest

Jerry Watkins and Angelina Russo

ARC Centre of Excellence for Creative Industries and Innovation
Queensland University of Technology
Tel/fax +61 7 3105 7353
jj.watkins@qut.edu.au

Abstract. Despite the proliferation of web-based news and information services, there remains a lack of online destinations from which to obtain reliable and authoritative cultural knowledge. In many countries, such knowledge is provided by cultural institutions such as museums and libraries. Recent discussion suggests that social media – including blogs, wikis and digital stories – may provide a creative solution to the ongoing interaction between cultural institutions and communities of interest. However, little applied research exists to demonstrate how social media can be established and maintained within museums and libraries, and what issues are raised within the institution by a more participatory approach to cultural communication. This paper highlights the implementation of a new program at the Australian Museum to train staff in social media production, in order to make the many thousands of objects and stories held within the Museum's collections more accessible and engaging to communities of interest.

Keywords: co-creativity; social media; digital cultural communication; human-computer interaction.

1   ICT Penetration Within Museums

Major state-funded museums in Australia, New Zealand and much of Europe continue to attract questions about their ongoing role: should they remain seemingly aloof organizations which concern themselves with collection, archiving and knowledge distribution; or should they seek to compete with the level of popular engagement offered by themes parks and the like in an effort to connect with visitors (in part, through the deployment of interactive multimedia)? As this debate is frequently revisited within both museum conferences and the culture pages of newspapers worldwide, this paper does not attempt to answer it. Rather, it examines current work in Australia which demonstrates how HCI and participatory design principles can help museums engage with communities of interest via social media.

The expansion of the museum into the online space is often focused on the implementation of content management systems and collection digitization projects. These programs seek to not only accelerate cataloguing procedures, but to also increase online access by visitors who do not normally visit site-specific collections.

D. Schuler (Ed.): Online Communities and Social Comput., HCII 2007, LNCS 4564, pp. 212–221, 2007.

This information transfer strategy does not seem to demonstrate any substantial differentiation from the Shannon & Weaver communication process model [1]. Arguably, the museum is accelerating its existing work practice using information and communication technology, rather than facing the rather tougher questions of how ICT has changed the cultural communication environment and the expectations of museum visitors. In terms of new models of digital distribution, ICT has certainly had an impact. Web-based cultural networks such as Australian Museums and Galleries Online (AMOL) link content across institutions, thus providing a distributed network of collection resources across Australia [2]. The Voyager Heritage Network has created a "museum without walls" to acts as a portal of museums in Northern Ontario USA, providing a social and historical document of the area [3]. Yet the many current ICT-based initiatives in content management systems and networking have not produced a satisfactory improvement in external interactions. In an apparent effort to move the museum to a higher level of engagement, a Museums Association report challenges museums to find new ways to broaden access and develop innovative relationships with audiences [4]. As well as housing and exhibiting physical collections, major museums and libraries have become hubs for formal and informal communities of interest through their substantial public and educational programs and some commentators suggest that digital media such as blogs, wikis and digital stories may provide a solution for cultural institutions wishing to interact with communities and audiences in more creative and lasting ways [5,6].

2   Cultural Institutions and Co-creativity

This research is based upon a major investigation being conducted by the Australian Research Council Centre of Excellence for Creative Industries and Innovation at Queensland University of Technology [7]. The *New Literacy, New Audiences* project examines the potential for museums and libraries to sustain and interact with online knowledge-based communities of interest using social media such as blogs, wikis and digital stories [8]. The research uses knowledge from human-computer interaction, museum communication and audience evaluation to question whether site-specific content can or even should expand its presence into the online space, and whether social media are a suitable vehicle for such expansion. A number of Australia's leading cultural institutions are research partners within the project, and they are amongst a small number of museums, galleries and libraries worldwide which are becoming aware that engaging both physical and online audiences in content creation activities is not only a route to increased visitation rates, but also a means by which to deepen the audience relationship significantly. As Gillard notes, 'cultural products or activities create audiences as people engage with them' [9] and to demonstrate this, social media products have been used to integrate audiences with a number of recent high-profile museum exhibitions including:

• The Museum of Modern Art (New York) retrospective of the Residents – an avant-garde multimedia group – which posted clips by finalists on YouTube and invited votes and comments from the public to help determine the final exhibition [10].

- Pace/MacGill Gallery's (New York) *Self-Portraitr* exhibition which included nearly 130,000 user-submitted photos via the Flickr content-sharing site [11]. The exhibition itself drew a younger-than-usual audience for the Gallery [12].

The MOMA example uses a social medium (in this case, YouTube) for a creative online interaction and we can speculate that in so doing the passive exhibition audience evolved into a community of interest (CoI) with an active and vocal participation in the final exhibition. The *Self-Portraitr* example demonstrates how the institution co-created an original exhibition based on digital content supplied by a cultural CoI. Not only did the institution listen and respond to this community (as in the MOMA example) but it went further by privileging and thereby validating community content within the institution. This innovative and arguably more democratic creative relationship between the cultural institution and its CoIs can be described using the term 'co-creativity'. Originally attributed to US-based interaction designer Abbe Don, Shedroff describes co-creative technologies as "those that offer assistance in the creation process. People are naturally creative and are almost always more interested in experiences that allow them to create instead of merely participate" [13]. Although there may be some question as to just how many people are "naturally creative", Shedroff's basic position is key to the concept of 'everyday creativity' being privileged by the institution through co-creation, as demonstrated by *Self-Portraitr* and as discussed in this paper. Within this discussion, co-creativity refers to both:

- The *philosophy* of increasing creative civic interaction by allowing the voices of individuals and communities to be heard within the cultural sphere.
- The *practice* of collaborative cultural digital media production by the cultural institution and its audiences.

Simply put – *why* should museums, galleries or libraries seek to engage audiences through digital content creation and distribution? And if it decides to adopt a co-creative philosophy, *how* can the institution translate this into practice?

3 Co-creativity and HCI

Co-creativity does not present the HCI research with 'hard' problems, to the extent that "criteria for their optimal solution" are not anticipated [14]. But neither is co-creative communication an applied research challenge that can be answered satisfactorily by heuristics alone. This research adopts an interdisciplinary approach which integrates knowledge from communication, interaction, education and organizational behavior; in the full knowledge that some unidisciplinary researchers are wary of interdisciplinary HCI approaches that integrate techniques from other knowledge bases without a full understanding of the originating discipline.

Creativity has been firmly linked to digital literacy in HCI literature: "One of the most important skills for almost everyone to have in the next decade and beyond will be those that allow us to create valuable, compelling, and empowering information and experiences for others. To do this, we must learn existing ways of organizing and presenting data and information and develop new ones" [13]. Beyond design-based

HCI questions, any examination of the possibilities and limitations for digital co-creativity within established cultural institutions also raises organizational and policy issues. Turpeinen describes the co-evolution of broadcasted, customized and community-created media as a paradigm within which active individuals and communities use computer-mediated networking to tell and exchange their stories and to enhance the interaction among member and their peers in other groups [15]. This form of community co-creation can both develop new paths for community knowledge and simultaneously enhance community life. Institutions which represent distributed cultural constituencies may have to work harder for audience share, and digital community co-creation programs can help the institution to the extent that such programs not only empower ground-up digital cultural creation, they also create new communities of interest. Institutional support for co-created knowledge bases is by no means a given: the recent accusations of indirect corporate tampering recently aimed at Wikipedia's XML definitions [16] may not persuade authoritative cultural institutions to open their online collections to semi-moderated community input.

4 Digital Literacy

One of the reasons that the Australian Museum is exploring co-creation is the fact that in 2004 it received a US$32 million state grant to fund a new extension, refurbish existing listed structures, and create two major new exhibitions. In order to inform the appropriate investment of this grant, the Museum's Audience Research Centre has made significant efforts to listen and respond to the voice of visitors and associated communities in the design of the new exhibitions [17].

Established in 1827, the Museum specializes in natural history and indigenous studies and is the oldest institution of its kind in Australia [2]. This heritage has resulted in a collection of 14.5 million specimens which in turn attract a monthly web visitation rate which regularly exceeds 1.5 million. Since the *quantity* of web visitors more than satisfies the Museum's public service criteria, management focus is being placed instead on the *quality* of online experience offered, especially to youth / informal learning communities. According to a 2004 internal survey, 63% of respondents described themselves as "educational visitors" to the Museum's site – which works out to at least 945,000 educational visits on a good month. In an effort to find out more about this substantial user group, in 2005 the Museum conducted a study into the use of educational websites by students and teachers. Five focus groups were conducted with students and teachers from a mix of both public and private institutions: primary school teachers, years 5-6; secondary teachers, year 7-10 (primarily science teacher/coordinators); students aged 13-16 years; and a mixed group of teachers with a focus on IT/computing specialists [18]. Some of the observations made by teachers dispel the myth of the digitally literate youth user:

Kids today have a surface level knowledge of technology, but if you scratch below the surface, they often don't have much more than that. There's a big misconception out there that they have this deep understanding of how the technology works, but they don't. They're consumers of technology, and that's probably not a good thing [Teacher, mixed group, male].

Basic critical ability in the selection and use of web-based information were also questioned during the focus groups. For example, many students in the study reported that search engines were easier and quicker to use for researching their homework and therefore preferred to books – often, the first site listed in by a search engine would be the one used by the student. As a centre for natural history, the Australian Museum is deeply involved with primary and secondary school curricula and has developed its relationship with these user groups within an informal participatory design framework. For example, in a study entitled *The Museum I'd Like*, school students were asked about how they wanted to engage with museums. The project culminated in a two-day *Kids' College* at which 30 students from mixed schools toured the Museum and briefed exhibition design teams on what they wanted to see in the refurbishment. This level of participation in museum exhibition design is rather unusual: major museums regularly ask child audiences to contribute to the design of aspects of exhibitions as users, testers or informants but rarely as design partners [19]. Analysis of the *Kids' College* suggested that

> While the students recognised the value of scientific information they also wanted information in the form of stories – they were looking for a human face to be inserted into the exhibits... A number of participants in the College indicated that they valued stories and anecdotes that illuminated any given exhibit [20].

The *Kids' College* study suggests that communication between the museum and the youth / informal learning communities of interest requires more than just efficient information transfer strategies. Informal learning messages can be enhanced through use of narrative, storytelling and the 'human face' – a lesson which has been ably demonstrated by the success of the *Crocodile Hunter* format.

5   Storytelling

The effectiveness of digital storytelling as an interactive tool is being tested by a few cultural institutions internationally which are seeking to form a co-creative link with communities of interest, both physical and online [21,22]. Community content creation is not a new field of study. Since the 1960s, major cultural instructions have broadened their programs to include audience interaction with content through education and a range of public programs [23], yet such interaction has previously been restricted to entertaining ways of using cultural content as part of educational programs, without genuine engagement with museum scholarship. Advances in social media are now providing communities of interest with a means to interact far more directly with museum collections, most notably through the rise of folksonomies (user-generated content tagging) as an alternative to fixed institutionally generated collection taxonomies. Although less 'visible' than arts projects such as *Self-Portraitr*, the challenge presented by folksonomies to traditional taxonomy-based collection organization is regarded as somewhat radical (and not particularly welcome) within some science-based curatorial circles.

If curators see folksonomy as radical, what are they to think of far more active forms of co-creative engagement such as digital storytelling? The digital storytelling process is characterized by a workshop in which a small group of participants are trained in digital literacy, narrative and content creation techniques in order to produce a short video piece. This consists of a condensed script, illustrated by a sequence of still images and accompanied by a voiceover; all created by the participant with minimal curatorial / editorial interference in order to encourage the participant to make and tell their own story, in their own words, using their own images and voice. This technique is fundamentally co-creative: the institution collaborates with the community in order to allow the latter to create their own digital cultural content. Digital storytelling is one form of social media that has been used successfully by a few institutions as a means of privileging community stories in the co-creation of social histories [24] but the implementation of such co-creative programs raises many operational issues, including:

- Sourcing and retaining skilled trainers, developing training materials.
- Hardware platforms, application selection.
- Content archiving, display and distribution.
- Communication models and feedback systems.

Previous research has dealt with design and implementation issues in some detail [25], but two major strategic questions remain:

- Philosophically, should a cultural institution tasked with relaying accurate cultural information in an authoritative voice even consider the use of semi-moderated popular social media such as digital storytelling or blogging?
- Organizationally, how does a cultural institution (particularly a science-orientated institution) embrace co-creative practice?

In answer to the philosophical question, an enthusiastic UK sector report firmly supports a shift towards a more co-creative cultural institution:

> In the past, museums, libraries and archives have been seen as suppliers, away from the action of creativity and occupying the supporting role of attracting workers to the creative industries. In truth, they are crucial in *inspiring* creativity [26].

Unfortunately an extended discussion on this issue is beyond the scope of this paper – suffice it to say that other recent research supports the adoption of co-creativity by cultural institutions [27]. But the organizational question is very relevant to HCI organizational behavior practitioners. Museums and libraries small and large act as hubs for dispersed communities of interest (CoIs) built around their content, collections and/or knowledge bases. The use of Internet to support online CoIs is particularly relevant in Australia, as most of the major cultural institutions are situated within state capitals which are difficult to access for regional and rural populations due to the country's vast size and low population density. Furthermore, the remote location of the country itself makes visitation by the international audience problematic. Therefore the successful implementation of online cultural communication could have particular value to Australian institutions. However, any such implementation is not straightforward due to the traditional site-specific nature of many institutions: the focus of staff is squarely on the preservation and exhibition of the physical collection. Therefore any technology initiative that might reduce visitation to the physical site could be frowned upon: this attitude is captured by Nie and Erbring in a rather extreme warning against online community: 'The Internet could be the ultimate isolating technology that further reduces our participation in communities even more than did automobiles and television before it' [28].

6 Co-creative Workshops

The Australian Museum is exploring the organizational ramifications of digital literacy through a series of internal co-creative workshops. Based on the digital storytelling format, the workshops train staff in script writing, creative production and editing in order to produce microdocumentaries which illustrate some previously unseen facet of the Museum's collections: in effect, bringing informal narrative and the 'human face' into museum communication, as suggested by the participants of the *Kids College*. Although off-the-shelf creative applications are a feature of the workshop (principally the use of Sony's Vegas video editing suite) the focus is firmly on team-based digital content creation techniques. A three-person team of writer, producer and editor is responsible for producing an original microdocumentary; a close creative collaboration is essential to devise and deliver the finished item within an accelerated two-day schedule. Through a focus on teamwork rather than technology, this creative digital literacy training has been extremely well received by previously techno-resistant participants, proving that "Learning to create content helps one to analyse that produced professionally by others; skills in analysis and evaluation open the doors to new uses of the Internet" [29].

Participatory design (PD) methodology has been selected to provide a framework to the investigation. PD is an evolution of user-centred design which considers the user as an equal collaborator within the design process. Recently, this methodology has been extended to both museum exhibition design [30] and library website design [31] from which a three-stage PD implementation framework has been adapted:

1. *Discovery:* gaining the trust of participants; exploring working practices, goals, values via participant observation; depth interviewing.
2. *Prototyping:* co-creative prototyping with participants to produce ideas, concepts, and new co-creative media forms for use within their institutions.
3. *Evaluation:* participants explore, evaluate and discuss comparative co-creative artefacts via surveys, focus groups and workshops.

Formal PD 'needs to be part of an *integrated design* that looks at work organization, job content, and the way technology is used to support these activities' [32] and the application of PD methodology to the Australian Museum workshops by the researchers has fulfilled this definition. In this project, due diligence has been very much a feature of stage (1), including the design and team selections for the co-creative workshops. These workshops constitute stage (2) of the PD application. Stage (3) has comprised formal internal evaluation of the efficacy of the co-creative workshops as a means to promote digital literacy: post-workshop surveys indicate that workshop participants strongly agree with this proposition. The next stage of evaluation will be formal focus groups conducted with potential target audience segments for the microdocumentaries produced in the co-creative workshops. These segments include parents of under-5s, teachers, and cultural adults.

The results of these evaluations will inform ongoing co-creative workshops. If the evaluations are positive, then the medium-term destinations for the microdocumentaries are the Museum's labyrinthine website and its new physical exhibitions. The operational strategy is to develop a core of digitally literate staff which will then collaborate with communities of interest already associated with the Museum to establish a sustainable program of co-creative communication using social media.

7 Summary

Across much of the Australian cultural sector, the principal mission of cultural institutions remains the production of site-specific physical exhibitions. This mission is entirely understandable when viewed through the tradition of ongoing cultural exhibition in well-populated urban locations, yet sits less comfortably within the wide geographic distribution of the Australian population. Although a growing desire to reach wider audiences via an expanded online presence is evident, such initiatives are tempered by the prohibitive cost of digitising existing collections optimised for physical exhibition. Significant amounts – if not the majority – of compelling cultural content remain inaccessible to communities and the general public. This paper opened with the dilemma of whether the museum should concern itself with collection, archiving and knowledge distribution' or seek to provide visitor experiences to compete with themes parks. It has even been suggested that "Museums are compromised institutions, caught between their twin desires for both authenticity and the spectacular" [33] – even though a designer might well argue that there is no reason why the museum cannot achieve both authenticity and spectacle.

The Australian Museum has used informal participatory design knowledge to guide the development of digital literacy within its own staff, as a preparatory step to engaging communities of interest in co-creative digital cultural communication. Schuler has argued that communities are distinguished by lively interaction and engagement on issues of mutual concern and that their well-being contributes to the well-being of the state as a whole. He proposed that ICT could play a role in community life by improving communication, economic opportunity, civic participation and education. His position extended to community-oriented electronic communication where community networks have a local focus [34]. But the relationship between institution and community has a far greater co-creative potential than the one-way provision of access and facilities. The digitally literate community not only has access to and knowledge of the tools to consume digital culture, it can co-create its own digital cultural artifacts with the institution. As creative technologies and practices become further embedded in cultural institutions, they have the potential to create new platforms for community engagement. This paper has argued that increasing digital literacy within cultural institutions could be integral to the further development of a co-creative relationship between institutions and communities of interest. As audiences expect higher levels of interactivity with content, social media provide a channel for communities and institutions to co-create new cultural experiences. It is hoped that the philosophy and practice of co-creativity can engage communities of interest in cultural participation as well as realize the civic opportunities afforded by digital literacy.

References

1. Mattelart, A., Mattelart, M.: Theories of communication: a short introduction, p. 186. Sage, London (1998)
2. Australian Museum Online (AMOL) (February 11, 2007) http://www.amol.org.au
3. Voyager Heritage Network (February 11, 2007) http://www.visitamuseum.com/en/about.asp
4. Wilkinson, H.: Collections for the Future, Museums Association. p. 36 (2005)
5. Trant, J.: Trust, audience and community: museums, libraries and identity. In: Trant, J. (ed.) Museums and the Web, Museums and the Web (2006)
6. Spadaccini, J.: Museums and Web 2.0. In: Spadaccini, J. (ed.) ideum (2006)
7. ARC Centre of Excellence for Creative Industries and Innovation (February 10, 2007) http://www.cci.edu.au/
8. New Literacy, New Audience, http://www.cci.edu.au/nla (February 10, 2007)
9. Gillard, P.: Museum Visitors as Audiences: Innovative Research for Online Museums. In: O'Regan, T., Balnaves, M., Sternberg, J. (eds.) Mobilising the Audience, University of Queensland Press: St Lucia, Queensland. p. xii, 363 p.177 (2002)
10. See for example http://www.youtube.com/watch?v=PdKHboldZIA
11. See for example http://www.flickr.com/photos/tags/selfportraitr/
12. LaValee, A.: Museums Try YouTube, Flickr To Find New Works for the Walls, in Wall Street Journal Online. New York (2006)
13. Shedroff, N.: Information Interaction Design: A Unified Field Theory of Design. In: Jacobson, R.E. (ed.) Information Design, p. 357. MIT Press, Cambridge, MA (1999)
14. Checkland in Long, J. and J. Dowell. Conceptions of the Discipline of HCI: Craft, Applied Science, and Engineering. In Proceedings of the Fifth Conference of the BCS HCI SIG. 1989. CUP (1989)
15. Turpeinen, M.: Co-Evolution of Broadcasted, Customized and Community-Created Media. In: Remit, L.G.F., H.T. (eds.) Broadcasting & Convergence: New Articulations of the Public Service 2003, Nordicom,Göteborg (2003)
16. Schofield, J.: Microsoftie tries to improve Wikipedia, indirectly. Guardian Unlimited, London (2007)
17. Australian Museum Audience Research Centre (February 10, 2007) http://www.amonline.net.au/amarc/index.htm
18. Kelly, L.: Developing educational websites: investigating internet use by students and teachers. In: Proceedings of Thinking, Evaluating, Rethinking, ICOM-CECA Conference, Rome: ICOM (2006)
19. Druin, A.: The Child as Learner, Critic, Inventor and Technology Design Partner: An Analysis of Three Years of Swedish Student Journals. International Journal for Technology and Design Education 12(3), 189–213 (2002)
20. Groundwater-Smith, S.: Millennials in Museums: Consulting Australian Adolescents when Designing for Learning. Invited paper presented to the Forum of Museum Directors, National Museum of History, Taipeh (October 2006)
21. Molnar, H., Meadows, M.: Songlines to Satellites: Indigenous communication in Australia, the South Pacific and Canada. Pluto Press, Sydney (2001)

22. Springer, J., Kajder, S., Borst Brazas, J.: Digital Storytelling at the National Gallery of Art. In Museums and the Web 2004. Toronto, Archives & Museum Informatics (2004)
23. Vergo, P.: The Reticent Object. In: Vergo, P. (ed.) The New Museology, pp. 41–59. Reaktion Books, London (1993)
24. Australian Centre for the Moving Image (February 11, 2007) http://www.acmi.net.au/digital_stories.htm
25. Watkins, J., Russo, A.: New media design for cultural institutions. In: Proceedings of the Conference on Designing for User eXperience, AIGA, San Francisco, USA (2005)
26. Holden, J., Jones, S.: Knowledge and Inspiration: the democratic face of culture. In: Demos (ed.) Museums, Libraries and Archives Council, London, p. 23 (2006)
27. Russo, A., et al.: How will social media affect museum communication? In: Nordic Digital Excellence in Museums (NODEM 06), Oslo (In press) (2006)
28. Nie and Erbring in Etzioni, A.: On Virtual, Democratic Communities. In: Feenberg, A., Barney, D.D. (eds.) Community in the digital age: philosophy and practice. Rowman & Littlefield: Lanham, Md. Oxford. p. 229 (2004)
29. Livingstone, S.: Media Literacy and the Challenge of New Information and Communication Technologies. The. Communication Review 7(3), 5 (2004)
30. Taxén, G.: Introducing Participatory Design in Museums. In: 8th Biennial Participatory Design Conference. Toronto, Canada (2004)
31. Nikolova-Houston, T.: Using Participatory Design to Improve Web Sites. In: Hoffman, D. (ed.) Computers in Libraries. Information Today, Inc. (2005)
32. Greenbaum, J.: A Design of One's Own: Towards Participatory Design in the United States. In: Schuler, D., Namioka, A. (eds.) Participatory design: principles and practices, p. 28. L. Erlbaum Associates, Hillsdale, NJ (1993)
33. Ames, M.: Museology Interrupted. Museum International 57(3), 44 (2005)
34. Schuler, D.: Community networks: building a new participatory medium. Communications of the ACM 1(37), 38–51 (1994)

A Study of Emotional and Rational Purchasing Behavior for Online Shopping

Lifen Yeh, Eric Min-Yang Wang, and Sheue-Ling Huang

Department of Industrial Engineering and Engineering Management
National Tsing Hua University, Hsinchu, Taiwan

Abstract. Emotion has gained much attention in product design over recent years. It is not surprised that the aesthetic appeal may determine the fate of a product, namely its success or failure in the market. Unlike the traditional marketing channel, websites provide a different opportunity for promoting the products to the potential customers who may know the products via a computer mediated website and its user interface. Previous studies have shown that website design features and usability can influence the willingness of the purchase. However, whether the product characteristics on the websites and the customers' attitudes (emotional thinking vs rational thinking) will affect the purchasing behavior is still unknown. In this study, the influence of the emotional appearances of the websites and the product characteristics as well as the user characteristics to the purchase behavior was examined. The findings suggest the emotional web appeal may not be able to affect the thinking style which may further enhance the purchasing intention of specific products. Further study on web appeal and web design strategies may be needed to identify and attract online customers.

Keywords: E-commerce, Emotional decision, Web appeal, Purchase behavior.

1 Introduction

According to Forrest Research, the US Internet commerce was 16.5 billion dollars in 2001, and expects to reach 35.1 billion dollars in 2011. As this growth continues, there is increasing interest and needs in understanding issues regarding online consumer behavior. Indeed, the online sales environment is different from the traditional market in which the face-to-face contact and the direct experience of the transaction are required in making purchase decisions. In the electronic commerce, or e-commerce, the buying and selling of products and services is computer mediated. Medium characteristics, consumer characteristics and product characteristics are important group factors to online consumer behaviors [2]. Among others, design elements are one of the major attributes of the medium characteristics. The purpose of this study is to identify what design strategies should have to enhance consumer's purchasing intention by examining the interaction of emotional on web design and product and consumer characteristics.

D. Schuler (Ed.): Online Communities and Social Comput., HCII 2007, LNCS 4564, pp. 222–227, 2007.
© Springer-Verlag Berlin Heidelberg 2007

2   Background and Research Proposition

Emotional and rational paradigms can apply in many different aspects of consumer decision-making process. From determining of the product characteristics to evaluation of the advertisement effectiveness and to understanding the styles the consumer process product information, some models were used for developing the strategies to attract consumers.

2.1   Rational and Emotional Paradigm on Product Type and Advertisement Appeal

The consumer's purchasing decision making process can vary widely among products. Vaughn [14] reviewed Foot, Cone, and Belding's FCB model, by which products were categorized with two different dimensions: involvement (high/low) and rationality/emotionality (think/feel). From these dimensions of FCB model, any product purchasing decision can be classified into one of the following four types, i.e., think/high, think/low, feel/high and feel/low. Typically, think/high products include large appliances, home appliances etc. Feel/high products include fashion, jewelry and apparel, etc. Products such as foods, drugs and house cleaning belong to think/low categories, and those which can help to create little personal pleasure, such as beers and desserts, are of feel/low group. Reliable measurement of FCB dimension was developed [11] and the scales were used to test candidate products in order for insuring the proper choice of product type.

On the other hand, appeals are used to enhance the attractiveness of products. Appeals in product advertisement can be considered as either emotional or rational [13]. Rational appeals can be seen as informative in nature and may be exemplified with information such as product components, availability, nutrition content, package details, price/value position, etc. Emotional appeals can be seen as psychological in nature and may stimulate either negative or positive emotion that changes purchasing desire [4]. It was hypothesized that the type of appeals works better when matching the type of products. The result of the study did show that the rational appeals work best for the thinking products and emotional appeals are more appropriate for feeling products.

2.2   User Characteristics

User characteristic will lead to variations of which people respond to an advertisement appeal. It was argued that when exposed to the same amount of emotional stimuli, people who are more emotional oriented will respond with a higher level of emotionality [7], and people who enjoy thinking more will process and evaluate the advertisement more deeply [10]. Based on the above findings, it is expected that the similar effects of the advertisement appeal will also be found for the web appeal. Thus, the following hypothesis was formulated.

H_1: People who process information by feeling (the feelers) are affected by the emotional web appeal and people who process information by thinking (thinkers) are not affected by the emotional web appeal.

2.3 Web Design

Web design plays an important role in online shopping, Fogg et al. [5] found that 46% of online consumers would judge the site's credibility based on the impression received from the web design. Like traditional retail channel, the atmosphere of web site is considered important for attracting and retaining online customers; therefore, the similar effects of real shop atmosphere are expected. [9]. This study expected the emotional web appeal would work in the same way as emotional advertisement appeal did for feel type products. The following hypothesis was formulated, accordingly.

H_1: Enhancing the emotional atmosphere of the web appeal will also enhance the emotional response of consumers to the feel type products.

3 Methodology

3.1 Experimental Design and Subjects

A test was conducted in the laboratory in order to find out if the hypotheses were acceptable. There were 32 participants whose ages ranged from 20 to 29 with gender balanced in this study. According to a survey done by Market Intelligence Center (2006), 56.9 percent of Internet users in Taiwan belonged to this age group. The participants were recruited from graduate students at the Department of Industrial Engineering and Engineering Management in National Tsing Hua University.

A 2* 2* 4 experiment design comprising of 2 levels of web appeal (low/high) and 2 levels of user's information processing style (thinking vs. feeling) and 4 levels of product types in FCB models were used in this study. User's information processing style and web design are between subject variables. Subjects of different information processing style groups were randomly assigned to either one of web design condition.

3.2 Manipulation of Web Design

In order to create different levels of emotional web appeal (low and high), five design experts were interviewed. Experts suggested including animated pictures and scenario images on the website to stir up the consumers' positive emotional response. They also addressed that animation should be used carefully, since it only attracts consumers at their first visit and may reduce the efficiency of the webpage. They also addressed that the structure of the web design should be the same as those online super stores. This would also be essential for the acceptance and the trust by online consumers. The two levels of web appeals were created based on the expert's comments, and both had the same page layout, product categories, tools, navigation structure and the same amount of information. The differences were the heading design and advertisement shown on the main page. The low emotional web appeal design was informative oriented (the web logo in the heading part and product image advertisement) and the high one showed more emotional tendency (the animated heading design and scenario type holiday advertisement). The colors of web were also considered because colors may produce emotional effects on people and, in general, warm colors are believed to be more exciting than the cold colors do. The orange color was selected for this experiment, since it could evoke emotions regarding home and make people feel comfortable [6].

3.3 Experimental Procedure

In order to classify subjects by their information processing styles, they were asked to answer the need for cognition (NFC) and the preference of affect (PFA) scales before the actual tests were started. This was due to the facts that construct of NFC has been found to be reliable for distinguishing individuals who enjoy more thinking [1] while the PFA has been proved also reliable for measuring the affective processing [12]. Only subject shows high thinking processing style (high NFC scores and low PFA sores) and high feeling processing style (Low NFC scores and high PFA scores) were interested and included in our study.

In the beginning of the test, subjects were exposed to one of the web appeal (low/high) then answered items related to their attitude toward the web design. Subjects rated each item on a scale of 1 to 7, where 1 represent to "strong disagree" and 7 is strong agree. Items about receiving of pleasant, attractive, pleased feeling, easy to use and willingness to buy product in the web were included for manipulation checking of web appeal.

After subjects answered those questions, they were given a short introduction about the next task. They were asked to find the specific product (NB->Think/high, watch->feel/high, battery->think/Low and cake->feel/low) each time and performed memory tasks after view the product page for 2 mins A free- recall task is used to measure the memory in this study. Since previous researche shows that pleasant material is associated with the increase of memory capability. We believe an emotional web appeal should increase the positive emotional response of people (make them more pleasant) and then to increase their memory capability. Subjects were given a maximum of 5 mins to complete the free- recall task, and after that they were told to record the product information as many as possible. Subjects need to go through all the 4 products, and the order of products were followed by the latin-square design rule to reduce the ordering effects. Further, subjects were asked to reconstruct the layout and graphics of the home page of the web sites. They were informed to draw everything they have seen. Finally, the demographic data of subjects were collected.

4 Result

The result of ANOVA showed that no significant difference was found in terms of pleasance, willingness to buy and easy to use regarding the low and high web appeals. The manipulation of web appeals did not work well enough as expected. The animated heading design and holiday advertisement only slightly increased the positive responses. For the attitude toward web attractiveness, the interaction is significant. (F=9.239, P=0.005). It was observed that feelers' opinions were opposite to those of the thinkers. The manipulation of emotional web appeal did work in attractiveness for feelers, however, it created negative responses to thinking style people.

For the memory tasks, the total items recalled did not show major difference on either user type or product type. The persuasive communication effects of emotional type advertisement were not found with the emotional web appeal.

The result of recalled tasks of the web design elements are shown in the Table 1.

Table 1. Percentages of subjects who correctly recalled the web design elements in the two levels of web condition

Item	Low (% of users)	High (% of users)
Name of web	44%	35%
Color	75%	56%
Heading design	19%	44%
Main advertisement	31%	81%
Wordings used in the heading	31%	50%

The animation and scenario type advertisement did increase awareness of some subjects, however, it was not the case for recalling the name of the web and the color used.

5 Discussion and Conclusion

The result shows that no strong relationship between emotional web appeal and purchasing intention of emotional consumers, which are measured by better memory on the product information. The result and conclusion can be highlighted as below.

1. Consumers spend much less time in online shops than traditional channels. When they visit the super stores, they usually focus on searching the product information and therefore pay less attention to the web appeal. And unlike the advertisement appeal are directly contribute to the product promoting, the web appeal is indirectly contributor.
2. The result of manipulation check shows only slightly effects on the deign manipulation. And in order to remain certain structure of web super stores, the available areas for manipulating web appeal is limited. Although animation heading design and scenario advertisement did increase the percentage of subjects correctly recalled. However, it did not make people feel the web more attractive and pleasant to visit. We should seek for more effective way and correct to enhance the emotional web appeal. Furthermore, the result of subject attitude of attractiveness also implies the fact that we know only little about what design strategies can enhance purchasing intention of consumers. And it might be related to the information processing style with which works for feelers but may not be necessarily the same for the thinkers. Further research requires to identify successful manipulation of emotional web appeal for different information processing style people.

References

1. Cacippo, J.T., Richard, E.P., Chuan, F.K.: The efficient assessment of need for cognition. Journal of personality assessment 38(3), 306–307 (1984)
2. Cheung, C.M.K., Zhu, L., Kwong, T., Chan, G.W.W., Limayem, M.: Online consumer behavior: a review and agenda for future research, 16th Bled eCommerce conference, Bled Solvenia, pp. 194–218 (June 2003)
3. Csikzentmihalyi, M.: Optimal experience: psychological experience of flow. Cambridge university press, London (1998)
4. Davies, M.: Developing combinations of message appeals for champaign management. European Journal of marketing 27(1), 45–63 (1993)
5. Fogg, B.J., Soohoo, C., Danielsen, D., Marable, L., Stanford, J., Tauber, E.: How Do People Evaluate a Web Site's Credibility? Results from a Large Study. Published by Consumer WebWatch (2002) Available at http://credibility.stanford.edu/mostcredible.html
6. Grossman, R.P., Wisenblit, J.Z.: What we know about consumers' color choice. Journal of marketing practice: Applied marketing science 5(3), 78–88 (1999)
7. Larsen, R., Doener, J.: Affect intensity as an individual difference characteristic. A Rew. J. Res. Pers. 21, 1–39 (1987)
8. Khalid, H.M., Helander, M.G.: A framework for affective consumer needs in product design. Theor. Issues Ergon. 5(1), 27–42 (2004)
9. Madu, C.N., Madu, A.: Dimensions of e-quality. International journal of quality & reliability management 19(3), 246–258T (2002)
10. Mantel, S.P., kardes, F.R.: The roe of direction of comparison, attribute-based processing, and attitude based processing in consumer preferences. J. consumer Res. 25, 35–52 (1999)
11. Ratchford, B.T.: New insight about the FCB grid. Journal of advertising research 27(4), 24–28 (1987)
12. Sojka, J.Z., Giese, J.: Think and /or feeling: an examination of interaction between processing style. Adv. Comsun Res. 24(4), 438–442 (1997)
13. Turley, L.W., Kelly, S.W.: A comparison of advertising content: Business to business versus consumer services : Journal of advertising. vol. 26(4), pp. 39-47 (1997)
14. Vaughn, R.: How advertising works: A planning model. Journal of advertising research 25(5), 27–33 (1980)

A Trust-Based Reputation System in Peer-to-Peer Grid

Zenggang Xiong[1,2], Yang Yang[1], Xuemin Zhang[2], Dairong Yu[1], and Li Liu[1]

[1] School of Information Engineering, University of Science and Technology Beijing, China
[2] Department of Computer Science, Xiaogan University, China
jkxxzg@163.com

Abstract. Grid computing and peer-to-peer computing are both hot topics at present. The convergence of the two systems is increasingly visible, and OGSA provides a framework for integrating grid and peer to peer. However, managing trust is a key issue for peer-to-peer grid. This paper proposes a novel trust-based reputation system for peer-to-peer grid, which is based on Bayesian theory. Theoretical analysis and simulations prove that the trust-based reputation system in peer-to-peer grid can improve the performance of cooperation among Gridpeers.

1 Introduction

During the past several decades, the processing speed of a computer has exponentially increased over one million times. A personal computer today is more powerful than a supercomputer ten years ago. However, today's computer, even the supercomputer, still cannot satisfy the increasing need of life sciences, physics etc. Therefore, the grid computing and peer-to-peer computing obtain development gradually. At present, grid and peer-to-peer are both hot topics respectively. However, the convergence of the two systems is increasingly visible: the two research communities started to acknowledge each other by forming multiple research groups that study the potential lessons that exchanged. P2P research focuses more and more on providing infrastructure and diversifying the set of applications; Grid research is starting to pay particular attention to increasing scalability[1][2].

Up to now, many grid models have been proposed, which are based on peer-to-peer technology[3][4][5]. These peer-to-peer grid models improve the performance of the traditional grid such as scalability, autonomy and dynamic. However, new challenges in peer-to-peer grid take place. Managing trust is a key issue for peer-to-peer grid, especially among Gridpeers. To address the trust problem in the peer-to-peer grid environment, this paper proposes a trust-based reputation system.

The rest of this paper is organized as follows. In section 2, we make a brief survey on the related works. Section 3 describes a trust-based reputation system in the peer-to-peer grid. Firstly, this section presents a peer-to-peer grid model, then a trust model based on Bayesian approach is introduced in the peer-to-peer grid environment. In section 4, we present a simulation to show that the performance of the model is better than interest-based model. Section 5 concludes the paper.

2 Related Works

Yang, B et al. present a super-peer network in [6]. Mastroianni, Carlo et al. extend super-peer network ideas and discusses a peer-to-peer grid model in [7]. According to

D. Schuler (Ed.): Online Communities and Social Comput., HCII 2007, LNCS 4564, pp. 228–235, 2007.

[8][9], the Grid computing paradigm is aimed at providing flexible, secure, coordinated resource sharing aiming dynamic collections of individuals, institutions and resources, and enabling communities to share geographically distributed resources as they pursue common goals.

The problems of managing trust in typical grid environments are discussed by Azzedin et al.[10] who define the notion of trust as consisting of identity trust and behavior trust. Alunkal, et al. [11] propose to build an infrastructure called "Grid Eigentrust" using a hierarchical model in which entities are connected to institutions which then form a "VO". They conclude with the realization of a "Reputation Service", however, without providing mechanisms that can automatically update trust values.

Apart from the typical grid, there are several proposals for managing trust and reputation in peer-to-peer system. Kamvar et al.[12] present the "EigenTrust" algorithm which evaluates the trust information provided by the peers according to their trustworthiness, using trust ratings for credibility, but their system is vulnerable to malice attacks. Wang [13] use "Bayesian Networks" for enabling peers to develop trust and reputation, especially with respect to the competence and capability of peers to offer high quality files and valuable recommendations in a P2P file sharing application, but it cannot give the analysis and evaluations in detail. Mui, et al.[18] present the well-known method of Bayesian estimation as the right probabilistic tool for assessing the future trusting performance based on the past interactions. Only direct interactions were studied. The question of recommendations was not considered.

3   A Trust-Based Reputation Model

Based on the related paper [14], we propose a peer-to-peer grid model, and Figure 1 shows this model. In the peer-to-peer grid, grid is divided into two layers. Underlying

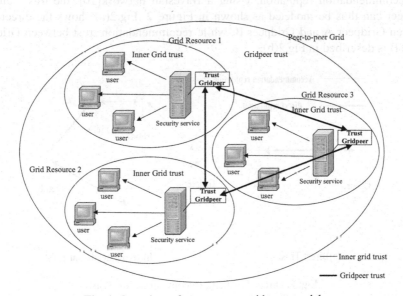

Fig. 1. Overview of peer-to-peer grid trust model

layer works by traditional grid model. On the other hand, the interaction among Gridpeers is implemented by peer to peer model. Gridpeer, according to [6], acts as Superpeer. The clients first request message from the Gridpeer by traditional grid model at local, if this Gridpeer cannot satisfy with the clients, then it forwards the request message to the other Gridpeers by peer-to-peer model. In this paper, we don't consider Inner Gridpeer trust, but only focuse on the trust among Gridpeers.

3.1 Basic Concept

According to [15], in the information system, trust can be defined as "the firm belief in the competence of an entity to act dependably and reliably within a specified context". Trust is usually specified in terms of a relationship between a "*trustor*", the subject that trusts a target entity, and a "*trustee*" (i.e., the entity that is trusted). Trust forms the basis for allowing a trustee to use or manipulate resources owned by a trustor or may influence a trustor's decision to use a service provided by a trustee.

In the peer-to-peer grid environment, when an entity makes decision, it is necessary to consider other entity's information and options about the specified entity. As above analyzed, this paper give the definition of trust in the peer-to-peer grid environment: *Trust* is the expectation of a certain Gridpeer which acting as entity, and the expectation depends on self-behavior of the Gridpeer, including direct reputation and recommendation reputation. The *direct reputation* specifies the past behavior of the Gridpeer in some context designated, and the *recommendation reputation* illuminates the information of interaction between the Gridpeer and the other Gridpeers.

As mentioned above, trust relations are classified into two kinds: direct reputation and recommendation reputation. Using a Bayesian network[16], the trust value of Gridpeer can thus be modeled as shown in Figure 2. Fig.2(a) shows the direct trust between Gridpeer A and Gridpeer B, while recommendation trust between Gridpeer A and B is described in Fig.2(b).

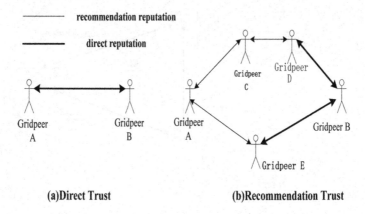

(a)Direct Trust   (b)Recommendation Trust

Fig. 2. Direct Trust and Recommendation Trust

In Fig.2(a), Gridpeer A directly evaluates the trust reputation of Gridpeer B through numerous collaborations with the Gridpeer B. Fig.2(b) shows the recommendation trust. Gridpeer A possesses the direct trust reputation about Gridpeer B through the recommendation of the other Gridpeer E, or possesses the trust reputation through the recommendation of the other Gridpeer C.

The Bayesian analysis is built on the basis of subjective probability, and Bayesian methods are very suitable for the trust assessment. This paper analyzes the probability of successful collaboration between two Gridpeers by Bayesian methods. And the trust model based on this method is also presented.

Trust is always connected with some specified context. For the sake of simplicity, we only consider a peer-to-peer grid system within the same context during a period of time. For two Gridpeers x and y, the successful cooperation probability between them is denoted by θ.There may have direct interactions between them, there may also have other intermediate Gridpeers and each of them has direct experiences with x and y. On the one hand, if there are direct interactions between x and y, we can obtain direct probability of successful cooperation, which is called direct reputation value, and denoted by θ_{dr}. On the other hand, if there is an intermediate Gridpeer z between x and y, and there are interactions between x and z, z and y, then we can also obtain an indirect probability of successful cooperation between x and y, which is called recommendation reputation value, and denoted by θ_{rr}. So, there are two kinds of probabilities of successful cooperation. We will combine these two kinds of probabilities to be the estimator of successful cooperation probability. That is,

$$\hat{\theta} = a\hat{\theta}_{dr} + b\hat{\theta}_{rr}. \qquad (1)$$

In which, a and b satisfy a, b$\in$ [0, 1], and a+b=1. They are weights for represent the importance of these two probabilities respectively and are decided by the personal characteristics of the Gridpeer x.

3.2 Direct Reputation Value and Recommendation Reputation Value

In order to estimate the direct reputation value, we use Bayesian theory to compute its estimator. So, we use the following formula to be its estimator:

$$\hat{\theta}_{dr} = E(Beta(\theta \mid \alpha + 1, \beta + 1)) = \frac{\alpha + 1}{\alpha + \beta + 2}, \qquad (2)$$

Where $0 < \theta < 1$ and $\alpha, \beta > 0$.

In which, α is the number of successful cooperation between Gridpeer x and Gridpeer y after n times interactions. β is the number of failure cooperation in the same context.

With respect to recommendation reputation value, using Bayesian theory, we obtain the estimator, which is,

$$\hat{\theta}_{rr} = E(Beta(\theta \mid \alpha_1 + \alpha_2 + 1, \beta_1 + \beta_2 + 1)) = \frac{\alpha_1 + \alpha_2 + 1}{n_1 + n_2 + 2}. \tag{3}$$

Where $n_1(n_2)$ is the number of interaction between Gridpeer x and Gridpeer z (Gridpeer z and Gridpeer y), $\alpha_1(\alpha_2)$ is the number of successful cooperation between Gridpeer x and Gridpeer z (Gridpeer z and Gridpeer y) after n times interactions;On the other hand, $\beta_1(\beta_2)$ is the number of failing cooperation between Gridpeer x and Gridpeer z (Gridpeer z and Gridpeer y) after n times interactions.

When the recommendation Gridpeer is more than one, it is easy to be inferred from Bayesian theory that the recommendation reputation value:

$$\hat{\theta}_{rr} = \frac{\sum \alpha + 1}{\sum (\alpha + \beta) + 2}. \tag{4}$$

3.3 The Analysis of Relationships Between Two Gridpeers

In the peer-to-peer grid system, the relationships between Gridpeer x and Gridpeer y can be sorted into 4 kinds with reference to what if there are recommendations and/or direct interactions between them. In the following, let's discuss how to get the final estimator Gridpeer x through analyzing the parameters of Beta distribution.

Table 1. The estimator of the 4 kinds of relationships

(Dr,Rr)	$\hat{\theta}_{dr}$	$\hat{\theta}_{rr}$	$\hat{\theta}$
(1,0)	$\dfrac{\alpha+1}{\alpha+\beta+2}$	0	$\hat{\theta}_{dr}$
(1,1)	$\dfrac{\alpha+1}{\alpha+\beta+2}$	$\dfrac{\sum \alpha+1}{\sum(\alpha+\beta)+2}$	$a\hat{\theta}_{dr}+b\hat{\theta}_{rr}$
(0,0)	1/2	0	1/2
(0,1)	1/2	$\dfrac{\sum \alpha+1}{\sum(\alpha+\beta)+2}$	$a\hat{\theta}_{dr}+b\hat{\theta}_{rr}$

Assume Dr=1(or 0) to represent there are (not) interactions between Gridpeer x and Gridpeer y. While let Rr=1(or 0) denote there is (not) an intermediate Gridpeer z between Gridpeer x and Gridpeer y. Then, the 4 kinds of relationships can be described as Table 1.

4 Simulation and Evaluation

We can use (1) to get the final estimator of successful cooperation probability under the same context, and it is a summary about past experience. On the other hand, it can be taken as an instructor of Gridpeer x's trusting in Gridpeer y to decide if Gridpeer x select Gridpeer y to be its partner in the future. What's more, it will form a relatively steady cooperation system with respect to Gridpeer. We use the algorithm, which is provided in [17], to aggregate the trust Cooperation.

We simulate our approach in a simulation of a file content sharing system in a peer-to-peer grid from original phex-like network in [5]. Every Gridpeer only knows other Gridpeers directly connected with it and a few file providers at the beginning. Our experiments involve 10 different file providers and 400 Gridpeers. Parameter a in formula (1) is set to 0.8. Each Gridpeer will gossip with other Gridpeers periodically to exchange their Bayesian networks. The total number of interactions is 1200 times.

The goal of the first experiment is to see if a Bayesian trust-based reputation mechanism helps Gridpeers to select file providers that match better their preferences. Therefore we compare the performance (in terms of percentage of successful recommendations) of a system consisting of Gridpeers with Bayesian trust model and a system consisting of Gridpeers that represent interest-based trust model[19]. Successful

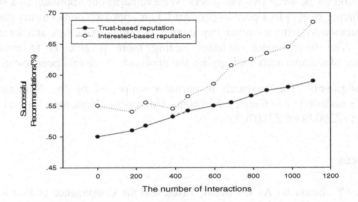

Fig. 3. Trust-based Reputation vs. Interest-based reputation

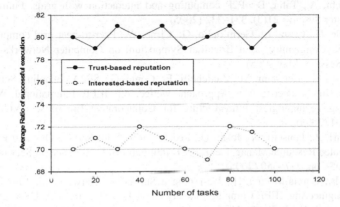

Fig. 4. Average ratio of successful execution with different Gridpeers

recommendations are those positive recommendations when Gridpeers are satisfied with interactions with file providers with good reputation value. If a Gridpeer gets a negative recommendation of a file provider, it will not interact with the file provider.

Figure 3 shows that the system using trust-based reputation performs better than the system with interest-based in terms of the percentage of successful recommenddations, especially when the number of interactions is very large.

The goal of the second experiment is to see the successful execution ratio in the peer-to-peer grid in the condition of different number of downloaded files, which is called tasks. Figure 4 shows that the trust-based mechanism is helpful when executing tasks than the interest-based mechanism.

5 Conclusions and Future Work

In this paper, we propose a trust-based reputation in peer-to-peer grid to solve the security problems between two Gridpeers. We evaluated our approach in a simulation of a file sharing system in a peer-to-peer grid. Our approach outperforms the interest-based reputation system; however, we cannot consider malicious attacks and fraud behaviors. The future work includes adding more parameters to evaluate the performance of the approach, and applies the approach to the real peer-to-peer grid.

Acknowledgments. This research is partially supported by the National Natural Science Foundation of China, Xiaogan University National Natural Science Foundation (Z2007039, Z2007042).

References

1. Foster, I.T., Iamnitchi, A.: On Death, Taxes, and the Convergence of Peer-to-Peer and Grid Computing. In: Kaashoek, M.F., Stoica, I. (eds.) IPTPS 2003. LNCS, vol. 2735, pp. 118–128. Springer, Heidelberg (2003)
2. Iamnitchi, A., Talia, D.: P2P computing and interaction with grids. Future Generation Computer Systems 21(3), 331–332 (2005)
3. Andrade, N., Costa, L., Germ'oglio, G., Cirne, W.: Peer-to-peer grid computing with the OurGrid Community. 23rd Brazilian Symposium on Computer Networks - IV Special Tools Session (May 2005)
4. Amoretti, M., Reggiani, M., Zanichelli, F., Conte, G.: SP2A: Enabling Service-Oriented Grids using a Peer-to-Peer Approach. wetice,14th IEEE International Workshops on Enabling Technologies: Infrastructure for Collaborative Enterprise (WETICE'05), pp. 301–304 (2005)
5. Uppuluri, P., Jabisetti, N., Joshi, U., Lee, Y.: P2P Grid: Service Oriented Framework for Distributed Resource Management. IEEE International Conference on Services Computing (SCC'05), pp. 347–350 (2005)
6. Yang, B., Garcia-Molina, H.: Designing a Super-Peer Network. In: 19th Int'l Conf. on Data Engineering, IEEE Computer Society Press, Los Alamitos, CA, USA (2003)
7. Mastroianni, C., Talia, D., Verta, O.: A super-peer model for resource discovery services in large-scale Grids. Future Generation Computer Systems 21(8), 1235–1248 (2005)

8. Foster, I., Kesselman, C. (eds.): The Grid: Blueprint for a New Computing Infrastructure, 2nd edn. Morgan Kaufmann, San Francisco (2004)
9. Foster I.: What is the grid? A Three Point Chkeklist. Daily News And Information For The Global Grid Community, vol 1(6) (July 22, 2002)
10. Azzedin, F., Maheswaran, M.: Evolving and Managing Trust in Grid Computing Systems. In: Conference on Electrical and Computer Engineering, Canada, pp. 1424–1429. IEEE Computer Society Press, Los Alamitos (2002)
11. Alunkal, B., Veljkovic, I., von Laszewski, G.: Reputation-Based Grid Resource Selection. Workshop on Adaptive Grid Middleware (AgridM), New Orleans, Louisiana, USA (2003)
12. Kamvar, S.D., Schlosser, M.T., Garcia-Molina, H.: The Eigentrust Algorithm for Reputation Management in P2P Networks. In: Proceedings of the Twelfth International World Wide Web Conference (WWW), Budapest, Hungary, pp. 640–651 (2003)
13. Wang, Y., Vassileva, J.: Bayesian Network-Based Trust Model. Web Intelligence, Halifax, Canada, pp. 372–378 (2003)
14. Montresor, A.: A robust protocol for building super peer overlay topologies. In: Proceedings of the International Conference on Peer-to-Peer Computing, Zurich, Switzerland (2004)
15. Grandison, T., Sloman, M.: A Survey of Trust in Internet Applications. vol. 3(4) of IEEE Communications Surveys & Tutorials (2000)
16. Heckerman, D.: A tutorial on learning with Bayesian networks.Technical Report MSR-TR-95-06, Microsoft Research (2004)
17. Shu-qin, Z., Shan-lin, L., Yong-tian, Y.: Trust Based P2P Topology Evolution. Mini.-Micro Systems 27(2), 246–250 (2006)
18. Mui, L., Mohtashemi, M., Halberstadt, A.: Computational model of trust and reputation. In: Proceedings of the 35th Hawaii International Conference on System Science(HICSS) (2002)
19. Sripanidkulchai, K., Maggs, B., Zhang, H.: Efficient content location using interest-based locality in peer-to-peer systems. IEEE INFOCOM 2003.Twenty-second Annual Joint Conference of the IEEE Computer and Communications Societies, pp. 2166–2176 (2003)

Part II

Knowledge, Collaboration, Learning and Local On-Line Communities

The Social Implications of an Assisted Living Reminder System

Bedoor K. AlShebli, Eric Gilbert, and Karrie Karahalios

{alshebli,egilber2,kkarahal}@cs.uiuc.edu

Abstract. We present the findings of an in situ field study conducted using our assisted living system, I-Living, that aims to enable seniors to live in a cost-effective manner independently. Basing the study on both interviews and diaries provided valuable and well-rounded data. Some of the main findings revealed that seniors will wear small health sensors if designed carefully. The study further reveals that delicate and complicated social structures influence the design space in such communities. The primary contribution of this paper is the pilot study conducted at an assisted living facility. It paints a compelling picture of day-to-day life in a healthcare institution and uncovers broad design implications that apply to a wide range of technologies.

Keywords: assisted living, pilot study, seniors, reminder system.

1 Introduction

Americans are living longer than ever before and want to enjoy their senior years with dignity and independence. Today, however, many people spend these years in healthcare facilities with less control over their daily routines. Developing systems that provide remote monitoring and diagnosis would free many people from institutions, thereby reducing financial costs and the need for constant supervision.

In this paper, we present the findings of a pilot study at an assisted living facility. By pairing interviews with diaries, our study contributes a compelling picture of life in a healthcare institution. We describe the social aspects and draw design implications for wearable health sensors and alert systems. In addition, we show designs of interfaces modeled on implications drawn from the study. Therefore, our primary contribution is the pilot study, as it uncovers broad design implications that apply to a wide range of technologies and benefits other practitioners in the field.

Our system, I-Living, [18], ultimately belongs in the home. However, to study its potential impact we focused on people who currently live in facilities but would live at home if given the option. I-Living currently acts as an alert system. It sends seniors reminders, such as medication and doctors' appointments. Its design, however, allows a variety of sensor devices and interfaces to come online via a flexible architecture.

The main goal of our project is to provide the elderly with the option of living independently with confidence and security. When fully realized, we hope I-Living will permit seniors to manage their own health at home in a cost-effective way. The work we present here is the first step towards achieving that goal.

D. Schuler (Ed.): Online Communities and Social Comput., HCII 2007, LNCS 4564, pp. 239–249, 2007.
© Springer-Verlag Berlin Heidelberg 2007

In the remainder of this paper, we discuss related work and its impact on our designs. We then draw a detailed picture of the living environment. We report our findings, concentrating on reminders and forgetfulness. Finally, we conclude with lessons learned from the study and future work informed by these lessons.

2 Related Work

The development of technologies for seniors is becoming increasingly popular. Many companies and universities are pursuing this field. For instance, in the Information Technology for Assisted Living at Home project [2] at the University of California at Berkeley, each user has his/her own Home Health System to monitor the health of the patient.

The Broadband Institute Residential Laboratory of the Aware Home Research Initiative (AHRI) [1] at Georgia Institute of Technology, is a three-story, 5040-square-foot home that functions as a living laboratory with the state-of-the-art facilities for broadband access and computing. Projects such as the Digital Family Portrait, [10], and Peek-A-Drawer,[16], were built to improve social relations between family members far apart. Other projects funded by the Aware Home, such as Memory Mirror [11], Cook's Collage [17] and InfoCanvas [9] focus on technologies designed to enable seniors to age in place and simplify their home and activity management.

The PlaceLab [8], a joint MIT and TIAX initiative, is a residential condominium installed with sensing components to help control and monitor activity in the environment. It has been designed to accommodate research into the viability and acceptance of wearable, physiological medical monitoring equipment and their related interfaces, including EKG, pulse oximetry, blood pressure, respiratory auscultation, weight, blood sugar levels, etc., in the context of daily living.

In [4], William Gaver examines different ways to keep the aging population closer to their local community. We look at some of our interfaces as complementing Gaver's efforts by focusing on finding ways to strengthen the relationship and interaction between seniors and their family and friends.

Ken Go's Familyware [5] is another way of reducing the social gap between small communities. However, it does not facilitate text-based, video, or audio mediated means of communication; rather, it supports sharing the "feeling of connection" by sharing objects, with simple signals, such as a child hugging or shaking a teddy bear.

Catherine Plaisant and Ben Schneiderman's personal medical history visualizations, Lifelines [13], inspired some of our more generic clinician interface designs, discussed in the future work section of the paper.

UbiMon [19], at the Imperial College London, addresses issues related to seniors using wearable and implantable sensors for distributed mobile monitoring. Implantable biosensors are used for post-surgical care and monitoring. These sensors can generally be placed inside the body during the operation with minimal additional cost.

Intel's Proactive Health lab [3] also has numerous projects aimed to help and study the needs of seniors dealing with cognitive decline, cancer, and cardiovascular disease.

The Center of Aging Services Technologies, [15], is a website that keeps track of ongoing technologies related to improving the aging experience and healthcare in the US. Also, other related projects are Philip's Personal Health Care Systems [12], British Telecom's House Care [14], and IBM's Personal Care Connect (PCC) [6].

The list goes on. However, due to lack of space we have decided to limit this section to only the universities and companies whose research is closely related to what we're doing and would benefit us in our research. As far as we could tell, we are one of very few to perform an in situ pilot study at an assisted living facility.

3 Method and Research Setting

We conducted semi-structured, one hour pre-interviews and post-interviews with 12 residents and 3 nurses in an assisted living facility. The interviews focused on the two key aspects: *wearable health sensors* and *alert systems*. The results of the pre-interview informed the design of out interfaces in the facility. The post-interview gave us feedback about the users' impressions of our technology.

To supplement the interviews, we supplied each participant with a diary. Participants recorded their thoughts and impressions when they felt it was appropriate. Diaries complement interviews by offsetting the effects of observers in an interview setting. In our case, the diaries enabled us to gain data that participants would have been reluctant to provide in an interview due to social pressures.

3.1 The Living Environment

Our pilot study took place at a working assisted living facility, in a large city in the Midwest, selected for its friendly and helpful atmosphere. We will refer to the facility as St. Ambrose[1]. It sits on a lush, green campus and serves about 140 residents. Residents stroll the grounds multiple times a day. A small chapel sits at the heart of the facility where residents attend the services held every morning and evening. In the afternoons, residents often gather in the community room to read organize activities or just chat over coffee. At mealtime, residents eat together in a large dining room.

The floor where a resident lives indicates their level of independence. The closer a resident lives to the nurses' station, the less independence they get. Residents living on the further floor often guard their independence closely, and tend to cover up each other's falls in the shower, since a bad fall could mean a move closer to the nurses.

3.2 The Residents

Most of the residents of St. Ambrose, and all of our participants, are retired nuns. The age of the residential participants ranged from 75 to 94, with an average age of 88. Most of our participants had spent some time teaching in a Catholic school, 1 participant spent 40 years as a nurse, and 3 participants had dedicated their careers to teaching hearing impaired students. Almost all of our participants hold a Masters

---

[1] We have changed the name of the facility to protect the identities of our participants.

degree. All of them demonstrated diligence and interest in the study. One participant called an author 5 days in a row to make sure that the system functioned properly. The residents continually impressed us with their articulate feedback. In one instance, a participant critiqued our interface from the perspective of a deaf person for over 30 minutes, and ended up connecting us by phone with an expert within St. Ambrose.

Some might argue that our participants do not represent the average target user. They do, however, represent the realities of doing field work. Their intelligence, enthusiasm, and insight have helped them provide us with much better feedback than expected. Such ability represents a significant strength of the participants in this study. Often a participant would not only tell us how the technology affected their life, but they would also analyze it from the perspective of other seniors with other disabilities. This served as a great aid at such an early stage in the design phase. Further research is required in this area to understand the diversity of user needs. Still, our study represents a significant first step in this design space.

3.3 The Nurses

Three nurses participated in our study. Their years of experience ranged from 3 to 20. Most of the time, one nurse serves all 140 residents. Therefore, they are usually very busy. During one 30 minute interview, an author counted 9 interruptions. Each interruption seemed to require a different skill from the nurse. In one case, a nurse in a different wing needed a reading about a resident. In another, St. Ambrose's director wanted to talk about a community event in the works. After the 8th interruption, the nurse apologized again and said, "It's always like this around here."

The nurses work in a small nurses' station. They use the station to prepare medication, store resident files and maintain awareness of the ongoing work. During a shift change, the outgoing nurse spends about 15 minutes telling the incoming nurse about the shift's major events. Most of these events revolve around the health of one of the residents. They discuss facts over a thick black binder that the nurses use to log their shifts. Soon after entering the nurses' station, we noticed that the nurses did not use a computer. In fact, a copier was the only electronic device visible in the room.

3.4 Existing Services

St. Ambrose is a very tight-knit community and residents often look out for one another. For example, a resident organizes a weekly car pool to the doctor's office, seeks out who should attend, and makes sure that everyone makes their appointment.

In terms of technology, St. Ambrose uses the intercom system the most. Nurses often communicate directly with residents by opening a channel to their room. They can access a resident's room by intercom at any time without having to ask the resident for permission. The facility's staff also uses the intercom to broadcast messages. Twice a day, a priest uses the intercom system to broadcast a prayer.

The nurses use the intercom to remind residents of their medication. If a resident forgets, the intercom is used again. If that fails, the nurse goes to the resident's room.

4 Pilot Study Pre-interview

4.1 Residents

Before conducting the pre-interview, state law required us to assess each resident's cognitive ability. To accomplish this, we conducted a Short Blessed Test with each resident [7]. The Short Blessed Test is a six-item test derived from the 26-item Blessed Test developed in 1968. It identifies cognitively impaired patients. The test asks residents to name the year, count backwards from 20 and recall a phrase from memory. All 12 residents passed the test and therefore continued with the study.

Participants were asked about their familiarity with technology. Surprisingly, only 2 of the 12 residents expressed some level of unease with technology.

4.2 Reminders at St. Ambrose

The staff at St. Ambrose already provides a set of routines to remind residents to accomplish certain tasks. A chime on the intercom system, for instance, reminds residents of mass. One resident commented, *"They really monitor people so they don't forget."* The facility established a rule stating that a resident gets one chance to prove they can self-medicate upon first entering. They are given two weeks of unsupervised access to their medication. If all goes well, they are allowed to self-medicate. If they fail the test, St. Ambrose takes control of their medication schedule.

(a)   (b)

Fig. 1. (a) A resident using the blood oximeter and the vital measurement reminder interface. (b) A.

However, during the interviews, participants voiced their concern about various situations or events in which they are failed to be reminded of. We categorized these situations as follows and addressed them when designing our interfaces:

- *Time:* Residents reported needing reminders for meals, meetings, and even the date. One participant even said that some residents will consider you a part of the staff if you can recall the date and time of day.
- *Things:* Participants confessed to misplacing their belongings regularly. One resident was known to often leave her walker at strange places around the facility.

- *Activities:* Some noted that they often forget to sign out of the facility or even check their voice-mail. Others forget trips, carpool events, and mundane activities like turning the lights off and wearing clean clothes. In one extreme case, a participant told us of a resident who unknowingly ate 3 pancakes and 4 muffins.
- *Place:* Residents often forget certain locations, such as their rooms or the chapel.

5 Interface Deployment and Interaction

Due to limited resources, we provided 2 of the residents with blood oximeter devices, computers and wireless networking (Figure 1(a)). The other 10 participants used placeholder objects that mimicked the dimensions of the blood oximeter sensor. The study ran for 2 weeks with the intention of using low-fidelity technology to gather preliminary data. Using the results, we intend to iterate our current interface designs, create new interfaces and perform a longer and more thorough study.

5.1 Reminder Interfaces

Currently, our system acts as an alert system. The nurses fill out an electronic form (Figure 2(a)) that schedules residents' reminders, such as check-up appointments, medication times and vital measurement readings throughout the day.

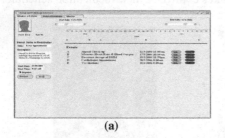
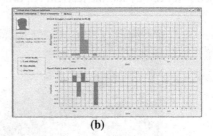

(a)   (b)

Fig. 2. (a) "Send a Reminder" tab on the clinician's interface. (b) Clinician's user interface showing the two vital sign measurements, blood oxygen and heart rate.

We began by modeling the interface after a regular prescription slip. The idea behind it was to ease the transition from the physical to the virtual world. However, a historical account was added to prevent errors like multiple reminders, along with a time line to enable the quick review of assigned reminders.

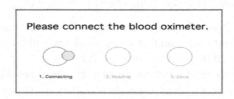

Fig. 3. Resident's vital measurement reminder interface

When a resident receives a reminder on her PC, as shown in Figure 1, she clips the blood oximeter on her finger. An interface (Figure 3) provides residents with directions and feedback throughout the three phases of the reading: connecting, reading and done. The nurses can then monitor the vital signs taken by the residents. The periodic readings submitted by the residents are retrieved from the ALSP (Assisted Living Service Provider) server and displayed in a two-way bar graph (Figure 2(b)). Nurses can view the data at three different time scales: the last 10, 30, or 365 days. The graph is used to display the readings, with the origin being the vital sign norm of the resident. The norm is provided by the resident's physician. By looking at the graphs, the nurses can immediately see whether the resident's heart rate level is above or below the norm and by how much. Should the readings suggest any abnormal behavior, nurses can issue appropriate medical instructions to the resident.

5.2 Placeholder Objects

We gave the remaining ten residents off-the-shelf pedometers, (Figure 1(b)) to act as placeholder devices. They wore them in the morning and took them off before bed. Our aim was to study where and how they wore the devices. We wanted to gauge the residents' reaction to its form and collect data regarding their everyday use. Residents were encouraged to modify the pedometers in any way they saw fit.

6 Results

6.1 Lessons Learned

After the two week study, post-interviews were conducted with the participants and the diaries were collected. Using the data gathered, we deduced the following:

- Residents were willing to wear the sensing apparatus, as long as it is unobtrusive.

  Nine of the ten residents wore the placeholder devices every single day of the two week study. One of the residents dropped hers in water and stopped wearing it for fear of compromising the study. We asked them to wear them however they saw fit. One resident fashioned the device into a necklace, while another fashioned it into a watch. However, we found that most wore them inside a pocket and wished they were thinner. One said, *"For the first two days that I wore the instrument, I was wearing a dress and a jacket. The instrument was bulky in the pocket of my jacket; I thought it was unsightly bulging that way. I was thinking how convenient it would be if tit was designed in a rectangle shape and was thin, then it would not bulge"* On the other hand, other residents feared losing the device because it was small.

  Many participants used the pedometer's text-to-speech features, as well, which reported steps taken, calories, etc. Several reported that the placeholder device made noise at inappropriate times. One resident said, *"I named my placeholder Josephine. It felt heavy and clumsy in my pocket. I would have liked it narrower. ... Josie talked to me in church."*

- There is a fear of breaking or dropping devices

  We found that some would leave the devices in their rooms when leaving the facility. Two dropped their devices in water. One let it dry and continued to use it as normal, while the other dropped out for fear of compromising the study. In a diary statement, a resident reported issues with wearing the device, saying: *"Even though it did not fall off my slacks band, I did not wear it for more than a half-day. Because I have a bladder disease, I use the rest room frequently and found it to be bothersome to be concerned each time the instrument would fall. ... On Fri. (June 23rd) I wore a jacket with shallow pockets. I placed the instrument in the pocket; it fell when I used the rest room and when I was having breakfast."*

- The monitoring interface was intuitive and encouraged further exploration

The two residents using the monitoring interface found the interface useful and very easy to use. They were very articulate in describing their experiences. Based on that, it was decided that the next version of the resident monitoring device will be a screen against a wall that provides alerts and shows pictures of their choosing at other times. This decision was a result of several interviews with one of the residents using the working device. *"Could you make it into a bed or chair side picture that's a screensaver of a relative. Don't make it a glaring outside object."*

The interface was created to be simple and not require any keyboard use by the residents. However, we found them wanting to delve further into their own data and willing to use a keyboard or touch screen. Also, more residents wanted to use the working prototype. In the future, we hope to equip more residents with working systems and with more devices such as scales and blood pressure units.

None of the residents were comfortable using a cell phone. Similarly, many felt the buttons on the placeholder objects were small and difficult to read. One resident mentioned that arthritis kept her from using the pedometer and asked to have the battery removed. Furthermore, the system was not fully trusted and at times did not go off when expected. One said, *"One went off at 11:45 p.m., and I was forced to get up. Is there someone in my room? Maybe a reason not to use a human voice at night"* This was due to wireless networking glitches the first few days of the study.

- Nurses want an interface that monitors more vital signs and provides privacy

The nurses' primary concern was displaying information they normally checked, such as blood pressure. Also, they were very busy with so many residents that privacy during discussions was a large complaint by the residents.

6.2   Social Factors Learned

During our short stay at St. Ambrose, we came to realize the existence of a very strong social network amongst the residents. For instance, the residents did not want reminders for every possible medication they should take. Some of them enjoy going to the nurse's station for medication and anticipate the social aspect of the gathering. Car pooling for doctor appointments was another time where the residents enjoyed socializing and catching up. Every Sunday, all the sisters went to mass and would socialize afterwards while waiting their turn to take the elevator. Furthermore, the residents try to organize a social event every afternoon or night, such as Friday night movies. Therefore, any engineering approach targeted at assisted living residents should reflect on these social aspects.

7 Future Work

7.1 Future Visualizations

Only one nurse is usually on duty at time. Due to that, the nursing staff are always overwhelmed. One of their main concerns with our system was that it might end up taking up even more of their time. They weren't very interested in the blood oximeters and didn't want data that wasn't in their job description. They wanted information they actually needed and would help save trips to residents rooms. Upon listening to these concerns, we decided to design two visualizations that could help them. One is to view the resident's health history and the other to show their current status at a glance.

Medical History's Visualization. This visualization (Figure 4(a)), inspired by Ben Schneiderman's Lifelines [13], is designed to help clinicians/nurses understand the resident's background/medical history in a timely manner. It shows the resident's medical history over a period of time and divides it into five main sections: *Illnesses, Medications, Doctors, Interventions,* and *Hospitalization.* By scrolling the bars on the top, the clinician can go back and forth in history to see the different times of illnesses.

Current Position and General Health Visualization. This visualization (Figure 4(b)) would help clinicians, family and friends check on the residents in a non time-consuming manner. It shows two main parameters:

- *the position of the user at the current time,* shown by the angle at which the resident's name appears in the visualization.
- *the general health condition of the user at the current time,* shown by location of the resident's name on the radius of the visualization. In other words, the closer the name is to green, the better their overall health condition is, and vice versa.

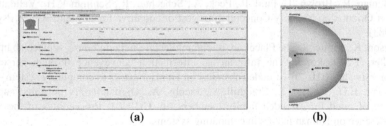

(a)   (b)

Fig. 4. (a) Resident Medical History visualization. (b) Position/General Health visualization.

7.2 Future Devices

Based on the social implications learned from this study, we found that some of the residents might be more accepting and comfortable in using devices that they have already are or have been using since their youth. They also wouldn't mind wearing any devices that might be common among a younger generation. Therefore, we hope to introduce devices that can be used by all ages, which would monitor health amongst other things.

7.3 Future User Studies

In the future, we hope to conduct a longer and more thorough ethnography. We hope to use a different set of users that might better represent what our average target user might be. Three facilities have already agreed to participate in our studies. The participants are closer to typical targeted end users with an average age of 78 and a more even gender distribution (55% female and 45% male). A more robust network will be installed using wireless range extenders, and more sensors will be used. Finally, we hope to install most, if not all, of the interfaces mentioned in this section.

References

1. Abowd, G., Price, E.: AwareHome: Georgia Institute of Technology: http://www.awarehome.gatech.edu/
2. Bajcsy, R.: ITALH: The Information Technology for Assisted Living at Home project. University of California at Berkeley. http://www.eecs.berkeley.edu/ eklund/projects/ITALH/
3. Dishman, E.: Proactive Health Laboratory. Intel. http://www.intel.com/research/prohealth/
4. Gaver, W.W., Dunne, A.: Project Realities: Conceptual Design for Cultural Effect. In: Proceedings of ACM CHI'99 Conference on Human Factors in Computing Systems, pp. 600–607 (1999)
5. Go, K., Carroll, J.M., Imamiya, A.: Familyware: communicating with someone you love. In: Proceedings of HOIT: Home-Oriented Informatics and Telematics (2000)
6. Husemann, D.: PCC: Personal Care Connect. IBM. http://www.zurich.ibm.com/pcc/
7. Katzman, R., Brown, T., Fuld, P., Peck, A., Schechter, R., Schimmel, H.: Validation of a short Orientation-Memory-Concentration Test of cognitive impairment. Am. J. Psychiatry (1983)
8. Larson, K., Intille, S. The PlaceLab. http://architecture.mit.edu/house_n/placelab.html
9. Miller, T., Stasko, J.: The InfoCanvas: information conveyance through personalized, expressive art. CHI '01 extended abstracts on Human factors in computing system
10. Mynatt, E.D., Rowan, J., Craighill, S., Jacobs, A.: Digital family portraits: supporting peace of mind for extended family members. In: CHI '01: Proceedings of the SIGCHI conference on Human factors in computing systems
11. Mynatt, E.D.: Memory Mirror. http://www-static.cc.gatech.edu/fce/ecl/projects/dejaVu/mm/index.html
12. Philips. Personal Health Care Systems: http://www.extra.research.philips.com/swa/cluster_phcs.html
13. Plaisant, C., Milash, B., Rose, A., Widoff, S., Schneiderman, B.: LifeLines: visualizing personal histories. In: CHI '96: Proceedings of the SIGCHI conference on Human factors in computing systems. Vancouver, British Columbia, Canada
14. Porteus, J., Brownsell, S.: House Care. British Telecom. http://www.housingcare.org/downloads/kbase/2334.pdf

15. Scritchfield, R.: CAST: Center of Aging Services Technologies. http://www.agingtech. org/
16. Siio, I., Rowan, J., Mynatt, E.: Peek-a-drawer: communication by furniture. CHI '02 extended abstracts on Human factors in computing systems. Minneapolis, Minnesota, USA
17. Tran, Q., Calcaterra, G., Mynatt, E.: Cook's Collage: Deja Vu Display for a Home Kitchen. In: Proceedings of HOIT: Home-Oriented Informatics and Telematics, pp. 15–32 (2005)
18. Wang, Q., Shin, W., Liu, X., Zeng, Z., Oh, C., AlShebli, B.K., Caccamo, M., Gunter, C.M., Gunter, E., Hou, J., Karahalios, K., Sha, L.: I-Living: An Open System Architecture for Assisted Living. In: Proceedings of IEEE SMC (2006)
19. Yang, G.: UbiMon: the Ubiquitous Monitoring Environment for Wearable and Implantable Sensors. Imperial University London. http://www.doc.ic.ac.uk/vip/ubimon/ home/index.html

Disaster-Response Information Sharing System Based on Cellular Phone with GPS

Masakatsu Aoki, Shunichi Yonemura, and Kenichiro Shimokura

NTT Cyber Solutions Laboratories, NTT Corporation, Hikari-no-oka 1-1, Yokosuka-City,
Kanagawa, 239-0847 Japan
`{aoki.masakatsu,yonemura.syunichi,k.shimokura}@lab.ntt.co.jp`

Abstract. In disasters, the victims must be provided with various bits of information. The information needed also changes with the situation. In this paper, we analyze the characteristics of such information and introduce an information sharing system. A prototype is developed around a cellular phone with GPS and its effectiveness is described.

Keywords: Disaster Information, Information Sharing System, Cellular Phone with GPS, meta-data.

1 Introduction

The victims of a disaster need various bits of information. Examples include disaster scale, safety areas, and rescue plans. Unfortunately, such information is now unevenly distributed among key spots such as safety areas. The information needed is too complex for reliable verbal transmission or bulletin boards. Because no fixed information structure can remain effective in the face of a disaster, victims receive only fragmentary and unreliable information. This confuses the victims and fails to minimize the damage.

This paper collects the features of disaster-response information. Next, we set the requirements to design a system that shares accurate information to respond to a disaster. A prototype of the information sharing system that is based on the requirements is described.

2 Information After a Disaster

After a disaster, the situation changes hourly, as does the information needed by the victim. In other words, one characteristic of disaster information is that it depends upon the current situation.

The information that the victim needs after a disaster, in this instance a large earthquake, is shown in Table 1.

D. Schuler (Ed.): Online Communities and Social Comput., HCII 2007, LNCS 4564, pp. 250–255, 2007.
© Springer-Verlag Berlin Heidelberg 2007

Table 1. Needed disaster response information (Earthquake)

						time: t
Disaster Information	*t -1*	*t 0*	*t 1*	*t 2*	*t 3*	*t 4*
A) Earthquake info.	*	***	***	**	*	
B) Aftershock info.			***	***	**	*
C) Evacuation info.			***	**	*	
D) Damage info.			*	**	**	*
E) Rescue info.			**	**	**	**
F) Life info.				**	***	***
G) Victim info.			**	***	**	*

"***" maximum need.

Time progression in disaster

Time	Situation	Passage of time
t -1	imminent earthquake	before time
t 0	earthquake occurrence	at the time
t 1	immediate aftermath of earthquake	after some hours
t 2	after a day of earthquake	after a day
t 3	after some day of earthquake	after some days
t 4	after earthquake	after a week ...

Disaster Information are following in Table 1.

A) Earthquake info.   : earthquake scale and tsunami forecast, etc.
B) Aftershock info.   : outlook for future earthquakes, etc.
C) Evacuation info.   : refuges and escape routes, etc.
D) Damage info.   : casualties and damage to buildings and lifelines, etc.
E) Rescue info.   : the rescuer necessary and the rescuer supply, etc.
F) Life info.   : restoration of lifeline, etc.
G) Victim info.   : safety of family, friends, and acquaintances etc.

2.1 Information Transmission

Currently, the main method of information passing in a disaster is mass-media, i.e. TV and radio. The same contents are passed to all receivers. Moreover, the information is tailored to suit large areas. The most useful information is very personal and has a limited shelf-life. The victim currently obtains such information by using "private-media" such as bulletin boards and word-of-mouth communication. Table 2 shows the suitability of the two media.

Some time after the disaster, the information that the victim needs becomes personal information. Mass media cannot be used to transmit such information.

When information is passed from person to person, it becomes distorted to the point of becoming a rumor. Because the source is ambiguous and the information is fragmentary, intermediary message passers often "supplement" the information.

Table 2. Media support for disaster response information

Information	mass-media	private-media	time period
A) Earthquake info.	**		$t0-t1$
B) Aftershock info.	**	*	$t1-t3$
C) Evacuation info.	*	**	$t1-t2$
D) Damage info.	**	**	$t2-t3$
E) Rescue info.	**	**	$t1-t4$
F) Life info.	*	***	$t2-$
G) Victim info.		***	$t1-$

"**" indicates a high degree of support.

We believe that information provided by the mass-media is reliable, but it is not timely nor is it sufficiently personalized. Information via private-media can be timely and sufficiently personalized, but the source cannot be trusted; it is necessary to validate the information.

2.2 Meta-data of Information

Information is generally validated by acquiring similar information from two or more sources that can be trusted. When there is no source or we judge authenticity from just the contents of the information itself, we need to determine:

- Who sent it? / Who said it?
- When was it sent? / When you heard it?
- Where is it? / What place?

If each point is clear, the authenticity of information is high. Authenticity is further raised by the addition of photographs and images that can validate the information objectively. In other words, information authenticity is increased by the addition of meta-data such as, Who, When, Where, and What (4W).

Information authentication consists of two parts. It is one to acquire supporting information from other source. The other is to appraise the information itself.

3 Implementation

Our approach to authenticating private channel information is to transmit meta-data with the information. We set the following requirements to designing the system.

1) Time resolution
Timely information must be sent hourly to keep up with the changing situation. Moreover, the information should be received properly.

2) Spatial resolution
Detailed location information must be given. It is hoped that the information is place that can be concrete, and specified.

3) Objectivity of event

Photographs and images that can objectively should be appended. For instance, it is easy to understand information to which the photograph is appended more than information on the text-only when reporting on a fire.

4) Usability interface

It is necessary to add the meta-data to information easily. Therefore, the system expects the interface that automatically adds the meta-data.

3.1 Prototype

A prototype of the system was constructed on a weblog. Weblogs are mainly used by for distributing personal information and are a type of diary with frequent updates. A very recent trend is the emergence of Moblogs (mobile weblogs); they are created and maintained by cellular phone users. Modern mobile phones make it possible to append locally-captured photographs and sound clips to an e-mail, so timely information entry via Moblogs is now possible. Furthermore, if the cellular phone offers a GPS (Global Positioning System) service, it is possible to acquire and append detailed location information (latitude and longitude). As shown in Figure 1, the prototype consists of

OS: Windows 2003 Server
Web Server: Apache
DB Server: MySQL
Weblog tool: WordPress ME [1]
Client terminal: A cellular phone with GPS / PC

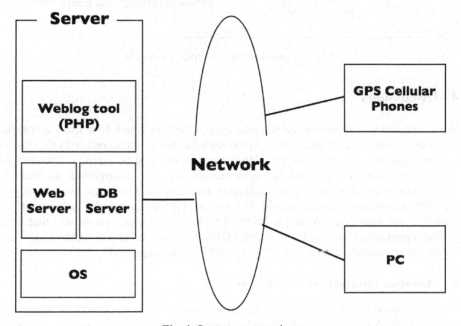

Fig. 1. System construction

Weblog posts were entered on a digital map based on the location information to confirm the information presented by the camera data (Figure 2). We used Googlemaps [2] as the digital map. In this prototype, the 4W meta-data is automatically added to allow authentication of the information as shown in Figure 2.

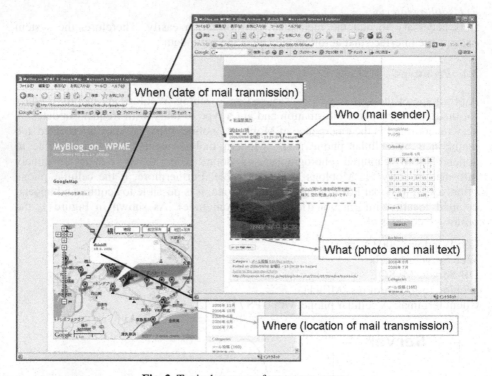

Fig. 2. Typical screens of prototype system

4 Discussions

We conducted an experiment on the prototype system in which four users employed the system over a two month period. Since each posting was stamped with the time of transmission, the temporal validity of the information could be verified. Photographs attached to each post effectively supplemented the text information, so that the description of the phenomenon was adequate and efficient. Outdoors, the accuracy of the GPS information was acceptable. Indoors, the GPS accuracy was rather poor and capture times were long. A simple problem with the prototype system was that three distinct operations were needed to acquire GPS coordinates, capture local images, and create the text message; usability of the system must be improved.

4.1 Location Information: GPS Limits

Some information sharing systems that uses cellular phones with GPS have been proposed [3]. Another approach visually shares information on a map in cooperation with GIS (Geographic Information System) [4]. Reports indicate that information accompanied by location data and photographs can transmit information more efficiently than text-based information. However, each approach assumes only outdoor use.

While many disasters involve outdoor responses, there are many cases in which indoor use is essential. Since the current GPS is rather ineffective indoors, we need to supplement GPS. One candidate is the system based on RFID (Radio Frequency Identification) tags.

4.2 Information Structure

In this paper, we proposed that information authenticity can be increased by the addition of 4W meta-data. The basic set of 4W information is essential but we need to consider higher data granularity. "Floor number" and "Apartment numbers" are needed for condominiums while, "Lane" is necessary for roads.

4.3 Interface

Our system uses the cellular phone as the information sending interface. The current prototype was created by simply concatenating several application programs so operation was rather clumsy and time consuming. Operation can be improved by altering the picture taking function so that GPS data and time are automatically appended to each photo. Given our goal of responding to disasters, the interface of the system must be as stress-free as possible.

5 Conclusion

This paper assessed the types and temporal attributes of information needed to respond to disasters. Next, we proposed an information sharing system for victims of disasters that uses meta-data (4W) to improve authenticity. A prototype system was constructed on a moblog foundation; the terminals are cellular phones with cameras and GPS functionality. We confirmed that our system is able to offer information sharing with some assurance of information authenticity. In the future, we will investigate how to increase information granularity by extending 4W, and improve the usability of the system.

References

1. WordPress ME http://wordpress.org/
2. Googlemaps http://maps.google.com/
3. Abe, A., Sasaki, T., Odashima, N.: GLI-BBS: A Groupware Based on Geographical Location Information for Field Workers. In: Proc 5th International Conference on Enterprise Information Systems, vol. 4, pp. 3–9 (2003)
4. Nakanishi, Y., Motoe, M., Matsukawa, S.: JIKUKAN-POEMER: Geographic Information System Using Camera Phone equipped with GPS, and Its Exhibition on a Street, Mobile HCI 2004 (6th International Conference on Human Computer Interaction with Mobile Devices and Services), Glasgow, Scotland (September 2004)

Tags for Citizens: Integrating Top-Down and Bottom-Up Classification in the Turin Municipality Website*

Franco Carcillo[1] and Luca Rosati[2]

[1] Turin Municipality website & assistant professor at University of Turin,
Via Meucci, 4, 10121 Torino, Italy
carcillo@comune.torino.it
[2] Information architect & assistant professor at University for Foreigners of Perugia,
via XX settembre 25, 06124 Perugia, Italy
luca@lucarosati.it

Abstract. Tags for citizens project aims to empower the citizens' experience within the Turin municipality website (http://www.comune.torino.it) integrating a standard top-down taxonomy with a bottom-up classification by tags. The top-down taxonomy has been conceived following the UK Integrated Public Sector Vocabulary (IPSV 2006 – an ISO 2788 fully compliant classification scheme) and empirically refined by usability tests with users and by log files monitoring. The bottom-up classification works as a social tagging system. The latter it is not simply added to the former, but completely integrated to it, in order to obtain a coherent system.

Keywords: eGovernment, Metadata, Information Architecture, Social Classification, Folksonomy, IPSV (Integrated Public Sector Vocabulary).

1 Introduction: The Best of Both Worlds

The collaborative tagging (or folksonomy) may be not only an alternative to the canonycal classification models born in librarianship field, but it may works as a valid complement of conventional taxonomies or facets. In such a way we can correct the intrinsic limits of each classification approach and enforce their benefits. Considering the wide range of mental models an e-gov site has to satisfy, this may take strong advantages by a "blended" approach.

So, the purpose of the project is to show how the flat keywords space of user-generated tags can be effectively mixed with a richer poly-hierarchical classification scheme to improve the system information architecture.

Besides enforcing order on the flat space of keywords, the blend of tags and taxonomy is able to empower the *information scent* [1] and the *berrypicking* [2] capabilities of the system. Every information architecture project refers to two different information axes [3]:

- a **vertical** (or paradigmatic) axis, i.e. the hierarchical relationship that each item of a system engages with the others.

---

* Though the article is the result of a common strength, Franco Carcillo wrote the paragraphs 1-2, Luca Rosati the paragraphs 3-4.

D. Schuler (Ed.): Online Communities and Social Comput., HCII 2007, LNCS 4564, pp. 256–264, 2007.
© Springer-Verlag Berlin Heidelberg 2007

- a **horizontal** (or syntagmatic) axis, i.e. the semantic, contiguity relationship that each item engages with the others.

In our case, the combination of tags and taxonomy allows for better management of both these axes:

- from the vertical or paradigmatic point of view, when a user is going to associate a keyword to a category of the taxonomy (in order to tag a resource), the system suggests similar tags or hierarchy of tags pertaining to the same category
- from the horizontal or syntagmatic point of view, at the same time, the system will allow the user to see all the other tags belonging to the same category.

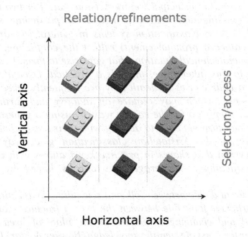

Fig. 1. The two axes of information architecture

Other main features will be:

- tags suggestion (by Ajax) during the tag assignation phase or during the keyword/tag insertion in the search engine
- hybrid search both by tags and keywords
- usage opportunity of compound tags or keywords
- tagging history.

2   Taxonomies and Folksonomies: Pros and Cons

> *My guess is that we have a folk theory of categorization itself. It says that things come in well-defined kinds, that the kinds are characterized by shared properties, and that there is one right taxonomy of the kinds.*
> *It is easier to show what is wrong with a scientific theory than with a folk theory. A folk theory defines common sense itself. When the folk theory and the technical theory converge, it gets even tougher to see where that theory gets in the way-or even that it is a theory at all (Lakoff) [4].*

Taxonomies are top-down classification systems designed by specialised staff and thus fairly centralised and accurate. They resemble the form of classification Lakoff calls "scientific theory", reflecting Aristotelian-type logic.[1]

On the other hand, folksonomies are bottom-up classification systems, created by users themselves by adding keywords. As they are distributed, these systems are not too accurate, but better reflect a user's viewpoint. They come closer to the classification model Lakoff calls "folk theory" - in this case comparable to the Eleanor Rosch prototype theory (more than to Aristotle).

However, in philosophical terms, no classification system can call itself completely scientific or completely empirical (folk). Any classification, even one starting out as scientific, tends to become folk, based on the empirical needs its use inevitably requires of it.

> So why do we sometimes appear in practice prototypical in our classifications, even if in principal we are Aristotelian? For two main reasons: because each classification system is tied to a particular set of coding practices; and because classification systems in general (we are not making this as an ex cathedra pronouncement) rellect the conflicting, contradictory motives of the sociotechnical situations that gave rise to them. [...]
>
> In addition to this inheritance, there is a practical Occam's razor. When doctors come to code causes of death they are frequently faced with a set of difficult judgments (which may require an autopsy and further diagnostic work). They can simply go for the easiest way, by using a generalized "other" category. They can then get back to dealing with their live patients [...]. So the classical beauty of the Aristotelian classification gives way to a fuzzier classification system that shares in practice key features with common sense prototype classifications – heterogeneous objects linked by metaphor or analogy. [...]
>
> There is no great divide between folk and scientilic classifications. Below, we discuss one particular fault line between the two: a fracture that is constantly being redelined and changing its nature as the plate of lived experience is subducted under the crust of scientific knowledge (Bowker & Star) [5].

All these considerations have led us to the idea of combining top-down and bottom-up classifications in order to both gain (so to say) the best of two worlds and – above all – to try to get a better picture, through folk classification, of citizens' mental models and correct the limits of top-down taxonomy.

Taxonomy and folksonomy can be seen as alternative, complementary tools and not opposing ones. Due to such individual peculiarities, each can be used in specific contexts with specific objectives.

2.1 Taxonomies Anatomy

Taxonomies are knowledge organisation and management systems made up of terms set out in a hierarchical tree-like structure. They exploit hierarchical-enumerative classification systems, from which they inevitably inherit qualities and defects.

---

[1] An Aristotelian classification works based on binary properties that the object being classified has or has not. Hence, at each classification level, you choose a group of these properties to decide on whether an object belongs or does not belong to a single class: e.g. a polygon belongs to the rectangle class if it has four sides, these sides are at right-angles and if the opposite sides are the same length.

Tree-like systems permit precision and order when classifying elements within a group, favouring a 'known-item seeking' approach. These same characteristics are also their limits.

- As they are top-down (creation and upkeep by a few experts or an institution), taxonomies are fairly centralised systems where any changes to be made can only be made from above.
- The strict precision of tree-like models often makes for excessive system rigidity and closure. Introducing new categories at any point in the system often requires changes being made to other parts and can only be done by whoever created the system.
- As they branch out deeply, tree systems tend to hide the more popular classes (those used by users to a greater extent) and 'push' them downwards.
- The hierarchical structure is highly suited to known-item seeking strategies (used by users who know what they are looking for), while it does not suit exploratory-seeking strategies (users who do not know what they are looking for, those browsing or non-expert users). Moreover, they do not help the berry-picking model type (see Par. 1) so typical of the web.

2.2 Folksonomies Anatomy

The strength of these systems lies not in their precision but their wide-scale popular use, i.e. people. Instead of making an effort to build classification systems suiting the users' mental model, you simply enable the users themselves – from below – to 'create' common, shared mental models, which emerge spontaneously (through a collaborative process and natural selection).

As a matter a fact, folksonomies should be called **distributed classification** systems. Folksonomies can also be used for analysis: to study the mental models of entire communities through the way their members describe (classify) a group of collected items. They can be used as support when processing categories, choosing favourite terms or setting up controlled vocabularies [6].

Critics of folksonomy mention the following main defects:

- Folksonomies are not precise either in terms of categorising or language. The risk is that of having many language variables for the same concept thus loss of control over vocabulary and its synonyms. It is also true that recent tag systems foresee a 'suggestion-based' system displaying tags linked to the one chosen. Moreover, to criticise this position we can turn to the Lakoff quote found in Par. 2: a classification system is always somewhat hybrid as its end is practical (what it is used for) and this inevitably mixes a logical-scientific base with strictly popular, empirical criteria.
- Tags used in folksonomies have no hierarchical structure whatsoever. There is no division into categories and sub-categories, whether in the hierarchical-enumerative sense or analytical-synthetic. Tags are a flat space of keywords. This objection – though essentially true – does not highlight the most innovative aspect of the phenomenon, which is not so much the flat mass of tags but their aggregation by users themselves.

- Folksonomies have low findability and are therefore more suited to exploratory seeking than known-item seeking.

As far as the positive or interesting aspects of folksonomies are concerned, we can list these advantages as follow.

- Above all, not all folksonomy limits are defects. If on the one hand you lose precision, on the other this loss is offset by an important number of benefits in terms of suggestions as to the representation and use of certain concepts by a large number of users, and thus on navigators' mental models. In this sense, folksonomies can be considered not only as classification systems but as support tools for designing the classification itself.
- Folksonomies are more suited to finding information (discoverability) than targeted searches (findability). Referring to models seen, we could say that folksonomies favour the **berry-picking** search model type, and strongly integrate the idea of **serendipity**.
- Inexpensiveness: tag systems are extremely economical to set up (in terms of both time and money), as all classification work is carried out by users successively.

3 "Tags for Citizens" Project: Classification Systems Components

3.1 The Taxonomy Layer: IPSV (Integrated Public Sector Vocabulary)

We are running a taxonomy redesign of the Turin Municapality website following the British standard IPSV (Integrated Public Sector Vocabulary) [7]. The Integrated Public Sector Vocabulary (IPSV) is a controlled vocabulary, also known as an 'encoding scheme' for populating the Subject element of the e-Government Metadata Standard (e-GMS). It should be used with all the electronic resources produced in the UK public sector, so that citizens may access them more easily. IPSV complies with ISO 2788 and BS 8723, the International and British Standards for monolingual thesauri.

The IPSV was developed with the backing of the Department for Communities and Local Government (DCLG) (formerly the Office of the Deputy Prime Minister) and the e-Government Unit (e-GU) of the Cabinet Office.

We have structured the redesign process into three steps:

- content inventory (mapping of the first two navigation levels of Turin Municipality website (www.comune.torino.it)
- comparison between the actual taxonomy, the IPSV model, and a sample of IPSV application (the UK Public Services website, www.direct.gov.uk) in order to extract the new top-down information architecture of Turin Municipality website
- a successive deeper comparison between the labels of the two systems in order to design a more coherent labelling system.

The matching results are shown in Table 1 below (we have not enough space to explain the taxonomy redesign procedure in detail).

Table 1. Comparison between the actual Turin Municipality website taxonomy, the IPSV model, and the UK Public Services website, www.direct.gov.uk

Turin website	IPSV	Direct.gov.uk
Ambiente e verde [Environment and green]	Environment	Environment and greener living
Casa e territorio [Home and territory]	Housing	Home and community
Commercio e impresa [Commerce and business]	Business and industry	Information for businesses [in the footer menu]
Cultura, sport e tempo libero [Culture, sport and leisure time]	Leisure and culture	Young people > Leisure
Formazione e Scuola [Education, training and school]	Education and skills	Education and learning
Lavoro e Orientamento [Work and orientation]	Employment, jobs and careers	Employment
Sanità e Servizi Sociali [Healthcare and social services]	Health, well-being and care	Health and well-being
Sicurezza cd emergenze [Safety and emergencies]	Public order, justice and rights > Security I Emergencies	In: Newsroom > Public safety [utilities menu]
Soldi e risparmio [Money and savings]	In: Economics and finance > Personal finance	Money, tax and benefits
Tasse e agevolazioni fiscali [Taxes and tax benefits]	In: Economics and finance > Tax	Money, tax and benefits
Trasporti e viabilità [Transport and roads]	Transport and infrastructure	Travel and transport
Jolly Item (e.g. Special: Olympic Games 2006)	--	--

3.2 The Folksonomy Layer

The folksonomy layer works as a speed classification/movement skin overlapping the taxonomy layer.

This system has two main aims.

• Allow users to save pages that interest them from the City of Turin website in a reserved area so as not to have to search for them each time (labelling them through tags). As such, tags become access shortcuts for frequent users.

- Furthermore, allow users who have not saved their "own pages" to use tags created by other users as complementary browsing tools to the taxonomy and search motor.

From the home page, the user can use the tags both as main tools to access content or to refine a search started through the standard taxonomy or search engine. User tags will be saved in a personal area on the website - with each user able to decide to what extent to make this information public: completely, partially or not at all.

These two forms of use correspond to two levels of interactivity:

- one more active, the former.
- one more passive, the latter.

The first form of use is for users who are more inclined to take part actively or used to using similar systems (e.g. Del.icio.us). The second is for those who, though more conservative, can be stimulated to change their behaviour by taking advantage of work done by other users.

3.2.1 Save and Find Functions

The system is displayed to users through two key functions in two boxes on the page (normally placed in the right-hand column) - see Fig. 2.

The Save function allows users to save the page in a personal bookmark (tagging it) to find it more easily later on. No registration will initially be required. Users will only need to tag the page and then will be subsequently requested to complete a brief registration. Alternatively, they can use the Delicious account (if they already have one) or another similar system.

The Find function allows users to find pages similar to, or linked to, the current one, through tag clouds. The system will visualise the tag/s (if available) other users used to tag the page and any other tags linked semantically to the first ones (e.g. "Whoever used this tag also used...", or "Whoever consulted this page also read..."). This function will also allow users to search for pages on a specific topic through the use of tags.

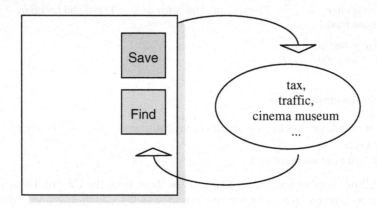

Fig. 2. Main functions of the folksonomy layer

4 Putting All Together

We said the folksonomy layer is not just added to the taxonomy one, but integrated with it. The synthesis happens in the tagging phase: during the tag inserting process. The system asks users to link tags to the site category taxonomy creating a link between the two classification layers. One tag can be associated to several categories at the same time.

Integration has further advantages in terms of system functionality.

- The user has two complementary access systems available: through taxonomy and tags.
- There can be interchange between the two systems: moving from taxonomy to tag and vice-versa, without interruption.

In greater detail, this enables:

- Showing (all) other tags belonging to a certain category when the user associates a tag to that category.
- Avoiding the tag flatness problem (tags on a single indistinct level), allowing macro-category grouping.
- Helping to solve (at least partly) the problem of synonyms.
- Monitoring the most frequently used tags and their correlation with categories to correct or integrate the taxonomy (the classification system created from above).
- Progressively absorbing into a meta-data or controlled vocabulary system tags going over a certain threshold of use (as happens in the BBC website).

> *BBC staff have suspected for many years that metadata could be the solution to guiding the audience through the site, but it has not been simple to find the right approach. [...]*
> *Maintenance costs and responsiveness [of the controlled vocabularies] were still a problem. A compromise solution (known as the metadata threshold) allows for free-text tagging that is absorbed into formal controlled vocabularies when enough content is tagged with that term. The solution aims to combine cheap and responsive tagging with unambiguous aggregation power. So far it has been very successful at slashing overheads. The controlled vocabulary, semi-automatic suggestions and metadata threshold were still coupled to the CMS, but the development of an application programming interface (API) should resolve the issue of tagging content being produced in different systems (Loasby) [8].*

References

1. Chi, E.H., Pirolli, P., Chen, K., Pitkow, J.: Using Information Scent to Model User Information Needs and Actions on the Web. In: Proceedings of the SIGCHI conference on Human Factors in Computing Systems, ACM Press, New York (2001), http://www2.parc.com/istl/projects/uir/publications/items/UIR-2001-07-Chi-CHI2001-InfoScentModel.pdf
2. Bates, M.: The Design of Browsing and Berrypicking Techniques for the Online Search Interface, UCLA (1989) http://www.gseis.ucla.edu/faculty/bates/berrypicking.html

3. Rosati, L.: I due assi dell'architettura dell'informazione [= The Two Axis of Information Architecture], Trovabile (2006) http://trovabile.org/articoli/assi-architettura-informazione
4. Lakoff, G.: Women, Fire and Dangerous Things: What Categories Reveal About Mind, p. 121. University of Chicago Press, Chicago (1987)
5. Bowker, G.C., Star, S.L.: Sorting Things Out: Classification and Its Consequences, pp. 64–67. MIT Press, Cambridge (1999)
6. Quintarelli, E.: Folksonomies: Power to the People, paper presented at the ISKO Italy-UniMIB meeting, ISKO Italia (2005) http://www.iskoi.org/doc/folksonomies.htm
7. UK Cabinet Office eGovernment Unit: IPSV-Integrated Public Sector Vocabulary, (2006) http://www.esd.org.uk/standards/ipsv/
8. Loasby, K.: Changing Approaches to Metadata at bbc.co.uk: From Chaos to Control and Then Letting Go Again, in ASIS&T Bulletin (October/November 2006) http://www.asis.org/Bulletin/Oct-06/loasby.html

Tracing Conceptual and Geospatial Diffusion of Knowledge

Chaomei Chen[1,2], Weizhong Zhu[1,2], Brian Tomaszewski[1,3], and Alan MacEachren[1,3]

[1] Northeast Visualization and Analytics Center (NEVAC)
[2] College of Information Science and Technology, Drexel University, Philadelphia, USA
[3] Department of Geography, Penn State University, State College, USA
chaomei.chen@cis.drexel.edu, wz32@drexel.edu, bmt139@psu.edu,
maceachren@psu.edu

Abstract. Understanding the dynamics of knowledge diffusion has profound theoretical and practical implications across a wide variety of domains, ranging from scientific disciplines to education and understanding emergent social phenomena. On the other hand, it involves many challenging issues due to the inherited complexity of knowledge diffusion. In this article, we describe a unifying framework that is designed to facilitate the study of knowledge diffusion through multiple geospatial and semantic perspectives. In particular, we address the role of intrinsic and extrinsic geospatial properties of underlying phenomena in understanding conceptual and geospatial diffusion of knowledge. We illustrate the use of visualizations of geographic distributions of terrorist incidents, the structural evolution of research networks on terrorism and avian flu, and concept-location relations extracted from news stories.

Keywords: knowledge diffusion, geographic mapping, collaboration networks, information visualization.

1 Introduction

Understanding the dynamics of knowledge diffusion has become increasingly challenging due to the overwhelming volume of data from multiple sources and the increasing complexity associated with multiple perspectives. The diffusion of knowledge and technical innovations involves individuals, groups, and communities at various stages. Knowledge diffusion in mass opinions is characterized by the emergence of consensus or the expansion of one thematic thesis across a given population. Research in fields such as social network analysis [1], citation mapping and information visualization [2] has addressed various issues concerning the structural complexity challenge. Research in knowledge discovery and data mining is also relevant, notably in the areas of concept drifts [3, 4], topic detection [5, 6], and change detection [7, 8].

The aim of this article is to introduce an integrative approach to tracing conceptual and geospatial aspects of knowledge diffusion so that one can explore knowledge diffusion from different perspectives in a consistent framework. Specifically, our approach is designed to improve our understanding of the structure, the growth, and the spread of knowledge. In this article, we focus on the role of intrinsic and extrinsic

D. Schuler (Ed.): Online Communities and Social Comput., HCII 2007, LNCS 4564, pp. 265–274, 2007.
© Springer-Verlag Berlin Heidelberg 2007

geospatial properties of an underlying knowledge diffusion process. An intrinsic geospatial property identifies the inherent geospatial nature of an event. For example, the location of an avian flu outbreak is intrinsic because it is essential to our knowledge of the event. In contrast, an extrinsic geospatial property is secondary to the understanding of a phenomenon. For example, the interest and expertise of a researcher may or may not have anything to do with the location of his/her institution. In this article, we describe a conceptual framework such that data from multiple sources with various degrees of geospatial relevance can be accessed and contrasted in a unifying analytic environment.

2 Related Work

The study of information diffusion is concerned with how and why people accept or reject a new idea. The simplest model of information diffusion is the "Magic Bullet" model, which is also known as the *hypodermic needle model*. In this model, an intended message is sent directly to a receiver and unconditionally accepted by the receiver. A more sophisticated model is the *two-step flow model*. It suggests that the spread of information from mass media to the society takes two steps. First, the information is filtered through opinion leaders, who then influence others. The classic example is that undecided voters before an election tend to vote the way their friends and colleagues voted later in the election [9]. Opinion leaders play a vital role in this model.

Rogers [10] explains how a new innovation or idea would spread through society in terms of adopters of five types. Innovators would be the first to accept the new idea, then early adopters, early majority, late majority, and finally laggards. Early adopters are usually social leaders, popular, and educated, whereas laggards tend to have neighbors and friends as their main sources of information and fear of debt. The adopter-based model has been modified to account for the spread of high tech products [11].

Knowledge diffusion within scientific communities has largely attributed to the role of invisible colleges [12]. The role of social networks in diffusion of technical innovations was identified in [13]. Studies of scientific collaboration networks found that co-authorship is the best predictor of subsequent citations [14]. There is a growing interest recently in how information spreads over web logs, or blogs [15].

Purely geographically driven diffusion paths are relatively straightforward to derive. In this article, we address the challenge of integrating geographic and semantic perspectives within a unifying framework such that users are able to explore salient patterns back and forth between a geographic space and a social-semantic space of knowledge. In particular, we focus on collaboration networks of individual researchers by co-authorship and geographic distributions of events in the physical world. Our goal is to combine the two potentially interrelated and complementary but so far inadequately integrated perspectives, namely geographic-centric and semantic-centric perspectives. Such integration is significant because of the societal nature of knowledge creation, information seeking and sense making, and the potential of advances in human-computer interaction to enable these processes.

3   Methods

Our approach consists of four major components: information extraction, geographic coding, constructing associative networks, and constructing thematic layers for geographic visualization (see Figure 1). We explain each component in terms of the example datasets used in this study.

3.1   Information Extraction

In this article, we consider two types of data in terms of the role of geospatial properties: Type-A, geographic properties are secondary, and Type-B, geographic properties are primary. Collaboration networks are an example of Type-A data because geographic properties of such networks are secondary in nature. Vertices in such networks are individual researchers in a specific knowledge domain, such as avian flu or terrorism. Edges in these networks are collaborative ties between researchers. The strength of a collaboration tie between two researchers is measured by how many times they published joint papers with each other. On the other hand, terrorist incidents, such as suicide bombing, kidnapping, and shooting, are an example of Type-B data. Geographic locations are essential in this case.

Several Type-A datasets were retrieved from the Web of Science, including research on terrorism (1990-2006), avian flu (2001-2006), and astrophysics (a subset known as Sloan Digital Sky Survey – SDSS) (1996-2006). We also collected 1,427 terrorist incidents as a Type-B dataset from a website maintained by the Israeli International Policy Institute for Counter-Terrorism (ICT[1]). These incidents took place between May 1980 and December 2002 world wide. Each incident is recorded with date, location, responsible terrorist organization, type of incident, causality, and a short description of the event (See Table 1).

Table 1. An example record from the ICT dataset

Date	*Sept 9, 2001*
Location	*Nhariya, Israel*
Attack Type	*Suicide Bomb*
Target	*Civilian*
Casualties	*3 Killed; 90 Injured*
Organization	*Hamas; Number of Terrorists: 1*
Description	*Three people were killed and some 90 injured, most lightly, in a suicide bombing near the Nahariya train station in Northern Israel. The terrorist, killed in the blast, waited nearby until the train arrived from Tel-Aviv and people were exiting the station, and then exploded the bomb he was carrying. Hamas claimed responsibility for the attack.*

3.2   Geographic Coding

Geographic coding identifies the altitude and longitude of an event or the institution of a researcher so that we can precisely locate the event or the institution on a

---

[1] http://www.ict.org.il/

geographic map through a thematic overlay. Locations in the USA are resolved by using zip codes, whereas locations outside the USA are resolved based on postal codes and direct name searches. We use the web services provided at www. geonames.org.

The successful rate of geocoding is high for Type-A datasets: 92.28% for the avian dataset (2001-2006), 95.98% for the terrorism dataset (1998-2003), and 96.53% for the SDSS dataset (2001-2006). However, the successful rate of 60.05% is relatively low for the Type-B dataset, i.e. terrorist incidents. Among the total of 846 locations in the terrorist event dataset, 62 are unspecified locations. Here are some examples of other types of problematic locations: 'enroute to London from Jedda," "outskirts of Jerusalem," "Atarot Industrial Zone," "Arc Royal aircraft carrier," and "Egyptian Border."

3.3 Collaboration Networks

An integration of conceptual networks with geospatial perspectives is illustrated with examples of collaboration networks of individual researchers. Such networks are derived from bibliographic records retrieved from the Web of Science. Each bibliographic record contains its authors, title, abstract, and a list of addresses of the authors. These authors are called co-authors. Co-authorship indicates the existence of a collaboration tie between co-authors. For example, a record shows that a 2006 article, entitled '*Avian influenza H5N1 in viverrids: implications for wildlife health and conservation,*' has coauthors from the following institutions:

> Univ Hong Kong, Dept Microbiol, Hong Kong, Peoples R China.
> Univ Hong Kong, Dept Pathol, Hong Kong, Peoples R China.
> Univ E Anglia, Ctr Ecol Evolut & Conservat, Norwich NR4 7TJ, Norfolk, England.
> World Hlth Org, Natl Inst Vet Res, Dept Virol, Hanoi, Vietnam.
> World Hlth Org, Communicable Dis Surveillance & Response Unit, Hanoi, Vietnam.
> Owstons Civet Conservat Program, Ninh Binh, Vietnam.
> Endangered Primate Rescue Ctr, Ninh Binh, Vietnam.

Altitudes and longitudes of cities such as Hong Kong, Norwich, Hanoi, and Ninh Binh would be resolved. These cities would be connected by lines in the 2006 model of the collaboration network. In this way, we expect to reveal collaboration patterns with reference to geospatial distributions.

3.4 Multiple Layers of Thematic Overlays

Once collaboration networks are constructed and geospatial details are retrieved, multiple layers of thematic overlays are produced so that they can be viewed with Google Earth. A useful way to explore the diffusion of knowledge over geographic boundaries is to compare and contrast thematic layers of adjacent time intervals. For example, one may identify the expansion of a collaboration network over time by tracking the locations of major hubs year by year. In addition, one can hide and show multiple layers by topic and look for cross-layer patterns.

The four layers in Figure 1 illustrate the benefit and flexibility for users to study the diffusion of conceptual patterns as well as geospatial patterns. These overlays show the expansion of the avian flu research network between 2003 and 2006 and spread among countries in Southeast Asia.

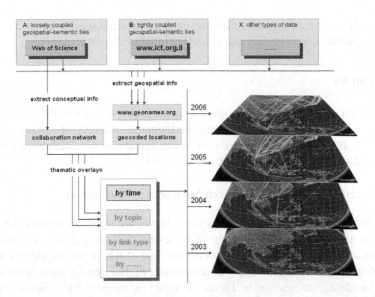

Fig. 1. A conceptual overview of our approach shows key components, processes, and results. The four thematic layers depict the growth of the avian flu research network in Southeast Asia.

Geospatial patterns play distinct roles in different conceptual spaces. The structure of a geographic space of researchers may not match the structure of a semantic space of knowledge because researchers do not always choose their collaborators based on geographic proximity. Furthermore, a geographic space of events, such as terrorist incidents or avian flu outbreaks, may or may not have anything to do with a geographic distribution of relevant expertise. For example, a group of researchers in Hong Kong publishing on avian flu may not imply a nearby avian flu outbreak. However, if researchers in several Southeast Asian countries were found to collaborate frequently with researchers in Memphis in the USA, such collaboration ties in a knowledge space could be particularly valuable because the absence of geographic proximity means that their connections seem to be unlikely in the geographic space. Facilitating users to explore patterns in two spaces can help users recognize and better understand patterns that may not be obvious if users only search in one space. The possibility of bridging geographic gaps via semantic proximity in a collaboration network is also encouraging for responders to terrorist incidents or avian flu outbreaks. For example, they would need to find not only experts on a specific subject but also experts who have knowledge of specific geographic areas. From a knowledge diffusion point of view, being able to see collaboration networks over a geographic map is the first step towards a deeper understanding of the interplay between knowledge and the context of its application.

The following examples demonstrate the use of different thematic layers to highlight potentially interesting patterns. These examples all have geospatial references. However, geospatial references in some of the datasets are essential to the underlying phenomena, but they are secondary in other datasets.

4 Examples

We first depict geospatial distributions of terrorist incidents such as suicide bombings, shooting, and kidnappings. Then we impose thematic overlays of research networks of terrorism. The second example illustrates the expansion of collaboration networks on avian influenza across Southeast Asian countries.

4.1 Terrorist Incidents and Research Networks on Terrorism

Figure 2 shows an example in which thematic layers are selected, namely the terrorist attack layer and the collaboration network layer of terrorism research. The occurrence of each incident is marked as a red translucent disc at where the incident took place. Thus multiple incidents in an area will accumulate higher density than geographically isolated incidents. As shown in Figure 2, Israel is marked by a dense cluster of incidents. The figure also shows a higher concentration of collaboration links in Europe, especially in Britain, than other areas. A few long lines across the globe indicate joint publications between Israeli researchers on terrorism and remote collaborators.

Fig. 2. Geographic distributions of terrorist incidents and research networks on terrorism

Figure 3 shows the details of a terrorist incident in Nahariya, Israel and a few collaboration links in the same timeframe, 2001. Terrorist incidents are shown as red markers, whereas research sites are depicted as greenish yellow markers.

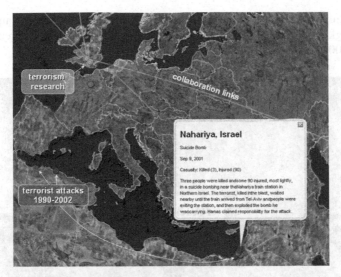

Fig. 3. Details of terrorist incidents are available by clicking on corresponding markers

Figure 4 illustrates the use of multiple themes simultaneously on the same map, including collaboration networks on three different subjects and terrorist incidents. This would make it easy for users to identify various interrelationships.

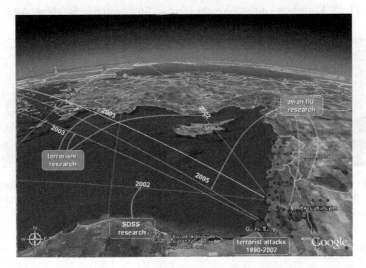

Fig. 4. Israel, as seen here, is the site of a large number of terrorist attacks. Multiple layers of thematic overlay also reveal other research activities in the areas of astronomy, avian flu, and terrorism in terms of collaboration links.

4.2 Avian Influenza

Figure 5 shows knowledge diffusion paths of avian flu research in Southeast Asian countries. The regional hubs of collaboration moved from Tokyo to Hong Kong, then reached Bankok and later on Jakarta. A strong collaboration triangle among Hong Kong, Bangkok, and Hà Noi emerged since 2004 and subsequently strengthened in 2005 and 2006.

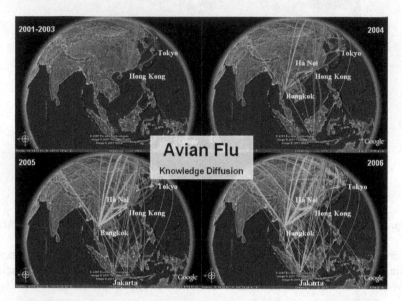

Fig. 5. Knowledge diffusion paths of avian flu research in Southeast Asia

Fig. 6. Left: Geographic locations computationally extracted from news articles about flooding in the mid-Western United States. Right: The detail of an abstract concept (National Hurricane Center) found in a news story and a related geographical location.

4.3 News Stories

News stories implicitly contain numerous geographic references such as towns, cities, and counties. Such information can be used to geographically contextualize situations such as disaster recoveries and humanitarian relief missions [16]. Figure 6 shows geographic locations computationally extracted from news articles about flooding in the mid-Western United States. Lines indicate connections between a news articles geographical origin and other geographical locations found in the article. Colors represent different individual news articles, thickness of line indicated the frequency of mention in the news article, transparency of a line indicates how old a story is (the older the story, the more transparent the line). Locations are plotted based on user-selected geographic scales allowing the user to view data at varying local, national, or international scales.

5 Conclusions

The work contributes to human-computer interaction in several ways: 1) It provides an intuitive and consistent framework to combine the visualization of concrete and abstract diffusion processes; 2) It introduces a potentially effective way to explore conceptual and geospatial diffusion of knowledge over time; and 3) This is a generic approach that can be applicable to a wide range of domains.

This is our ongoing effort to facilitate the understanding of dynamic and complex information processes and sense making activities involving large volumes of information, which is applicable to understanding online communities and social phenomena. Research on geocoding of locations derived from implicit geographic data sources will focus o establishing a document's geographic origin [17], examining multiple geo-spatial contexts within a document [18], improved disambiguation of geographic names [19, 20],and improved matching of abstract concepts with geographical locations [21, 22].

Future research directions include exploratory visual analytics methods that support comprehensive analysis of three-way spatial, temporal, and semantic relationships that are embedded (and potentially) hidden in these rich data sources. One strategy we will adapt is the *group, select, and filter* methodology in which analysts can select arbitrary subsets of entities in multivariate space to explore the cross-connections [23]. We have demonstrated the integration of two types of thematic perspectives in this article. Integrating spatial data with non-spatial data is an even more challenging area of research for future research.

Acknowledgments. The work is in part supported by the National Visualization and Analytics Center (NVAC) through the Northeast Visualization and Analytics Center (NEVAC) and the National Science Foundation under grant IIS-0612129.

References

1. Wasserman, S., Faust, K.: Social Network Analysis: Methods and Applications. Cambridge University Press, Cambridge (1994)
2. Chen, C.: CiteSpace II: Detecting and visualizing emerging trends and transient patterns in scientific literature. J. Am. Soc. Inf. Sci. Technol. 57, 359–377 (2006)
3. Klinkenberg, R., Renz, I.: Adaptive information filtering: learning in the presence of concept drifts. In: Klinkenberg, R., Renz, I. (eds.) Learning for Text Categorization, pp. 33–40. AAAI Press, Menlo Park, CA (1998)
4. Tsymbal, A., Pechenizkiy, M., Cunningham, P., Puuronen, S.: Dynamic integration of classifiers for tracking concept drift in antibiotic resistance data. Technical Report TCD-CS2005-26. Department of Computer Science, Trinity College, Dublin, Ireland (2005)

5. Morinaga, S., Yamanishi, K.: Tracking dynamics of topic trends using a finite mixture model. In: KDD'04, pp. 811–816. ACM, Seattle, Washington (2004)
6. Steyvers, M., Smyth, P., Rosen-Zvi, M., Griffiths, T.: Probabilistic author-topic models for information discovery. In: KDD'04, pp. 306–315. ACM, Seattle,Washington (2004)
7. Kleinberg, J.: Bursty and hierarchical structure in streams. Proceedings of the 8th ACM SIGKDD International Conference on Knowledge Discovery and Data Mining, pp. 91–101. ACM Press, Edmonton, Alberta, Canada (2002)
8. Kumar, R., Novak, J., Raghavan, P., Tomkins, A.: On the Bursty Evolution of Blogspace. WWW2003, Budapest, Hungary, p. 477 (2003)
9. Lazarsfeld, P.F., Berelson, B., Gaudet, H.: The people's choice: How the voter makes up his mind in a presidential campaign. Columbia University Press, New York (1944)
10. Rogers, E.: Diffusion of Innovations. The Free Press, New York (1962)
11. Moore, G.: Crossing the Chasm. Harper Business, New York (1991)
12. Crane, D.: Invisible Colleges: Diffusion of Knowledge in Scientific Communities. University of Chicago Press, Chicago, Illinois (1972)
13. Singh, J.: Social networks as determinants of knowledge diffusion patterns. Vol. 2004 (2004)
14. Newman, M.: The structure of scientic collaboration networks. Natl. Acad. Sci, vol. 98, pp. 404–409, USA (2001b)
15. Gruhl, D., Guha, R., Liben-Nowell, D., Tomkins, A.: Information diffusion through blogspace. In: Proceedings of the 13th international conference on World Wide Web, New York, NY, pp. 491–501 (2004)
16. Mubareka, S., Khudhairy, D.A., Bonn, F., Aoun, S.: Standardising and mapping open-source information for crisis regions: the case of post-conflict Iraq. Disasters 29, 237–254 (2005)
17. Amitay, E., Har'El, N., Sivan, R., Soffer, A.: Web-a-Where: Geotagging Web Content. In: SIGIR'04. ACM, Sheffield, South Yorkshire, UK, pp. 273–280 (2004)
18. Graupmann, J., Schenkel, R.: GeoSphereSearch: Context-Aware Geographic Web Search. In: SIGIR '06. Workshop on Geographic Information Retrieval, ACM, Seattle, WA, USA (2006)
19. Wang, X.: Robust utilization of context in word sense disambiguation. In: Dey, A.K., Kokinov, B., Leake, D.B., Turner, R. (eds.) CONTEXT 2005. LNCS (LNAI), vol. 3554, pp. 529–541. Springer, Heidelberg (2005)
20. Rauch, E., Bukatin, M., Baker, K.: A confidence-based framework for disambiguating geographic terms. In: Proceedings of the HTL/NAACL Workshop on The Analysis of Geographic References (2003)
21. Liu, X., Pezanowski, S., MacEachren, A.M.: Bridging forms of knowledge for crisis management: Concept maps to Geographic maps. In: Kraak, M.-J. (ed.): ICA Commission on Visualization and Virtual Environments (2006)
22. Mitra, P., Pan, C.: Extracting Semantic Networks among Named Entities from Websites. International Conference of the Association of Computational Linguistics (submitted)
23. Weaver, C., Fyfe, D., Robinson, A., Holdsworth, D., Peuquet, D., MacEachren, A.M.: Visual analysis of historic hotel visitation patterns. Information Visualization (2007)

The Differences Between the Influences of Synchronous and Asynchronous Modes on Collaborative Learning Project of Industrial Design

Wenzhi Chen[1,2] and Manlai You[2]

[1] Department of Industrial Design, Chang Gung University, Taiwan
[2] Graduate School of Design, National Yunlin University of Science and Technology
wenzhi@mail.cgu.edu.tw, youm@yuntech.edu.tw

Abstract. Understanding communication in collaborative design is helpful for development and selection of communication software and technology in design project. The aim of this article attempts to explore the differences between the influences of synchronous and asynchronous modes on collaborative design learning projects. Two experiment projects were conducted, and the participation record and the content of communication were collected. Both quantitative and content analysis methods used in order to indicate the attributions of different communication mode. Results of this study showed that there have differences in participation and communication pattern between the synchronous and asynchronous modes on collaborative learning project. It should be noted that this study is restricted to the size of sample and uncertain variables. The future research is obviously required.

Keywords: collaborative design, computer mediated communication (CMC), industrial design.

1 Introduction

In recent years considerable concern has arisen over the computer (Internet) support collaborative design. Many researchers and educators have using the tele-communication technology to conduct or mediate the collaborative design projects. The forms of computer mediated communication (CMC) can be synchronous or asynchronous, and the channel (content) can be multi-media, include the text, audio, and video etc. Communication is a critical success factor in design [7]. It is important to understand the communication processes for improvement of communication. Although there has been some research done on analysis and compare the face-to-face and the computer-mediated-communication modes on collaborative design, little is known about the differences between the influences of synchronous and asynchronous modes on collaborative design.

The purpose of this study is to understand the participation and communication pattern in synchronous and asynchronous modes to better determine the influence of difference communication mode on collaborative design. Such research is still in its infancy, but it may have a contribution to make to understand the CMC and the online collaborative design.

D. Schuler (Ed.): Online Communities and Social Comput., HCII 2007, LNCS 4564, pp. 275–283, 2007.

2 Analysis of Online Design Communication

Since 1990s, numerous models of virtual design studio have been introduced [1, 10], and most of them focused on collaborative design. But the results and the influences of using the Internet and information technology in design education still need to be research and prove [8]. Communication is an important factor of successful design, whether in face-to-face or virtual design studio. The analysis of the design communication can help to better understanding of the design process. There are several strategies for studying design behavior include the think-aloud protocols, content analysis, process isolation and situated studies [3], in which the content analysis is contributed to analysis the content of CMC to provide a rich data for researching and understanding online design and learning [6, 9].

Simoff & Maher [11] proposed various approaches to study the communication in online collaborative design included the text analysis, data mining, and visualization of the content. Gabriel & Maher [4, 5] based on protocol analysis method, proposed a coding scheme (Figure 1) development by using data, external and theory-generated structures in order to code verbal design representations in collaborative design.

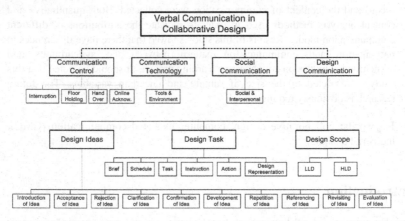

Fig. 1. A hierarchical tree of the coding scheme: verbal communication in collaborative design [Gabriel & Maher, 2002, p.206]

Simoff & Maher [11] and Gabriel & Maher [4, 5] provide various approaches to analysis the communication content for researching and understanding the collaborative design. The approach for this research was referred with those approaches with empirical data to explore the participation and communication pattern in online collaborative design learning project.

3 Method

Two experiments collaborative design learning project were conducted to collect the data and content analysis used to explore the participation and communication of different CMC modes on collaborative design learning projects.

3.1 Experiment Projects

The participants in this study were 33 undergraduate students majored in industrial design in two universities in Taiwan, the National Yunlin University of Science and Technology (NYUST) and Chang Gung University (CGU). The variables of the projects are list in Table 1. In project A, NYUST and CGU used the same schedule and design theme, and used synchronous as primary communication mode. There are 13 volunteers from the NYUST and CGU participated the project and cross group into two teams. Project B used asynchronous as primary communication mode and 20 volunteers from the both universities were paired grouped into 10 teams. But the schedule and design theme is different. Both projects emphasize the collaboration in concept design phase. The participants were asked to communication and exchange the ideas once per week at lease, and every participant had to propose their own design solution by themselves finally.

Both projects used "CoCreaThink Design (http://thinkdesign.cgu.edu.tw)" [2] as the platform for communication and share the design documents. The synchronous mode provides the video-conference, e-whiteboard, text chat, and file-sharing functions. The asynchronous use the forum that with attach function as the main communication channel. Causing the bandwidth and quality of the Internet, the project A using the text based chat with file sharing function as the main communication channel finally.

Table 1. The list of variables for the 2 experiment projects

Project	A (Synchronous mode)	B (Asynchronous mode)
Theme	CGU/NYUST: Healthy product	CGU: Hair Dryer NYUST: Cultural gift
Participants	CGU: 7 NYUST: 6	CGU: 10 NYUST: 10
Grouping	Cross group into 2 teams	Pair group into 10 teams
Period	NYUST/CGU: 10 weeks	CGU: 8 weeks NYUST: 6 weeks
requirements	Collaborative in design research and ideation phase, every one should propose the design solution by themselves	Collaborative in design research and ideation phase, every one should propose the design solution by themselves
Collaboration	Concept design	Concept design
Collaborative method	One meeting per week using the CMC (text based chat with file sharing)	Discussion and share the concept and ideas by post the message in the online forum
Platform & Functions	CoCreaThink Design Studio Text based Chat, file-sharing	CoCreaThink Design Classroom Forum that provide the attachment function

3.2 Data Collection

All the data were collected by the MS SQL server of *CoCreaThink Design* platform. The record of the users' participation and the content of communication were collected for future analysis.

3.3 Data Analysis

Both quantitative statistic and content analysis were performed. The analysis used the SPSS statistical software package. First, descriptive statistics of the participation record were computed. Next, the communication content was coded by the coding scheme referred with Gabriel & Maher [5]. Finally, the content coding also was calculated and tested.

3.4 Coding Scheme and Coding

In order to explore the communication pattern of difference CMC modes in online collaborative design learning project, the coding scheme that proposed by Gabriel & Maher [5] for analysis the verbal communication in collaborative design (Figure 1) were used. Gabriel & Maher's scheme has 4 categories and several levels. Figure 2 show the categories and level that this study focuses on. Table 2 illustrated the categories, code, and description of the coding scheme. The detail of the scheme can find in Gabriel & Maher's [5] article.

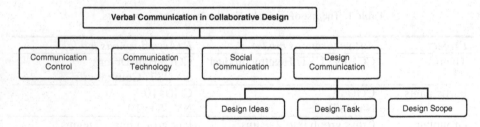

Fig. 2. The coding scheme used in this study

Table 2. The categories, code, and description of the coding scheme

Category	Code	Description
Communication control	CC	Communication control includes statements made by the designers to hold the floor, to interrupt, to acknowledge presence, and to hand over communication to the other person.
Communication Technology	CT	A data derived structure, looks at discussions held between participants related to the use of the tools and the collaborative environment.
Social Communication	SC	Communication content dealing with interpersonal relationships.
Design Communication	DC	Communication content dealing with the design representation and activities.

Table 2. (*Continued*)

Design Ideas	DI	Includes introduction, acceptance, rejection, clarification, confirmation, development, and repetition, evaluation of idea, and referencing and revisiting an idea.
Design Task	DT	Includes brief, schedule, task, action, and design representation.
Design Scope	DS	Includes low-level design and high-level design.

4 Results

The results of the participation and communication pattern were description in follow. Because the condition and data of the each project were not equally, the percentage was used in order to normalize the value.

4.1 Synchronous Mode

The analysis of the participation includes the frequency of login, contribution of content, and frequency of reading of sharing files. The result of participation analysis is shown as Figure 3. The frequency of login was distributed in every week, and had higher percentages in week 1-5. The contribution of content was increased in the week 2, then kept stable, and dramatically went down at week 5. The frequency of reading of sharing files that participants uploaded was centered on middle and final stages of the process.

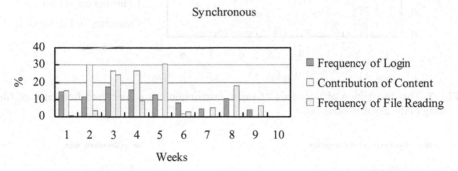

Fig. 3. The distribution of frequency of login, contribution of content and frequency of file reading of the synchronous mode

The percentage of the coded text segments, across the 4 primary coding categories and sub-categories of design communication is presented in Figure 4. The most text segments deal with the *design communication* (46.83%) and *social communication* (41.96%). In *design communication* category, the percentage of *design ideas* (71.70%) is higher than the *design task* (24.67%) and *design scope* (3.63%).

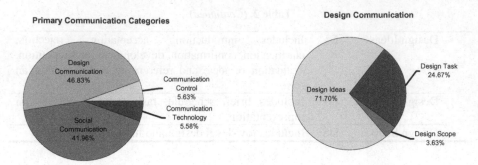

Fig. 4. Percentage of the 4 primary coding categories, and sub-categories of design communication of the synchronous mode

4.2 Asynchronous Mode

The result of participation analysis of the asynchronous mode is shown as Figure 5. The percentage of frequency of login was higher in week 1-2, then dramatic decrease. The distribution of the contribution of content is similar to frequency of login. The percentage of the frequency of file reading was high in week 1-2, then went down dramatically, and increased since week 4.

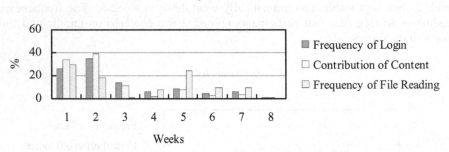

Fig. 5. The distribution of frequency of login, contribution of content and frequency of file reading of the asynchronous mode

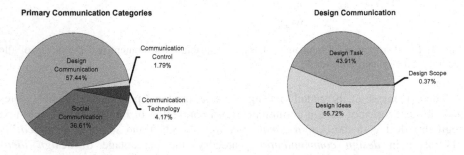

Fig. 6. Percentage of the 4 primary coding categories, and sub-categories of design communication of the asynchronous mode

Figure 6 presented the result of the content coded. In primary communication categories, there were 57.44% content deal with the *design communication*, and 36.61% focus on *social communication*, 4.17% on *communication technology*, and 1.79% on *communication control*. In *design communication* category, 55.72% deal with *design ideas* and 43.91% with *design task*, only 0.37% focus on *design scope*.

4.3 The Differences Between Synchronous and Asynchronous Modes

According the results of participation and communication analysis and observation through the project, there are some differences between the synchronous and asynchronous modes.

Participation. There are several differences between synchronous and asynchronous modes in participation. The participants' login central on the particular date of the team meeting and to continues, and the contribution of content is stable in synchronous mode. In asynchronous mode, the frequency of login is distributed, and the contribution of content is high in initial stage then decrease dramatically.

The frequency of login was dramatic decrease and the interval of login was increase in the asynchronous mode. The more likely explanation is the uncertainness of the feedback. The fewer of the feedback and long time for wait reply will affect the motivation of the participation.

The utterance and the contribution of words of synchronous mode are more stable than asynchronous mode. The contribution of the content seems to be closely connected to the frequency of login. Despite the uncertainness of the feedback, the schedule and the requirement of the project may be the reason for, too.

The frequency of files reading was centered on middle and a later stage in synchronous mode, and centered on the initial and later stage in asynchronous mode. The average time of reading in the initial stage is longer than other stage in asynchronous mode and more stable in synchronous mode.

Communication Pattern. In the results of communication pattern, the percentage of *communication control* was significant difference between asynchronous and synchronous mode. The *social communication* was stable appear during the progress of project both in asynchronous and synchronous mode. In *design communication* level, more *design ideas* segment contributed in synchronous mode, and more *design task* segments was dealt with in asynchronous.

In the synchronous mode there were fewer text segments deal with the *design communication* and more segments concerned with *communication control*, *communication technology*, and *social communication*. The results of the ANOVA showed a significant difference between synchronous and asynchronous in *communication control* ($F=11.619$, $p < 0.05$), and no significant different in other 3 communication categories.

Observation of the projects progress founded that the *social communication* and *communication technology* continuously occurred, and the *communication control* was appeared in the initial stage of project in synchronous. The *design communication* and *social communication* continuously occurred, and the *communication control* and *communication technology* were fragmental appeared in asynchronous mode.

5 Concluding Remarks

This paper presents the results of the participation and communication pattern of synchronous and asynchronous modes on collaborative learning project of industrial design. The results support the conclusion that there have differences in participation and communication pattern between the influences of synchronous and asynchronous modes on collaborative learning project.

These results may be explained by considering the motivation and attitude of participants, and the planning or setting of the project. It needs the more precise research to clear prove. In addition, it is important to emphasize that the data collected from the real learning project may limit the interpretations, and the study involved only two experiment projects, the results cannot be generalized. This study has taken a step in the direction of understanding the difference between synchronous and asynchronous CMC mode on collaborative learning project. The future research will provide more detailed results which may differentiate these views from one another.

Acknowledgements. This research was partially supported by a grant from the National Science Council (NSC) (NSC 92-2520-S-182-002 & 90-2218-E-182-004). Additionally, the authors wish to express their appreciation to all the teachers and students who participated in the experiment courses.

References

1. Broadfoot, O., Bennett, R.: Design Studios: Online? Comparing traditional face-to-face Design Studio education with modern internet-based design studios, AUC Conference 2003. (2003) Retrieved July 22, 2005, from http://auc.uow.edu.au/conf/conf03/papers/AUC_DV2003_Broadfoot.pdf
2. Chen, W., You, M.: A framework for the development of online design learning environment. In: Proceedings of the 6th Asian Design Conference: Integration of Knowledge, Kansei, and Industrial Power (CD ROM), October 14-17, Tsukuba, Japan, I-01 (2003)
3. Craig, D.L.: Stalking home faber: a comparison of research strategies for studying design behavior. In: Eastman, C.M., McCracken, W.M., Newsletter, W.C (eds.) Design knowing and learning: cognition in design education, Elsevier, pp. 13–36. Elsevier, Amsterdam (2001)
4. Gabriel, G., Maher, M.L.: An Analysis of Design Communication with and Without Computer Mediation. In: Scrivener, S.A.R., Ball, L.J., Woodcock, A. (eds.) Collaborative Design, Springer, London (2000)
5. Gabriel, G.C., Maher, M.L.: Coding and modelling communication in architectural collaborative design. Automation in Construction 11, 199–211 (2002)
6. Gerbic, P., Stacey, E.: A purposive approach to content analysis: Designing analytical frameworks. The. Internet and Higher Education 8, 45–59 (2005)
7. Maier, A.M., Eckert, C.M., Clarkson, P.J.: Identifying requirements for communication support: A maturity grid-inspired approach. Expert Systems with Applications 31, 63–672 (2006)

8. McCormick, R.: Collaboration: The Challenge of ICT. International Journal of Technology and Design Education 14, 159–176 (2004)
9. Naidu, S., Järvelä, S.: Analyzing CMC content for what? Computers & Education. Computers & Education 46, 96–103 (2006)
10. Schnabel, M.A., Kvan, T., Kruijff, E., Donath, D.: The First Virtual Environment Design Studio. In: The proceedings of 19th ECAADE-conference, pp. 394–400 (2001)
11. Simoff, S.J., Maher, M.L.: Analysing participation in collaborative design environments. Design Studies 21, 119–144 (2000)

Self-Awareness in a Computer Supported Collaborative Learning Environment

Kwangsu Cho and Moon-Heum Cho

221A Townsend Hall, School of Information Science & Learning Technologies,
University of Missouri, Columbia, MO 65211, USA
chokw@missouri.edu, mckr7@mizzou.edu

Abstract. The purpose of this study was to examine the role of self-awareness (SA) interfaces implemented for writing skill improvement in a computer supported collaborative writing environment called SWoRD [7]. Visualization interfaces to improve SA were developed for SWoRD. Students were provided with opportunities to self-monitor and self-evaluate their writing with the use of multiple peer feedback. The study results show that although all the students did not develop their SA with the interfaces, the students who developed SA drastically improved their writing skills compared to those who did not enhance SA. Finally, the results are discussed and future research topics are suggested.

Keywords: Self-awareness, Peer feedback, Peer review, Writing, CSCL, SWoRD, Self-monitoring.

1 Introduction

While writing is considered as one of the most important skills that learners are expected to master for professional as well as academic success, being able to write well is a fundamental skill that most students lack across any ages in the U.S. and also very likely in other countries [21]. Although the U.S. National Commission on Writing consisting of more than 4,300 schools and colleges in the U.S. declares of great urgency the increased emphasis on writing at all levels of education, instructors avoid writing instructions [21]. Instructors are simply overwhelmed by a daunting challenge of reviewing and giving grades on student papers. Therefore, students have few opportunities to practice writing.

Our purpose is to examine the role of self-awareness (SA) interfaces implemented for writing skill improvement in a computer supported collaborative writing environment. The SA interfaces are theoretically based on self-regulated learning and collaborative learning that were found to be robust in improving writing skills. In specific, we address two major questions as follows: 1) Does the computer supported self-monitoring system influence SA? and 2) Are the SA changes related to writing quality improvement?

1.1 Self-Awareness

SA is defined as students' consciousness about their writing processes and their use of writing strategies [22]. It seems that SA may be activated by self-evaluation via

D. Schuler (Ed.): Online Communities and Social Comput., HCII 2007, LNCS 4564, pp. 284–291, 2007.

self-monitoring (SM) on the use of learning strategies and processes [4], [27], [29]. SA manages students' self-regulated writing activities [4], [19], [27]. For example, SA contributes to students' metacognitive assessment of the validity and usefulness of their learning strategies.

Existing research seems to agree upon the positive role of SA in learning and also in writing improvement [5], [15], [29]. It was found that SA is one of the most important characteristics of the successful writers. They are aware of their own limitations, necessary processes, and ways to improve their writing. In addition, SA is found to make writers strategically function when working on their writing [14], [16], [24], [27], [29], [31].

Writers' SA is activated through self-regulated learning processes such as goal setting or planning, monitoring, and evaluation and reflection [27], [29]. More specifically, successful writers set goals or plans for writing. Once they set goals, they regularly monitor their writing processes. Based on their monitoring results, self-regulated writers self-evaluate and self-reflect and produce SA about what they are doing and what they need to improve their writing quality. The activation process of SA implies that providing students opportunities to self-monitor and self-evaluate is important.

1.2 Peer Feedback as a Way to Activate SA

While SA is critical in learning to write, inaccurate SA may undermine its positive role in writing improvement [18]. When student writers overestimate or underestimate their writing quality, their inaccurate SA may hinder the students from setting realistic goals and using appropriate learning strategies. Thus, inaccurate SA may have students deviate from an established route to writing improvement.

Providing students with opportunities having feedback is one of the most commonly used methods to improve SA [15], [25]. Feedback enables student writers to view their own writing from various reader perspectives. By checking feedback, student writers may improve self-monitoring on their own writing, generating reliable SA. Therefore, it can be inferred that providing feedback to students is an effective way to be used to promote students' SA.

Despite the effectiveness of feedback as a way to promote students' SA, instructors avoid providing students with feedback on student writing. This is simply because reading and giving feedback on student writing is time and effort demanding especially in a large class setting [7], [9]. As an alternative to this unfortunate situation, multiple peer feedback has been implemented in writing education. Cho and his colleagues found that multiple peer feedback is more effective in improving writing than expert feedback in education settings as well as in organizational settings [6], [7]. Also, Fallahi, Wood, Austad, and Fallahi found students experiencing peer reviews significantly improved their writing skills in terms of grammar, writing style, mechanics, and referencing [11]. Furthermore, Cho, Schunn, and Wilson found multiple peer evaluations are highly reliable and also valid as instructor evaluations [9].

In addition to peer feedback, revision opportunities may help students improve their SA. Successful writers use self-monitoring and self-evaluation process while they are engaged in revision processes. Based on feedback from others, writers may successfully self-monitor how their own writing evaluation is different from others as well as self-reflect how they improve their writing after comparing their own evaluations with those from others. This comparison may enable writers to revise their plans or goals to activate proper cognitive and metacognitive writing strategies.

1.3 SA Interface Design

Based on the literature review, Cho and Schunn developed visualization interfaces to improve SA in SWoRD (Scaffolded Writing and Rewriting in the Discipline), a web-based hybrid intelligent system supporting reciprocal peer reviewing of writing where each student plays two roles, one of writer and one of reviewer [7].

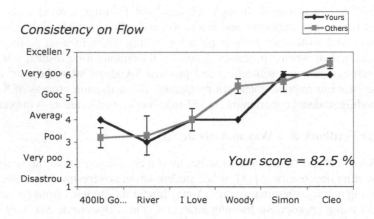

Fig. 1. An example SA interface in SWoRD

Two types of interfaces were designed to promote SA; one is for SA on their own writing and the other is for SA on their reviewing. First, SA interfaces on their writing were designed to use self-monitoring by comparing self-evaluations with peer evaluations on their own writing [2], [24], [26], [30]. The other type of the SA interfaces on reviewing was designed to allow each reviewer to compare their evaluations with other evaluations on the same papers. Figure 1 shows an example of the reviewer support interface activating SA for a reviewer. The interface visualizes the extent to which a reviewer's evaluation is consistent with that of others who reviewed the same papers. The pattern in Figure 1 shows that the reviewer's grades are consistent with those of others, while there is a visually significant difference with 400lb Gorilla. Pseudo names such as 400lb Gorilla or River are used to keep students from identifying reviewers. Also, if a reviewer clicks on the author name, then the reviewer can read both her own review and others' reviews on the same writing.

In sum, this study is to investigate the role of the SA interfaces in improving writing skills. We examine this question with a large number of participants in universities in the U.S., unlike the past SA research conducted with a small number of elementary or adolescent students [14], [20], [28]. This endows the study with strong generalizability. In addition, this study may be characterized with subject matter courses unlike most of the previous studies using writing courses.

2 Method

2.1 Participants

Data were collected from three research universities in the U.S. across 16 courses including various genres of writing tasks (i.e., cognitive psychology, cognitive science, physics, and healthy psychology). 603 students participated in the research for course credits and used the SWoRD system for their course activities. Typically writing and reviewing together accounted for approximately 40% of the final course grade in each course.

2.2 Writing Task

The exact writing task assigned to students varied across the courses, as one would expect across courses from many different disciplines. The required length of the assigned papers varied from shorter (5-to-8 pages) to longer papers (10-to-15 pages). Paper genres included 1) the introduction section to a research paper; 2) a proposal for an application to real life of a research findings; 3) a critique of a research paper read for class; and 4) a proposal for a new research study.

2.3 Self-Monitoring (SM)

SM is defined as an absolute difference between self-evaluation (SE) and other evaluation (OE) and on their writing. If the difference is closer to zero, a learner is assumed to have better self-monitoring. OE stands for an average of other evaluations and SE stands for an average self-evaluation. Students had SE and OE on the first writing and also on their revised writing.

$$SM = | SE - OE |. \tag{1}$$

2.4 Self-Awareness (SA)

SA is defined as a difference between the first self-monitoring (SM_{t1}) and the second self-monitoring (SM_{t2}). If the SA value is positive, it is assumed that SA occurs. Positive values means students self-monitoring gap between others and self are reduced the second time. SM_{t1} stands for the total differences between the first other evaluation and the first self-evaluation. SM_{t2} is the total difference between the second other evaluation and the second self-evaluation.

$$SA = SM_{t1} - SM_{t2}. \tag{2}$$

2.5 Procedure

The experiment followed the built-in processes in SWoRD. After each instructor set their writing and reviewing assignments, due dates, and assignment policies, all of the remaining procedures were managed online by SWoRD. First, student writers turned in their first drafts and did self-evaluations on the seven-point rating scale (1: Disastrous to

7: Excellent). Then individual student reviewers reviewed a set of peer drafts randomly assigned by the system. The reviewers used the same rating scale. Then, the writers received peer evaluations and revised their writing. After the writers submitted the revised writing and did their self-evaluations, the system asked the same reviewers who evaluated the first drafts to review the revised/final drafts. Finally, the writers received peer reviews from their reviewers.

3   Results

First, we examined if SA would develop over time with the SA interface. The mean of SA1 was 3.04 (SD = 2.6), and that of SA2 was 3.32 (SD = 3.1), respectively. In fact SA was decreased from SA1 to SA2, t (602) =-2.23, p < .05. Further research is necessary to explain the decrease of SA. Thus, overall the participants' SA was not found to be improved.

To address the second question, the role of individual difference with SA was investigated. As shown in Figure 2, the writing quality was enhanced with students whose SA was improved over time, M = 2.2, SD= 2.09, while the writing quality was not improved with students whose SA was not improved for non-SA, M = -.18, SD = 3.10. The mean difference between the SA and non-SA group was statistically significant, F(1, 601) = 119.92, MSE=7.11, p < .001. A large effect size was estimated, d = .93. This result shows that SA positively influences writing quality improvement.

In addition, the Pearson Correlation was computed to analyze the association between, SA change and the writing quality improvement. The correlation was statistically significant, r (602) = .66, p <.001, showing SA change and writing quality improvement are highly associated.

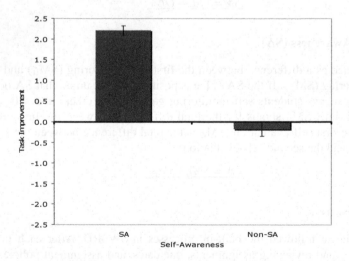

Fig. 2. Individual difference of SA and writing quality improvement

4 Discussion

The results show that although all the students did not develop their SA with the interfaces, learners who enhanced SA drastically improved their writing compared to those who did not develop SA. The results are consistent with Graham and Harris's self-regulated strategy development (SRSD) model that self-regulated writing positively influences writing performance [12]. For example, Graham, Harris, and Mason found that students who received SRSD training significantly improved their writing in their post-test as well as outperformed those who did not receive SRSD training in terms of number of writing length, story element, persuasive elements, and quality [13].

Although this study found the impact of SA on writing improvement, the role of the SA interfaces seems less stable than hypothesized because some students greatly benefited from the SA interfaces while others did not. One of the possible explanations is that students' unfamiliarity of the SA interface may be attributed to the non-improvement of SA. For example, Azevedo using the think-aloud method compared students' self-regulated learning experiences between a computer supported scaffolding environment and a human-agent supported scaffolding environment [1]. It was found that students in the computer environment are less likely to activate self-regulated learning strategies than those in the human-agent environment. The study implied that if students are not familiar with new interfaces, they are less likely to activate self-regulated learning strategies even if the system provides them with effective self-regulation scaffolding. Therefore, it can be inferred that students who were not familiar with the SA interfaces in this study might not know how to use peer feedback to monitor their own writing. Future research is necessary to test this assumption.

In addition, in this study we did not provide explicit instructions on SM and SA. This approach is somewhat different from the previous research on self-regulated learning that emphasizes explicit training of self-regulated learning strategies [14], [17], [32]. Therefore, explicit instructions on SM and SA strategies might result in more positive findings with the SA interfaces.

The research findings have several implications. First, the results empirically verified that SA is important for students' writing improvement in that students whose SA was effectively activated outperformed those whose SA was not activated. According to self-regulated learning theories, skillful self-regulated writers tend to be correctly aware of their own learning [18], [27], [29].

Second, the research findings might be attributed to students' developmental differences of epistemological beliefs. Research on epistemological belief argues that students' beliefs about knowledge sources are related to learning strategy use [3], [10], [23]. If students are leery of peer evaluations because the most typical evaluation source is experts and instructors, the students may not value peer feedback, which in turn may lead to inaccurate self-awareness for their self-regulated writing [7]. By contrast, if they value peer evaluations, the students may take advantage of using peer evaluations to enhance their SA for self-regulated writing. Consistently past research supports this reasoning. For example, Schommer found that students who have naïve epistemological beliefs knowledge tended to avoid effective learning strategies [23]. Also Bråten and Strømsø found a negative relationship between certain types of knowledge beliefs and the use of metacognitive self-regulated learning strategies [3].

They commonly found sophisticated epistemological beliefs are associated with deep level self-regulated learning strategies such as self-monitoring and self-evaluation.

Acknowledgement. This research was supported by the grants from the Andrew Mellon Foundation, the University of Pittsburgh Provost Office, and the Korea Education Research and Information Service to the first author. We thank Carla Bates for her comments on an earlier draft.

References

1. Azevedo, R.: Using Hypermedia as a Metacognitive Tool for Enhancing Student Learning? The Role of Self-Regualted Learning. Educational Psycholoigst 40(4), 199–209 (2005)
2. Bandra, A.: Social Foundations of Thought and Action: A Social Cognitive Theory. Prentice Hall, Englewood Cliffs, New Jersey (1986)
3. Bråten, I., Strømsø, H.I.: The Relationship between Epistemological Beliefs, Implicit Theories of Intelligence, and Self-Regulated Learning among Norwegian Postsecondary Students. British Journal of Educational Psychology 75, 539–565 (2005)
4. Butler, D.L., Winne, P.H.: Feedback and Self-Regulated Learning: A Theoretical Synthesis. Review of Educational Research 65(3), 245–281 (1995)
5. Cho, K., Chang, K., Kye, B. A.: Next-Generation E-Learning Model Based on Learners' Interest, Motivation, and Flow. Korean Education Research and Information Services (2005)
6. Cho, K., Chung, T. R., King, W. R., Schunn, C. D.: Peer-Based Computer-Supported Knowledge Refinement: An Empirical Investigation. Communications of the ACM (in press)
7. Cho, K., Schunn, C.D.: Scaffolded Writing and Rewriting in the Discipline: A Web-Based Reciprocal Peer Review System. Computers & Education 48(3), 409–426 (2007)
8. Cho, K., Schunn, C.D., Lesgold, A.: Comprehension Monitoring and Repairing in Distance Collaboration. In the Proceedings of the 24th Annual Conference of the Cognitive Science Society. Erlbaum, Mahwah New Jersey (2002)
9. Cho, K., Schunn, C., Wilson, R.: Validity and Reliability of Scaffolded Peer Assessment of Writing from Instructor and Student Perspectives. Journal of Educational Psychology 98(4), 891–901 (2006)
10. Dahl, T. I., Bals, M., Turi, A. L.: Are student's beliefs about knowledge and learning associated with their reported use of learning strategies? British Journal of Educational Psychology, 257–273 (2005)
11. Fallahi, C.R., Wood, R.M., Austad, C.S., Fallahi, H.A: A Program for Improving Undergraduate Psychology Students' Basic Writing Skills. Teaching of Psychology 33(3), 171–175 (2006)
12. Graham, S., Harris, K.R.: Self-Regulated Strategy Development: Helping Students with Learning Problems Develop as Writers. Elementary School Journal 94, 169–182 (1993)
13. Graham, S., Harris, K.R., Mason, L.: Improving the Writing Performance, Knowledge, and Self-Efficacy of Struggling Young Writers: The Effects of Self-Regulated Strategy Development. Contemporary Educational Psychology 30, 207–241 (2005)
14. Graham, S., Harris, K. R., Troia, G. A. Writing and Self-regulation: Cases from the Self-Regulated Strategy Development model. In: Schunk, D. Zimmerman, B. (eds.): Self-Regulated Learning: From Teaching to Self-Reflective Practice. Guilford New York, pp. 20–41 (1998)

15. Hacker, D., Cho, K.: Other-Regulated to Self-Regulated Writing: A Web-Based Approach to Peer Revision. (Unpublished manuscript) (2006)
16. Hayes, J.R., Flower, L.S.: Identifying the Organization of Writing Processes. In: Gregg, L.W., Steinberg, R. (eds.) Cognitive Processes in Writing, pp. 3–30. Erlbaum, Hillsdale New Jersey (1980)
17. Ley, K., Young, D.B.: Instructional Principles for Self-Regulation. ETR&D 49(2), 93–103 (2001)
18. McCaslin, M., Hickey, D.T.: Self-Regulated Learning and Academic Achievement: A Vygotskian View. In: Zimmerman, B.J., Schunk, D.H. (eds.) Self-Regulated Learning and Academic Achievement, pp. 153–189. Lawrence Erlbaum Associates, Hillsdale New Jersey (2001)
19. McComb, B.: Self-Regulated Learning and Academic Achievement: A Phenomenological View. In: Zimmerman, B.J., Schunk, D.H. (eds.) Self-Regulated Learning and Academic Achievement, pp. 67–124. Lawrence Erlbaum Associates, Hillsdale New Jersey (2001)
20. Mooney, P., Ryan, J.B., Uhing, B.M., Reid, R., Epstein, M.H.A: A Review of Self-Management Interventions Targeting Academic Outcomes for Students with Emotional and Behavioral Disorders. Journal of Behavioral Education 14(3), 203–221 (2005)
21. National Commission on Writing in American School and Colleges. The Neglected 'R': The Need for a Writing Revolution. Retrieved November 12, 2006 from (2003) http://www.writingcommission.org/report.html
22. Schraw, G.: Promoting General Metacognitive Awareness. Instructional Science 26, 113–125 (1998)
23. Schommer, M.: Effects of Belief about the Nature of Knowledge on Comprehension. Journal of Educational Psychology 82(3), 498–504 (1990)
24. Schunk, D. H., Zimmerman, B. J. Developing Self-efficacious Readers and Writers: The Role of Social and Self-regulatory Processes. In: Guthrie, J. T., Wigfield, A. (eds.): Reading for Engagement: Motivating Readers through Integrated Instruction. International Reading Association New York, pp.34–50 (1997)
25. Sitko, B. M. Knowing How to Write: Metacognition and Writing Instruction. In: Hacker, D. J., Dunlosky, J., Graesser, A. C. (eds.): Metacognition in Educational Theory and Practice, pp. 93–115, LEA New Jersey (1998)
26. Vygotsky, L.S.: Mind and Society: The Development of Higher Mental Processes. Harvard University Press, Cambridge MA (1978)
27. Winne, P. H., Hadwin, A. F. Studying as Self-Regulated Learning. In: Hacker, D. J., Dunlosky, J., Graesser, A. C. (eds.): Metacognition in Educational Theory and Practice. LEA New Jersey, pp. 277–304 (1998)
28. Wong, B.Y.L.: Writing Strategies Instruction for Expository Essays for Adolescents with and without Learning Disabilities. Topics In Language Disorders. pp. 29–44 (August 2000)
29. Zimmerman, B.J.: Becoming a Self-Regulated Learner: An Overview. Theory Into Practice 41(2), 64–70 (2002)
30. Zimmerman, B., Kitsantas, A.: Acquiring Writing Revision and Self-Regulatory Skill through Observation and Emulation. Journal of Educational Psychology 94(4), 660–668 (2002)
31. Zimmerman, B., Risemberg, R.: Becoming a Self-Regulated Writer: A Social Cognitive Perspective. Contemporary Educational Psychology 22, 73–101 (1997)
32. Zimmerman, B. J., Bonner, S., Kovach, R.: Developing Self-Regulated Learners: Beyond Achievement to Self-Efficacy. American Psychological Association Washington DC (1996)

How to See the Beauty That Is Not There : The Aesthetic Element of Programming in the Computer-Based Media Art

Hyunkyoung Cho and Joonsung Yoon

Dept. of Digital Media, Soongsil Univ., 511 Sangdo-dong,
Dongjak-gu, 156-743 Seoul, Korea
{mailcho,jsy}@ssu.ac.kr

Abstract. This study is to define aesthetic elements of the programming in the computer-based media art. It can be explained as the totality of the concept and reality in the respect of collaboration of art and science. The programming as aesthetic object deconstructs the traditional notion of art that the aesthetic value is determined by the aesthetic attitude. The code is not just for the computer programming, but for the pleasure. The artistic and creative 'Open Code' must be at the cost of the death of the code closed in a signified, and it lives, improves and changes through additional new functions or algorithms. Like the conceptual art, the programming is both a dematerialization of the object and an immaterialized meaning. It leads us to change the seat of a subject as a signifier. Therefore, 'The beauty of program that is not there' becomes more viable when it involves the application of aesthetics.

Keywords: beauty, aesthetic object, code reading, open code, subject.

1 Introduction

The goal of this study is to define aesthetic elements of the programming in the computer-based media art. It calls for a reconsideration of the art and the beauty in new media, and leads to the central research questions: What is the beauty of the computer-based media art? , Is there an aesthetic in the programming? , How to combine art and science?

The computer-based media art implies no internal constraint on what works of art and the beauty are, so that one can no longer tell if something is a work of art or not. Theodor Adorno states, the computer-based media art is "self-evident that nothing concerning art is self-evident any more, not its inner life, not its relation to the world, not even its right to exist."[1] Adorno's recognition does not mean that it is arbitrary whether something is a work of art, but only that traditional criteria are no longer applied.[2] Therefore, the computer-based media art has only self-evident so far as an endless losing of self -evident.

---

[1] Theodor W. Adorno, Aesthetic Theory (Minnesota: Minnesota Univ. Press, 1998) 19.
[2] Arthur C. Danto, The Abuse of Beauty (Illinois: Open Court Publishing Company, 2003) 17.

D. Schuler (Ed.): Online Communities and Social Comput., HCII 2007, LNCS 4564, pp. 292–300, 2007.

TX-Transform is one of examples for losing of self-evident. This digital film art work makes the time axis (t) and the space axis (x) to be transposed each other (Fig.1 and Fig.2). Generating filmic sequence of the objects is no longer fixed through spatial presence but rather as a condition over the time. As a new technique converging art and science, *TX-Transform* shows us 'time-images' that we can never see. Furthermore, it is more upgraded with installation art work, so called automat, *TX-Transformator* creates an interactive and astonishing new perception in real time (Fig.2).

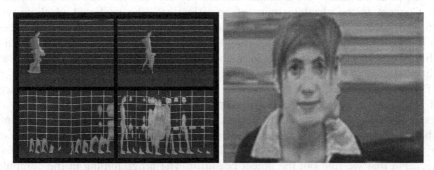

Fig. 1. 1. Concept and Idea: Martin Reinhart and Virgil Wiedrich, 2.Software: Georg Dorffner, 3.Hardware: Georg Hirzinger, *TX-Transform* , 2000

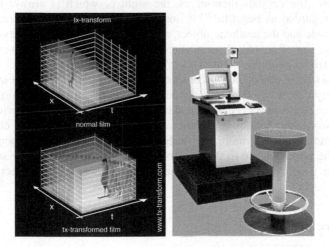

Fig. 2. The fundamental notions of TX-programming and *TX-Transformator* , 2000

In these computer-based media art, what has changed is that the art cannot be identified as a restricted set of objects, since anything one can think of might be a work of art, and what accounts for this status cannot be a matter of simple recognition. It is the reason that many people say 'there are not there,' and put aside the beauty of the computer-based media art as unconceivable something. The beauty, however, can be thought as a topic that is understandable, since it is only specific way of expressing and representing the object, and stands open throughout every respect of conceptual thinking. Thus, the computer-based media art and the beauty are consistent with the radical openness that has overtaken the traditional domain and definition, and it absolutely depends on a level of philosophical discourses.

2 Beauty of Aesthetic Object

G. W. F. Hegel defines that "the beauty is the Idea of the beauty" and "the beauty can be grasped as the Idea."[3] He distinguishes sharply between the Idea and the Concept. The Concept is the absolute unity of specifications, the mediated ideal unity of particular factors. The Idea reveals itself in the real (actual) existence of the Concept, and it is the immediate totality (including the infinity in itself) of the Concept with its reality. Therefore, the beauty becomes the Idea as the totality of the Concept and reality.

The computer-based media art also can be explained as the totality of the Concept and reality in the respect of collaboration of art and science. Since, the beauty has respect of the shape in its rest as well as movement, regardless of its purposed fullness in the satisfaction of needs, and the accidental nature. From this point of view, we will say not that what will be called beauty lies in our subjective consideration of the object, but that we find out the object beautiful. The programming in the computer-based media art exactly represents this term that the beauty is obtained in the shape.

Sigmund Freud spoke, "the love of beauty is a perfect example of a feeling with inhabited aim...the genitals themselves, the sight of which is always exciting, are hardly ever regarded as beautiful."[4] It implies that the beauty is separated from the aesthetic attitude and the aesthetic object, and that we only get the beauty when we do not depict the site of sexual pleasure directly. Today, the beauty, however, is being originating from genitals themselves. The programming as an invisible and immaterial aesthetic object in the computer-based media art is the genital, and the beauty entirely dues to it. This term deconstructs the traditional notion of art that the aesthetic value (the beauty) is determined by the aesthetic attitude (experience).

In other word, the beauty is not the artist or the viewer, but the object creates values or meanings. Furthermore, the reversed attest can be found in Jacques Lacan's assertion, "the pre-existence to the seen of a given-to-be-seen" as the subversion of the Cartesian Cogito (the certainty of the existence) which the subject apprehends himself as thought.[5]

3 Pleasure of Code

3.1 From Code Writing to Code Reading

For a long time, the program has been regarded as a practical tool. Every program was code writing and it was merely the expression in computer language of a series of

---

[3] G. W. F. Hegel, Aesthetics, trans. T. M. Knox (London: Oxford University Press, 1975) 106.
[4] Sigmund Freud, Civilization and Its Discontents, trans. James Strachey (New York: W.W. Norton & Company, 2005) 33.
[5] Jacques Lacan, The Four Fundamental Concepts of Psychoanalysis, ed. Jacques-Alain Miller, trans. Alan Sheridan (New York: W.W. Norton & Company, 1998) 74.

actions that the computer needed to take in order to solve a problem. And what is really important in the programming was always how efficiently they ran on a computer.

Since the growth of open source software, the view has been changed gradually from writing codes to reading codes. That is, the code is not just for the computer. It can be enjoyable, and some programmers are emerging as artists using those codes. Actually, many programming artists show us both ways of art works and of their codes. We can enjoy them at once and furthermore, make others own the art work through downloading their opened source codes (Fig. 3).

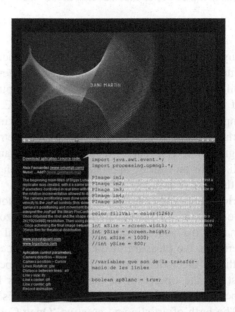

Fig. 3. Art work and code download: 1. Osman Khan, *Net worth,* 2004, 2. Aleix Fernandez, *Yo Soy La Juani,* 2006, http://processing.org

We can read the code purely for our own pleasure. The pleasure corresponds to Roland Barthes's 'the Pleasure of the Text'. The shift from writing codes to reading codes is related to Barthes's "from literature work to text as arbitrary signs."[6] It defines that the text itself plays as one plays a game and the reader plays twice over as a practice which re-reproduces it. In short, the text requires that one tries to abolish the distance between writing and reading.[7]

These 'development of literary criticisms' show us how to expand the code, and how to recognize and appreciate the beautiful as well as the useful. Like the text, the program consists of codes. The code can be treated as a sign that follows the

---

[6] Roland Barthes, The Pleasure of the Text, trans. Richard Miller (New York: Hill and Wang, 1975) 51.
[7] Roland Barthes,Image-Music-Text, trans. Stephen Heath (New York: Hill and Wang, 1977) 162.

semiological order. A sign's value is determined by both its paradigmatic and syntagmatic associations. Ferdinand de Saussure describes it as an associative relationship in which one sign enjoys all the other signs in the same system. On the one hand, the paradigmatic dimension can be predicated based on "a similarity between two signs at the level of signifier, the signified or both."[8] The paradigmatic dimension is supported by the human memory system, not by the discourse. On the other hand, the syntagmatic dimension can be realized in discourse, and it is a combination of signs. In the computer-based media art, the program as associative relationship of codes also reveals those two dimensions simultaneously.

3.2 Closed Code and Open Code

Many studies have approached aesthetic elements of the program. In 2002, 'Aesthetic Computing Manifesto' was announced and aesthetic computing was defined as "the application of art theory and practice to computing."[9] As early as 1974, the author of 'Art of Computer Programming,' Donald E. Kunth wrote, "when I speak about computer programming as an art, I am thinking primarily of it as an art form in an aesthetic sense. It can be like composing poetry or music."[10] He firmly believed that programming can reach literary proportions and it is more artistic than most people realize. His pioneering approach evokes that the program doesn't originally have to be for the sake of utility.

However, classic notion of the code has not paid attention to these aspects of the code, and it was a completely blockade zone, since many software companies managed the source code with an industrial secret which all rights are reserved. Therefore, the pleasure of the code can be accomplished throughout abolition of the myth that the coder as the author is the only person in the program and the code only exist for the operation of the computer. As long as we merely view the code as something practical, we will never see a flourish of it.

The birth of artistic and creative 'Open Code' must be at the cost of the death of the code closed in a signified. This 'Closed Code' only operates in its function like that the work of the literary can be seen in a bookshop and can be held in one's hand. Whereas, like a literary text as an arbitrary signs in the movement of a discourse, the artistic and creative 'Open Code' lives, improves and changes through additional new functions or algorithms.

The interactive art work of Aleix Fernandez, *Yo Soy La Juani* was made using an open source software, *Processing* (Fig.4). It is exhibiting in the internet, and we can download the work's source code. The work is repeatedly creating more complex figures. Parameters for movements of line and camera directions are controlled in real time with the keyboard and mouse of the user. Moreover, the user can record it and have the recorded animation as an art work of one's own. Actually, one of them has been used for the beginning main title of a film.

---

[8] Kaja Silverman, The Subject of Semiotics (New York: Oxford Univ. Press, 1984) 10.
[9] The Dagstuhl Aesthetic Computing Workshop, "Aesthetic Computing Manifesto." (Leonardo36, No.4,2003) 225.
[10] Donald E. Kunth, Art of Computer Programming (New Jersey: Addison-Wesley, 1979) 670.

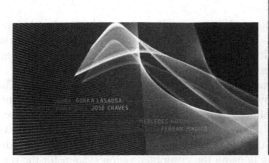

Fig. 4. Aleix Fernandez, *Yo Soy La Juani*, 2006. Still image and Film Poster.

3.3 Emptiness of Code

The code itself can be artistic. Since a textual section of the program has both denotative as well as connotative signifiers. Thus, the program structures and its mathematical orders even seem a kind of conceptual artworks. Conceptual art can be defined as the "appreciation for a work of art because of its meaning, in which the presentation of shape, colour and materials has no value with out the intentions of the work." [11] Therefore, 'its meaning' becomes the machine that makes the art. [12] It indicates that the idea behind the artwork or the mean of production is more important than the finished work or its fixed appearance.

Like conceptual art, the programming itself is both a dematerialization of the object and an immaterialized meaning, since it can both operate without materiality and can describe the material as well as the immaterial. Therefore, some programmers even define that "(the code) appears in the Buddhist teaching on Emptiness, which asserts that all thing interdependently with all other things, both materially and conceptually." [13]

The artistic and creative 'Open Code' is, however, not simply inserting well-written comments. To recognize the code as a pleasure is the key to success. Every programming language is a collection of words and symbols (syntax) with a set of rules defining their uses (semantics). It allows people to convert their ideas into codes in different ways. The artistic and creative 'Open Code' offers the possibility of activating our own models and inventing newness. It is needed not because commercial software tools are insufficient, but because someone has to "picks the meaningful signal from the noise." [14]

---

[11] Joseph Kosuth, Art After Philosophy and After: Collected Writing, 1966-1990(Cambridge: MIT Press, 1991).
[12] Paul Fishwick, Jane Prophet, Perspectives on Aesthetic Computing (Leonardo, Vol. 38, No.2, P 133-141, 2005) 136.
[13] John Maeda, Creative Code (New York: Thames & Hudson, 2004) 228.
[14] John Maeda, Creative Code (New York: Thames & Hudson, 2004) 46.

4 Real Subject

Strange Convergence exhibition (2006) questions, who the real subject is in computer-based media art. [15] The exhibition pronounced diverse discourses on convergence of art and technology. Every work was based on the programming, and completed by the interaction between the work and the participant.

In the computer-based interactive art, there are two ways of interaction. The first interaction is accomplished by 'the visible' as a direct (physical) movement of participant in a specific site (gallery or museum) (Fig.5), and the second interaction is originated from 'the invisible' as an indirect movement of unspecified individuals (information retrieval of the user in internet) (Fig.6). For example, *Human gets everything and loses everything* is using the computer vision system for the real-time processing. The camera recognizes a participant's movement as the input source image, and the projector projects the result on the screen (Fig.5). *Dewey with 10 fingers* is continuously moving by counting how many *Google* users are searching for specific information in real-time. In short, the original input source of this work is information or amount of information retrieval result (Fig.6).

Fig. 5. Jaehwa Kim, *Human gets everything and loses everything,* 2006

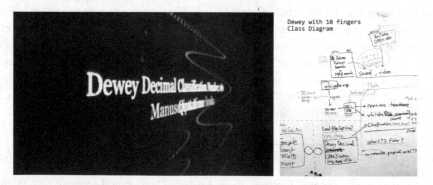

Fig. 6. Yonggeun Kim, *Dewey with 10 fingers,* 2006

---

[15] 'Strange Convergence' Exhibition, Space Mass, Seoul, Korea, 2006.

In these art works, who is the real subject? Marcel Proust's 'In Search of Lost Time' is a recollection of unconscious memories.[16] While it is a first-person novel, the subject 'I' in the novel is a strange and ambiguous being. The speaker 'I' traverses the consciousness and the unconsciousness as an unconscious 'I'. In volume1 'Swann's Way' of the novel, 'I' feel an indefinable pleasure when 'I' eat a piece of madeleine. The pleasure comes from the memory that is immanent in the mental state rather than the taste itself, finally drawing 'me' the memory of childhood. As the unconscious 'I' of the novel, the program in the computer-based media art freely operates an aesthetic experience of the viewer.

Specially, the interactive art rightly reflects this situation. In the interactive art, the artist is replaced with 'the provider' that offers the interface and the playground, and that the viewer is the indispensable 'participant' as a part of the work. The art work becomes a result of interaction between the work and the participant. Whatever happens, it is alone a moment of endless change that has never a similarity so far as working. At that time, what produces and provides a real-time interaction is the program as a real subject of the work. The participant merely spends an aesthetic experience in the process of an input and output by the program.

The program as a real subject calls up Edgar Allen Poe's mystery, "The purloined letter" that the subject of the novel keeps changing by the letter as a real subject or a signifier.[17] Like the letter, the program also leads us to change the seat of a subject as a participant; that is, so called, inter-subjectivity. Furthermore, the program as a real subject is a kind of signifier, and it builds "the synchronic network as it appears in the diachrony of preferential effects."[18] In other word, the program of interactive art stands for the art work as synchronic network that consists of each different participant's experiences as diachrony. And it has both ways of the presence and the absence, the material and the immaterial.

5 Conclusion

Programming is a process of ultimate abstraction. It is the abstract representation of the programmer's thoughts on how to interpret and manipulate the real world. When a thought is translated into a program, it loses the ability to live with vagueness that thoughts normally employ. Conversely, the program, however, reflects our own patterns of thinking.[19] It shows us the other side of ourselves that we have never seen. In this point, the aesthetic element in the program gets the originality. Hegel pointed out, "in one respect, the originality is the most personal inner life of artist, yet on the other hand it reveals the nature of object and the special character of thing itself."[20]

The originality of the programming in computer-based media art should be considered as 'the nature of object' and 'personal inner life of artist' at the same time,

---

[16] Marcel Proust, In Search of Lost Time, trans. C.K. Scott Moncrieff & Terence Kilmartin (New York: The Modern Library, 2003) 60.

[17] Edgar Allen Poe, "The purloined letter" Short stories of Edgar Allen Poe(New York:Vintage Books,1975).

[18] Jacques Lacan, The Seminar of Jacques Lacan, ed. Jacques-Alain Miller, trans. Sylvana Tomaselli (Cambridge: Cambridge Univ. Press, 1988) 67.

[19] Daniel Kohanski, The philosophical Programmer (New York: ST. Martin's Press, 1998) 186.

[20] G. W. F. Hegel, Aesthetics, trans. T. M. Knox (London: Oxford Univ. Press, 1975) 294.

because the program is both a science and an art, and it makes them nicely complementary each other. Therefore, 'The beauty of program that is not there' becomes more viable when it involves the application of aesthetics. Within a 'technosphere' which we lives in a technological context, looking for 'the beauty that is not there' is inevitable fate or reality.

Acknowledgments. This work was supported by Soongsil University Research Fund.

References

1. Adorno, T.W.: Aesthetic Theory. Minnesota P, Minnesota (1998)
2. Barthes, R.: Image-Music-Text. Trans.Stephen Heath. Hill and Wang, New York (1977)
3. Barthes, R.:The Pleasure of the Text. Trans.Richard Miller. Hill and Wang, New York (1975)
4. Danto, A. C.: The Abuse of Beauty. Open Court Publishing Company, Illinois (2003)
5. Freud, S.: Civilization and Its Discontents. Trans. James Strachey. W.W. Noton & Company, New York (2005)
6. Hegel, G. W. F.: Aesthetics. Trans. T. M. Knox. Oxford P, London (1975)
7. Kosuth, J.: Art After Philosophy And After: Collected Writing, pp. 1966–1990. MIT Press, Cambridge (1998)
8. Kohanski, D.: The philosophical Programmer. ST. Martin's P, New York (1998)
9. Kunth, D.E.: Art of Computer Programming. Addison-Wesley, New Jersey (1979)
10. Maeda, J.: Creative Code. Thames & Hudson, New York (2004)
11. Lacan, J.: The Four Fundamental Concepts of Psychoanlysis. In: Miller, J.-A., Sheridan, A. (ed.) Trans. W.W. Norton & Company, New York (1998)
12. Lacan, J.: The Seminar of Lacan, J., Miller, J.-A., (ed.) Trans. Tomaselli, S., Cambridge Press, Cambridge (1988)
13. Poe, E. A.: The purloined letter" Short stories of Edgar Allen Poe. Vintage Books, New York (1975)
14. Proust, M.: In Search of Lost Time. Trans. Scott Moncrieff, C.K., Kilmartin, T., The Modern Library, New York (2003)
15. Silverman, K.: The Subject of Semiotics. Oxford Press, London (1984)
16. Yoon, J., Kim, J.: The interactive Artwork as the Aesthetic Object, vol. 4326. Springer, Berlin (2006)
17. The Dagstuhl Aesthetic Computing Workshop, Aesthetic Computing Manifesto, Leonardo36, No.4, MIT Press, Cambridge (2003)
18. Fishwick, P., Prophet, J.: Perspectives on Aesthetic Computing. In: Leonardo, vol. 38(2), MIT Press, Cambridge (2005)
19. http://www.processing.org

CNA² – Communications and Community; Neighborhoods and Networks; Action and Analysis: Concepts and Methods for Community Technology Research

Peter Day and Clair Farenden

CNA Project, CIRN, Watts 604, University of Brighton, Moulsecoomb, Brighton & Hove,
England, UK, BN2 4GJ
p.day@btinternet.com

1 Introduction

The purpose of this paper is to examine the challenges and opportunities of employing ICT in a community building/development context through a critical reflection of the experiences of the Community Network Analysis (CNA) and ICT research project[1] in the Poets Corner community of Brighton and Hove, UK. Grounded in community networking, community development and community learning theories, the CNA project aimed to: investigate impacts of ICT on the network ties and social cohesion of community groups; whilst exploring the uses of network technologies in stimulating social capital and promoting community development in Poets Corner.

In order to address these aims we developed a participatory action research (PAR) methodology [36], and utilised ICT in ways similar to the UNESCO approach of ethnographic action research (EAR). That is to say that we provided "a flexible and adaptable approach to researching and developing ICT projects.....within a broad and embedded understanding of local contexts and needs" [34, p103]. The rationale of this approach was to generate knowledge of community ICT applications that could be used to support and sustain community development processes. This meant that CNA possessed a dual purpose. One was to investigate the potential influence of ICT on social capital and social cohesion in community networks. The second was to design, implement and develop a community communication space (CCS) in partnership with representatives from the community infrastructure. The next section situates CNA within its theoretical and conceptual environment by locating it in community development and community informatics knowledgebases.

2 Situating the Research Through Blended Literature

In 1955, the UN defined community development as, "a process designed to create conditions of economic and social progress for the whole community with its active participation and the fullest possible reliance on the community's initiative" [35, p6].

[1] Economic & Social Research Council (ESRC) - People at the Centre of Communication & Information Technology (PACCIT) research programme (Grant RES-328-25-0012).

D. Schuler (Ed.): Online Communities and Social Comput., HCII 2007, LNCS 4564, pp. 301–314, 2007.

For many community developers, this has meant formulating strategies and planning activities—with communities—that met the needs of the community at a specific point in time [1, 19]. Smith puts this into context by contending that community development should concentrate on improving local democracy; promoting mutual aid; encouraging local networks; and supporting communal coherence [32].

Around the millennium, community informatics (CI) emerged as an academic construct that concerned itself with investigating community-based ICT applications [15, 20]. However, CI is not the sole preserve of academic researchers. It has an inherent practice-based component, which focuses on the application of ICT in support of community processes and to achieve community objectives [16]. What CI currently lacks is a distinctive research agenda that lays down a clear direction or development path. It has been suggested, and this is a viewpoint with which the CNA team concurs, that CI "emphasizes a grassroots perspective whereby community members are centrally involved in the application of ICTs for community development" [20, p.4]. Because community development takes place in the everyday environment of people's lives and is built on processes of empowerment and participation that enable communities to question their realities and affect action for change [23], a question emerges as to whether the use of ICT by communities can make a significant contribution to community development. Answering this question through research requires the development of community engagement strategies built on trust and mutual respect. Such relationships do not appear over night. They take time and effort to build and more time and effort to nurture and to sustain.

In building such relationships, community informatics researchers must acknowledge the potential danger of power imbalances, even in the most well intentioned community research projects. Put simply, power is "the ability to get someone to do something he or she would not ordinarily do" [2, p10]. From a community research perspective, the question of validity—"whether you are measuring what you think you think you are measuring" [33, p32]—becomes a factor. If the processes, outcomes and results of community research can not be 1) understood, and 2) used by the community, then it is not valid as community development research. Such a situation can only be developed through mutual power sharing and open, honest and respectful dialogue in the community research partnership.

2.1 Community Networking and ICT

Community-type organisation is a feature of all human societies, and studies of humans and other higher primates suggest that we share an inherent sociability, a willingness to connect and to cooperate. [13, p.1]

Pointing to relationships between social networks and their role in structuring modern community life, Gilchrist illustrates an interesting sociological constant. Regardless of changes in the structure and organization of society, humanity has, down the ages, adapted to social change and continued—sometimes in the face of extreme adversity—to socialize, develop relationships, plan events and organize activities in the name of community. The desire for community, whatever form it takes, is a feature of human behavior. The communicative behavior of networking referred to by Gilchrist is the glue, or social cohesion, that forms and sustains community.

In a seminal text on the emergence of 'new', i.e. ICT based community networks, Schuler explains that community networks existed as a sociological concept—i.e. community communication patterns and relationships—long before the web-based community networks we know today emerged [29]. From this perspective community networks are important factors in the community development environment. Interestingly however community networks are increasingly referred to as technological artifacts and appear to be understood in terms of the connectivity they give to ICT (e.g. [17]) rather than the community building links to social capital they afford within communities.

Establishing what lies at the heart of community networking, i.e. the purpose and nature of the social relationships within communities and their attendant processes of communication, is central to understanding community [7]. It provides a starting point for addressing the challenges that accompany the design, development and sustainability of technology mediated community networks. Put simply, knowledge of what shapes and energizes community life is pivotal to developing effective community networks. Connected through dialogue, community activists give purpose to social capital. They influence community norms; develop trust and sustain community networks. If community technology activists and researchers engage with communities in ways appropriate to community needs then ICT can impact significantly on building and sustaining social capital in community networks [10].

2.2 Social Capital – Communicative Networks of Trust and Purpose

Of course, making and sustaining social network relationships can be problematic. Communities are contested spaces comprising difference and diversity [23]. Conflicts can and do arise. Celebrating and respecting diversity through the promotion of a culture of shared communication, shared values and shared knowledge, or social cohesion [14], is a big step toward building healthy communities. However, establishing and maintaining social connectivity can be challenging. Social cohesion requires "stocks of social trust, norms, and networks that people can draw upon to solve common problems" [31] known as social capital. Putnam suggests that, "social capital calls attention to the fact that civic virtue is most powerful when embedded in a sense network of reciprocal social relations" [26, p.19]. However, as with any other forms of capital, its value is found in the purpose to which it is put. The capacity of people connected in community networks to communicate with one another and use their knowledge to identify problems, plan agenda, agree and execute actions, and evaluate outcomes is what Schuler calls 'civic intelligence' [30]. A theory that "describes the capacity that organizations and society use to "make sense" of information and events and craft responses to environmental and other challenges collectively" [9, p.34].

A growing body of literature relating to ICT, social capital and community capacity is emerging. However, much of the studies from which it draws are still in their infancy. Hypothesizing that ICT will affect both bonding and bridging social capital, Gaved and Anderson warn that the analyses that currently exist, based as they often are on surveys conducted only 6 – 12 months into an initiative's lifecycle, are "often too shallow and too soon" [11, p.8]. If, as Resnick suggests, "social capital is a residual or side effect of social interactions and an enabler of future interactions" [27] then those communities with existing stocks of social capital are likely to benefit more from initiatives that enrich social capital [10]. One of the distinct challenges facing the CNA project was to identify whether ICT might contribute to building stocks of social capital in a community such as Poets Corner, where social capital stocks had been in atrophy for a number of years.

3 Insights into a Community Informatics Methodology for Community Development

Before reflecting on the project methodology and community development activities, we pause to clarify CNA's interpretation of the term 'ICT'. Focusing on the information and communication assets of Poets Corner, it became clear that we had to adjust our understanding of ICT and adapt it to that of the community. Of course, interpretations or understanding vary in the community. We have met people with very advanced ICT literacy skills and others with basic or no skills at all. Even in a small, resource poor community like Poets Corner, information is required, acquired, stored, distributed and exploited in numbers of ways and communications takes place at various levels using different media. As we learnt more about the communications of Poets Corner we decided to interpret ICT in a broader sense than initially intended. We determined to include all modes of community communication that the community used or were interested in using. A community newsletter entitled the West Hove News (WHN) illustrates the necessity. We soon learnt that WHN was a pivotal community communication medium serving as an important source of community information and knowledge exchange. In Poets Corner, WHN is an important community ICT. In order to understand ICT in the community it is necessary to understand the media that the community uses as well as the processes of communication.

We adopted what the Community Development Foundation (CDF) describes as an 'involvement ready' model [4] to determine research partnership involvement. Preliminary interviews suggested that the community infrastructure, i.e. the groups, clubs, associations and organizations, would provide partners most capable of participating. This approach provided an interesting focus for the project. Chee contends that most studies of this nature are focused at the individual level [5]. This presents community from individualistic rather than collective perspectives. Concentrating on networks in the community infrastructure enables a broader understanding of the structure and organization of community life to emerge, which in turn will provide opportunities for situated or contextualized research into the individual and familial components of community networks to be conducted later.

CNA methodology comprised 4 components of investigation into community network development: 1) community profiling; 2) social network analysis (SNA); 3) participatory learning workshops (PLWs); and 4) community communication space (CCS). Although presented as separate entities, the interaction and overlap between the elements is significant.

3.1 The CNA Community Profile

Community profiles are community development tools used to describe a process or processes of community knowledge generation about a specific area or community, in which particular emphasis is placed on community perceptions in order to identify and address problems in the community [18]. Conducting a community profile had a duality of purpose for the CNA team. One was to map the community infrastructure and create a database of the community assets which could be used by the community^2 [21]. The other was to identify the information and communication needs of the community infrastructure. Both purposes were achieved using a number of techniques: exploiting existing information sources, e.g. census and neighborhood renewal surveys; in-depth interviews using story-telling techniques [37]; reflective and scenario workshops; transect walks with local historians and community activists; observation of community meetings—formal and informal—and engagement in diverse community activities. Encouraging community participation in these profiling techniques provided access to insights into the social fabric of community life that would otherwise have been hidden from exogenous researchers. Enabling people to tell their stories, precipitated a process of 'critical consciousness' [23] within the community infrastructure that enabled reflection on existing community practices and highlighted the need for improved social networking.

Poets Corner, forms a large part of the Portland Road and Clarendon Neighborhood Renewal Area, and comprises just over 100 community organizations, groups, clubs and associations. Despite the best efforts of community development agencies, the grass-roots community and voluntary sector has witnessed a weakening of social relationships between organizations and an apparent growth in territorial tensions. Communications within the community infrastructure are relatively poor and shrinking resources have meant that dialogue with the community is at times almost non-existent. Organizations and networks that should be collaborating with one another often regard themselves as competitors for resources and there is some evidence of a culture of distrust emerging between some groups.

However, there are also positives in this local story. The old community forum (West Hove Forum) which had stagnated and became moribund due to political infighting and factionalism was re-established as the Portland Road and Clarendon Forum under the auspices of a community development agency—the Trust for Developing Communities. Evidence from the first few meetings points to a desire to bridge division within the community infrastructure and collaborate for the collective good. A recent community workshop organized by CNA acknowledged the problem of local distrust and tribalism and expressed a desire to find ways of working together and improving community communications.

Of the 104 groups, clubs, associations, etc. in Poets Corner 3 main clusters and 6 smaller clusters were identified through the mapping exercise. These clusters, or affiliation networks, appear to be built around parent organizations, e.g. community associations and faith based organizations. Affiliation is based on organizational support mechanisms and the availability of physical space to support activities. A

---

^{2} The database was used by a local community development to inform the community infrastructure of the relaunch of a community forum, which had been moribund for some time. The forum is currently flourishing.

number of isolated nodes and dyadic networks, such as the infant and junior schools, were also identified. The network interactions of the schools tend to be with parents, children and the public sector. Connectivity with the community infrastructure has been limited in the past but both schools now have representatives on the newly launched forum.

'Informal' network structures in the community tend to be more open and dynamic than their 'formal' counterparts but are also more transient. Networking often occurs in public spaces, e.g. Stoneham Park, local pubs and coffee shops, or serendipitous street meetings. This agora 'effect' provides opportunity for knowledge exchange, and comfort and support contacts to be made. Communication transactions tend to be both self-organizing and mutually reinforcing, especially where familial and/or friendship ties predominate. The centrality of Stoneham Park makes it an ideal informal communal meeting and activity space, where networks of informal associations gradually evolve. Repeated recognition, shared or parallel activities, nodding acknowledgement of presence, anonymous conversations en passant, name exchanges and gossip often lead to friendship networks developing. Informal, or weak, neighborhood network ties [12] are formed through an accumulation of social interaction; initiated for no specific social purpose other than the human need to communicate and interact. In other words, through communication rooted in the fabric and practice of neighborhood life.

The nature of informal networks in Poets Corner appears to fall into two categories – spontaneous and planned. Spontaneous informal networks tend to be unstructured and spur-of-the-moment. During the collection of personal narratives we learnt that a local cat had gone missing. Neighbors immediately organized a search of the area. In another street, learning of the arrival of a new family, neighbors collectively left bags of clothes and toys on their doorstep as a welcoming gesture. People visiting each other's homes for a chat and coffee: reinforcing and developing social bonds, illustrates the spontaneous nature of informal community networks. Planned informal networks are more structured and preconceived but have no formal membership. A curry club—where participants get together to try new curry recipes and socialize—is organized at irregular intervals by email, and a book club—run along much the same lines as the curry club—is organized by mobile phone. Circles of baby-sitters and parents requiring 'sitters' that evolved through the local grapevine are maintained by landline telephone, SMS text messaging and face to face contacts. Key holder groups, formed by neighbors in the same street, where spare keys are cut and distributed in case of need or emergency (especially among the elderly) are another example of organized but informal networks in the community. Networking activities such as these illustrate that people are increasingly comfortable using communication technologies such as email and mobile telephony to support their network structures and facilitate communicative exchanges.

3.2 Social Network Analysis (SNA)

The project's use of a SNA approach was intended to encourage community partners to think about the effectiveness of their network relationships by getting them to reflect on: 1) the nature of their ties within the infrastructure, and 2) the significance of communications to community activities and practices. Data collection involved surveys of two significant areas of community communication activity – firstly, the organization of the family fun day and summer festival, and secondly a more comprehensive investigation of communication patterns within the community infrastructure.

The first survey focused on communication within the family fun day organizing committee and who they spoke to in the broader community infrastructure. The survey also questioned why and how they communicated, together with their preferred communication media. Our main objective was to use network data to illustrate the communication patterns occurring during the organization of the community's biggest event of the year. Because social network analysis uses graphical images to represent social realities we were able to use these visualizations as aids to stimulate critical reflection of the communication processes. Providing the opportunity for community groups to reflect on and discuss their community communication behavior proved to be an essential element in the community network learning process. For example, we were able to show how the organizing committee had developed excellent connectivity within the committee itself but that communications with the community infrastructure were fairly ineffective. In fact, the organizing committee was a clique which emanated mainly from the Poets Corner Residents Society (PCRS) and was at the time of the survey, dependent on individuals for communicating with non PCRS groups in Poets Corner. Since this survey was conducted, the organizing committee, whist not an ideal model of inclusivity has become a more openly participative body in the community.

The second survey collected data on formal network relationships within the community infrastructure. The intention here was to build a representation of the community network structure and organization by plotting transactional exchanges, i.e. communication, in a way that illustrates in graphical form the connecting elements and nodes [6] in the community network. Frequency, purpose and mode of communications were also identified in order to stimulate critical reflection of existing communication and relationship patterns within the infrastructure at large.

A separate paper is required in order to provide a detailed discussion of the community infrastructure network survey. However, 2 points of interest arise that contribute to the point here. The first is that the survey confirmed the findings of the mapping exercise regarding the structure of the community infrastructure, i.e. it comprises 3 large clusters or affiliate networks; 6 smaller clusters; a dyadic network and a number of individual community entities. The majority of communication takes place within clusters, providing some evidence of bonding social capital, although a detailed analysis reveals a more complex picture. Evidence of bridging social capital exists but much of this occurs during formal monthly or bi-monthly community meetings such as the Portland Road and Clarendon community forum or community safety meetings and is undertaken by one or two key stakeholders, or hubs, from each cluster. Whilst these hubs, i.e. highly connected elements of a network [6], provide the shortest routes between clusters and are effective community communicators, they are also what Csermely describes as keystone species [6]. Their removal from the communication ecology of a community could result in the fragmentation of the community network.   Bridging social capital is more widespread during the planning and organization of the Fun Day and summer festival.

The survey provides interesting evidence about the significance of linking social capital. Even groups with limited community relationships indicated the importance of their connections to exogenous community development and neighborhood renewal resources and funds and government agencies and offices. The CNA team subsequently developed working relationships with the Neighborhood Renewal team, the Trust for Developing Communities and Brighton & Hove Community Initiatives and has established themselves as members of the Portland Road & Clarendon Forum with a view to ensuring that all CNA actions and activities are transparent and contribute to community attempts to build social cohesion in the community.

3.3 Participatory Learning Workshops (PLWs)

PLWs afford interactive ICT learning spaces which provide and share knowledge of, and skills in, the use of network technologies. Traditional community ICT training courses often lack social or community contextualization and are typically driven by performance indicators and targets. Training is often task based and aimed at individual users rather than members or participants in a community network. The PLW rationale acknowledges 2 main considerations. Firstly, learning is contextual and affected by the environment in which it occurs [22, 3]. Secondly, social interaction is a crucial component of learning. PLWs provide spaces for diverse community stakeholders to situate their engagement with ICT in a community context. They actively encourage open participation and knowledge sharing through social networking and dialogue [24].

The type of technologies introduced during PLWs, together with other community learning needs, are determined by community participants prior to the workshops— underlining the importance of dialogue between researchers and community. Workshops are designed to stimulate critical reflection of the social appropriation of technologies and encourage community networking. This is achieved by workshops: 1) employing participatory and interactive learning techniques, 2) working at the community's pace, 3) working with technologies and applications that the community wants to learn, and 4) wherever possible, using content generated by workshop participants.

As the project developed so hybrid PLWs evolved to meet community needs, which were extending beyond the static environment of the Talkshop[3] ICT suite. Mobile PLWs emerged because people were not always able to attend the Talkshop workshops. In order not to exclude these people we utilized wifi networked laptops to take the workshops to the community at time and locations appropriate to their needs. The second factor was technology related. A significant proportion of participants expressed an interest in learning to use digital cameras and digital camcorders. Some wanted to learn how to use their mobile (cell) phones and portable media players to generate content. Mobile PLWs enabled us to facilitate situating community learning in community contexts, and enabled community groups to generate their own digital content.

---

[3] Talkshop is a small community centre – converted by local people from a disused council storage building in a rundown 'park' inhabited at the time by drug dealers and disillusioned youth. Stoneham Park has since been reclaimed by the community and is a thriving community space.

A third type of PLW evolved during the project—the scenario PLW. These workshops are built on the philosophy of open participation, knowledge sharing, social networking and dialogue found in the other PLWs in order to find a collective solution to community problems. An issue or question facing the community is presented as a scenario to participants who, drawing on their own knowledgebase, collaborate to find solutions. Due to the diversity of participants this usually requires some effort in establishing common ground before solutions can be identified. Scenario PLWs are an excellent way of highlighting the significance and potential impact of social networking in both theory and practice.

During the first round of PLWs we worked with a range of community groups to develop their skills in recording and archiving the activities that have taken place during the summer festival as well as other community events e.g. local history walks, holistic health days, tai chi in the park, poetry, art and music. Digital video, photography and podcasting have proved popular activities in the community and we are planning to work with interested parties to create digital community story maps for the community as part of the CCS.

3.4 Community Communications Space (CCS) – A Prototype

The purpose of the CCS is to provide ICT mediated support for community networking activities. During the design and implementation of the prototype we sought to achieve this by embedding it as an integral part of the community infrastructure and community activities. However, such an approach is accompanied by various levels of complexity that present challenges to both researcher and community participant. Firstly, achieving consensus for a project across the community can be problematic. Building the necessary levels of trust and respect with the community to create effective partnerships takes time and effort—and these resources are usually at a premium in both academic and community sectors. Balancing the competing demands of program funders and community partners is no simple matter and there is a very real danger of researchers getting caught up in the day to day excitement of community life and losing sight of the fact that the investigation is a funded research project—we have probably been guilty of this on occasion. Impatience can add to complexity. There have been times when people have appeared to forget what the partnership agreed to do, i.e. create an online environment which would underpin and be used for community development. It is important to understand that as spaces of diversity and difference, communities, like people, learn at different speeds. They also engage in different ways and accommodating difference and diversity is not always straightforward. The choice of technical platform also added to the complexity as at times we were left with inadequate technical knowledge. Ensuring appropriate levels of technical support is essential before commencing a project such as this. When we set out, we believed we had the support we needed but circumstances change and for the remaining social scientists and community practitioners with reasonable levels of techno-savvy, the technology proved to be a big problem at times. Earlier, we clarified what we meant by the phrase 'ICT' in terms of our engagement with community groups and activities. Because CNA aimed to: investigate impacts of ICT on the network ties and social cohesion of community groups; whilst exploring the uses of network technologies in stimulating social capital and promoting community development in Poets Corner, it is also necessary to explain how we approach ICT as an element of data analysis.

Within community informatics a considerable literature exists that focuses on the use of ICT as tools supporting community activities (see e.g. [8, 28]. Indeed, in this study we refer to ICT appropriated in support of community activities. In this sense the CCS can be understood as a tool supporting community activity. However, presenting the CCS as a tool paints a limited picture of its versatility. Intended to support community communications, as well as the social and organizational activities of community groups, the CCS is much more than a simple tool. It supports information transfer and knowledge sharing and can be used to generate community content and community contexts. The CCS supports community communication and social networking. In this way ICT is understood as space or environment [25] in which people engage in dialogue, network with one another and develop relationships in a virtual world. Although a fuller picture of the CCS is now emerging, the CCS is still more than a combination of tools and virtual environments. One of the purposes of the project was to work with the community to design, implement and develop a community prototype and although this phase of the project has just ended, it is far too early to evaluate it in terms of its direct impact on social capital [11]. This does not mean, however that the CCS can not be analyzed in terms of social capital.

In order to analyze the affects of ICT on network ties, social cohesion and social capital, it is necessary to understand how effective the processes of utilizing ICT in a community development context have been. CNA is ostensibly a project about processes—community development processes; community networking processes; community learning processes; community communication processes and community technology processes—Resnick's model of social capital forms and facilitated interactions [27] therefore provides us with a useful framework for understanding ICT as process. That is to say the process or processes that connect people through situated community ICT learning; for purposes of information sharing, communication, participation, network ties strengthening and trust building.

The components of the CNA methodology referred to previously were used to collect data and engage the community in designing a digital environment that meets the needs of those engaged in the initiative at that time. Yet it needs to be flexible enough to adapt to and accommodate the changing needs of additional participants as the initiative's diffusion throughout the community expands. For example, whichever format the PLWs took, we always sought to ensure they provided space for community discussion of CCS design considerations and needs, which informed the planning, design, implementation and ongoing development of the CCS prototype. Built on the Plone open source, content management system (CMS), the prototype has gone through a number of iterations as PLW participants have learnt to use it and numbers engaging with the project have increased. Enabling all the usual group pages, blogs, notice boards, visitor pages, local diaries and news facilities that you might expect from a community web site, the CCS also supports video and audio podcasting, digital story-telling, digital art, poetry and music activities. Discussion forums are being added to support the community development/building processes currently underway through the Portland Road and Clarendon Community Forum referred to earlier. A range of social networking applications are also being considered.

4 Conclusion

During our work in Poets Corner we encountered a strong desire to share stories and meaning in the community. More than that however, we discovered an eagerness to learn how communication technologies might assist in supporting and sustaining community activities. As the CCS moves into a community diffusion phase we are exploring innovative and creative ways of developing community voice and memory initiatives that promote community networking. If technology mediated community networks are to support the diversity found in community environments, then community informatics practitioners and researchers must focus on the design and development of safe and welcoming spaces that encourage and facilitate participation and engagement. Enabling people to interact with one another by constructing narratives and sharing meaning in convivial environments is central to effective community networking.

In order to address some of the fears about technology that exist in communities, ICT must be seen to be relevant to the needs and interests of community life. The community technology environment must be accessible to all and use language that encourages common ground thinking in determining community uses. Local communities need to feel in control of technologies rather controlled by them. When CNA engages with community groups we contextualize ICT in ways that relate to their environments and activities. Learning about the community environment, its practices and its relationships is paramount. Conducting community profiles and speaking to people, is not only a great way of breaking the ice between researcher and community, but provides knowledge crucial to the effective design of community networks.

Participants from all sections of Poets Corner have understood the need for improved communications within the community infrastructure and with the community at large. Information about what the community needs and wants from the community infrastructure has become a significant issue for many groups in the area. Although ESRC funding for CNA has now ended, we have secured funding through the Brighton and Sussex Community Knowledge Exchange (BSCKE), to conduct a community-based participatory research (CBPR) project undertaking a community needs assessment of the Portland Road and Clarendon Neighborhood Renewal Area and to present the results in the form of tag clouds on the CCS. In an additional outcome, following agreement in principle of a number of community groups, we are currently exploring the possibility of establishing CNA as a community sector organization or charity.

During our time in Poets Corner, we have, in keeping with our contractual obligations to ESRC, generated knowledge contributing to the body of academic knowledge in the field of community informatics. In addition and in keeping with our ethical responsibilities to our community partners, we have generated knowledge and processes that will support community development and community networking. The CNA methodology has:

1. Demonstrated that the use of personal narratives—story-telling—is a useful tool for facilitating critical consciousness of the community environment, which in turn is paramount for building effective community development practices and strategies.
2. Shown that communities are interested in learning how to use and apply ICT that are appropriate to their needs. Technologies such as digital camcorders and cameras,

mobile phones, PDAs and iPods are particularly useful in providing support for community voice and memory activities. It is activities such as these that often provide the contextualizing 'hooks' or act as a catalyst for communities wanting to learn about the archiving and distribution capacities of other ICT. In addition to this we have shown that by collaborating with others to appropriate ICT for community purpose, communities can build and increase their stocks of social capital.

3. Developed a suite of PLWs to support community learning that situated and contextualized in the day to day realities of the community environment. PLWs are grounded in a philosophy of information sharing, open participation, social networking and dialogue.

4. Highlighted how, through the use of social network analysis techniques, critical awareness of community communication patterns can assist in understanding the strengths and weaknesses of a community's social relationships. This in turn can lead to improved communication, common knowledge, community identity, shared values, obligations, roles and norms and trust.

5. Illustrated how, despite an inherent focus in academic circles on the significance of bridging and bonding social capital, 'linking' social capital also plays an increasingly crucial role in sustaining the community infrastructure. An important lesson that we as CI researcher take away from this project is to engage with community development and government agencies; seek to raise awareness of, and support for, community networking activities; and commence dialogue about how CI can support community development.

In closing, we reiterate the 3 key points from the literature that we hope will stimulate further discussion. The first is that to be valid, community informatics research must be of use to the community in which the researchers are engaged. In this respect, we concur with Keeble and Loader [20] who contend that the community informatics research agenda must emphasize grass-roots needs and perspectives. For the CNA team, this means locating the application of ICT, and associated learning processes, within a community development context. By community development we mean development that occurs in the everyday lives of the community environment and is based on processes of empowerment and participation [23]. Secondly, designing, implementing and developing technology mediated community networks requires a grounded understanding of the social network structures, organization and communication processes that comprise the community environment. Finally, the capacity of people in community networks to communicate with each other in order to share knowledge and collectively solve community problems is a crucial component of civic intelligence [30]. Finding ways of assisting communities to develop their capacity to shape and sustain their own community networks should be an integral part of all community research partnerships.

References

1. Alinsky, S.D.: Rules for Radicals. Random House, New York (1971)
2. Biklen, D.P.: Community Organizing: Theory and Practice. Prentice-Hall, Englewood Cliffs, NJ (1983)

3. Boettcher, J.: Ten Core Principles for Designing Effective Learning Environments: Insights from Brain Research and Pedagogical Theory. Innovate. 3(3) (2007) http://www.innovateonline.info/index.php?view=article&id=54
4. Chanan, G., Garratt, C., West, A.: The New Community Strategies: How to Involve Local People. London: Community Development Foundation (2000)
5. Chee, K.H.: Zoom In – Zoom Out: Understanding community participation through the lenses of rational choice, social capital and age stratification. The Journal of Community Work and Development, (8), pp. 27–43 (2006)
6. Csermely, P.: Weak Link: Stabilizers of Complex Systems from Proteins to Social Networks. Springer, Berlin (2006)
7. Day, P.: Community Networks: Building and Sustaining Community Relationships. In: Schuler, D. (ed.) Liberating Voices! A Pattern Language for Communication Revolution, MIT Press, Cambridge, MA (2007)
8. Day, P., Harris, K.: Down-to-Earth Vision: Community Based IT Initiatives and Social Inclusion, [The Commit Report]. IBM/CDF, London(1997)
9. Day, P., Schuler, D.: Community Practice in the Network Society: Pathways Toward Civic Intelligence. In: Purcell, P. (ed.) Networked Neighbourhoods: The Connected Community in Context, pp. 19–46. Springer, Heidelberg (2006)
10. ESRC, ICT, social capital and voluntary action. ESRC Seminar Series – Mapping the public policy landscape. ESRC: London (2006)
11. Gaved, M., Anderson, B.: The impact of local ICT initiatives on social capital and quality of life. Chimera Working Paper 2006-6, University of Essex, Colchester (2006)
12. Granvetter, M.: The strength of weak ties. American Journal of Sociology. 81, 1287–1303 (1973)
13. Gilchrist, A.: The Well-Connected Community: A networking approach to community development. The Policy Press, Bristol (2004)
14. Gill, K.S.: Knowledge Networking and Social Cohesion in the Information Society. A Study for the European Commission. Brighton: SEAKE Centre, University of Brighton (1997)
15. Gurstein, M.: Community Informatics: Enabling community uses of information and communications technology. In: Gurstein, M. (ed.) Community Informatics: Enabling communities with information and communication technologies. Hershey, PA, Idea Group, pp. 1–31 (2000)
16. Gurstein, M.: Community Informatics: What is Community Informatics. In: Gurstein, M., et al. (eds.) Community Networking and Community Informatics: Prospects, Approaches, Instruments. St. Petersburg: Instruments/Textbooks (2003)
17. Halcyon Consultants, 2003. Wired up Communities Programme 2000 – 2003: Final Report to the Department for Education and Skills (December 2003) http://www.intelligent communities.org.uk/
18. Hawtin, M., Hughes, G., Percy-Smith, J.: Community Profiling: auditing social needs. Open University Press, Buckingham (1994)
19. Jones, B.: Taking Action: Community Development Strategies and Tactics. CDPractice – Promoting Principles of Good Practice. No. 3. (1995) http://comm-dev.org/
20. Keeble, L., Loader, B.: Community Informatics: Shaping computer-mediated social relations. Routledge, London (2001)
21. Kretzmann, J.P., McKnight, J.L.: Building Communities from the Inside Out: A Path Toward Finding and Mobilizing a Community's Assets. ACTA Publications, Chicago, IL (1998)

22. Lave, J., Wenger, E.: Situated Learning: Legitimate Peripheral Participation. Cambridge University Press, Cambridge, UK (1990)
23. Ledwith, M.: Community Development – A critical approach. BASW/Polity Press, Bristol (2005)
24. Neilsen, C.: Community learning: creating a sustainable future through critical awareness. Development Bulletin 58, 102–105 (2002)
25. Preece, J.: Online Communities: Designing Usability, Supporting Sociability. Wiley, Chichester (2000)
26. Putnam, R.D.: Bowling Alone. The collapse and revival of American community, Simon and Schuster, New York (2000)
27. Resnick, P.: Beyond Bowling Together: SocioTechnical Capital. In: Carroll, J.M. (ed.) HCI in the New Millennium, pp. 247–272. Addison-Wesley, Reading (2002)
28. Shearman, C.: Local Connections: Making the Net Work for Neighbourhood Renewal. London: Communities Online (1999)
29. Schuler, D.: New Community Networks: Wired for Change. Harlow, Addison-Wesley, UK (1996)
30. Schuler, D.: Cultivating society's civic intelligence: patterns for a new "world brain". Journal of Society, Information and Communication 4(2), 157–181 (2001)
31. Sirianni, C., Friedland, L.: Civic Innovation and American Democracy. Change, vol. 29(1) (January-February 1997) //www.cpn.org/crm/essays/innovation.html
32. Smith, M.: Community development. The encyclopeadia of informal education. (2006) http://www.infed.org/community/b-comdv.htm
33. Stoecker, R.: Research Methods for Community Change. Sage, London (2005)
34. Tacchi, J., Slater, D., Hearn, G.: Ethnographic Action Research. New Delhi: UNESCO (2003)
35. United Nations, Social Progress through Community Development. New York: United Nations (1955)
36. Wadsworth, Y.: What is Participatory Action Research? Action Research Interna-tional (1998) http://www.scu.edu.au/schools/gcm/ar/ari/p-ywadsworth98.html
37. Waller, S.: Story-Telling And Community Visioning: Tools For Sustainability. Background Paper for the State Sustainability Strategy, Sustainability Policy Unit, Department for the Premier and Cabinet (2003) http://www.sustainability.dpc.wa.gov.au/docs/BGPapers/Waller%20S%20-%20Storytelling.pdf#search=%22story-telling%20waller%22

Toward Machine Therapy: Parapraxis of Machine Design and Use

Kelly Dobson

MIT Media Lab, Computing Culture Group, Massachusetts Institute of Technology
20 Ames Street, E15-020d, Cambridge MA 02139, USA
monster@media.mit.edu

Abstract. Machine Therapy is a new methodology combining art, design, psychodynamics, and engineering work in ways that access and reveal the vital relevance of subconscious elements of human-machine interactions. In this paper I present examples of empathic relationships with domestic appliances, roles of wearable and prosthetic apparatuses, and instances of evocative visceral robots that interact with people's understandings of themselves and each other. The Machine Therapy projects facilitate unusual explorations of the parapraxis of machine design and use. These usually unconscious elements of our interactions with machines critically affect our sense of self and our shared development.

Keywords: Machine Therapy, human-robot interaction, human-machine interaction, autonomic, parapraxis, body, organ.

1 Introduction

On a typical afternoon during my first year at MIT I was walking down Massachusetts Avenue and came across a jackhammer in use, tearing up the street. It had been a particularly frustrating morning and my reaction to the sound of the jackhammer was, unusually, one of immediate relief. I found in it a safe place to scream. Standing on the sidewalk nearby I let it out, safely hidden in the acoustic overload of the machine in use. It felt great. And no one seemed to notice.

I began experiencing all construction machines as opportunities to make some exploratory sounds with my voice while feeling safe doing so. I began to visit the various construction sites of the Big Dig project going on in Boston at the time. With many of the machines I could find a vocal resonance with tones and harmonics of their motors. Much like singing the same pitch with another person, often I could not separate my voice from the sound of a machine that I was trying to sound with. I thereby experienced the machine as a sort of body extension, as part of me and under the visceral control of my voice. At other times the machine seemed to be pulling me along into expressions, leading and facilitating my vocalizations. I learned more than I can write in this short paper. But I will begin. One aspect I must mention is that the construction workers and machine operators who spend their days and often nights with these machines welcomed me and these explorations and even would introduce me to different machines at different parts of the sites when they found them

D. Schuler (Ed.): Online Communities and Social Comput., HCII 2007, LNCS 4564, pp. 315–323, 2007.

interesting and thought that I might find them interesting to sound with. Individually, many confided in me that they too have often made sounds with the machines.

The explorations of expression that came along with vocally and viscerally relating with the construction machines enabled non-normative but useful takes on machines in public spaces and myself in public spaces. This unusual example catalyzed a series of projects and ideas, some of which I want to introduce in this paper.

To begin, I will briefly review a couple of concepts from psychoanalytic theory, namely object relations and transitional objects. Then, I will talk about the different reflective affordances of various categories of objects and machines. Finally, I will use these topics to ground the introduction of Companion Projects, a new series of autonomically sensate and viscerally active machines.

2 Objects

The processes of making objects and of perceiving objects are never neutral. That is, every time we make something we do so from our mostly subconscious set of assumptions and desires and perspectives that are thereby inscribed into the thing we are making. This cannot be avoided. We perceive and make things in this manner to some extent out of necessity. It is how we are able to engage and communicate with the world, with each other, and with ourselves. We can, however, become more aware of some of what we may be accustomed to take for granted in our approaches to things and machines.

2.1 Object Relations Theory

People use things and other people, and parts of things and parts of other people, to know about themselves. Whenever we perceive someone or something we are in a process of reflecting from this other something that is meaningful to us. Melanie Klein posited that part objects could be used in this manner, too.

2.2 Transitional Objects

There are special experiences within object relations that D.W. Winnicott termed transitional phenomena [3]. Winnicott explains, through his primary example of the relating between an infant and the infant's mother or primary caregiver, the developmental phases characteristic of a transitional object relationship that enable the individual infant to develop their own ego and sense of self awareness and ability to relate to other things and people in the world. The newborn does not yet have a sense of it being a distinct self and instead perceives all things as continuous and part of its full being and under its omnipotent control. In order to develop a secure sense of self and body boundaries and relations with other people and things who is able to be gently introduced to the disillusionment of this conception by careful and just in the right time weaning of the infant and separation of elements like the mother that the baby can learn to perceive as separate but in relation to the baby's self. Even in adult life we have transitional objects and phenomena that aid us in understanding ourselves, our bodies, and our social and political voices and agency in the world. Because in transitional phenomena the infant for a while is able to perceive no boundary between the object and themselves, I am especially interested in adults in objects that can be easily taken on as part of the self. The new projects that are the final section of this paper are about machines designed to be just this.

2.3 Bodies in Pieces

The machines of the industrial factories in the US and England that Marx writes about in Das Kapital are distillations of the earlier generation of workers' human body parts in action. Arms churning wheels are now hundreds of metal mechanical arms churning wheels while a person looks on to make sure the machines have power and run smoothly. This person witnesses their own body in action distilled into the machine, multiplied, and dissociated from their own desire.

At the same time that human body parts become design inspiration and distilled into machines, machines become design inspiration and built as human body parts: the artificial heart, mechanical prostheses, personal digital assistants as auxiliary brains.

With cultural and technological development we have become accustomed to our bodies in pieces, if not literally at least imaginatively. Our body parts and organs are separable and able to be related to by a person both as part of one's self and as separable from one's self at the same time. This non-neutral element of our contemporary experience of embodiment has special affordances.

In explorations of technological devices taken on as armor or training transitional objects, I have engaged in a series called Wearable Body Organs. I mention them here briefly just to ground the Companion Projects that end this paper in past work also about autonomic communication, organs, and personal therapy via body-based machines. They include ScreamBody, a portable space for screaming that silences the person's scream at time of scream to let them feel safe screaming at any time, but also records it for later release when, where, and how the person chooses. Another is HoldBody, which can inflate to actuate a self administered hug or string holding. And others in development now include CryBody which will function autonomically to help let crying happen when a person feels they need to but have been unable.

Fig. 1. Wearable Body Organs are a series of wearable apparatuses I am building also under the theme of Machine Therapy. They address needs not addressed by mass marketed devices. These include the need to scream or vocalize (ScreamBody), the need to be hugged or held (HoldBody), among others. ScreamBody is designed to resemble and serve the function of a set of surrogate lungs.

2.4 Puppets, Automata, and Companion Robots

Puppets, automata, and companion robots, often in the form of anthropomorphic whole creatures, enable a extension of our anthropomorphic reflections of other onto self as described in object relations to wider than human ranges. They enable this by the observable fact that they are not tied to the same laws of gravity (marionettes on strings are pulled upwards and merely alight on the ground) or human self consciousness.

In a machine modeled to resemble a whole organism, versus a machine modeled to resemble a part or organ of some unknown whole, there are different expectations implied. For a person interacting with an anthropomorphized companion robot, the relationship between the person and the machine is in some ways more akin to that between the person and a whole creature or another person. The person may, for example, easily identify elements and modes of behavior of the machine that resonate cognitively and socially with the person's own experience of themselves in the world. Though the machines may have relative (to humans) impoverished social vocabularies and demonstrations of personality, intention, self-awareness, and social awareness, they have enough that people can immediately identify and interact with them on emotional and cognitive levels [2].

Machines that are not by design intentionally anthropomorphic also facilitate reflections of self that can be body-based and meaningful. These meanings may be autonomic and subconscious more often than cognitively perceived and this may aid in the hallucination as the machine as part of the self.

3 Parapraxis of Machine Design

The word parapraxis is used in the context of psychoanalysis to refer to the slips of the tongue and other side events that may reveal unconscious motivations or repressed desires. I am applying its meaning here to machine design and use to discuss the side elements of machines that have been often subconsciously relevant in design and use. Especially focusing on the visceral elements including sound, infrasound, heat, movements, I have been looking for the parapractic elements in our everyday devices and machines and finding them everywhere. For example, laptops are warm as a side effect of their design but this warmth is something that helps people become endeared to their laptops. Car sounds were at first side elements but eventually designers and manufacturers and car enthusiasts began to design the sounds and even patent them (Harley Davidson, Ferrari).

When one uses a blender at home the cat darts and hides under the bed, the baby screams and cries, but the aggressive sound of the violent action taking place may otherwise go unnoticed by those present. Foregrounding the viscerally major element of a kitchen blender's violent sound in the making and using of Blendie is a way of bringing into awareness one example of very significant aspects of machines that often goes unnoticed consciously because it is not part of the intended purpose.

Fig. 2. Blendie is a re-appropriated vintage blender that instead of responding to the turning of knobs or pressing of buttons, requires the person to make the sound of its motor in action with their own voice. If the person is able to make a good enough human approximation of the pitches and roughness of the blender sound, Blendie will try to spin its own motor at the right speed to attain harmonic resonance with the dominant pitch the person is making.

A person with a very different vocal apparatus compared to the sound making apparatus of a machine cannot possibly make the same sounds a machine makes. This is clear in digital signal analyses of human and machine sounds. We hypothesized that people will nevertheless make somewhat predictable voiced expressions when trying to express the sounds of different machines [3]. We trained a machine learning model based on the recordings of eight people trying to individually vocally imitate five machines including a blender, a vacuum cleaner, a drill, a coffee maker, and a sewing machine. Our hypothesis turned out to be statistically verified and more work is underway to explore the sound relationships between existing domestic machines and people further.

Next, however, I want to turn to introducing a series of machines designed after all of these others with a foregrounding of elements that are often parapractic elements: sound, electromagnetic radiation, and rhythmic movement.

4 Companion Projects

Understanding that autonomic interaction is vitally relevant in machine use, we can design machines to facilitate visceral affects and autonomic therapy.

Three types of organ-like autonomically sensate and actuating machines named Umo, Amo, and Omo are currently under development. In this section I will discuss some of the design decisions and material choices going into each machine.

Fig. 3. My early sketches of Companion Projects sometimes imagined them with soft fur-like surfaces, but in the interest of allowing them to be perceived as being ambivalently between organ-like parts and complete organic wholes, I later re-imagined to have hairless outer surfaces.

Fig. 4. Umo, Amo, and Omo are each about lap-sized and comfortable for people of all sizes to hold. They weigh between six and nine pounds. They are soon to be adopted and to go out into the world and develop relationships – the next stage of the research project.

4.1 Umo

Umo is designed to listen to its surroundings and to incorporate these sounds into its ever-changing development of its own purr. It responds through its visceral purring in relation to the sounds that it is sensing in close to real-time and that it has sensed in the past.

Fig. 5. As illustrated in the design sketches and first physical prototype, Umo is shaped organically and has a soft rubber squeezable outer layer . It is lap-sized, as seen in Figure 4.

The background research for Umo included acoustic and infrasonic digital signal processing and analysis using recordings gathered from seven domestic cats and ten domestic machines that people describe as "purring," including cars, sewing machines, washing machines, air conditioners, and refrigerators.

Fig. 6. Sofie Lexington Whitman the cat and a washing machine in a local laundromat are among the subjects recorded with a dual microphone stethoscope built for this research.

Looking at different components of the sounds, such as the modulation spectral centroid, dominant pitch estimation, aperiodicity, power estimation over frames, and time-based modulation, a considered decision about which components of the sounds are consistent or correlative between the different machines and cats can be made. This in turn informs the design of how Umo develops its sounds over time.

4.2 Amo

Amo is designed to monitor the heart rate variation of the person holding it via electrode-based sensors build into its surface and in turn to modulate its own pseudo-heart beat variation manifested as an electromagnetic field around Amo. This

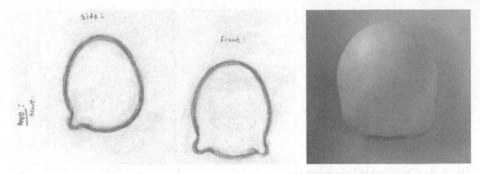

Fig. 7. Amo has two protruding areas in the first design that have been made more subtly distinct that in the early drawings. The protrusions have been purposefully designed to invite hands to rest on them. They house electrodes for sensing heart beat through hand contact.

electromagnetic field is modeled to mimic that of a human heart in different affective states.

4.3 Omo

Omo is a breathing object. It can sense the breathing of a person holding it via integrated quantum tunneling composite pressure sensors arrayed in its rubber outer layer. It performs signal processing on these sensor values to make a mapping of the breath of the person. It can then match its own breathing rate and pattern and phase to that of the breath of the person. It can also slowly change once entrained, and thereby slowly influence and effect change in the breathing of the person.

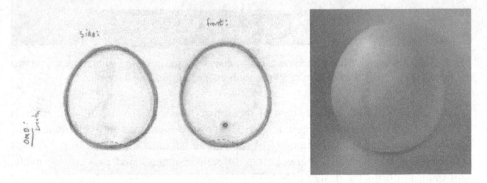

Fig. 8. Omo

The rubber orifice through which Omo breathes is designed to guide the air flow in a way that effects breath-like sounds when Omo expands and contracts its inner mechanical diaphragm.

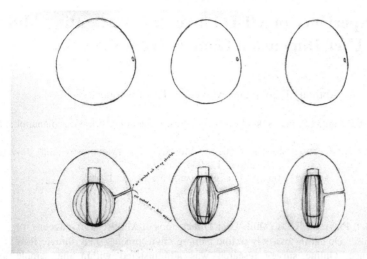

Fig. 9. Early sketches of the breathing of Omo show an air –tight bladder that is morphed in shape by mechanical elements to pull in and push out air, thus changing the overall shape and size of Omo in relation to its breath. The small air tube through which the air travels has been redesigned, along with the breathing bladder itself, to produce more breath-like variations of sound as Omo breathes different breath patterns.

5 Evaluation and Conclusions

The studies of people relating person-to-machine with these new organ-like companion projects are just beginning now. By the time of HCII 2007 this summer there will be much more to report.

Acknowledgments. Special thanks to the whole of the Computing Culture Group past and present at the MIT Media Lab, as well as Professor Roz Picard and Professor Edith Ackermann for feedback and fruitful conversations about the work discussed in this paper.

References

1. Dobson, K., Whitman, B., Ellis, D.: Learning auditory models of machine voices. In: Proceedings of the 2005 Workshop on Applications of Signal Processing in Audio and Acoustics (WASPAA.) Mohonk, NY (2005)
2. Fong, T., Nourbakhsh, I., Dautenhahn, K.: A survey of socially interactive robots. Robotics and Autonomous Systems 42(3-4), 143–166 (2003)
3. Winnicott, D.W.: Playing and Reality, Routledge, New York (1971)

Flow Experience of MUD Players: Investigating Multi-User Dimension Gamers from the USA

Anthony Faiola[1] and Alexander E. Voiskounsky[2]

[1] 535 West Michigan Street, School of Informatics, Indiana University, Indianapolis, IN
USA
[2] 8/5 Mokhovaya St., Psychology Department, Moscow M.V. Lomonosov State University,
Moscow, 125009, Russia
afaiola@iupui.edu, vae-msu@mail.ru

Abstract. Playing MUDs (Multi-User Dimensions or Multi-User Dungeons, or Multi-User Domain), text-only online gaming environments, may initiate flow experience. Online survey research was administered within the sample population of 13,662 MUD players from the United States of America, using the specially designed questionnaire with four categories of questions related to: flow experience, experience in playing MUDs, interaction patterns, and demographics. Replies of respondents (N = 287) fit a five factor model. All the correlations between the factors are significant (p < 0.05). Since players experienced flow while MUDding, it was proposed that flow is one of the sources of the long-time attractiveness for MUD players.

Keywords: play, online, flow, MMORPG, MUD, interaction, structural equation modeling.

1 Introduction

Every online community embodies both technological and social choices that impact those citizens or members of the community. MUDs (Multi-User Dimensions, or also Multi-User Dungeons or Multi-User Domains) are one such online community comprised of text-only environments that allow multiple users, or gamers, access to a shared database of rooms, exits, and other objects. MUDs are virtual environments, usually in the form of an adventure game that is either original or based on fantasy books or movies. Each gamer browses and manipulates this database from inside one of those rooms, while moving from room to room through the exits that connect them.

Although we might call a MUD an electronically-generated virtual reality, it does not have any two or three-dimensional computer graphics for its users to orient themselves as they move about their description-based spaces [6], as seen in today's MMORPGs (Massively Multiplayer Online Role Playing Game). In the typical MUD environment, gamers type their commands through a standard computer keyboard and receive back feedback in unformatted text on their display screen. Being quite crude in comparison to today's sophisticated and highly animated computer graphic systems, the MUD graphic user interface is quite reminiscent of computer games like Adventure and Zork.

D. Schuler (Ed.): Online Communities and Social Comput., HCII 2007, LNCS 4564, pp. 324–333, 2007.
© Springer-Verlag Berlin Heidelberg 2007

An important point to note is that MUDs are online role-play group games in which hundreds of players are simultaneously online. The players' goals include the development to the maximal level of characters of their choosing to represent them in all the situations taking place during the game. Other goals are connected with interaction patterns within the players' communities. Strong human ties and friendly relations are common within the communities of MUDders: competitive players use the advantage of intense communications (in the text-only mode) during playing sessions.

Since their origin a quarter of a century ago, the communities of MUDders have been investigated in a limited way. As a result, our research focuses on the flow experience of gamers while playing MUDs, and is a continuation of previous flow experience studies that dealt with communities of Russian and French MUD players [16,17].

2 Background Research on MUD Gaming Behavior

This review is limited to some of the major theoretical views and empirical findings on the behavior of MUD players, and not on video and/or computer gamers in general. The earliest studies regarding MUD players investigated disinhibition, i.e., the loss or reduction of an inhibition, as well as general friendly attitudes and openness [13]. Some of these problems are still of high importance for gaming researchers. For example, the effects of disinhibition have been recently discussed within the broader context of Web related behavior [7]. An empirical typology of MUDders developed by Bartle [1] is based on two crossing axes, namely "acting with" (i.e., interacting) vs. "acting on", and "emphasis on players" vs. "emphasis on the environment". Bartle states that it is important for the vitality of the MUD environment that it have a balance of the four types of players (i.e., achievers, killers, socialisers, and explorers) in his typology.

Utz [15] found that 76.6% of respondents report they have had virtual relations with fellow MUDders. Using cluster analysis with three attitudinal scales (role-play, game, and skepticism), Utz [15] was also able to differentiate four types of players, including: 1) role-players – those interested in playing roles; 2) gamers – those interested in having adventures and playing games; 3) virtuals – those interested either in online meetings with partners and in chatting with them, or in development of virtual environments; and 4) sceptics – those disinterested in most of the features of MUDs and refusing to identify themselves with any group of MUDders.

The work of Turkle [14] has also brought to the fore findings that establish the phenomena of virtual relations specifically among MUD players in the areas of culture and metaphor, and interpersonal and personal relationships. These relationships include friendship and romance, intimacy and deception. She has described how online gamers find ways to construct their identities online as personae, with an extensive development of their self-concepts. She has also paid special interest to gender issues and gender swapping, i.e., the MUDders experience of gender role playing other than in real life. Turkle holds that in virtual space the boundaries between one's real life and virtual life have been significantly eroded, e.g., she depicts MUDders who simultaneously play several roles, such as those of a courageous young man, a timid young man, and an attractive girl.

In addition to role playing, Salvay [12] also compared MUDs with virtual environments for psychodrama. Both promote personal and social growth, largely due to the effect that is gained by changes in players' positions, roles, characters, ways of behavior and related changes in feelings, affects and emotions. As part of social learning theory, Lee [8] suggested that self-efficacy, i.e., self-realization of one's capabilities to deal with and to oppose real-life problems, is a major psychological dimension inherent in MUD-related behavioral analysis. Lee argues that according to the effects of the MUD experience, certain parameters of self-efficacy can be measured.

3   Flow Experience in the MUD Environment

Although MUD communities are not a new form of online gaming, there is still much that can be learned from the way their members interact and communicate. Additional research is needed to investigate how these communities function as precursors to today's more advanced MUDs and MMORGs that consist of sophisticated three-dimensional graphics.

Flow experience, initiated by Csikszentmihalyi [4, 5], has been heavily used by researchers such as McKenna and Lee [9] in investigating MUDs. As Csikszrnymihalyi notes, processes of pursuing a desired or cherished result are sometimes more pleasing and self-rewarding than the result itself, i.e., when and if it is gained. Csikszentmihalyi described this "positive experience" as one's "flowing from one moment to the next, in which he is in control of his actions, and in which there is a little distinction between self and environment, between stimulus and response, between past, present, and future" [5].

The researchers also found that flow might accompany almost every type of human behavior. Major characteristics of flow are: temporary loss of self-consciousness and sense of time; high concentration on the task and high level of control over it; objectives becoming clear and distinct; actions merging with awareness, experiences bringing full satisfaction and worth doing for their own sake (or motivated intrinsically); and immediate feedback. What is especially important is that flow rests upon the precise matching between the available skills and the task challenges [4].

The dimensions listed above make it tempting to find out whether the overwhelming devotion of MUDders to the process of playing might be partly or fully explained in terms of flow experience. Indeed, gamers usually feel satisfaction while MUDding. Moreover, during their MUDding experience they often keep control over the gaming tasks while the complexity of those tasks might be dynamically changing. In addition, gaming task objectives might be quantified, feedback is close to immediate, the sense of time is most often altered, concentration and awareness are reportedly very high, and motivation is certainly intrinsic.

McKenna and Lee [9] have shown that MUDding fits the flow model and that social interaction while playing MUDs is inseparable from the flow experience. Researchers have also shown that flow experience and interaction patterns collaborate in forming long-term attachments to certain online games [3]. The highest level of involvement in MUDding was noted to take place at the moment when the gaming environment is neither too simple nor complex [11]. Decisions made in these environments tend to be optimal due to a balance between the players' skills and task challenges. According to Csikszentmihalyi [4], such a balance is both effective and welcomed as a means of experiencing flow.

The construct of flow experience is being increasingly investigated within ICT research, but to the best of our knowledge, there are only a few studies of flow patterns within communities of MUD players. McKenna and Lee [9] supported the view that MUDders experience flow, and that flow is positively related to the players' communicative patterns. Supposedly, these findings might provide a valid explanation of the long (lasting over a quarter of a century) popularity of MUDs among gamers. In a recent paper it is shown that flow is one of several constructs (along with personal and social communication patterns and loyalty) explaining behavior of those who play the same online games over a long period of time [3]. Although the process of text-only MUDding has not changed that much over the last two decades, with thousands of devoted MUD players, an updated investigation is still warranted to compare with past studies done by McKenna and Lee [9] ten years ago and others [16, 17].

The goal of the current research was first to determine the factors influencing behavior patterns of MUD players from the United States of America (USA), flow experience being one of several factors observed. Based on past findings related to MUD flow experiences (outlined above), we selected a set of dimensions that we refer to as a "flow dialect," which describes a flow pattern typical of MUD players.

4 Methodology

There are currently thousands of MUDs available online, with new MUDs being added and old ones closing annually. Yahoo Groups along has 825 different MUD groups that range in membership from five to over 2000 members. From our computation, we estimated that there is a total population of MUD users that exceeds 100,000 players worldwide. We define MUD players or gamers as individuals who login at their favorite MUD site, communicate by means of online chat with other members of that MUD environment, explore the areas, solve puzzles or other challenging riddles, and/or create new items, as well as reshape their own online characters. Although English is the official language in the majority of MUDs among MUDders from diverse geographic location, more and more MUDs are developing in other European and Asian countries.

4.1 Participants

To recruit MUD players for our study we placed an invitation for volunteers on five Yahoo MUD User Groups, having a total membership of 3662 members. Because Yahoo lists the groups according to size, with the largest first, we selected the five largest. Next, we sent invitations for volunteers to members located at twelve MUD sites, which we estimated to have approximately 10,000 members.[1] We selected these twelve as they appeared through a Google search for MUD sites. In sum,

---

[1] Yahoo User Groups: DRauctioneer, DRPlats, codersclub, retromudclub, DRList; and MUD sites: hsoi.com, topmudsites.com, hexonyx.com, topsmaugmuds.com, game.org, mudmagic.com, mud-connect.com, saugus.net, coremud.org, dartmud.com, armageddon.org, mudconnector.com

approximately 13,662 MUD players received our invitation. From this population, 650 took the survey, with 520 completing the survey, i.e., 4% of the total approximated recipients of the invitation. Of those that completed the survey, 375 were players from the USA, which was the focus of our data analysis. Of the 375 from the USA 87 responses were found to be corrupted, leaving us with 287 good responses. Interesting to note is that when comparing male to female respondents to the invitation, 15% of USA respondents were female as opposed to outside the USA, which was 21%. We opened our survey on January 30, 2007 and closed it on February 7, 2007, because we reached our target goal of 350 MUD participants from the USA. The age of respondents ranged from 14 to 50+, with the greatest group being 21-25 at 52%, and the remaining groups at: 19% (15-20), 20% (31-40), and 9% (41-50+). The highest reported amount of regular time spent per week was 25 hours among 17% of the participants, with the least reported number of hours being under three hours at 21% of the participants.

4.2 Questionnaire and Data Analysis

The main method for collecting data on flow experience is putting questions to the members of selected samples. Asking open-ended questions means interviewing respondents, which includes retrospective reports about flow-like experiences within any type of a respondent's behavior. When multiple-choice questionnaires are used, there are two main approaches. The first is using questions that refer to possible dimensions of flow-like experiences, reported retrospectively. The other is in the form of a questionnaire that is administered at random moments in an attempt catch respondents in the act of experiencing flow, i.e., when connected with the distant game server. At this time they are able to respond according to their instantaneous experience. This is the Experience Sampling Method, used by Csikszentmihalyi and his colleagues.

We used neither of these methods because they usually allow only a limited sample of users to be contacted. We preferred to increase the number of possible respondents (sample size) to be more representative of the population. Moreover, one of our research goals was to investigate a range of factors influencing the behavior of MUD players. Thus, the questionnaire included questions on flow, as well as issues which stand outside the flow experience. The online questionnaire was composed of 39 multiple-choice questions based on information gained from formative research. Specifically, we designed our questionnaire by reviewing the work of other MUD studies on flow experience [9, 10, 16, 17].

Thirty-one questions were asked in order to gain greater understanding of the dynamics of player perception involved in MUDding, with the remaining questions being demographic. Specifically, our questionnaire was composed of four categories of questions: flow experience (12 Likert questions), experience in playing MUDs (12 questions), interaction patterns within the game (9 Likert questions), and demographics (3 questions).[2] The questionnaire was delivered using the online survey service Zoomerang.

---

[2] Flow experience, included question numbers: 1-7, 11, 13-14, 17, 28; experience in playing MUDs, included question numbers: 8-9, 12, 15, 18, 27, 29-31, 37-39; interaction patterns within the game, included question numbers: 10, 19-26; demographics, included question numbers: 33-35.

Regarding our data analysis, in our study we used the traditional method of handling survey data with factor analysis. Thus, our research was entirely quantitative. Processing of research results involved four stages: 1) analysis of demography and parameters referring to online gaming experience in the samples of MUD players; 2) statistical analysis of the questionnaires' items (calculation of the means for each item); 3) explorative factor analysis, targeted at stemming all the parameters into factors; and 4) scale reliability analysis for each determined factor.

5 Findings

The total number of the self-selected respondents from the USA was 375; 88 of them provided incorrect data by selecting several reply variants; thus, the replies of 287 USA respondents were analyzed. The average MUD player respondent was male (78.75%), age 26, a college student (62.37%), with eight years of experience in playing MUDs, and playing about seven hours per week.

All the questionnaire items were analyzed referring to the parameters of flow at the second stage of the analysis. The calculated means are presented in Table 1. Based on these means, we are able to characterize briefly the sample of the USA respondents. The sample consists of players who are interested in MUDs, feel inspiration and enthusiasm while playing, investigate unknown areas of a game, are active and do not feel constant pressure. They are fond of interaction with other players and frequently establish close relations. They often lose sense of time, and find themselves engaged in gaming sessions longer than they planned. They prefer to achieve success while playing and most often believe that MUD is nothing more than a game, although some respondents report that they mix real-life and within-game situations. Their attention is focused on a game; they control messages coming from other players. They do their best to supervise the situations in which their characters are acting and often reflect on the play after it is finished.

Table 1. Survey question with means

#	Question	Mean
1	I often feel anxious while MUDding.	2.26
2	While MUDding I often feel (active/passive)	2,27
3	I frequently lose track of time while MUDding.	3.79
4	When interacting with other MUD players, I lose track of time.	3,74
5	I always control the situation while MUDding.	2.86
6	While MUDding I am always in high spirits.	2,97
7	I take MUD as a game, i.e., I stay in reality while playing	3.89
8	I am extremely interested in playing MUDs.	4,00
9	I sometimes spend more time in the MUD than planned.	4.10
10	The possibility of interacting with other players attracts me to MUDding	4,01
11	Nothing can distract me from MUDding.	1.82
12	I am interested in exploring new areas of the MUD, that I have not experienced before.	4,14
13	When in the MUD, my attention is focused on the game.	3.89
14	I feel constantly stressed while MUDding.	1,66
15	My aim is to be successful in MUDding.	3.33
16	I experience negative emotions connected with situations within a MUD.	2,70

Table 1. (*Continued*)

17	I am so involved in MUDding that I take it as reality.	1.55
18	My aim in MUDding is to develop the chosen character to its possible extreme.	3,54
19	I often replay the same episode of the MUD (with the same character) several times just for pleasure.	2.76
20	I often replay the same episode of the MUD (with the same character) several times for reaching the result.	2,97
21	When grouping with other players in MUD I often take a position of a leader.	3.40
22	While interacting in MUD I often make close friends.	3,74
23	I play MUDs because it's important for me to be in a group of people sharing the same interest.	3.01
24	While interacting with other players in MUD, I feel confident.	3,92
25	I pay particular attention to chatting and messages from other MUD players.	3.78
26	Talking to other players adds interest to MUDding.	4,36
27	After MUDding I often think over the game.	3.39
28	It's difficult for me to stay focused on the game while MUDding.	1,95
29	While playing MUD I prefer to use familiar behaviors.	3.59
30	I choose MUD games in which I know how to succeed.	2,98
31	I don't replay the same episode several times.	2.97

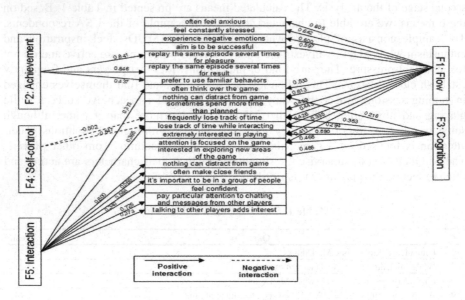

Fig. 1. Factor Analysis Schematic

On the third stage of the analysis while using explorative factor analysis (with the Direct Oblimin and the Cronbach's alpha), we developed a factor model for the USA sample presented, which shows the factor loadings for each question. (See Figure 1.) This figure also shows a five-factor model.

- Factor 1 (F1) can be called **Flow**. This factor includes the following parameters: spending more time in game than planned due to losing track of time while gaming and within-play interacting; feeling that nothing can distract from the game; taking MUD as reality; thinking over the game; feeling deep interest in the processes of playing; and focused attention. Also, quite often, this factor includes heavily loaded parameters referring to negative effects from MUDding, such as anxiety, constant stress, and an experience of negative emotions. These effects may be referred to as the high responsibility the respondents feel toward within-game situations: the greater the experience, the higher the responsibility. Indeed, the question sounds like that: "negative emotions connected with situations within a MUD." That means, negative feelings and anxiety are situational.

- F2 might be called **Achievement.** The parameters included in this factor are: the replay of the same episode for pleasure and for reaching the result by choosing familiar behaviors.
- F3 might be called **Cognition**; it includes parameters of being extremely interested in playing and interested while exploring new areas of the MUD, being focused on the game, losing track of time while exploring and while interacting with other players so that nothing can distract from the gaming behavior.
- F4 might be called **Self Control;** it includes parameters such as not losing track of time while playing and while interacting with other players in MUD.
- F5 might be called **Interaction** – it includes parameters of interest toward interaction with other players, frequent establishment of close connections and making friends, feeling confident, being in constant control over messages coming from fellow players, the desire to find oneself united in a group of people sharing the same interests, having lost the sense of time while communicating within MUDs and keeping interest while interacting and thinking over the game when the game session is over.

6 Discussion and Conclusion

As a type of an online game, it would be expected that text-only MUDs would eventually be replaced by much more technologically up-to-date MMORPGs, as mentioned above. This is because their worlds are enriched with three-dimensional graphics that provide a far more comprehensive cognitive stimulation. However, the current study shows this is not the case. During only a few days as many as 520 survey responses were received (although only 287 were analyzed in the paper); this indicates that MUDs have remained popular in the USA.

Moreover, our findings showed that the sample of respondents were non-traditional, i.e., the overwhelming majority reported playing MUDs five years or more (with a median of eight years), and for relatively short periods of time (with a median of one hour per day, with 70% playing less than two hours per day). Thus, we suggest that the respondents in this sample are experienced gamers who have continued to play MUDs for many years as a challenging form of sport or hobby. This, we hold, corresponds to the findings of McKenna and Lee [9], who found that experienced MUD players were not hard players, i.e., playing for long periods of time each day.

In summary, we found that factors F2 (Achievement), F3 (Cognition) and F5 (Interaction) were common for almost any reasonable sample of MUD players. For example, these factors also characterized Russian and French MUDders, as observed in earlier studies by the second author and his colleagues. However, it was not the same with the rest of the factors. The Self Control (F4) factor may be thought of as being peculiar to this unusual sample of high-level players who keep constant control of the time intervals allocated to MUDding. Flow as factor F1 was expected (based on the Russian sample of MUDders); however, F1 also included parameters that referred to both the (positive) flow experience and to negative emotions. The latter is, as we have already suggested, situational. Since flow is a major factor, the respondents are believed to go on MUDding for years in order to keep and to renew the feeling of their flow experience. We suggest that this feeling is habitual and desired. At the same time, it does not appear to save respondents from situational stress or negative emotions that might emerge while MUD playing. Perhaps, one could surmise that they feel guilty allocating time to a well-known game. Whatever the exact nature of the negative emotions, when combined with the parameters of flow, they represent a very special "dialect" of the flow experience. It is also possible that this "dialect' does not transpire that often and might be peculiar to this unusual sample of experienced players.

Finally, the instrument used in the study proved to be valid, and the chosen procedure has also proven capable of providing meaningful results. This study supports the assertion that flow experience, as well as achievements, cognition and interaction, are among the strongest reasons for the long-term playing of MUDs by thousands of players throughout the USA.

References

1. Bartle, R.: Hearts, clubs, diamonds, spades: Players who suit MUDs. Journal of MUD Research, 1(1) (1996) Retrieved from http://www.brandeis.edu/pubs/jove/HTML/v1/bartle.html
2. Chen, H., Wigand, R.T., Nilan, M.S.: Exploring web users' optimal flow experiences. Information Technology & People 13(4), 263–281 (2000)
3. Choi, D., Kim, J.: Why people continue to play online games: In search of critical design factors to increase customer loyalty to online contents. CyberPsychology & Behavior 7(1), 11–24 (2004)
4. Csikszentmihalyi, M.: Flow: The psychology of optimal experience. New York: Harper and Row (1990)
5. Csikszentmihalyi, M.: Beyond boredom and anxiety: Experiencing flow in work and play. Jossey-Bass, San-Francisco (Original work published 1975) (2000)
6. Curtis, P.: Excerpt from mudding: Social phenomena in text-based virtual realities. In: Stefik, M. (ed.) Internet Dreams: Archetypes, Myths and Metaphors, Cambridge, MA
7. Joinson, A.N.: Understanding the psychology of internet behaviour: Virtual worlds, real lives. Houndmills, Hampshire, UK and New York, NY: Palgrave Macmillan (2003)
8. Lee, K.M.: MUD and self efficacy. Education Media International 37(3), 177–183 (2000)
9. McKenna, K., Lee, S.: A love affair with MUDs: Flow and social interaction in multi-user dungeons (1995) Retrieved from
http://www.fragment.nl/mirror/various/McKenna_et_al.nd.A_love_affair_with_muds.html
10. Novak, T.P., Hoffman, D.L.P.: Measuring the flow experience among web users. Paper Presented at Interval Research Corporation (July 3, 1997) Retrieved from http://sloan.ucr.edu/blog/uploads/papers/Measuring%20the%20Flow%20Experience%20Among%20Web%20Users%20[Hoffman,%20Novak%20-%20July%201997].pdf

11. Reinberg, F., Engeser, S., Vollmeyer, R.: Measuring components of flow: The flow-shot-scale. Paper presented at the 1st International Positive Psychology Summit, Washington, DC (2002)
12. Salvay, Y.: Multi-User Domains: Sociodramatic Conflict Resolution (2002) Retrieved from http://www.geocities.com/ysalvay/sociodramaticmuds.html
13. Sempsey, J.J.: Psyber psychology: A literary review pertaining to the psycho/social aspects of multi-user dimensions in cyberspace. Journal of MUD Research, vol. 2(1) (1997) Retrieved from http://www.brandeis.edu/pubs/jove/HTML/v2/sempsey.html
14. Turkle, S.: Life on the screen: Identity in the age of the Internet. Touchstone Book, New York (1997)
15. Utz, S.: Social information processing in MUDs: The development of friendships in virtual worlds. Journal of Online Behavior, 1(1) (2000) Retrieved from http://www.behavior.net/JOB/v1n1/utz.html
16. Voiskounsky, A.E., Mitina, O.V., Avetisova, A.A.: Communicative patterns and flow experience of MUD players. International Journal of Advanced Media and Communication 1(1), 5–25 (2005)
17. Voiskounsky, A.E., Mitina, O.V., Avetisova, A.A.: Flow experience and interaction: Investigation of Francophone online gamers. In: Sudweeds, F., Hrachovec, H., Ess, C. (eds.) Proceedings of Cultural Attitudes Towards Communication and Technology 2006, pp. 385–398. Tartu, Estonia (2006)

Unveiling the Structure: Effects of Social Feedback on Communication Activity in Online Multiplayer Videogames

Luciano Gamberini, Francesco Martino, Fabiola Scarpetta, Andrea Spoto,
and Anna Spagnolli

Human Technology Lab
Department of General Psychology
University of Padova - Italy
{luciano.gamberini,andreaspoto,fabiola.scarpetta}@gmail.com
{francesco.martino,anna.spagnolli}@unipd.it

Abstract. Feedback intervention in computer-mediated situations can be interpreted as a way to augment communication. According to this idea, this study investigates the effect of providing a group with a Social Network Analysis-based feedback on communication in an on-line game where players talk to each other via textual chat. Three different situations across two different sessions were compared: an Informed Group with a correct feedback, a not-Informed Group with no feedback and a mis-Informed group with an incorrect feedback. Results show that giving correct information increases the related dimensions of communication, while the absence of feedback and the incorrect feedback were not accompanied by any significant modification.

Keywords: social network analysis, feedback, augmented communication, cooperative online game.

1 Introduction

Feedback is a well known resource for increasing people's motivation and performance, as highlighted by several models such as Cybernetic or Control Theory [1], Goal-Setting Theory [2] and Social Learning Theory [3]. When feedback is provided intentionally by an agent different from the one performing the activity, and consists of information that is not the spontaneous byproduct of the ongoing task, then we have a special kind of procedure called Feedback Intervention [4]. It is defined as a series of "actions, taken by (an) external agent(s) to provide information regarding some aspect(s) of one's task performance (p. 255)". By extending this definition to other processes than just 'performance' and including technology as one possible 'external agent' providing the feedback, feedback intervention emerges as a strategy of augmented interaction. Information on the quality or quantity of interaction is provided to the users by way of technical devices incorporated in the mediated environment where the activity takes place. In this case, technology is employed to enrich the communicative process with cues that would not be offered by the original

D. Schuler (Ed.): Online Communities and Social Comput., HCII 2007, LNCS 4564, pp. 334–341, 2007.

setting [as in 5, 6], instead of just trying to imitate the characteristic of face-to-face communication.

This study presented here is part of an EU-funded Integrated Project called 'PASION' (Psychologically Augmented Social Interaction Over Networks) [7], aiming at augmenting mediated interaction by making more evident the status of the larger social network to which the individuals contribute with their actions. This first experiment investigates the usage of feedback based on Social Network Analysis (SNA) [8] and its effects on the communicational structure of the users.

1.1 Feedback Effectiveness

Different studies have observed the way in which feedback on a certain dimension of group-mediated activity is able to affect users' behavior. Losada, Sanchez and Noble gave their participant a complex feedback about collaborative exchanges in two different tasks (a list ranking task and an in-basket simulation) with or without a computer-supported collaborative environment. They found that feedback was able to reverse the difference in the socio-emotional behavior produced in mediated and non-mediated environments: this behavior tended to decrease in mediated environments, except when a feedback was provided [9]. Di Micco, Pandolfo and Bender [10] used a display during an information-sharing task to illustrate the users' participation rates. They found that in some groups the participation rate changed in a direction connected with the evaluation implicit in the feedback. Zumbach, Schönemann and Reimann (2005) studied a problem-solving task executed by dyads through an HTML-based collaborative system. Each episode of collaborative behaviors was detected by a human observer, and immediately displayed on the participants' monitors, along with an appraisal. The task type (homogeneous versus distributed resources) and the provision of feedback (with/without) were manipulated. The highest amount of collaborative events was detected in the condition with distributed resources and with feedback [11].

These three studies converge on the result that feedback presentation is able to produce a change in those aspects of the performance that are covered by the feedback. However, they also suggest the need to pay attention to the nature of the feedback provided, for instance its accuracy [10] and complexity [9]. Classic psychological studies on feedback offer some specific recommendations in this respect. Ilgen, Fisher and Taylor in their review underline the role of credibility [12]. Kluger and DeNisi, on the basis of an extensive meta-analysis of 131 papers, suggested that feedback works by drawing user's attention to one of three levels: task-motivation, task-learning and meta-task (self). When both goal and feedback are clear, optimal usage of a feedback occurs when the processing remains on the task-motivation level, with the user trying to find a way to fill the standard-feedback gap. Finally, they suggested that feedback providing specific and detailed information on the way in which the task must be executed facilitates learning insofar as it is congruent with the task and helps reject erroneous hypotheses. In the case of a collaborative tasks, feedback at a group level may provide that kind of congruent information that increases the overall performance, since the individual contributions would become more precise, and appropriate to the actual status of the activity. To this respect, there is some empirical evidence that the best feedback is able to link the individual actions to the group status without separating the two kinds of information. Zander and Wolfe [13] found that individual and group feedback together were more effective than either feedback alone. DeShon, Kozlowsi, Shmidt, Milner and Wiechman [14] were interested in tasks requiring both individual and team effort allocation ('discretionary tasks'), in the assumption that they represent the most recurrent form of tasks in real-life groups. They found that the highest level of individual and team-oriented performance occurred when team members received a single, focused source of feedback, but stressed that the feedback they provided did not allow to relate the individual performance to the team one, and this prevented participants from knowing how to use the two kinds of information.

In the present study, we resorted to an SNA-based feedback, which is able to position the individual user within the group structure and dynamics. SNA is a formal theory based on networks of relations among social actors [8]: social actors are treated as nodes in the network, and relations among them are represented as ties or links. SNA can provide valuable tools to describe, evaluate, and visualize the quantity and quality of social relations, and for this reason it has been applied to the analysis of work organizations [15], and, recently, to on-line communication [16,17,18,19]. Some research in particular focuses on the use of SNA feedback in mediated environments. Isbell, Kearns, Singh, Shelton & Stone (2006) showed that a 'bot' with the ability to give social dyadic relation statistics (e.g. "who loves me", and so on) and provide social ranking increased social participation in the LambdaMoo in which it was introduced [20]. Morris [21] found a way to increase elderly people's self-awareness and confidence in the possibility of improving their social life by way of a social-network display to control their own social activity. Authors found that participants were able to draw attention to the part of the network with fewer contacts, that they were able to cope with this problem and that they were more socially active.

Our goal with the study presented here is to devise an experiment in order to test specifically whether providing SNA indexes to people involved in a group task is able to change their behavior and to do it in a way related to the content of the feedback.

2 Method

To investigate a common form of a mediated collaborative task, we used an on-line treasure-hunt game, built with the open-source cooperative multiplayer graphical game called 'Crossfire' [22]. Eight participants were assigned a PC station and an avatar each, with which they could operate in the same digital environment. They could talk to each other exclusively via Skype® textual chat (figure 1). The aim of the game was for the group to find and pick up seven special objects hidden in the environment during a forty-minute game session. In addition to the hunt, participants had to keep their avatars alive by picking up some food placed in the game environment.

Simple commands were implemented: the four directional arrows moved the avatars, the "a" keystroke picked up objects or allowed one to enter/exit buildings, the left button of the mouse highlighted the name of other avatars actually present in the screen, and the right button of the mouse picked up the special objects. Players were

Fig. 1. A screenshot from the game interface (left) and a picture of the game session (right)

instructed to make use of the cues spread across the environment containing some directions to the 'treasures', and to communicate; they were made aware of the large extension of the environment (too large to be explored alone in 40 minutes) and that the score was calculated on the group as a whole.

2.1 Participants

Participants were twenty-four Psychology students at the University of Padova aged 24, 88 on average (standard deviation 2.96). The proportion of males and females in all groups was the same (one male every three females). All participants were accustomed to using computers and instant messaging software but none of them was an expert videogame user.

2.2 Procedure

Participants played during two game sessions a week apart. The first session was preceded by a five minutes practice to get familiar with the commands, the game rules and the digital environment. In the two sessions, the game scenarios were different, but had the same extension. Also, the special objects were distributed in different places, but with the same ratio. In order to avoid biases due to participants' previous relationships, each participant was assigned a nick name by the experimenters. Players were requested not to reveal their avatars' identity until the end of the whole study. A member of the research team supervised each session to warrant its regularity.

2.3 Experimental Design

To test the effect of SNA feedback on participants' activity, a two-factor experimental design was applied, with a two-level between-subjects factor called "feedback" ('Informed' versus 'not-Informed' groups) and a two-level within-subjects factor called "session". The feedback consisted of histograms representing the results of the SNA conducted on the first session data, and was provided to participants in the 'with feedback' conditions a few minutes before the beginning of the second session.

In addition, to make sure that it was not just the provision of a feedback to cause an effect regardless of the feedback content, we introduced a third condition in which participants were provided with a false feedback ('Misinformed' group). The data of this group were analyzed separately because of its late introduction in the design.

2.4 Data Collection and Feedback Construction

The data collected were the log files of each dyadic conversation occurring within the game session in the instant messaging software. From the chat logs we identified two different kinds of information used to calculate SNA indexes. The first data were the thread-starting requests, namely messages starting a thread of subsequent messages on the same topic. This measure is boolean, from A to B (ArB=1, else ArB = 0), or from B to A (BrA=1, else BrA = 0). The second data from the chat logs were the number of messages sent and received by each participant.

On the basis of these data we built two different types of matrices in order to perform a SNA. With the "thread starting requests" we filled in a Boolean matrix for each session, composed of eight rows and eight columns; the number of messages was inserted in valued matrices with 8 rows and 8 columns for each session. On these two types of matrices, Ucinet software [23] calculated two kinds of indexes, 'dyad-based reciprocity' and 'degree-centrality' respectively. The former represents the mutuality of choices in a network, and ranges from 0 to 1, the latter represents the amount of communication received by a single person in the network.

Centrality and reciprocity of each player were the kind of feedback returned to the Informed and Mis-Informed group. No feedback on performance was given.

3 Data Analysis and Results

3.1 Results

In order to test the effect of the feedback on the communicational behavior we performed an ANOVA for mixed models to verify the difference between and within the Informed and the Not-informed group in the number of messages received by each participant. The ANOVA performed on the valued matrices shows that there is a significant increase of messages received by participants in the Informed Group between the first and the second session ($F_{2,14} = 8.5$; $p<.05$). In figure 2, the trends of the in-degree values in the two sessions for the informed versus not informed group are shown.

Two t-tests for paired samples have been performed on the data from the Boolean matrix in order to test the difference in reciprocity between the two sessions. We found that there is a significant difference between the two sessions in the Informed group ($t_7 = 2.85$; $p<.05$) while there is no significant difference in the Not-Informed group. Figure 3 shows the trends of reciprocity in the two groups under analysis.

A particular non-parametric t-test [24] has been performed to test the significance of the difference between first and second sessions in the three groups (Informed, Not-Informed and Mis-Informed). The technique used to carry out this kind of analysis is the 'bootstrap', a very powerful kind of analysis that mixes together the SNA indexes and the more traditional statistical inferential methods. The test was

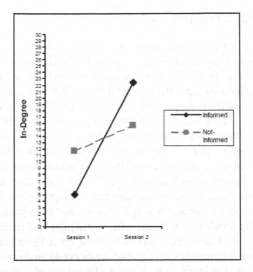

Fig. 2. Trends in in-degree centrality in the Informed and Not-Informed groups in the first and the second session

performed on density values and indicates that there was a significant difference between density of the two sessions for the Informed group ($t_{14} = 3.46$; $p < .01$) while there is no difference for the Not-Informed and the Misinformed group.

As to performance, the Informed group showed a 150% increase in the number of goblets found; the Not-Informed group showed a 20% increase; the Misinformed group presents a 20% decrease. This data suggests that providing correct feedback on the communication flow could have improved performance. However, further research is needed to confirm this interpretation.

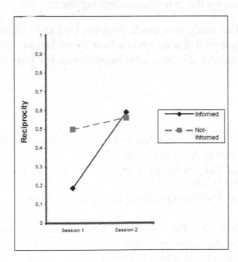

Fig. 3. Trends in dyad-based reciprocity among the Informed and Not-Informed groups in the first and the second session

4 Discussion and Conclusions

The analysis showed that the social feedback on density and reciprocity provided to a network of people is accompanied by an increase in the flow of communication in the network. Not only did feedback have a decisive influence on the quantity of communication acts (density and degree-centrality), but also on the organization of the communication, with an improved symmetry in the so-called 'thread-starting requests' (reciprocity). This means that the increase was not due to practice alone since all groups underwent two game sessions, but only the Informed one showed an increased communication flow in the second one. If all members of the informed group in our study increased and improved their communication, then this may imply that the reported dimension was perceived as relevant to the task, and the presentation of the scores was perceived as an encouragement to improve on that dimensions. On the contrary, the incorrect feedback was not able to change communication activity in a significant way; this result is consistent with some previous research [10] where the feedback perceived as inaccurate was not able to trigger any change in the participants' behavior. This means that participants could make a distinction between accurate and inaccurate feedback, which has to be taken into account when planning to implement a system to augment communication.

Another interesting result was the variation of performance. The intensification of the communication flow in the Informed Group did not interfere with its performance, since the number of goblets found had a dramatic increase absent in the other conditions. The reason for this improvement, however, is not clear. It may be an effect of the strict connection between communication and performance in this specific kind of task, or a consequence of a halo effect of the feedback, which may have affected several behaviors relevant to the task.

We can conclude by saying that showing SNA indexes of communication can provide a means for community building, in the sense that increasing the awareness of the individual's impact on the group dynamics may be a tacit yet effective encouragement to intensify the connections among them.

Acknowledgments. The study was made possible by the EU funding of the PASION (Psychologically Augmented Social Interaction Over Networks) Project, FP6 - IST program - reference number 27654 - scheduled to run for four years (January 2006 - December 2009).

References

1. Carver, C.S., Scheier, M.F.: Attention and self regulation: A control theory to human behavior. Springer-Verlag, New York (1981)
2. Locke, E.A., Latham, G.P.: A theory of goal setting and task performance. Prentice Hall, Englewood Cliffs, NJ (1990)
3. Bandura, A.: Social learning theory of aggression. Journal of Communication, 28(3) (1978)
4. Kluger, A.N., DeNisi, A.: The effects of feedback interventions on performance: A historical review, a meta-analysis, and a preliminary feedback intervention theory. Psychological Bulletin 119(2), 254–284 (1996)

5. Lee, J., Jun, S., Forlizzi, J., Hudson, S.E.: New forms of interaction: Using kinetic typography to convey emotion in text-based interpersonal communication. In: Proceedings of 6th ACM conference on Designing Interactive systems (2006)
6. Danninger, M., Vertegaal, R., Siewiorek, D.P., Mamuji, A.: Using social geometry to manage interruptions and co-worker attention in office environments. In: Proceedings of, Conference on Graphics Interface, ACM International Conference Proceeding Series, vol. 112, pp. 211–218 (2005)
7. Brugnoli, M.C., Morabito, F., Walker, R., Davide, F.: The PASION Project: Psychologically Augmented Social Interaction Over Networks. PsychNology Journal 4(1), 103–116 (2006)
8. Wasserman, S., Faust, K.: Social Network Analysis. Methods and Applications. Cambridge University Press, Cambridge, MA (1994)
9. Losada, M., Sanchez, P., Noble, E.E.: Collaborative technology and group process feedback: Their impact on interactive sequences in meetings. In: Proceedings of the, ACM Conference on Computer-Supported Cooperative Work, pp. 53–64 (1990)
10. DiMicco, J.M., Pandolfo, A., Bender, W.: Influencing group participation with a shared display. In: Proceedings of the, ACM Conference on Computer Supported Cooperative Work, pp. 614–623 (2004)
11. Zumbach, J., Schonemann, J., Reimann, P.: Analyzing and supporting collaboration in cooperative computer-mediated communication. In: Proceedings of the 2005 Conference on Computer Support for Collaborative Learning. International Society of the Learning Science (2005)
12. Ilgen, D.R., Fisher, C., Taylor, M.S.: Consequences of individual feedback on behavior in organizations. Journal of Applied Psychology 64(4), 349–371 (1979)
13. Zander, A., Wolfe, D.: Administrative rewards and coordination among committee members. Administrative Science Quarterly 9, 50–69 (1964)
14. DeShon, R.P., Kozlowski, S.W.J., Schmidt, A.M., Milner, K.R., Wiechmann, D.: A multiple-goal, multilevel model of feedback effects on the regulation of individual and team performance. Journal of Applied Psychology 89(6), 1035–1056 (2004)
15. Cross, R., Borgatti, S.P., Parker, A.: Making invisible work visible: Using social network analysis to support strategic collaboration. California Management Review 44(2), 25–46 (2002)
16. Wellman, B.: For a social network analysis of computer networks: A sociological perspective on collaborative work and virtual community. In: Proceedings of the, ACM SIGCPR/SIGMIS Conference on Computer Personnel Research, pp. 1–11 (1996)
17. Park, H.W.: Hyperlink Network Analysis: A new method for the study of social structure on the Web. Connections 25(1), 49–61 (2003)
18. Donath, J., Boyd, D.: Public displays of connection. BT Technology Journal 22(4), 71–82 (2004)
19. Martino, F., Spoto, A.: Social Network Analysis: a brief theoretical review and further perspectives in the study of information technology. PsychNology 4(1), 53–86 (2006)
20. Isbell, C.L.I., Kearns, M., Kormannn, D., Singh, S., Stone, P.: Cobot in LamdaMOO: An adaptive social statistics agent. Autonomous Agents and Multi-Agent Systems 13(3), 327–354 (2000)
21. Morris, M.E.: Social networks as health feedback displays. IEEE Internet Computing 9(5), 29–37 (2005)
22. http://crossfire.real-time.com/
23. Borgatti, S.P., Everett, M.G., Freeman, L.C.: Ucinet for Windows: Software for Social Network Analysis. Analytic Technologies, Harvard, MA (2002)
24. Snijders, T.A.B., Borgatti, S.P.: Non-parametric standard errors and test for network statistics. Connections 22(2), 61–70 (1999)

Habitat Computing: Towards the Creation of Tech-Enabled Mexican Neighborhoods

Victor M. Gonzalez[1], Luis A. Castro[1], and Kenneth L. Kraemer[2]

[1] Manchester Business School, University of Manchester, United Kingdom
[2] Paul Merage School of Business, University of California, Irvine, USA
{vmgonz,luis.castro-quiroa}@manchester.ac.uk,
kkraemer@uci.edu

Abstract. The use of personal computers and Internet at home is becoming more and more common in some developing countries such as Mexico, where affordable prices and credit plans have contributed to this trend. Undoubtedly, the presence of information technology in the households has effects in the life of families and their communities; however how beneficial these effects are depends on the way technology is contextualized to support domestic and community practices. Achieving a proper contextualization is the goal of what we call *habitat computing*. This paper presents the case of Real del Sol, a housing community in Mexico where an implementation of habitat computing is being developed. Houses are built with Internet access and personal computers as part of their basic infrastructure. We analyze here the role, usage and development of the Real del Sol community intranet, which is a key element on supporting the vision of the project.

Keywords: Community Intranets, Security cameras, Online Shopping.

1 Introduction

The use of personal computers and Internet at home is becoming more and more common in some developing countries such as Mexico, where affordable prices and credit plans have contributed to this trend. A study conducted by the Mexican Association of Internet , in 2005, revealed that about 20 million Mexicans had some form of internet access, from which 43% reported to have it at home [1]. According to Mexican Institute of Statistics, the growth of Internet access at home increased 20% in 2005 with respect to the previous year [2]. These figures reflect a scenario where, without reaching the rates of penetration experienced in the developed world, the uptake of computer technology and internet access in Mexico is real and palpable. In parallel, in the last few years, Mexico has experienced a sustained investment to build housing complexes that are affordable, especially for low and middle-level income people. Through credit plans and mortgages, more people have been able to afford their own house. These two aspects do not reveal an idealistic scenario where both digital and housing divides have been eliminated; Mexico is far from that. Instead, we believe that they reveal a set of conditions where technologies are likely to impact the very conceptual bases of what we understand for homes and more generally neighborhoods; a vision that we refer here as *habitat computing*.

D. Schuler (Ed.): Online Communities and Social Comput., HCII 2007, LNCS 4564, pp. 342–351, 2007.
© Springer-Verlag Berlin Heidelberg 2007

This paper presents results of a study conducted to understand the practicalities of implementing a vision of habitat computing in a Mexican neighborhood. In the city of Tecamac, in Mexico, Real Paraiso Residencial, a housing company, in partnership with Conectha, an Internet Service Provider, built a residential complex (Real del Sol) consisting of about 2000 houses equipped with a personal computer and broadband internet access. The analysis presented here focuses on the characteristics of the community intranet technology and the usage of the computer and online services during the first year of use. Although we did find that the adoption and domestication of information technologies achieved in Tecamac is still minimum it was possible to identify the reasons for this, as well as many areas where further development is likely to produce a greater impact.

The rest of the paper is organized in the following way: Section 2 presents a definition of habitat computing and refers to previous studies to set the background and motivation for this study. Section 3 provides details about the case study and the research methodology. Section 4 presents the characteristics and services supported by the community intranet used in Real de Sol. Section 5 discusses the current state of technology usage at Real del Sol as well as our findings with regards to the main factors facilitating or preventing the uptake of the community intranet. Finally, section 6 closes the paper with some conclusions and discussion of results.

2 Defining Habitat Computing and Related Studies

Undoubtedly, the presence of information technology in the households has effects in the life of families and their neighborhoods; however how beneficial these effects are depends on the way technology is contextualized to support domestic and community practices. To contextualize, or domesticate, information technology means to integrate it to the household practices in a natural way [3]. This level and type of natural integration constitutes what we call *habitat computing*. Many communication technologies such as the telephone, television, or postal mail have achieved that level of integration, becoming constitutive elements defining what most of us consider being a home. Their constitutive nature can be seen on the way in which many domestic routines (e.g. season greetings cards preparation) and the very architecture of the household (e.g. TV rooms) have been shaped by their characteristics. Similarly, we believe that by adapting information technologies to support the practical and everyday needs of families and their housing communities we can materialize successful scenarios of habitat computing. Obviously, the challenge becomes to identify those needs, but more important to create solutions that respond to them in an unobtrusive, natural and simple way. Furthermore, we argue that fundamental and practical changes in household practices can be realized if instead of following paths leading to automation, assisted living and smart homes, designers take an approach that aims at supporting more 'down to earth' needs and, at the same time, assume that it will be for its sustained usage that information technology will find its way to become domesticated.

Many previous studies have been conducted within the context of information and communication technology usage at home and neighborhoods. Among them, the experiences of Blacksburg, Virginia in the US, gave clear indications that the adaptation of information technologies can give people at local neighborhoods new opportunities for social interaction, trade, information exchange, identity development and social cohesion [4]. Similarly, other studies have explored the uptake of computer and Internet at home and have identified benefits derived from their usage such as support on children education, cost savings in communication, increased opportunities for merchant comparison and shopping, as well as the new channels for entertainment and amusement [5]. Clearly, the uptake of computer technology at home is not exempt of challenges. A number of studies have reported that lacking critical mass, good quality content, and open participation, can prevent successful implementation of technologies supporting community neighborhoods [6-7]. Within the context of home, Venkatesh et al [5] reported that current computer technologies, being designed for individuals rather than families, cause problems and challenges in domestic settings, and that future designs should pay attention to the requirements for everyday living.

Following the line of studies on community networks [5-9] and home telematics [10], we believe that more investigation has to be conducted to expand our understanding of scenarios where information technology integration is the result of an orchestrated strategy to create habitat computing. This scenario is different to other where technology integration is a result of academic initiative or just a result of accidental circumstances. In scenarios that aim at promoting and implementing habitat computing, computers and Internet access are seen as part of the constitutive elements of the home and neighborhoods and therefore consider ubiquitous utilities like gas, water or electricity. We were motivated to understand such scenario as it was experienced in a housing complex in Mexico were designers took the perspective outlined above.

3   Characteristics of the Study and Methodology

At the end of February 2006, with the support of Real Paraiso Residencial and Conectha we conducted a set of ethnographic interviews with families living in or about to move to Real del Sol. A number of people were identified as likely to accept taking part in the study and then were contacted. Those voluntarily accepting where then scheduled for an interview.

A total of 34 individuals were interviewed covering 27 households averaging 3 members per family (87 individuals in total). Interviewees have a variety of occupations, from journalists to primary school teacher and from house keepers to tourist agents. The interviews were semi-structured and covered a set of topics including the factors motivating the purchase of the houses, the experience of moving in, the relationships with the neighbors and the rest of the community, their use of the technology to support domestic practices as well as perspectives on how to make the technology more useful. Each interview lasted an average of 45 minutes and was conducted in their houses. Just in two cases interviews were conducted at Conectha's offices, as the informants had not yet moved to their properties by the time of the interviews. The interviews were complemented with a number of observations of the community and informal interviews with staff from both Conectha and Real Paraiso Residencial, as well as with people from the Ojo de Agua community (not living at Real del Sol), including taxi drivers, shop owners and security staff. The data collected were then analyzed using a comparative approach aiming at identifying patterns among the responses and producing an integrated set of findings.

4 Habitat Computing: The Case of Real del Sol

At the beginning of 2005, Real Paraiso Residencial and Conectha started the construction of their first housing complex guided by a concept called "Habitat of Seventh Generation" o G7 Habitat. They defined G7 Habitat as a household concept that emerges from sixth previous generations experienced by the domestic household. Under this design concept, Information and Communications Technologies (ICTs) play not just a strategic role, but one where they are intrinsically linked and embedded to the basic idea of a household. Upfront, they envisioned houses where Internet access was one more of the core utilities, as opposed to an optional service. They aimed at having all houses with at least one personal computer connected to the Internet and with access to a set of local services around the G7 Habitat concept. To achieve this, Conectha designed and built a community intranet portal. This section describes the characteristics of that intranet.

4.1 The Houses and the Community

Real del Sol housing development is located in the city of Tecámac, in the State of Mexico. Although Tecámac is not part of the metropolitan area of Mexico City, it is close enough as to allow a reasonable commute to the city (approximately an hour trip, with good traffic conditions). The majority of residents work in Mexico City.

Fig. 1. A typical house in Real del Sol (Privada Ananke); view of common areas

The design of the houses followed a Californian style that aims at distinguishing each property: No two adjacent houses have the same designs emphasizing individuality and diversity. Compared with similar complexes within the same range of prices, the housing development at Real de Sol, is more aesthetic and well integrated. The development counts with two small parks, basketball courts, a primary school, a kindergarten, and other communal areas. To facilitate organization, the development is organized in *privadas*, groups of ten or twenty houses that are separated of the rest with gates. People in the *privadas* share some green areas and services (trash bins sections). Figure 1 shows a picture of a house in Real del Sol and a partial view of one of the communal gardens. Each house counts with all standard services (water, electricity, gas), including Internet access thorough a wireless network that allows speeds up to 384 Kbps. Some of the houses also include a personal computer for free or it is offered by Conectha at preferential prices. The houses are about 30 square meters or more, with 2-4 bedrooms and a range of prices starting at $25,000. Most owners purchased the properties through credit plans and mortgages offered by private and government agencies.

Fig. 2. Community Intranet in Real del Sol

4.2 Real del Sol Intranet and E-Mail

Through their home computers, neighbors of Real del Sol have access to a set of services in the community intranet designed by Conectha. The intranet is operated and maintained by Conectha's staff, and there is not direct way for neighbors to modify their contents. In spite of that, neighbors are encouraged to provide content of common interest that then is published by the webmaster. Figure 2 shows a screenshot of the Intranet.

Each resident is given an e-mail account that he or she can access through the community intranet. Conectha aimed e-mail as one of the forms of contact between Real del Sol and the residents, and among the residents. No additional accounts are provided to other residents in the same household.

Real del Sol's intranet services are only accessible to residents of the development through a personal account and password. Through a simplified menu, users can select different services including access to security cameras, community information, contract information, educational content, on-line ordering of grocery and other products. Beyond these local services, the intranet provides links to external sources such as job banks, adult education, and entertainment.

4.3 Security Cameras System

With a rampant increment in the number of kidnappings, burglaries and other forms of crime in the urban Mexican neighborhoods, having safe and secure housing environments is a priority for most people. Attending that need, the developers installed a set of video cameras all over the complex. Through the cameras, residents are able to monitor the activity outside their properties as well as four communal areas.

Fig. 3. Images from cameras in Real del Sol community intranet

Each *privada* has one camera placed at the rear of the parking lot to maximize the visual field captured. Through the community intranet, a resident can have access to the cameras which captures color images in real time. The frame rate is not fast enough to perceive sudden movements of people, but it is still useful to monitor activity. Cameras operate 24/7 and are not monitored by professional security staff. Because its web-interface, cameras can be monitored by people from anywhere, including their workplaces.

4.4 Shopping Portal and Discount Traders

The community intranet provides two main commercial services: online shopping and discount traders. A number of small local companies in the communities of Tecamac and Ojo de Agua, including a pharmacy, butchery, and a convenience store established a contract with Conectha to provide the services to the residents of Real del Sol through the intranet. Each business was given a computer and wireless connection to Conectha network that they use to update their product stock, receive and process orders. Figure 4 shows the interface of the shopping portal used by residents to order products from the convenience store. As opposed to other scenarios where transactions are done with credit or debit cards, the transactions in Real de Sol are in cash. People order their products online and then the shop delivers the goods by bike or motorbike and charges the costumer in cash at their door.

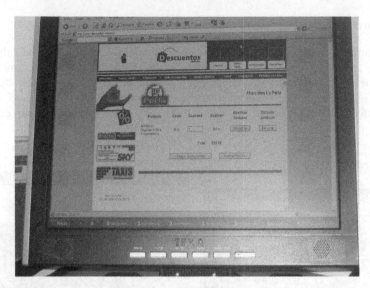

Fig. 4. The shopping portal and discount service

Many other local businesses participate in the commercial section of the intranet by providing discounts coupons to local residents. A matrix of add contains discounts from shops selling a variety of products including furniture, clothing, phone, electronics, food, baby, kitchen, and garden items. Companies advertising their coupons on the intranet, also receive advice from Conectha personnel with regards to marketing and promoting their products.

5   Results and Findings

Based on the analysis of our interviews and field observations, we were able to identify some aspects that are facilitating or preventing the uptake of the community intranet provide by Conectha. This section discusses the findings.

5.1   Current Uptake of Community Intranet

Before coming to Real del Sol, most of the interviewees had used a computer and surfed on the Web via dial-up Internet access. Consequently, for them the difference was on having internet access 24/7. With this type of access people were able to keep their computer on and do things such as having open Instant Messenger chat sessions all day, or having access to Stream Radio or similar services. Most of the informants reported using the Internet to stay in touch with family and friends, but many others also indicated they use it for work-related communications. Some self-employed informants reported that the all-day Internet service helps them to stay connected with clients or providers whenever it was necessary.

In contrast with internet usage in general, the actual reported usage of the community intranet was minimum. People did not check the content regularly, and even were unaware of some of the services provided. We found that most of them knew that an intranet was operating and its content was interesting and valuable, but at the same time, they did not have a motivation to regularly consult it.

In general, we can argue that people do make use of the services provided although not often with the aim they were conceived. Instead, people have tailored the services to their own needs of communication and organization. The actual usage is discussed in the following lines.

5.2 Factors Facilitating or Preventing the Uptake of Community Intranet

Electronic communication was a service that most informants identified as a benefit of having Internet at home, but not necessarily associated as one of the services that make use through the community intranet. Given the limitation of space in the e-mail account provided by Conectha, and the availability of free services such as Yahoo or MSN, people were eventually abandoning the usage of Conectha e-mail account. Furthermore, the e-mail account was often left aside to post messages to the community as users perceived their neighbors as not regular users of the service. Interestingly, when informants were requested their contact information they provided e-mail addresses different to the ones provided by Conectha. These findings indicate that despite that e-mail might be a commodity that could be included as part of the Intranet services, the current pervasiveness of e-mail usage makes very unlikely that people will switch to use it as there are plenty of strong alternatives to compete with.

We also found that security cameras experienced a reduced usage, and when used they were not used as originally envisioned by designers. Residents were able to watch their properties while away and mainly before moving in. Because many of the future residents were provided with access to surveillance video cameras before moving in they were enabled to follow up the erection of the house as the construction moved on. Some of them, after moving in, were using the cameras not only to 'keep an eye' on their home but also for showing their homes off to their relatives and friends. The lack of usage as security tools could be mainly due because of the limited functionality of the cameras and they did not record any activity. Furthermore, people realized that no professional security staff was monitoring the cameras and even if they decided to monitor them by themselves, the level of detail and quality of the image was not optimal. Because no video-recording was done, the possibility of analysis in case of robberies was eliminated.

In contrast, the local shopping service as simple as it might seem was very adequate to the needs of people. Through the commercial link informants reported to have brought products form a local pharmacy, and a small convenience store. This service was particularly relevant and useful during the initial stage when families were settling in because they did not know what other alternatives were around and did not have time to look for them. However, once they became familiar with the area, the usage of online shopping and some discount coupons declined.

5.3 Expected Evolution of Domestication of Community Intranet

The domestication of the community intranet by February 2006 was clearly scarce among neighbors. However, it does not mean that the service is not working. It is working, but in a different way that expected by designers. Based on our interviews we can anticipate some changes will occur with the community intranet that can produce a higher level of domestication. Our study revealed that some distinction has to be made between those services that can be beneficial during the process of moving in and those that people will use once they settle in. Consequently, we expect more of the latter services being created and adopted. People mentioned some services that could be valuable at the latter stage, among them medical services, stationery stores and an eBay-like web site to enable neighbors to sale used items among them. Some neighbors expressed plans to start the latter service, and personnel from Conectha mentioned similar idea.

Given the concerns with regards security it is likely that this need will be attended either through cooperation among neighbors or as a service from Conectha. Some neighbors expressed that they will contract more and better security cameras from Conectha. Some other are planning to install alarms and other security devices in their *privada*. The relevance of this aspect is likely to place a major role on communication and organization among neighbors.

We found that the needs of communication among neighbors could be fulfilled in a better way. Given the scarce use of Conectha e-mail account, the lack of awareness regarding the e-mail addresses of their neighbors, and the fact that not everybody even owns a computer, residents have fulfilled their communication needs with pieces of paper posted on the houses' front doors and public places such as the school. Some reported that they were planning to collect e-mail addresses and eventually, once enough critical mass is reached, we can expect that e-mail will be more relevant for communication among residents. Conectha, has also discussed ideas with regards encouraging the use of the Web site as an electronic posting service together with a public display such as the ones used in most banks (i.e. led-based displays).

Overall, we believe that lacking full participation in the content creation of the community intranet is preventing its adoption by residents. This situation is likely to change as Conectha is planning modification to the intranet that would make possible that scenario.

6 Conclusions

We present results from a study of an implementation of habitat computing in Mexico and focus on the analysis of the community intranet uptake. A main conclusion of our study is that further attention has to be placed on the changing nature of the needs regarding community intranet usage. We showed how some needs are more relevant at certain times, which demands from designers to provide adaptive applications. The findings indicate that the adoption of the community intranet is still minimal among residents, however we believe that based on the plans of Conectha and those of the residents, the domestication of the intranet will more palpable in the near future.

Acknowledgments. We wish to express our gratitude to all families in Real del Sol participating in our study as well as to the people of Real Paraiso Residencial and Conectha for their support. This study was made possible by a grant from The University of California Institute for Mexico and the United States (UC MEXUS).

References

1. AMIPCI (2005) Hábitos de los Usuarios de Internet en México 2005 (October 2005)
2. INEGI (2005) Encuesta Nacional sobre Disponibilidad y Uso de Tecnologías de la Información en los Hogares (November 2005)
3. Kraut, R.E., Brynin, M., Kiesler, S.: Computers, Phones, and the Internet: Domesticating Information Technology. Oxford University Press, NY (2006)
4. Carroll, J., Rosson, M.: Developing the Blacksburg Electronic Village. Communications of the ACM 39(12), 69–74 (1996)
5. Venkatesh, A., Stolzoff, N., Shih, E., Mazumdar, S.: The Home of the Future: An Ethnographic Study of New Information Technologies in the Home. Advances in Consumer Research XXVIII, Valdosta, Georgia: Association for Consumer Research, 2001, pp. 88–96 (2001)
6. Foth, M., Brereton, M.: Enabling local interaction and personalized networking in residential communities through action research and participatory design. In: Hyland, P., Vrazilic, L. (eds.) Proceeding of OZCHI 2004: NSW: University of Wollongong (2004)
7. Pinkett, R.: Community Technology and Community Building: Early Results form the Creating Community Connections Project. The. Information Society 19(5), 365–379 (2003)
8. Foth, M.: Analyzing the factors influencing the successful design and uptake of interactive systems to support social networks in urban neighborhoods. International Journal of Technology and Human Interaction, 2(2) (2006)
9. Gurstein, M.: Community informatics, community networks and strategies for flexible networking. In: Keeble, L., Loader, B.D. (eds.) Community informatics: Shaping Computer-Mediated Social Relations, pp. 263–283. Routledge, New York (2001)
10. Venkatesh, A., Chen, S., Gonzalez, V.: A Study of a Southern California Wired Community: Where Technology Meets Social Utopianism. In: Proceedings of Human-Computer Interaction 10th International Conference, June 22-27, 2003 Crete, Greece (2003)

Fostering Knowledge Mode Conversion in New Product Development Environment

Eduardo González[1], David Guerra-Zubiaga[1], and Manuel Contero[2]

[1] Institute of Technology and Higher Studies of Monterrey, Center of Innovation in Design and Technology, Ave. Garza Sada 2501, 64849 Monterrey, Mexico
{egm,david.guerra}@itesm.mx
[2] Polytechnic University of Valencia, School of Industrial Engineering, Camino de Vera s/n, 46022 Valencia, Spain
mcontero@degi.upv.es

Abstract. The creation of new knowledge that comes from Knowledge Mode Conversion (KMC) activities improves New Product Development (NPD) activities. However, there is still limited understanding of "how" a Knowledge Mode Conversion activity varies using collaborative and conversational technologies to improve product development performance. The main contribution of this research is to establish a set of indicators that can be used as guides to help identify effective Knowledge Mode Conversion activities that can be useful for organizations whose performance rely upon effective new product development activities. These indicators are obtained evaluating and comparing documents stored in a Product Data Management System (PDM) for differing levels of semantic significance, applying Latent Semantic Analysis (LSA). This provides a linkage between New Knowledge creation and the development of Capabilities for KMC, and a better understanding of "how" design teams improve their performance.

Keywords: Knowledge Mode Conversion, Latent Semantic Analysis, Collaborative Engineering, Knowledge sharing, Product Design.

1 Introduction

Knowledge creation at New Product Development (NPD) process is a key strategy that helps enterprises to survive in a global and highly competitive market. As manufacturers realize that they must compete globally, they recognize that developing and launching better new products is a critical issue. While Product Lifecycle Management (PLM) applications are core to this initiative, success will be determined by how well manufacturers assess the most critical underlying processes and resources. According to a report [14] from "AMR Research" a consulting firm focused on supply chain and enterprise-wide manufacturing applications:

- 95% of new consumer products ('96-'01) lost money or broke even.
- Median new vehicle development costs are $500 million higher than best in class.
- Poor NPD costs apparel makers 30% of annual revenue in markdowns.
- Food retailers spend $957K per store on new products that fail.

D. Schuler (Ed.): Online Communities and Social Comput., HCII 2007, LNCS 4564, pp. 352–361, 2007.

In dealing with the necessity to generate an effective method for the creation of new knowledge within NPD, it is needed to support the knowledge transfer capability[16].

This capability has been viewed as critical for competitive advantage [1]. It has been referred to as "integrative capability" [2] and a "core competence" [3] business.

This growth in importance of the NPD process points us towards the need to consider a way of monitoring this process, taking the Knowledge Creation derived from KMC activities as the main variable to track during the NPD stages.

This paper reports a research over several years conducted at ITESM University by undergraduate design teams. The paper provides indicators showing proper Virtual Collaborative monitoring and Conversational technologies supporting knowledge transfer and combined capabilities that result in an effective method for KMC.

The design process is considered a socio-technical activity, and the design team acts as the mechanism for knowledge mobilization. This research establish a way for measuring the ability of individuals involved in design project teams, to come together to create, share, maintain and combine their individual knowledge, and transform that knowledge into new knowledge [4,12,17].

2 Background

A key issue in conceptualizing a KMC for the NPD would be the definition of what Nonaka described as "tacit" knowledge and the description of the process that transform "tacit" into the "explicit" or possibly organized knowledge [5]. According to Nonaka, knowledge is created through a continuous dialog between tacit and explicit knowledge, this concept implies that the flow of information between tacit and explicit knowledge foster the Knowledge Mode Conversion.

Explicit knowledge is defined as knowledge that can be transmitted in formal, systematic language, whereas tacit knowledge refers to knowledge that has an individual character and is therefore difficult to formalize and communicate [4]. Nonaka presented four modes of Knowledge Conversion between tacit and explicit:

- Socialization (tacit to tacit),
- Internalization (explicit to tacit),
- Externalization (tacit to explicit), and
- Combination (explicit to explicit).

Figure 1 shows the graphical representation of Nonaka's Knowledge Spiral. Socialization represents the interaction between individuals. Combination involves combining explicit knowledge through meeting and conversation or using information systems. Internalization converts explicit knowledge into tacit knowledge and externalization converts tacit knowledge into explicit knowledge.

Organizational knowledge creation takes place when all four modes of knowledge conversion form a continual cycle triggered by such actions as team interactions, dialogue, metaphors, coordination, documentation, experimentation, and learning by doing, etc. Organizational knowledge creation can be viewed as an upward spiral process from the individual level to the collective group level, and then to the organizational level, sometimes to the inter-organizational level. [9]

Conversational knowledge creation emerged as a popular way for NPD to create knowledge in the context of KMC. With a collaborative environment, individuals share knowledge through dialog with questions and answers. KMC model of knowledge creation is different from other models, where knowledge is for instance created through abstraction or aggregation of information [6, 16].

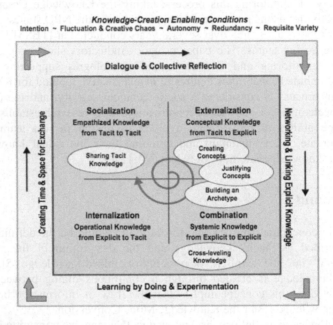

Fig. 1. A graphic depiction of Nonaka's & Takeuchi's theory on knowledge creation [9]

There is evidence shown by Agogino, that shared understanding is produced in the NPD process. Semantic coherence concerning the meaning related to a written text, can be understood as a property of a set of related descriptions, but it can also be understood as a property of a single description with respect to a set of descriptions whose semantic coherence has been established, and we can also derivate the semantic coherence of a set of descriptions as determined by their pair-wise coherence. The coherence metric applied in this research is based on the cosine measurement, which is appropriate for measuring the pair-wise coherence of documents consecutive in time to detect the change in coherence over discrete periods of time [15, 8].

In the context of characterizing design team performance, semantic coherence levels have been measured in all stages of a design team process [7, 17]. The present research is based in the idea that, it is possible to measure the semantic coherence levels for documents identified as strongly associated with Knowledge Modes [9] and knowledge modeling [16].

3 Research Method

The general approach to this research involves the capture of documents generated within a design team, working on a collaborative project consisting in the creation of an unmanned air vehicle. The project involves the participation of more than 30 undergraduate students of different disciplines over a 3-year period that uses "Central Desktop" [7] as the Product Data Management (PDM) platform. According to the nature of the data contained in the documents of the PDM system, it was decided to use LSA as one of the methods of this research.

The main idea behind LSA for analyzing the cognitive processes underlying, modes of knowledge conversion on documents, is that by looking at the entire range of words chosen in a wide variety of texts; patterns will emerge in terms of word choice, as well as word and document meaning. LSA is a statistical technique for extracting and inferring relations of expected contextual usage of words in a given document. For this matter it was decided to perform a semantic analyses in the documents identified as typically used in the supporting technologies for each KMC described by Brohman [11] in Table 1.

Table 1. Modes of knowledge creation and supporting technologies

Mode	Interplay Relationship	Definition	Information System
Socialization	Tacit to Tacit	Conversion of tacit knowledge to new tacit knowledge through social interactions and shared experience among organizational members.	Computer-mediated communication
Combination	Explicit to Explicit	Creation of new explicit knowledge by merging, categorizing, reclassifying, and synthesizing existing explicit knowledge.	Data warehousing, data mining, document repositories, and software agents
Externalization	Tacit to Explicit	Creation of new explicit knowledge from tacit knowledge by supporting beliefs, paradigms, and view-points with codified evidence.	Collaboration, coordination, & (e.g., GSS)
Internalization	Explicit to Tacit	Creation of new tacit knowledge from explicit knowledge by understanding and learning from reports or discussion.	Intranets

First thing to apply LSA is to present the text that is going to be analyzed as a matrix in which each row stands for a singular word and each column stands for a given text or other context. The intersections contain the frequency with which the word of its row appears in the given text denoted by its column. After that, the intersection values are weighted by a function that expresses both the word's importance in the particular portion of text and the degree to which the word type carries information in the domain of the general text. Then LSA applies statistical inferences to determine the semantic coherence [3]. We can observe from Figure 2 that LSA applies Singular Value Decomposition (SVD) to the matrix. In SVD, a rectangular matrix is decomposed into the product of three other matrices. One component matrix describes the original row entities as vectors of derived orthogonal factor values, another describes the original column entities in the same way, and the third is a diagonal matrix containing scaling values such that when the three components are matrix-multiplied, the original matrix is reconstructed.

It has been established three methods [3] to calculate coherence trough measuring shared semantic similarity between design team documentation. These measures can be obtained performing one of the following operations on the associated high dimensional vectorial representation of text and terms on a semantic space:

- **Dot Product** $\qquad x.y = \sum_{i=1}^{N} x_i y_i$

- **Cosine** $\qquad \cos(\theta_{xy}) = \dfrac{x.y}{|x|\|y\|}$

- **Euclidean** $\qquad euclid(x,y) = \sqrt{\sum_{i=1}^{N}(x_i - y_i)^2}$

According to Landauer [3] a Semantic Space section, is a mathematical representation of a large body of text. Every term, every text, and every novel combination of terms has a high dimensional vector representation. When you compare two terms you compare the cosine of the angle between the vectors representing the terms.

The present research employed the cosine method to compare semantic similarities and used the "LSA @ CU Boulder" [13] web software application to perform the corresponding analysis (see Figure 3 for a screenshot of this application).

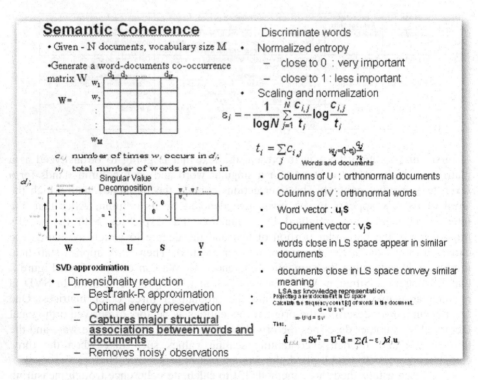

Fig. 2. Algorithmic structure of the LSA technique. Based on [4] and [8].

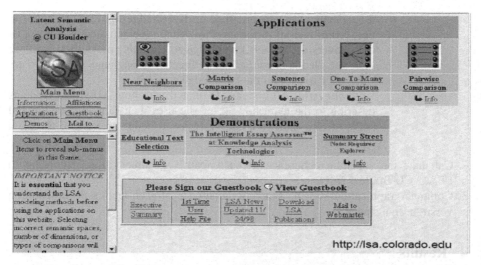

Fig. 3. Latent Semantic Analysis@ CU Boulder [13]

The following method was employed to measure semantic coherence:

1. Documents of each design team are grouped and categorized using the information system technologies identified as typically used for each KMC described in Table 1. For this matter the following criteria for categorization of documents had been used:

   - Documents in the Socialization Knowledge Mode are those that are elaborated as a result of team activities of shared experience.

     In our case: All documents related with how students learned from mentors or professors through a process of observation and repetition. In the building of the unmanned aerial vehicle that required new processes and their implementation. Each team developed documents related to the new work practices and routines to integrate and make sense of the NPD.

   - Documents in the Combination Knowledge Mode are those that are elaborated as a result of a process by which explicit knowledge held by individuals is shared.

     In our case: All documents related with how students interacted around the process of designing the unmanned air vehicle. Students had to combine knowledge about how best to integrate the aerial vehicle during formal or informal meetings.

   - Documents in the Internalization Knowledge Mode are those that are elaborated as a result of the traditional concept of learning process. However, because in this case explicit knowledge is converted to tacit, it is the process or action that enables the conversion. In the case of a new technology tool, the act of using the tool enables the internalization of knowledge.

     In our case: All documents related with how students improve their knowledge and skills of new hardware and software

- Documents in the Externalization Knowledge Mode as an opposite case from Internalization are those that are elaborated as a result of the conversion of tacit knowledge to explicit knowledge. Because tacit knowledge is not definable directly in language, metaphors are often used to explain the knowledge concept.

  In our case: All documents related with how individual students describe to the team how he or she uses their new knowledge and skills of new hardware and software to better perform in the team activities.

2. Calculate the semantic coherence of each team's documentation, according to LSA @ CU Boulder software.
3. Compute graphical data of the semantic coherence of each team's documentation versus design stages.

4 Results

In order to characterize the design team performance, documents identified as typically used in a Knowledge Mode, as described in the previous point, were analyzed to obtain a measure of semantic coherence using LSA. This not only gave us a measure trough all stages of the NPD, but also gave us the opportunity to zoom-in the Knowledge Creation Process proposed by Nonaka.

Text from documents was analyzed using the "Sentence Comparison Method Interface" of LSA @ CU Boulder. The interface allows you to compare the similarity of sequential sentences within a particular LSA space. Each sentence is compared to next sentence. The program will automatically parse the input into sentences [13].

The result of the application of this interface is a measure of the semantic coherence within the text analyzed. The measures of coherence for all documents used by the design teams in all the design stages were collected and used to compute graphical data.

The data of semantic coherence between three design teams was compared not only taking in a count the design stages, but also the Knowledge Modes described by Nonaka.

A key result from this study is the determination of a method for collaborative-based environments that identifies which product development activities promote the growth of coherence levels in knowledge modes. This method facilitates to monitor activities that can be indicators of semantic significance that promote KMC. The presence of increasing significance, in KMC, during the design process is desirable.

In the other hand, decreasing in semantic significance in product development activities denote disruption and disfunctionality as already observed by Agonino [7].

The difference between this research and other previously released is that with this new proposed approach it is possible to track coherence measures within the Knowledge Modes. In this way, design teams could monitor, in a collaborative-based environment, which product development activities within its supporting technologies promote higher semantic coherence levels.

Table 2. Team data of coherence media for Knowledge Modes

week	TA Soc	TA Ext	TA Comb	TA Intern	TB Soc	TB Ext	TB Comb	TB Intern	TC Soc	TC Ext	TC Comb	TC Intern	
w1	0.1	0.31	0.32	-0.15	-0.14	-0.13	-0.16	-0.15	0.14	-0.11	0.2	0.15	DESIGN STAGES
w2	-0.22	0.33	0.35	-0.1	-0.22	0.33	-0.12	-0.18	-0.13	0.22	0.25	-0.21	
w3	0.31	0.36	0.54	0.13	-0.1	-0.12	0.45	-0.32	0.22	0.12	0.33	0.14	
w4	-0.25	0.33	0.65	0.28	-0.25	0.17	0.22	0.28	0.35	0.43	0.45	0.18	
w5	0.33	0.44	0.62	-0.22	0.16	0.34	0.62	-0.12	0.33	0.44	0.32	0.32	
w6	0.33	0.56	0.54	0.26	0.23	0.56	0.45	0.46	0.23	0.66	-0.14	-0.23	Concept Design
w7	0.3	0.22	0.67	0.22	0.33	0.82	0.34	0.39	0.23	0.62	0.23	0.31	
w8	0.25	0.42	0.86	0.13	0.22	0.45	0.24	0.13	0.46	0.55	0.86	0.33	
w9	0.56	0.75	0.77	0.14	0.76	0.55	0.85	0.24	0.55	0.74	0.92	0.24	
w10	0.31	0.92	0.34	-0.25	0.51	0.72	0.77	0.25	0.41	0.88	0.43	0.65	Preliminary Design
w11	0.6	0.92	0.89	0.45	0.66	0.52	0.89	0.55	0.45	0.9	0.66	0.75	
w12	0.24	0.95	0.95	0.54	0.27	0.88	0.77	0.39	0.74	0.89	0.85	0.43	
w13	0.66	0.87	0.88	0.48	0.56	0.66	0.73	0.5	0.66	0.87	0.76	0.81	
w14	0.54	0.91	0.88	0.33	0.49	0.9	0.77	0.63	0.78	0.81	0.85	0.83	Final Design

In our case, we anticipated through observing Socialization Knowledge Mode coherence measures of design teams (as seen on Table 2), the need to trigger interaction activities where our students could learn from observation and imitation of a professor, tutor or instructor. For this matter a manufacturing facilities was created where a professional instructor constructed with our students special parts for the aerial vehicle, with the purpose of facilitating this kind of knowledge sharing.

In the other hand, it was also promoted activities to obtain a collective reflection on how the new skills and abilities related to the use of new hardware and software tools, were improving each individual performance toward the improvement of the performance of the whole team. These collective reflection activities were inducing growing in coherence for both Externalization and Internalization Knowledge Mode, but for this last Mode, activities of hands-on learning by doing of the new hardware and software tools were also implemented.

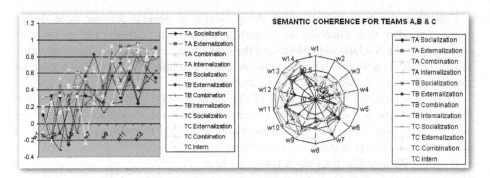

Fig. 4. Coherence variation in time of Knowledge Mode level

Activities with the intention to grow coherence measures for the Combination Knowledge Mode were deployed with the purpose of coordinate the work of the different sections within a design team. These activities considered the way teams were connecting existing or previous knowledge or data with other explicit knowledge in the project of the NPD.

In our research, was observed that coherence levels grow over each design stage, but also was observed a correlation between the growing in coherence in the Socialization Mode and the grow of coherence in the Externalization Mode, but with a slight delay in time (see Figure 4 and Table 2).

So once this sequence was observed work was focused on measuring the correlation between coherence grow in a particular Knowledge Mode and the growing of the coherence in the next and sequential Knowledge Mode.

5   Conclusions

This paper has surveyed the following activities that can trigger Knowledge Mode Conversion in the processes underlying organizational knowledge creation using the Nonaka model and that in an empirical way were detected to improve the semantic coherence measures for the Knowledge Mode:

* Activities to learn from observation and imitation of a professor, tutor or instructor.
* Activities to obtain a collective reflection on how the new skills and abilities related to the use of new hardware and software tools, were improving each individual performance.
* Activities of collective reflection on how new knowledge and skills of individuals promote better team performance.
* Activities of hands-on, learning by doing of new hardware and software tools.
* Activities with the purpose to coordinate the work within teams that consider the way teams connect existing or previous knowledge or data with other explicit knowledge in their design projects.

Coherence levels grew over each design stage in general for our three design teams, but also was observed an empirical correlation between the growing in coherence in the Socialization Mode and the grow of coherence in the Externalization Mode, but with a slight delay in time. A good example of this is the coherence measures for team A (see Figure 4 and Table 2).

There is a tendency to have cycles of divergent thinking following of convergent process all through the whole new process development as already observed by Agonino [7]. The coherence measurements are expected to grow as the process is passing from a divergent stage to a convergent one.

It would be possible for design teams, to keep a monitoring of their Knowledge Mode Semantic Coherence Level in real time, for the progress in their documents, as well as their web based design activities that are all important potential indicators of a design team's performance within a New Product Development Process.

Acknowledgments. The authors acknowledge the support received by the Instituto Tecnológico y de Estudios Superiores de Monterrey (ITESM) through the Research Chairs in Autotronics. Additional support for this work has been provided by the IBM SUR GRANT.

References

1. Wagner, C.: Wiki: A Technology for Conversational Knowledge Management and Group Collaboration. Communication of the Association for Information Systems 13, 265–289 (2004)
2. Nonaka, I.: A Dynamic Theory of Organizational Knowledge Creation. Organization Science 5(1), 14–37 (1994)
3. Landauer, T.K., Foltz, P.W., Laham, D.: Introduction to Latent Semantic Analysis. Discourse Processes 25, 259–284 (1998)
4. Guerra-Zubiaga, D.: A Manufacturing Model to Enable Knowledge Maintenance in Decision Support Systems. Ph.D. Thesis, Loughborough University (2004)
5. Prahalad, C.K., Hamel, G.: The Core Competence of the Corporation. Harvard Business Review 68, 79–91 (1990)
6. http://www.centraldesktop.com
7. Hill, A., Song, S., Dong, A., Agogino, A.M.: A Document Analysis Method for Characterizing Design Team Performance. Journal of Mechanical Design 126(3), 378–385 (2004)
8. Hill, A., Song, S., Dong, A., Agogino, A.M.: Identifying Shared Understanding in Design using Document Analysis. In: Proceedings of the 13th International Conference on Design Theory and Methodology. ASME, Pittsburgh, Pennsylvania (2001)
9. Nonaka, I., Takeuchi, H.: The Knowledge-Creating Company. Oxford University Press, Oxford (1995)
10. http://www.zipfer.com
11. Brohman M.K.: Knowledge Creation Opportunities in the Data Mining Process. In: Proceedings of the 39th Hawaii International Conference on System Sciences. vol. 8, pp. 170c (2006)
12. Guerra-Zubiaga, D., Donato, L., Ramírez, R., Contero, M.: Knowledge Sharing to Support Collaborative Engineering at PLM Environment. In: Reimer, U., Karagiannis, D. (eds.) PAKM 2006. LNCS (LNAI), vol. 4333, pp. 86–96. Springer, Heidelberg (2006)
13. http://lsa.colorado.edu
14. AMR Research, Inc. www.amrresearch.com Source: CSFB/HOLT: Deloitte Consulting Analyses, from The Innovator's Solution, Christiansen and Raynor (2003)
15. Voina, C.: Principles of Semantic Coherence in Concept Learning. In: Proc. of the Singapore Int. Conference. on Intelligent Control and Instrumentation, vol. 2, pp. 736–739 (1992)
16. Guerra, D., Young, R.: A Manufacturing Model to Enable Knowledge Maintenance in Decision Support Systems. In: 33 Annual Conference of North American Manufacturing Research Institution of Society of Manufacturing Engineering (NAMRI/SME), Columbia University, NY, vol. 33-1, pp. 203–210 (2005)
17. Young, R., Cutting-Decelle, A., Guerra, D., Gunendran, G., Das, B., Cochran, S.: Sharing Manufacturing Information and Knowledge in Design Decision Support. In: Bramley, A., Brissaud, D., Coutellier, D., McMahon, C. (eds.) Advanced Integrated Design and Manufacturing in Mechanical Engineering, pp. 173–185. Springer, Heidelberg (2005)

Social Rewarding in Wiki Systems –
Motivating the Community

Bernhard Hoisl[1], Wolfgang Aigner[2], and Silvia Miksch[2]

[1] Institute of Software Technology and Interactive Systems, Vienna University of Technology,
Favoritenstr. 9-11/188, 1040 Vienna, Austria
e0252748@student.tuwien.ac.at
[2] Department of Information and Knowledge Engineering, Danube University Krems,
Dr.-Karl-Dorrek-Str. 30, 3500 Krems, Austria
{wolfgang.aigner,silvia.miksch}@donau-uni.ac.at

Abstract. Online communities have something in common: their success rise and fall with the participation rate of active users. In this paper we focus on social rewarding mechanisms that generate benefits for users in order to achieve a higher contribution rate in a wiki system. In an online community, social rewarding is in the majority of cases based on accentuation of the most active members. As money cannot be used as a motivating factor others like status, power, acceptance, and glory have to be employed. We explain different social rewarding mechanisms which aim to meet these needs of users. Furthermore, we implemented a number of methods within the MediaWiki system, where social rewarding criteria are satisfied by generating a ranking of most active members.

Keywords: Social Rewarding, Wiki, Online Communities, Motivation, Participation, Contribution.

1 Introduction

Wikipedia – the most famous free encyclopaedia – has grown to the biggest wiki community site where hundreds of thousands of users all around the world post and edit articles in many different languages. The tremendous contribution rate on Wikipedia has led to many problems, like wrong information, copyright violations, or users' misbehaviour, for example, spammers or trolls [16]. Other online communities beside Wikipedia have massive troubles motivating users to participate actively. We are going to present techniques where the fundamental problem of both – reaching a critical mass of active users – are addressed.

On the one hand, Wikipedia has the problem that published information is not checked for its accuracy and legality by a formal process of reviewing. There has to be a large and heavily involved community which is cross-checking and proofing information for its correctness voluntarily. However, the operators of Wikipedia have not only a social but also a legal responsibility to publish only correct and faultless information to assure their creditability. On the other hand, many online communities have troubles motivating enough users to build an active community. Participation of

D. Schuler (Ed.): Online Communities and Social Comput., HCII 2007, LNCS 4564, pp. 362–371, 2007.
© Springer-Verlag Berlin Heidelberg 2007

members is the key factor for a successful online community, and that is why good motivating factors are essential.

As information provided over the Internet is treated like public goods, problems like free riding[1] or social loafing[2] arise. In Wikipedia users are not charged in proportion to their use, therefore it appears rational for people to view articles without contributing anything on their own. If we assume an economic point of view it can be said that a user has costs by publishing an article to Wikipedia (e.g., information acquisition and presentation costs or Internet connection costs) and therefore she/he wants something in return. Extending the benefit for a user so that it exceeds her/his costs is a good starting point to increase participation. With this contribution we are going to focus on an approach to motivate users to participate actively in an online community by making use of a number of different social rewarding techniques [8].

To classify our approach, we will give an overview of related work in the next section. Section 3 will explain the developed social rewarding techniques while section 4 gives an insight on the calculation process of these methods. Section 5 covers the visual appearance of the authors' ranking and the implementation is summarized in section 6. A conclusion is drawn in section 7 containing an outlook on future work.

2 Related Work

There are numerous books and articles about the wiki phenomenon (e.g., [5, 11, 14, 18]). However, most work focuses on technical details, like installing and running a wiki or the revisioning system and its vantages for collaborative information development. Unfortunately, too little attention is paid to investigate users' behaviour in online communities. Some research is done to explain the problem of free riding [1, 6] which is likely to occur in times of the Internet and shared information platforms. There are also studies about communication activities of users in virtual communities [17], but the focus is not on motivational factors for users of online communities.

Which factors are motivating for a human being, was already discussed by Abraham Maslow and his hierarchy of human needs theory [13]. In an article about using social psychology to motivate contributions to online communities [10] an experiment took place where the problems of under-contribution and social loafing were addressed. In the article, as predicted by theory, individuals contributed when they were reminded of their uniqueness and when they were given specific and challenging goals. As other predictions were disconfirmed, results of the experiment

---

[1] In this case, free riding means that a user shoulders less than a fair share of the costs of the whole information production of a wiki [3]. If everybody contributes the same value of information to a wiki, nobody free rides. One of the biggest problems is that the value of an information resource to an individual is very subjective and hard to determine.

[2] Social loafing is the phenomenon that persons make less effort to achieve a goal when they work in a group than when they work alone [9]. As the least articles in Wikipedia (like in nearly every other wiki) are written by only one user but in a team the problem of social loafing is likely to occur. The answer to social loafing are motivational factors which are partly solved in the MediaWiki software by the possibility to see which sections of an article belongs to which author. So, a contribution is linked to an author's name and can therefore be evaluated.

have to be interpreted carefully. An article from the same co-authors [12] focusing on a related topic, tried to manipulate two factors to increase participation in online communities: *similarity* – how similar group members' contributions were and *uniqueness* – how unique members' contributions were within the group. As a result both factors positively influenced participation.

Our approach to increase users' participation in a wiki is based on accentuation and reputation [15]. By motivating many users we want to increase the community so that cross-checking takes place and false information is automatically sorted out. That such an approach of member-maintained communities increases the quantity and quality of contributions was affirmed [4] and empirically tested on Wikipedia [2].

3   Social Rewarding Techniques

In this paper we present social rewarding mechanisms that generate benefits for the users in order to achieve a higher contribution rate in a wiki community. In our case, social reward refers to something that causes a behaviour to increase in intensity. In an online community, social rewarding is in the majority of cases based on accentuation of the most active members. As money cannot be used as a motivating factor, others like status, power, acceptance, and glory have to be employed. We explain different social rewarding methods which aim to meet these needs of users.

The techniques presented are focussing primarily on automatic investigations of quantitative and qualitative characteristics of published articles. As a proof of concept, three social rewarding mechanisms were implemented using the software MediaWiki[3] (which is also used by Wikipedia). Most active members are accentuated by applying these social rewarding methods to calculate a ranking of authors:

- *Amount of References* – This social rewarding method uses Google's SOAP search API to build an index quality number based on three different criteria: the size of a reference, the number of links pointing to this reference and the number of links pointing to the specific article.
- *Rating of Articles* – A user centric evaluation of articles published is still missing in the MediaWiki software. We have implemented an open rating system where users can vote for or against an article (and optionally leave a comment) by making use of a predefined pointing scale.
- *Most Viewed Articles* – Visits of users are counted working with configured parameters.

The two most important criteria for our choice were, on the one hand, to find a good mixture of different methods and, on the other hand, the level of complexity of the implementation process in MediaWiki.

We believe that using a couple of different social rewarding mechanisms will result in better findings for two reasons. The first reason is because data will be retrieved from different sources. Combining these data should result in a better and more plausible result than any other technique alone. The second reason is that many different data sources make it hard for an author to betray. If we only count users' hits

---

[3] http://www.mediawiki.org

it is obvious that authors would try to cheat by visiting their own articles a lot more often than other ones. Of course there have to be control mechanisms, like preventing authors to be counted as visitors of their own articles. But too many restrictions can falsify the *real* behaviour of users which we are trying to measure.

3.1 Amount of References

As in the case of the Wikipedia encyclopaedia the value of an article grows with the amount and quality of used references. An approach to an automated quality check of Internet resources was realized by the help of one of the world's largest search engines: Google. Google can help to detect the quality of an article by figuring out how much sites are linked to a cited reference[4]. If many sites are linking to an Internet resource cited as a reference and this links themselves have a high number on links to them, then information displayed on this site must have at least a basic level of plausibility (this concept is the basis for Google's search algorithm named *PageRank* [7]).

Besides the number of links to a reference another criterion – the size of the reference – is used[5]. We assume that a reference with thousands of sub-sites can be more trusted than a home-made personal web-site with only three pages.

A more global idea is counting the links to a wiki article from outside. By using Google we cannot only check references within articles, but also figure out how many sites outside the wiki are pointing to an article. If there are thousands of links to an article it is likely that this article is valuable to many people. The higher the amount of links to an article is, the higher is the frequency of visitors and readers. Many links are also an indicator for good quality of an article.

Our calculation is influenced by these three directly presented criteria: the number of links pointing to a reference, the size of this reference and the number of links pointing to the specific wiki article. Now a quality index number of an article can be generated which can be used for a basic classification of the references as more or less credibly and which can indicate the publicity of the article. So at least an initial quality check of Internet resources can be realized by using Google's PageRank technique. This attempt tries to rank articles not only by means of quantitative characteristics but also qualitative ones.

3.2 Rating of Articles

To distinguish good written articles from bad ones, the user has the possibility to vote for or against it. This is done by asking only one simple question with standardized answer alternatives. Answer possibilities could be: *Yes/No* ("Did you like the article?"); *-5 to +5* ("How relevant was the information shown in this article to you?") or something similar to that. A text field is inserted giving the user the chance to write in what she/he liked/disliked. So the rating points are quantitatively calculated while the author also gets a personal qualitative feedback.

---

[4] Entering *link:http://www.tuwien.ac.at* as a search term will result in showing all pages linking to this address.
[5] By inserting *site:http://www.tuwien.ac.at* as a search term the number of sub-sites belonging to this address will be returned.

The rating results are inserted in the discussion page of the article. Users and especially the author her-/himself can have a quick overview why users rated the article positively or negatively. As a next step the author could rewrite the article based on the ideas of the users (certainly users can do this also on their own). In the discussion page the author has the possibility to post answers upon users' comments, thus giving her/him the chance for a justification.

Other aspects that have to be considered are the number of minimal votes needed for a representative result and some sort of protection against multiple votes.

3.3 Most Viewed Articles

The idea behind a list of most viewed articles is that when an article is viewed by many people it is either (1) very informative and very well written with good background knowledge of the author, or (2) it has a highly interesting theme for a broad range of people. If we assume case one then it can be said that articles which have a high rate of hits or visits help to achieve a good reputation for their authors.

A list of most viewed articles can be an overall list of most viewed articles ever, separated by a certain amount of time, or they can be categorized by their topic. A list of most viewed articles ever can be a good idea, although there will certainly not be very much fluctuation among the top articles in the list. To avoid this behaviour most viewed articles of the month or week can be a solution.

The following section explains how these directly presented social rewarding methods are combined to find out most active users.

4   Calculation

As said before our developed social rewarding techniques are focussing on accentuation of the most active members in a community. This is done by highlighting the most productive authors in a ranking. In the former chapter we introduced the social rewarding methods which are used for the calculation of such a listing. Now it is time to explain the two-step calculation process.

4.1   Revision Basis

Each of the three social rewarding mechanisms computes points for a single revision[6] of every article. This is done by comparing the value of the specific revision with the average value of all revisions in the wiki (see equation 1).

$$avg_{Rj} = \frac{\sum_{i=1}^{n} r_{ij}}{n}. \tag{1}$$

R is a set of all revisions where r_{ij} is the value of the j social rewarding mechanism of revision i:

---

[6] Every change made to an article results in a new revision.

$$R_i = \{r_{i1}, r_{i2}, r_{i3,\dots,} r_{ij}; 1 \le j \le 3\}. \tag{2}$$

For example, for the social rewarding technique *Most Viewed Articles* all visits to a revision are counted. Let us assume article *A* in revision *7* has *20* views. The average value of views of all revisions is *30*. So revision *7* of article *A* has only *66.67%* of the overall average views. As we want to credit every revision with a certain amount of points according to their visits, a scale must be predefined to set the intervals. In our scale a value of *66.67%* would be graded with *2* out of *5* points[7].

This example of point assignment is done for every revision and for every social rewarding method. For mechanism *Rating of Articles* users vote for an article by assigning *0* to *5* points. For the technique *Amount of References* the number of links pointing to a reference, the size of this reference and the number of links pointing to the specific article are used as variables. These three criteria are weighted according to users' settings and are compared to a mean value calculated over all revisions.

In the end of the first computation step for every social rewarding method and for every revision points are assigned according to predefined scales. These values are weighted and summed up to an overall value per revision. By looking at equation 3 it can be seen that p_{r_i} are the summed up points for revision *i* for every social rewarding method *j* weighted against w_j (which has to be defined in the configuration file).

$$p_{r_i} = \sum_{j=1}^{3} \frac{r_{ij}}{avg_{Rj}} * w_j . \tag{3}$$

The allocation of points of revisions to authors is done in the next step.

4.2 Author Basis

As a revision is linked to exactly one author it is now possible to sum up all points of every revision an author has written. This is done by using two methods to weight the result: the length of the edit and the creation time of a revision.

A modified set of *R* is created where r'_{ik} is revision *k* of article *i* (equation 4).

$$R'_i = \{r'_{i1}, r'_{i2}, r'_{i3}, \dots, r'_{ik}\}. \tag{4}$$

We assume that the more different a new revision is compared to the former one, the more important were the changes made. It does not matter, if a new revision is extended or shortened – a surplus in content quality is assumed[8]. The difference from one revision to another is counted in bytes. Using equation 5 we get an overall value of size changes from all revisions *k* from an article *i* (where $s_{r'_{ik}}$ is the specific size change from one revision to the former one).

$$S_{r_i} = \sum_{k=1}^{n} \underbrace{abs\left[size\left(r'_{ik}\right) - size\left(r'_{i(k-1)}\right)\right]}_{s_{r'_{ik}}}. \tag{5}$$

---

[7] These examples use a scale from *0* (worst) to *5* (best) points, but it can be defined as wanted.
[8] That means we factor out flamers, trolls etc.

The second assumption is that newer revisions count more than older ones. We believe that newer revisions have up-to-date topics and therefore should be weighted higher than ones written long ago. Equation 6 sums up the relative amount of time for all revisions k for an article i ($t_{r'_{ik}}$ is the relative amount of time for one revision).

$$T_{r_i} = \sum_{k=1}^{n} \underbrace{time\left(r'_{ik}\right) - firstTime\left(r'_i\right)}_{t'_{ik}}.$$ (6)

For all revisions of every article, the differentiation to the former revision, and its age according to the creation date of the article are saved (equation 5 and 6).

Equation 7 defines a subset A of revisions belonging to one author. This means that only revisions from the specific author for whom the calculation takes place are considered. So, for example, $s_{a_{ik}}$ (in equation 8) is the size change from one revision of the author which is divided by the overall size change of all revisions of the article to get a percentage value.

$$A \subseteq R'.$$ (7)

In equation 8 for every revision belonging to an author and every criterion (size and time) percentage values are generated which are weighted using a predefined scale (w_S and w_T). Then these two values are multiplied with the specific points calculated in the first step for this revision (p_{r_k}) and both values are summed up. The outcome is a new weighted value for every revision ($p_{a_{ik}}$) which has to be summed up for all articles belonging to an author (p_A).

$$p_A = \sum_{i=1}^{n} \sum_{k=1}^{m} \underbrace{\frac{s_{a_{ik}}}{S'_{r_i}} * w_S * p_{r_k} + \frac{t_{a_{ik}}}{T'_{r_i}} * w_T * p_{r_k}}_{p_{a_{ik}}}.$$ (8)

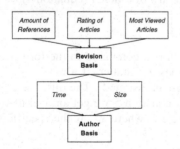

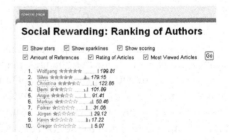

Social Rewarding: Ranking of Authors

Fig. 1. Two-step calculation process. At first points are computed on a revision basis using the three described social rewarding methods. In a second step the points are weighted according to time and size factors and summed up for an author.

Fig. 2. Screenshot of ranking of authors. Besides the authors' names, stars and sparklines can be seen. The numbers on the right are the achieved scores according to the calculation of the social rewarding methods.

This procedure has to be done for all authors, so that in the end every author has one value assigned which is the basis for displaying the ranking. Fig. 1 gives an overview of the two-step calculation process described in this section.

5   Ranking of Authors

For displaying results, various authors' rankings can be generated where the most active one will see her-/himself on the first place (Fig. 2). To support shown results, two well-known data visualization techniques are used: *stars* and *sparklines* [19].

5.1 Stars

Using stars to generate a ranking is well known and an established way to give a quick indication on how good or bad something is. Large Internet sites, like eBay or Amazon and many forum applications use stars as graphical expressions. We recommend using a five star scaling to show the participation rate of a user (displaying half-stars can be activated additionally). As stars are computed on the basis of the participation rate of all other members of the community, they are a good indication for the overall contribution rate of a user.

5.2 Sparklines

Sparklines are *"small, high-resolution graphics embedded in a context of words, numbers, images. Sparklines are data-intense, design-simple, word-sized graphics. Sparklines have obvious applications for financial and economic data, by tracking changes over time, showing overall trend as well as local detail"* [19].

In this work sparklines are used to show the participation rate of a user over a certain period of time split by predefined intervals. Therefore, the contribution rate is calculated using the three social rewarding mechanisms described earlier. We have chosen sparklines mainly because of their good integration in a context of words and their simplicity. The appearance, intervals, heights, widths, spaces, and colours of the sparklines can be customized by the user.

6   Implementation

We implemented our developed social rewarding techniques as an extension in the MediaWiki system. For setting up the extension a configuration file is used where all variables belonging to our package can be configured (~*100*).

As the computation of the authors' ranking depends strongly on the amount of articles, revisions, and authors it can be very time consuming. Therefore, a caching algorithm was implemented so that the calculation does not have to be done upon every single request. Caching data can either be saved on the file system or in the database. By selecting the latter a history of authors' ranking can be generated.

Most functions of the extension were implemented to be displayed as so-called *SpecialPages*. But also some self-defined markups can be inserted into an article to display information provided by our package. At last, hooks are used for collecting necessary data for the computation process.

7   Conclusion and Future Work

Because under-contribution is a serious problem for many online communities, we have tried in this paper to give an insight on how to motivate users by means of social rewarding techniques. We based our work on the accentuation of most active members in a wiki. To find these users we generated an authors' ranking by making use of calculated points of three developed social rewarding mechanisms: *Amount of References*, *Rating of Articles*, and *Most Viewed Articles*. Several weighting variables influence the ranking. Some of them are configurable; others rely on the quantity, quality, and novelty of the authors' text. Besides the ranking, stars and sparklines are used to visualize the results. As an implementation platform we have chosen MediaWiki in which our social rewarding mechanisms where integrated.

Our approach can be seen as a starting point to develop mechanisms to the important issue of motivating users to participate actively in a wiki system. In no other online community the participation rate of users is more important than in a wiki, because there producers and consumers of the good (namely information) are the same. If too less users produce content and only free ride a wiki community will cannibalize itself. We think that our implementation of social rewarding techniques as a mixture of several methods is a good way to create qualitative high results which are necessary to generate non-monetary incentives for users. Nevertheless, it is a failure to think that mechanisms we have described in this paper will be sufficient to motivate enough people to form an active community to participate in every wiki. Users must have an intrinsic motivation to contribute to a wiki which with our developed techniques can only be stimulated.

Our project is not publicly released yet and therefore empirical data is not available. For this reason, we are currently planning to evaluate our implemented concepts in a larger setting.

References

1. Adar, E., Huberman, B.A.: Free Riding on Gnutella. Xerox Palo Alto Research Center (2000)
2. Chesney, T.: An Empirical Examination of Wikipedia's Credibility. First Monday, vol. 11(11) (2006)
3. Cornes, R., Sandler, T.: The Theory of Externalities, Public Goods and Club Goods, 2nd edn. Cambridge Univ. Press, Cambridge (1996)
4. Cosley, D., Frankowski, D., Kiesler, S., et al.: How Oversight Improves Member-Maintained Communities. CommunityLab (2005)
5. Ebersbach, A., Glaser, M., Heigl, R.: Wiki: Web Collaboration. Springer, Heidelberg (2005)
6. Feldman, M., Papadimitriou, C., Chuang, J., et al.: Free-Riding and Whitewashing in Peer-to-Peer Systems. School of Information Management and Systems, UC Berkeley (2004)
7. Google Technology (Retrieved on 2007-02-15) http://www.google.com/technology/

8. Hoisl, B.: Social Rewarding in Online Communities - A Focus on Wiki Systems. Master thesis, Vienna University of Technology (2007) (To be published)
9. Jackson, J.M., Harkins, S.G.: Equity in Effort: An Explanation of the Social Loafing Effect. Journal of Personality and Social Psychology 49, 1199–1206 (1985)
10. Kimberly, L., Beenen, G., Ludford, P., et al.: Using Social Psychology to Motivate Contributions to Online Communities. CommunityLab (2004)
11. Leuf, B., Cunningham, W.: The Wiki Way: Quick Collaboration on the Web. Addison-Wesley Professional, London (2001)
12. Ludford, P., Cosley, D., Frankowski, D., et al.: Think Different: Increasing Online Community Participation Using Uniqueness and Group Dissimilarity. University of Minnesota, Department of Computer Science and Engineering (2004)
13. Maslow, A.H.: Motivation and Personality. 3rd edn. HarperCollins Publishers (1987)
14. McFederies, P.: Technically Speaking: It's A Wiki, Wiki World. IEEE Spectrum 43, 88 (2006)
15. Resnick, P., Zeckhauser, R., Friedman, E., et al.: Reputation Systems: Facilitating Trust in Internet Interactions. Communications of the ACM 43(12), 45–48 (2000)
16. Sanger, L.: Why Wikipedia Must Jettison Its Anti-Elitism. (Retrieved on 2007-02-15) (2004) http://www.kuro5hin.org/story/2004/12/30/142458/25 Kuro5hin
17. Schoberth, T., Preece, J., Heinzl, A.: Online Communities: A Longitude Analysis of Communication Activities. Working Paper in Information Systems (2003)
18. Tapscott, D., Williams, A.D.: Wikinomics: How Mass Collaboration Changes Everything. Portfolio (2006)
19. Tufte, E.R.: Beautiful Evidence. Graphics Press, pp. 7– 19 (2006)

Integrating Digital Library Resources in Elementary School Classrooms – A Case Study of Social Study Instruction

Kuo Hung Huang

Department of E-learning Design and Management
National Chiayi University, Taiwan
kuohung@mail.ncyu.edu.tw

Abstract. In Taiwan, integrating the computer technology with instruction has been becoming a major effort of the Ministry of Education to improve the quality of the education. However, teachers' willingness and capabilities to use these digital learning resources will have an important impact on the outcomes of the policy. The purpose of this paper is to study the educational applications of the digital library resources in elementary school. Combining the WWW technologies and the Internet resources of National Digital Archives, a web-based learning environment was implemented for classroom instruction. Teachers first developed several learning activities based the framework of situated learning, and then integrated these digital resources in the classroom instruction. The researcher-collected data of learning activities to evaluated the students' achievement and teachers' professional development. The results indicated that, in addition to factual knowledge, students had the opportunities to practice variety of skills such as teamwork, information searching and organization, presentation, and discussion. The teacher also comprehended the meanings and process of constructive learning by supporting students' learning with digital resources and technologies.

1 Introduction

Social studies have been a course in need of improvement in instruction. Most teachers nowadays still spend most of the class time on factual recitation. Rote memorization has been taken as the only way to teach or learn the content of social studies. This paper discusses a project of creative learning, funded by the National Digital Archives Project, aiming to develop a model of social studies instruction to encourage students to learn actively by using the digital resources from the digital archives [1].

2 Project

Based on the framework of situated learning, the researcher first collected the digital archives related to the local city and then hyper linked to a web-based electronic

D. Schuler (Ed.): Online Communities and Social Comput., HCII 2007, LNCS 4564, pp. 372–374, 2007.

map [2]. The users can also select a thematic representation, an automatic combination of layers of maps. The thematic representation was selected and tested as a better view to comprehend the information about a specific topic about Chiayi. (Figure 1).

Fig. 1. The data of the archives are displayed on a local map. Users interact with the web pages to retrieve and display the information through the Flash components.

3 Instruction

The research was conducted in an elementary school. The subjects were 32 fourth-grade students. The teacher integrated the electronic map and digital archives in the classroom instruction. After being familiar with the resources, the students were divided into several groups to complete their own project. The project for each group was to construct a thematic map based on the electronic map and digital resources. Students in each group participated the activities of discussing the theme, distributing tasks, collecting data, constructing map, and preparing a slide to present their works. (Figure 2).

The teacher was convinced of the educational advantages of the digital archives. Seeing the students working together as a team, she realized that the digital archives playing the role of mediating student's active learning. In addition to the factual knowledge, commented by the teacher, the students learned how to learn by doing.

374   K.H. Huang

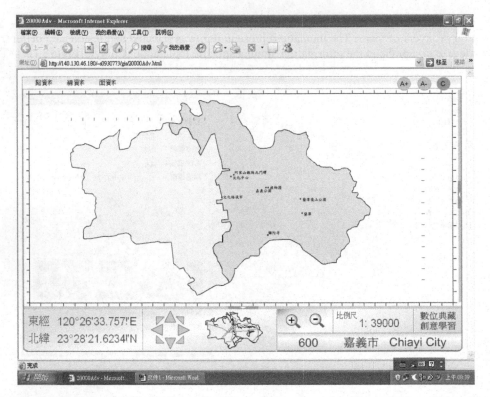

Fig. 2. A work by a group of students. The theme of the map was the eight ancient beautiful spots in Chiayi.

4   Conclusion

Although the research outcome is primitive, this research results revealed the educational application of digital archives is positive to the constructive learning. By cooperating with the teachers, a more mature, suitable approach of instruction will be developed in the future.

References

1. NDAP: NDAP Introduction (2003) Accessed at http://www.ndap.org.tw/Introduction/ index_en.shtml
2. Huang, K.-H., Tsai, C., Cheng, C.-C.: Information Visualization of the Digital Archives: Implementing an Exploratory Learning Environment with GIS Interface. In: Proceedings of 2005 International Conference of Active Media Technology, Japan (2005)

Managing Fairness: Reward Distribution in a Self-organized Online Game Player Community

Chyng-Yang Jang

University of Texas at Arlington, BOX 19107, Arlington, TX 76019, USA
cyjang@uta.edu

Abstract. Reward distribution is essential to the wellbeing of self-organized online game player communities. This paper adopted a case-study approach to investigate how a particular player community managed fairness in sharing rewards among members. The results found that the community primarily relied on a raid point based auction system for reward distribution. Perceived fairness was managed as various written policies focusing on two dimensions: behavior regulation and resource management. The guiding principles of fairness management were identified and articulated. So was the role of structural features of the game and the community in triggering policy discussion. Finally, the implications for future research was discussed.

Keywords: Fairness, Distributive justice, Online community, MMORPG.

1 Introduction

How to fairly distribute rewards resulting from collective works has been a central issue for organizations. Rooted in the social exchange theories [1, 12], past research found that higher perceived fairness in compensation led to higher job performance, trust, organizational citizenship behavior, benefits satisfaction, and lower turnover intention [2, 3, 11, 13]. These effects of perceived fairness are especially important to voluntary online communities. These communities depend on members' citizenship behavior and continuous participation. Fair return on members' efforts is essential to ensure further contribution. On the other hand, any unjust distribution of collective gains may lead to frustration, reduced participation, or even migration to other communities. Therefore, management of reward distribution is critical for the survival and success of online communities. This study aims to investigate how people manage distributive fairness in virtual communities.

Of particular interest are those self-organized online communities for playing massively multiplayer online role playing games (MMORPGs). These communities usually contain a task component of accomplishing in-game missions and constantly produce tangible outcomes via group efforts. Reward distribution is, therefore, a more significant issue to them.

Playing MMORPGs has become increasingly popular recently. In early 2007, one of the top MMORPG game titles, World of Warcraft (WoW), reported to reach 8 million subscribers in four continents across seven different language versions [4]. The subscription revenue of MMORPGs was estimated to be more than a billion in

D. Schuler (Ed.): Online Communities and Social Comput., HCII 2007, LNCS 4564, pp. 375–384, 2007.

2005 [7]. This rapid adoption rate makes MMORPG not only a worthwhile industry but also an increasingly visible research target.

As previous studies suggested, different from playing traditional single player computer games, participating in MMORPGs is primarily a social experience [5, 10, 15]. Particularly, in many role-playing based MMORPGs, games are deliberately set so difficult that players have to collaborate in order to complete in-game missions. To this end, thousands of self-organized player communities have been established to develop a stable collaborative relationship among a smaller set of players. These communities usually organize a number of in-game trips, or raids, to dungeons to fight the monsters and acquire resources, such as weapons, armors, and other artifacts, to fulfill game quests. Members of a player community are, therefore, engaged in an exchange relationship that allows them to contribute and be compensated. As previous research pointed out, one fundamental aspect of social exchange is distributive justice [Adams, 1965 #15;], which refers to the fairness in sharing rewards. Perceived fairness among exchange partners is essential to a social relationship. Perceived inequity was reported to be associated with dissatisfaction and group conflict [16]. In this light, how battleground rewards are shared among raid participants becomes a central issue for the long-term health of a player community. The purpose of this study is to examine the mechanisms of managing distributive fairness in virtual communities and the factors that influence the development of such mechanisms.

2 Perceived Fairness in Organizations

In an extensive body of research on fairness in organizational settings, two types of justice have been identified: distributive justice and procedural justice [11]. As mentioned above, distributive justice refers to the perceived fairness in sharing collective rewards. Literature suggests three rules governing the perceived fairness in outcome distribution: equity, equality, and need [6].

The rule of equity emphasizes on the comparison of input and outcomes. It implies that team members should receive rewards in proportion to their contribution to the team task. The rule of equality, on the other hand, suggests allocating equal amount of reward to all parties regardless of their inputs. Finally the principle of need dictates that reward distribution should be based on relative need of each party. Supports for all three rules functioning in organizations were found in both organizational research and social psychological studies [6].

While this study focuses on the distributive justice, procedural justice plays a role in the community's debates on fairness. Procedural justice concerns the decision making process of reward allocation. It was suggested that decisions on group outcome distribution should be made with consistency and accuracy, and avoid personal bias [9].

This study adopted the three governing principles of distributive justice as well as the concept of procedural justice as guidance for its investigation on reward distribution and fairness management in virtual communities.

3 Method

3.1 Data Collection

This study employed a case study methodology. An active WoW player community, also called "guild", agreed to participate in the study. It will be referred to as DX in this paper. The game, WoW, was selected due to its 39.7% market share [18]. DX was established right before the release of WoW in the fall of 2004. Currently, DX has more than 70 active members from Australia, Europe, and the US. DX members are very active. In a typical week, there are usually two to four guild-organized raids. For each raid, a team will be assembled which usually consists of 20 to 40 members depending on the setting of the dungeon to be visited. For this case study, multiple types of data have been collected. Seven semi-structured interviews were conducted with the guild officers and members. Each interview lasted 30 to 60 minutes. The author also observed live game playing. Finally, the guild discussion archive on the Web was examined.

3.2 Overview of World of Warcraft

WoW is a role-playing game based on the popular Warcraft series. When entering the game, players create virtual characters to explore the fantasyland. During the creation of their characters, players can choose from eight different races and ten different classes. Each race and class has its own special combination of capabilities and skills. Some of them are good at fighting in close range; some of them are specialized in spell casting from a distance. Once the characters are chosen, players can then begin their adventures involving learning skills, acquiring better equipments, fighting monsters, and pursuing quests. However, embedded in the design of the races and classes is the interdependence among players. Individual players have to team up to form a strong enough collective in order to complete major quests or conquering main dungeons. However, the undertaking of a raid is not a casual act. It requires carefully planning and executing among participating players. These teamwork processes occur not only during the actual fighting with monsters, but also before and after each mission. The success of a raid hinges on team coordination and member commitment [8].

4 Reward Distribution in DX

Each time a team goes to a dungeon, it may acquire multiple game items from killed monsters. These items, also called "loots", can enhance the capabilities of a character or fulfill game quests. They can also be sold to other players for in-game currencies or even real dollars. In addition to these material outcomes, participating in the guild also yield social and psychological rewards. Social rewards include various types of social capital such as status, reputation, trust, and friendship. The primary source of psychological reward is the enjoyment of playing the game. While participating in a guild is important to enjoy particular aspects of the game, the guild does not involved in the distribution of the fun of playing. This report will focus on the distribution of material and social rewards.

4.1 Material Rewards Distribution: The Raid Point and Auction System

DX currently uses a raid point and auction system to document the efforts of raid participants and distribute game items gained in raids. Under this system, each raid participant is awarded a specific amount of raid points for the time they spent in a guild-organized raid. Typically, participants can earn one point per hour. These raid points are then used in bidding for loots. Most items gained in a raid are distributed to raid participants via auction. These raid points are also accumulative. For the most part, a common pool approach is adopted in which raid points earned across raids and dungeons are added together. It allows members to "save" their efforts and "spend" them for desired items at a later time and/or in a different dungeon.

From the distributive justice perspective, this raid point and auction system provides a delicate balance among the equity and equality principles. The fact that everyone earns the same amount of raid points for their participation well represents the equality principle. On the other hand, the auction mechanism offers players a great degree of control of their own rewards. It supports the equity rule by allowing raid participant to decide what a fair return is for their efforts.

In addition, the common pool approach is a particular kind of implementation of the raid point system. It implies three types of equality regarding player contributions: equality across players, equality across time, and equality across dungeons. First, everyone's contribution to a raid mission is the same, and, therefore, everyone earns raid points by the same hourly rate. Second, the time spent at a given dungeon is worth the same no matter when the raid occurs. Third, the time spent at a given dungeon is worth the same as the time spent in another dungeon. For the common raid point pool approach to work, all three types of equality need to be accepted by the guild members. However, each of the three types of equality has its own challenge and requires policy remedy.

Contribution equality across players is in general accepted by guild members due to the interdependent nature between different character classes and the difficulty of objective evaluation. However, there are a number of policies aiming at regulating raid-related behaviors. These policies can be seen as attempts to ensure a minimum quality of individual performance.

Contribution equality across time holds most of the cases excepting when a dungeon is new. It requires a lot of time and efforts for DX to figure out the most effective and efficient strategy for conquer a new dungeon. During the exploring stage, failed raid trips were common and, as a result, little loots are gained. To compensate for the low return on game items, DX constantly award extra bonus points for trips to new dungeons.

Finally, contribution equality across dungeon is the one that has been challenged most often, especially when the differences between dungeons widen. Please see below in subsection 5.2 for further discussion.

4.2 Social Rewards Distribution

In addition to the social relationships cultivated via participating in guild activities, DX provides a couple of explicit social rewards. First, experienced and interested players may be promoted to raid leaders who will be responsible to make tactical decisions during a raid and expect all raid participants to follow. Currently, new raid leaders are nominated and consented by the guild leadership. Second, DX also awards its members who accumulate the highest total raid points with a valuable unique game item in recognition of their contributions to the guild. This recognition can be seen to compensate the inability of the auction system to provide fair return for excessive contribution.

5 Fairness Management

The management of fairness regarding reward distribution is most clearly manifested in various guild policies and norms. Through the proposition, discussion, and revision of related policies, the perceived fairness was negotiated, debated, and confirmed. Of particular interest are those policies addressing two distinct dimensions: behavior regulation and resource management. The dimension of behavior regulation deals with the contribution aspect in an exchange relationship. The resource management policies address issues in the distribution aspect. This section will begin by identifying policy categories within each dimension. Following, the emerging principles in framing policy debates will be articulated. Finally, the structural features of the game environment and the guild that triggered policy discussion will be discussed.

5.1 Behavior Regulation

As discussed above, the way DX implemented its raid point system implies that everyone's stay in a dungeon makes the same level of contribution to the raid mission. Therefore, each participant is awarded the same amount of raid points. To ensure the performance equality across players, it is necessary to control the quality of input by raid participants. To this end, DX has established policies on issues related to qualification, attendance, and obedience.

Qualification policies concern the membership status. To be admitted to DX, applicants need to participate in the guild activities for a four-week observation period, be sponsored by four guild members, and be voted in by guild members on a super majority ground (80%). As researchers suggested, personnel selection was important in facilitating trust relationship in virtual organizations [14]. By choosing those who are trustworthy to work with, the group reduces the risk of receiving sub-optimal input. DX's tight membership admission policy works in the same manner. It attempts to control the most important input of raid missions – the players.

In addition to personnel control, DX also adopts various policies to regulate raid-related behaviors. Due to the highly interdependent nature of raid task, attendance is one of the most important aspects of raid coordination. DX offers sign-up raid point bonus to encourage the disclosure of availability as well as commitment from interested members. The guild also applies raid point penalties to those who reserve a spot but do not show up at the raid time or those who leave the raid early.

Moreover, all raid team members are asked to unconditionally follow the order of the raid leader. Conquering a dungeon consists of a series of battles with monsters. Each battle may require a different strategy detailing the division of labors, the position of each player, and the timing of every move. This delicate and complicate endeavor can easily fail due to one player's uncoordinated action. As a preventive measure, a severe penalty will be applied to those who do not adhere to the leader's instructions.

Overall, these behavior-regulating policies aim to ensure the contribution by each raid participant to meet a minimum standard. They provide important support for implementing the equality rule in the raid point system.

5.2 Resource Management

Resource management policies deal with the distribution of group outcomes. While there are several advantages of relying on auction for sharing rewards, there are also a number of potential market failures. To address the pitfalls, DX established rules covering three different aspects of outcome distribution: market segregation, item filter, and pricing. Each will be discussed below.

First, the issue of market segregation is directly related to the common raid point approach, and , more specifically, the contribution equality across dungeons. In WoW, each dungeon offers different class-specific items. A player may never find suitable equipment to his or her character class in a dungeon and, therefore, there is little incentive for the player to visit that particular dungeon. One common raid point pool resolves this participation issue by allowing players to spend their raid points across different dungeons. However, this arrangement also makes the time spent in easier dungeons equivalent to time spent in harder ones. When the differences between dungeons increase, it becomes more difficult to hold this particular arrangement. Indeed, DX set up a separate pool for a specific dungeon where only 20-member teams are allowed instead of the normal 40-person groups. The expansion set, which offers new tier of game items and lowers team size limit, also brought a couple of changes. For the new 25-person team events, DX establish another new raid point pool. As for the 10-person event, it was decided that the participants themselves without the guild intervention would determine loots.

Second, while most items acquired in a raid are distributed via auction, there are several exceptions. As mentioned earlier, certain unique items may be reserved and offered as social rewards for top performing members. In addition, the distribution of "legendary" items, which are rare and powerful, does not subject to the auction. Instead, they are decided by the guild leadership. Moreover, game items with specific utilities to raid missions will also be shielded from the auction and deposited to a guild repository for later use. Together, these rules work as filters between the loot items and the auction system to address a potential market problem -- the auction procedure sends items to players who value them the most rather than those who can produce the most impacts to the guild raids. Therefore, to the benefit of the guild, certain items are not distributed via bidding, but, instead, exchanged for commitment to future guild activities. The following policy regarding the Warlock Bag fully illustrates the point.

> "The core leather for the warlock soul shard bags will be given out to warlocks for free, [...] This only applies to mains who are active in raids [...] Further, they will be expected to bring the bag to raids *full* of shards."

Third, another intervention to the auction market in DX is its minimum bid policy. The minimum bid policy was implemented at the end of 2005. Prior to that, anyone could bid an item for as little as one raid point. In a well-explored dungeon, bidding competition was low since most veterans had collected all the loots they wanted. As a result, new members could acquire equipments with very low cost. However, it also led to increasing bidding pressure in new dungeons because all the raid points saved by the new comers could be used to compete for new equipments. This was perceived as "unfair" by the veterans as articulated in the quote below.

> "I am more than happy for anyone new to get all their items for 1 [raid point] or even for free, so in that regard I am happy for them not to have to work as hard as others have for those items. The issue has solely been that in return for us giving them free loot, we have to work even harder to get loot ourselves."

In response, a tiered minimum bid system was implemented with the lowest bid increased to 10 raid points. As the guild leader justifying the new policy, it was claimed that "minimum bids even the field so that there is some time/reward investment even if you're the only one that needs a given item." In other words, the minimum bid policy is a compromise between the need principle and the equity principle.

5.3 Guiding Principles

Upon examining the community discussion on policies related to reward distribution, six norms or arguments had been mentioned repeatedly. The three rules of distributive justice were evident in its implementation of the raid point system and related policies as discussed above. In addition, procedural justice, task efficiency and effectiveness, as well as community identity also emerged as main factors shaping perceived fairness. These ideas provided guiding frameworks in which fairness was negotiated and consented.

Procedural justice concerns about the process of distributing group outcomes. All guild members should be subject to the same process and regulations. The guild has frequently cited this principle and resisted suggestions to deal with negative behaviors on case-by-case bases. For example, in the discussion of the leaving early penalty, one guild officer stated, "general guild policies are much better than singling individuals out arbitrarily. [...] It's really hard to be objective and fair with that sort of policy in place." A number of members also expressed similar emphasis on procedural justice and posted comments like this one: "everyone is put on the same level and given the same penalties which is fair. ... Everyone in DA should be given equal punishment just as we all get equal bonuses."

In addition, how raids can be run effectively and efficiently is also an important factor to be considered for both behavior regulation and resource management policies. Opportunistic or anti-disciplinary behaviors may cause extra coordination efforts, extra waiting time of teammates, and even the whole raid to fail. As one DX member put it in discussing the leaving early penalty, "right now, only the raid is paying the price for a choice you get to make. I think it's perfectly acceptable to have both parties suffer a bit." That is to say, if people cause the cost of raid to increase or the expected outcomes to decrease, they need to pay for it. By the same token, people who can reduce the raid cost or increase the likelihood of raid success should be compensated by the guild. This argument also lends support to the item filter policies discussed above.

Moreover, how the guild perceives itself has direct impacts on how fairness is calculated. For example, whether or not a community adopts a hardcore (vs. casual) guild identity relates to the level of participation expected from each member, and, therefore, influences the perceived deservedness of rewards. When a community adopts an identity of "free trade", it prides itself on facilitating individual growth via collective help. As a result, the community will stash away resources to distribute to members with relatively under-developed game characters. The fairness of this exchange is based on the need principle and evaluated against potential future contribution from the beneficiaries to the community.

DX identifies itself as "a raiding guild, but not a powergamer guild" in its official charter document. This particular community identity was constantly mentioned in the debates of policies. For example, before the implementation of the raid point bidding system, many guild members voiced their objection based on the believe that the system would turn the guild from a "laid-back, easy-going" one to a "a 'professional' hardcore gamer guild." Arguments based on the guild identity also appeared in the discussion of leaving early penalty. One dissent member proposed a looser version with a comment saying "even then it sounds like we're getting too hardcore for my liking". Another member also posted to question the fitness between the guild identity and this stricter behavior regulation: "didn't you say we are not a hardcore guild? [...] why should a NON hardcore guild take away our points? Hmmmmmmmm" Overall, different community identities prompt people to consider the issue of fairness differently and may favor different distribution principles.

5.4 Structural Factors

Guild policies did not rise in a void. Often times they were proposed in response to changes in the guild or the game. In particular, four structural features of the game environment, including task characteristics, raid team size, reward tiers, and loot placement, were observed to give rise to various policies. Task characteristic is an important factor. As discussed above, high level of task interdependence of raid activity is part of the reason to accept performance equality across players.

Additionally, uneven loot placement across dungeons furthers the interdependence among players. As mentioned above, many game items are class specific. However, any given dungeon does not offer loots to all classes. This uneven allocation requires members to help each other out even if it means to visit dungeons with little reward expectation. Consequently, it supports the contribution equality across dungeons.

Moreover, changes in raid team size and loot tiers may create significant differences between dungeons to challenge the assumption of contribution equality across dungeons and trigger market segregation as discussed above.

Evidence also demonstrates the importance of structural features of the guild, such as guild size and member structure. When a guild grows bigger, more formal organization is needed [17]. Managing fairness via returning personal favors or turn taking within a small clan is not adequate for a large community. Indeed, in the discussion prior to the implementation of the raid point system, several members advocated the view that "with a guild this size we really need a bit more structure." The size of the guild necessitated formal structure to handle reward distribution.

In addition, the composition of group members also matters. The idea of a raid point system was thought to be disadvantageous to casual players. The different perspectives on fairness were made clear by both the casual player and serious gamer camps in the discussion. Similarly, new comers and veterans split their opinions on the minimum bid policy. While veterans thought minimum bids were fair price to ask, new guild members considered themselves unfairly taxed to protect veterans' bidding advantage. The evidence indicates that member composition and relative political power of each member subgroup will then influence how different perspectives can be merged to guide the design and implementation of reward distribution policies.

6 Conclusion

This study provides a snapshot on how an online gamer community managed fairness in reward distribution. Several contributions are made to further our understanding in this area. First, the implementation of a formal reward distribution system reflects particular distribution principles. Additionally, results showed that how the guild manages fairness is constantly evolving in the form of new policy initiation or policy revisions. Various community policies regarding behavior regulation and resource management were introduced to patch up potential pitfalls of the reward distribution system and fine-tune fairness management. Second, in addition to equity, equality, and need, three additional guiding principles emerged in fairness debates were identified including procedural justice, task efficiency and effectiveness, and community identity. Third, a number of structural features of the game environment as well as the guild were recognized to have impacts on policy choices related to fairness management.

Overall, the findings identify important aspects of fairness management in virtual communities. They can serve as a blueprint for future studies. Further research is needed to expand the catalog in each aspect, as well as validate the findings in large population. Additionally, considering the importance of player communities to individual players' game experience [17], it is imperative for game developers to provide better help to player communities. This study can also serve as basis to generate propositions to further the development of game community support.

References

1. Adams, J.S.: Inequity in social exchange. In: Berkowitz, L. (ed.) Advances in Experimental Social Psychology, pp. 267–299. Academic Press, New York (1965)
2. Alexander, S., Ruderman, M..: The role of procedural and distributive justice in organizational behavior. Social Justice Research 1(2), 177–198 (1987)
3. Arnold, T., Spell, C.S.: The relationship betweeen justice and benefits satisfaction. Journal of Business & Psychology 20(4), 599–620 (2006)
4. Blizzard, E.: World of Warcraft surpasses 8 million subscribers worldwide (2007)
5. Brown, B., Bell, M.: CSCW at play: ' There' as a collaborative virtual environment. In: CSCW'04, ACM, Chicago, Illinois, USA (2004)

6. Cohen, R.L.: Distributive justice:Theory & research. Social Justice Research 1, 19–40 (1987)
7. Intellegence, D.: Who will benefit from the growth of online game subscription revenue (2006)
8. Jang, C.-Y.: Supporting collaborative fighting – A case study of a massively multiplayer online game user community. In: 7th Asian Pacific Computer Human Interaction Conference, Taipei, Taiwan (2006)
9. Leventhal, G.S.: What should be done with equity theory? New approaches to the study of fairness in social relationship. In: Gergen, K.J., Greenberg, M.S., Willis, R.H. (eds.) Social Exchange: Advances in Theory and Research, pp. 27–55. Plenum, New York (1981)
10. Lin, H., Sun, C.-T., Tinn, H.-H.: Exploring clan culture: Social enclaves and cooperation in online gaming. In: Level Up Conference, Utrecht, The Netherlands (2003)
11. McFarlin, D., Sweeney, P.D.: Distributive justice and procedural justice as predictors of satisfaction with personal and organizational outcomes. Academy of Management Journal 35(3), 626–637 (1992)
12. Molm, L.D.: Theories of social exchange and exchange networks. In: Ritzer, G., Smart, B. (eds.) Handbook of social theory, pp. 260–272. Sage, London (2001)
13. Moorman, R.H.: Relationship between organizational justice and organizational citizenship behaviors: Do fairness perceptions influence employee citizenship? Journal of Applied Psychology 76(6), 845–855 (1991)
14. O'Leary, M.W.J., Orlikowski, W.J., Yates, J.: Distributed work over the centuries: Trust and Control in the Hudson's Bay company, 1670-1826. In: Hinds, P., Kiesler, S. (eds.) Distributed Work, pp. 27–54. MIT Press, Cambridge, MA (2002)
15. Seay, A.F., et al.: Project Massive 1.0: Organizational commitment, sociability and extraversion in massively multiplayer online games. In: Level-Up, Utrecht: Digital Games Research Association (2003)
16. Wall, J.V.D., Nolan, L.L.: Small group conflict: A look at equity, satisfaction, and styles of conflict management. Small Group Research 18(2), 188–211 (1987)
17. Williams, D., et al.: From tree house to barricks: The social life of guilds in World of Warcraft. Games and Culture 1(4), 338–361 (2006)
18. www.mmogchart.com Market Share by MMOG (2006)

Mobile Social Software for the Developing World

Beth E. Kolko[1], Erica Johnson[2], and Emma Rose[1]

[1] Department of Technical Communication, University of Washington, Seattle, WA
[2] Department of Political Science, University of Washington, Seattle, WA
{bkolko,ejj3,ejrose}@u.washington.edu

Abstract. This paper discusses how the importance of social networks for performing everyday tasks in the developing world leads to new considerations of the utility of social networking software (SNS). The paper presents some results from a multi-year, multi-method study in Central Asia that tracks patterns of technology adoption and adaptation, as well as shifts in media consumption and information seeking. Our results suggest SNS is a particularly compelling approach in resource-constrained environments (broadly defined) as a way to leverage and systematize the ad hoc processes people develop to navigate their everyday lives and information ecology.

Keywords: Mobile phones, Internet use, technology adoption, Central Asia, social networks, social networking software, information seeking.

1 Introduction

This paper explores the importance of traditional social networks and trust in sources of information in order to inform the design of mobile social software applications in digitally emergent societies. This work is part of a multi-year study of information and communication technologies (ICTs) and their usage in Central Asia, specifically the countries of Kazakhstan, Kyrgyzstan, Tajikistan, and Uzbekistan. This project, the Central Asia + Information and Communications Technologies Project (CAICT), began with exploratory work in Uzbekistan in 2000, and has since expanded to the general region. The CAICT project uses a multi-method approach that incorporates broad social surveys, interviews, ethnographic observation, policy monitoring, web archiving, monitoring and analysis of chat sites, focus groups, and design ethnography. The fine-grained understanding of ICT usage patterns that emerges from this work provides background information that can inform innovative design approaches to new hardware, software, and services for the developing world. In particular, the results presented in this paper focus on pre-existing patterns of ICT usage and relate those findings to how social networks function in offline contexts— in particular, to how people get information and what information sources they trust. The real-world dependency on social networks that has emerged as a theme throughout this research points to the value of developing applications that leverage social relationships in a variety of ways. To further explore this emerging trend, we conducted a design ethnography in Kyrgyzstan in July 2006. The design ethnography

D. Schuler (Ed.): Online Communities and Social Comput., HCII 2007, LNCS 4564, pp. 385–394, 2007.
© Springer-Verlag Berlin Heidelberg 2007

activities were specifically aimed at exploring both the functional importance of social networks in people's lives across multiple domains as well as gaining a more nuanced understanding of the ICT ecology within which they live.

2 Methodology

Most of the findings reported here are based on a broad social survey that was conducted throughout Central Asia in January–March 2006 and based on pilot survey work in Uzbekistan in 2002–2003 and in Kyrgyzstan in 2003–2004. The CAICT project designed the survey instrument and contracted the survey firm BRIF Research Group, located in Almaty, Kazakhstan, to administer the survey. The survey was administered to 4,000 respondents, aged 15 and older: 1,000 subjects in each of four countries: Kazakhstan, Kyrgyzstan, Tajikistan, and Uzbekistan. The survey sample was based on census information on age, gender, ethnicity, and geographic location released by the government of each country. The sample includes 50 sampling locations, and 12–29 respondents were interviewed in urban and rural areas from several regions of each country.

In addition to exploring patterns of ICT adoption and adaptation in Central Asia, the survey also focuses on the information ecology of individuals, their patterns of different media usage, and issues of trust in sources. The survey was administered in Russian and other regional/national languages to residents throughout each country. In addition to the general sampling scheme, a three-stage process was used to select respondents:

- Probability Proportional to Size sample of Primary Sampling Units (PSU);
- Consecutive random sampling of households in determined PSU;
- Selection of a respondent using Kish Grid method.

Because Internet use rates in the region tend to be quite low, most of the questions are geared for the general population and address information seeking behavior and communication patterns across traditional media. The survey also contains questions about attitudes towards the Internet, which were administered to all respondents. A separate section on Internet usage patterns was administered only to respondents who indicated they use the Internet.

This research is also supported by ethnographic observation conducted by members of the U.S. research team and local researchers and focused primarily on public use of ICTs. Observational data includes field notes and photographs and is used to provide explanatory background with respect to everyday life in the region and technology use.

As mentioned above, much of the survey focuses on social networks and information channels, and results from multiple data collection activities of the project indicate that better understanding the web of connections within which people live can productively inform approaches to technology design. Our work throughout this project demonstrates that looking at resource-constrained environments reveals certain patterns related to dependency on social networks. This finding is relevant for a variety of resource-constrained environments, and Central Asia is an excellent site for such an investigation because of the interplay of resource issues; the region can be characterized as both an emerging economic market and an information-poor environment. Our findings here open up the question of whether resource-constrained environments are in fact sites where people are more dependent on social networks; this question is outside the scope of this paper, but it is especially interesting in light of how resource constraint becomes an issue in the developed world as we move from the desktop computer to small screen and mobile computing devices.

3 Theoretical Framework

3.1 Social Networks and Post-Soviet Society

Environments vary in their information ecology. Central Asian societies are traditionally characterized by heavy reliance on social networks to acquire information, personal favors, jobs, and consumer goods. In these traditional social networks, the people one knows are important avenues to information, assistance, and goods [1], [2], [3]. Social networks typically consist of extended family, neighbors, and close personal relationships, such as classmates, and are less commonly associated with impersonal ties. Despite the many modernization processes of the Soviet system, the reliance on close and personal social ties actually increased during the Soviet era as society became atomized and distrustful due to the terroristic policies of the communist party and Soviet secret police [4]. Neighborhood committees, traditional community institutions of self-help and dispute arbitration in several of the post-Soviet Central Asian countries, were co-opted by the state during the Soviet era [5], and this co-optation continues today or has discredited and caused the disintegration of the traditional neighborhood networks. As a result of these Soviet legacies, very personalized patterns of social networking became vital for access to information and opportunities in the Soviet era. These types of social networks remain significant today.

These traditional social networks distribute information about local and international news, goods, and services, and they provide important alternatives to tightly regulated state information services. Throughout the Central Asian region, the local governments control the information available in local news media and only report positive or non-controversial stories.[1] Moreover, decaying Soviet telecommunications infrastructure limits the access households have to information. For example, even in urban areas some households still do not have phone lines, and the situation is much worse in rural areas where entire villages may not have landline telephone access. According to data from the International Telecommunication Union, for example, fixed line penetration through the Commonwealth of Independent States is only 37 percent of that in Western Europe [7]. In urban areas, the Internet is present, but expensive and inconvenient, as most use occurs at public access sites such as Internet cafes. Indeed, 48.7 percent of survey respondents who use the Internet indicated that they *usually* do so from Internet cafes. Thus, local residents rely heavily on family and friends for "real" news, a practice that leads to confusion, muddied transmission of information, and rumor, even about

---

[1] In fact, Reporters without Borders has rated Central Asian governments among the world's lowest in press and Internet freedoms, even labeling several of the local governments "enemies of the Internet" [6].

critically important local events such as Kyrgyzstan's Tulip Revolution in March 2005 and the Andijon uprising in Uzbekistan in May 2005. However, mobile phone technologies are rapidly spreading throughout the urban and rural areas of Central Asia [8], and, given the pattern of technology adoption that is emerging, it seems possible that social networking applications for mobile phones could critically contribute to improving access to information and networks for local residents. Fig. 1 compares technology usage across the four countries surveyed, and it demonstrates that mobile phone usage significantly outstrips that of Internet.

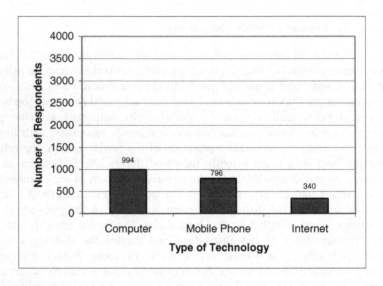

Fig. 1. Number of respondents who indicated using computers, mobile phones, and Internet in Central Asia; N=4,000

Within this context of social structure and technology use, since the collapse of the Soviet Union, western aid programs have devoted concerted efforts to construct the more diffuse types of social networks through the promotion of civil society institutions, such as non-governmental organizations, associations, and clubs.[2] While initially seen as crucial to the post-communist political and economic transitions, these new organizations are also seen as important counterpoints to clan ties and radical Islamic mobilization, which threaten stability in the Central Asian region. In practice, these new organizations are often more responsive to international agendas and donors than to the needs of the local communities [11], [12], [13]. They do not, therefore, supplant the social networks with which individuals navigate their communities. Nevertheless, they have begun to establish important elements of a professionalized "third sector" that might eventually serve as liaisons between state agencies and societal interests. In addition, these organizations are also seen to develop and deepen the impersonal social networks that social networking software

---

[2] These efforts are theoretically motivated by an understanding of a robust civil society as an essential underpinning of successful democratic and economic systems [9], [10].

applications might enhance. In some ways these new organizations are an offline version of what social networking software can be: an externalized resource that aggregates resources for individuals.

3.2 Social Network Software

The critical importance of social networks in post-Soviet Central Asian society reveals an opportunity to imagine the ways in which these existing social networks can be supported by technology. Social network software or services (SNS), broadly conceptualized, refer to the ways in which information and communication technologies are used to leverage, articulate, and extend social networks. The emergence and subsequent growth of SNS has garnered much attention from the media and from researchers, but, more importantly, the rise in use and adoption of SNS by vast numbers of people worldwide highlights its significance and potential.

Currently the most popular types of SNS are web-based and focus primarily on socializing activities. As web-based systems, they are designed and optimized for desktop use. By their current implementation, we can extrapolate that the intended audiences of these sites are individuals with large groups of friends and a significant amount of time to devote to socializing with peers. Based on patterns of use that imply long amounts of time spent on these sites, we can also state that users either own or have access to computers with continuous Internet connections. Some examples of SNS web sites that facilitate socializing—that is, creating and maintaining friendships and seeking dating partners—include Orkut, MySpace, and Friendster [14], which provide ways for individuals to create and share profiles and link between profiles. In doing so, these users explicate existing and expanding social networks that exist both on and offline. Other SNS focus membership around existing established offline communities. For example, in its first iteration, the site Facebook tied membership specifically to established offline communities in the form of educational institutions, like a college or university. Access to the social network was contingent on and restricted to members of an offline community. Research conducted on Facebook found that members used the community network for social searching—looking for a particular person who was already known to them in the offline community, rather than social browsing—looking to meet strangers in the network [15].

A small but growing number of sites are utilizing SNS applications for purposes beyond socializing and friendship building. For example, sites that provide job postings, recruiting, and networking opportunities like Jobster and LinkedIn allow individuals to connect via social networks for the purpose of career advancement. In the United States, the site Prosper.com facilitates lending and borrowing outside of conventional banking systems. Other sites provide alternative social formations, such as meetup.com or provide recommendations of events, like upcoming.org. What has not been fully investigated is how these uses of SNS that push beyond mere socializing can impact or transform traditional structures or practices in people's everyday lives.

The web-based SNS examples above highlight the ways in which ICTs can mediate and enhance social networks. Considering the mobile phone as such a technology is relevant since its basic functionality as a device is one that emphasizes social connections. Mobile devices are social devices, according to Bleeker, "in the degree to which they mediate social relationships, social networks and manage the circulation of culture that sustains such networks." [16] SNS for Mobile, or Mobile Social Software (MoSoSo), examples include applications that allow users to share their location and find others in their immediate or extended social network and broadcast messages, such as Dodgeball, Twitter, or Slam. While these examples are contingent on users checking in or letting the system know their location, other examples of MoSoSo leverage more robust, yet potentially intrusive, situationally-aware technologies such as GPS, phone towers, and Bluetooth which allow individuals to be notified if they are within geographic proximity to others in their network. Some examples include Reno [17], which provides mobile enabled information for parties attempting to rendezvous, and Jabberwocky [18], which ascertains a sense of "familiar strangers" by scanning for nearby mobile phones and Bluetooth-enabled devices to illuminate someone who may be recognizable but who an individual has not spoken to. Finally, the product Serendipity [19] provides a combination of user-created profiles, as we have seen on friendship enhancing websites with situational awareness technologies, to provide matches of individuals who share commonality based on defined attributes and a geographic similarity by being in the same room or building.

As demonstrated above, the genre of SNS provides a variety of opportunities for technology to support social interactions. These interactions are limited to contexts replete with information technology infrastructure and resources. By understanding particular characteristics of lifestyle and usage patterns, and investigating new locations and situations, we can imagine new ways that technology, and in particular, mobile technology, can facilitate meaningful social interactions. Central Asia, with its emerging digital infrastructure and low levels of impersonal social networks, is a prime location for testing new approaches to SNS applications.

4 Study Findings

This section reports findings from the project's 2006 survey. We discuss evidence of the local importance and trustworthiness of social networks and other information sources and the implications for SNS applications.

4.1 Use and Trustworthiness of Information Sources in Central Asia

As discussed above, personal social networks are important sources of information for individuals in Central Asia. A substantial component of our survey was designed to compare the importance of these networks with other types of information sources. In a 2003 pilot test of the survey in Uzbekistan, respondents were asked to rate the importance of information sources such as family, friends and neighbors, television, radio, newspapers, and the Internet on a five point scale (with 1=extremely unimportant and 5=extremely important). Compiling 2003 pilot data and 2006 survey results on Uzbekistan, Wei et al. [20] find that, for Uzbeks, friends and family are second only to television as critical information sources, and that rural residents rely heavily on state television as their only regular information resource from non-local, non-personal sources. Given the bias of government sanctioned media, finding alternative sources of news and information through social mobile software could have important implications for the Central Asian populations.

The 2006 survey conducted throughout four countries of Central Asia asked respondents to state their opinions on the trustworthiness of a variety of personal and media information sources (very trustworthy, trustworthy, untrustworthy, very untrustworthy). Respondents were also asked to report whether they had consulted these information sources within the past week in a variety of domain areas, including health, information about elected officials and official services, commercial purchases, religious news, and local news items. As Fig. 2 and Table 1 below indicate, personal social networks are important information sources throughout the region.

While, generally, all sources of information are seen as trustworthy, personal networks are viewed as most trustworthy. Indeed, nearly 100 percent of respondents rate family as very trustworthy or trustworthy, nearly 90 percent rate friends as very trustworthy or trustworthy, and nearly 80 percent rate neighbors as very trustworthy or trustworthy. By contrast, television, newspapers, radio, and the Internet were seen as less trustworthy sources of information.

In another block of questions, respondents were asked how frequently they used various sources to find information about a variety of topics. These questions provide domain-specific insight into information-seeking patterns (See Table 1). Television was the most commonly consulted source of information, but, as Fig. 2 indicates, information from personal social networks is seen as more reliable and honest.

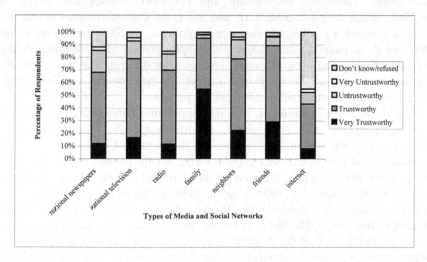

Fig. 2. Trustworthiness of media and social networks as information sources; N=4,000

Table 1. Percentage of respondents who indicated using various sources to find information in six domain areas in the preceding week; N=4,000

Information Source	Local news	Something to buy	Health issue	Elected official	Official service	Religious news
Television	67.6	26.2	40.0	35.1	28.0	36.1
Family	35.8	31.2	34.7	12.4	22.8	21.6
Friends or Neighbors	38.9	26.0	23.4	13.7	20.9	24.9
Newspaper	32.8	14.7	18.3	15.4	12.8	10.0
Radio	26.1	9.0	13.8	12.4	9.7	11.5

5 Discussion

The findings reported above suggest that in digitally emergent Central Asia, social networks are still critically important, but television and other new sources of information and communication technologies can play important supplemental roles. Designing new electronic information sources and social networking applications is more involved than enabling old behaviors with new media. It is necessary to think about a system that leverages experience with social networks and that also takes into account a collective awareness of which information to trust and which viewed more skeptically. Additionally, the survey data indicates that one's "social network" is not a clearly defined entity, even when it is a resource upon which one relies significantly. In other words, the utility of the social network does not correlate with its uniformity. The data in Table 1 demonstrate that "family" and "friends or neighbors" are relied upon in quite different patterns depending on the domain of information under consideration. There are overlapping and concentric circles that define how individuals utilize their social network, and this is the kind of complexity that makes the social network a challenging resource to replicate via SNS. In seeking to better understand these nuances, our design ethnography probed for a detailed picture of what parts of the social network people leveraged for different life tasks. Discussion of those results is beyond the scope of this paper, but they are critical to informing the SNS design guidelines that will result from our project.

As we consider the potential of SNS, it is important to understand the meaning of technology adoption patterns in terms of actual usage. As Fig. 1 demonstrated, mobile use is higher than Internet use in the region. Consequently, it seems important to consider how social networks and mobile phones might productively interact rather than focusing attention on desktop applications. However, it is also important to note here that mobile applications in the developing world are not synonymous with the mobile web. Indeed, there are tremendously innovative applications that use SMS, and it is crucial to recognize the extremely low usage rates of the mobile web in the developing world. In seems much more productive to consider developing mobile applications that dovetail with the existing mobile usage patterns in such regions.

6 Conclusion

This paper has sought to explain some of the underlying societal issues that contribute to a population with strong reliance on personal social networks and to illustrate how such patterns of information seeking can be leveraged by social software. Our goal has been to demonstrate that in resource constrained situations such as those found in the developing world (although not exclusively there), people develop extensive and agile networks of varying levels that allow them to navigate their world successfully.

Coupled with the rapid uptake of mobile phone technology in the developing world and the growing popularity of Internet-based SNS, it seems apparent that social networking applications developed for mobile phones would leverage both existing technology usage patterns and information seeking patterns in the developing world. It is also clear that there are many exigencies beyond socializing that can drive users to MoSoSo. Social networks are already a multiplier for accomplishing tasks; building software to further leverage that relationship could potentially provide significant resources to the populations in question. The key is to situate such applications firmly within an understanding of what drives a reliance on social networks and of how people currently use the technology to which they have access.

References

1. Kandiyoti, D.: Rural Livelihoods and Social Networks in Uzbekistan: Perspectives from Andijan. Central Asian Survey 17(4), 561–578 (1998)
2. Stevens, D.: The Concept and Importance of Social Capital: An Aid to Understanding Uzbekistan in to the 21st Century. Journal of Central Asian Studies 2(2), 42–46 (1998)
3. Kuehnast, K., Nora D.: Better a hundred friends than a hundred rubles? Social networks in transition—the Kyrgyz Republic. World Bank Working Paper #39 (2004)
4. Jowitt, K.: New World Disorder: The Leninist Extinction. University of California Press, Berkeley (1992)
5. Kamp, M.: Mahalla Committees and Social Welfare in Uzbekistan. In: Luong, P.J. (ed.) The Transformation of Central Asia: States and Societies from Soviet Rule to Independence, Cornell University Press, Ithaca (2004)
6. Reporters Sans Frontiers (2004) 2004 Annual Repor http://www.rsf.org
7. International Telecommunication Union (2005) Europe and CIS's telecommunication/ICT markets and trends: 9.
   http://www.itu.int/ITU-D/ict/statistics/at_glance/Europe_RPM_2005.pdf
8. Wei, C., Kolko, B.: Studying mobile phone use in context: Cultural, political, and economic dimensions of mobile phone use. In: Proceedings of the 2005 International Professional Communication Conference, Limerick, Ireland, July 10-13, pp. 205–212. IEEE, Piscataway, NJ (2005)
9. de Tocqueville, A., Reeve, H., Spencer, J.C.: Democracy in America. G. Dearborn & Co, New York (1838)
10. Putnam, R.D.: Making Democracy Work: Civic Traditions in Modern Italy. Princeton University Press, Princeton, NJ (1993)
11. Mendelson, S.E., Glenn, J.K. (eds.): The Power and Limits of NGOs: A Critical Look at Building Democracy in Eastern Europe and Eurasia. Columbia University Press, New York (2002)

12. Henderson, S.L.: Selling Civil Society: Western Aid and the Nongovernmental Organization Sector in Russia. Comparative Political Studies 35(2), 139–167 (2002)
13. Howard, M.M.: The Weakness of Civil Society in Post-Communist Europe. Cambridge University Press, New York (2003)
14. Boyd, D.: Friendster and Publicly Articulated Social Networks. In: Conference on Human Factors and Computing Systems (CHI 2004), April 24-29, pp. 24–29. ACM, Vienna (2004)
15. Lampe, C., Ellison, N., Steinfield, C.: A face(book) in the crowd: social Searching vs. social browsing. In: Proceedings of the 2006 conference on Computer supported cooperative work, Banff, Alberta, Canada, November 04-08, ACM, New York (2006)
16. Bleecker, J.: What's your social doing in my mobile? Design Patterns for Mobile Social Software. In: WWW2006 Workshop "MobEA IV—Empowering the Mobile Web." May 23, 2006, Edinburgh Scotland (2006)
17. Smith, I.: Social-Mobile Applications. IEEE Computer 38(4), 84–85 (2005)
18. Paulos, E., Goodman, E.: The Familiar Stranger: Anxiety, Comfort, and Play in Public Places. In: Proc. Human Factors in Computing Systems (CHI 2004), pp. 223–230. ACM Press, New York (2004)
19. Eagle, N., Pentland, A.: Social serendipity: mobilizing social software. Pervasive Computing 4(2), 28–34 (2005)
20. Wei, C.Y., Spyridakis, J.H., Kolko, B.E.: 2006, Information-Seeking in Digitally Emergent Society: A Case of Old Wine in New Bottles? (Unpublished paper, In preparation)

An E-Health Community of Practice: Online Communication in an E-Health Service Delivery Environment

Elsa Marziali[1] and Tira Cohene[2]

[1] 246 Bloor Street, University of Toronto, Toronto, Ontario M5S 1A1, Canada
elsa.marziali@utoronto.ca
[2] Microsoft
tirac@windows.microsoft.com

Abstract. Results of a series of studies of consumer response to online interactive communication and video-based technologies for the delivery of health care services are presented. The studies include development, evaluation and usability studies of two interactive, video conferencing web sites; Caring for Others© [CFO] designed for older adults caring for a family member with a chronic disease, and Caring for Me© [CFM] designed to support an e-health program for obese adolescents. Stages of web site development, usability analyses, and evaluation of consumer response to the customized e-health programs are reported.

Keywords: E-health, Internet, interactive communication, health risks, benefits.

1 Introduction

Advances in computer and communication technologies have made it possible to provide, world wide, information and health support programs to consumers. However, computer-based health support systems are provided in an unregulated digital world. Despite the fact that government health jurisdictions and health professional organizations have developed guidelines for the development of technology-based health service programs there is no regulatory body or monitoring system that holds organizations accountable for the authenticity of health information provided or the standards of health services provided. [1], [2]. Consumer guidelines for evaluating the risks associated with the adoption of web-based health information and therapies have been developed, but the frequency with which they are accessed and applied is unknown [3]. Consequently, the consumer of web-based health information may be at risk for negative health outcomes due to a) the inaccuracy of the information, b) consumer use of information in ways that compromise prescribed treatments, and c) consumer purchase of health remedies that, despite claims on the web, are ineffective and may interact negatively with prescribed medications [4], [5]. These potential negative consequences for consumers can be avoided when health professionals adhere to evidence-based protocols for the development, implementation, and evaluation of

D. Schuler (Ed.): Online Communities and Social Comput., HCII 2007, LNCS 4564, pp. 395–405, 2007.

Internet-based health information and therapy programs. In addition, specific characteristics of different consumer groups need to be taken into account when building e-health programs and protocols.

2 Background

There are many challenges to the design, development, and implementation of Internet-based health care interventions that target the needs of consumer groups with specific health care needs. The problems are compounded when a) the consumers, as for example older adults, have had little to no prior computer usage experience and possess even less knowledge about the complexities of the Internet; b) the authenticity of the health information exchanged is unknown; c) consumer identity and health information is unprotected; and d) the health benefits of the using the Internet to access and exchange information are unknown. In the development of any Internet-based health care program emphasis needs to be placed on knowing the needs/abilities of the end users. Older adults approach the Internet with motivations, knowledge, and skills that differ from younger adults and adolescents. Seniors in their seventies and eighties may not have used computers prior to retirement and may reject the idea of acquiring new skills late in life. In contrast, most adolescents are highly skilled and have considerable experience in accessing the Internet and using an array of software for communication, uploading and downloading content, playing games, and engaging in virtual reality space. Thus, the design, content development, and functionality of web-based healthcare programs must address the end users' prior experiences with using technology as well as consumer-specific barriers to full engagement with any e-health program of care. Older adults are the fastest growing novices to computer use and they access the Internet in increasing numbers, largely to obtain health-related information and for travel planning. In conjunction with the incremental use of computers by seniors, software developers have begun to address the common characteristics of aging that frequently impede the older adult's effective use of technology. Failing eyesight, problems with muscle coordination, lags in learning, and retaining new concepts and behaviors contribute to seniors' difficulties with managing computer hardware and software. Significant advances have been made to modify hardware and screen interface to accommodate the limitations of persons with physical disabilities (e.g. Microsoft Assistive Technology; Apple Computer Worldwide Disabilities Solutions Group; IBM National Support Center for Persons with Disabilities [6]). However these technical enhancements do not insure efficient and unambiguous communication between an older adult and a healthcare provider when the Internet is used as the platform for the exchange of information. Preferable is a technology-based environment that replicates, in large measure, the typical clinic-based face-to-face encounter between a professional care provider and patient. In other words, when health information is communicated using computer-Internet technology how is it interpreted and applied? What are the risks for misinterpretation and subsequent negative health consequences for the patient? Do patients involved in e-health programs benefit in ways comparable to clinic-based health care programs?

Despite the fact that the Internet supports thousands of web sites with information about health, disease, and remedies, the interpretation of numerous web-based versions of disease diagnoses and treatments, and judgments as to their authenticity, are the responsibility of the consumer. Yet little is known about how Internet-based health information is understood or applied by individuals to manage their health concerns. The Spry Organization (www.spry.org) [3] has generated guidelines for judging the merits of health information web sites but the effectiveness of the guidelines in helping consumers distinguish between accurate and faulty information is unknown. In addition to being at risk of accessing inaccurate information, older adults may be especially vulnerable to persuasive advertisements about the benefits of unregulated remedies frequently promoted by vendors who develop and support many health information web sites [4]. The challenges in designing e-health programs for adolescents diverge significantly from those that need to be addressed when providing healthcare for seniors via the Internet. Adolescents have the technical knowledge and skills and in most instances surpass those of the professional health care providers with whom they communicate. For the adolescent consumer the challenge is to design web pages and content that will capture and maintain their interest for the duration of the e-health intervention program. There are also risks to consider when dialogue between the adolescent and the health care provider is dependent on Internet-based communication tools such as text messaging, voice over IP, or video meetings. Given the adolescent's developmental propensity to mistrust adults, the possibilities for miscommunication, misunderstanding, and imprecise communication are many. Furthermore, adolescents are more vulnerable to the views of peers in situations where they are risk of being perceived as being 'different'. Consequently e-health programs that use chat rooms or group video conferencing tools need to include options for securing anonymity when building the web platform for delivering health care interventions to adolescents.

3 System Development

Our initial e-health program was developed to address the needs of spousal caregivers of older adults with chronic disease (Alzheimer's, Parkinson, Stroke). The aim was to replicate in an Internet environment the typical clinic-based support group programs provided for caregivers. A password protected website Caring for Others© [CFO] was built based on usability guidelines (Web Content Accessibility Guidelines, 1999 [7]; Web Accessibility Initiative (WAI), 2003 [8]) that specify design criteria for older adult users. It includes large, obvious icon images and uncluttered pages with subtle color contrasts. Use of the keyboard is minimized. The web site provides links to a) online disease-specific handbooks that provide information about each disease, it's course and it's management as well as self care strategies for the caregiver; b) an e-mail link with pull-down list of e-mail addresses for peer group members (within disease groups) and health care providers; c) a threaded discussion forum; d) a video conferencing link for one-on-one communication; and e) a video conferencing link for group interactions. Parallel with the development of the web site, a simplified computer training manual was developed with a primary emphasis on strategies for negotiating the web site links. Through an iterative test, re-test process we obtained usability feedback from caregivers in a computer lab format. Based on participants' responses we modified both the web site and training manual. The aim throughout was to simplify the steps for accessing and negotiating the web site links. In particular, the initial design and modifications to the web site addressed the physical and behavioral characteristics of older adults that could potentially impede ease in accessing and negotiating the web site. This approach was especially important for addressing the concerns of spousal caregivers who had not used computers previously.

Web Site Technical Development: The Caring for Others© [CFO] website offers innovative features not seen before on websites for seniors and was built in a Microsoft environment that utilizes traditional ASP (Active Server Pages) for much of the functionality. Latterly, ASP.NET was incorporated in the final version. To meet the security needs of the user, access information is stored in a Microsoft Access database that can easily be upsized to a Microsoft SQL Server database when necessary. Beyond the traditional form-based functionality, the CFO website also offers video-conferencing, and video chat interaction. The video components were built using Macromedia's Flash Communication Server. This technology allowed us to build our own video conferencing environment that did not require any client desktop software installation. The user only required the free Macromedia plug-in in order to use the video conferencing and video chat components. The Flash Communication Server acts as the hub that manages the incoming and outgoing streams. The conferencing component was built with efficiency and ease-of-use as primary goals so as to meet the unique challenges experienced by the caregiver users. The number of streams has been kept to a minimum with only one outgoing stream at any one time and this is controlled by the conference facilitator. As many as nine viewing streams can be assigned. The outgoing stream is passed around by the facilitator to whoever is the live speaker, while the remaining participants view the central stream. The active window picture located in the centre of the screen (160 by 120 pixels) has high resolution and little to no lag in the voice component. The active window is surrounded by video snapshots of the participants and facilitator. The video components of the web site require high speed Internet connections for all users. In addition to the video communication components, the site offers access to disease specific educational materials, a threaded discussion forum, a personal message centre, a conferencing scheduling application, a contact form, personal profiles, video streaming, and a complete administration component that allows maintenance over all aspects of the site. The web site includes libraries of educational materials – power point presentations and videos. Currently, six videos portraying care giving scenarios for caregivers of dementia patients are available for viewing at times convenient to the participant. The web site database is used to log traffic throughout the site for research purposes. We also customized a tool that allows the researchers to review the recorded conferences. The video footage is downloaded and burned to a CD that includes functionality for 'coding' the video footage. With SAVI Viewer developed by MeLogic (www.savisys.com) [9] it is possible to score, comment, or code at precise moments in the video. The Caring for Me© [CFM] web site is a modified version of the CFO web site. The same features are available – information handbooks specific to the needs of the particular consumer group, the threaded discussion forum, the e-mail and the video conferencing links. The CFM has been customized according to the characteristics of each user group. It has been used with isolated, community dwelling older adults needing social connection and monitoring of health status.

Currently it is being modified for an obese adolescent group. The e-mail feature has been omitted since adolescents have independent e-mail addresses and can choose whether or not to disclose them to other teenagers in their e-health support group. In the video conferencing mode the adolescent participant has the option of having their own picture posted (as is the practice with the older adult user groups) or substitute an avatar of their choosing. During video conferencing sessions the avatar would appear in the circle and move in and out of the active window while the voice of the adolescent would be heard. Two other features have been added to the CFM customized for the adolescent group. Six animations of typical scenarios involving obese adolescents and their peers have been developed. These will be available for streaming by the facilitator during specific video conferencing sessions. The animated scenarios can be viewed as vehicles for stimulating active exchange of information among the group participants. A second feature consists of personal eating patterns and activity diary imbedded in the web site. A list of foods color coded as to their caloric values is provided so that the adolescent can enter the color code with each entry of food consumed throughout the day. Similarly, the adolescent can choose from a list of physical activities with estimates of calories burned to record daily activities. Only the adolescent will have access to the diary and can choose whether or not to share it with the other group members. Parallel with the e-health support group program for the adolescents, Internet-based video conferencing support groups will be offered to their parents using the CFM web site. For this program we have included an information handbook for the parents with a focus on the health risks of adolescent obesity as well as strategies for changing family life patterns that will enable the adolescent to alter his/her own eating patterns and activity choices.

Web Site Security: To insure security of the web site users and content we decided to make the CFO web site accessible only through the use of unique passwords for each user. Consequently the web site is not and will never be available in the public Internet domain. Within the web site there are three levels of security; the site administrator has access to all links and user groups, the professional facilitators have access only to the members within the groups that they facilitate, and the participants have access only to the members within their own group. All e-mail messages, threaded discussion text, and video conference sessions are encrypted and stored on the server. Subsequently, all information is copied to CDs and stored in locked cabinets for analyses. Following data analyses all electronic data is destroyed.

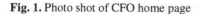

Fig. 1. Photo shot of CFO home page   Photo shot of video conf group

System Evaluation: Usability: Following the completion of the first caregiver online support group a usability study was implemented. Each of the five participants were interviewed and asked to respond to a series of questions about specific web site features and their ease of use. Overall, the participants found the large icons, color contrasts, and uncluttered pages easy to follow. Also the large 'GO' buttons insured that they could move forward and backwards without getting 'lost'. Because of the number of incoming and outgoing streams during the video conferencing meeting there were lags and sometimes a participant would be 'bounced' out of the session requiring them to log on again. This proved to be very frustrating for the participants. Frequently the problem with maintaining contact with the web site was due to Internet server used by the participant. Multiple Internet server providers were used by the participants depending on location and consequently were out of the control of the web master and the server hosting the CFO web site. From the participants' feedback some features of the web site were modified. A major change had to do with adding the participants' pictures to the page that supported the group video conferencing. In the first version of the video conferencing link each participant followed instructions to take their picture (web cam mounted) prior to entering the group. The picture then appeared in a circle surrounding the central active window. This step in the process proved to be challenging frequently resulting in errors, frustration and 'giving up' with regard to participating that day. This feedback resulted in a modification where we now archive pictures of all of the participants so that when they enter the video conferencing group their picture is programmed to appear in the circle surrounding the active window. In summary, the usability study following the initial pilot trial of the Internet supported video conferencing support group was essential for making important modifications to the web site.

System Evaluation: Older Adult Response: The initial pilot study with older adult caregivers yielded the following: the modified version of the CFO web site, an Intervention Training Manual and a Computer Training Manual. These program products were developed to insure that during the next phase of evaluation of the e-health program the procedures would be carried out reliably. A feasibility study was implemented with the goal of evaluating the responses of a cohort of caregivers to using the Internet to obtain health information and participate in a video conferencing support group. The study was located in two remote areas of two Canadian provinces. Thirty four caregiver-care recipient dyads were recruited (17 at each site with 5 to 6 caregivers of persons in each of three disease groups – Alzheimer, Parkinson and stroke). With informed, signed consent the caregivers agreed to baseline and follow up interviews as well as having the video conferencing sessions archived for subsequent analyses. Technicians at each site installed equipment (computer, video camera, audio headset and high-speed Internet connection) in the homes of all participants and provided two computer training sessions using the project Computer Training Manual. Using the Intervention Training Manual a clinician at each site was trained to carry out the intervention. To insure reliable adherence to the model of intervention the facilitators received weekly supervision using televideo conferencing facilities at each of the participating sites. Subsequent to the 10 facilitated sessions, in each group a member assumed the facilitator role and the groups continued to meet weekly for an additional period of three months. Research assistants interviewed the caregiver participants in their homes prior to participating in the online group intervention and six months later. At follow up they were asked to comment on their experiences with using computers for communicating with other caregivers in a support group and to compare this experience with meeting in face-to-face groups.

Data analyses included content coding of the archived video sessions to insure that the online intervention had been carried out reliably according to the strategies specified in the Intervention Training Manual. Two raters independently coded a sample of video recorded sessions from each group. Inter rater agreement ranged between 85 and 90%. The results showed that each facilitator carried out the online intervention within each group in a reliable fashion. In addition, an open coding method applied to the archived video sessions of each group was used for extracting salient themes across phases of each of the participant groups. These analyses yielded four major themes a) group bonding and mutual acknowledgement and respect for the collective knowledge about their relatives' disease and coping capacities, b) insights into personal emotional and cognitive processing barriers that interfered with managing their lives in the context of care giving, c) processing the meanings of the changing relationship with the dependent relative, and d) anticipatory mourning of the loss of the relative as reflected in planning transfer to a long term care facility. These themes replicated those observed in clinic-based face-to-face support groups for caregivers of persons with chronic diseases. Of particular note was the fact that the group members formed positive bonds with each other despite the limitations of the video conferencing mode that allowed only one person at a time in the active window.

In follow up interviews we asked about the participants' response to the website. Seventy-eight percent indicated that the web site was very easy to use, for example, "Yes, because I think I was taught pretty well"; "It was clearly laid out"; and "It was very easy, very user friendly". When asked what they liked most about the website, some of the caregivers responded, "That it was accessible...a lot of great information and being able to have visual contact with other group members"; "One of the things I liked was the larger print" and "The meetings that we had on the website were terrific". When asked what they liked least about the website, they referred to initial frustrations in accessing the website due to problems at the server end. When subsequently the website was transferred to a provider that specialized in supporting Macromedia Flash Communication Server the problems in linking with the video conferencing mode were eliminated.

We computed the frequencies for total logins by each of the caregiver user groups as well as the frequencies of use of each of the web site links over a period of eight months. The total logins ranged between 2500 (Dementia group) and 5000 (Stroke group). Once logged onto the website the frequencies with which the links were accessed ranged between 15,000 (Dementia group) and 19,000 (Parkinson group). These results show that, on average, all users (N=34) accessed the web site links 15.6 times a day (2.1 logons per caregiver per day) with frequent use of the links during each login episode (on average 5 links per login). The most frequently used link was to the disease-specific handbooks, followed by e-mail, and video-conferencing (either duplex or group). As expected, overall use of the web site increased over time.

With respect to using video conferencing to communicate with each other the participants were asked to describe their reactions to using the video conferencing mode. Ninety-six percent indicated that they liked being able to see and hear the other members in the group during the video conferencing sessions. One participant noted, "Yes, definitely. It's easier to connect with them if you can see and hear them". Ninety-five percent of the caregivers found the experience of using the Internet to participate in a support group very positive or moderately positive. For example, some of their responses were "I think it's great...it seemed much easier to get to know them than in person. In reality, I wouldn't have talked as much"; "Definitely, I think so...you knew you were going to have that every week, you knew you were going to see them"; and "I felt like I got to know them and I've been continuing to stay in touch with them".

Approximately half of the caregivers had never used a computer before participating in the project. Ninety-one percent of these indicated that they had gained considerable skill in using the computer. Primarily, they used the computer for participating in the group conferences, sending emails, playing computer card games and accessing the Internet. Eighty-two percent reported that they now felt either very comfortable or moderately comfortable using the computer. One participant noted, "I'm pretty good at it...there's lots I have to learn yet but it will come gradually". Eighty-two percent felt the training they obtained at the beginning of the project was sufficient in order to feel comfortable in accessing and negotiating the project web site. The other 18% received help from family and friends for several weeks following the formal training sessions and eventually were sufficiently skilled in using the hardware and accessing the CFO web site.

At six month follow up, over 90% of the caregivers reported benefiting from their participation in the virtual support group either "extremely" or "very" positively. Examples of participant responses follow: "It's been really a positive learning experience and avenue through which you could express feelings that others understood, express your day-to-day involvement with living with someone who has Alzheimer's". "Participating in this project during the past year has meant a great deal to me and could be aptly described as my lifeline". "I found encouragement, inspiration, humor, honesty; it was a safe place to vent my feelings, share ideas, explore options". "When providing round the clock care, there is not a whole lot of time to deal with one's emotions and they tend to get buried alive. Sooner or later they surface....anger, guilt, frustration, grief. No longer did I feel so isolated as I quickly found out that other caregivers shared these feelings". "Being able to connect with one another in the comfort of our homes at any time of day or night is a very effective, non-intrusive and reassuring way to communicate...as well, the information provided on the website was excellent and a vital component of this project and I feel would be of great benefit if it could be distributed to all caregivers" [10].

System Evaluation: Adolescent Response: The features of the CFM web site for use by obese adolescents and their parents are in the process of being evaluated. The information handbooks for each group (adolescents and their parents) have been completed and reflect the views of experts in the field of health care for obese adolescents. For the adolescent group we chose language and graphics that would appeal to teenagers. Versions of the handbook were reviewed by several adolescents and modified according to their feedback. Similarly, the animations have been built to reflect obese adolescents' challenges in communicating with peers. In a focus group format we have shown the animations and solicited feedback from health care professionals who provide services to obese adolescents. Their observations and suggestions resulted in further modifications of the animations. The personalized food and activity diary is in the process of being developed. Color coding of food caloric values and calories burned by activity level have been used by professional health care providers with populations of obese adolescents. For our purposes we will transfer this information to our web based diary module and subsequently evaluate its effectiveness in helping obese adolescents to alter life style behaviors.

Professional Ethics and Standards in an E-health Service Delivery Environment: During the development and evaluation of our e-health programs we were concerned with a) insuring the accuracy of the health information that we generated and shared with the project participants; b) how the information would be interpreted and used; and c) whether the Internet-based health support program would reflect the same standards of practice evident in face-to-face delivery of health care services. Early in the project we conducted a systematic review of published studies of technology-based interventions delivered to older adults in their homes [11]. The purpose of the review was to determine whether or not adherence to professional practice standards and implementation of research ethics procedures were discussed in reports of studies of e-health service programs. We found that the most common ethical issues addressed included, informed consent (50%), presence of a mechanism for monitoring subjects (43%), confidentiality protection (28%), and a mechanism for contacting the health provider (25%). Among the interventions provided via the Internet, the use of a password (24%), securing data (22%), and encryption (10%) were most commonly reported. As expected, very few of the articles (4%) reported using any theoretical framework or practice standards for guiding the delivery of the service or intervention online. We extract reports of randomized controlled trials of e-health program (N=26) in order to take at closer look at the monitoring of professional practice standards. The analyses showed that 42% (11/26) provided some details as to procedures used for insuring reliable adherence to a specified model of intervention. Only 38% (10/26) reported using protocol guidelines for delivering the intervention, 19% (5/26) provided information about training the clinician prior to beginning the trial, and 12% (3/26) indicated that the clinician received supervision for the duration of the trial. None of the studies reported independent assessment of archived interactions between provider and patient to demonstrate whether the intervention had been delivered reliably according to protocol. Ten studies (38%) provided no information as to the use of strategies for insuring adherence to intervention protocol. These analyses guided our approach to the development and implementation of our e-health programs. We insured that the identity of the participants would be protected through the use of a password protected web site as the platform for engaging in the exchange of information. As described above, levels of protection were built into the web site such that individual participants would be known only to their own groups members and the professional facilitator. Firewalls and encryption were used to protect against any attempts by non participants to access information on the web site. Furthermore, all interactive information generated on the web site (threaded discussion, e-mail, video conferencing) was backed up on the servers and removed daily from the web site. The accuracy of the information handbooks provided online to the participants was monitored according to feedback following reviews by health specialists in each disease area. We were able to clarify inaccurate interpretations of the health information in the weekly meetings with the participants. We were able to monitor the health of the participants by maintaining e-mail contact as well as scheduling one-on-one video meetings when needed.

In terms of professional standards of practice we developed intervention training manuals to insure that the intervention would be carried out reliably and subsequently we coded the support group sessions to insure that the intervention had been delivered as intended. Similarly, the computer training manuals that we developed insured that each participant would be trained to negotiate the web site in a consistent manner. Furthermore, technicians were available throughout the project in order to provide assistance and trouble shoot with each participant whenever equipment or software problems arose.

4 Conclusion

With the rapid development of web applications that can support the exchange of health information and the delivery of health care programs, it will be increasingly feasible for health professionals to use the Internet to provide disease-specific information and standard therapies for specified disease group. In order to insure the accuracy of the information and its interpretation by consumers medical experts will need to evaluate the quality of the information for accuracy and clarity of presentation. In interactive modes of service delivery via the Internet health professionals will need to develop valid and reliable intervention protocols. Protection of patient information and client privacy within an Internet service delivery environment will need to be supported. The use of password-protected web site access, encryption, and firewalls should be mandatory for any exchange of information between a healthcare provider and consumer. Similarly, consumers have the right to know that the services they receive in a technology-based environment meet the highest professional standards of health care. Currently there is no regulating system for monitoring the credentials of the providers, and whether evidence-based models of therapy are used. Ultimately, an e-health regulatory body to which health professionals can be held accountable will be required to protect consumers, especially older adults who may be more vulnerable when receiving technology-based services. In summary, answers to the questions raised can be addressed only through research initiatives focused on demonstrating that both high quality health care information programs and secured consumer privacy can be provided when technology is used to deliver health care services.

References

1. American Psychological Association. APA Statement on Services by Telephone, Teleconferencing, and Internet (1997) http://www.apa.org/ethics/stmnt01.html
2. National Initiative for Telehealth. National Initiative for Telehealth Framework of Guidelines. Ottawa, NIFTE (2003)
3. Spry Foundation. Guide to Evaluating Health Information on the World Wide Web. http://www.spry.org
4. Gustafson, D.H., Robinson, T.N., Ansley, D., Adler, L., Flatley Brennan, P.: Consumers and Evaluations of Interactive Health Communication Applications. Am. J. Prev. Med. 16, 23–29 (1999)

5. Eng, T.R., Gustafson, D.H., Henderson, J., Jimison, H., Patrick, K.: Introduction to Evaluation of Interactive Health Communication Applications. Am. J. Prev. Med. 16, 10–15 (1999)
6. Microsoft Assistive Technology, www.microsoft.com/enable/ Apple Computer Worldwide Disabilities Solutions Group, www.apple.com.accessibility/ IBM National Support Center for Persons with Disabilities, www-03.ibm.com/able/
7. Web Content Accessibility Guidelines 1.0 W3C Recommendation (1999) http://www.w3.org/TR/1999/WAI-WEBCONTENT-19990505
8. Web Accessibility Initiative (WAI) (2003), www.w3.org/WAI
9. SAVI Viewer developed by MeLogic www.savisys.com
10. Marziali, E., Donahue, P.: Caring for Others: Internet, Video Conferencing Group Intervention for Family Caregivers of Older Adults with Neurodegenerative Disease. Gerontologist 46, 398–403 (2006)
11. Marziali, E., Dergal, J., McCleary, L.: A Systematic Review of Practice Standards and Research Ethics in Technology-Based Home Health Care Intervention Programs for Older Adults. J of Aging and Health 17, 679–696 (2005)

A Framework for Inter-organizational Collaboration Using Communication and Knowledge Management Tools

Paul Nuschke and Xiaochun Jiang

North Carolina A&T State University, Department of Industrial and Systems Engineering,
1601 East Market Street, Greensboro, NC
paul.nuschke@yahoo.com, xjiang@ncat.edu

Abstract. Organizations are often involved in joint ventures or coalitions with multiple, diverse partners. While the ability to communicate across organizational boundaries is important to their success, the organizations may have different cultures, processes, and jargon which inhibit their ability to effectively collaborate. The objective of this paper is to identify a framework that enables organizations to communicate complex knowledge across organizational boundaries. It leverages communication and knowledge management tools such as the wiki, and calls for more integration between these tools.

Keywords: HCI, collaboration, wiki, online community, bulletin board, blog, transcriber, organizations, knowledge management.

1 Introduction

Consider the following scenario: your agency is working with organizations all around the world to develop a strategy to combat AIDS in the developing world. The organizations have different cultural, social, and technological backgrounds. Most of the people involved have other projects and busy schedules, making face-to-face meetings, or even teleconferences, rare and not fully attended. With different backgrounds, training, and terminology, even if parties talk, will they be able to understand one another? What technology and processes can you use to help these collaborations?

At the heart of collaboration are conversations between the people involved. In order to have conversations with people across the world, people need communication tools which suit both their needs and the context in which they will be used. For example, in some cases people want to be able to have meetings using an audio conferencing system. In other cases, people from all over the world may not be able to hold such conferences, but they can use e-mail and bulletin boards. A collaboration framework should be able to handle both cases.

The success of conversations is often said to depend on the degree of common knowledge between the people involved. For example, if an electrical engineer tried to explain electromagnetism to an artist, they may not get very far because there isn't much common knowledge between the two. Research in the field of knowledge

D. Schuler (Ed.): Online Communities and Social Comput., HCII 2007, LNCS 4564, pp. 406–415, 2007.

management has yielded many insights into how to strategically manage knowledge in organizations. The knowledge management tools that have been developed can be used to bridge the common knowledge gap between people.

When many people are working together, it is often called a community of practice. Research into communities of practice reveals potential problems and advantages of such communities. Finding ways to support the communities of practice, and their inherent complexity, will be an important part of the framework.

2 Collaboration and Communities of Practice

Since collaboration between multiple organizations is a difficult undertaking, it is reasonable to ask, why do they even attempt to collaborate? According to Hardy, Phillips, & Lawrence, there are three types of potential advantages: knowledge creation, political, and strategic [1]. Knowledge creation will be discussed later, but essentially organizations can learn from one another, or they can create new knowledge. Politically, the organizations involved are inevitably linked through social structures. This web of relationships has a significant impact on the ability of organizations to act as they would like to act, and to influence other organizations and policies. Strategically, the organizations may be looking to secure resources that they cannot develop internally without significant effort. Such resources may include equipment, knowledge, experience, skills, manpower, money, or relationships.

Communities of practice are formed when groups discuss shared goals or practices (or collaborate). If one or more communities primarily interact online, they are also called an online community. Researching communities of practice is inherently difficult because communities may take months to form, and their lifecycle may last for years. The two most popular methods for studying communities of practice are ethnographic case studies [2] and laboratory research [3]. Since case studies are difficult to generalize, and laboratory research cannot replicate the scale involved when hundreds of people collaborate, the collaborative frameworks that have been developed using this type of research often underestimate the complexity, dynamics, and lack of constraints inherent in real-world problems. Carroll, Rosson, Convertino, & Ganoe's framework accounts for dynamic collaboration and also provides a convenient way in which to view issues related to supporting collaboration [4]. Three facets of this framework include common ground, community of practice, and human development.

Common Ground. Common ground can be defined as mutual knowledge, beliefs, and assumptions, on which all collective action is built [5]. Common ground has been used to explain communication and conversations. Preece and Maloney-Krichmar give an example of two people (A & B) talking about another person's daughter. To understand one another, they must understand that they are talking about the child playing outside and not the one in the room [6]. "Grounding" is used to describe the process of acquiring this understanding. It is often done informally and sometimes unconsciously through gestures such as nods, and phrases such as "uh-huh." In the example above, person A may wave informally towards the playground to indicate which child they are referring to. Some gestures signal agreement or understanding, while others signal confusion or lack of understanding, and correct interpretation of these signals help people arrive at a shared understanding. Grounding is heavily influenced by first five factors listed in Table 1.

Table 1. Factors that Affect Communications and Grounding (Adapted from [6])

Factor	Description
Co-presence	People in same physical space
Visibility	People can see one another
Audibility	People can hear one another
Co-temporality	People experience conversation at roughly the same time
Simultaneity	People take turns in order
Reviewability	People can review messages
Revisability	People can revise messages

Since communication mediums differ along these dimensions, the type of medium will therefore affect grounding. Though face-to-face conversations are often held up as the gold standard in supporting common ground, other methods can actually provide more support, depending on the situation. For example, King found a positive correlation between the number of months a group of recovering addicts used an electronic bulletin board and the average duration of their recovery. While this correlation is not proof, King theorized that bulletin broads provide two key necessities for recovering addicts: anonymity and having time to reflect before replying ("reviewability") [7]. In any case, supporting ways for community members to find common ground is an important and often neglected step in community formation.

Communities of Practice. The term communities of practice likely came from Etienne Wenger, though as he says, the concept is not new [8]. Communities of practice are evident in all walks of life, either through local artist communities, engineers discussing software development on the web, or parents discussing child rearing at sporting events.

According to Wenger, communities of practice have many immediate and long-term benefits for organizations. In the short term, organizations gain by improving the quality of decisions, finding answers more quickly, and getting more perspectives on problems. In the long term, they gain by facilitating new capabilities and alliances, increasing the ability to think strategically about employee knowledge and capabilities, reduction of group "silos," and better retention of talent [8]. From the strategic point of view, communities of practice enable "distributed cognition," which essentially means that the group is able to pool knowledge and collectively achieve more than they would be able to on their own [9].

Online communities, instead of or in addition to interacting in person, interact through the Internet using one or more tools. Communication tools are often broken down by time (same vs. different) and place (local vs. distributed), where each combination requires a different tool. For example, two people meeting face-to-face and sharing graphs and figures clearly have different needs than ten scientists working in various nations across the world (and in different time zones). Ellis, Gibbs, & Rein use a time-place matrix (Table 2) in order to show the possibilities [10]. "Same time" communications such as the telephone are often called "synchronous," whereas communications that occur across time (e.g., email or discussion boards) are called "asynchronous."

Table 2. Time / Place Collaboration Matrix (adapted from [10])

	Same Time	Different Time
Same Place	**Synchronous local** Face-to-face	**Asynchronous local** Team scheduling, group calendars
Different Place	**Synchronous, Distributed** Telephone, Instant Messaging, video or audio conferencing	**Asynchronous, Distributed** Pull: Newsgroup, discussion board, blog, wiki, online community Push: Email, list-server

In addition to time and place, communication tools vary by whether the sender "pushes" the information (e.g., using a list-server) or whether the receiver "pulls" it (e.g., using bulletin boards). The distinction is potentially important if, for example, the user is waiting on important information. In a pull technology, they must continually check the information source. In a push technology, it is automatically delivered to them.

Alberts and Hayes also characterize the degree of "smartness" required by the user sending communications through each technology [11]. For instance, the telephone (a one-to-one communication) is considered a "smart, smart push," which means the person sending a message must know that the message is important (the first smart); they must know who might also consider it important (the second smart); and then they push the message by calling that person. The broadcast (a one-to-many communication) is considered "smart push," because the sender does not need to know who might want the message (everyone will receive it). However, this places an additional burden on all of the receivers, as they must receive and screen more messages. E-mail is flexible because it can be sent to one person, like the telephone, select groups of people, or everyone (like the broadcast). The central point for Alberts and Hayes is that any networked environment should include several technologies so that all needs are met.

The factors that affect communication (Table 1) are part of the larger context in which a communication tool must be used. For example, even though e-mail is a reviewable and distributed technology, it will be difficult for someone that is traveling to send an e-mail. Most often, they will use a telephone because they can easily communicate the essential information. Each technology, be it e-mail, bulletin boards, or the telephone, has certain contexts in which it is particularly useful and usable and certain contexts in which it is not. Consequently, integrating multiple technologies is necessary in order to assure that all relevant contexts are supported.

Human Development. People change over time, often as a result of their interaction with communities. One key theory to explain this is Vygotsky's zone of proximal development. In the theory, a person has a certain amount of knowledge and skills, but that person also has the capacity to quickly gain new knowledge and skills through the interaction with more capable or knowledgeable peers [12]. Communities of practice can benefit individual learning by providing a place for this proximal development to occur [9]. In addition, members benefit by getting immediate help to problems, access to experts, confidence that their ideas have been adequately vetted, and a sense of belonging or participation. In the long term, they may have a larger network to rely on for job opportunities, a better professional reputation, and a better understanding of their field [8].

3 Knowledge Management

At the most basic level, knowledge is built on data: raw numbers, observations, or pure stimuli, before any interpretation has been done or meaning has been assigned. If the data is meaningful, it is typically given the name "information." Knowledge, then, is information that has been put into a framework in a person's mind, or as Nanoka says, "justified, true belief" [13]. Knowledge management is "a range of practices and techniques used by organizations to identify, represent and distribute knowledge, know-how, expertise, intellectual capital and other forms of knowledge for leverage, reuse and transfer of knowledge and learning across the organization" [14].

The importance of knowledge in industry and government has increased substantially since Peter Drucker first wrote about "knowledge workers" in 1959 [15]. The increased importance of information and knowledge on workers today has led to a surge of interest and research in knowledge management. In this research, knowledge management is necessary in order to assure that collaborators involved in complex projects have enough common knowledge in order to fulfill their goals while working together.

In his book, Rollett describes several key processes of knowledge management, which include: assessing, maintaining, integrating, organizing, creating, and transferring [16]. Assessing refers to the assignment of value or quality to knowledge. For example, is the knowledge relevant, accurate, comprehensive, and timely? Integrating refers the degree to which the knowledge is integrated into the work of an organization. It refers to both how well the knowledge is captured by systems and how much it is used once it has been captured. If knowledge is not integrated with the work of an organization, then it will not be used as often.

Organizing refers to how the knowledge is organized. Some knowledge may be easier to find if placed in a hierarchy, linked to from other documents, or tagged with keywords. Organization can present significant barriers to using knowledge management systems. For example, on a company intranet, information may be located on many different servers, written by different teams, having different headings, permissions settings, search engines, and interfaces. Thus organization is critical. Maintaining refers to the review, correction, preservation, and eventual removal of knowledge from both human minds and from the technological knowledge repositories. Maintenance is far from trivial. As will be discussed later in this section, maintenance is one of the bottlenecks in the design of current knowledge management systems.

One popular way to look at the process of creating and transferring knowledge is to use Nanoka's "spiral of knowledge" framework [13]. Like many other researchers, Nanoka splits knowledge into two types: explicit and tacit knowledge. Explicit knowledge is typically defined as factual knowledge, while tacit knowledge is defined as procedural knowledge or know-how. Nanoka describes the process of creating new knowledge as a transfer from one type of knowledge to another, in one of four processes: socialization, externalization, internalization, and combination. From the knowledge management perspective, it is important to support as many, if not all, of these knowledge creation processes.

Because of all of the processes involved in knowledge management, it is rare that one application can handle them all. The typical approach is to use different applications for different tasks. For instance, data mining tools may be used to extract knowledge from large values of data. Another approach is to use groupware and document management systems to manage knowledge. Improving these systems is often done by looking for better ways to index the content, providing ways to search it, and by providing links between content [17].

Wagner claims that there are several bottlenecks to traditional knowledge management that software fails to address: narrow bandwidth, acquisition latency, knowledge inaccuracy, and maintenance trap [18]. Knowledge management tools often have a narrow bandwidth to capture knowledge from its source (e.g., experts, documents, and transactions). Acquisition latency refers to the delay from when knowledge has been captured and when it can be shared. For example, consider the publication process: it can take weeks, months, or years for the results to become available. Knowledge inaccuracy refers to mistakes that may be made, and which are often very difficult to correct (again, publications are fairly permanent once they are distributed). Such publications can also become out-of-date rather quickly. Finally, maintenance trap refers to the problem that as more knowledge is captured, more has to be kept up-to-date [18]. Wagner proposes the wiki as a potential solution for these bottlenecks.

4 The Framework

A diagram representing key aspects of the framework for inter-organizational collaboration is shown in Fig. 1. Though the diagram only contains two collaborators, the framework is extensible to thousands of people. The devices adjacent to each collaborator represent possible choices which they can use to access the framework. The "Asynchronous Tools" are the methods collaborators can use, beyond phones, to communicate with one another. In addition, using a computer, the collaborators can interface with the portal directly ("Pull").

Portal. A portal is simply a web page, often customized for each individual user, which allows people to access many other web pages and applications. In this framework, the "portal" provides a customized view into the knowledge and communication tools, and it is the gateway to access much of the functionality of the framework.

One important characteristic of the portal is that it is very flexible. With a single link, an entire application can be launched from the portal. In other cases, using standards such as Real Simple Syndication (RSS), the portal can integrate information from multiple sources at once, including news, e-mail, new entries in the communication tool, weather updates, etc. Consequently, entire applications (or views to those applications) can be added to the framework with minimal intrusion on the user. However, providing points of integration for those new applications with existing applications will be a necessary development task.

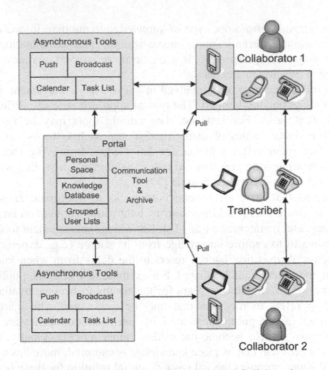

Fig. 1. Framework for Inter-Organizational Collaboration

Communication Tool and Archive. At the very heart of the portal and the framework is the communication tool and archive (e.g., a bulletin board). This component must provide a place for collaborators to hold new discussions and to view discussions that have occurred in the past. Such an archive must assure that messages or communications are both revisable and reviewable. One key aspect of such an archive is that it provides some amount of inherent organization, as well as ways for collaborators to find needed information as easily as possible. For example, collaborators should be able to perform searches, browse by organization or user or hierarchy, or possibly search by tag words. Other tools may be explored, such as a tracking tool which suggests potentially relevant topics to the user based on the people posting to it or the information contained in it.

Knowledge Database. For collaboration to work between organizations, the people involved must become familiar with processes and procedures, language, documents, terminology, and acronyms used by other organizations. A knowledge database (such as a wiki) can help reduce problems related to the lack of familiarity between organizations. However, for a knowledge database to work, it must support the knowledge management processes (e.g,. creating, maintaining), and it must be tightly integrated with the communication tools.

Perhaps the best way to couple a knowledge database with a communication tool is to explicitly link from the communication tool to the database any time a word or concept arises that is contained in the database. In this way, users are not required to know that the term is contained in the database; if they are using a computer, then they could simply click a link and read about the concept.

Supporting the knowledge management processes requires attention to both the functionality in the application and the policies related to the use of the application. For example, the application should make it easy for people to transfer their existing knowledge into the database. If policies restrict who can enter the knowledge too severely, then the time it takes to implement such a knowledge database would be adversely affected (due to the "narrow bandwidth").

Transcriber. Because collaborators may need to talk synchronously with one another (e.g., via telephone), an important component to the framework is the presence of a transcriber. This person can transcribe conversations, take notes, or use tools such dialog mapping [19] to assist in converting synchronous conversations into a digital form that can be communicated to many people or saved for later. For small collaborations, this person may be a secretary. In larger collaborations, it is more critical and likely more feasible to hire one or more transcribers.

Suppose for example that fifteen people are holding an audio conference and that the information will be important to many other people. The transcriber can record the conversation, transcribe it live, or take notes that can be used to summarize the conversation. One the meeting is complete, the transcriber can enter the summary into the communication tool, adding tag words or setting priority levels.

Grouped User Lists. Grouped user lists are important for both the distribution of messages in the framework, and for controlling security and permissions for the framework. Integration of the grouped lists with the other components of the framework is critical. For example, the grouped lists could support the communication tool by being tied to discussion forums. The grouped lists should also be flexible enough to accommodate people who need to setup lists on the fly.

Personal Space. The personal space provides a place for people to include either personal (e.g., a picture, favorite links) or professional information about themselves (e.g., their main skills). While this may seem like a trivial and low priority need, helping collaborators find common ground is an important goal in any collaborative activity. For example, pictures could help collaborators recognize one another should they meet in person. Some personal information could be automatically supplied by the organizations involved. For example, the training, title, and awards of each employee could be imported from company databases.

Asynchronous Tools. This framework looks to take existing technology and incorporate or integrate it in the best way possible to fulfill the communication needs of collaborators. In addition to the synchronous communication methods (telephone), people should have a variety of asynchronous methods at their disposal, including push and pull type interactions, and one-to-one and broadcast message distribution.

Push technologies such as e-mail are useful because people have to exert less effort in order to be notified of new information. One disadvantage of push technologies is that they can push too much information, making it difficult for people to find the information they really want to know. Pull technologies are needed so that people can find information on their own time. Since most people already have a one-to-one communication method (e-mail), the framework instead needs to help people find e-mail addresses for other collaborators. E-mail programs are relatively poor at helping people setup lists for broadcasting messages. The grouped user lists mentioned previously should allow them to quickly access existing and setup new lists.

Calendars and task lists could be very useful for project-oriented collaborations or when timelines are critical. For example, two existing project collaboration applications, Base Camp (basecamphq.com) and Central Desktop (centraldesktop.com), make heavy use of calendars and task lists to help collaborators meet deadlines. The calendar and task lists, together with the communication tool, grouped user lists, and knowledge database, provide a concise and yet very powerful framework that can assist inter-organizational collaboration.

Integration. Though integration is not listed in the framework diagram, it is perhaps the key to the framework. Too often, tools are developed separately with little regard for how they might support one another. By integrating the knowledge management and communication tools, both tools are improved. The knowledge management tool can be used more, and the communication tool will support discussions better.

5 Future Work

The next step is in this research is to implement the main components of the framework, including the communication tools and knowledge database. While such an implementation could be useful almost immediately, it would also benefit from more analysis using case studies and laboratory experiments.

References

1. Hardy, C., Phillips, N., Lawrence, T.B.: Resources, Knowledge and Influence: The Organizational Effects of Interorganizational Collaboration. Journal of Management Studies, 40(2) (2003)
2. van Baalen, P., Bloemhof-Ruwaard, J., van Heck, E.: Knowledge Sharing in an Emerging Network of Practice: The Role of a Knowledge Portal. European Management Journal 23(3), 300–314 (2005)
3. Lochbaum, K., Psotka, J., Streeter, L.: Harnessing the power of peers. In: Interservice/Industry, Simulation and Education Conference (I/ITSEC). Orlando, FL(2002)
4. Carroll, J.M., et al.: Awareness and teamwork in computer-supported collaborations. Interacting with Computers 18(1), 21–46 (2006)
5. Clark, H.H., Brenna, S.E.: Grounding in communication. In: Resnick, L., Levine, J.M., Teasley, S.D. (eds.) Perspectives on socially shared cognition, APA, Washington, DC (1991)
6. Preece, J., Maloney-Krichmar, D.: Online Communities: Focusing on Sociability and Usability. In: Jacko, J., Sears, A. (eds.) Handbook of Human-Computer Interaction, pp. 596–620. Lawrence Erlbaum Associates Inc, Mahwah, NJ (2003)

7. King, S.: Analysis of electronic support groups for recovering addicts. Interpersonal Computer and Technology: An. Electronic Journal for the 21st Century (IPCT) 2(3), 47–56 (1994)
8. Wenger, E., McDermott, R., Snyder, W.M.: Cultivating communities of practice: a guide to managing knowledge. Harvard Business School Press, Boston, MA (2002)
9. Davenport, E., Hall, H.: Organizational knowledge and communities of practice. In: Cronin, B. (ed.) Annual review of information science and technology, Information Today, Medford, NJ. pp. 171–227 (2002)
10. Ellis, C.A., Gibbs, S.J., Rein, G.L.: Groupware: some issues and experiences. Communications of the ACM 34(1), 39–58 (1991)
11. Alberts, D.S., Hayes, R.E.: Power to the edge. Information Age Transformation Series. CCRP Publication Series (2003)
12. Vygotsky, L.S.: Mind and society. In: The development of higher mental processes, Harvard University Press, Cambridge, MA (1978)
13. Nonaka, I., Takeuchi, H., Umemoto, K.: Theory of organizational knowledge creation. International Journal of Technology Management 11(7-8), 833 (1996)
14. Wikipedia. Knowledge management (2006) [cited 2006 September 14th]; Available from: http://en.wikipedia.org/wiki/Knowledge_management
15. Drucker, P.: Landmarks of tomorrow: a report on the new "post-modern" world (1959)
16. Rollett, H.: Knowledge management processes and technologies. Kluwer Academic Publishers, Boston, MA (2003)
17. Holsapple, C.W., Joshi, K.D.: Knowledge management: a threefold framework. The. Information Society 18(1), 47–64 (2002)
18. Wagner, C.: Breaking the knowledge acquisition bottleneck through conversational knowledge management. Information Resources Management Journal 19(1), 70–83 (2006)
19. Conklin, J.: Dialog mapping: an approach for wicked problems. 2003: CogNexus Institute.

A Mobile Portfolio to Support Communities of Practice in Science Education

Oriel Herrera[1], Sergio F. Ochoa[2], Andrés Neyem[2], Maurizio Betti[3],
Roberto Aldunate[4], and David A. Fuller[5]

[1] Informatics Engineering School, Universidad Católica de Temuco,
Manuel Montt 56, Temuco, Chile
oherrera@uctemuco.cl
[2] Computer Science Department, Universidad de Chile,
Blanco Encalada 2120, Santiago, Chile
{sochoa, aneyem}@dcc.uchile.cl
[3] Education Department, Universidad Católica de Temuco,
Manuel Montt 56, Temuco, Chile
mbetti@uct.cl
[4] Department of Civil and Environmental Engineering, University of Illinois,
205 N Mathews Av.,Urbana, Illinois, USA
aldurate@uiuc.edu
[5] Computer Science Department, Pontificia Universidad Católica de Chile,
V. Mackenna 4860, Santiago, Chile
dfuller@ing.puc.cl

Abstract. Practice activities are a key issue for science education students. Typically, these activities are carried out by a community of practice (practicing students and professors) using physical or centralized electronic portfolios. However, these alternatives are limited when the community members need to share the portfolio resources, any time and anywhere. This limitation is also present when support for high interactivity among these persons is required. This paper presents a new kind of portfolio which is able to work in autonomous, client-server, and peer-to-peer manners. This mobile portfolio is fully distributed; therefore, it improves the flexibility to conduct interactions or share portfolio resources among the members of a community of practice. The functionality and stability of the tool have been tested by the developers and the results obtained are encouraging. The use of this distributed portfolio is expected to help science students and professors to enhance practice activities, interactions and interchange of experiences and resources.

Keywords: Mobile Workspaces, Mobile Portfolios, Communities of Practice, Education.

1 Introduction

Practice activities are key issues in science education studies. These activities transform theoretical knowledge into specific actions. Dewey stated that theoretical knowledge and its application are strongly related; therefore the learning process takes place

D. Schuler (Ed.): Online Communities and Social Comput., HCII 2007, LNCS 4564, pp. 416–425, 2007.

mainly during practice activities [1]. This learning process involves identifying and overcoming the challenges that a community of practice (practicing students and professors) has to face in order to reach a significant goal. This learning approach is aligned with the situated experience theory [2] and social practice theory [3], [4]. In addition, the learning is part of the formative design processes usually applied in several professions [5].

The Universidad Catolica de Temuco, Chile, has used practice activities in early stages of the science education studies. The obtained results have been very positive [6]. These practice activities become more important in later stages of the students' studies, provided they are dedicated to these activities full-time.

Typically, these students work during 3 or 4 hours daily in an Educational Center assigned by the University. There, they put all their knowledge into practice and become more confident about their actions. A supervisor guides and monitors the activities of the practicing students (see Fig. 1). In this scenario the students can also use a senior teacher to validate their activities or interchange experiences. Interactions with peer students are useful to validate ideas or gain knowledge about a specific issue.

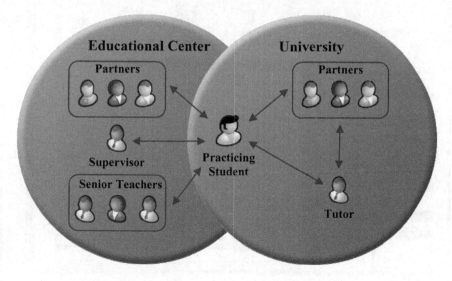

Fig. 1. Type of interactions between a practicing student and the rest of the actors

At the same time, these students can interact with peers and with their tutor in the university scenario. The tutor is the main person responsible for the practitioners' instruction and guidance. They are all part of a community of practice in charge of carrying out a global instruction process for a specific student group. These communities are characterized by a strong negotiation of the meaning of practical experiences [2], [9].

In order to show their progress in the practice activities, each student implements a "portfolio". The creation and maintenance of these portfolios involves: planning, activities execution, and creation of documents and records related to the performed activities [7]. All evidence that a student collects during the practice activities is stored in said portfolio. This evidence is classified according to a national cataloging system [8].

Currently these portfolios are implemented as a physical file, which is the least expensive solution, more easily adopted by any organization or student. Unfortunately, the physical portfolios have several operative limitations in sharing the information they contain: making a copy of a document is not easy and it could be a slow process, delivering a document requires having the sender and receiver in a face to face situation, and the delivery process may also be unreliable and/or slow (e.g. post mail). These are just some of the reasons why sharing physical documents is not the best option. In order to overcome these limitations, the authors created a digital portfolio, following the client-server paradigm.

Fig. 2. Tutors' view of the online portfolios

This portfolio is a shared space where the students can store public and private digital information. Students' public information can be seen only by peers, tutors or supervisors. The information in the public space can be commented on and copied into the portfolio of any student, tutor, or supervisor. Fig. 2 shows the view of the tutors' functionalities implemented in the online portfolio.

Although this tool helps solve several problems of the physical portfolios, some important limitations can not be overcome. An example of this is the software capability to allow access to shared information if a server is not available. Flexibility is an important requirement for any solution intending to be appropriate for supporting the interaction among the community members. Therefore, the solution should support the interaction almost anytime and anywhere.

Mobile computing technology and wireless networks could help community members overcome the current limitations in sharing experiences and accessing portfolio information. For this reason, this paper presents a mobile portfolio to enhance collaborative learning and interaction among communities of practices in science education.

The rest of the paper is organized as follows. Section 2 defines interaction problems among community members. Section 3 presents related work. Section 4 describes features of the implemented mobile portfolio that support interactions among these actors. Finally, section 5 presents the conclusions and future work.

2 Problem Definition

In science education, the student instruction process is characterized by a high degree of social interaction. Such interactions can be categorized as formal or informal.

Formal interactions. These interactions are carried out between the practicing student and the supervisor in order to determine the real progress in the student portfolio. They involve a supervisor and a group of practicing students. This type of interaction is also carried out in group meetings where the students share experiences. There, the supervisor helps students to understand specific situations or to organize the discussions. Formal interactions can also be carried out between the practicing students and senior professors that belong to the educational institution where the students are practicing. These professors help the student to understand and assimilate the lessons learned, and to make possible corrections in the practical activities the student is conducting.

Informal interactions. These interactions are present when a practicing student meets with his/her peers in the educational center. These interactions are usually focused on interchanging experiences and conducting a pre-validation of these experiences. Informal interactions are also conducted by the educational center's professors when they provide students with practical situations and lessons to be learned during the time period they instruct other students.

All these interactions could provide new material for the student portfolio, instances for sharing information or portfolio review. By analyzing the interactions among students, supervisor and tutors, and the diversity of places where such interaction can be performed, it is clear that a new supporting tool is required by the community members. The online portfolio [7] is not appropriate to support ad-hoc meetings. Provided that said solution depends on a central server that stores the students' portfolios, the distributed access to these resources depends on the server availability. However, having centralized information allows professors to get updated information about all the students' portfolios.

This paper presents an extension to the online portfolio in order to allow both centralized and decentralized access to and distribution of portfolio information. Each portfolio is now an autonomous unit which can be connected to a server or the portfolio of any student on-demand. The coherence of the information is maintained through data synchronization operations, which are executed on-demand. This functionality extension is focused on supporting sharing information, because in face to face meetings, it does not make sense to use computer supported interaction tools except those for data sharing and data synchronization.

3 Related Work

Several experiences and instructional strategies have reported the use of portfolios to support instructional activities. However, most of them involve the use of physical portfolios. Advances in information and communication technologies have allowed translating the metaphor of physical portfolios to digital portfolios [11], [12]. Then, digital portfolios have been extended to virtual portfolios, allowing not only preparing and storing digital documents and records, but also supporting interaction among the actors of the instructional scenario [13]. These functionalities have an impact on the way that communities of practice carry out their activities. More and more groupware tools have been included in these portfolios in order to improve the flexibility of the work in these communities [16]. However, some key requirements such as the support for ad-hoc meetings are still pending.

The use of these virtual portfolios has overcome the limit of educational scenarios. Currently, it is possible to see experiences of using these products in work scenarios such as: police departments [14], K-12 educational institutions [15], and businesses [17], [18], [19].

Most of the available solutions implement virtual portfolios using centralized components [20]. However, distributed and ad-hoc access to the resources is required, for example, during a trip or while sitting in a waiting room, in order to provide more flexibility for interactions. The next section presents the virtual environment that was designed to provide more flexibility to interactions among practicing students, tutors and supervisors in both educational centers and universities.

4 Mobile Portfolio

The implemented virtual space is the result of the reengineering process done to the online portfolio shown in Figure 2. Although the look and feel of the tool is the same, it has been completely redesigned in order to support synchronous and asynchronous work of practicing students and professors (tutors and supervisors). The portfolio has been transformed into an autonomous and mobile entity which can be used in synchronous and asynchronous work scenarios. The portfolio information now has two master copies that need to be synchronized. A copy is stored in the server and the other in the mobile computing devices used by the student/professor/tutor. The information of both portfolio copies can be copied or shared with any other portfolio of a community member on-demand. A student can work offline on his/her desktop PC, Laptop or Tablet PC and then, he/she can synchronize the updated information with the master copy stored in the server. The online portfolio becomes mobile. Although the information included in the portfolio can be in any digital format (e.g. PDF, gif, jpeg, .doc and .xls), each file has a XML descriptor that registers the metadata about the current version of the file and its cataloging information. These file descriptors are copied (as attached files) every time a copy of a portfolio resource is carried out.

The mobile portfolio allows students to share its information with other peer computers (of students or professors) without intermediary servers. It allows students to carry the portfolio all the time and meet with peers and professors in any place (e.g. coffee shops, parks or any other physical place) and at any time. It does not matter if there is network communication support or not. In such cases, the portfolio implements a Mobile Ad-hoc NETwork (MANET).

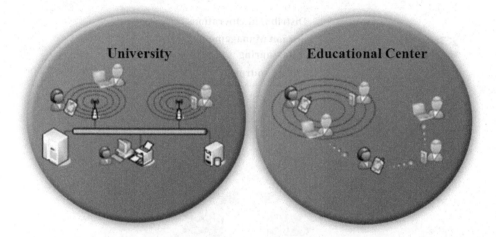

Fig. 3. Interaction scenario using the mobile portfolio

Typically, the work inside the university can be done in a synchronous or asynchronous way (Fig. 3). If the work is asynchronous, the XML descriptors are used to synchronize the portfolio information between the client and server. These descriptors can also be used to synchronize portfolio contents between two users. In case of synchronous work, an updated copy of the portfolio is always available in the server. Professors can use his/her portfolio module to access all public resources stored in the server.

When students are in the educational center doing practice activities they can use a local copy of the portfolio to record experiences, add/updates to the documents and conduct ad-hoc meetings with peers and professors (Fig. 3). The mobile portfolio implementation provides more flexibility to the students' work mainly when they are in scenarios without networking services. Provided that the portfolio is stored locally in the mobile devices, students and professors can be on the move as much as they need, and the resources will be available all the time. Provided that the mobile portfolio can store its resources into a mobile computing device (e.g. Laptop or TabletPC), the resources can be easily shared and distributed to other users, even if such users are not located in the same place or are working at the same time. These mobile portfolios can be used as intermediaries to support sharing information among users that are not co-located.

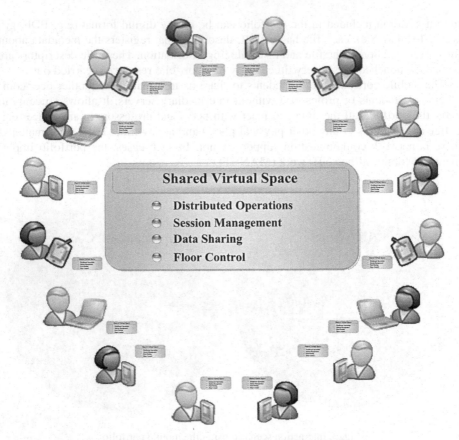

Fig. 4. Services provided by the mobile portfolio

The mobile portfolio implements five main services (Fig. 4): distributed operation, session management, data sharing, floor control management and on-demand synchronization. The *distributed operations* currently implemented are: annotations (comments) in shared PDF and MS word documents, presentations using PPT files. These operations require synchronous communication among the users involved in the interaction process.

The *session management* supports closed (private) and open sessions. They do not require the presence of a server. This functionality allows students and professors to carry out ad-hoc meetings almost anytime and anywhere. Each portfolio has a public and a private storage space. The private space can be accessed by the owner of the portfolio only. Usually, it contains unconcluded work or preliminary ideas. The public storage space represents the official portfolio. It includes all documents that are visible to other users. Functionalities to share and synchronize these documents are part of the portfolio *data sharing* capabilities.

Finally, the *floor control* functionalities allow users in a work session to follow a free (i.e. peer-to-peer) or master-slave (i.e. client-server) interaction protocol. This functionality could be used, for example, to carry out a distributed presentation in an ad-hoc work meeting.

This strategy of integrating coupled and uncoupled portfolios facilitates the interaction among members of a community of practice. Wenger [2] defined three main features for a community of practice: common community goals (portfolio goals), committed community members and a shared repertory (public storage space). The mobile portfolio supports the third feature, which is the only one applicable to this product.

The mobile portfolio was implemented by using C# and reusing part of the functionalities available in the .NET framework and the OneNote libraries. It included the use of COM components to implement shared objects attached to shared documents, such as comments and synchronous data delivery (e.g. distributed presentations). Provided that the shared files are modified mainly by the authors, the data consistency of the public storage space follows the Unix semantic policy [21]. All functionalities of networking, data synchronization, and session management embedded in the mobile portfolio are the same as that implemented in the PASIR platform [22], [23].

The mobile portfolio has been tested in a simulated scenario at the University of Chile. Five persons (mobile users) from the Computer Science Department were involved in such tests. These activities wanted to identify capabilities and limitations of the mobile portfolio when it is isolated (disconnected), connected to a MANET or connected to an infrastructure-based wired/wireless network. The obtained results show the application is able to work in these three scenarios with an acceptable performance. The application functionalities were available at all times in the three scenarios. The data synchronization process worked well in client-server and peer-to-peer connections. These results are not surprising. They can be explained because the new functionalities of the portfolio were implemented mainly by reusing tested components that are part of PASIR. Therefore, the real challenge for the mobile portfolio is to show that it is useful and usable by members of communities of practice to support their practice activities in science education.

5 Conclusions and Future Work

One of the most important activities carried out by educational science students during the instructional process are the practice activities. These activities are more enriching and attractive when they are conducted through a community of practice. The use of portfolios is a common practice to support students' practice activities. These portfolios can be physical or computer-supported. The first ones have well-known limitations that have been discussed in the literature [11], [12]. The second ones are the evolution of the physical portfolios. The digital (or computer-supported) portfolios have tried to overcome the limitations of the previous ones. Unfortunately, most of these digital portfolios involve centralized components which limit its applicability when no communication infrastructure or access to a server is available.

This paper presents a mobile portfolio which can work in both peer-to-peer and client-server scenarios. The services provided by this platform allow members of a community of practice to interact almost anytime and anyplace. Provided that the mobile portfolios can locally store the resources they contain, the resources can be easily shared with other users, even if users are not working at the same time and place.

Currently, the implemented application is stable, but no formal experimentations have been done with real practicing students or professors. However, several tests have been performed by the developers in order to validate the flexibility, availability and functionalities provided by the tool. The obtained results are encouraging. Although the system has shown good results during the tests (in terms of functionality and stability), its real contribution can only be defined by the final users. Therefore, the next step in this research work involves using the mobile portfolio to support real communities of practice in Educational Centers and Universities.

Acknowledgments. This work was partially supported by Fondecyt (Chile), grant N°: 11060467 and by MECESUP (Chile) Project N°: UCH0109.

References

1. Dewey, J.: The School and Society. University of Chicago Press, Chicago, Illinois (1915)
2. Wenger, E.: Communities of practice: Learning, meaning and identity. Cambridge University Press, Cambridge UK (1999)
3. Engeström, Y.: Learning by expanding. Orienta-Konsultit, Helsinki Finland (1987)
4. Vygotsky, L.S.: Mind and Society: the Development of Higher Psychological Processes. Harvard University Press, Cambridge UK (1987)
5. Schon, D.A.: Educating the Reflective Practitioner: Toward a New Design for Teaching and Learning in the Professions. Jossey-Bass Publishers, San Francisco, CA (1987)
6. Inostroza, G.: The practice: the engine of the teachers' instruction (in Spanish). Olmen, Santiago de Chile (1999)
7. Betti, M., Mellado, M.E.: Using TICs in the initial instruction of teachers: the on-line portfolios and the communities of practice/learning (in Spanish). Pensamiento Educativo 35, 311–330 (2004)
8. Chilean Education Ministry: Standards to Perform the Initial Instruction of Teachers (in Spanish). High Education Division, Santiago, Chile (2001)
9. Brown, A., Campione, J.: Psychological theory and the design of innovative learning environments. In: Schauble, L., Glaser, R. (eds.) Innovations in Learning: New Environments for Education, pp. 289–325. Lawrence Erlbaum, Mahwah (1996)
10. Herrera, O., Fuller, D.: Shared Knowledge: the Result of Negotiation in Non-Hierarchical Environments. In: Fuks, H., Lukosch, S., Salgado, A.C. (eds.) CRIWG 2005 LNCS, vol. 3706, pp. 255–262. Springer, Heidelberg (2005)
11. Pardieck, S., McMullen, D.: Development of a Digital Portfolio System for Preservice Teachers. In: Proc. of the 17th World Conference on Educational Multimedia, Hypermedia and Telecommunications, Montreal, Canada, pp. 2306–2310 (2005)
12. Spendlove, D., Hopper, M.: Using 'electronic portfolios' to challenge current orthodoxies in the presentation of an initial teacher training design and technology activity. International Journal of Technology and Design Education 16(2), 177–191 (2006)
13. Sorensen, E., Tolsby, H., Dirckinck-Holmfeld, L.: Virtual Portfolios for Collaboration in Distributed Web-Based Learning. In: Proc. of the 13th World Conference on Educational Multimedia, Hypermedia and Telecommunications, Denver, USA, pp. 1840–1845 (2002)

14. De Laat, M.: Network and Content Analysis in an Online Community Discourse. In: Proceedings of the 4th Computer Support for Collaborative Learning (CSCL), Boulder, Colorado, USA, pp. 625–626 (2002)
15. Stahl, G.: Groupware goes to school. In: Haake, J.M., Pino, J.A. (eds.) CRIWG 2002 LNCS, vol. 2440, pp. 7–24. Springer, Heidelberg (2002)
16. Suthers, D.: Supporting and Changing Practices of Multiple Communities. In: Proc. of the 6th International Conference of the Learning Sciences, Los Angeles, California, USA, pp. 537–544 (2004)
17. Choi, M.: Communities of practice: an alternative learning model for knowledge creation. British Journal of Educational Technology 37(1), 143–146 (2006)
18. Hildreth, P., Kimble, C., Wright, P.: Communities of Practice in the Distributed International Environment. The. Journal of Knowledge Management 4(1), 27–37 (2000)
19. Vasconcelos, J., Castro, P., Gens, P., Kimble, K.: Knowledge Management in Non-Governmental Organisations: A Partnership for the Future. In: Proceedings of the 7th International Conference on Enterprise Information Systems (ICEIS), Miami, USA, pp. 24–28 (2005)
20. Sorensen, E.K., Takle, E.S., Taber, M.R., Fils, D.: CSCL Structuring the Past, Present and Future through Virtual Portfolios. In: Dirckinck-Holmfeld, L., Fibiger, B. (eds.) Learning in Virtual Environments, Samfundslitteratur Press (2002)
21. Accetta, M., Baron, R., Bolosky, W., Golub, D., Rashid, R., Tevanian, A., Young, M.: Mach: a new kernel foundation for UNIX development. In: Proc. of the USENIX Summer Conference, Altanta, GA, USA, pp. 93–113 (1986)
22. Neyem, A., Ochoa, S.F., Guerrero, L.A., Pino, J.A.: Sharing Information Resources in Mobile Ad-hoc Networks. In: Fuks, H., Lukosch, S., Salgado, A.C. (eds.) CRIWG 2005 LNCS, vol. 3706, pp. 351–358. Springer-Verlag, Heidelberg (2005)
23. Neyem, A., Ochoa, S.F., Pino, J.A.: Supporting Mobile Collaboration with Service-Oriented Mobile Units. In: Dimitriadis, Y.A., Zigurs, I., Gómez-Sánchez, E. (eds.) Groupware: Design, Implementation, and Use. Lecture Notes of Computer Science, vol. 4154, pp. 228–245. Springer-Verlag, Heidelberg (2006)

Sociability Design Guidelines for the Online Gaming Community: Role Play and Reciprocity

Yu Chieh Pan, Liangwen Kuo, and Jim Jiunde Lee

Graduate Institute of Communication Studies
No.1001, Dasyue Rd., Hsinchu City 300, Taiwan (R.O.C)
National Chiao Tung University
tracypan0705@gmail.com

Abstract. This study connects two different perspectives, HCI and CMC, and attempts to develop sociability design guidelines for the online community. According to the literature, the results of previous studies related to sociability are either too general or are lacking in focus. Role play and reciprocity are important factors influencing the dynamics of the online community because they can keep the community to development positively and keep the community in the order. The research questions for this study originated from the theoretical framework which combines role play process ideas of impression management with role play models.

Keywords: sociability, role play, reciprocity, design guideline.

1 Introduction

This paper begins with a discussion of the importance of social factors in groupware development. As Human Computer Interaction Design has gradually put more emphasis on situation and cultural factors, it may be practical to refer to related research from Computer Mediated Communication (CMC), and apply the results to a study of sociability. After reviewing previous studies of CMC, it is clear that role play and reciprocity have a close relationship to the online community. As a result, the main purpose of this study is to identify how the design of the website can create appropriate role play activities and reciprocity.

Impression management [4] and role play models [1] can complement each other. By integrating these two theories, a set of semi-structured interview questions was developed, while the methodology used in this study was based on case studies and contextual inquiry. Finally, the effects of role play and reciprocity in "Gamer" will be discussed, and the results will be mapped to the results of earlier studies.

2 Literature Review

2.1 The Importance of Social Factors in the Development of Groupware

The design of groupware is complicated because it needs to consider the interaction within the groups, and different factors in different situations. Grudin (1994) briefly

D. Schuler (Ed.): Online Communities and Social Comput., HCII 2007, LNCS 4564, pp. 426–434, 2007.
© Springer-Verlag Berlin Heidelberg 2007

summarized the origin of groupware and why groupware is successful. In his definition, "groupware" represents software applications which can help groups share documents and information easily. Besides, it also helps groups to accomplish common tasks. Group members have different interests, values, goals, responsibilities and roles and groupware need to coordinate these. It is due to these factors that groupware design is so complicated.

Grudin (1994) considered that social motivation factors are the main issue of groupware study, and that they are also the key to making a groupware design successful. Whether or not groupware is accepted by its target users depends on the common social dynamics. However, these issues are rarely obvious or static. Users' behavior will be oriented by tradition, personal characteristics and the people around them. Therefore, being aware of personal priorities is also important for the designer.

2.2 "Sociability" from the Perspective of CMC

2.2.1 Definitions of Sociability: Broad View vs. Narrow View
According to the Oxford English dictionary, "sociability" refers to a characteristic of an environment which makes people want to make friends with each other, keep company with others, and communicate with others in a friendly way. This explanation is similar to Rutter and Smith's. From the perspective of sociology, Rutter and Smith found that the study of sociability began with the paper written by Georg Simmel in 1911. Simmel put emphasis on human interaction rather than personal characteristics. Therefore, Rutter and Smith considered that sociability, according to Simmel, is a "purer" feature. In other words, it is togetherness which is important in our lives, and it is others' company which makes us happy.

However, when it comes to website design, sociability is defined differently. To speak concretely, sociability is a social strategy and technical structure. It can support the common goals and interaction processes in the online communities [2], [10].

As can be seen from the above discussion, sociability can have both a broad and a narrow definition. The narrow definition may aid and expand the broad definition. However, the definition of sociability in HCI lacks humanity, culture and is also task-oriented. Therefore, it may not satisfy the demands of online community. Consequently, this study redefines sociability as "The sociability-related strategy and technical structure which can promote an intimate relationship, friendly communication process and togetherness in the group, and which supports group collaboration to achieve the common goals".

2.2.2 The Importance of Role Play and Reciprocity
Role play and reciprocity are essential to group dynamics. Reciprocity is a basic feature of the online community, and it is also the key point that can make a community successful or not [9]. On the other hand, the online community can be managed and controlled effectively by taking advantage of role play [9]. Besides, one of the barriers to the development of the online community is the conflict of benefits, but the concordance of role play will improve this problem [5]. Therefore, a good groupware design which uses the concept of role play should make each member play their role well, and ensure that they understand the values, norms and responsibilities of the community.

As to the influence of roles in games, they not only affect personality but can also be used to predict user's behavior [6]. In other words, players with different levels, occupations and races will have different personalities. Consequently, if roles in the online community are related to roles in games, the differences between players and members in the online community will decrease. Therefore, we may take advantage of roles in games to help us manage the members' behavior in the online community.

Roles are created by interaction, and adhere to the norms and values of a community. Besides, role play still needs other resources to support it. Coordinated role play systems will decrease the conflict within the community. As a result, if we can design a website taking into consideration these differences, members in the online community will be able to communicate more efficiently.

2.3 Role Play and Reciprocity

2.3.1 Role Categories

Maloney-Krichmar and Preece (2005) applied 27 different membership roles, as identified by Benne and Sheats (1948), to analyze the dynamics of groups. Different perspectives and types of group require different categories of roles [3], [12], [6]. Of the various categories of roles, Benne and Sheats' (1948) are more complete than those of others. Besides, we can tell the level of reciprocity between members by identifying the role played by each member. Benne and Sheats (1948) clearly identified Group Membership Roles which include three main types: task roles, socio-emotional roles and individualistic roles. Under these three main types are a total of 27 different kinds of roles. Among these roles, are some which are related to the concept of reciprocity, namely information giver, initiator, opinion giver, elaborator, energizer and encourager. The definitions of these roles are given in Figure 2 [3].

Although researchers from different disciplines have discussed the processes and phenomena of role play, there is still a lack of role play theory to support the explanation of these studies. Therefore, in the next section, theater theory [4] and the role play model [1] will be integrated.

Table 1. Group Membership Roles as developed by Benne and Sheats (1948)

Task Roles	Definitions
Information giver	provides data and facts
Initiator	suggests novel ideas
Opinion giver	provides ideas, values and feelings
Elaborator	provides examples, rehearsal and instruction
Energizer	When members are not willing to discuss, energizer will encourage them and make them keep working.
Socio-Emotional Roles	
Encourager	Encourages creation of ideas and expresses a friendly attitude.

2.3.2 Theoretical Framework: Impression Management and the Role Play Model

One of the ideas in Goffman's theatre theory (1959) is impression management. According to Goffman's opinions, role is considered to be the process of growing, and he argues that a role will finally become a part of our personality. Role is formed from the interaction of interpersonal relationships, and it is also a natural phenomenon. In contrast, Ashforth (2001) studied role from the perspective of organizational management, focusing on efficiency. The role play model he developed provides the motivation for role play. In his linear model, people may finally leave their role and experience role transition. This model can help us understand and analyze the process of role play. However, it ignores other factors such as human interaction and interpersonal relationships.

Although these two theories have some differences, they both deal with situation and role identity. Therefore, they can complement each other and become the framework of this study. For example, Goffman considered that "setting" is the tool to define the situation, while Ashforth considered that roles can steadily develop in a strong situation. Situation refers to furniture, setting, decoration and other background items. It should provide stage scenes and properties to make players play in that environment. A "strong" situation has three characteristics: members understand the same role in the same way; they know what behavior is appropriate; it can provide some functions to support members' behavior.

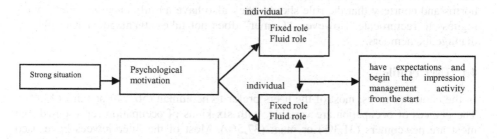

Fig. 1. Dynamic model of role play

Based on Goffman and Ashforth's theories, we can synthesize a dynamic model of role playing (Fig.3). That is to say, the situation will be the trigger to provide individuals with the motivation to play the role. Besides, a role has two forms, fixed and fluid. If a role's inner characteristics can express consistent and continuing images through the outside expression tools, this can be considered as great impression management. To rely on impression management, role play activities can help us maintain or create good social relationships [4].

3 Methodology

The methodology used in this study combines the concepts of case study and contextual inquiry. "Gamer" is the largest online game-community in Taiwan, and it applies the metaphors of race and game-related occupations to manage its users. In the recruiting section, this study cooperated with "Gamer", and the recruiting propaganda was posted on the homepage of its website. The subjects included 8 females and 8 males who are all users of "Gamer", and who use "Gamer" at least 4 times a month.

The results of the interviews were analyzed using task analysis, and based on the results, four models were defined: artifact model, physical model, sequence model and culture model. Of these, the culture model was the most effective model in the study. The sociability guidelines of this research are compared with past related guidelines in the concluding section of this paper.

During the process of interviewing the users, the interviewees were asked to use a laptop which could connect to the "gamer" website. The interviewer started the interviews according to the semi-structured interview questions and a questionnaire filled out by the interviewee previously. In addition to recording the audio, the operation image of the computer was also recorded using the software "Camtatasia Studio 3.0".

4   Results and Analysis

According to cross analysis, both role play and reciprocity were found to affect the development of sociability, and the effect of role play was especially obvious. Besides, it was found that one of the factors which influences reciprocity is related to trust. Moreover, it was also found that people use personal front, such as user's level and outlook of the role, to judge whether someone is worthy of trust or not. The norms and courtesy that the role should obey also have an influence on others' willingness to reciprocate. However, "Gamer" does not take advantage of role play to manage its members.

4.1   User Profile

In the choice of races, most of the users prefer to be human (56.3%) or fairy (43.8%). The choices of occupation are variable, with six kinds of occupation represented, but most are newcomers (31.3%) or magi (37.5%). Most of the interviewees have used "Gamer" for between 1 and 5 years (68.9%). In the evaluation of the role of reciprocity, the main roles identified were information giver (62%), opinion giver (56.3%) and encourager (62.5%). Overall, the subjects evaluated "Gamer" as a website with characteristics of friendliness (62.6%), goal satisfaction (68.8%) and togetherness (56.3%).

4.2   Role Play

According to the results of the interviews, there are three ways in which the sociability of a website can be enhanced, namely by promoting group cooperation, by using communication tools and by building norms to decrease communication problems.

To promote positive group cooperation experiences, both, planned and unplanned activities can be used. Beginners and the webmasters play important roles in both types of activities. Planned cooperation will actively provide topic-related information. However, unplanned cooperation relies on unspoken consensus. This type of cooperation will sometimes be deleted by the webmaster because it has no relationship to the topic. This seems to be the trade-off need to be balanced.

Using communication tools and building up the norms of the roles will decrease communication problems. That is to say, the communication tool themselves are related to sociability. From the perspective of motivation, some subjects use email to avoid conflict. Therefore, using email can often help to reduce paper battles.

Enforcing the norms effectively can make the website operate in concordance. Sometimes people feel impatient because the communication lacks efficiency. Therefore it is important to set up rules and enhance the function of article searches so that the whole website will keep in order.

Maintaining good social relationships and a nice atmosphere can be improved in three ways: by creating chatting topics, by making people feel that they are respected, and by making them feel comfortable. When people share their image designs, they can increase their chatting topics. Unique role image designs will make others feel curious. If they see that another roles' style is similar to theirs, they will feel curious and want to contact those people. When it comes to how to make people feel respected, communication efficiency is important. People will want to talk more when the communication efficiency is good. Besides, users will feel comfortable when their rating points are enhanced, when responses to their articles increase, and when they receive other short messages eg. for their birthday. The ideas for the last two experiences come from BBS and other online game communities. Besides, people will feel especially comfortable in one to one interaction.

4.3 Reciprocity

Reciprocity has to achieve community efficiency and confirm user's existence of identity. Some users want to know who has given them GP. GP is presented by number, and users will give GP to others when they appreciate their article. Besides, when users win in some virtual competition held by the website they will gain GP too. However, the system does not satisfy this demand. Therefore, to maintain communication efficiency, "Gamer" sacrifices the existence of its members and takes away the right to communicate with others. Consequently, from the perspective of website design, it is critical to guarantee both reciprocity and communication efficiency. Efficiency can be achieved by using symbols to express support. Besides, people can know who is supporting them, which can also increase the social interaction.

4.4 The Problems of "Role Play" in "Gamer"

The subjects identified a number of reasons that make them want to use the functions of career and race. These motivations are: fun, showing off, feeling bored, admiring others' outlook, and building a personal unique style.

The expectation to role can be categorized into "attacking" and "aiding", and it is similar to the expectation to role in the game. However, roles in the website cannot be mapped to roles in the game. Users are influenced by the games they have played before, and their thinking about the roles in "Gamer" is related to the functions and features of their role in the game. When the website can not satisfy the users' expectations, the function of the role in the website does not affect their behavior.

Ambiguity of the roles results in imitation and conflict between the roles and the images. In the world of gaming, there are always some characteristics that everybody likes, but imitation will interrupt the effect of the role play functions in the website. Moreover, if the users are over-focused on their images, the function cannot help them to influence their social relationships. The more blurred the roles are, the more limited the roles' learning and effect will be. These are also problems in "Gamer".

5 Conclusion

Figures 5 and 6 summarize the sociability design guidelines developed in this study and the guidelines for sociability which were developed by other researchers in the past. According to the main goals and sub-goals, the tables below show that social strategies and technical structure are related to sociability. Based on the literature, the importance of role play and reciprocity can also be affirmed from different kinds of online communities.

6 Future Research Suggestions

Although studies in the past have not shown the relationship between reciprocity and sociability, this study shows that they do influence each other. The users also have two different viewpoints. One of the points of view suggests that giving others help has no relationship with interpersonal relationships. However, some people consider that helping each other can increase the chance of interaction. Therefore, the relationship between reciprocity and sociability still needs further research.

Table 2. Summary of the sociability design guidelines related to role play

Main goal	Sub-goal	Social Strategies and Technical Structure	
		Social Strategies	Technical Structure
Group Cooperation	Prolong Group Cooperation	Provide sources to aid the collaboration. Reward users according to their level of contribution.	Establish a reward system. Open space for group activities unrelated to the topic.
			Environment has structure to support group cooperation [1].
		Allow the members to reply in a humorous way [11].	
Reduce communication problems	Prevent negative emotion from spreading.	Take advantage of one to one communication tools such as email.	Add a short message function and place this function in a clear and convenient place.
	Reduce user's feelings of impatience.	Enhance the efficiency of communication and reading.	Empower search functions such as search of full text. Provide an instant messaging service.
	Perform role rules effectively.	Remind users of the rules. Remind users in a definite way with appropriate frequency.	Show the reasons why some users are punished. Implement membership exams and occupation transfer exams.
		Develop values ,norms, and control processes that are agreed upon by all members [10].	

Table 2. (*Continued*)

Build good social relationships	Build an intimate and friendly environment.	Set up some funny and interesting topics on a timely basis.	Use a voting system to help the group make decisions. Group users with a common sense of beauty.
	Create a supportive environment	Users can get others' encouragement effectively, especially through one-to-one communication.	Show the ratings of the points of the personal information file, numbers of the replying articles and congratulation messages.
	Make users feel respected.	Make users reply to new articles or to articles that have had no replies.	Put new articles or articles that have had no replies in an obvious place.
	Make new friends.	Increase chatting topics. Help users to enhance the quality of their articles.	Let users visit others' role images freely. Let users know who supports and encourages them.
			Provide more visible communication tools [2].

Table 3. Summary of the sociability design guidelines related to reciprocity

Main goal	Sub-goals	Social Strategies and Technical Structure	
		Social Strategies	Technical Structure
Increase chances of reciprocity	Create contact chances and motivation.	Put emphasis on communication efficiency and users' sense of being.	Create symbols to show support and encouragement. Users have right to choose to reveal their identity or not.
	Enhance level of trust.	Provide indexes for users to refer to the level of trust of an article or other users.	Use trust-related indexes such as the number of the posted texts, number of log ins, rate of points of the personal information file, outlook of the role, level identified by the website and other special identities such as webmaster and rank in virtual activities.
		Maintain appropriateness of discussion content.	Assign a moderator. People who reply to articles should be approved by the authority or have qualifications [12].
	Enhance willingness of reciprocity.	Strengthen Netiquette.	When users need to post an article asking for help, the system may provide some model sentences.
		Develop values, norms and control processes that are agreed on by all members [10].	

The scale of the website may have an important influence on role play activities. From Goffman's perspective (1959), the definition of impression management is the ability and process to manage the image. Ashforth (2001) believes that a strong situation is important. If it is difficult to be impressed by the same person many times, it is also difficult to deal with impression management. In other words, sociability may vary according to the scale of the website.

References

1. Ashforth, B.E.: Role transitions in organizational life: an identity-based perspective. Lawrence Erlbaum Associates, NJ (2001)
2. Barab, S.A. , Makinster, J.G., Moore, J.A., Cunningham, D.J., & The ILF Design Team.: Designing and Building an On-line Community: The Struggle to Support Sociability in the Inquiry Learning Forum. ETR& D, vol. 49(4), pp. 71–96 (2001)
3. Benne, K.D., Sheats, P.: Functional Roles of Group Members. Journal of Sociological Issues 2, 42–47 (1948)
4. Goffman, E.: The presentation of self in everyday life. Doubleday, NY (1959)
5. Grudin, J.: Eight challenges for developers. Communications of the ACM 37(1), 93–105 (1994)
6. Kozinet, R.V.: E-Tribalized Marketing?: The Strategic Implications of Virtual Communities of Consumption. European Management Journal 17, 252–264 (1999)
7. Li, C.J., Yang, T.A.: A Research of Performance and Personality of On-line Game Players in "Lineage". Kaohsiung Normal University Journal 19(3), 85–104 (2005)
8. Maloney-Krichmar, D., Preece, J.: A multilevel analysis of sociability, usability and community dynamics in an on-line health community, ACM Transactions on Computer-Human Interaction (TOCHI), vol. 12(2) (2005)
9. Oxford English Dictionary Online [Online]. Available http://dictionary.oed.com/
10. Preece, J., Maloney-Krichmar, D.: Fundamentals, evolving technologies, and emerging applications:HCI hand book Online communities focusing on sociability and usability. In: Jacko, J.A., Sears, A. (eds.) The human-computer interaction handbook, Lawrence Erlbaum Associates, Mahwah, NJ (2003)
11. Preece, J.: Online communities: Usability, Sociability, Theory and Methods. In: Earnshaw, R., Guedj, R., Van Dam, A., Vince, T. (eds.) Frontiers of Human-Centred Computing, Online Communities and Virtual Environments, pp. 263–277. Springer, Heidelberg (2001)
12. Rutter, J., Smith, G.: (s/d). [Online]. Available: http://www.cric.ac.uk/cric/ Jason_Rutter/papers/Ritual.Pdf Yi, H.H. (ed.) The factors that influence the trust between members in the virtual community. National Chung Cheng University Department of Business Administration (2002)
13. Yang, T.Y.: Members' role and interaction in virtual community. National Chung Cheng University Department of Business Administration (2000)

CINeSPACE: Interactive Access to Cultural Heritage While On-The-Move

Pedro Santos[1], André Stork[1], Maria Teresa Linaza[2], Oliver Machui[3],
Don McIntyre[4], and Elisabeth Jorge[5]

[1] Fraunhofer-IGD, A2
{Pedro.Santos,Andre.Stork}@igd.fhg.de
[2] VICOMTech
mtlinaza@vicomtech.es
[3] Trivisio GmbH
machui@trivisio.de
[4] Lighthouse
don.mcintyre@urbanlearningspace.com
[5] Fomento de San Sebastián
Elisabeth_Jorge@donostia.org

Abstract. Films are unquestionably a part of Cultural Heritage. Problems of current systems for accessing Cultural Heritage resources which deal with film objects include some of the following aspects: Distributed sources which store huge amounts of information; different formats of the contents ranging from traditional ones such as paper to advanced multimedia objects; and finally, and what is more crucial for the content providers, lack of systems which support currently the needs of the user such as enriched content, interaction with the information, usability, and exchange of experiences with other users. Taking into account these gaps detected by some European cities with a strong connection with the film sector, CINeSPACE a European research project aims at designing and implementing a mobile rich media collaborative information exchange platform, scalable, accessible through a wide variety of networks, and therefore, interoperable and Location-Based for the promotion of Film Heritage, going beyond the current state of the art. CINeSPACE enables users to interact with Location-Based multimedia contents while navigating a city. Audiovisual information will be delivered through a unique and portable low-cost wireless high definition near-to-the-eye display and audio phones. CINeSPACE will also comprise a small camera able to record or send what the user is "seeing". This information can be uploaded to a database through a WLAN hot spot or a 3G connection in order to create collaborative experiences with other end users. This paper presents the current status of development of the project.

1 Introduction

As stated by the UNESCO, films (whether they are documentaries or fiction, plastic or video) are unquestionably a part of the Cultural Heritage of the humanity whose vocation is to grow each day while respecting pluralism. Cinema, besides being a technical support in constant evolution, has been a novel form of expression for creative thoughts and feelings, a conveyor of dreams and emotions, and an instrument

D. Schuler (Ed.): Online Communities and Social Comput., HCII 2007, LNCS 4564, pp. 435–444, 2007.

of the imagination as well as a witness of instants, places and visions situated in time and space, and hence an incomparable aid to memory. Nevertheless, nowadays, digitalization, access and preservation of Cultural Heritage has been mainly addressed to cultural objects, related to literature, history or architecture, forgetting other important kind of Cultural Heritage like cinema. Film Heritage as part of the overall concept of Cultural Heritage is very important by itself, but also has a strong potential as means for promoting the traditional cultural objects like architecture, history, literature or cultural diversity.

As stated in a previous analysis made by the cities taking part in CINeSPACE, film contents can be used to promote access to urban and cultural objects through new interactive and creative experiences. However, there are still many problems for accessing Urban, Film and Cultural Heritage of a city:

- Cities own big amounts of information from different sources (history, monuments,
- museums, natural environments, traditions, cultural agenda or film archives).
- All multimedia content has different formats (text, pictures, audio, video, reality, film).
- The content is distributed among different databases and providers (City Council, cultural
- institutions, film archives).
- Concerning the needs of the tourists to these Film cities, there are currently some lacks
- that are not covered.

  - A guide or map may not include enough detailed information to cater for the
  - interest area or domain (Cultural Heritage, architecture, film scenarios).
  - Within a sightseeing tour, the breadth and depth of information is often limited.
  - Information drawn from the Internet is often time consuming to collect and
  - assimilate.
  - PDA displays and multimedia mobile-phones have limited resolution and field-of-view.

- Tourists and even citizens of the cities have great difficulty to communicate their own
- experiences to other people.
- It is difficult for tourists to share multimedia content with other possible users.

Fig. 1. The CINeSPACE Approach

2 Approach

The general objective of creating a mobile interactive rich media platform to support collaborative information exchange for the promotion of film tourism and cultural heritage is reflected in the following technical approaches:

- To provide a rich media software delivery platform, capable of distributing Location-Based specific information related to Urban, Film and Cultural Heritage. In addition, users will not only be able to experience but create visual information while "on-the-move".
- To integrate and go beyond the existing standards in order to provide semantic access using standard ontologies to multimedia indexed cultural content using MPEG-based standards in novel scenarios such as film tourism, cinema professionals and citizens.
- To create an integrated, wireless, lightweight, high definition wearable Head Mounted Display, combined with compression/decompression audio/video streaming hardware and a wireless network connection.
- To create a hybrid outdoor tracking system using a combination of different tracking techniques (GPS, image processing and inertial sensors) to enhance the precision of pose estimation to allow for Augmented Reality content.
- To explore the application of collaborative mobile information technologies to deliver and create rich media information based on the location of the user within urban spaces.
- To validate the platform through three pilot experiences in three cities: Venice, San Sebastián and Glasgow, each one oriented to the three possible end users of the platform.

The CINeSPACE system is addressing the following target users:

- Film tourism: People that choose a tourist destination due to its relationship with cinema (famous International Film Festivals, shooting locations).
- Cinema professionals: Film producers that want to know possible stages and film facilities of some interesting urban environments.
- Citizens: Citizens of the cities that have stories to tell and most have a longing to understand more about their own 'home'

3 Adaptive Media Services

CineSpace represents a heterogeneous computing environment. The pervasive use of networks and the Internet by all segments of modern society means that the number of connected computing resources is growing tremendously. To make CineSpace available to a broad audience we have the opportunity and the need for heterogeneous computing systems to effectively utilize these resources in novel ways.

Adaptive Media Services in the Application Service Level provide the link between the end-user devices and content providing rich media services in CineSpace.

Users can access CineSpace through the specific CineSpace device or individual mobile devices ranging from mobile phones, PDAs to Laptop Computers which are connected over a variety of different network connections from UMTS to WLAN. In addition CineSpace content can be accessed from stationary devices such as home computers and workstations.

The key to connect users with different user skills or data retrieval needs and different devices communicating over different connections is context-awareness.

3.1 Context Awareness

Context-awareness is any information that can be used to characterize the situation of an entity, where an entity can be a person, place, physical or computational object or the use of context to provide task-relevant information and/or services to a user, wherever they may be through the ability of a computing device or program to sense, react to, or adapt to the environment in which it is running.

In order words an application can exhibit three important context-awareness behaviours, namely:

1. The presentation of information and services to a user (display context).
2. The automatic execution of a service (context-sensing) and
3. The tagging of context to information for later retrieval.

In addition there are a couple of general problems associated with distributed computing especially under heterogeneous conditions. The most crucial are those on mobile devices. These include:

- Limited I/O capabilities (and most often difficult to used input modalities)
- Tiny displays for content presentation
- Resource constraints (like energy supply and data storage)
- Unreliable and bit error-prone wireless connections

Apart from the aforementioned problems associated to mobile devices, other typical problem areas are network and user-centred problems. For instance, a major problem is, choosing a platform-independent User Interface Description Language (UIDL) for content presentation across the spectrum of device technologies available on the market. Another issue is the lack of appropriate modelling techniques for dynamically choosing an optimal communication protocol at runtime for each device which requests content from a server or a web service provider.

Furthermore, in most environments other issues like authentication, security, privacy and trust also pose significant problems. Then there is the challenge of providing context-ware and location-based services in situations where there is either incomplete or inaccurate information of the user's environmental conditions.

Therefore CineSpace needs a framework based on a device-independent specification and a model-view-controller paradigm that uses a strategy for separating implementation logic from rendering logic.

4 Content Management

The system has been designed to be client device and platform independent. Another requirement has been web accessibility. Taking this into account, Web services have been chosen as the interface of the system. Web services provide interoperability between different platforms and programming languages and they have client libraries available for most of them.

The main inputs received by the system will be IDs of the users, locations and profiles. With this information, the system will maintain the state of each user and deliver the content that best fits the requirements of the user.

Figure 2 displays the proposed architecture for the Rich Media Servers. Several levels have been defined, which will be explained in the following sections.

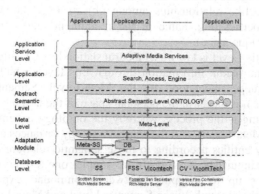

Fig. 2. CINeSPACE System Design

4.1 Application Level

The Application Level will be in charge of delivering the contents, managing the queries from the users. The first time a user logs into the system, his/her profile will be loaded or created if it does not exist. This level will manage the state of each user, tracking what they send and receive, managing the relationships between users and asking for the content to deliver.

The profile will be used to include personalization functionalities into the system. The georeference information will be the key factor to retrieve the content to be delivered, but other aspects of the personalization will include language, device, areas of interest or demographic data.

A simplified example of the performance of this level will be the following.

- The Application Level receives through the web service a query telling that the user 123 is on the position 43°18'53.86"N, 1°59'35.45"W (La Concha beach in San Sebastian) and has the CINeSPACE device.
- It checks the state of the user, validating he/she has the rights to use the system and is in a state where videos should be shown.
- It checks the profile of the user and notices that the user is mostly interested in romantic films, is 30-35 years old and speaks Spanish.
- The Application Level requests videos of romantic films, if possible with Spanish audio or at least subtitles and if available, the ones, that have more probability to be well known for a 30-35 years old person.
- The Application Level gets the video and sends it to the user after checking the user has the rights to watch it.

4.2 Semantic Level

Abstract Semantic Level is located between the Application Level and Meta-Level (see Fig. 2). It includes an ontology which refers to an engineering artefact, made up basically by a specific vocabulary used to describe a certain reality and a set of explicit assumptions regarding the intended meaning of the vocabulary.

Vocabulary of terms includes objects, concepts and words, e.g. city, monument. It is not enough naming the terms of the vocabulary but rather more information about them is necessary, like relationships among objects (e.g. monument of the city), attributes and properties (e.g. name of the monument) and constraints (e.g. each monument has a unique name).

Abstract Semantic Level is known as the translation level. Using the search engine, users will query the media information through this level, which will translate the queries to a language understood by the Meta-Level. Semantic Level is more appealing to user as it is closer to the personal space of the user.

Ontology mapping is the process whereby the ontology is semantically related at conceptual level (Meta-Level), and the source ontology instances are transformed into the target ontology entities according to those semantic relations. Different kinds of mappings are distinguished starting from simple one-to-one mappings between classes and values up to mappings between compound expressions. Ontology mapping is the technical step between Semantic Level and Meta-Level.

Besides defining a concrete ontology for CINeSPACE project, some existing ontologies will be integrated. In this case, we will combine CIDOC Conceptual Reference Model (CIDOC CRM) and International Federation of Information Technology and Travel & Tourism (IFITT) ontologies with the ontology created for CINeSPACE. Therefore, MPEG-7 will be used for describing the features of multimedia content (audio-video records, shooting shorts, interviews), CIDOC- CRM as an domain ontology for Cultural Heritage information or IFFIT RMSIG which provides a reference model for modelling electronic tourism markets (gastronomy, accommodation). There are still other information types, such as curiosities, film extras, folklore and intangible heritage, location and production guides, facilities) that should be fit in any extension of the previously defined standards.

The CIDOC CRM approximates relevant expert conceptualisations underlying major documentation and metadata formats of material cultural heritage and beyond. It also provides an extensible vocabulary and an extensible structure about possible states of affairs as a unique reference in order to transform and merge data of different structures and to drive queries (mediation). And finally, it is not a fusion of existing formats, but a product of expert insight and intensive interdisciplinary work. As such, it builds on a meta-schema of fundamental categories and causal relationships with explanatory power.

IFITT implement a methodology for harmonizing electronic tourism markets. This methodology has to take into consideration the following requirements:

- Interoperability of different electronic markets or systems, independent of their physical representation
- Flexibility and extendibility (to be adaptable to specific requirements or changes)

Its reference model focuses on the modelling of market processes and tourism services on a conceptual level, independent of their physical representation (e.g.

representation as XML documents or distributed objects). Instead of specifying details of the physical model (e.g. XML DTDs or IDL descriptions), the conceptual model describes semantic aspects of electronic tourism markets, i.e., entities and their relationships.

4.3 Meta-level

Meta-Level manages the connection between metadata and information of the databases. Metadata can be defined as *data about data*. Although this is the most common definition, there are many others more sophisticated, as "metadata is structured, encoded data that describe characteristics of information-bearing entities to aid in the identification, discovery, assessment, and management of the described entities".

Therefore, metadata has an essential role in multimedia content management through media content lifecycle (create, manage and distribution/transact) and is critical for describing essential aspects of multimedia content, including main topics, author, language, events, scenes, objects, times, places, rights, packaging, access control, content adaptation, and so forth. Conformity with open metadata standards will be vital for multimedia content management systems (see Figure 3) to allow faster design and implementation, interoperability with broad field of competitive standards-based tools and systems, and leveraging of rich set of standards-based technologies for critical functions such as content extraction, advanced search, and personalization.

Some main requirements are essential in order to get a group of effective metadata, such as standardised structural elements ("fields") and structure, and standardised encoding of structure and data (authorities). The system has some requirements which have to be captured when defying the metadata. These main aspects are the following ones:

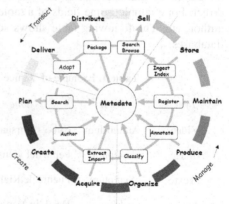

Fig. 3. Meta Content Lifecycle

- Localization using georeference, specifying latitude and altitude of the audio, text, image or video information (Location-based services).
- Identification of the visitor via personalization, related to the usage of the Content Management (Users customizing).
- Visual appearance in relation to colour (black and white or colour) and to final viewer device (pocket pc/PDA or magnifiers) (Visual appearance).

Information search results will depend on the city (Glasgow, San Sebastián and Venice). When the visitor is in San Sebastián, he/she will not be able to access any information neither from Glasgow nor from Venice. Therefore, the system must be aware of the location of the user. The first requirement provides that information. Perhaps, some visitors do not want to view more than once a certain image or video, so it is necessary to maintain a tracing of their visits. All these actions described are based on the following aspects of the first requirement:

- Events, scenes, objects, times, places. User customizing refers to the type of information that will be provided to the final user. There can be a hierarchy of users. This way, some visitors of a level-hierarchy will be able to view particular information but no lower-level users.
- Rights, access control, main topic, author, publication, language. The language spoken in each city of the project is different, so city tourists, film directors etc. maybe do not understand any of the language of the cities, even if they want to use the system. Besides, images can be black and white or coloured; the final device is composed by two main parts (magnifiers and pocket pc or pda) and the information can be shown into any of them, and so forth. It is clear that more adaptation is necessary.
- Content adaptation. As said before, each city (Glasgow, Venice and San Sebastián) will have its own database with a distributed database architecture. There are two different situations of data provided by the city manager: Glasgow as a city with a database and meta-level created, and San Sebastián and Venice as cities without any database or meta-level created.

Therefore, an uniform Meta-Level among three databases and Semantic Level is needed. As the cases of San Sebastián and Venice are similar, we will design their databases so that the translation between the Meta-Level and all the databases is direct. For example, some fields of a table of the databases could be type, name, year, author, etc. The following table shows some tables of Venice's and San Sebastian's databases.

Table 1. Example of Venice's and San Sebastian's databases

Type	What	Name	...	Year	Author
Video	Auditorium	Cubo - Kursaal	...	1999	Rafael Moneo
Image	Sculpture	Peine del viento	...	1977	Eduardo Txillida
Text	Sculpture	Puente de Rialto	...	1352	Antonio Da Ponte
Audio	Film	Death in Venice	...	1971	Thomas Mann (Book) Luchino Visconti (Film)

In these cases, the Meta-Level will have some metadata related to the type of information presented, the name, the date of creation, the author of the work, etc. so that the connection between the databases of Venice and/or San Sebastian and the Meta-Level is transparent.

On the other hand, Glasgow is a particular case. They have already a big multimedia repository and a Meta-Level for that repository too. So, another level between the Meta-Level and the Semantic Level has to appear to support this particular situation. Otherwise, if that level had not been created, the system would not be homogenous.

4.4 Adaptation Module

The multimedia repository of Glasgow has already a Meta-Level defined to its database, but the Meta-Level has been defined for the specific work of Scottish Screen. Thus, the system requirements force to define some new metadata related to Location-based services, users customizing or visual appearance. This new metadata will be stored in a new database so that the actual module will be made up by the existing meta-level and the new database designed for the metadata not taken into account before.

This action will not affect to the connection of the multimedia databases. On the other hand, it will make easier the connection with the general Meta-Level because we get the same metadata defined in the next level for the remaining databases.

4.5 Performance of the System

The process starts (see Figure 4) with the storage of multimedia information in the Rich-Media Server for each city. Firstly, geographical description is needed as an important part of the metadata. Afterwards, low level features for the multimedia content including structural and semantic aspects will be indexed. In such a way, some MPEG-7 files will describe all multimedia information.

The CINeSPACE system is not focused on the indexing stages, so that each of the city partners of the project will be in charge of collecting the necessary information to create the metadata. The system will allow to store and access this metadata.

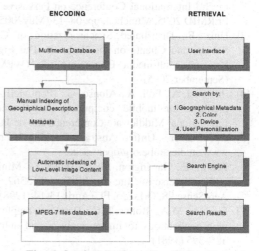

Fig. 4. Logical Performance of the Content

On the other hand, the user of the system will retrieve information. Users could search by three concepts: georeference, personalization and visual appearance. Search by georeference means the device will show multimedia information around her/his actual location. Customer personalization allows filtering the information to which the user has rights to visualize. And visual appearance can be performed with colour (black and white or colour) and/or the final device (PDA or magnifiers). After configuring it, search engine returns the results.

5 Conclusion

The system design has been concluded. In the next step the consortium will analyze which kind of hardware to use for the mobile outdoor application and if there will be one or more specialized CineSpace Gadgets. We will try to also support common end user devices such as mobile phones or PDAs which will be able to connect to the CineSpace system. To take advantage of the flexible CineSpace design we plan to make complete tours available to users as session logs of where they have been and which annotations they took. We think that the CineSpace system presents a useful add-on to film tourism in many cities as well as for film professionals.

Acknowledgements. This work is partially funded by European Commission Grant CineSpace IST-2005-034990.

References

[1] Gadh, Prabhu, Su, C.: Middleware for Multimedia Mobile Collaborative System. IEEE ComSoc sponsored 3rd annual wireless Telecommunication Symposium (2004)

[2] Hinz, F.: Context Modelling for Device- and Location-Aware Mobile Web Applications. In: 3rd International Conference on Pervasive Computing (Pervasive 2005), Workshop: PERMID 2005, München, pp. 08–13 (May2005)

[3] Hinz, F.: Distributed Synchronization of Context Modelling Mechanisms between Servers and Clients on the Web. In: The Eigth International Conference on Wireless Personal Multimedia Communication (WPMC'05), Aalborg, Denmark, pp. 18–22 (September 2005)

[4] Popovici, A., Frei, A., Alonso, G.: [PopoviciFA:03] [published] A proactive middleware platform for mobile computing. In: Proceedings of the 4th ACM/IFIP/USENIX International Middleware Conference Rio de Janeiro, Brazil, (June 16-20, 2003)

[5] Opentracker - Unfied Abstract Tracking Interface (Last Visited: 01.01.2007) Website: www.studierstube.org/opentracker

[6] Foxlin, E., Harrington, M., Altshuler,Y.: Miniature 6-DOF inertial system for tracking HMDs. Intersense, Inc. In: SPIE, vol. 3362, Helmet and Head-Mounted Displays III, AeroSense 98, Orlando, FL (April 13-14, 1998)

[7] Fischler, M.A., Bolles, R.C.: Random sample consensus: A paradigm for model fitting with applications to image analysis and automated cartography. Comm. ACM 24(6), 381–395 (1981)

[8] Lowe, D.G.: Three-Dimensional Object Recognition from Single Two-Dimensional Image. Artificial Intelligence 31, 355–395 (1987)

[9] Stricker, D.: Markerloses optisches Tracking. Dissertation, pp. 89–141 (November 2002)

[10] Jurie, F., Dhome, M.: A Simple and Efficient Template Matching Algorithm. In: International Conference on Computer Vision, pp. 544–549 (2001)

[11] Michaël, A., Gilles, S., Marie-Odile, B.: Handling Uncertain Sensor Data in Vision-Based Camera Tracking. ISMAR, pp. 58–67 (2004)

[12] Wexler, Y., Fitzgibbon, A.W., Zisserman, A.: Learning epipolar geometry from image sequences, Computer Vision and Pattern Recognition, 2003. Proceedings. 2003 IEEE Computer Society Conference on vol. 2, pp. 18–20 June 2003 Page(s): II - 209-16 vol.2 (2003)

The Hidden Order of Wikipedia

Fernanda B. Viégas, Martin Wattenberg, and Matthew M. McKeon

Visual Communication Lab, IBM Research, 1 Rogers St,
Cambridge, MA 02142, USA
{viegasf,mwatten,mmmckeon}@us.ibm.com

Abstract. We examine the procedural side of Wikipedia, the well-known internet encyclopedia. Despite the lack of structure in the underlying wiki technology, users abide by hundreds of rules and follow well-defined processes. Our
case study is the Featured Article (FA) process, one of the best established procedures on the site. We analyze the FA process through the theoretical framework of commons governance, and demonstrate how this process blends
elements of traditional workflow with peer production. We conclude that rather
than encouraging anarchy, many aspects of wiki technology lend themselves to
the collective creation of formalized process and policy.

Keywords: Wikipedia, Governance, Commons, Peer Production.

1 Introduction

Wikipedia, the online encyclopedia that anyone can edit, has become one of the most
visited sites on the web. A common question is how such apparently useful content
can be generated by an army of distributed volunteer editors. This paper discusses
part of the answer: despite the seeming potential for anarchy or chaos, a sophisticated
set of processes have emerged.

Every day the Wikipedia front page presents a "Featured Article" (FA). Consider
the trajectory of one such article, on AIDS, which was featured on June 15 2006.
Before appearing on the front page, the article underwent a lengthy process of peer
review. It was nominated as a Featured Article Candidate (FAC) on 20 March 2006.
Before nomination, it had gone through a separate peer review to help improve its
quality. The article was also part of the "Medicine Collaboration of the Week" project, where members focus their attention on a given medicine-related article per
week. The FAC review process itself involved 18 different users and amassed 61
posts. In these posts there were references to seven of Wikipedia's guidelines and the
entire review process lasted 20 days.

Such a complex and bureaucratic process runs counter to naïve depictions of
Wikipedia as an anarchic space. The site boasts myriad guidelines, policies and rules.
Moreover, a series of formal processes, of which the FA procedure is a prime example, are starting to materialize. Analyzing the organizational principles behind these
emerging processes can help us better understand the inner workings of Wikipedia.
The emergence of these processes is, we believe, just as interesting—and "magical"—
as the emergence of high-quality articles.

D. Schuler (Ed.): Online Communities and Social Comput., HCII 2007, LNCS 4564, pp. 445–454, 2007.

The paper starts with a review of related academic work on online communities. This review leads us to the work of two scholars who have framed our analysis of process in Wikipedia: Yochai Benkler's study of online peer production [1,2] and Elinor Ostrom's review of collective action and governance in offline communities [14, 15]. After laying out this intellectual framework, we plunge into a detailed investigation of the FA process in Wikipedia: how it works, how it relates to Wikipedia's policies and guidelines, and what it tells us about formal processes on the site. We finish with a discussion of how the structure of the FA process relates to Benkler's and Ostrom's principles. We conclude that rather than encouraging anarchy, many aspects of wiki technology lend themselves to the group creation of workflows and process.

2 Related Work

In the 1980s and earlier, online communities consisted mainly of conversation. People came together in Usenet, chatrooms, IRC channels, and even MUDs primarily to talk to each other. With the exception of MUDs, interaction was exclusively conversational and scholarship on these environments reflected the focus on conversation [4, 7, 13].

Online communities today include social networking sites, wikis, and social bookmarking tools. While conversation remains important, the production of a variety of goods has become a vital aspect of these communities. Code, encyclopedic entries, massive websites, and even game economies exist today. In response, online communities scholarship has expanded to encompass new inquiry areas such as economics and law [10].

To examine the governance structure of Wikipedia, this paper draws on the literature of regulation in commons-based communities. Our main sources are Yochai Benkler's work on commons-based peer-production and Elinor Ostrom's work on commons-based governance. After an overview of this theory, we then focus on the FA process in Wikipedia and its relation to Ostrom and Benkler's work.

2.1 Commons-Based Peer Production

One of the best-studied examples of online collaborative production is open source software. Researchers have examined both the development process [12] and the incentive structures [9]. Of particular interest is a framework proposed by Yochai Benkler encompassing open-source development, Wikipedia, and several other online systems. Benkler suggests these systems represent a new form of economic organization, distinct from either firms or markets: commons-based peer-production [1]. Unlike other organizational methods—such as the market and the firm—peer production depends on individual action that is self-selected and decentralized rather than hierarchically assigned. Individuals make their own choices with regard to resources managed as a commons.

Benkler defines two evolutionary phases that successful commons-based communities typically go through:

1. Creating content (utterance):
   This is the initial phase where large, complex tasks are broken into small, independent modules. This phase is marked by providing contributors with a wealth of tasks that can be achieved individually, in uncoordinated fashion.

2. Quality control (relevance/accreditation):
This second phase is characterized by a concerted effort on quality assurance. How can we know that the content produced by widely dispersed individuals is not nonsense? In this phase, the community must define standards and create low-cost quality control mechanisms.

Scholars are starting to investigate the nature of work coordination and quality assurance in Wikipedia. Stvilia et al. investigated how Wikipedians improve the quality of entries through discussions in Talk pages [18]. Viégas and colleagues have examined the role of Talk pages in group coordination and policy enforcement [20].

2.2 Governing the Commons Offline

Online communities are not the only place where one finds commons-based communities. In fact, the challenges of commons-based governance are not new. There is a broad literature about the evolution of institutions for collective action in the offline world, where communities have had to self-organize and govern for millennia. Elinor Ostrom's work [14,15] analyzes the principles behind successful, self-governed common-pool resources communities (CPRs). She has looked at communal tenure in a variety of settings, including high mountain forests in Japan, commons-based irrigation institutions in Spain and the Philipines, and inshore fisheries in Turkey and Sri Lanka. For centuries, these communities of farmers, villagers, and fishermen have successfully found ways to manage shared natural resources—forests, rivers, fisheries, timber—without relying on centralized authority.

Some challenges faced by these offline, self-governed communities are similar to the challenges faced today by their online counterparts: creation of rules, monitoring mechanisms, arbitration, and conflict resolution. Ostrom proposes a list of eight organizational principles found in long-enduring CPR institutions. As a first step, we focus on four principles which seem natural to map to the online space. A detailed consideration of the other principles is an important area for future research.

1. **Congruence between rules and local conditions:** instead of relying on "one-size-fits-all" regulation, rules must be intimately associated with the particularities of the resources they regulate. For instance, a community of farmers who depend on a river for irrigating their crops will need to devise rules that fit the particular geographical profile of their region and river as opposed to relying on some "generic" set of rules for irrigation.

2. **Collective-choice arrangements:** most individuals affected by the operational rules should be able to participate in modifying these rules and the cost of altering rules should be kept low.

3. **Monitoring:** Individuals who monitor the commons should be accountable to the rest of the community.

4. **Conflict-resolution mechanisms:** community members should have rapid access to low-cost local arenas to resolve conflicts.

Whereas Benkler's work addresses the importance of coordination and information flow in online peer-production, Ostrom's principles show us how commons-based communities can be successful in self-organization and self-governance. Her principles give us a framework with which to examine and situate coordination processes in Wikipedia.

3 Case Study: Featured Articles

To examine the interplay of rules, processes, and governance in Wikipedia in depth, we concentrated on one of the best established and most visible processes on the English site: the FA process [22]. As mentioned above, an FA, is an article that appears prominently on the main Wikipedia page. There is only one FA at a time, changing once a day. Selecting these articles is a delicate matter: quality is important, since they represent the public face of Wikipedia. At the same time, many more articles are suggested for FAs than can be accommodated. Choosing which articles should be featured is a challenge in collective action, and it turns out that a process has evolved in response.

We gathered information on the FA process through several avenues. An important aspect of Wikipedia is that procedures and the guidelines that drive them are described in detail on publicly accessible pages. Furthermore, much of the discussion surrounding the creation of the guidelines is available via so-called "Talk" pages. Thus the point of departure for our investigation was a careful reading of FAs, FA reviews, guideline pages, and discussion pages attached to guidelines.

To augment this examination, we conducted an extended interview, via email and telephone, with one of the key players in the FA process, Mark Pellegrini, the director of the front-page Featured Articles. This interview was useful both for confirming facts we had learned from reading the history of the process as well as providing some of the organizational "backstory" of the process.

Over the years, the standards for promoting an article to FA status have increased dramatically. In the beginning, for instance, there was no requirement that an article must contain inline citations. Moreover, requirements for topic comprehensiveness have become stricter. In fact, the criteria have evolved so much that over 200 of the early FAs have been demoted because they do not meet current FA criteria.

Before an article can be promoted to FA status, it needs to be nominated as a Featured Article Candidate (FAC). Anyone can nominate an article as an FAC. Nominations are public and nominators are expected to make an effort to address any objections that editors raise during the review process (see "FAC review" in figure 1). For instance, if an editor objects to the prose style of the lead section of the article, the nominator is expected to rewrite it. When nominators have worked on the article prior to nomination, they are supposed to mark it a "self-nomination."

A nomination summarizes the state of the article, For example:

Daniel Boone: Self-nomination. Listed as a "good article", assessed as "A-class" by Wikipedia WikiProject Military History, has gone through a couple of peer reviews. The article is based on the major 20th century biographies, with points of disagreement between historians noted in the text or footnotes, especially regarding the issue of history versus folklore, a central concern in Boone historiography. All comments are welcome; hope you enjoy reading it. —Joan 16:43, 18 September 2006 (UTC)

Supporting and objecting

For a nomination to be promoted to FA status, consensus must be reached that the article meets the FA criteria. Anyone is allowed to participate in the process of reviewing an FAC and votes of support or opposition need to be backed by explicit reasoning. Objections have to be actionable, in the sense that they have a clear way of being addressed; if nothing can be done in principle to address the objection, the FA Director may ignore it. An example of an actionable objection is:

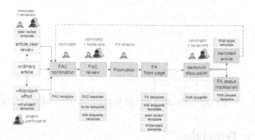

Fig. 1. Diagram of steps in the Featured Article process. Before an article is nominated as an FAC, it tends to undergo significant editing—it is not uncommon for articles to have gone through a separate peer review or have been the focus of a Wikiproject. Once the article is nominated, it enters the FA pipeline, which includes a review and, hopefully, promotion. All along, templates communicate the status of the article to contributors and readers.

Nagorno-Karabakh War→ Object: massively undercited; many large portions of text—and even direct quotes!—have no citations. More generally, I'm concerned that almost all the references seem to be newspaper articles, even though a number of books dealing with the topic (including those listed as "Further reading", for example) are not used as sources. -Jason 19:07, 16 September 2006 (UTC)

The FA Director determines whether there is consensus on promoting or rejecting an FAC. If actionable objections have not been resolved or consensus for promotion has not been reached, a nomination may be removed from the list and archived. The FA Director determines the timing of the process for each nomination. The FAC process generally takes at least 5 days.

Articles can lose their FA status over time ("demotion discussion," Figure 1). While this may seem natural since entries change over time, articles usually lose FA standing not because of edits but because they the FA criteria have become stricter. FAs are demoted through a consensus derived through discussion on the FA Removal Candidates page. A user has to nominate the entry for demotion, which initiates a review process.

That FA entries can be downgraded because of sub-standard quality is a testament to the evolution of the FA process. As of September 2006, 238 articles had lost featured status, while eight had been re-promoted.

Several automation tools have been created for the FA process. One looks for common problems of syntax and style, for example the use of "weasel words" and automatically creates a to-do list for the page. A second, the cite.php module, created in 2005, helps with various aspects of creating inline citations. Before the module existed,

creating such citations was awkward; the introduction of the module has been mentioned as an enabling factor for the current strict requirements for citations.

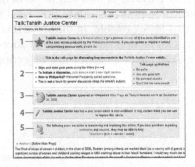

Fig. 2. Screenshot of templates at the top of the discussion page of an FA

Workflow Markers: Templates

The FAC process can be thought of as the workflow necessary to promote an article
to FA status. There is a series of steps that the article must undergo and a sequence of
tasks involved in the procedure (Fig. 1). Keeping track of this progression can be
hard. To solve this problem, Wikipedians have devised a way to communicate the
status of an article: *templates*. A template is a piece of wiki code that creates a visual
marker—often a text box with a different background color from that of normal text
(Fig. 2)—usually placed near the top of a page. In the context of the FA process, templates often alert Wikipedia readers and contributors to the current status of an article.
For instance, templates can include navigation aids, warnings that a page is currently
being featured on the home page, or that content is sub-standard.

A page can have several templates and any contributor is free to add templates to
pages. In fact, templates are so important that they have their own namespace and are
used on pages throughout the encyclopedia. Templates that provide information only
of service to editors belong on an article's talk page. These are the kinds of templates
that aid the FAC review process.

Editors use templates to keep contributors informed of the current status of the entry. In figure 2, for example, template (1) says this article is an FA, (2) lists Talk page
guidelines and briefly explains Talk page editing etiquette, (3) documents the date
when the article appeared on Wikipedia's Main Page, (4) indicates that the article has
had a peer review which is now archived, and (5) lists users who are active in maintaining and improving this article.

A special kind of template is particularly useful for editors during the FAC process: the to-do list. As its name implies, this template lists improvements that are suggested for the article. The list is maintained by editors, writers, reviewers or readers as
a way to focus collaborative efforts.

Users can add templates to their personal watchlists, so they are notified any time
that template is added to a new page. Articles with a to-do template, for instance, are
automatically inserted into the list of articles with To do's, which attracts additional
editors. When a to-do is finished, editors strike it out to mark the progress.

4 Discussion

The FA process consists of a well-documented series of steps organized around an artifact—an article—which is modified, approved, or rejected. The process for moving through individual steps is rule-bound, guided by a large set of written policies. In fact, the FA endeavor starts to sound very much like a modern-day, enterprise workflow process. It is not, however. Here we discuss the FA process in light of Benkler's and Ostrom's work.

Benkler: Peer-production and Peer-Process

Two aspects of the FA process are unusual. First, several roles in the process are filled by crowds of self-identified individuals. The editors of the article, the reviewers, and the people who vote on whether the article meets FA criteria are volunteers and there is no preset limit on the number who may participate. The second unusual aspect is the non-hierarchical flow of information, where some people signal that work is needed—through the use of templates—and other people pick up the signal and act on it. While there is a FA Director, he relies completely on volunteers and is not a "boss."

This arrangement resonates with Benkler's claims about the first phase of commons-based peer production and the importance of breaking large, complex tasks are into small, independent modules. In this case, the independent modules are the small edits and votes needed to move an article along in the FA promotion process. As soon as someone adds an "FAC template" to a page, volunteers will find that page and may decide to review the article. These individuals may have no previous connection with the article, and they may never look at it again in the future, but they will spend time reviewing it.

At the same time, however, the FA process does not belong entirely in Benkler's first phase because its raison d'être is quality assurance. So here is an interesting hybrid of both of Benkler's phases: a process that coordinates individuals' efforts around quality assurance (phase II), while doing so in a distributed manner that relies on independent modules—"five-minute increments of human attention" (phase I). Part of the FA success is likely due to the fact that individuals can easily step in and out of the process at any point. It is a "peer-process:" a completely distributed, yet coordinated and formalized, procedure.

Ostrom: Policy and Self-Governance

Another key reason why the FA process runs smoothly is Wikipedia's extensive body of rules and guidelines (as of September 2006, 75 general guidelines and 119 style guidelines covering text presentation and formatting). The policies were written by the community to address a set of problems that is common to all efforts to organize collective action: creation of institutions, monitoring mechanisms, arbitration, and conflict resolution. These are exactly the challenges faced by the self-governing communities studied by Elinor Ostrom that succeeded in managing natural resources . There is an impressive degree of overlap between what happens on Wikipedia and the design principles that Ostrom extracted from. offline, communities.

That Wikipedians have independently arrived at some of the same governance answers as in offline communities suggests some of these principles are universal. Conversely, an analysis of which principles do not hold in Wikipedia may inform us about what is particular to online self-governance. Here we describe how four of Ostrom's principles translate directly to the context of Wikipedia: congruence between rules and local conditions, collective-choice arrangements, low-cost monitoring, and conflict-resolution mechanisms. We then add a new hypothesis, that the persistent, public nature of work and debate on Wikipedia is a key to the success of peer process and briefly discuss the role of templates as workflow markers.

Congruence between rules and local conditions: There is close interaction between rule shaping and what is happening "in the field" in Wikipedia. An example of this interaction is the adaptation of the article size rule to the new reality of the FA requirements. Originally, FA criteria did not require references and citations explicitly. Adding properly linked citations was an awkward manual process. Now, the standard FA must have inline citations and a comprehensive coverage of its subject matter. This change has been accompanied both by accommodations in code (the cite.php module that eases the manual labor) and in rules: page size now refers only to the prose in the main body of the article, disregarding references and citations.

Collective-choice arrangements: This principle means that most individuals affected by operational rules can participate in modifying the rules. This is true of Wikipedia where rules are publicly discussed and established. Anyone can participate in the debate about rules and policies. Moreover, the costs of changing rules is low, at least from a technical perspective—anyone can post suggestions to a talk page and make the case for why a given rule needs to change. The low barriers for participation mean that regulations are not set in stone and can be adapted to better fit the intention of the community.

An important convention for collective choice in Wikipedia is polling. Indeed, the culture of Wikipedia seems to encourage polling as a means of building consensus and voting as a way of making a choice. This mechanism has been important in the development of the FA review procedure, starting with the original vote to delegate authority to the FA Director to make changes to the home page.

Monitoring: Ostrom posits that a well-governed community needs to have low-cost monitoring capabilities to prevent free riding or other antisocial, negative behavior. While this concern certainly holds for Wikipedia in general and the FA process in particular, the element of online asynchronous work done by ad hoc volunteers adds additional considerations to the notion of monitoring.

Consider the role that users' watchlists play in monitoring activity. Not only do they allow editors to quickly address harm done to the site, they also provides users with a way of organizing editing activity. The interaction between watchlists and templates transforms a monitoring mechanism into a tool for work coordination.

For instance, in the FA process, the templates allow participants to see at a glance the status of an article, thus providing visibility into the progress of the process. An additional technical point is that by adding templates to a watchlist a user is able to see all pages newly tagged with that template. This fact is crucial to the functioning of the FA process: merely by tagging an article with the appropriate template, a user can attract the attention of a crowd of volunteers willing to participate in the process.

Easily-accessible, persistent public documentation and conflict management: the persistent and public nature of transactions on the site helps users coordinate actions and resolve disputes. In fact, having accessible records is so crucial for the community that most communication between users happens publicly on the site [16]. Although Wikipedians use mailing lists, they are encouraged to keep most communication within the confines of the public site. This approach creates a transparent system of record keeping that is easy to refer and link to. In turn, these easy-to-access records are invaluable for the evolution of governance. The FA process provides several examples of persistent archives. During editing activity, our findings show that it is common for editors to refer to a many different guideline pages. These guidelines provide common ground for participants, help resolve arguments, and ensure consistency across instances of the process.

A second simple example is given by the FA Director [16]. One commonly requested change to the process is to protect a page on the day it is a FA, to defend against the expected onslaught of vandalism. After much debate, it was decided not to take this step, yet new users consistently ask for it to be implemented. The FA Director reports that he simply posted the reasoning behind the debate on his user page, creating a document he could refer people to when the question arises.

Technology: Two pieces of technology conspire to make the sort of peer-process we find in Wikipedia possible. On one hand, the persistence of wiki records means that all steps of the process are continuously documents and available. On the other hand, Wikipedians' creative use of templates means that tight coordination of activity does not impose any type of workflow overhead on participants.

5 Conclusion

The vast number of policies in Wikipedia and the existence of robust, formal processes such as FA, indicate that governance is a thriving aspect of this community. The fact that these policies and processes have been devised and modified over time according to a set of collective-choice rules makes Wikipedia a fascinating example of self-governing institutions. In fact, Wikipedia's formalized processes, such as FA, seem to share several of the design principles found by Ostrom in offline, self-governed communities around the world [15].

First, Wikipedia's rules are tightly bound to particular technical aspects of the site and are therefore "localized," instead of generic solutions. Second, they are collective-choice arrangements where everyone may participate in modifying the rules. Third, monitoring the actions of others is facilitated by the technology available. In fact, we identify Wikipedians' use of templates as being one of the driving technological factors of the success of the FA process. Finally, in contrast with many offline communities, Wikipedia's records are persistent, public, and easily available online. We believe this is the second technological element driving both the creation and the adoption of norms and guidelines on the site.

A large part of the increase in coordination and regulation efforts in Wikipedia is due to the need of defining quality standards and assuring quality control in entries. The FA process is the poster child of this endeavor. We find that this process represents a hybrid of Benkler's two evolutionary phases in successful commons-based communities: the

FA process directly addresses quality assurance at the same time that it is structured to allow complex coordination tasks to be broken into small, independent modules. In other words, FAs ensure quality using peer-production mechanisms, and this characteristic is likely a key to their success in Wikipedia.

References

1. Benkler, Y.: Coase's Penguin, or, Linux and The Nature of the Firm. The Yale Law Journal, 12(3) (December 2002)
2. Benkler, Y.: The Wealth of Networks: How Social Production Transforms Markets and Freedom. Yale Press (2006)
3. Bryant, S., Forte, A., Bruckman, A.: Becoming Wikipedian: Transformation of Participation in a Collaborative Online Encyclopedia. In: Proceedings of GROUP (2005)
4. Cherny, L.: Conversation and Community. CSLI Pub (1999)
5. Emigh, W., Herring, S.: Collaborative authoring on the Web: A genre analysis of online encyclopedias. In: Proceedings of HICSS-38 (2005)
6. Forte, A., Bruckman, A.: Why do People Write for Wikipedia? Incentives to Contribute to Open-Content Publishing. GROUP 05.
7. Herring, S.: Interactional coherence in CMC. HICSS 32 (1999)
8. Holloway, T., Bozicevic, M., Börner, K.: Analyzing and Visualizing the Semantic Coverage of Wikipedia and Its Authors. Submitted to Complexity (2005)
9. Lakhani, K., Wolf, R.: Why Hackers Do What They Do: Understanding Motivation and Effort in Free/Open Source Software Projects. In: Perspectives on Free and Open Source Software, MIT Press, Cambridge, MA (2005)
10. Lessig, L.: The Law of the Horse: What Cyberlaw Might Teach, 113 Harvard Law Review 501 (1999)
11. Lih, A.: Wikipedia as Participatory Journalism: Reliable Sources? Metrics for Evaluating Collaborative Media as a News Source. In: Proceedings of the Fifth International Symposium on Online Journalism (2004)
12. Mockus, A., Fielding, R., Herbsleb, J.: Two Case Studies of Open Source Software Development: Apache and Mozilla. ACM Trans. Software Engineering and Methodology 11(3), 309–346 (2002)
13. Nonnecke, B., Preece, J.: Lurker Demographics: Counting the Silent. CHI (2000)
14. Ostrom, E.: Governing the Commons: The Evolution of Institutions for Collective Action. Cambridge University Press, New York (1990)
15. Ostrom, E.: Collective Action and the Evolution of Social Norms. Journal of Economic Perspectives 14(3), 137–158 (2000)
16. Pellegrini, M.: (Featured Article Director), personal communication (September 2006)
17. Sartwell, C.: Wikipedia: See 'Information,' 'Amazing, Anarchy.' Los Angeles Times, (May 4, 2005)
18. Stvilia, B., Twidale, M., Gasser, L., Smith, L.: Information Quality Discussions in Wikipedia. Technical Report ISRN UIUCLIS–2005/2+CSCW (2005)
19. Viégas, F., Wattenberg, M., Dave, K.: Studying Cooperation and Conflict between Authors with history flow Visualizations. In: Proceedings of SIGCHI (2004)
20. Viégas, F., Wattenberg, M., Kriss, J., van Ham, F.: Talk Before You Type: Coordination in Wikipedia. HICSS-40
21. Wales, J.: Wikimania Keynote Address. Cambridge, MA (2006)
22. http://en.wikipedia.org/wiki/Wikipedia:Featured_articles

Major HCI Challenges for
Open Source Software Adoption and Development

Nikos Viorres, Papadopoulos Xenofon, Modestos Stavrakis,
Evangelos Vlachogiannis, Panayiotis Koutsabasis, and John Darzentas

University of the Aegean - Department of Product and Systems Design Engineering,
Hermoupolis, Syros, Greece, GR – 84100
nviorres@aegea.gr, xenofon@syros.aegean.gr, modestos@aegean.gr,
evlach@aegean.gr, kgp@aegean.gr, idarz@aegean.gr

Abstract. The aim of the paper is to identify and discuss major challenges for OSS from an HCI perspective, so as to aid the adoption and development processes for end-users, developers and organizations. The paper focuses on four important HCI concerns: product usability, support for user and development communities, accessibility and software usability and proposes areas for further research on the basis of related work and own experiences.

1 Introduction

Over the last ten years, OSS (Open Source Software) has experienced widespread recognition and adoption. Supported by the ever-growing internet penetration in both developed and developing countries and the constant momentum-gaining on-line communities, the model has stimulated the interest of not only visionaries, developers, academics and small organizations around the world, but also of large enterprises [11] [30]. The Open Source Definition [18] declares a set of conditions, which can be used to determine whether a software license can be thought of as open source. Briefly, these are related to: the provision of source code, free distribution, the allowance of redistribution of modifications, the protection of the author's original code, the dismissal of discriminations and license-specific conditions.

With respect to the OSS popularity/adoption, there are some very impressive figures. Netcraft's surveys[1] show a sustained market share above 65% for the Apache web server and 33%[2] for Sendmail. GNU/Linux commands greater than 50% market share for infrastructure applications like file/print servers, cache/firewall [12]. In addition, various Open Source programming languages like PHP, Python and Perl, exhibit phenomenal popularity among web developers. There is a variety of reasons for the notified popularity of OSS, including the quality and reliability of OSS products, the rapid release schedules, the reduced cost of OSS development and ownership [11], as well as flexibility and benefits from open standards support.

---

[1] Netcraft – Web server survey archives 2006.
[2] http://www.securityspace.com/s_survey/data/man.200611/mxsurvey.html

D. Schuler (Ed.): Online Communities and Social Comput., HCII 2007, LNCS 4564, pp. 455–464, 2007.
© Springer-Verlag Berlin Heidelberg 2007

The widespread recognition and adoption of OSS and its paradigm has attracted significant attention from the user, developer, academic and industry communities. Users are interested in adopting OSS solutions to seek for potential better alternatives to proprietary software, reduce the costs, and even participate in OSS activities and communities. Developers have various incentives [14], including ethical and educational reasons, rapid development cycles, high reusability, and the ability to make a profit while gaining reputation and at the same time get enjoyment out of it (the freedom of choice). The software industry has already found business models to exploit Open Source (Red Hat, IBM, etc.), while on the other hand proprietary software companies are carefully considering the OSS both as a potential business model and as a valid development process (Sun/Java, Microsoft). Finally, researchers and academics are looking into the ways that OSS has influenced software development in general [26] and are exploring means to contribute, evaluate and explain OSS, in terms of its workings, advantages (business and technological), as well as identify potential limitations and inhibiting factors.

Various research efforts have tried to identify challenges and potential limitations of OSS and contribute towards its progress. Some notable areas of concern include, collaboration issues [1] [6], organizational and community issues [6] [5]; [25], security [20] [7], code quality [28] [27] and product quality in general [21]. A group of problems that has attracted limited attention is related to the multidisciplinary field of Human Computer Interaction (HCI), with various concerns and focuses including usability of software, communication, collaboration and more generally interaction issues in the OSS communities. However, an analytic enquiry to the HCI issues related to OSS in an inclusive manner, is of great importance towards the improvement of both the software products and the interaction in OSS communities.

The aim of the paper is to identify and discuss major challenges for OSS from an HCI perspective, so as to aid the adoption and development processes for end-users, developers and organizations.

The paper is structured as follows: section 2 presents the related work and scope. Section 3 presents major OSS challenges from an HCI perspective emphasizing at: product usability, support for user and development communities, accessibility and software usability. Section 4 presents the authors own experiences in developing OSS projects. Finally section 5 presents the conclusions.

2   Related Work and Scope

The penetration and popularity of OSS needs to be considered in relation to the audience that OSS addressees. Firstly, projects such as the Apache HTTP project, Sendmail, BIND (DNS) and various Linux installments can be considered as infrastructure software. Secondly, there is a variety of popular OSS products that qualify as development frameworks (various Apache Software Foundation products), APIs and tools (eclipse), which are addressed to the development communities and whose primary goal is to assist in the design, development and production of software. Last but not least, cases of great success of OSS that are addressed to end users, such as applications and desktop implementations include the Mozilla Firefox, having gained a considerable market share from Microsoft's IE; and OpenOffice, having attracted interest by individuals and corporations due to its free distribution and support of open standards.

Although the design and development lifecycle of open source projects cannot be classified in a unique and all-encompassing way, due to their number and the diversity in their size, purpose and architecture [25], several traits can be identified. Most such projects make limited use of long established software engineering directives and practices such as formal design procedures, specifications, testing and prototyping of a system [31] [16]. Instead, they often adopt a bottom-up approach that focuses on the development of individual components, while the complete model of the system is formulated along the way, where emphasis is given to technical performance, instead of user interface and information presentation issues [10].

A common challenge for the adoption of open source software lays to a perception of its inadequacy vis-à-vis the technological state of the art. This ranges from Linux sometimes limited support for leading-edge or specialized hardware to the acclaimed reduced functionality of open source programs compared to their close-source competitors. Whether a misconception, a distorted image presented by competitors or a valid argument, this subject, its extent and the reasons behind it are hotly debated topics and positions tend to be biased.

A similar issue is relevant to the interoperability between OSS and mainstream applications. It is a fact that the open source community advocates and actively promotes the use of open standards and open formats, both as from an ideological standpoint and as a means to promote both interoperability and variety in the development of available products. However several proprietary or closed formats dominate today's desktop market and the legislature is often invoked in an attempt to actively exempt open source software from achieving a higher degree of integration and interoperability with the market standards. Apart from creating the ideal landscape for passionate debate between sides, these factors introduce additional challenges for the adoption of open source software by end users. It is possible that end users might encounter difficulties importing and exporting their data when they attempt to migrate to an open source equivalent of their previous application, or to keep both applications working in parallel (such as in the case of OpenOffice support for MS Office documents). Users who adopt the Linux operating system need to check the availability of drivers for their hardware, and expert opinion is not always readily available.

Finally, a matter of significant importance in relation to OSS adoption and development is related to issues that concern HCI's multidisciplinary perspective. The assumption that HCI related problems could constitute inhibitors in both widespread OSS adoption and development is not without merit [17]. Indeed, the success of projects that target end-users, such as desktop-applications, may be correlated to corporate support and industry-practices regarding usability. Typical examples in support of this claim are Mozilla Firefox, which engaged User Interface designers in the community [29], Apple's OS X that employed a proprietary interface to an otherwise OSS and OpenOffice.org that is sponsored by Sun and is backed by the StarOffice HCI experts [4]. Thus, an examination of OSS from the inclusive HCI perspective for the identification of problems and concerns that could affect both the adoption and development of OSS products is deemed plausible.

3 Major OSS Challenges from an HCI Perspective

The identification of the major challenges and concerns of OSS related to HCI – presented here - in combination to empirical findings (discussed in chapter 4) allows us to acknowledge a number of important areas of concern for HCI in OSS development and use. These areas are positioned at various levels of abstraction with respect to OSS, and concern: the usability of the product, the support of OS communities, the notion of accessibility and software engineering usability.

3.1 Product Usability

The approach to software usability by HCI strongly supports the philosophy of user centered design. The notion is that typical end-users should be actively involved throughout the software lifecycle in order to produce software products that best match their requirements. However, this approach to the lifecycle of design and development indicates a potential problematic integration to open source communities and practices, which could inhibit the vision of widespread desktop replacement of proprietary software [22].

Nichols and Twidale [17] perform a review regarding the usability of OSS and discuss how the characteristics of open source development affect it. The major issues they identified include; the absence of usability experts, OSS development incentives which bias towards improvements in functionality instead of usability, the bottom-up OSS approach and the lack of resources. To encounter these problems they suggest various methods, techniques and approaches, such as corporate involvement, the development of automated evaluation methods and usability infrastructures (similar to bug-issuing and resolving tools), and involvement of a variety of stakeholders including end-users, experts and academics.

In [3] the introduction of usability practices to popular OSS products, such as Gnome, OpenOffice.org and NetBeans is discussed. Some of the biggest challenges they discovered are the communication between developers, the confusion regarding the target user audience, process problems (including methodological and problem reporting tactics) and the resumption of responsibility within the community. More recently, [17] attempt to explain how the majority of OSS currently addresses issues of usability with respect to the widely identified challenges. Their reported findings suggest that current systems for reporting usability problems are difficult to use by users, and when they do get used the meaning is often lost due to increased complexity with issues related to the analysis of the problems and proposal of solutions/re-designs. As a solution they propose methods to simplify such procedures and may be summarized to:

- Improving bug reporting, by widening participation through lowering effort, cultural and technical barriers
- Improving the analysis of usability-related problems by the community, by applying HCI theoretical principles, comparisons with established interfaces and engaging the reporter to a discussion
- Supporting argumentation for resolving usability related issues.

3.2 Support for User and Development Communities

In research literature, it is widely acknowledged that the model(s) of collaboration in OSS communities differ significantly from established norms in computer-mediated collaboration [32]. The production of high quality software by OSS communities in a spatially distributed environment, using processes and models that are radically different form typical software engineering principles and methodologies, has been a strong incentive to examine how these communities interact through technology. In general researchers have concluded that the models of collaboration in OSS communities differ significantly from established norms in computer-mediated collaboration.

Mahendarn [15] notified the interactions occurring through code in the OSS communities, indicating a potential problem with examining separately the communication-social perspective and material/results occurring in OSS. In order to overcome these problems, some researchers have adopted an ecological view of the world (OSS community domain) that focuses on the relationships of people and material [19].

From a collaboration perspective, OSS stakeholders coordinate their activities in three information spaces [23] [9] [2], namely:

- the implementation space i.e. the source code
- the documentation space, which consists of the documentation, the web resources that contain information about the project, the information in the code versioning systems and various issue tracking systems.
- the discussion space, which consists of mailing lists (developers-users), forums, emails and blogs (to a lesser extent).

The information spaces are supported by tools that mediate the coordination and communication throughout the projects lifecycle. Predominantly, these tools are OSS products themselves and are provided by the community that embraces the project. With respect to the correlation between the quality of these tools and the technical infrastructure in general to the project's outcome [23] perform an evaluation of their proposed methodological framework for socio-cognitive analysis of collaborative design of OSS (a combination of ethnographic methods and computational tools to analyze interactions) on the Python community and find evidence of an "inverse Conway's Law" [24] that could explain how the technical structure of the software might directly influence the social and governance structure of the project.

3.3 Accessibility

From an ethical point of view Open Source concept is strongly related with accessibility expressed as the "right to access for all". From a design and development viewpoint OSS relation to accessibility is twofold. Firstly, it involves Open Standards, which are used widely to ensure the interoperability of services and maximize access to resources. Secondly, the embodiment of accessibility in OSS design; currently we see a move towards the inclusion of accessibility features into systems, tools and the programming languages themselves as system wide core functionalities (e.g. KDE, GNONE and Java Accessibility). To respond to such a requirement Crombie et al [8] argue for the need of a unifying and inclusive approach to open source information systems and introduce the so called "(Open Source) Accessible Information Processing" approach. The aim of such an approach is to synchronize various efforts in the accessibility arena and offer them to end-users and business as a 'package'. This package would include explicit knowledge about the exact requirements and implementation of these requirements as practical and re-usable approached that codify accessible information. Their usage by the community will be continually fed back (communication from scratch concept).

The requirement for a unified approach is imperative, considering that to date, despite the large variety of accessibility APIs, standards and software in OSS, the majority of disabled users prefer proprietary software due to availability of accessibility applications in combination to assistive technology compatibility.

3.4 Software Usability

The open source movement has offered programmers a vast wealth of free, readily available tools, several of which are used to develop new open source projects or enhance current ones, including the projects of the tools themselves. In that way, a positive feedback loop is created that leads to the enrichment and enhancement of the entire open source codebase. The influx of new developers and their involvement with existing open source projects is crucial for their expansion and level of maturity [16].

It is thus imperative that software development tools, having such an important role in the maintenance and expansion of the open source codebase, conform to high quality standards, both from a software engineering [28] and an HCI perspective. [17] suggest that the usability of open source software such as compiles and file editors present no usability challenges; however, our experience in extended use of such tools indicates that they present several of the HCI-related issues ascribed to less specialized software. Furthermore, it highlights a few additional challenges.

- The highly modular approach, typical of most OOS development tools, increases the complexity of both installing, using and maintaining them.
- The latest releases of several OOS development tools do not adhere to the backwards compatibility principle, even in the case of minor version upgrades, which occur at a high rate.
- The documentation is often limited or fragmented, spread among several sources (forums, white papers, personal web pages, source code).

According to [24] and our own experience, the quality from an HCI perspective seems to have a significant correlation to the overall quality of an open source project. Therefore, addressing the concerns expressed here in respect to development tools is likely to benefit both the open source community and the end users of OSS.

4 Experiences with OSS Development Projects

In this section, the authors' experience from participation in OSS projects is briefly presented in relevance to the identified HCI challenges.

4.1 E-Class

E-class is a platform developed the Greek Universities Network as a fork of the Claroline platform, an online collaborative learning platform, widely used in academic institutes around the world. It is open source software, based on PHP and MySQL. We have been using *e-class* in the Department of Product & Systems Design Engineering since 2002, as the core of our asynchronous e-learning platform. It is part of our everyday academic life and currently contains 110 courses, 58 registered tutors and 570 registered students. During this time, we have added functionality and improved its user interface to better suit the needs of our students and faculty members. In addition, we have participated in projects related to installing, configuring and further developing the latest Claroline release (1.8) for several universities and technical institutes in Greece. The HCI challenges we encountered by adopting both systems as developers, administrators and end users included:

- The usability of both platforms from the students' perspective has been adequate; a recent internal survey has produced several suggestions for improvement.
- The perspective of tutors varies. E-class has been developed by an institution focused on the Greek academic institutes, and seems better tailored to their needs and way of operation. It is noteworthy that the users' requirements during the demonstration of the Claroline platform to course instructors frequently and consistently included modifications already present in the e-class version.
- The documentation of e-class is adequate, and each page contains a link to online context-sensitive help. As to version 1.8, Claroline's context-sensitive help is limited to a few tools and its Greek translation is very poor. Information in the official Claroline forums is partly in French, posing language barriers to our users.
- Neither platform complies with the W3C WCAG 1.0 accessibility guidelines, although a relevant effort is underway by the Claroline development team. However, similar efforts undertaken by our development team for both the Claroline and the e-class platforms are seriously hampered by the lack of accessibility considerations in the initial design, leading to the need for major code rewriting and even redesign of some components.
- From a development perspective, the source codes of both projects present some interesting (and fairly uncommon) challenges. It appears to be the result of several programmers working during the span of several years with no imposed standards, coding conventions or preplanned architecture. Several variable names and database fields are in French. Parts of the code are of different quality and maturity level. These quirks did not prove major obstacles, but Claroline is a fairly simple system from a software engineering perspective; we see this diversion from established programming best practices as negative and we already witness its impact as we work towards the accessibility of the e-class platform.

From the above case we can see that whenever the HCI principles were taken into consideration (cases b and c), the end result was more satisfying to the users. Furthermore, it is apparent that by involving the user into the design and development process the rest of the challenges may be addressed.

4.2 E-University

E-University (http://e-university.gunet.gr) is a national project that aims to design and develop electronic infrastructures for Greek universities. All these activities are under development as portlets which are going to be hosted from each University's portal. A common academic portal will be a gateway to all Universities portals. All aforementioned portals will be based on a common customizable portal infrastructure that is being developed by the project. A fundamental requirement of this project is accessibility. At this time, e-University subproject responsible for designing and developing the portal infrastructure is at the development phase using Apache Jetspeed 2 open source portal. It is interesting to go through HCI issues that have been faced and relate to the design and development based on such an open source framework:

- First of all, while investigating the possible software framework implementations; even if Jetspeed seemed a very interesting implementation there were some concerns about the status of the project. Jetspeed 2 was on a pre-release stage comparing with the mature Jetpseed 1, but the promising features were tempting. This introduced an increased risk, but the fact that the community was highly active was a decisive factor for its selection.
- An important accessibility problem met to most of open-source portal implementation was the usage of HTML for the layout portlets and portal. Jetspeed-2 makes an improvement by replacing HTML tables with CSS technology.
- Jetspeed 2, by conforming to JSR-168 portlet specifications, makes use of standard CSS classes for the distinctive portlet elements. This approach helps avoid accessibility problems. Nevertheless, these were not enough for an accessible portal. Further improvements were developed by the authors including inter-portlet navigation mechanism and CMS editor improvements.
- Jetspeed 2 introduces decorators and layouts. Both are mechanism to develop portlets and portal user interface following the MVC pattern (i.e. using Velocity, JSP, XSLT)
- Jetspeed 2 provides a flexible profiler and capabilities mechanism that allows the developer to build up personalization and adaptation mechanisms.
- Documentation for the use and development of Jetspeed 2 was a major problem. This was strengthened by the complexity of the architecture itself, but also with the development tools.

5 Conclusions

If OSS products are to exploit their full potential in terms of widespread acceptance, they need to systematically address HCI concerns into their design process. Current research focuses on finding more suitable ways for involving end-users in the development process and supporting constructive analysis and resolution by developers. The support of collaboration (communication, coordination, cooperation) among OSS participants needs to be further investigated, mainly in terms of community (tool) support. The influence of established communities which provide ready-made collaboration support via a plethora of tools, is deemed as very important in ensuring a smooth start-up process and critical mass generation. Lastly, accessibility is a significant aspect for OSS, which currently from a technological and standards point of view, exhibits unrealized potential. The requirement for a unified approach is imperative, an approach that would both strengthen the OSS's appeal and bring it even closer to its philosophical roots.

Acknowledgements. This work has been partially supported by the EUREKA F-JEWEL project.

References

1. Ankolekar, A., Herbsleb, J.D., Sycara, K.: Addressing Challenges to Open Source Collaboration With the Semantic Web. In: 3rd Workshop on Open Source Software Engineering (2003)
2. Barcellini, F., Détienne, F., Burkhardt, J.M., Sack, W.: Thematic coherence and quotation practices in OSS design-oriented online discussions. In: Schmidt, K., Pendergast, M., Ackerman, M., et Mark G. (eds.) Proceedings of the, International ACM SIGGROUP conference on supporting group work (2005b), pp. 177–186 (2005)
3. Benson, C., Muller-Prove, M., Mzourek, J.: Professional usability in open source projects: GNOME, OpenOffice.org, NetBeans. In: Extended Abstracts of the Conference on Human Factors and Computing Systems, pp. 1083–1084. ACM Press, New York (2004)
4. Benson, C.: Meeting the challenge of open source usability. Interfaces: 9–12 Number 59 (2004)
5. Bergquist, M., Ljungberg, J.: The power of gifts: organizing social relationships in open source communities. Information Systems Journal 11, 305–320 (2001)
6. Bezroukov, N.: Open Source Software as a Special Type of Academic Research. First Monday (4:10) (1999)
7. Bradbury, D.: Documentation dearth undermines open source security. Infosecurity Today, 1(5), 6 (2004)
8. Crombie, D., Lenoir, R., McKenzie, N.: Communication from scratch: towards accessible open source information systems. The First International Conference on Open Source Systems Genova, Italy (July 11–15, 2005)
9. Ducheneaut, N.: Socialization in an Open Source Software Community: A Socio-Technical Analysis. Journal of Computer Supported Collaborative Work. 14, 323–368 (2005)
10. Feller, J., Fitzgerald, B.: A Framework Analysis of the Open Source Software Development Paradigm. In: Orlikowski, W.J., Weill, P., Ang, S., Krcmar, H.C., DeGross, J.I. (eds.) Proceedings of the 21st Annual International Conference on Information Systems,Brisbane, Queensland, Australia, pp. 58–69 (2000)
11. Feller, J., Fitzgerald, B.: Understanding Open Source Software Development, Harlow, Essex, UK, Pearson Education (2001)
12. Gartner note: Open Source Software Hype Cycle 2004, Gartner note #G00120900 (June 2004)
13. Kelly, B., Dunning, A., Rahtz, S., Hollins, P., Phipps, L.: A Contextual Framework For Standards. WWW 2006 Edinburgh, Scotland 22-26 May 2006. Conference Proceedings, Special Interest Tracks, Posters and Workshops (CD ROM)
14. Lerner, J., Tirole, J.: Some Simple Economics of Open Source. Journal of Industrial Economics 50(2), 197–234 (2002) Available at SSRN: http://ssrn.com/abstract=313493

15. Mahendran, D.: Serpents and Primitives: An ethnographic excursion into an Open Source community. Master's Thesis, School of Information Management and Systems, UC Berkeley (2002)
16. Mockus, A., Fielding, R.T., Herbsleb, J.: Two Case Studies of Open Source Software Development: Apache and Mozilla. ACM Trans. Software Engineering and Methodology 11(3), 309–346 (2002)
17. Nichols, D.M., Twidale, M.B.: The usability of open source software. First Monday 8(1) (2005) http://firstmonday.org/issues/issue8 1/nichols/
18. Open Source Initiative: Open Source Definition (v1.9) (Accessed 10/01/2007) http://www.opensource.org/docs/definition.php
19. Osterlie, T.: In the Network: Distributed Control in Gentoo Linux. In: Proceedings of the 4th International Workshop on Open Source Software Engineering, Edinburgh, Scotland, pp. 76–81 (2004)
20. Payne C.: On the security of open source software - Information Systems Journal, 12, 61–78 (2001)
21. Porter, A., Yilmaz, C., Memon, A. M., Krishna, A. S., Schmidt, D.C., Gokhale, A.: Techniques and processes for improving the quality and performance of open-source software in Software Process. Improvement and Practice (Wiley) vol. 11(2) (2006)
22. Raymond, E.S.: The Cathedral and the Bazaar. First Monday, vol. 3(3) (March 1998) at http://firstmonday.org/issues/issue3_3/raymond/
23. Sack, W., Détienne, F., Ducheneaut, N., Burkhardt, J., Mahendran, D., Barcellini, F.: A Methodological Framework for Socio-Cognitive Analyses of Collaborative Design of Open Source Software. Comput. Supported Coop. Work 15(2-3), 229–250 (2006)
24. Sack, W., Ducheneaut, N., Mahendran, D., Detienne, F., Burkhardt, J.M.: Social Architecture and Technological Determinism in Open Source Software Development. International 4S Conference: Social Studies of Science and Society, Atlanta, GA (2003)
25. Scacchi, W.: When Is Free/Open Source Software Development Faster, Better and Cheaper than Software Engineering? In: Koch, S. (ed.) Free/Open Source Software Development (2004)
26. Spinellis, D., Szyperski, C.: Guest Editors' Introduction: How Is Open Source Affecting Software Development? IEEE Software 21(1), 28–33 (2004)
27. Spinellis, D.: Code Quality: The Open Source Perspective. Addison Wesley, Reading (2006)
28. Stamelos, I., Angelis, L., Oikonomou, A., Bleris, G.: Code quality analysis in open source software development – Information Systems Journal, 12, 43–60 (2002)
29. Trudelle, P.: Shall we dance? Ten lessons learned from netscape's flirtation with open source UI development. Open Source MeetsUsability Workshop, Conference on Human Factors in Computer Systems - CHI 2002 (2002)
30. VA Software whitepaper, SOURCEFORFE (2004), Leveraging Open Source Processes and Techniques in the Enterprise (November 2004) (Accessed at October 25, 2006) http://sourceforge.aservo.com/Leveraging_Open_Source_Processes_in_the_Enterprise_-_VA_Software.pdf
31. Vixie, P.: Software engineering. In Open Sources: Voices from the Open Source Revolution. Dibona, C., Ockman, S., Stone, M. (eds.) O'Reilly, Sebastopol, Calif, pp. 91–100 (1999)
32. Yamauchi, Y., Yokozawa, M., Shinohara, T., Ishida, T.: Collaboration with Lean Media: how open-source software succeeds. In: Proceedings of the 2000 ACM conference on Computer supported cooperative work, pp. 329–338 (2000)

Open Source Communities in China (Mainland): An Overview

Yi Wang[1], Fan Li[2], and Jiguang Song[3]

[1] Dept.of Computer Science and Engineering, Shanghai Jiaotong University,
200240 Shanghai, P.R.China
yi_wang@sjtu.edu.cn
[2] School of Management, Zhejiang University (Zijingang), 310058 Hangzhou, P.R.China
shelleylf@gmail.com
[3] School of Software Engineering, Beihang University, 100083 Beijing, P.R.China
aiquanshui@126.com

Abstract. Open Source Software development has been an important software development way in last decade. Meanwhile, the Open Source Communities also grow fast in these years and become more and more important. This paper presents a preliminary study to China's Open Source Communities. We provide some descriptive results according our survey and point out some problems threatening the further developments of China's Open Source Communities. We also provide a model for assessing the maturity of the Open source comm.-unity. A case study about one typical China Open Source Community also provided.

1 Introduction

1.1 Motivation

In recent several years, open source movement and community-driven software development have been popular in software industry. Many of these projects won great success, for example Apache [1], Ubuntu [2] [3] and so on. In China, open source development also has been a hot topic. It has also been attracted many scholars' interest [4]. However, quite a few studies has focused on these online communities that driven these software developments. This paper provides some preliminary research in this area.

Studying the properties of Open Source Communities is important. It can provide better understanding of community-driven software development to the open source software developers. It is helpful in building a vibrant community, and facilitates efficient communications within the community. And ultimately, increases the productivity of software and provides more reliable and usable software. Besides, for Open Source Communities in China are mostly in their startup phase, researches on this area can help them a lot in their further developments.

We first give a brief introduction of our data source and Categories of Open Source Communities in China in Section 1.2 and 1.3. Then a descriptive analysis of the

D. Schuler (Ed.): Online Communities and Social Comput., HCII 2007, LNCS 4564, pp. 465–474, 2007.

communities in our survey is presented in Section 2. A preliminary model to assess the Open Source Communities' maturity is given in Section 3. Maturity Index (MI) also defined in this section. Section 4 is a case study of a typical China Open Source Community (Woodpecker Pythonic). Related works and Conclusion are described in Section 5 and 6 respectively. The future work is included in section 7.

1.2 Data Source

The data of this research mainly comes from three sources:

- Questionnaires mailed to 300 members of 10 Open Source Communities (listed in the end of this paper) in China. And then, we got 216 replies.
- Open materials available on the Internet.
- Related data in some projects' bug report archives, email archives, and the CVS repositories.
- The authors' personal experiences as Open Source Community leaders.

1.3 Categories of Open Source Communities in China

The Open Source Communities in China can be divided into three categories, they are: (1) Branches of international communities, 2 in our survey, for example, Ubuntu China. (2) Local Open Source Communities, 8 in our survey, for example, Woodpecker. In this paper, the focus is mainly on the latter category. The reason is that branches of international communities are more influence by their superior communities that do not locate in China.

2 Descriptive Analysis

We first provide descriptive analysis of the Open Source Communities in China according the data we gathered. The descriptive analysis can bring the direct understanding of current China's Open Source Communities. We discuss the Venues, structure, governance, financial support, and license selection of China's Open Source Communities in this section.

2.1 Venues

Venues refer to the places where communities' activities take place. Any online communities, no matter their sizes, must have at least one regular venue, open source communities also are not exceptions. However, Open Source Communities are not *Pure* online communities, some activities also occurs in our real life not only just in the virtual digital world. We discuss these two kinds' venues respectively in the following.

2.1.1 Online Venues

For the Open Source Community's members do not live in one location, they can not meet other members as soon as they want. The online venues satisfy this demand of instant communications. Typical online Venues include mailing lists, web forums, instant message software (IM), IRC channels, and so on. Figure 1 describes the use of these venues in China's Open Source Communities.

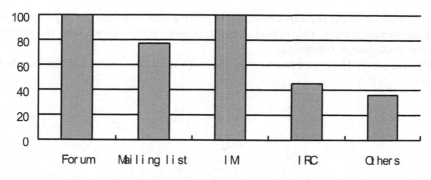

Fig. 1. The use of different online venues

From figure 1, we can find that China's Open Source Communities' members are more like to use web forums and instant message software while mailing lists and IRC are extremely popular in Open Source Communities have European and North American backgrounds.

2.1.2 Offline Venues

Offline Venues vary a lot according their scale, from several persons meetings to nation-wide conferences. For example, Ubuntu (A typical worldwide Open Source Community) holds several worldwide conferences and organize lots of small workshops. However, Open Communities in China seldom hold large-scale conferences. In our survey, no one of these 8 local communities has held this kind conference. Besides, most of them even do not plan to do so. The chief reason is the lack of necessary expenditure. However, there are some regular offline meeting among developers living in the same city and these core developers.

2.2 Structure

Every member in the community has his/her role, so we can build the community's structure according the members' role. The structure of Open Source Community is very important because of the structure shows out the composition of the community's members. Compared to other online communities in other forms, the Open Source Communities need more contributors. A health Open Source Community should be in Onion-Shaped Structure, while an unhealthy one is not.

2.2.1 Onion-Shaped Structure

Here we use the roles defined by Crowston and Howison [5].The members of Open source community can be divided as follow:

1. *Core developers* (members): This group can be quite small—three to ten is adequate for most projects. This group includes founders, project leaders and release coordinators. Every person in this group is familiar with others. Their main task is decision-making.

2. *Co-developers* (members): They are people who provide code for review by core developers; they are the main force in development process.

3. *Active users*: These persons contribute by testing new releases, posting bug reports, writing documentation, and, provide help to passive users—those who use the code without contributing themselves.
4. *Passive users*: They are persons who use software without any contributions to the project.

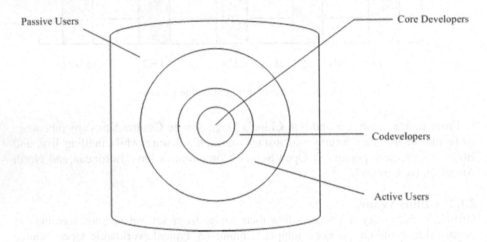

Fig. 2. The Onion-Shaped Structure is consisted by *core developers, codevelopers, and active users*. To keep a community's health, the numbers of active users is essential.

We show the Onion-Shaped Structure in figure 2. In this figure, we point out the role of different members and describe their relations. From this figure, we can find that the circle represents *active users* should be wide enough.

2.2.2 Structure of Communities in Current China

In our survey, most of intervi-ewees admit their communities in lack of active users. So they can not get enough testing and bug reports for their software. In some degree, the structure looks like an Onion loses its Scarfskin.

The reason is not the lack of users but most users download the software are silent users. For example, we have tracked an email client-tool (it has an obvious bug) for six months in an experiment. It was downloaded over 300 times. However, we get only 7 reports of this bug till now. This experiment proves that communities in China need to pay more efforts in building their own active users groups.

2.3 Governance

The Open Source Community looks like a human society in some sense. The governance of it also follows the two ways of our real world. One is the Centralized while another is the Democratic. The table 1 describes these two different governance models.

We are surprising by that the centralized governance is dominant in most communities in our survey. In the 8 local communities, only one chooses the democratic governance. We think this may result from the tradition of Chinese politics. The explicit reasons need further investigation.

Table 1. The comparision between the democratic governance and the centrilized governance

	The Democratic	The Centralized
Leadership	By election	Not appointed by the public
Important decisions	Make by the whole community	Make by a small group or some individuals
Advantages	Better engagement, The decisions may be more rational, Better atmosphere in the Community. Better intendance to leaders' personal actions.	High efficiency
Disadvantages	Some times low efficiency	Limits the engagement, The decisions may cause great disagreement, No or little intendance to leaders' personal actions

2.4 Financial Supports

Considering Open Source movement as communistic dream is nothing more than superficial [6]. Financial assistant is essential for any kinds of software development. Some communities affiliated with enterprises while others are pure voluntary organizations. The former do not need to care about money. But things are totally different for the latter. They must raise enough money for their survival and development.

Domestic enterprises have little interests in providing financial supports for Open Source Communities. In our survey, 8 local communities are all in lack of money in some degree. Only one (WiseReal) has a company as its perpetual supporter. Two of them even have to rely on members' personal donations and their financial states are extremely bad. As we mentioned in section 3.1.2, many communities can not hold offline activities for lacking of money.

2.5 Licenses

Source license models fall into three general categories [7]:

1. *Free*: the program can be freely modified and redistributed;
2. *Copyleft*: the owner gives up intellectual property and private licensing;
3. *GPL-compatible*: licenses are legally linked to the GPL licensing structure.

In practice, there are exists hundreds models of licenses. The 10 Open Source Communities in our survey mainly use 5 License models. We summarize them in the table 2, the last column show the number of communities use the license respectively.

Table 2. The Use and basic information about the Open Source License

License	Free software	Open source	Copyleft	GPL-com	Num. of use
GPL	Yes	Yes	Yes	Yes	2
LGPL	Yes	Yes	Partial	Yes	3
CCPL	Yes	Yes	Partial	Yes	1
M/NPL	Yes	Yes	No	No	1
BSD	Yes	Yes	No	No	3

2.6 Summary

Based on above descriptive analysis, we can easily find out the problems faced by most China's Open Source Communities. These are:

1. Lack offline activities as additions for online activities;
2. Do not provide support of other languages;
3. The structure is not reasonable for the lack of active users;
4. The governance mechanism needs some reformations;
5. Lack necessary financial supports, enterprises are not interested in supporting Open Source Communities in finance.

3 China's Open Source Communities' Life Cycle

Communities experience several phase before their totally maturity. These are: *Startup Phase, Grow Phase and Mature Phase* [8]. Therefore, to a great extent, describing the life cycle of the community equals to defining its maturity degree.

3.1 Maturity Index (MI)

For a specified Open Source Community, the paper presents a model to assess its maturity. We define Maturity Index (MI) to describe a community maturity degree. Each MI corresponds with a series of conditions as table 3. For a community, if its MI is 3, it must at least fulfill the conditions MI3 corresponds.

Table 3. The MI assessment system. MI has four grades, each related to some conditions we specifies in the right of table 3.

MI	Conditions Must Be Fulfilled
1	Has been found with some goals; Only do a few simple things; Has some core members.
2	Has built its own online infrastructure; Has formed its fundamental guidelines; Has attracted some members, but these members do not have explicit roles; Has basic governances; Has regular meetings within core members; Do not have adequate funds.

Table 3. (*Continued*)

3	Easy to access for potential contributors and users; Has systemized community and project guidelines; Has enough members with different roles; Has regular meetings within core members and other developers; The communications between members are frequent; In lack of financial supports, but not severe; The community's governance is in working order;
4	Easy to access for potential contributors and users; Easy to use by members; Has a systemized and comprehensive community and project guidelines; The members have formed an Onion-Shaped community, according their different roles; Has many efficient means for members to communicate in public and private. Has regular meeting in different levers. For example, within or between teams and the whole community; The community runs smooth with efficient governance; Has stable financial supports, can raise enough money; Has some activities offline; Has detailed plans for future development.

3.2 MI of the Communities in Our Survey

According this model, no one of these 8 Local communities' MI fulfills the standard of MI4. Following table shows the distribution of their MIs:

Table 4. MI of the Communities in Our Survey

MI	Num. of Comm.
1	*One*
2	*Two*
3	*Five*
4	*Zero*

3.3 Summary

We are regretted to find that no one can fulfill the standard of MI4. This means there are quite a few Open Source Community can be considered as a *mature* community in China. These communities still need to improve themselves in many aspects.

4 Case Studies

We examine a typical China Open Source Community in this section. One author of this paper is among the founders of it. So we can get precise and abundance information about it. This is Woodpecker Pythonic [9], which is an Open Source Community trying to build applications using Python (A popular programming Language in open source world).

Following table show some basic information about Woodpecker Pythonic:

Table 5. Some basic information about the Woodpecker Pythonic community, includes its goal, main venues, and so on

Founded Date	June 2004
Main Goal	Python based software development
Main Venues	Web forum, IM, Wikis
Languages	Chinese (simplified)
No. of members	Over 1000 registered users, but the real contributors less than 100
Role of members	Explicit, but in lack of active users
Funded by	Members' donation, Training and service fee
Financial Status	Not very good
Governance	Centralized.
Licenses	LGPL
Document	Code of Conduct and some others
Meeting	Regular meeting on the Internet

According the Maturity Assess Model we provide in above section, the MI of Woodpecker Pythonic community is 3. The reason are: (1) they have venues for users to engage and make their contribution easily, (2) they have some formal document, (3) they have lot of users and their roles is explicit, (4) they have some channels to get financial support. Besides, the lack of active users and abundance money make it can not be a MI4 community.

5 Related Works

Till now the research on this area is extremely limited. Most Open Source researchers' interests are topics related to the software development process but not the topics related to the communities. Crowston and Howison [5] did some exploration on this filed. They defined the role of Open Source Community's members and provide a health model for assess a community's health. Our work is mainly focus on some basic statistic information about the China's Open Source Communities and builds a model to assess their maturity in order to describe their life cycle.

6 Concluding Remarks

The paper provides some preliminary research results of China's Open Source Communities. We can find that these Communities are not very mature and face many problems. This paper points out some of this problems through the survey we conducted. This paper also provides a model to assess an Open Source Community's maturity. The model use MI to describe the life cycle of a community. Each MI corresponds to a series conditions. At last, the paper also provides a brief case study.

7 Future Work

In future, we want to refine our works in following aspects:

1. Do more empirical studies about China's Open Source Communities;
2. Refine our assess model to make it more reasonable and comprehensive;
3. Build a dynamic model for Open Source Community's development process for guiding China's Open Source Communities' development;
4. Extend our models to the Open Source Community not just mainly located in China.
5. Provide efficient solutions for the problems faced by the Open Source Communities.

Acknowledgements. The authors thank the help of these 10 communities Members. They also want to show their appreciates to following persons: they are Miss Peng Qiu, Mr Bing Bai, Mr Jun Xie, Mr Defeng Guo and Mr Min Zhang for their constructive suggestions. We are also grateful to the anonymous referees of the extend abstract of this paper.

References

1. Apache Home Page http://www.apache.org/
2. Ubuntu Home Page http://www.ubuntu.org/
3. Mako Hill, B., et al.: The Official Ubuntu Book. Prentice Hall, Englewood Cliffs (2006)
4. Bezroukov, N.: Open Source Software Development as a Special Kind of Academic Research http://firstmonday.org/issues/issue4_10/bezroukov
5. Crowston, Howison.: Assessing the Health of Open Source Communities, IEEE computer, pp. 89–91 (May 2006)
6. Glass, R.L.: A Look at the Economics of Open Source: Is open source the future of the software field or a passing fad? Communications of The. ACM 47(2), 25–27 (2004)
7. Wei Wu, M., Dar Lin, Y.: Open Source Software Development: An Overview, IEEE computer, pp. 33–38 (June 2001)
8. West, J., O' Mahony, S.: Contrasting Community Building in Sponsored and Community Founded Open Source Projects. In: Proceedings of the 38th Hawaii International Conference on System Sciences (2005)
9. Woodpecker Pythonic Home Page http://www.woodpecker.org.cn

Appendix: The 10 Open Source Communities in Our Survey

1 Branches of International Communities

Ubuntu Chinese Team: http://forum.ubuntu.org.cn/
Debian Chinese: http://www.debian.org/index.zh-cn.html

2 Local Open Source Communities

C3CRM: http://www.c3crm.com/
Extmail: http://www.extmail.org/
JiuJie: http://www.inlsd.org/
Linuxfans Club: http://www.linuxfans.org/
LUPA: http://www.lupaworld.com/
Rnby Chinese: http://rubycn.ce-lab.net/
Udclub China: http://cn.udclub.com/
WiseReal: http://www.wisereal.com.cn/bmb/
Woodpecker Pythonic: http://www.woodpecker.org.cn/

Cooperation and Competition Dynamics in an Online Game Community

Ruixi Yuan, Li Zhao, and Wenyu Wang

Center for Intelligent and Networked Systems, Department of Automation, Tsinghua
University, Beijing, China
ryuan@tsinghua.edu.cn, zhaoli04@mails.tsinghua.edu.cn

Abstract. Cooperation and competition are important subjects in social and
economical studies. Similar dynamics exists in large-scale online communities.
In this paper, we present a quantitative study on the cooperation and competition dynamics of an online gaming community. During a period of four months,
we collected a total of over one million data points in an open game room with
an online gaming site (www.ourgame.com.cn) for a popular card game "upgrade". The "upgrade" game room provided us an excellent environment to observe how cooperative and competitive relationships are formed in an online
community. Through the statistical analysis, we obtain the probability for players with different score tags forming cooperative and competitive relationships
with each other. Our analysis shows that all players exhibit preferential bias in
their partner selection process, but shows little bias in their selection of competitors. Further, the cooperation bias is the strongest in both the low score and
high score ends of the player population. We also discuss the effect of such
preferential bias on the population distributions in the game community. To our
knowledge, this is the first large-scale quantitative study on the cooperation dynamics in online gaming community. The online game community environment
offers us a great proxy to study the same dynamics that is difficult to investigate
in the real world social environment. The large, statistically significant amount
of data enables us to develop and test many hypotheses.

Keywords: communities, game, cooperation, competition, and preferential
bias.

1 Introduction

1.1 Background

Competition and cooperation dynamics has long been the subject of game theory and
economic studies, [e.g. 1, 2]. In the past two decades, how cooperation might arise
and evolve in a competitive environment has attracted increasing attentions. For example, the iterated prisoner's dilemma (IPD) game has been the subject of numerous
theoretical and experimental studies [3]. Most notably the work of Robert Axelrod
[2,4,5] has shown that cooperation can emerge as a norm in an environment comprising individually selfish entities. Additionally, the introduction of an arbitrary tag and

D. Schuler (Ed.): Online Communities and Social Comput., HCII 2007, LNCS 4564, pp. 475–484, 2007.

its effect of the evolution of cooperation have been extensively studied using computer simulation [6,7]. It is shown that tag induced partner selection bias can greatly facilitate the emergence of cooperation even without direct or indirect reciprocity [7]. However, how an arbitrary tag affects the partner and opponent selection process in a real world environment with both cooperation and competition is still unclear.

Large-scale online communities offer us great environments to study the social and economical behavior of large population. First, it is relatively easy to find large virtual communities that evolve rapidly through cooperation and competition. Second, online data acquisition can be automated and large amount of data obtainable in a relatively short amount of time. Third, the pseudo-anonymous nature of online environment encourages users to display their true behaviors, not revealing their identities in the real world. Hence, the study of online community offers great opportunity to understand a wide range of social, economical and network systems.

1.2 Related Works

While the online virtual community represents a great opportunity for the research on social interaction and behavior, much of the research has focused on improving human-computer interaction [e.g. 8, 9], or the how the electronic media is changing the human-human interaction [e.g. 10, 11]. Fewer research have focused on using the online communities as observation environments for the study of human interactions and behaviors.

Closer to our work, there are several recent researches in human computer interaction that have paid attention on virtual communities including online dating [12,13], online game [14], and online social environment [15]. Andrew T. Fiore and Judith S. Donath [12, 13] have discussed how people choose their romantic relationship with others in online dating system and propose the intrinsic factors for successful attraction. The factors involve physical features, odors, economic status, hobbies, and so on. they serve as tags in preferential partner selection for each individual. However, these tags are static and remain unchanged throughout the process of the courtship. Furthermore, the distinct values (e.g. gender, race) does not offer continuous ranges for more detailed analysis. Authors in [14, 15] studied online game environment; explored both the promises and inadequacies of online gaming environment in studying the social interactions. Barry Brown and Marek Bell studied an online environment in [16] and made a case for improving the social interaction by better integrating multiple sensory methods.

1.3 Our Study and Main Contributions

In this paper, we present the study of large online game rooms at a highly popular gaming website in China (www.ourgame.com.cn). Over one million of cooperation and competition pairing data points are collected from the game rooms where thousands of players congregate. Through the statistical analysis of the collected paring, we obtain the probability for players with score "S1" in cooperative relationships with other players with score "S2" (the players' score is described in detail in section 2). This probability is then compared with the "expected" probability for purely random relationship forming. Our analysis showed that all players exhibit preferential bias in their partner selection process. That is, players tend to form cooperation relationship with others with similar scores. Further, the preferential bias is the strongest in both the low score and high score ends of the game room, and the bias is the weakest in the middle of the score range. In the meantime, players are much less selective in the choice of opponents.

To our knowledge, our paper is the first study on cooperation and competition dynamics from large-scale online communities. For the first time, the quantitative values of preferential bias with respect to the degree of similarity are obtained. Analysis also showed that the value and trend of the bias plays a critical role in the population evolution of the game system. As online communities a proxy for real-world environments, such study should also be applicable in real social and economical environments.

2 The "Upgrade" Game Community

The "upgrade" game is a popular card game played throughout China. It involves four players; two players form a partnership and play against the partnership of the other two players. The winning depends on both the cards being dealt and the quality of cooperation between the partners.

The "Ourgame" site (www.ourgame.com.cn) is one of the most popular online game sites in China. It enables players all across the country to form partnerships and play against each other online. The computer is responsible for dealing the cards and calculates score after the completion of each game as well as supplying information of each player in the communities. Each player online is identified by a unique ID (an ASCII string) and has the following attributes.

Score: An integer used to record player's historical wins and loses . Players gain positive score when they win the game and gain negative score when they lose. Winning a game usually causes the score increase by one and losing a game resulted the score decrease by one.

Historical rounds: The number of rounds this player has played.

Upon logon, a player is presented with multiple game rooms, each with a limit of 300 participants. The player enters the game room by clicking the room's link. Each room contains 100 game tables which are adequate to hold all the players in the room playing games. Each game table has four seats (East, West, North and South). Seating at the opposite end of the table means the willingness to form a cooperative relationship. When a table has seated four players, and all agrees to proceed to playing (by raising the virtual hand), the game begins. There are two types of game rooms: open game rooms and advanced game rooms. The open games are open to everyone regardless of their score and historical rounds. The advanced game rooms are only open to players with scores greater then 30 and historical rounds greater than 50. Figure 1 shows a section of the open game room with eight tables.

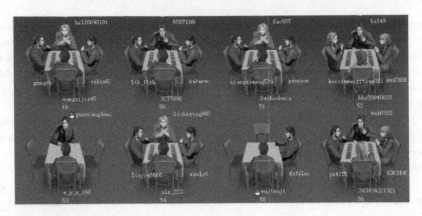

Fig. 1. A section of the game room where 8 tables are displayed, tables 49, 50, 51, 52, 54 and 56 have four players seated and have already begun to play. Table 53 has two players sitting opposite, signaling their willingness to form a cooperative relationship. Table 55 has two players sitting adjacent to each other, signaling their willingness to form a competitive relationship.

As shown in figure 1, six game tables are already occupied with ongoing games. Two table have only two players, and waiting for others to join. One table (table 53) has two players sitting at the opposite sides, meaning that they are willing to cooperate and waiting another pair to join. Another table (table 55) has two players sitting at the adjacent sides, signaling their willingness to form a competitive relationship. A player may choose to join a partially filled table or simply sit at an empty table and waiting for others to join. When a new player joins a table, the existing players may choose to leave if he/she is not satisfied with the resulting cooperative and competitive relationships.

Clearly, a round of game requires two successful cooperative relationships (E-W, N-S) and four successful competitive relationships (E-N, E-S, W-N, and W-S). A player is entitled to leave the table if the player is not satisfied with any of the relationships. A player can make his/her decision based on many factors. Usually, the accumulative score is the most important factor.

In order to automate the data collection, we wrote our own data collection robot. The robot periodically logs onto the game site and enters the game room. Each time it enters the game room; it records all the players in the game room, including those already in play, and those still waiting to form relationships. To avoid duplicate sampling, we choose the periodic interval of 6 minutes, which is a sufficient duration to complete a round of game and allow old relationship to dissolve and new relationship to form. During the period between March 2005 and July 2005, we successfully collected data from a total of 5890 open game rooms. The aggregated total data points is 1,007,248 player×round data points. Table 1 shows some statistics of the collected data points.

The population distribution across the score range is for the players with historical rounds > 50, and is shown in Fig. 2. It has a peak at score 0, because 0 is the default assigned score for all the new players. There is a sharp drop of players at the score of 30. When a player's score reaches 30, he/she is eligible to enter advanced game rooms and probable leaves the open game room.

Table 1. The statistics for the 1 million collected data points

Number of distinct player × round	Total number of distinct players	Number of players with historical rounds > 50	Number of players with observed rounds > 50
1007248	192315	129121	2800

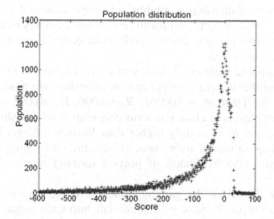

Fig. 2. The population distribution across the score range for players with more than 50 historical rounds in the open game room. The default score value 0 for all players produced the peak at 0. The sharp drop at 30 is caused by players leaving the open game room for advanced game room when they become eligible with score 30.

3 Cooperation and Competition Bias

We are interested in the dynamics of how players interact with each other. Most notably, how does one player decide to form cooperative or competitive relationship with each other? The collected raw data from the game room showed the players in cooperative and competitive relationships, as well as those in the game room waiting. However, it does not directly tell the likelihood of forming relationship when one player meets another player. Therefore, we must infer the likelihood from the existing relationships and their distributions. Our analytical approach is describes below.

3.1 Analytical Approach

We first divide the players in the game room into fixed score range classes. For each class of players, we compare the actual numbers of successful relationships with the expected numbers with random selections.

Suppose player class i of has n_i players and player class j of has n_j players. If the players chose partners at random, then the total number of cooperative relationships formed between class i and class j should be proportional to $n_i \times n_j$. From the game room data, we can obtain the actual numbers of cooperative relationships between class i and class j as C_{ij}. (obviously, C_{ij} equals C_{ji}) Next, we compute the value $R_{ij} = C_{ij} \div (n_i \times n_i)$, and R_{ij} is then averaged across all the game room data. We denote the ensemble average $<R_{ij}>$ as the preferential bias strength between class i and j. For special cases with relationship formation within the same class, the normalization factor is $n_i \times (n_i-1)/2$ instead of n_i^2. The reason is that when 2 players both in the same class form cooperative relationship, 2 choices by different players actually happened, but only 1 cooperation relationship is established so we increased C_{ii} by 1, which is likely only 1 player's takes effect. Comparatively, when 2 players in different classes become partners, the two players' choices will make both C_{ij} and C_{ji} increase, thus each player's choice takes effect.

As an example, suppose there are 3 classes of players i, j and k, and each class has 100 players. If the number of actual cooperative relationships are observed as $C_{ii} = 30$, $C_{ij} = 60$ and $C_{ik} = 30$. Then, $R_{ii} \approx 0.0061$, $R_{ij} = 0.006$. $R_{ik} = 0.003$. Obviously, it is twice more likely for players in class i to form cooperative relationships with players in class j than in class k. R_{ii} is slightly higher than R_{ij} since a player has a relatively smaller selection range in his/her own class. Hence, the preferential bias strength is directly proportional to the likelihood of players forming relationships with each other.

For the collected data from the gaming community, we divide the entire score spectrum into fixed ranges. Players with score fall into each range are then in the same class. It is worth noting that the value of the score range may affect the calculation. Obviously, if the score range is too wide (the extreme being the entire score range as a single class), it cannot capture the fine granularity of the preferential strength. On the other hand, if the score range is too narrow (the extreme being a single exact value), the number of players in the range is not sufficient to have statistical significance. We have experimented with a wide range of values for the score range, and found that the results are stable as long as there is sufficient number of players within each class. The results in the next subsection are obtained with a score range of 50.

3.2   Preferential Bias Strengths for Cooperation

Using the collected data from the game community, we computed the preferential bias strength for cooperative relationship formation. Fig. 3 shows the contour plot for the cooperative preferential bias strength for the game community. The preferential bias is the strongest along the diagonal. This is easy to understand as players tends to form cooperative relationship with other at the same score level. What is surprising in our finding is that the bias is stronger in both the high and low end of the score ranges, but weaker in the middle. Note the two big peaks at (50, 50) and (-150, -150), and relative flatness between in between. Hence the players in the middle range are less discriminatory against players in both high and low end of the spectrum. A cross section at for the contour plot at value 50 is shown in Fig. 4. The trend of the preferential bias exhibits non-linear descends from the peak. The exact form for the preferential bias as a function of the score differential is also important and will be the subject of a separate research.

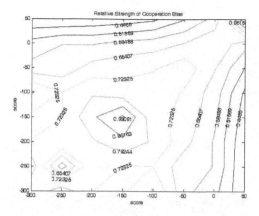

Fig. 3. The contour plot for preferential bias strength in cooperative relationship formation. The strength is normalized so that the large value is normalized to 1. Two large peaks are obtained at (50,50) and (-150, -150).

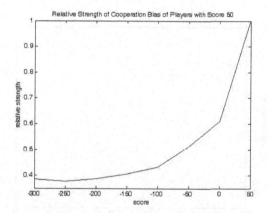

Fig. 4. The preferential bias strength in cooperation for players in score range (0,50]

3.3 Preferential Bias Strengths for Competition

The same computation can be carried out for the competitive relationship formation. Fig. 5 shows the contour plot for the competitive preferential bias strength for the same game community. Unlike the cooperative bias, we find that the bias is much weaker in the forming of competitive relationships for all players regardless of their score range. This is also surprising as one might expect players will also be careful in choosing their opponents. Obviously, the players are much more selective in choosing their partners than their opponents. A cross section at for the contour plot at value 50 is shown in Fig. 6. One can observe that the smaller variations (from 0.84 to 1.00) of the preferential bias, and the exhibits a somewhat linear trend when the score differentials are large.

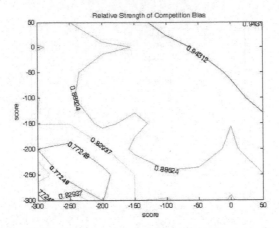

Fig. 5. The contour plot for preferential bias strength in competitive relationship formation. The strength is normalized so that the large value is normalized to 1. There are no obvious peaks in the figure.

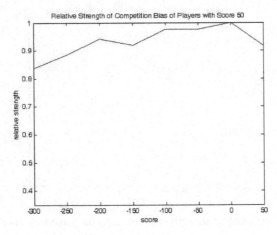

Fig. 6. The preferential bias strength in competition for players in score range (0,50]

4 Discussion and Summary

Two surprising, yet understandable conclusions were found from the analysis of game room data. First, there exists strong preferential bias in forming cooperative relations among players. However, the preferential bias strength is not uniform across the score spectrum. Rather, the bias is the strongest in both the high and low end of the player population, while players in the middle exhibit weak preferential bias. Second, there is little preferential bias in forming competitive relationships for players regardless of their score ranges. Players are much more tolerant towards their opponents' score differences.

It is very important that the preferential bias in the middle score range is weak, as the middle population serves to bridge the players in the high and low end scores. This contributed the prosperity of the game room community. Theoretically, if the preferential bias is strong throughout the entire score range for cooperative and competitive relationships, the game community will be fragmented into different sub-communities, each only contain a small number of players with narrow score ranges. This will lead to the collapse of entire community.

During our study of the game room, we observed that finding the right partner could be a relatively long process. This is directly caused by the selection bias, which narrows down the potential partner set, especially for players in the two extreme ends. However, such long waiting time could also contribute to the reduction of preferential bias, as the discriminatory behavior reduces the chance of game participation. When the perceived cost of lost opportunity outweighs the risk of losing a game, a player may choose to form a cooperative relationship that is imperfect.

We believe that the preferential bias in selecting cooperative partners is one of the most fundamental aspects for interactions in virtual communities. Such preferential bias is also prevalent in real world social and economical environments. Many previous cooperation dynamics study (e.g. iterated prisoners' games) has assumed uniform preferential bias. Our Quantitative study showed that such assumptions are not accurate. Detailed understanding of the preferential bias will also enable us to better design and implement policies that foster the prosperity of both virtual and real communities.

The gaming dynamics of online communities offer us a great proxy to study the same dynamics that is difficult to investigate in the real world social environment. The large, statistically significant amount of data enables us to develop and test many hypotheses. In particular, the cooperation dynamics and its effect on population distribution evolution warrant further study. Other topics, such the quantitative range of human perception on score differential are also meaningful and can find its way into social and economical area.

References

1. Camerer, C.F., Loewenstein, G., Rabin, M.: Behavioral Economics: Past, Present, Future. In: Advances in Behavioral Economics, Princeton University Press, Princeton, NJ (2003)
2. Axelrod, R.: The Evolution of Cooperation. Basic Books, New York (1984)
3. O'Riordan, C.: Iterated Prisoner's Dilemma: A Review. Technical Report No. NUIG-IT-260601, National University of Ireland, (2001)
4. Axelrod, R., Dion, D.: The Further Evolution of Cooperation. Science 242, 1385–1390 (1988)
5. Riolo, Cohen, M.D., Axelrod, R.: Evolution of Cooperation without Reciprocity. Nature 414, 441–443 (2001)
6. Holland, J.: The Effect of Lables (Tags) on Social Interactions. Santa Fe Institute Working Paper 93-10-064, Sante Fe, New Mexico (1994)
7. Riolo, R.L.: The Effect of Tag Mediated Selection of Partners in Evolving Populations Playing the Prisoner's Dilemma. Sante Fe Institute Working Paper 97-02-016, Sante Fe, New Mexico (1997)

8. Grossman, T., Balakrishnan, R.: The Bubble Cursor: Enhancing Target Acquisition by Dynamic Resizing of the Cursor's Activation Area. CHI 2005 (2005)
9. Aoki, P.: Making Space for Stories: Ambiguity in the Design of Personal Communication Systems. CHI 2005 (2005)
10. Mantovani, F.: Cyber-attraction "The emergence of computer-mediated communication in the development of interpersonal relationships". In: Anolli, L., Ciceri, R., Riva, G. (eds.) Say not to say: New perspectives on miscommunication, IOS Press, Amsterdam (2001)
11. Rashid, A.M., Ling, K., Tassone, R.D., Resnick, P., Kraut, R., Riedl, J.: Motivating Participation by Displaying the Value of Contribution. CHI 2006 (2006)
12. Fiore, A.T., Donath, J.S.: Online Personals: An Overview. CHI 2004 (2004)
13. Fiore, A.T., Donath, J.S.: Homophily in Online Dating: When Do You Like Someone Like Yourself?' CHI 2005 (2005)
14. Papargyris, A., Poulymenakou, A.: Learning to fly in persistent digital worlds: The case of massively multiplayer online role playing games. ACM SIGGROUP Bulletin 25(1), 41–49 (2005)
15. Golder, S.A., Donath, J.S.: Hiding and Revealing in Online Poker Games. CHI 2004 (2004)
16. Brown, B., Bell, M.: Social Interaction in "There". CHI 2004 (2004)

Rural Internet Centre (RIC) as Catalysts for Building Knowledge-Based Society – The Case of Northern States of Malaysia

Nor Iadah Yusop, Zahurin Mat Aji, Huda Ibrahim, Rafidah Abd. Razak, and Wan Rozaini Sheik Osman

Faculty of Information Technology
Universiti Utara Malaysia
06010 UUM Sintok, Kedah, Malaysia
{noriadah,zahurin,huda753,rafidah,rozai174}@uum.edu.my

Abstract. The creation of Rural Internet Centre (RIC) by the Malaysian government was to provide opportunity and to empower the rural communities in Malaysia. The RIC provides IT skills training and knowledge acquisition programs to the rural community in Malaysia, including women, the elderly, and children. RIC was launched in March 2000 with two centers: Sungai Ayer Tawar in Selangor and Kanowit in Sarawak. By 2006, 42 RICs have been implemented in thirteen states in the country (KTAK, 2006). The Ministry of Energy, Water and Communications (MEWC), Malaysia Post Berhad and Maju Sedunia Digital (MSD) are responsible for the project. The Malaysian government aim to set up 240 centres by the year 2010 which will eventually reaching an estimated 2.8 million members of the rural communities. The management of the centre's operations and activities are given to the local communities. This creates opportunities to the locals to be employed and also provide the chance for acquisition of IT related skills and qualifications. This paper aims at providing an overview over the current RICs implementation with respect to supporting Malaysia government's aspiration towards building the knowledge-based society by the year 2020. RICs could function as the catalyst to achieve this objective. The initial findings on RICs current situations in Northern of Malaysia show that the centres can be further enhanced in order to function as desired.

1 Introduction

The World Science Forum (2003) defines knowledge-based society as "an innovative and life-long learning society, which possesses a community of scholars, researchers, engineers, technicians, research networks, and firms engaged in research and in production of high-technology goods and service provision". The Knowledge Society in Europe (Knowledge Society Homepage) characterize knowledge-based society as the society who believe that "the most valuable asset is investment in intangible, human and social capital and that the key factors are knowledge and creativity". To build such society, they must be equipped "with the ability to generate and capture new knowledge and to access, absorb, share and efficiently use information, knowledge,

D. Schuler (Ed.): Online Communities and Social Comput., HCII 2007, LNCS 4564, pp. 485–490, 2007.
© Springer-Verlag Berlin Heidelberg 2007

data, and communication" (European Community and some Asian countries: http://www.sciforum.hu/knowledge_based_society.html). These definitions imply on knowledge creation and production, usage and diffusion, as well as protection, while information and communication technological (ICT) tools allow access to human knowledge. "Knowledge is used to empower and enrich people culturally and materially, and to build a sustainable society" (World Science Forum, 2003), and "the advent of a knowledge-based society requires improved means of communicating and using knowledge and opportunities for lifelong learning" (Citizens and Governance in a knowledge based society: http://ec.europa.eu/research/fp6/index_en.cfm?p=7).

In this sense, we do agree with the European Community and some Asian countries (http://www.sciforum.hu/knowledge_based_society.html) that says "knowledge and information are viewed as global public goods, and they are tools to enrich the learning environment, support everyday experience, and augment instructional resources." To prepare the people to live and work in such society, ICT skills are deemed necessary. Thus, people from all walks of life are of no exception, and the question posed in (http://www.sciforum.hu/knowledge_based_society.html) on whether "building a knowledge-based society seems to have a geographical speciality" is also relevant in Malaysian context, urban and rural. Evers (2001) had mentioned that "Malaysia, or at least its government, has made the move towards a knowledge–based society and economy its primary target". Dr Mahathir (cited in Evers, 2001) did point out that, "... in our pursuit towards developing K-economy, knowledge has to replace labour and capital as the key factors of production of our economy. The challenge for Malaysia is to develop this knowledge amongst our citizens so that our success will be due to the contribution of Malaysian talents and knowledge workers". Hence, Malaysia's dream on knowledge-based society will stay put as a dream if issues on digital divide amongst urban and rural communities remain. Thus, in this respect, ICT plays very important role in bridging the digital divide in realizing the dream.

Apart from being a key enabler for regional and rural success especially in economic and business development, O'Neil (2002) and Thompson (2005) stated that ICT "has also been linked to the aspiration of community empowerment where dimensions include revitalising a sense of community, building regional capacity, enhancing democracy and increasing social capital". Among the initiatives taken to reduce the digital gap is the establishment of multi-purpose community centre (MPCC) or telecentre (Van Belle & Trusler, 2005). Similar establishment in Malaysia began with turning rural post offices into community Internet classes, and second, creating mini-cyber-cafes through people and corporations. The former project, which started with three pilot sites (Kota Marudu in Sabah, Bau in Sarawak and Sungai Air Tawar in Selangor), were run by Pos Malaysia Berhad (the national mail delivery agency). Each site was equipped with five to seven computers and this number remains until now. To train the orang asli (aborigines) youth and adult community leaders in the use of the Internet and IT equipment, the Community Communication Centre (Komas) that acts an alternative media organization was established (Shom Teoh, 2006). This project emphasized on people and a corporation's participation. The corporations will provide the capital (including the infrastructure (comprising of five PCs and two wireless connections over a VSAT - very small aperture terminal)), and the community will produce the required energy and ideas to encourage the project. Initiatives of this nature have been proven practical by many developing countries, including countries with weak IT infrastructure.

In general, to formalize these initiatives three approaches have been taken by the Malaysian government: top-down, down-up, and top-down-up (UNESCAP, 2006). Top-down model is initiated by the central government, down-up model is initiated by non-governmental organizations with some collaboration with community-based organizations and government agencies, and the top-down-up is initiated by government, but implemented with strong community participation. Examples of top-down projects are Pusat Internet Desa (Rural Internet Centre – RIC), Medan InfoDesa (MID), Kedai.com, SchoolNet, Universal Service Provision (USP) program, MIMOS projects (Mobile Internet Unit and AgriBazaar), and State government projects. Down-up projects are mostly funded by the Demonstrator Application Grant Scheme (DAGS) include sm@sy, CyberCare, TaniNet, e-Pekak, T-Centre, AKIS/PadiNet, and e-Bario. Top-down-up projects include e-WargaKota, Eagle's Net, Warga Emas Network, Pesarajaya, and e-Upcom. However, the implementation of these Community e-Centres (CeCs) experienced a number of difficulties.

Two studies by the JICA Study Team on RICs initiated by the Ministry of Energy, Water and Communications (MEWC) conducted in March 2003 revealed that the pilot CeCs suffered from various problems: lack of full-time supervisor, improper physical environment, inadequate maintenance and repair, inadequate publicity of CeCs, low updating frequency of the local homepage, inadequate IT training, resulting in inability to use CeCs by residents with low IT literacy (cited in Noor Bathi, 2005). Hazita et. al (2007) also highlighted one of the problems faced by the RICs users is the inability of the administrators to support them in using the centres' facilities. This is due to the fact that the administrators were not provided with sufficient training in IT. Pertaining to publicity of the centres, Mohd Nizam (2005b) and Wan Rozaini et. al (2007) findings are consistent with the JICA Study Team's. Hence, they also suggested that the government needs to put more effort to ensure a larger percentage of rural community aware of the establishment of these centres.

This paper provides an overview over the current RICs implementation with respect to supporting Malaysia government's aspiration towards building the knowledge-based society by the year 2020.

2 Challenges in Rural Internet Centres (RICs) Implementation

Rural Internet Centre (RIC) is one of the projects set-up by the Malaysian government to bring the Internet to small towns and rural communities in Malaysia, and is run by the MEWC, Malaysia Post Berhad and Maju Sedunia Digital (MSD). The government aims to set up 240 centres by the year 2010 which will eventually reaching an estimated 2.8 million members of the rural communities. This aim corresponds to the government's aspiration to achieve fully developed nation in the year 2020.

RIC projects were launched in March 2000 with two centers: Sungai Ayer Tawar in Selangor and Kanowit in Sarawak. By 2006, 42 Rural Internet Centres (RICs) have been implemented in thirteen states in the country (KTAK, 2006). RIC provides IT skills training and knowledge acquisition programs to the rural community in Malaysia, including women, the elderly, and children. The number of RICs in each state and the types of facilities, activities and services provided in each centre are dependent on the size of states.

The studies on RICs in Selangor (Mohd Nizam, 2005a; Mohd Nizam, 2005b) and in Kedah and Perlis (Wan Rozaini et. al, 2007) have shown that the implementation of the centres in that states has been well accepted by the local communities. The centres do not only give the communities an access to the Internet, but also improve their knowledge and skills in ICT. The numbers of RIC users and visitors have increased every day. The centres however, do not have enough ICT resources, for example, PCs, printers, and other peripheral devices. Each centre is only equipped with be-tween five to seven PCs. The centres also have a limited number of staff to administer the RICs. Mohd Nizam's (2005a) study finally concluded that RICs in Selangor and other states should be given more spaces and resources in order to achieve the RICs' objectives.

The assessment of the current RIC operations and usage indicates that the RICs have attracted the interest of the youth compared to the other age categories (Wan Rozaini et. al, 2007; Ezhar et. al, 2007; Hazita et. al, 2007). In terms of gender, they also found that the number of male and female administrators, as well as users, is almost equivalent. Wan Rozaini et. al (2007) found that the Malays outlay the other races as the RICs' administrators and users because the communities surrounding the RICs are mainly the Malays. Similarly, Ezhar et. al (2007) found that the Bidayuh features the majority of users since they are the main race in rural Sarawak. These provide an early indication that the RICs are mainly used by the main races surround-ing the RICs.

The management of the centre's operations and activities are given to the local communities. This creates opportunities to the locals to be employed and also provide the chance for acquisition of IT related skills and qualifications. The RICs are man-aged by full-time administrators. Wan Rozaini et. al (2007) found that almost 46 per-cents of them are Diploma holders, 27 percents has certificates and the rest with Bachelor and Masters degree. However, these figures do not depict the scenario of entire RICs administrators since the study is conducted only for RICs in Kedah and Perlis. Certificate holders feature the majority users (Ezhar et. al, 2007; Wan Rozaini et. al, 2007).

Regarding the RICs' operations, all studied RICs operate between 8.30 a.m. to 5.30 p.m. on weekdays (Mohd Nizam, 2005b; Wan Rozaini et. al, 2007; Hazita et. al, 2007). All RICs have the basic ICT facilities such as printers, scanners, and internet access. Apart from that, many RICs are equipped also with photocopy and fax ma-chine, LCD projector, digital camera, and reference books. The users also suggested that the number of computers as well as other basic facilities is increased as the cur-rent number is insufficient, and the operation hours be extended (Mohd Nizam, 2005b; Wan Rozaini et. al, 2007; Hazita et. al, 2007). These are proposed to allow participation of more users.

Studies by Wan Rozaini et. al (2007) and Hazita et. al (2007) agreed that the com-mon training provided by the RICs include basic computer classes, basic Internet, introduction to Windows and Microsoft Office. In addition, Wan Rozaini et. al (2007) found that webpage development course is also offered. Wan Rozaini et. al (2007) also indicate that among the services provided include giving advices on computer purchase, computer selling and servicing, card printing and writing official letter, e-procurement services, and posting advertisement in webpage.

3 Conclusion and Recommendations

The current RICs' infrastructure and facilities are enough to support their basic operations. However, to offer better services to the communities, these facilities need to be continuously upgraded and improved. Furthermore, to equip the administrators with sufficient skills and abilities, series of training have to be given, either IT related or not. Training modules as suggested by Murray et. al (2001) (cited in UNESCAP (2006) are communication and development, the role of CeCs in development, the role of the CeCs managers/ coordinator, basic business and financial skill, information production skills, needs assessment skills and evaluation (research method), training skills, participation skills, human resource management, and marketing and public relation skills should be taken into consideration to support the government effort in building knowledge-based society. Similarly, continuous trainings that suit communities (user) of different groups and levels should be provided.

To enhance the communities' awareness about the establishment of RICs, aggressive publicity in collaboration with respective agencies and non-government organizations (NGOs) needs to be undertaken through various means such as electronic media, newspapers, and road show to attract a larger percentage of users. In conjunction with the establishment of International Telecommunication Union Asia Pacific Centre in Universiti Utara Malaysia (ITU UUM ASP-CoE) for Rural ICT Development Programme, it can be used as a platform to promote RICs at local and international level. In relation to that, appropriate awareness programs have to be planned and designed.

Regarding the RICs' web pages, the template is provided by the MSD and the maintenance is done by the administrators. However, there are differences in the design and content of each RIC's web pages. Some are mainly informational in which they provide only basic information about the RICs committees, local communities' activities, background of the location, and little information on business opportunities and other e-commerce links. In contrast, some do have additional advanced sections that enable users to link to various online applications especially e-government services such as National Registration Department (JPN), e-procurement, Motor Vehicle Department (JPJ), registrar of commerce, and institutions of higher education. On this account, an effort should be taken to create a standard design so that the targeted communities will get equal opportunities to relevant information and thus bridge the digital gap. In relation to this, analysis of the users' requirements is deemed necessary to enable suitable information or content be included in the websites.

Another important issue related to RIC is its sustainability. For instance, Songan et. al (2004) mentioned that ICTs cannot just be "dropped" in the rural village but need to be accompanied by training and education to be successful and sustainable. Among the aspects outlined in UNESCAP (2006) report include human resource, financial, and social sustainability. In terms of human resource, training of trainers and training of the community members must be carried out. This will create a pool of knowledgeable people from the rural community that can continuously assist the operations of RICs. Currently the RICs are funded by the federal government (Wan Rozaini et. al, 2007). To be financially independent of government funding, the communities must be able to generate their own source of income. This has been proven to work for the e-Bario project (UNESCAP, 2006). This exercise will inculcate the sense of ownership among the community. As a result, it will contribute to the sustainability of the centre. Social sustainability is necessary to ensure the RIC is relevant and continually used by the community. Therefore, the RIC services and activities need to be monitored and evaluated to ensure they are relevant to people from all walks of life. In addition, the use of RICs need to be supervised to avoid unethical and illegal activities.

References

Citizens and Governance in a knowledge based society [14 /01/2007] http://ec.europa.eu/research/fp6/index_en.cfm?p=7

Tamam, E., Ismail, N., anak Kasa, A.: Pola Pencarian Maklumat dalam Kalangan Belia di Pusat Internet Desa (PID) Sarawak, Presented at the E-Community Research Center Colloquium 2007, 8 February, Universiti Kebangsaan Malaysia, Malaysia (2007)

Azman, H., Setapa, S.H., Mustafa, J., Rizan, T.N., Maasum, T.M., Zabidi, N.A., Ibrahim, K., Norwati, Md., Amir, Z.: Peranan Pusat e-komuniti terhadap Pembangunan Kemahiran: eLiterasi di Kalangan Warga Belia Luar Bandar. Presented at the E-Community Research Center Colloquium 2007, 8 February, Universiti Kebangsaan Malaysia, Malaysia (2007)

Knowledge Society Homepage [14 /01/2007] http://ec.europa.eu/employment_social/knowledge_society/index_en.htm

KTAK , Portal Komuniti Desa (2006) [4 October 2006] http://idesa.net.my

Omar, M.N.: Dasar Perlaksanaan Inisiatif 'Internet Desa': Cabaran dan Implikasi dalam mengurangkan jaringan digital di Malaysia. In: Presented at Workshop 'Membudayakan Masyarakat Jaringan: Cabaran dan Batasan', 16 Jun, Universiti Kebangsaan Malaysia (UKM) (2005a)

Omar, M.N.: Information and Communication Technology Policies in Malaysia: Analysis on Government Measures to Minimise the Digital Divide. In: Proceedings of National E-Community Seminar 2005, Universiti Kebangsaan Malaysia, (December 6-7, 2005b)

Badarudin, N.B.: Draft Rural ICT Guidebook – Based on Malaysian Experience, presented at Regional Meeting on Effective Design and Delivery of Rural Community ICT Services by UNESCAP/INTAN, 28-30 November 2005, INTAN Bukit Kiara, Kuala Lumpur, Malaysia (2005)

Shom, T.: Rethinking the Digital Divide. The Star Online (March 2, 2006)

Songan, P., Ab Hamid, K., Yeo, A., Gnaniah, J., Zen, H.: Community Informatics: Challenges in Bridging the Digital Divide. In: Khalid, H.M., Helander, M.G., Yeo, A.W. (ed.) Work with Computing System 2004. Damai Science, Kuala Lumpur (2004)

UNESCAP, Guidebook on Developing Community e-Centres in Rural Areas: Based on the Malaysian Experience. United Nations Economic and Social Commission for Asia and the Pacific (2006)

Van Belle, J.P., Trusler, J.: An Interpretivist Case Study of a South African Rural Multi-Purpose Community Centre. The Journal of Community Informatics, 1(2) (2005) [14/02/2007] http://www.ci-journal.net/index.php/ciej/article/view/231

Osman, W.R.S., Aji, Z.M., Ibrahim, H., Yusop, N.I., Othman, N.: Ke Arah Memperkasakan Komuniti Luar Bandar: Penilaian Situasi Semasa Pusat Internet Desa (PID). Presented at the E-Community Research Center Colloquium 2007, 8 February, Universiti Kebangsaan Malaysia, Malaysia (2007)

World Science Forum, Budapest, Knowledge and Society, 8-10 November 2003 Budapest, Hungary [17/01/07] http://www.sciforum.hu/index.php?image=update&content=up_knowledge_based_society

SISN: A Toolkit for Augmenting Expertise Sharing Via Social Networks

Jun Zhang[1], Yang Ye[2], Mark S. Ackerman[3], and Yan Qu[4]

[1]School of Information, University of Michigan
[2]Department of Linguistics, University of Michigan
[2]EECS and School of Information, University of Michigan
[4]College of Information Studies, University of Maryland

Abstract. The current study attempts to address the social-technical gap by developing a toolkit that can help information seekers to search for expertise and seek information via their social networks. The focus of the current study is technical development of a toolkit that supports expertise sharing via social networks. Once such a toolkit is in place, it can facilitate researches that are more concerned with applications in social and organizational perspectives. Following a proposed full-fledged social network-powered expert searching and information sharing framework on the theoretical side, the study then reports a toolkit of Seeking Information via Social Networks (SISN), which is a general-purpose toolkit for social network-based information sharing applications that combines techniques in information retrieval, social network, and peer-to-peer system.

Keywords: expertise sharing, social networks.

1 Introduction

Information seeking plays a central role in people's daily work and life. Although the past decade has seen a thriving success of information seeking via web-based search engines, information seeking through one's social network has proven a more personalized, context-based, interactive hence more efficient way to accomplish the task, compared to a web or formal documents search. Most organizations have their own informational network structures, which are connected by various communication channels, such an email, IM, etc. Typically, these informational network structures do not provide direct support for information seeking via one's social network. Despite the effort of researchers to develop different systems to support the ad-hoc information seeking behaviors, the research community has yet to bridge the gap between social network-driven information seeking and the advent of the web and internet in this information era. This gap motivates research on developing different systems to integrate these ad-hoc information seeking and expert searching into the existing network structures.

Motivated by the gap discussed above, the current paper draws upon early studies and attempts to address the social-technical gap by developing a toolkit that embraces

D. Schuler (Ed.): Online Communities and Social Comput., HCII 2007, LNCS 4564, pp. 491–500, 2007.

the key components for building social network-based information sharing systems and can help information seekers to search for expertise and seek information via their social networks. The focus of the current study is technical development of a toolkit that supports expertise sharing via social networks. Once such a toolkit is in place, it can facilitate research that is more concerned with applications in social and organizational perspectives. Towards this end, on the theoretical side, we propose the key modules that should be embraced by a full-fledged social network-powered expert searching and information sharing framework. We then report on a toolkit of Seeking Information via Social Networks (SISN) on top of the conceptual discussions, which is a general-purpose toolkit for social network-based information sharing applications that combines techniques in information retrieval, social network, and peer-to-peer system.

The paper is organized as follows: Section 2 reviews previous work. Section 3 reviews the core modules that are indispensable in a social network-powered expert searching and information sharing system and propose such a framework. Section 4 elaborates on the architecture of SISN, a general-purpose toolkit that implements the modules proposed in the previous section. Section 5 concludes the paper and remarks on future work.

2   Related Work

Past decade has seen a series of studies investigating systems to help people or organizations identify experts. Such systems are usually called expertise finders or expertise location engines, among which the most well known ones include Who-Knows [10], ContactFinder [7], Answer Garden [1], IKNOW [4] and Expertise Recommender [8].

Another type of systems focuses on connecting people and enabling them to share information, such systems are termed referral systems seeking to leverage the social network within an organization or community and facilitate information seeking, represented by Yenta [5], ReferralWeb [6], and the commercial systems from Tacit and Microsoft. The systems attempt to emulate the way how people find information through their social contacts in real life. They endow the users with flexible control with regard to what to share and with whom to share.

Previous research has shown that expertise searching involves a range of perspectives, each one having multiple solutions. Each solution comes with certain benefits as well as limitations. The choice of a specific solution often depends on the target of the system as well as the context in which the system will be deployed. In many situations, the optimal solution may be a hybrid approach combining multiple methods.

Recently, the Web 2.0 trend has triggered an avalanche of new opportunities for large scale expertise sharing. For instance, various social websites (e.g. MySpace and Facebook) and online communities open up new ways for people to network. Conceptually, new social network-based expertise systems could be built to make use of these new resources. We believe a toolkit that takes into account the lessons learned from previous expertise finder systems and referral systems can better facilitate the development of such systems. This paper reports our pilot study in this line of research, and we focus on social network related mechanisms at the current stage.

3 Searching Expertise in Social Networks

Expert searching in social networks is a challenging take in that it requires a smooth integration of technologies from different fields. Generally speaking, a social networked-based experts searching system should consist of the following components:

- A collection of users with their expertise being represented by their profiles
- A social network that connects the users and place them along the query/referral/answer pipeline
- A collection of searching strategies to spread the query/referral efficiently across different user groups
- A coupling of the system with daily communication channels (e.g. IM and Email) to provide a convenient interface between the major parties involved in the information seeking process

Below we discuss these crucial components in details.

3.1 Expertise Profiling

One general way of profiling people in knowledge sharing systems is to use an ontology. An ontology is a hierarchical data structure containing all the relevant entities within a specific domain. Although there are some domain-specific topologies, they are typically too limited for the purpose of knowledge sharing. An alternative way is to automatically profile people by indexing their daily documents and generating a list of keyword vectors from these documents.

A challenge of keywords profiling is the lack of common terminologies among different user groups, which is more evident when the information seeker and the experts are from different fields. Furthermore, compared to the ontology approach, keywords profiling may suffer from a sparseness problem in the case where there is no exact match for the keywords.

To improve the automatic indexing method and combat keywords sparseness problem, it is helpful to automatically classify the documents or keywords into several knowledge domains.

At last, a person's knowledge is not limited to what he knows, but also whom he knows [9]. To this end, it is important to employ a transactive memory [11], which is an important vehicle for leveraging knowledge networks and gaining access to others knowledge sources for tasks that cannot be accomplished by individuals. Therefore, in one's profile, it is beneficial to include functions supporting the collection and storage of such memories.

3.2 Extracting Social Networks

Toward building a social network-based knowledge system, organizations should dynamically learn the network from people's communication patterns, such as frequency, longevity, and reciprocity of the emails or IMs of a user [12]. An IM crawler can extract the buddy list from the IM application. Other crawlers can also be implemented in parallel to collect other information. A network generated from such a process is an ego-network, in which the user is located at the center of the network and his social contacts are directly linked to him.

Once a number of individual ego-networks are extracted and connected via certain distance or similarity calibration, a pure peer-to-peer network topology is constructed. In such a network, nobody knows the complete topology of the network for the reason that all the processes are conducted locally and the results are stored only in the user's own machine. Individual users usually only know their direct social contacts. The network is flat and everybody is equally weighted in the network. In such a situation, local network searching algorithms could be applied but in a limited fashion.

Social networks in organizations, however, are usually not flat. Nodes with high centralities, such as the group managers, generally play more important networking roles. Previous research indicates that such nodes are usually the keys for faster social network searching, because they either span across the boundaries of different social groups or are connected to the largest number of nodes in their local groups [3]. It is therefore desirable to have analysis functions to help identify these important nodes.

In some organizations, it is possible to get a snapshot of the whole network topology. In this situation, a centrality analyzer is used to calculate different centrality measures of each node directly, after which we can determine the important nodes in the network and design the searching algorithm accordingly.

When we cannot get any network information besides one's ego-network, the dynamic learning analyzer can be used to induce other nodes' networking importance by analyzing the past searching history. In such a scenario, the network will start with a flat network where every node is equal. During the information searching process, an agent will cache queries as well as the query/referral chains that have passed it After some time, certain nodes will prove to be more prominent because they appear in many of the query chains. If such nodes become obvious, the agent can update its belief of the importance of these nodes.

3.3 Query Spreading Strategies

Different from an expertise database, social network-based expertise sharing systems usually use a peer-to-peer structure, in which expertise profiles are stored in users' local machines. It is therefore crucial to develop strategies that can efficiently spread the queries in the social network. Note querying a social network is not a straightforward breadth-first problem. It is a combination of approximating, broking, and requerying processes.

In our early studies [13], we proposed and tested three families of query spreading strategies: general broadcast, information scent, and network structure-based heuristic search. We reported on the advantages and limitations of each strategy. General broadcast is the fastest but too costly, because it involves a huge number of people in the network. It was also observed that a network structure-based heuristic search using highly connected social hubs (people with a lot of connections) is very efficient for query spreading. However, these social hubs are also high-level executives in the organization, thus increasing the access barriers. In contrast, the information scent strategy picks the person who has the highest match score between the query and one's profile as referral. Although it is less efficient than the strategy based on using social hubs, it performs reasonably well.

3.4 Media Coupling

To better facilitate query negotiating and reformulating processes, it is desirable to couple the system with certain communication channels such as IM or email. IM is an ideal channel in the sense that it provides quick turnarounds and requires less social expectation and pressure for formality. It minimizes the social cost involved in an information seeking action. IM's status indicator as well as many other features also can help information seekers judge the availability of the brokers and experts and make expertise seeking a more fun activity.

4 The Toolkit of Seeking Information Via Social Networks (SISN)

Section 3 describes the crucial elements that are indispensable in the construction of a system of searching expertise via social networks at the conceptual level. The current section implements the conceptual modules and packages them into a general-purpose toolkit, Seeking Information via Social Networks (SISN), which can be tailored to support social network-based information sharing applications. SISN embraces a wide diversity of techniques in information retrieval, social networks, and peer-to-peer systems. It supports constructing a searchable social network based on people's daily communication patterns, automatically propagates queries, and tightly couples with daily communication channels for the full cycle of the querying/broking/helping pipeline.

SISN is built entirely in Java and runs on all platforms that support Java 2. In the rest of the section, we will provide an overview of the architecture of the toolkit, followed by elaborations of the details of implementing the individual modules.

4.1 The Architecture Flow of SISN

In designing the architecture of SISN, we carefully couple the modules in the toolkit to the conceptual elements in the framework discussed in Section 3. Figure 1 illustrates the architecture flow of SISN. As shown in the flow chart, the toolkit takes users' raw documents as input, walks through different modules along the pipeline, and delivers the end products via IMs or emails.

4.2 Information Profiling

Information profiling is the first step once the raw documents of the users are input to the SISN. Information profiling in SISN is realized via an indexer and a categorizer.

Indexer. The document indexer is implemented using the Lucene indexing API with several application extensions for handling different file formats. The current version of indexer can index PDF, Word, HTML, Browser Bookmarks, and email archives. The indexing results are presented in the form of a list of weighted keywords vectors. The results are ready for direct query matching.

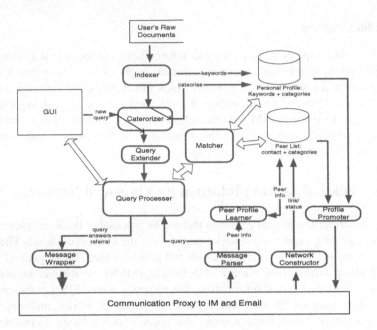

Fig. 1. The Architecture of SISN

Each type of documents is indexed separately depending on their privacy sensitivity as well as their relevance to people's expertise. Thus, it provides a great amount of flexibility for later access control and expertise valuing implementations. For instance, a user can select to share only the keywords generated from his emails with his closest friends while sharing the keywords generated from his publications publicly. Furthermore, a developer can give higher weight to keywords appearing in one's publications than one's bookmark pages, for the reason that those keywords might better reflect expertise.

An indexing editor is also provided to support further editing of profiling keywords for end users.

By the time of writing this paper, several desktop searching APIs are provided by Google and Microsoft, and an alternative indexing solution could be using these APIs because they can index a wider range of document types quickly. The indexer of SISN is implemented relatively in an independent fashion such that it could be replaced in future developments if necessary.

Categorizer. The document categorizer succeeds the indexer and is implemented as an automatic classifier using Dewey Decimal Classification method. It groups the documents provided by the users into different categories.

A user's profile is a combination of the categories of documents that a user contributes. This user profile is also called category level profile, which partly reflects the user's expertise domains. It can be used to facilitate directed information searching process in social networks.

In addition to the input documents, the categorizer is also used by the query extender, which will be described later in the section. When a user types in a new query, the categorizer will try to classify the query into a hierarchical class based on the keywords in the query.

4.3 Social Network Module

The social network module connects the users in various social groups and places them along the query/referral/answer channel. It is essentially the module that makes information seeking different from a web-based question answering practice. The social network module of SISN consists of a network constructor and a profile promoter.

Network Constructor. The network constructor of SISN is the component that extracts individual network topology from people's daily communication patterns. It has a collection of crawlers that can automatically analyze messaging archives from the users' communication logs and automatically generate the networks.

Profile Promoter and Peer Profile Learner. The profile promoter is used for an agent to broadcast its category level profile to its directly connected neighbors. It broadcasts once a day, such that each agent will have a cache of what types of knowledge its neighbors possess. There are two major reasons of sharing only the category level profile, one being privacy concerns and the other being the storage cost.

Coupled with the profile promoter, SISN also features a peer profile learner, which is the receiver of the messages sent by the profile promoter in the neighborhood. It collects all the messages, upon which it then builds a peer information table in the agent's profile.

4.4 Searching and Referral Strategy Module

Query Extender. The query extender extends a short question query into a hierarchal question with the assist of the categorizer. There are two reasons for extending a query: first, it facilitates the hierarchical search because the query is itself hierarchical; second, if the original query is too vague or too general, its higher-level category query might still be able to identify a person close to the targeting field, who can help reformulate the query to be more informative.

Query Processor and Query Matcher. The query processor and the matcher are the key elements of the SISN toolkit, the efficiency of which largely decides the match quality of the information needed by the expertise seeker and the returned information.

The query matcher computes the similarity between a query and the expertise profiles of the users. If no match is found, it will compute the similarity between the query categories and the peer's category level profile cached in this agent. In the case of a found category level match, a possible referral path is picked and the query processor will decide how to spread the referral message accordingly.

The query processor implements the various query-spreading strategies that we discussed in Section 3.

4.5 Communication Proxy

Once the different modules of the toolkit are in place, it is important to provide channels enabling the users to conveniently reach out for help and respond to queries. Such channels include quick turnaround web-based communication mechanisms such as IM and email. To this end, SISN also features a message wrapper, a message parser and a message proxy. These three help integrate other SISN components into everyday communications.

The message wrapper wraps a SISN specific message into a general IM or email message. Then the communication proxy will send out this message as a general instant message or an email, the choice between which depends on the user's general applications.

Figure 2 shows an example of a query message wrapped in an IM message.

The message type specifies the type of an SISN message. There are three message types: profile promoting (0), query (1), and querying result notice (2). When a new query is generated by a user, it will be assigned a unique QueryID such that it will not be processed multiple times by the same referral agent in case it comes from different paths. TTL is the time-to-live of the message. This number specifies the number of hops the message can travel in the referral network. The question ontology represents the domains from which the information seeker wants to get the answer. The question is the details of the actual question typed in by the user.

The messaging proxy monitors a user's incoming messages continuously. It scans the starting line of the message. Once it finds the SISN marker, it will trigger the message parser to parse the message. Then the message parser will decide the type of the message and generate related information to send to other components.

IM Message Header	**From:** jun@jabber.com **To:** tester@myjabber.net **Time:** 11:24:31 Oct 2004
IM Message Body (SISN Message)	__##SISN Message Marker -- **Message Type:** 1 **QueryID:** mike@jabber.com_064303 **Asker:** jun@jabber.com **Priority**: 1 **Path:** mike@jabber.com;jun@jabber.com **TTL:** 6 -- **Ontology:** computer science, visualization **Question:** How can we do acoustic visualization?

Fig. 2. An Example of a Query Message Wrapped in an IM Message

5 Discussions and Future Work

The current study draws upon research issues from information retrieval, expertise sharing, and social network studies. We implemented a peer-to-peer toolkit that provides various crucial functions for an information seeking task with the flexibility of both operating in isolation and being integrated into higher level information sharing framework. We believe that, by providing a general-purpose toolkit as a platform for sharing and seeking expertise via social networks, the current work helps us advance towards narrowing the gap between the social and technical perspectives of social network-based information seeking, i.e. the gap "between what we have to do socially and what computer science as a field knows how to do technically" [2]. We have good reasons to believe that upon a mature and optimized implementation of platforms of the kind proposed in the current study, information seeking and expertise sharing will advance towards greater efficacy with better personalization.

Looking to future work, we plan to invite a pool of test users of the SISN toolkit, whose feedback will help identify places for improvement with regard to the following aspects: a more robust design to accommodate domain-specific tailoring of the system; a smoother connection between the different modules in the pipeline; and, a more optimistic classification taxonomy so the categorizer can better represent the expertise domain of the users. We also look forward to integrating the toolkit into existent web-based online community tools to assist social network-based information and expertise seeking.

Acknowledgements. This work was supported in part by the National Science Foundation (IIS-0325347). The authors would also like to thank George Furnas Michael Cohen, and our research group colleagues.

References

1. Ackerman, M.S.: Augmenting organizational memory: A field study of answer garden. ACM Transactions on Information Systems 16(3), 203–224 (1998)
2. Ackerman, M.S.: The intellectual challenge of CSCW: The gap between social requirements and technical feasibility. Human-Computer Interaction 15(2-3), 179–203 (2000)
3. Adamic, L., Adar, E.: How to search a social network.Social Networks, 27(3) (2005)
4. Contractor, N., Zink, D., et al.: IKNOW: A tool to assist and study the creation, maintenance, and dissolution of knowledge networks. In: Ishida, T. (ed.) Community Computing and Support Systems. LNCS, vol. 1519, pp. 201–217. Springer, Heidelberg (1998)
5. Foner, L.N.Y.: A multi-agent, referral-based matchmaking system. In: Proceedings of the first international conference on Autonomous agents, Marina del Rey, California, United States, ACM Press, New York (1997)
6. Kautz, H., Selman, B., et al.: Referral Web: combining social networks and collaborative filter. Commun. ACM 40(3), 63–65 (1997)
7. Krulwich, B., Burkey, C.: ContactFinder agent: answering bulletin board questions with referrals. In: The 1996 13th National Conference on Artificial Intelligence, Portland, OR, USA (1996)

8. McDonald, D.W., Ackerman, M.S.: Expertise recommender: a flexible recommendation system and architecture. In: Proceedings of the 2000 ACM conference on Computer supported cooperative work, Philadelphia, Pennsylvania, United States, ACM Press, New York (2000)
9. Nardi, B.A., Whittaker, S., et al.: It's Not What You Know, It's Who You Know: Work in the Information Age, First Monday 5 (2000)
10. Streeter, L., Lochbaum, K.: Who Knows: A System Based on Automatic Representation of Semantic Structure. In: Proceedings of RIAO (1988)
11. Wegner, D.M.: Transactive memory: A contemporary analysis of the group mind. Theories of group behavior, pp. 185–208 (1987)
12. Whittaker, S., Jones, Q., Terveen, L.: Contact management: identifying contacts to support long-term communication. In: Proceedings of CSCW '02, pp. 216–225. ACM Press, New York (2002)
13. Zhang, J., Ackerman, M.S.: Searching for expertise in social networks: a simulation of potential strategies. In: Proceedings of GROUP'05, ACM Press, New York (2005)

WikiTable: A New Tool for Collaborative Authoring and Data Management

Xianjun Sam Zheng, Ilian Sapundshiev, and Robert Rauschenberger

Siemens Corporate Research
755 College Road East
Princeton, NJ 08540, USA
{sam.zheng,sapundshiev.ilian.ext,
robert.rauschenberger}@siemens.com

Abstract. Tables are an efficient tool for organizing complex data. Even though they are pervasively used in all kinds of documentation, current implementations of tables often limit the power of data management because generally they do not support concurrent collaborative authoring; they only allow keyword search, which typically yields poor search performance; and transporting tables among different applications is cumbersome. We present a new table tool, WikiTable, which permits multiple users to work on the same table simultaneously. The content of each table is stored in a database, which enables accurate data inquiry. More importantly, WikiTable is highly portable, permitting easy integration with other applications, such as Wikis or Blogs. An effort to apply the WikiTable in a global collaboration project of software development is also discussed.

Keywords: Tables, spreadsheet, Wiki, collaborative authoring, data organization, sharing, and management.

1 Introduction

Tables are a powerful tool for organizing complex data. They exploit the structuring of data into two-dimensional arrays, which permit not only the alignment of the data along two separate dimensions, but also make joint membership at intersections of categories along orthogonal dimensions explicit [7,11]. Even though spreadsheet applications (e.g., Excel) are designed with powerful functions for manipulating quantitative data, many tables are created only containing plain texts or qualitative contents. These tables are pervasively used in a variety of documentation, such as contact lists, schedules, project status reports, and software requirement documents. Moreover, these tables are often used by multiple teams at various geographical locations.

However, several major constrains of the current table implementation inhibit the power of effective data management. First, conventional tables do not support collaborative authoring. A user working on a single cell of the table will typically result in the table being locked for concurrent modification by a second user. This inefficiency is exacerbated when a large table requires the input from many users. Furthermore, even

D. Schuler (Ed.): Online Communities and Social Comput., HCII 2007, LNCS 4564, pp. 501–508, 2007.

though items in the table are interrelated, they are not semantically coded. As a result, this only permits a keyword search through the entire document, typically yielding poor search performance. Lastly, transporting tables among different applications is cumbersome. This is partially because the table format is mixed with its contents, and there is no single format that universally supports different applications.

Here, we present a new table tool, WikiTable, which permits collaborative authoring, allowing multiple users to work on the same table simultaneously. The content of each table is stored in a database, which also contains the semantic information for each cell item in the table; therefore, this supports accurate data searching and inquiry. More importantly, the WikiTable is a highly portable tool. It can be easily integrated into other applications, such as Wikis or Blogs. This provides a means for the user to access and modify the table contents without concerns about format compatibility. In addition, the user interface of the WikiTable is implemented with AJAX technology, which enables direct manipulation of the table.

In this paper, we first discuss why table is a powerful tool for data organization. Then we review the current implementations of tables and describe the limitations. We elaborate our approach to implement this new tool, WikiTable. We discuss our design considerations in architecture, integration as well as the user interface. This follows by a use case, which shows the benefits of using the WikiTable in a global software development project for document sharing and management. We conclude with a summary and the future directions.

2   Motivation and Related Work

The tabular organization of discrete items – first physical items, then abstract data – has a long history that dates back at least to the middle ages, in which tables (as in: the piece of furniture) with checkered cloth coverings were used to count money [ref.: Wikipedia: "table", 10]. In its modern instantiation – the spreadsheet – the tabular organization of discrete items retained its function in the services of accounting but moved away from the literal "table" to a two-dimensional array on paper. The arrangement of data in a two-dimensional array has inherent benefits that likely contributed to its popularity and longevity: Apart from making category membership explicit, the table (or spreadsheet) permits an immediate apprehension of the logical relationship between categories on orthogonal dimensions by encoding an "AND" relationship that pivots around items that are contained in cells at the intersection of a particular table row and a particular table column. For example, in a table with "size" as one dimension and "vertebrates" as the other, "elephant" will find itself in the cell at the intersection of "large" AND "mammal" because it simultaneously belongs to both of these categories. Similarly, a table permits the immediate apprehension of "OR" relationships, as mammals can be either "large" OR "small;" and large vertebrates can include "mammals" OR "fish" (in the case of sharks, for example).

The table furthermore capitalizes on one of the most basic metaphors used in human cognition: space – the other being time. Spatial layouts are essential for survival (e.g., finding "home" after a hunt); they have served as mnemonics for ages (e.g., method of loci); and they even form the basis of the most common visualization of time: the calendar. It should not be further surprising, therefore, that tables enjoy a particular and enduring popularity. In an important parallel to physical terrains, where we ascend elevations to gain an overview over the layout of the landscape, spreadsheets permit us to take a step back and appreciate the global pattern of entries, rather than focusing on small details. These global patterns can often be as meaningful as the individual cell entries. In the periodic table of elements, for example, the fact that certain regions of the table remain blank has important implications for the nature of the elements, their physical properties and the principles that govern them.

There are many software products that support the creation of tables, such as VisiCalc, Lotus 1-2-3, Excel, etc. These software products allow users to harness all of the beneficial qualities of tables. In addition, they integrate a multitude of features and functions that are intended to make spreadsheets an even more powerful tool. Modern spreadsheets, for example, can perform text manipulation (concatenation, letter string search, etc.), statistical computations (means, standard deviations, t-tests, etc.), algorithmic operations (addition, subtraction, division, etc.), and many other functions. They plot data in graphs, integrate visual basic and macro functions, and support a host of formatting parameters. Novice users and experts alike use spreadsheets in a large variety of fields ranging from accounting to zoology.

In this wealth of options, what has become increasingly obscured, however, are the basic virtues of tables expounded above. Spreadsheets have become so loaded with features that the applications themselves have bloated into very large software packages with tremendous overhead. Although all of these features are certainly useful (or they would presumably have been pruned in subsequent releases), tabular representations of information in and of themselves already possess considerable value. Under many circumstances, therefore, it may be desirable to have a 'stripped down' version of the spreadsheet used largely for the inherent benefits of two-dimensional data organization. The concept presented in the following is intended as exactly that.

2.1 Wiki and Collaborative Authoring

Although spreadsheets are useful for maintaining, organizing, and even sharing data, current instantiations are less amenable to collaborative authoring. In part, the limitations on cooperative authoring are a consequence of the complexity of the operations that can be performed on the cells of a spreadsheet, which often involve links and references to other cells. References are possible to other cells in the same spreadsheet, across spreadsheets or even to other 'workbooks' that, in turn, contain several spreadsheets, which comprise numerous cells that may have mutual links. If one author alters the contents of a given cell, this modification could result in a whole cascade of changes to the contents of linked cells, which depend on the original cell(s) their contents. Another author, unaware of these altered mutual dependencies, may similarly modify cells that are linked to other cells, resulting in abject chaos. For good reasons, therefore, present spreadsheet applications lock spreadsheets that have already been opened by another user for modification.

The emergence of what has been referred to as Web 2.0 [9] has demonstrated that it is valuable to rely on a 'collective intelligence' to produce content that is the result of multiple users concurrently working on the same document(s). To facilitate and support such collaborative authoring, new online tools have been developed, the most successful of which is the so-called Wiki [4, 10]. All authors work on the same document, which, importantly, is displayed via the web, so that every co-author has dynamic visual access to the same, shared text. Unlike traditional web authoring using HTML, the Wiki requires no special knowledge of a dedicated markup language, nor does the Wiki require authors to edit the web document offline and upload the result. Modifications can be made directly on the Wiki itself. To a large extent, this mitigates the issue of mutually interfering modifications, as encountered with the current spreadsheet applications, and as described above.

2.2 Combining the Two: WikiTables

Based on these considerations, it occurred to us that the strengths of both Wikis and tables should be harnessed by stripping tables of all the excesses that rendered them into spreadsheets (however useful these may be in some contexts) and combining the two concepts into a single tool – the WikiTable. In the WikiTable, individual cells can be modified independently of one another (see below). In part, this independence can be achieved because cells do not make reference to one another except in the linguistic sense (in the same way this paragraph makes reference to the preceding paragraphs) [11]. This absence of mutual links exists, of course, by design and should be regarded as one of the strengths of the WikiTable. Multiple authors can therefore work on the same table concurrently, each on a single cell at a time. Authoring of the cells occurs in exactly the same manner as with the standard Wiki. The entire application becomes very light and flexible. In essence, a WikiTable can be mutated into any repository of information that fulfills a commonly negotiated, gradually emerging need or goal. Co-authors no longer need to wait until some other user has completed his or her changes to the document; copies of the document no longer need to be disseminated by e-mail to all the stakeholders. Instead, everyone works on the same document, and changes are immediately posted to the same location on the web, visible to all. In accordance with its flexibility, the WikiTable can also become integrated into more formal structures and serve the function of a multi-authored sketchpad within this host application. In this case, in essence, it becomes something akin to a portlet: a dedicated application viewed within the context of a larger assembly, the portal.

3   Implementation

3.1   Architecture

The WikiTable is a web-based application. On the client-side WikiTable relies on web-browsers such as Internet Explorer or Firefox. The JavaScript support in these browsers should be enabled, because it is essential for the AJAX (Asynchronous JavaScript and XML) technology we used. AJAX is a novel web technique that makes a web page feel more responsive by exchanging small amounts of data with the web-server without the need to reload the whole page. In order to utilize the AJAX technique in a more common way, we used a JavaScript library called Prototype[6]. On the server-side the WikiTable requires a database server and a web server with PHP-support. During the development we used a standard Apache web server. We used MySQL as a database, but because the database design is not sophisticated, other databases could be easily integrated.

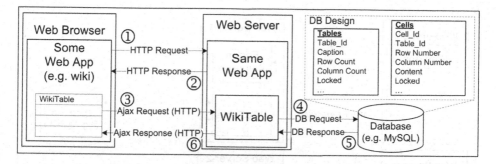

Fig. 1. The architecture and the database design of the WikiTable tool

Figure 1 shows a typical configuration of the WikiTable. The numbers indicate the order of the steps to display WikiTable in a web page. A web browser makes a request (1) to a web server for a web page, which contains one or more WikiTables. The web server returns the contents of the web page (2), which, for now, contains only a reference to a WikiPage. Once the web page is loaded by the browser, a JavaScript function is started. This function uses the DOM-functionality to find all the html-elements having the following structure <div id="wt_?????">some text</div> and extracts the following string: "?????." This string is the WikiTable's unique ID in the database. For every ID found, an AJAX request (3) is started. The server-side script of the WikiTable receives the request, checks if the ID is correct, and holds the appropriate data from the database (4 and 5). Once the WikiTable script has received the data, it constructs the HTML-Table-code, which is then sent to the browser (6). A Javascript function injects this piece of code in the appropriate place on the web page.

A key feature of WikiTable is to support collaborative authoring. To achieve this, we increased the granularity of the locked content while editing, from the usual whole-table granularity to a single cell. This makes a table editable by many users simultaneously, as long as every user works on a different cell. This feature has shaped the database design of the application (see Figure 1, the dashed rectangle in the top right position), which basically consists of two database tables. The first one contains metadata for every WikiTable, such as its caption, unique ID, number of columns and rows, and other information. Every row of the second database table represents a single cell in a WikiTable. It contains, among other things, the unique ID of the cell, its contents, the unique id of the WikiTable to which the cell belongs, and its position in that table (i.e., the number of the row and the column).

3.2 Integration

Another important characteristic of this tool is its easy integration with currently popular web applications, such as Wikis, Content Management Systems, Forums and Blogs. By using AJAX-technology, we implemented WikiTable as a thin, lightweight layer that could be easily integrated in the aforementioned types of web applications.

Currently, we have a MediaWiki integration. MediaWiki[5] is the wiki engine serving the popular Wikipedia Project.

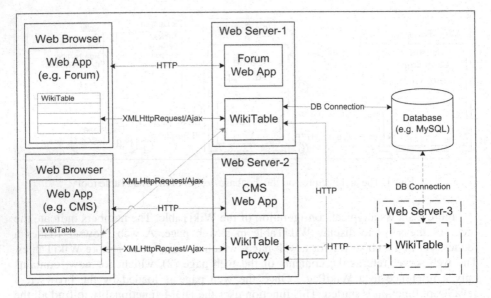

Fig. 2. The architecture of the WikiTable integration with different web applications

Figure 2 shows an integration of the WikiTable tool in two web applications, running on different web servers. Owing to security restrictions, most of the current web browsers do not allow their Javascript implementation to make a connection to a web server located on a different domain than the original one. There is a workaround for this restriction, which is known as Cross Domain AJAX Calls, and which is discussed in [8]. This is the reason we utilized a script called 'WikiTable Proxy' on every further web server that hosts web applications with WikiTables. This allows us to manage all the WikiTables from a central place, which, in Figure 2, is web server 1. An optional configuration could be the use of a dedicated web server (web server 3 in Figure 2), which hosts the WikiTable tool and manages all the requests from the WikiTable proxies hosted by web servers such as web server 2 in Figure 2.

3.3 User Interface

The user interface design is at a very early stage. Figure 3 is a screenshot of the current user interface; here, the WikiTable is integrated in MediaWiki. Area number 1 in the Figure is the title of the WikiTable. The two buttons following the title are: [e] Editability, toggles the editablilty of the table; and [o], New Window, displays the table in a new window (e.g., for printing). Every column and row of a WikiTable has its own header (areas 2 and 6), which is only visible in the editing mode. In the column header, clicking '«' will switch the position of the current column with the previous one, '-' will remove the column, '+' will add a new column after the current column and '»' will switch the current column with the next one. By clicking on a cell

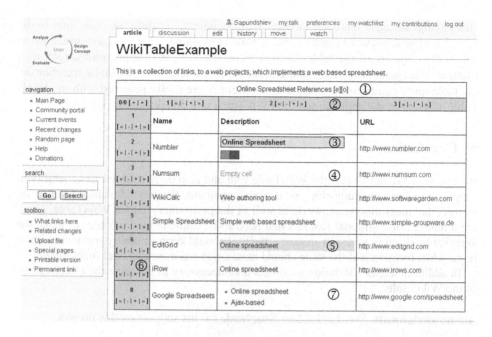

Fig. 3. An example of the UI of WikiTable integrated with the popular wiki engine, MediaWiki

from the table, the contents of cell become editable (cp. area 3). This functionality is known as "edit in place." Clicking the green rectangle confirms the changes, the red one discards them. Cells with no content display a grayed out text, "Empty cell" (cp. area 4). Area 5 shows a cell with a yellow background; this denotes that the current cell is currently being edited by somebody else. A cell may contain MediaWiki syntax as well; this is the case for the cell labeled as area 7. Here we used "*Online spreadsheet *AJAX-based" to achieve the bullet points.

All the described manipulation happens dynamically while utilizing the AJAX functionality, which we mentioned in the Architecture section. No reloading of the hosting wiki page is needed (cp. steps (3)-(6) from Figure 1).

4 Application Scenario

WikiTable can potentially be used in many application domains that require collaborative documentation sharing and management, such as software development, medical information management, and building information management. A good example is the Global Studio Project [2], which was initiated by Siemens Corporate Research. This project comprises six development teams located around the globe (US, Germany, Brazil, China, etc.). A Wiki site has been set up to facilitate information sharing and collaboration among these teams. Many documents, such as project plans, status reports, software requirements, etc. are organized in tables. However, without the WikiTable, the coordination of data input and editing among multiple users is challenging. Because there are thousands of documents, finding the right item in the table based on a keyword search is rather time consuming. There are also situations in which the contents of the tables needed to be used in other applications, such as a Content Management System, and current table implementations make transporting the table quite cumbersome. Yet, these challenges are easily resolved with the Wiki-Table. Currently, the application of the WikTable into this project is ongoing.

5 Conclusion

In sum, we have developed the WikiTable tool and also demonstrated its capability to support collaborative authoring and data management. We have developed the architecture, the integration framework, as well as the preliminary UI for WikiTable. There are a number of additional features that need to be implemented in order to make the WikiTable a mature tool. For instance, the tool should support table export and import (e.g., XML format), and the table should have some basic spreadsheet functionality.

In addition, a user validation session is also necessary to examine the effectiveness of the WikiTable.

Acknowledgments. We thank Claus Knapheide for his support on this project.

References

1. Bachmann, F., Merson, P.: Experience Using the Web-Based Tool Wiki for Architecture Documentation. Technical Note CMU/SEI-2005-TN-041
2. Ducasse, S., Renggli, L., Wuyts, R.: SmallWiki: a meta-described collaborative content management system. In: Proc. of the 2005 WikiSym, pp. 75–82. ACM Press, New York (2005)
3. Haake, A., Lukosch, S., Schümmer, T.: Wiki-templates: adding structure support to wikis on demand. In: Proc. of the 2005 WikiSym, pp. 41–51. ACM Press, New York (2005)
4. Leuf, B., Cunningham, W.: The Wiki Way. Addison-Wesley, Reading (2001)
5. MediaWiki – http://www.mediawiki.org
6. Prototype – JavaScript Framework http://prototype.conio.net
7. Silbernhorn, H.: TabulaMagica – An Integrated Approach to Manage Complex Tables. In: Proc. of DocEng, Atlanta, Georgia (2001)
8. Use a Web Proxy for Cross-Domain XMLHttpRequest Calls http://developer.yahoo.com/javascript/howto-proxy.html
9. What Is Web 2.0. http://www.oreillynet.com/pub/ a/oreilly/tim/news/2005/09/30/what-is-web-20.html
10. Wikipedia – http://www.wikipedia.org
11. Xia, S., Sun, D., Sun, C., Chen, D.A: Collaborative Table Editing Technique Based on Transparent Adaptation. In: OTM Conferences pp. 576–592 (2005)

Towards Building a Math Discourse Community: Investigating Collaborative Information Behavior

Nan Zhou and Gerry Stahl

College of Information Science and Technology, Drexel University, Philadelphia
PA 19104, USA
{nan.zhou,gerry.stahl}@ischool.drexel.edu

Abstract. We reported a study that analyzes collaborative information behavior of small groups in an online math discourse community. Taking group as the unit of analysis, we analyzed the social interactions of participants engaged in collaborative math problem solving and examined how they seek for information in such context. Participants look for information oriented to the procedure, problem, context, and social aspects. Various resources and methods are observed being used by participants to satisfy their information needs. These findings help us understand social interactions and online communities.

Keywords: Collaborative Information Behavior, Online Community, Computer-Supported Collaborative Learning, Conversation Analysis.

1 Introduction

Recent years have seen the growing emergence of online communities of various purposes and forms of organization. Developing online communities involves two issues: usability and sociability [1]. While usability concerns how human interact with computer technology, sociability is more concerned with supporting social interaction. More research is still need to understand online communities especially the social interactions to address the sociability issue, which is important for designers in order to develop healthy and sustaining online communities. This calls for a closer examination of participants' practices within the communities.

Participants of online communities often engage in all sorts of information seeking and information sharing activities, especially in communities with educational purposes. Information behavior has been a topic of central interest of information science. Though lots of research has been conducted on understanding human information behavior in various contexts [2],[3],[4],[5],[6], collaborative information behavior is relatively less studied and thus not very well understood. In this paper, we report a study that analyzes information behavior of small groups of young participants (6-12 graders) in an online community engaged in math problem solving collaboratively. The study is situated in a larger research agenda of the *Virtual Math Teams* project[1], an on-going research effort conducted to evolve an online math discourse community. Researchers from different disciplines (including information science, math education, anthropology, communication, etc) are working together

---

[1] www.mathforum.org/vmt

D. Schuler (Ed.): Online Communities and Social Comput., HCII 2007, LNCS 4564, pp. 509–518, 2007.
© Springer-Verlag Berlin Heidelberg 2007

designing a service extending the Math Forum's[2] Problem of the Week service to support collaborative learning and knowledge building [7] within this community. A central research aim of the project is to develop a systematic understanding of how math discourse takes place in an online chat environment [8].

In the study presented in this paper, we focus on analyzing collaborative information behavior of small groups within the VMT virtual environment. More specifically, we have looked at how participants in a small group negotiate and construct their information needs when engaged in math problem solving. We have examined what information they are looking for, what resources they use to find the information, and how they satisfy their information needs. These findings will be presented through detailed micro-level data analysis of a few short example excerpts. We then discuss the findings and their implications for building online communities.

2 Data Collection and Research Methods

We believe students can learn math better and more effectively when they talk about math with their peers. Bringing learners together can challenge them to understand other people's perspectives and to explain and defend their own ideas. It also helps to stimulate and build important comprehension, collaboration and reflection skills. The VMT project offers K-12 students such an opportunity by providing chat rooms for small groups of them to meet online and discuss math. Such discussion is organized as one hour long session, where 3 to 5 students in one chat room are provided a math problem that is designed to stimulate mathematical thinking. One facilitator will be there to get them started but it is up to the group to figure out the math. We have conducted around 50 sessions under naturalistic setting using online synchronous environments, from *AOL Instant Messaging* (AIM) early on to *VMT Chat*, a sophisticated chat environment specifically designed for the needs of the community. The *VMT Chat* provides a shared whiteboard with drawing facilities and features such as referencing tool that participants can use to make explicit reference to text postings and objects on the whiteboard. The conversations and other activities are preserved in the system for later access or examination.

Ethnomethodology, founded by Garfinkel [9], is a branch of sociology that studies the routine ways by which actions, including talk-in-interaction, are performed to constitute the intersubjective reality of social life. Harvey Sacks [10], who worked closely with Garfinkel, developed a related methodological approach for the close analysis of ordinary talk-in-interaction called *conversation analysis*. We have applied an ethnomethodologically-informed approach that combines aspects of conversation analysis and ethnomethodolgy to analyze information practices of participants within the VMT virtual community. This approach stresses close examination of interactional data at a micro level, to identify and describe the observable methods participants use to make sense of their interactions for themselves and each other.

3 Data Analysis and Findings

In this section, we show our analysis of a few sample excerpts from participants' transcripts which demonstrate different aspects of information behavior of VMT

---

[2] www.mathforum.org

participants. Taking the group as the unit of analysis, we've approached analyzing the data from an interactional perspective and looked closely at the social interactions taking place within the group.

3.1 Seeking Information to Make Sense of the Surroundings

A typical VMT chat session usually opens like what we can see in the following excerpt of transcript: participants log in the room and greet each other. Usually there is a facilitator present in the room to get participants started on working on the problem. In the following excerpt that lasts less than 2 minutes after the second participant (bwan) joined, we can see the unfolding of the interaction. Facilitator "Gerry" started by greeting everyone and identified himself as the "VMT guide". A participant with the handle name "Aznx" had the question regarding the identity of the person who appears as "Gerry". Bwan responded to the question using his own vocabulary and recognized "Gerry" as an admin (short for administrator). Gerry continued to provide information to the participants: the goal of today's session is "mainly to get to know the VMT system". There is also a comment on the rules or norms of the session *"So we can't have our own friends"* and information provided on identifying participants themselves: *"hey three of us are from miller"*. By greeting each other, identifying each other, and establishing the goal of the session, along with using abbreviation (lol, which usually is used as short for "laugh out loud") and emoticon (=)), the interaction unfolds in a friendly and lighthearted way and participants organize themselves into a position that is ready to move on to the next step of the session.

Excerpt 1.

Line #	Handle	Message	TimeStamp
1	Gerry	joins the room	06.17.35
2	bwan	joins the room	06.23.13
3	Aznx	joins the room	06.23.14
4	Qsilver	joins the room	06.23.14
5	bwan	hi	06.23.18
6	Aznx	Hi	06.23.23
7	Qsilver	hey	06.23.28
8	Aznx	So we can't have our own friends?	06.23.35
9	bwan	nope	06.23.40
10	bwan	lol	06.23.49
11	Qsilver	hey three of us are from miller	06.23.52
12	Gerry	Hi everyone!	06.23.55
13	bwan	oh	06.24.03
14	Gorry	I am your VMT guide today	06.24.06
15	Aznx	How?	06.24.06
16	Qsilver	nvrmind	06.24.12
17	Qsilver	two of us	06.24.13
18	Aznx	Who's Gerry?	06.24.13
19	bwan	admin	06.24.19
20	Aznx	Yeah. =)	06.24.19
21	Qsilver	Hello Gerry!	06.24.45
22	Gerry	Today's session is mainly to get to know the VMT system	06.24.59

As a new user of the system, one thing that probably is noticeably different about the environment from other chat systems is the whiteboard with drawing functions and other features. Coming into such an environment they are not familiar with, participants usually explore the system and get themselves oriented. They need to find out how to get around the system, how to use certain functionalities, etc. In order to satisfy these information needs, participants either try to figure out by experimenting by themselves or seek help from the group, including the peer participants and the facilitator. By identifying himself as "VMT guide" of the session earlier, Gerry positions himself as someone who knows better about the system than other participants and thus will be able to provide information regarding the use of the system. This identity and position has been acknowledged by the participants (e.g. bwan told Aznx that Gerry is the admin), which put them in the position of information seeker. In line 23, Aznx posed a question regarding how to use the whiteboard, whereas bwan started making reference to the whiteboard as a step of exploring how to use it.

Excerpt 2.

23	Aznx	So, how do you use the whiteboard?	06.25.18	
24	Gerry	I will answer your questions as you start to do things	06.25.51	
25	bwan	asdfadsf	06.25.59	Reference to whiteboard
26	bwan		06.25.59	
27	bwan	ok	06.26.15	
28	Gerry	The whiteboard is a shared area for drawing and textboxes	06.26.27	

Along the session, after participants are oriented to their task, they encounter the need for information on using the system from time to time. Participants frequently engage in such information seeking and information giving in their interactions.

3.2 Negotiation of Information Needs

One important type of information participants in a VMT chat session frequently find they are in need of is that related to solving the problem, which may include certain math information, and strategies or resources for tackling the problem. Facing a math problem, participants usually need to do the work of understanding the problem, identifying what is known and what they need to know in order to solve it. Such work is accomplished collaboratively through the interactions within the group. Participants often achieve the identification of information needs by negotiation. In the following excerpt, three participants (two 9 graders and one 11 grader) are working on a geometry problem:

> *If two equilateral triangles have edgelengths of 9 cubits and 12 cubits, what's the edgelength of the equilateral triangle whose area is equal to the sum of the areas of the other two?*

This example demonstrates the process of negotiating the information needs for solving the problem, which in this case happens to be a smooth one. AVR starts identifying what they need to know by proposing that they should "start with the formula for the area of a triangle". This is acknowledged by SUP. AVR continues by providing the formula. By putting this information out, followed by "I believe", AVR is calling for assessment from other participants. PIN indicates his explicit agreement with AVR's proposal and information being provided by saying "yes", "i concur". Instead of providing an agreement, SUP starts moving to the next step as finding the base and height, which the formula is built upon. By making such movement, SUP implicitly accepts what AVR is proposing. This short process of negotiation establishes the need of the group regarding solving the problem.

Excerpt 3.

AVR	Okay, I think we should start with the formula for the area of a triangle	8:21:46
SUP	ok	8:22:17
AVR	A = 1/2bh	8:22:28
AVR	I believe	8:22:31
PIN	yes	8:22:35
PIN	i concue	8:22:37
PIN	concur*	8:22:39
AVR	then find the area of each triangle	8:22:42
AVR	oh, wait	8:22:54
SUP	the base and heigth are 9 and 12 right?	8:23:03

3.3   Seeking Information on Math Problems

We prefer the term information inquiry than information seeking question because of the fact that a posting not formulated in the form of question can sometimes be treated as seeking information. It is the way a posting is read and treated by the group that makes it recognizable as an inquiry for information from an analytical and interactional point of view. This is also how an information inquiry is made publicly visible and recognizable through the interactions to us as researchers.   Many information inquires take the form of a question that seeks an answer which is information with relatively fixed boundaries. For example:

HOL: do you know the equation to find area of a cylinder?
AME: BaseArea times height

The question of HOL is clearly read as a call for information. The answer to the "do you know" question could legitimately be "yes, I do". But by recognizing it as seeking for information, AME provides the equation "BaseArea times height" in response to the question. In other cases, a posting may not appear as an information seeking question if judged from the form it is taking. It is however taken up by other participants as information inquiry and consequentially results in the action of providing information. The following excerpt (4) is from the same chat session as Excerpt 3. AVR's posting in the first line can be read as proposing what the group needs to do. From how it is responded by the other two participants PIN and SUP, the posting is doing the work of organizing the group to think about how to find the height: both PIN and SUP propose their way of finding the height, which is in a sense treating AVR's posting as a *how* question, that is, "how do we figure out the height?". PIN's response "I know how" brings AVR's interest in finding it out. By asking "how?", AVR shifts her position to one seeking information from the one (PIN) who claims to have the information to give. It needs to be pointed out that the sequence that postings appear in a chat environment may be distorted from the sequence of postings being composed and posted due to the nature of computer-mediated synchronous communication [11]. More than one participant could start "talking" at the same time due to the different turn-taking mechanism afforded by such communication and the time one utterance gets posted depends on the time it arrives the server that handles the messages. This is what happens in line 62 and 63, which have exactly the same time stamp. AVR asks "how" at line 64 clearly because she hasn't seen PIN's posting on line 63. This short excerpt demonstrates how a posting that doesn't appear in the form of a question can also be an information inquiry from an analytical point of view.

Excerpt 4.

60	AVR	i think we have to figure out the height by ourselves	8:23:27
61	AVR	if possible	8:23:29
62	PIN	i know how	8:24:05
63	PIN	draw the altitude'	8:24:09
64	AVR	how?	8:24:09
65	AVR	right	8:24:15
66	SUP	proportions?	8:24:19

In the next five minutes or so into the chat, the participants take up PIN's proposal on how to find out the height and go about actually "finding it". At 8:27:17, PIN asks "anyone remember formula for 30/60/90 triangle?" as a clear question seeking the formula from the group. The notion of 30/60/90 triangle is questioned by the other two participants and they decide they are dealing with 60/60/60 triangle. The following excerpt shows an information inquiry seeking a formula (line 108) is put on the table, which calls the response and action of other participants. AVR admits her deficiency of knowledge on this manner ("I have no idea") but acknowledges the usefulness of such information (line 110). The first attempt to seek information from the group fails. A proposal to turn to external resource is brought in by PIN: "search google", which is reified by AVR's action: "that's what I'm doing".

Excerpt 5.

108	SUP	is there a formula for a 60/60/60?	8:29:04
109	AVR	I have no idea	8:29:12
110	AVR	I think once we find the formula it should be pretty easy	8:29:20
111	AVR	I don't think there's a formula, though	8:29:24
112	PIN	search google	8:29:27
113	AVR	I think we find it some other way	8:29:29
114	AVR	that's what I'm doing	8:29:31

This practice is commonly observed in such collaborative sessions where participants work together to solve a problem. They usually take the group as a primary resource for information and often first turn to the group for help when encountering an information need. If the group is not able to provide the needed information, they may use external resources such as online search. This is what happens in this particular example as we discussed above.

3.4 Seeking and Providing Personal and Contextual Information

When participants in a group are communicating in a chat environment and trying to accomplish the task, all the interactions are achieved through the text postings, drawings on the shared whiteboard, awareness messages, etc., whatever is made available and visible for them in the system. Being in such a virtual environment, people are technically interacting with messages and activities shown on the screen. They are doing so because they are aware that there is a real person they are interacting with. In a virtual community, the feeling of social presence and co-presence [12] is important for meaningful communication. Participants engaged in a chat session often need information about others being present for establishing identify or for the sake of socializing. They employ different methods to find out what they need to know as well as provide information to others. This usually happens sometime into the session or after they worked on the problem for a while. In the following chat excerpt, REA is asking PIN a question about his math level. Immediately prior to this conversation, REA proposed that they "might have to use law of sines", which PIN reckoned that (his class) "haven't learned yet". This brought up PIN's inquiry on what it (law of sines) says and the two participants MCP and REA both provided their version of the law of sines. After this little episode of information inquiry and information giving, it seems natural that REA wants to find out PIN's math level, which is what is taking place in the following excerpt.

Excerpt 6.

REA	where are you in math	8:56:12
PIN	uhh	8:56:28
PIN	like level?	8:56:38
REA	yeah geo., alge, or algebra 2	8:57:11
PIN	ohhh	8:57:15
PIN	geometry honors	8:57:19
PIN	freshman	8:57:27
REA	what grade	8:58:03
PIN	9	8:58:13
REA	i am in 6 th	8:58:28
REA	grade	8:58:32

REA also provides information of his own grade level as a reciprocal action, which makes such information exchange recognizable as socializing. This brief moment of socializing may help establishing their identity to each other and thus bring the sense of co-presence in such a virtual environment. Participants therefore can feel that they are interacting with real people and build the feeling of being in a community. A few minutes after this episode, the two participants PIN and REA along with the third one MCP had casual chat on their school life and the tests they will be dealing with. Something noticeable is that REA explicitly calls MCP to check his presence, which is a message to invite him into this socializing conversation.

Teenagers nowadays in the US are a generation brought up with computer technologies. They are very apt users of online chats. There are certain practices and conventions that have been developed for online chatting within this young population. Naturally the participants at VMT bring in such practices and norms they are already familiar with. Among those, some are methods of seeking and providing information to construct the context of interaction and feeling of co-presence. Emoticons and abbreviations are frequently seen being used in the chat as ways to convey emotions and tones to the text posting. Participants also use ** to quote a message that describes to the group what one is doing. For example:

Excerpt 7.

AVR	**begins to scribble on paper**	8:20:36
AVR	or should I not do that?	8:20:47
PIN	doesnt matter	8:21:11
AVR	got it	8:21:25
AVR	**proceeds with scribbling..**	8:21:31

Providing such contextual information is important not only because it builds the sense of presence but also plays significant roles in facilitating the collaboration process by bringing the group up to date of one's status in working on the problem.

4 Discussion of Findings and Implications

Procedure-Oriented Information. When participants come to the VMT environment and work with their peers on math problem solving, their goal is to do the math in a group and have fun doing this. This is done by interacting with other participants through the particular environment. They first of all need to orient themselves to the environment and the task, that is to say, they have to make sense of their surroundings to be able to do the collaboration and problem solving. For most participants, the task of discussing math in a chat environment and work collaboratively on solving a math problem is relatively a new thing which they are not familiar with. Usually a facilitator is there to provide participants information on what they are supposed to do, procedures of the task, some technical issues of using the system, and norms of doing the chat. For example, the facilitator would say: "Here are four guidelines that we'll use tonight.1. During the session, share ideas about how to solve the problem...". Participants find out the information they need to make sense of the environment and the task by asking questions or experimenting the functionalities on their own.

Problem-Oriented Information. This is mainly about mathematics information. Since the main purpose of participants being here is to explore math problems together, the need for math information is often prominent during the process. Given the problem, they need to identify from the problem description what is known and what they still need to know. Such needs are negotiated and constructed together collaboratively. There are different resources participants use to seek information to satisfy the identified needs. The group they are working with is always one primary resource they seek help from. Very often, they turn to external resources such as google or the Math Forum online resources ff the group is not able to provide needed information. They also try to use their previous work in VMT or what's learned before in class: "What can we use that we already know?", "using the formula from yesterday's problem", "Since we're both in Spanish class, are you saying something what the Aztecs made?".

There are different methods observed participants use to seek information. Some information inquiries are in the form of a straightforward question such as "what does itmeans by edglengths?[3]" or "do you know the equation to find area of a cylinder?". Some postings in the chat do not appear in a question but they are taken up and treated by others as information inquiries. Some of them are formulated as a call for proposals, which are responded by participants with proposing strategies or information. Sometimes they result in actions taken in finding needed information. Participants also ask an information seeking question along with providing an alternative answer, which calls for assessment work of the group. Sometimes participants seek information by providing information. These methods are important for doing social interaction and collaboration thus worth closer examination.

Context-Oriented Information. During the collaborative session, participants need to constantly make sense of what is going on around them. They need find information to establish others' identity. They need information on the status of the work to keep themselves updated. A question like "bwang, what are we doing?" is seeking such information so the participant can be in sync with rest of the group. Participants are also quite apt at providing contextual information to others. Such information seeking and giving help making the collaboration process smooth.

Socially-Oriented Information. Apart from doing problem solving, participants sometimes also go "off topic" and socialize. They want to find out more about people they are interacting with. They are interested in finding out what math level and which grade the other is in, where the person is from, the school life, and math experience, etc. Socializing is an important and necessary part of the conversation from the perspective of evolving a community. Information about the participants helps to build the identity in the community and increase the sense of social presence. This finding encourages us to explore the need of building user profiles and what information to include in them. It helps us to recognize participants' needs for socializing and make us think how they should be supported by our facilitation. We want to create an environment where participants can fulfill what they want to do and have enjoyable experience of doing math collaboratively. This environment also needs to be safe for our young users, maybe by protecting their personal information and identity. It still remains a question how to develop policies for such community that would meet users' needs but also satisfy other goals such as safety.

Conclusions. In this paper, we presented our analysis of collaborative information behavior of an online math community where small groups of participants are working on solving math problems together. We looked closely at their social interactions and identified what information participants are looking for, what resources they use to find the information, and how they achieve these. By analyzing what activities participants do in such environment, we are able to understand better

---

[3] All the quotes are original from transcripts of VMT sessions.

their information and social practices. Participants have various information needs in this particular situation. How they formulate and direct an information inquiry is consequential on their interactions. There are different methods participants use to seek information. Some information inquires are successfully answered and some are not. Maybe there are certain features that make an information inquiry better than another. How can we build an environment that better supports participants' information practices? This study demonstrates the potential of understanding an online community from analyzing their information behavior. The findings have implications on how to design and support such a math discourse community.

Acknowledgments. This research is supported by the NSF grants awarded to the second author for digital library services (NSDL), innovative technologies (ITR/IERI) and the science of learning (SLC).

References

1. Preece, J.: Online Communities: Designing Usability, Supporting Sociability. John Wiley & Sons, Chichester, UK (2000)
2. Belkin, N.J.: Anomalous States of Knowledge as Basis for Information Retrieval. Canadian Journal of Information Science 5, 133–143 (1980)
3. Dervin, B.: An overview of sense-making research: concepts, methods, and results to date. In: paper presented at the Annual Meeting of the International Communication Association, Dallas, TX (1983)
4. Wilson, T.D.: Human information behavior. Information science, 3(2) (2000)
5. Kuhlthau, C.C.: Seeking Meaning: A Process Approach to Library and Information Services, 2nd edn. Libraries Unlimited (2004)
6. Fisher, K.E., Erdelez, S., McKechnie, E.F. (eds.): Theories of information behavior. Medford, NJ, Information Today (2005)
7. Scardamalia, M., Bereiter, C.: Computer support for knowledge-building communities. The Journal of Learning Sciences 3(3), 265–283 (1994)
8. Stahl, G.: Group cognition: Computer support for building collaborative knowledge. MIT Press, Cambridge, MA (2006)
9. Garfinkel, H.: Studies in ethnomethodology. Prentice-Hall, Englewood Cliffs, NJ (1967)
10. Sacks, H., Schegloff, E., Jefferson, G.: A simplest systematics for the organization of turn-taking in conversation. Language 50, 697–735 (1974)
11. Garcia, A., Jacobs, J.B.: The Eyes of the Beholder: Understanding the Turn-Taking System in Quasi-Synchronous Computer-Mediated Communication. Research on language and social interaction 32(4), 337–367 (1999)
12. Zhao, S.: Toward a taxonomy of copresence. Presence; teleoperators and virtual environments 12(5), 445–455 (2003)

Author Index

Lecture Notes in Computer Science

For information about Vols. 1–4483

please contact your bookseller or Springer

Vol. 4529: P. Melin, O. Castillo, L.T. Aguilar, J. Kacprzyk, W. Pedrycz (Eds.), Foundations of Fuzzy Logic and Soft Computing. XIX, 830 pages. 2007. (Sublibrary LNAI).

Vol. 4528: J. Mira, J.R. Álvarez (Eds.), Nature Inspired Problem-Solving Methods in Knowledge Engineering, Part II. XXII, 650 pages. 2007.

Vol. 4527: J. Mira, J.R. Álvarez (Eds.), Bio-inspired Modeling of Cognitive Tasks, Part I. XXII, 630 pages. 2007.

Vol. 4526: M. Malek, M. Reitenspieß, A. van Moorsel (Eds.), Service Availability. X, 155 pages. 2007.

Vol. 4525: C. Demetrescu (Ed.), Experimental Algorithms. XIII, 448 pages. 2007.

Vol. 4524: M. Marchiori, J.Z. Pan, C.d.S. Marie (Eds.), Web Reasoning and Rule Systems. XI, 382 pages. 2007.

Vol. 4523: Y.-H. Lee, H.-N. Kim, J. Kim, Y. Park, L.T. Yang, S.W. Kim (Eds.), Embedded Software and Systems. XIX, 829 pages. 2007.

Vol. 4522: B.K. Ersbøll, K.S. Pedersen (Eds.), Image Analysis. XVIII, 989 pages. 2007.

Vol. 4521: J. Katz, M. Yung (Eds.), Applied Cryptography and Network Security. XIII, 498 pages. 2007.

Vol. 4519: E. Franconi, M. Kifer, W. May (Eds.), The Semantic Web: Research and Applications. XVIII, 830 pages. 2007.

Vol. 4517: F. Boavida, E. Monteiro, S. Mascolo, Y. Koucheryavy (Eds.), Wired/Wireless Internet Communications. XIV, 382 pages. 2007.

Vol. 4516: L. Mason, T. Drwiega, J. Yan (Eds.), Managing Traffic Performance in Converged Networks. XXIII, 1191 pages. 2007.

Vol. 4515: M. Naor (Ed.), Advances in Cryptology - EUROCRYPT 2007. XIII, 591 pages. 2007.

Vol. 4514: S.N. Artemov, A. Nerode (Eds.), Logical Foundations of Computer Science. XI, 513 pages. 2007.

Vol. 4513: M. Fischetti, D.P. Williamson (Eds.), Integer Programming and Combinatorial Optimization. IX, 500 pages. 2007.

Vol. 4511: C. Conati, K. McCoy, G. Paliouras (Eds.), User Modeling 2007. XVI, 487 pages. 2007. (Sublibrary LNAI).

Vol. 4510: P. Van Hentenryck, L. Wolsey (Eds.), Integration of AI and OR Techniques in Constraint Programming for Combinatorial Optimization Problems. X, 391 pages. 2007.

Vol. 4509: Z. Kobti, D. Wu (Eds.), Advances in Artificial Intelligence. XII, 552 pages. 2007. (Sublibrary LNAI).

Vol. 4508: M.-Y. Kao, X.-Y. Li (Eds.), Algorithmic Aspects in Information and Management. VIII, 428 pages. 2007.

Vol. 4507: F. Sandoval, A. Prieto, J. Cabestany, M. Graña (Eds.), Computational and Ambient Intelligence. XXVI, 1167 pages. 2007.

Vol. 4506: D. Zeng, I. Gotham, K. Komatsu, C. Lynch, M. Thurmond, D. Madigan, B. Lober, J. Kvach, H. Chen (Eds.), Intelligence and Security Informatics: Biosurveillance. XI, 234 pages. 2007.

Vol. 4505: G. Dong, X. Lin, W. Wang, Y. Yang, J.X. Yu (Eds.), Advances in Data and Web Management. XXII, 896 pages. 2007.

Vol. 4504: J. Huang, R. Kowalczyk, Z. Maamar, D. Martin, I. Müller, S. Stoutenburg, K.P. Sycara (Eds.), Service-Oriented Computing: Agents, Semantics, and Engineering. X, 175 pages. 2007.

Vol. 4501: J. Marques-Silva, K.A. Sakallah (Eds.), Theory and Applications of Satisfiability Testing – SAT 2007. XI, 384 pages. 2007.

Vol. 4500: N. Streitz, A. Kameas, I. Mavrommati (Eds.), The Disappearing Computer. XVIII, 304 pages. 2007.

Vol. 4499: Y.Q. Shi (Ed.), Transactions on Data Hiding and Multimedia Security II. IX, 117 pages. 2007.

Vol. 4498: N. Abdennahder, F. Kordon (Eds.), Reliable Software Technologies – Ada Europe 2007. XII, 247 pages. 2007.

Vol. 4497: S.B. Cooper, B. Löwe, A. Sorbi (Eds.), Computation and Logic in the Real World. XVIII, 826 pages. 2007.

Vol. 4496: N.T. Nguyen, A. Grzech, R.J. Howlett, L.C. Jain (Eds.), Agent and Multi-Agent Systems: Technologies and Applications. XXI, 1046 pages. 2007. (Sublibrary LNAI).

Vol. 4495: J. Krogstie, A. Opdahl, G. Sindre (Eds.), Advanced Information Systems Engineering. XVI, 606 pages. 2007.

Vol. 4494: H. Jin, O.F. Rana, Y. Pan, V.K. Prasanna (Eds.), Algorithms and Architectures for Parallel Processing. XIV, 508 pages. 2007.

Vol. 4493: D. Liu, S. Fei, Z. Hou, H. Zhang, C. Sun (Eds.), Advances in Neural Networks – ISNN 2007, Part III. XXVI, 1215 pages. 2007.

Vol. 4492: D. Liu, S. Fei, Z. Hou, H. Zhang, C. Sun (Eds.), Advances in Neural Networks – ISNN 2007, Part II. XXVII, 1321 pages. 2007.

Vol. 4491: D. Liu, S. Fei, Z.-G. Hou, H. Zhang, C. Sun (Eds.), Advances in Neural Networks – ISNN 2007, Part I. LIV, 1365 pages. 2007.

Vol. 4490: Y. Shi, G.D. van Albada, J. Dongarra, P.M.A. Sloot (Eds.), Computational Science – ICCS 2007, Part IV. XXXVII, 1211 pages. 2007.

Vol. 4489: Y. Shi, G.D. van Albada, J. Dongarra, P.M.A. Sloot (Eds.), Computational Science – ICCS 2007, Part III. XXXVII, 1257 pages. 2007.

Vol. 4488: Y. Shi, G.D. van Albada, J. Dongarra, P.M.A. Sloot (Eds.), Computational Science – ICCS 2007, Part II. XXXV, 1251 pages. 2007.

Vol. 4487: Y. Shi, G.D. van Albada, J. Dongarra, P.M.A. Sloot (Eds.), Computational Science – ICCS 2007, Part I. LXXXI, 1275 pages. 2007.

Vol. 4486: M. Bernardo, J. Hillston (Eds.), Formal Methods for Performance Evaluation. VII, 469 pages. 2007.

Vol. 4485: F. Sgallari, A. Murli, N. Paragios (Eds.), Scale Space and Variational Methods in Computer Vision. XV, 931 pages. 2007.

Vol. 4484: J.-Y. Cai, S.B. Cooper, H. Zhu (Eds.), Theory and Applications of Models of Computation. XIII, 772 pages. 2007.